THE COMMON LAW OF OBLIGATIONS

The development of the law of obligations across the common law world has been, and continues to be, a story of unity and divergence. Its common origins continue to exert a powerful stabilising influence, carried forward by a methodology that places heavy weight on the historical foundations of legal principles. Divergence is, however, produced by numerous factors, including national and international human rights instruments, local statutory regimes, civil law influences, regional harmonisation, local circumstances and values and different political and legal cultures. The essays in this collection explore the forces that produce divergence, the countervailing forces that generate cohesion and consistency in the common law of obligations, and the influence that the major common law jurisdictions continue to exert over one another in this area of law.

The chapters in this book were originally presented at the Seventh Biennial Conference on the Law of Obligations held in Hong Kong in July 2014. A second collection, entitled *Divergences in Private Law* (ISBN: 9781782256601), will focus on particular departures from the common law mainstream and the causes and effects of those deviations.

The Common Law of Obligations

Divergence and Unity

Edited by
Andrew Robertson
and
Michael Tilbury

HART PUBLISHING
OXFORD AND PORTLAND, OREGON
2018

Hart Publishing
An imprint of Bloomsbury Publishing Plc

Hart Publishing Ltd
Kemp House
Chawley Park
Cumnor Hill
Oxford OX2 9PH
UK

Bloomsbury Publishing Plc
50 Bedford Square
London
WC1B 3DP
UK

www.hartpub.co.uk
www.bloomsbury.com

Published in North America (US and Canada) by
Hart Publishing
c/o International Specialized Book Services
920 NE 58th Avenue, Suite 300
Portland, OR 97213-3786
USA

www.isbs.com

First published in hardback, 2016
Paperback edition, 2018

British Library Cataloguing-in-Publication Data
A catalogue record for this book is available from the British Library.

ISBN: PB: 978-1-50992-111-9
HB: 978-1-78225-656-4

Library of Congress Cataloging-in-Publication Data

Names: Conference on the Law of Obligations (7th : 2014 : Honkong) | Robertson, Andrew, 1966– editor. | Tilbury, M. J. (Michael J.), editor.

Title: The common law of obligations : divergence and unity / Edited by Andrew Robertson and Michael Tilbury.

Description: Oxford : Hart Publishing, 2016. | Includes bibliographical references and index.

Identifiers: LCCN 2015039087 | ISBN 9781782256564 (hardback : alk. paper)

Subjects: LCSH: Obligations (Law)—Congresses. | Civil law—Congresses. | Common law—Congresses.

Classification: LCC K830.A6 D585 2016 | DDC 346.02—dc23 LC record available at http://lccn.loc.gov/2015039087

Typeset by Compuscript Ltd, Shannon

PREFACE

This book had its origins in the Seventh Biennial Conference on the Law of Obligations (Obligations VII), which was co-hosted by the Faculty of Law at the University of Hong Kong and Melbourne Law School and held in Hong Kong on 15–18 July 2014. Another volume from the Conference, *Divergences in Private Law*, explores a related set of issues and will be published simultaneously.

We are very grateful to the Faculty of Law at the University of Hong Kong and Melbourne Law School for supporting the Conference. Particular thanks are due to Carolyn Evans and Michael Crommelin, respectively the Dean and former Dean of Melbourne Law School. The existence of the Obligations conference series owes a great deal to Michael Crommelin's warm encouragement and unstinting support from the outset in 2001. Both Michael Crommelin and Carolyn Evans have provided enthusiastic and wholehearted support for the series in general, and for this particular collaboration with the Faculty of Law at the University of Hong Kong. We are also very grateful to Michael Hor and Johannes Chan, respectively the Dean and former Dean of the Faculty of Law at the University of Hong Kong, for their generous support for the Obligations VII Conference.

Our thanks also go to the staff at the Faculty of Law at the University of Hong Kong, led by the extraordinary Priscilla Wong—and including especially Daisy Lai and Tristan Wong—for the great care they took to make the Conference run smoothly and efficiently and ensure that delegates were very well looked after. We also thank Eddie Leung and Alan Tsang for their efficient and attentive IT and web support.

Thanks are also due to Hart Publishing, Cambridge University Press and Kerry Holdings for their sponsorship of the Conference.

Finally, we thank all who participated in the Obligations VII Conference for enthusiastically embracing the conference theme and contributing to the conversation that is, in part, recorded in this book.

Andrew Robertson and Michael Tilbury
June 2015

CONTENTS

LIST OF CONTRIBUTORS

TT Arvind is a Professor of Law at Newcastle Law School.

Allan Beever is a Professor of Law at Auckland University of Technology.

Andrew Burrows is Professor of the Law of England and a Fellow of All Souls College at the University of Oxford.

Peter Cane is a Distinguished Professor at the Australian National University.

Niamh Connolly is an Assistant Professor at Trinity College, Dublin School of Law.

Dame Sian Elias is Chief Justice of New Zealand.

Paul Finn is a Professorial Fellow at Melbourne Law School and a former judge of the Federal Court of Australia.

Paula Giliker is Professor of Comparative Law, University of Bristol.

Goh Yihan is an Associate Professor of Law at Singapore Management University.

James Goudkamp is a Fellow of Keble College, Oxford, an Associate Professor in the Oxford Law Faculty, an Honorary Senior Research Fellow in the Faculty of Law at the University of Western Australia and an Honorary Principal Fellow in the School of Law, University of Wollongong.

Sir Anthony Mason is a former Chief Justice of the High Court of Australia and a Non-Permanent Judge of the Hong Kong Court of Final Appeal.

John Murphy is a Professor of Law at Lancaster University and a Stipendiary Visiting Professor at the Chinese University of Hong Kong.

Dan Priel is an Associate Professor at Osgoode Hall Law School, York University.

Andrew Robertson is a Professor of Law at the University of Melbourne.

Michael Tilbury is a Professorial Fellow at Melbourne Law School, formerly Kerry Holdings Professor in Private Law at the University of Hong Kong.

Sarah Worthington is Downing Professor of the Laws of England and Fellow of Trinity College at the University of Cambridge and a Professorial Fellow at Melbourne Law School.

TABLE OF CASES

All decisions of the Privy Council are cited in the Table as UK cases.

United Kingdom

Australia

Canada

Court of Justice of the European Union

European Court of Human Rights

Hong Kong

India

Ireland (Republic of)

New Zealand

Nigeria

Sierra Leone

Singapore

South Africa (Republic of)

United States of America

TABLE OF LEGISLATION

United Kingdom

Statutory Instruments

Australia

Canada

European Union

Treaties

Directives

Regulations

France

India

Ireland (Republic of)

Malaysia

New Zealand

Nigeria

Sierra Leone

Singapore

South Africa

Trinidad and Tobago

United States of America

TABLE OF INTERNATIONAL INSTRUMENTS

1

Unity, Divergence and Convergence in the Common Law of Obligations

ANDREW ROBERTSON AND MICHAEL TILBURY

The development of the law of obligations across the common law world has been, and continues to be, a complicated story of unity, divergence and convergence. The common law jurisdictions of the United States broke away early and developed their own distinctive version of the common law. In major Commonwealth jurisdictions the common law of obligations for some time remained relatively uniform as a result of a number of different forces, some more formal and direct than others. The law of contract, tort, equity and restitution in these jurisdictions was held together: first, by the view that the common law remained essentially a single body of law; secondly, by the Privy Council acting as the ultimate appellate court for many jurisdictions; thirdly, by courts outside England treating decisions of the House of Lords as binding and, later, with deference. While those formal ties have loosened their grip over time, other less formal factors continue to play a unifying role.

The story of unity, divergence and convergence in the common law, as well as the theoretical underpinnings of that story, are addressed in the essays in this book, particularly in the context of the common law of obligations.

I. Unity

'Unity' has various shades of meaning. Two different kinds of 'unity' in the common law are referred to in this chapter: first, unity in the sense of a uniform, single body of law and, secondly, unity in the sense of a significant underlying commonality between bodies of law which differ in their particulars. To speak of the 'unity' of the common law in the first sense is to speak principally of the period in which the Judicial Committee of the Privy Council was the final appellate court from the countries comprising the British Empire and Commonwealth. By reason of the doctrine of precedent, all these countries were bound to follow the law set out in the 'advices' of the Privy Council. As James Goudkamp and John Murphy point out, the then prevailing declaratory theory of law meant that the Council understood its function as being to ensure the unity of the common law as far as was possible.[1] Because

[1] James Goudkamp and John Murphy, 'Divergent Evolution in the Law of Torts: Jurisdictional Isolation, Jurisprudential Divergence and Explanatory Theories', ch 13 of this volume.

the Judicial Committee was largely comprised of judges who sat at the same time in the House of Lords, decisions of the House of Lords were also generally regarded as binding on the courts of the territories for which the Privy Council was the final court of appeal. The result was that it was the English version of the common law that defined the uniform common law.

The unity of the common law throughout the Empire and Commonwealth, and the supremacy of the English version of the common law, was subject to four qualifications. First, and most obviously, not all the jurisdictions from which the Privy Council heard appeals were common law jurisdictions. In such cases, the Privy Council had to apply the local law, whether it was civil law or Hindu law or Islamic law. Notwithstanding some use of local judges in such appeals, the Privy Council inevitably applied local law through English eyes, and this could result in local dissatisfaction. In his contribution to this volume, Andrew Burrows points out that, in the past, the House of Lords as the final court of appeal from Scotland (a mixed jurisdiction), has been criticised as promoting 'an unwarranted Anglicisation of Scots law', a criticism that has extended to the Scottish Law Lords.[2] South Africa provides an example of the 'Anglicisation' of its law by the Privy Council in a decision in the early 1930s, in which the Privy Council brought the Roman-Dutch common law of South Africa into line with the English law relating to penalties.[3] A South African judge later referred to the Privy Council decision as a 'blemish on our legal system which militates against good faith, trust and business morality'.[4] The decision was overturned by legislation in 1962.[5]

Secondly, the application of English law was subject to valid local statutory provisions. Paul Finn notes early local dissatisfaction in Australia, Canada and New Zealand with the Privy Council's record in interpreting local statutes, and cites the example of a special sitting of New Zealand's Court of Appeal at which the Chief Justice referred to the Privy Council's record of acting under a 'misapprehension or an ignorance of our local laws', adding that the Council 'knows not our statutes, or our conveyancing terms, or our history'.[6] Dissatisfaction was particularly acute in cases where the statute involved was, effectively, the territory's Constitution. This proved a long-running sore in Canada where the Privy Council's favouring of the powers of the provinces at the expense of the federal government represented a 'pre-conceived, but ill-informed, notion of the proper form of a federal system'.[7]

Thirdly, however expressed, and whether expressed in relation to judge-made law or statute, effect was only given to English law so far as local circumstances permitted.[8] Whatever the exact import of this qualification, it is clear, as Goh Yihan points out in respect

[2] Andrew Burrows, 'The Influence of Comparative Law on the English Law of Obligations', ch 2 of this volume.

[3] *Pearl Assurance Co v Union Government* 1934 AD 560 (PC).

[4] *Tobacco Manufacturers Committee v Jacob Green and Sons* 1953 (3) SA 480 (AD) 493 (Van den Heever JA).

[5] Conventional Penalties Act 1962 (SA).

[6] Sir Robert Stout, quoted by T Arnold, 'Update on the Supreme Court', paper presented at the New Zealand Legal Research Foundation Annual General Meeting on 7 August 2003, available at www.crownlaw.govt.nz/uploads/UpdateSC.pdf. See also KJ Keith, 'The Unity of the Common Law and the Ending of Appeals to the Privy Council' (2005) 54 *ICLQ* 197.

[7] Paul Finn, 'Unity then Divergence: The Privy Council, the Common Laws of England and the Common Laws of Canada, Australia and New Zealand', ch 3 of this volume. Sir Owen Dixon thought it important to keep the Privy Council away from decisions relating to federalism on the basis that those who did not live in a federation did not understand it: *O'Sullivan v Noarlunga Meat Ltd (No 2)* (1956) 94 CLR 367, 375.

[8] See K Roberts-Wray, *Commonwealth and Colonial Law* (London, Stevens & Sons, 1966) 544–57.

of Singapore, that it was not sufficient to provide the basis for the development of a local jurisprudence distinct from English law.[9]

Fourthly, the unity that the Privy Council was able to bring to the common law was a formal one. Not every case went, or was going to go, on appeal to the Privy Council. This meant that local courts could arrive at acceptable solutions applying traditional common law techniques such as reinterpreting English decisions or simply distinguishing them. Writing about the historical development of Australian law, Bruce Kercher has pointed out that it is too simple to assume that the High Court of Australia simply copied the English common law in the first 50 or 60 years of its existence.[10] Moreover, there were bodies of law that may have flourished in local courts at a time at which that law was simply not the subject of a great deal of attention or litigation in England. An example is the development of equity jurisprudence in New South Wales in the course of the twentieth century, made possible by the long delay in introducing the Judicature reforms in that state.[11] This helped to foster a particular 'Australian' attitude to equity at a time when equity jurisprudence in England was, in Finn's words 'petrified, if not forgotten'.[12] It follows that the common law may not in fact have been entirely uniform throughout the British Empire and Commonwealth even during the period in which the Privy Council exercised ultimate control over its development.

Ultimately, the unity of the common law that existed in the period of the Privy Council's supremacy was overwhelmed by forces that produce divergence. Foremost among those factors was the establishment of local ultimate appellate courts and the abolition of appeals to the Privy Council in several major common law jurisdictions. That development was accompanied by an abandonment of the practice of invariably following decisions of the House of Lords, and a broader decline in the deference and precedential weight accorded to decisions of English courts.

There is not, however, a simple causal link between the breakdown in the unity of the common law and the ending of Privy Council appeals. Finn illustrates this by reference to the experience of the three major common law jurisdictions that form a focus of the discussion in this book, namely, Canada, Australia and New Zealand.[13] The process of abolishing appeals to the Privy Council was completed in Canada in 1949, yet, for much of the next two decades, the Supreme Court of Canada continued to bear the appearance of an English court applying English law in Canada. In contrast, in Australia, where the process of dismantling appeals to the Privy Council was only completed in 1986, it was clear from about 1975 that the development of the common law in Australia was not constrained by English authority. Again, while the abolition of Privy Council appeals only occurred in New Zealand in 2003, it was clear by the 1980s that a distinct common law of New Zealand was developing.

What this illustrates is that, apart from the abolition of Privy Council control, at least one other ingredient was necessary to the development of distinct common laws in Australia, Canada and New Zealand—the motivation and desire to do so. That came as local

[9] Goh Yihan, 'A Conscious Effort to Develop a "Different" Common Law of Obligations: A Possible Endeavour?', ch 4 of this volume.

[10] B Kercher, *An Unruly Child: A History of Law in Australia* (St Leonards, Allen & Unwin, 1995) 169–71.

[11] See M Leeming, 'Equity, the Judicature Acts and Restitution' (2011) 5 *Journal of Equity* 199, 216–22.

[12] Finn, above n 7.

[13] ibid.

judges witnessed their own jurisdictions assume their independent identities among the nations of the world as the sun set on the British Empire. It involved a change in mindset. Judges had to free themselves from the shackles of what Kercher has called an 'internalised imperialism',[14] so that the English imprimatur on developments in local common laws was no longer seen as necessary. Canadian, Australian and New Zealand experience also shows that the process of the localisation of common law was facilitated by judicial champions, notably, Bora Laskin and Brian Dickson in Canada, Anthony Mason and William Deane in Australia, and Robin Cooke in New Zealand.[15] In contrast, the change of judicial attitude in Singapore seems to have been more of a co-operative programme of the executive government, the legislature and the judiciary, and was manifested in the enactment of the Application of English Law Act in 1991 and a number of complimentary measures.[16]

Of course, there remain aspects of the inherited law in which common law jurisdictions have maintained commonality, whether in doctrine, taxonomy, underlying approaches, philosophies, principles or policies. As Goh's empirical study shows, that commonality is manifest in the principal reason for the citation of foreign (especially English) cases in Singapore courts, including in the law of obligations, namely, the acknowledgment of the origin of the rule or principle in question. It also explains the reason why Singaporean cases themselves are most cited by courts that share Singapore's common legal heritage, namely, the courts in Australia, England and Hong Kong.[17]

Even where the common law of obligations has not remained entirely uniform at the level of doctrines and rules, an underlying unity may nevertheless be identified. One example of this is the fundamental commitment to party autonomy, which shapes numerous doctrines in the common law of contract, explored in Chapter 14 by Sarah Worthington.[18] Worthington argues that it is only in very limited circumstances that the common law's commitment to party autonomy is trumped by the need to give effect to other social values. She argues that the penalties jurisdiction constitutes an unjustified interference with party autonomy, but in this regard stands alone in the common law of contract, where autonomy otherwise reigns supreme. This argument will no doubt find favour in jurisdictions like Hong Kong (a financial centre) and Singapore (a potential centre of international commercial dispute resolution), which are anxious to develop reputations as jurisdictions that, like England, are strong supporters of party autonomy. On the other hand, the recent expansion of the penalties jurisdiction in Australia appears to throw a strict view of party autonomy open to question.[19] Referring to a pattern of remedial legislation in Australia dealing with unconscionable conduct, unfair terms and unjust transactions, the High Court suggested that there was a 'need for caution in dealing with the unwritten law as if *laissez faire* notions of an untrammelled freedom of contract provide a universal legal value'.[20] At the same time, the Court appeared to endorse one of its own recent decisions[21] in which it had recognised that the penalties jurisdiction was exceptional because of its interference with freedom of contract.[22]

[14] Kercher, above n 10, 163.
[15] Finn, above n 7.
[16] Goh, above n 9.
[17] ibid.
[18] Sarah Worthington, 'Common Law Values: The Role of Party Autonomy in Private Law', ch 14 of this volume.
[19] *Andrews v Australia and New Zealand Banking Group Ltd* [2012] HCA 30, (2102) 247 CLR 205.
[20] ibid [5].
[21] ibid [15].
[22] *Ringrow Pty Ltd v BP Australia Pty Ltd* [2005] HCA 71, (2005) 224 CLR 656 [31]–[32].

II. Divergence

The forces causing divergence between common law jurisdictions are revealed in the reasons that led to local dissatisfaction with the Privy Council as the final court of appeal for common law jurisdictions. The central force was the conviction that the House of Lords or the Privy Council had, in a number of cases on appeal from overseas jurisdictions, simply gotten the (local) law wrong. There is nothing unusual about this. Appellate courts operating independently of one another will sometimes simply adopt different views as to what justice or policy requires in particular circumstances, particularly in relation to questions that are finely balanced. Inevitably, issue will be taken with the articulation of doctrine and the results in particular cases, particularly where the approach does not accord with views taken in other appellate courts, especially if a majority view is challenged in dissenting judgments. Disagreement and dissent of this nature are an essential part of the development of the common law. They do not result in a change in the hierarchy of courts. Local dissatisfaction with the unified common law model did. This was because its central theme came to be that the Privy Council got local law wrong because it had applied English law.

As Finn points out, the problem was that the English version of the common law was parochial, one that was inappropriate (for whatever reason) in local circumstances or offended local values.[23] In the context of the law of obligations, Finn argues that inappropriateness centred on an unduly formal approach to traditional doctrines that were productive of injustice, and on the failure to exact appropriate standards of conduct in relationships and dealings. The response, at least in Australia, Canada and New Zealand, was to move away from legal formalism, requiring transparent reasoning and rational reasons; and to develop what were seen as appropriate standards of conduct, informed by community standards. Although there are differences between the three jurisdictions, the results of this response include the unconscionable dealings doctrine; the emergence of equitable estoppel; the expansion of fiduciary law beyond the protection of economic interests; the acceptance of the remedial constructive trust; the development of the remedy of equitable compensation; and the uncoupling of compensation and liability. A commonality running through these cases in the three jurisdictions is a concern with 'equity' and 'justice', sometimes expressed in the language of 'unconscionability' or 'fairness'.

The inappropriateness of English law to local conditions can sometimes be identified more particularly than this. Goh gives examples from Singapore that are ultimately attributable to Singapore's chronic land shortage:[24] first, the extension of the right to support for land to include buildings on the land, notwithstanding *Dalton v Angus*,[25] in order to promote careful building practices in view of high density land use throughout Singapore; secondly, the imposition of liability for pure economic loss on property developers for defectively constructed buildings, contrary to *Murphy v Brentwood District Council*,[26] in order to protect the investment in high-cost real property which is the single most important investment that a Singaporean is likely to make in his or her lifetime; thirdly, the creation of a tort

[23] Finn, above n 7.
[24] Goh, above n 9.
[25] (1881) 6 App Cas 740 (HL).
[26] [1991] 1 AC 398 (HL).

of harassment to respond to human interaction in an area of high population density. The second of these examples was supported by reference to Commonwealth authority that had already departed from the English view:[27] the third itself provoked the development of a like tort in Hong Kong,[28] another small jurisdiction with high population density.

It is probably impossible to encapsulate in a meaningful universal formula the general circumstances in which local courts take the view that the English (or any other) version of the common law is inappropriate. In 1967, when the Privy Council accepted that the High Court of Australia could refuse to follow a restatement of English law, it did so on the basis that the area of law in question (the availability of exemplary damages) was a matter 'considerably … of domestic or internal significance', which was well settled in Australia, and which should be settled by local policy, since this was an area of law largely fashioned by judicial opinion.[29] This, of course, left open the question how to identify matters of 'domestic or internal significance' and, indeed, why the availability of exemplary damages was an example of such a matter. One suspects that the Privy Council may have had sympathy with the High Court of Australia's stance because the Council was itself less than convinced by the English restatement of the law of exemplary damages, as subsequent developments in English law demonstrate.[30]

One circumstance in which the English (or any other) version of the common law cannot be applied, and where divergence necessarily exists between common law jurisdictions, is where a local statute applies directly to cover the issue before the court and that statute is at odds with the common law. Statute also has the potential to effect divergence in the common law in another way: where a court takes the view that it must develop its common law by analogy to the statute or by reference to the policy underlying the statute. In his contribution to this volume, Sir Anthony Mason investigates the approach of Australian courts to this issue.[31] Unlike the New Zealand courts which have tended to view common law and statute as forming one legal order,[32] Mason points out that Australian courts have been reluctant to apply statutes by analogy or to hold that their underlying policy must now dictate the development of the common law. Mason's essay suggests that there are reasons to think that this aspect of the relationship between common law and statute will not be a major source of divergence between common law jurisdictions: first, because there are a number of technical reasons why such development is complex, including the determination of the scope of the statute; its intended relationship to the common law; the effects of statutory amendment; and the influence that a statute of one part of a federation can have on a general common law of the federation; more generally, because it is often difficult to determine the policies that do underpin statute, not least because there may be a lack of authoritative materials to do so. Moreover, there is a risk that the development of

[27] See E Peel and J Goudkamp, *Winfield and Jolowicz on Tort* 19th edn (London, Sweet & Maxwell, 2014) [10-053].

[28] *Lau Tat Wai v Yip Lai Kuen Joey* [2013] HKCFI 639, [2013] 2 HKLRD 1197.

[29] *Australian Consolidated Press Ltd v Uren* [1969] 1 AC 590 (PC) 641, 642–43.

[30] These include a rebellion by the English Court of Appeal (see H McGregor, *McGregor on Damages* 19th edn (London, Sweet & Maxwell, 2014) [13–003]), and a revival of support for exemplary damages: ibid [13-006]–[13-008].

[31] Anthony Mason, 'A Judicial Perspective on the Development of Common Law Doctrine in the Light of Statute Law', ch 6 of this volume.

[32] See Sian Elias, 'Public Actors and Private Obligations: A Judicial Perspective', ch 7 of this volume.

common law by reference to statute may freeze the common law at a point in time, or lead to incoherence in the law—and, whatever it means, coherence does present a potential hurdle to reliance on statute as a source of the development of the common law. Underlying the general reluctance to develop the common law by reference to statute is also the courts' desire to avoid straying into the legislative arena. While acknowledging that judges are now more willing to recast the common law than they once were, Mason has reservations about Andrew Burrows' view[33] that it is now an abandonment of judicial responsibility for judges to refuse to develop the common law on the ground that the development under consideration should be left to the legislature. Mason regards this as too absolute where there is unresolved political controversy about changes in the law; where changes in the law require inquiries that courts cannot undertake; and where the legal system of a particular jurisdiction takes a narrow view of judicial power.

Statutes (and treaties) that create regional arrangements which have consequences for the law of participating common law jurisdictions are, potentially, an obvious source of divergence between the laws of common law jurisdictions. In Chapter 5, Paula Giliker considers the effect of European law on English law, in particular, its potential to control and shape tort law and policy.[34] She points to the fact that a European law of strict liability has replaced negligence in product liability claims in England, and to the creation of state liability for breach of EU law. At the same time Giliker points out that there are factors that minimise the impact of European law on tort law. One is the nature of the intervention of European law in England: European law can be passed off as local initiative, and the European Court of Justice leaves to local courts a large degree of control over the development of the law. Another is the view that the English judges have of themselves: they are common law (or global) judges, not European judges. The shared legal heritage of the common law ensures that UK judges prefer to engage with material from other common law jurisdictions, illustrating the point made by some comparative lawyers that a bias for the familiar is more common than a search for the best solution. The empirical studies in this volume support this point. Burrows' study leads him to conclude that it is a 'myth' to assume that the comparative interest of English law has shifted from common law to civil law jurisdictions in the law of obligations;[35] while Goh's study shows that, in the years covered by his survey, Singapore courts made reference only to cases from other common law jurisdictions, at least in cases concerned with the law of obligations.[36] Giliker draws attention to what she sees as dangers in the current English comparative approach: its limitation to a select 'old Commonwealth club' and a potential failure to engage with materials from other jurisdictions on issues where it is imperative to do so.

A closely related topic is the potential of human rights law to create divergence between common law jurisdictions. In the United Kingdom this arises through the courts' engagement with the European Convention on Fundamental Rights and Freedoms via the Human Rights Act 1998 (UK), and, in other Commonwealth jurisdictions, through constitutional

[33] See A Burrows, 'The Relationship between Common Law and Statute in the Law of Obligations' (2012) 128 *LQR* 232.

[34] Paula Giliker, 'A Common Law of Tort: Is there a European Rift in the Common Law Family?', ch 5 of this volume.

[35] Burrows, above n 2.

[36] Goh, above n 9.

or statutory instruments. In the context of the law of obligations, the impact of this influence is likely to be felt most acutely in tort law. Giliker points out, however, that the UK courts generally retain their control over the development of tort law and policy by drawing a clear separation between claims in tort law and under the Human Rights Act,[37] as attested by the recent decision of the Supreme Court in *Michael v Chief Constable of South Wales Police*.[38] The development of privacy law is an exception to this. Here the law has clearly been developed in the United Kingdom under the influence of the Human Rights Act. In their contribution to this volume, James Goudkamp and John Murphy expand on this by drawing attention to the differences that now exist in the law of privacy between various Commonwealth jurisdictions.[39]

III. Convergence

We have seen that a number of factors, linked in time particularly to the decline of British power and influence in the world, have resulted, and continue to result, in once formally uniform common law jurisdictions around the world asserting their legal independence. These factors have resulted in divergences in the laws of common law jurisdictions. Goudkamp and Murphy[40] argue that this jurisdictional isolation and divergence is 'self-sustaining' and a 'runaway phenomenon', meaning that the laws of the various jurisdictions will grow ever further apart, each being less relevant to the others in the development of their respective common laws. The early separation of the United States from the United Kingdom is testimony to this. For Goudkamp and Murphy one result of this will be to diminish the likelihood of discovering a universal theory of tort law, which is already proving difficult enough.

It is clear, however, that this has not yet happened. It is undoubtedly true that with jurisdictional isolation comes a concentration on, even a pride in, and perhaps a flowering of, local jurisprudence. Goh's empirical study shows how the Singapore courts increasingly cited their own decisions once their legal independence was clearly established.[41] This enabled the imported law to 'be cultivated with an acute awareness of the soil into which it had been transplated'[42]—with all that implied. The words quoted in the last sentence are those of Justice Andrew Phang. But the same judge was later to say, in the Singapore Court of Appeal, that, in today's interconnected world, 'local courts ought to eschew parochialism' in the development of the law.[43]

This points to the fact that, just as there are, and have been, factors driving divergence, so there are factors that promote convergence. Internationalisation or globalisation is an obvious one, especially in the area of commercial law, widely defined.[44] Indeed, the same

[37] Giliker, above n 34.

[38] *Michael v Chief Constable of South Wales Police* [2015] UKSC 2, [2015] 2 WLR 343 [123]–[128], [130] (Lord Toulson), cf [196] (Lady Hale).

[39] Goudkamp and Murphy, above n 1.

[40] ibid.

[41] Goh, above n 9.

[42] *Tang Kin Hwa v Traditional Chinese Medicine Practitioners Board* [2005] 4 SLR(R) 604 (SGHC) [27].

[43] *Man Financial (S) (Pte) Ltd v Wong Bark Chaun David* [2008] 1 SLR(R) 663 (SGCA) [132].

[44] Consider Goh's empirical study, above n 9.

factors that promote divergence may also promote convergence. The EU law that potentially creates divergences between the English common law and the common law of other jurisdictions may also potentially result in convergence between English law and the civil laws of the European Union. And, just as common laws may diverge where it is inappropriate for whatever reason that the common law of one common law jurisdiction should be the same as that in another, so there may be situations in which it is appropriate that one common law jurisdiction should borrow from another. Hong Kong's adoption of Singapore's harassment tort, which has already been mentioned,[45] is an example of this.

It should also be noted that *some* convergence between common law jurisdictions may be achieved in the recognition of the need to develop the common law judicially, notwithstanding differences in the details of that development. Goudkamp and Murphy draw attention to two developments in the common law that illustrate this: defences in defamation and privacy.[46] The demand for law reform in these areas arose in the jurisdictions concerned at around the same time. Although, as Goudkamp and Murphy point out, there were, inevitably, a variety of responses from the jurisdictions concerned taking into account their constitutional structures or statutory laws, all the jurisdictions achieved a convergence in the need to develop the common law in these two areas for the purposes of providing a 'responsible journalism' defence in defamation in order to accommodate modern understandings of freedom of expression; and of responding to demands for greater protection of individual privacy than was possible in existing torts. The independent recognition by common law courts in various jurisdictions of the need for the judicial development of the law in these areas is, no doubt, attributable to the strength of the underlying unity of the common law.

Dame Sian Elias draws our attention to how this underlying unity (including the structure, values and methodology of the common law) can, potentially, promote not only convergence between common law jurisdictions but also between bodies of law that are traditionally recognized as distinct.[47] In her chapter in this volume, she addresses the responses of common law jurisdictions to the understanding of the relationship between private and public law that has arisen, and continues to develop, since the emergence of modern administrative law. Having regard to the nature and responsibilities of government and public bodies, Elias regards that relationship as requiring recognition by private law of what is 'public' *and* of the importance of enforcing 'private rights'—both in such a way that 'the law of obligations should not cede the ground to public law'. In disputes in the law of obligations, this means that the courts must have regard to the fact, where relevant, that one of the parties is a public actor, while at the same time recognising 'the private interests that are involved in correction of wrongs or the fulfilment of promises or the redress of what is unfair or unreasonable and unconscionable'. This is reinforced at the level of remedies: remedies in private law are available as of course (whereas those in judicial review proceedings are discretionary) and are generally unconstrained by separation of powers deference (again, unlike in judicial review proceedings). Elias investigates the implications of her approach in a number of areas of the law of obligations at the interface of private and public law, including: the extent to which implication of contractual terms of fairness, reasonableness and good faith should be informed by public law principles; the

[45] Above n 28.
[46] Goudkamp and Murphy, above n 1.
[47] Elias, above n 32.

reach of fiduciary obligations; and the extent to which compensation for breach of certain torts should overlap with, or be informed by the principles that govern, the assessment of compensation for breach of a corresponding right in applicable human rights law. While the underlying values of the common law in these and other areas may seem to point generally in the direction of convergence, the search for the best solution to particular disputes in individual common law jurisdictions will inevitably be affected by local values. These values may be found in local legislation, and their application may result in divergences with other common law jurisdictions. For example, New Zealand conditions, including the force of New Zealand statute law, justified the refusal of the New Zealand courts to follow the decision of the House of Lords in *Murphy v Brentwood District Council*,[48] preferring to maintain the liability of local authorities to purchasers of a defectively constructed building for pure economic loss resulting from the local authority's negligence in exercising its statutory functions of approval or inspection.[49]

Of course, in searching for the best solution in controversial cases such as this, common law courts are now able to draw on the decisions of all other common law jurisdictions. What Burrows[50] and Goh[51] demonstrate in their empirical studies is that, beyond the United States, the courts of jurisdictionally independent common law countries are frequently consulting each other—and to a greater extent than they did in the period of the formal unity of the common law. Leaving aside situations in which the purpose of citation is simply to acknowledge the origin of a rule or principle in the common law or to embellish a judgment with further authority, common law courts cite one another, and analyse each others' judgments, to provide a basis for the development of their own common laws, which may, of course, involve a rejection of developments elsewhere. Burrows points out that it is hardly surprising that this should happen in the English courts. In the past, the Privy Council has been a court that had to engage in comparative jurisprudence. It continues to do so. What has changed since the period of formal unity of the common law came to an end is that the Privy Council and the Supreme Court are now involved in a dialogue of equals with the common laws of the jurisdictions that they formerly controlled. This means, among other things, that English law may follow developments in other common law jurisdictions in preference to existing English law. A good example is the recent decision in *FHR European Ventures LLP v Cedar Capital Properties LLC*,[52] where the Supreme Court followed the courts in other common law jurisdictions in deciding that, contrary to the English authorities, a bribe or secret commission received by an agent is held on constructive trust for the principal.

IV. Theories of Unity, Divergence and Convergence

What, then, are the respective merits and underlying drivers of unity, convergence and divergence? Should divergence in the common law of obligations be viewed with regret,

[48] *Murphy v Brentwood District Council* [1998] 1 AC 398 (HL).
[49] *Invercargill City Council v Hamlin* [1996] AC 624 (PC).
[50] Burrows, above n 2.
[51] Goh, above n 9.
[52] *FHR European Ventures LLP v Cedar Capital Partners LLC* [2014] UKSC 45, [2015] 1 AC 250.

or viewed positively, as a manifestation of independence as different jurisdictions adapt the common law to local circumstances and make independent choices in relation to hard questions? Is an increasing divergence inevitable, or are there forces that, at a deep level, hold the common law together? This volume provides a range of different responses to, and perspectives on, these normative and predictive questions.

The divergences between the common law of the United States and those of Commonwealth countries are particularly wide. In their landmark study *Form and Substance in Anglo-American Law*, Atiyah and Summers analysed the distinctive type of reasoning employed in the United States, which inclines more towards matters of substance (morality, economics and politics), while English law inclines more towards form (the application of rules without direct regard to considerations of justice or the consequences of particular decisions).[53] The divide identified by Atiyah and Summers is borne out by Peter Cane's analysis of the divergence between US, English and Australian law in relation to the influence of sovereign immunity on liability in tort.[54] Sovereign immunity remains largely intact in the United States, has been abrogated by extensive exceptions in English law, and has effectively been abolished in Australian law. Cane sees the US approach as reflecting a public law model of tort liability, in which tort liability effectively represents just one of a number of tools for controlling and constraining the exercise of public power. In England and Australia, on the other hand, the tort liability of public authorities follows a private law model which is concerned with redressing wrongs, and which serves the same functions as the tort liability of individuals. The reasons for that divergence are of particular interest. Cane notes and rejects the explanation that the US position is based on a historical misunderstanding by US judges of English law, preferring the view that it is based on different understandings of the relationships between, and respective responsibilities of, different arms of government and, more deeply, on different conceptions of law. The public law model reflects an instrumentalist understanding of law, which sees it as a means to various ends, while the private law model reflects a non-consequentialist view, which sees public authority liability as an institutional analogue of interpersonal justice.

Dan Priel analyses the divide between US and Commonwealth common law at an even deeper level.[55] His analysis not only points to the basis of that particular divergence, but also offers an explanation as to why attitudes to divergence differ so widely, with some resisting divergence and others celebrating it. Priel argues that our attitude to divergence depends on our understanding of the authority of the common law. On its face the common law appears undemocratic, since it is made by unelected judges. Broadly, there are three ways in which the common law can be seen to have legitimate authority in spite of that appearance. The first approach sees the appearance as deceptive and the common law as fundamentally democratic on the basis that, even if it is not all produced directly by elected representatives, the common law is the product of state institutions operating under democratic control. Law made by the judiciary can on this view be seen as akin to delegated legislation. Secondly, it may be thought the authority of the common law is not dependent

[53] PS Atiyah and RS Summers, *Form and Substance in Anglo-American Law: A Comparative Study in Legal Reasoning, Legal Theory and Legal Institutions* (Oxford, Clarendon Press, 1987).

[54] Peter Cane, 'The Tort Liability of Public Authorities: A Comparative Analysis', ch 8 of this volume.

[55] Dan Priel, 'The Philosophies of the Common Law and their Implications: Common Law Divergences, Public Authority Liability and the Future of a Common Law World', ch 11 of this volume.

on the state, but on the conformity of its content to an external standard of morality or natural law. The third approach denies that democracy is the only legitimate source of authority, and sees the authority of the common law as grounded in tradition rather than in the authority of the state.

If, following the first view, we see the common law as fundamentally democratic, then unity across jurisdictions may in some respects be an empirical fact but it is not an ideal for which the law does or should aim. The common law, like statute law, is fundamentally local. This democratic understanding of the authority of the common law has long held sway in the United States, and this is reflected in a number of distinctive features of US law, including the practice of electing judges. If, on the second view, we see the authority of the common law as grounded in morality or natural law then we should see (or aim for) universal convergence, not only within the common law but across all legal systems. On this view the common law, like civil law, is fundamentally universal. If, in accordance with the third view, the authority of the common law is grounded in tradition, then common law jurisdictions should aim to maintain unity with each other, and have no reason to converge with civil law. Priel suggests that that divergence between common law systems will inevitably increase as support for the traditional view of the authority of the common law wanes.

Allan Beever strongly embraces the second model of the common law's authority identified by Dan Priel, and analyses divergence from the point of view of that understanding.[56] Beever sees divergence in the common law as something that is legitimate and desirable, on the one hand, while being regrettable and something to be avoided on the other. The reason for this is that, for Beever, the law aims at a universal moral truth, but we cannot be sure what that truth is. Divergence is desirable because independent common law jurisdictions can engage in experiments in legal justice which ultimately strengthen the common law. Since all jurisdictions are aiming at the same thing, which is universal moral justice, then when two diverge at least one of them must be wrong. Understood in this light, divergences involve disharmony and manifest error, but may be understood as steps on the path towards the perfection of legal justice.

In Chapter 9, Niamh Connolly studies divergence and convergence in the common law through varying attitudes towards public authority liability.[57] Like Peter Cane, Connolly observes the convergence between English and Australian law in this area, but Connolly sees the movement in those jurisdictions as part of a broader trend across the common law world towards the acceptance of government liability. From Connolly's broader perspective, the United States can be seen even more clearly as an outlier. The other major common law jurisdictions, though advancing in different ways and moving forward at different times, can all be seen to be on convergent paths towards the abolition of governmental immunity. Connolly attributes this convergence to a shared understanding of private law which is grounded in morality and respect for the individual, and which values freedom and equality very highly. This shared conception of private law is inherently hostile to the idea of immunities, which frustrate interpersonal justice and arbitrarily and unjustifiably subordinate individual interests to collective interests. The dismantling of government immunities reflects a shift in legal culture from the nineteenth to the twentieth century in which there

[56] Allan Beever, 'How to Have a Common Private Law: The Presuppositions of Legal Conversation', ch 10 of this volume.

[57] Niamh Connolly, 'We'll Meet Again: Convergence in the Private Law Treatment of Public Law Bodies', ch 9 of this volume.

is an increased concern to do justice in individual cases, and a growing reluctance to apply formal rules which may operate unjustly. Connolly also suggests that the rise of the corporation has brought with it a greater comfort with institutional responsibility and accountability, and an understanding that artificial persons are proper targets for liability. These shifts in private law have gone hand in hand with an increased concern in public law with the control of state power and the protection of individual interests.

TT Arvind argues that common law jurisdictions are converging in another direction altogether, which is the direction of a retreat from the common law of obligations, and a shift in emphasis towards other bodies of law.[58] Arvind sees this trend in the heightened concern in public authority liability cases about the imposition of private law standards interfering with the functioning of public bodies; in the rise of specific statutory regulatory regimes usurping the role of the common law of obligations; and in statutory provisions undermining or restricting common law causes of action. Arvind sees common law jurisdictions moving together in these respects, but sees the common law of obligations as a whole diverging dramatically from its own past. Arvind's answer to this tendency is that we need to bring the state back into our understanding and analysis of the common law of obligations, recognising its role as a form of governance and the functions it serves.

V. Conclusion

It is clear from the essays in this collection that the relations between the bodies of law of independent common law jurisdictions are far from straightforward. Those relations can only be understood in light of their history, since in some respects their interactions continue to be influenced by reactions to past events. Beyond this, the relations are appropriately described in terms of divergence and convergence. Neither is, however, inevitable. In some cases, local circumstances (including the force of statutory law) may dictate divergent solutions in different jurisdictions. In others, the unifying values and methodology of the common law may argue in favour of convergence. One thing is clear: the courts of common law jurisdictions can learn from one another. Speaking for the UK Supreme Court, Lord Neuberger has recently said:[59]

> As overseas countries secede from the jurisdiction of the Privy Council, it is inevitable that inconsistencies in the common law will develop between different jurisdictions. However, it seems to us highly desirable for all those jurisdictions to learn from each other, and at least to lean in favour of harmonising the development of the common law around the world.

[58] TT Arvind, 'Obligations, Governance and Society: Bringing the State Back In', ch 12 of this volume.

[59] *FHR European Ventures LLP v Cedar Capital Partners LLC* [2014] UKSC 45, [2015] AC 250 [45].

2

The Influence of Comparative Law on the English Law of Obligations

ANDREW BURROWS*

Those familiar with my work will know that I am essentially a doctrinal English lawyer concerned with practical legal scholarship. So this chapter on comparative law, which has at its heart an empirical survey, is not exactly within my comfort zone. Nevertheless when I looked at the stated comparative law themes of the Obligations VII Conference in 2014, it forcibly struck me, and I am ashamed to admit it, that I simply did not know how much use is being made of comparative law, including comparative common law, by English courts in relation to the law of obligations. I also thought that an examination of this topic would fit very well, at a high level of generality, with the themes of the conference. So for better or for worse this is a chapter on the influence of comparative law, especially comparative common law, on the English law of obligations.

I. Introduction

In a foreword to a book entitled *French for Lawyers*[1] in 1997 Lord Woolf MR wrote the following:

> [T]here was a time when English lawyers, if they were prepared to seek help from another jurisdiction, would only look to other common law jurisdictions. This is now changing. The House of Lords and the judiciary in general now recognise that civil jurisdictions have much to offer … there is, I believe, a real process of harmonisation between the civil and common law legal systems.

Professor Kötz in the 1998 third edition of his great co-authored work, Zweigert and Kötz's *An Introduction to Comparative Law*, wrote this:[2] 'Courts in England … and other

* I would like to thank Andrew Robertson and Michael Tilbury for inviting me to speak at Obligations VII in Hong Kong and for their superb organisation of a memorable conference. I would also like to thank Sophia Hurst, formerly of Brasenose College, for her invaluable research assistance. I am extremely grateful to Professor Keith Stanton of Bristol University for sending me, and allowing me to use, the raw data of his pioneering survey of the use of comparative law in tort cases by the House of Lords and Supreme Court 1990–2013. This survey underpins his article 'Comparative Law in the House of Lords and Supreme Court' (2013) 42 *Common Law World Review* 269.

[1] D Ditner and E Steiner, *French for Lawyers* (London, Hodder Arnold H & S, 1997).

[2] K Zweigert and H Kötz, *An Introduction to Comparative Law* (Oxford, OUP, 1998) 19. As regards English law, the text goes on to refer to judgments of Lord Goff and Lord Bingham.

commonwealth countries have long made reciprocal reference to each other's decisions and are now invoking continental law to a remarkable degree'. More recently, and more generally, Mads Andenas and Duncan Fairgrieve have written that 'Courts make use of comparative law, and make open reference to it, to an unprecedented extent'.[3]

It is in the light of those claims that the central part of the chapter comprises a survey of the last 25 years of decisions in the House of Lords and UK Supreme Court which seeks to assess the influence of comparative common and civil law on the English law of tort, contract and unjust enrichment. In the context of the law of obligations, answers are sought to questions such as the following. How commonplace is the use of comparative law in the United Kingdom's highest court? Is it accurate to regard our Supreme Court judges as being influenced as much today by civil law as by the law in common law systems? Should English practitioners and law students be spending more time considering comparative material?

However, I want to begin by looking at the 'one common law' model and its demise in the second half of the twentieth century. This is crucial historical background because, until that demise, there was no scope for, for example, comparative Australian common law influencing English law: Australian common law and English common law were one and the same.

II. The 'One Common Law' and Its Demise

'One Common Law'

In the early part of the twentieth century, the British Commonwealth was united by a model of law which largely rested on there being 'one common law' which was English law. Decisions of the House of Lords were in practice, if not in form, treated as binding and the highest court for appeals from Commonwealth courts outside the United Kingdom was the Privy Council sitting in London and largely comprised of Law Lords.

So Justice Michael Kirby has written of Australia and New Zealand: 'For a large part of the twentieth century a self-imposed tradition of largely unquestioning adherence to House of Lords decisions existed in both Australia and New Zealand'.[4] In 1943, in *Piro v W Foster & Co Ltd*,[5] Chief Justice Latham in the High Court of Australia, while acknowledging that House of Lords decisions were not technically binding, went on:

> [I]t should now be formally decided that it will be a wise general rule of practice that in cases of clear conflict between a decision of the House of Lords and of the High Court, this court, and other courts in Australia, should follow a decision of the House of Lords upon matters of general legal principle.[6]

[3] In G Canivet, M Andenas and D Fairgrieve (eds), *Comparative Law before the Courts* (London, BIICL, 2004) xxvii.

[4] M Kirby, 'The Old Commonwealth: Australia and New Zealand' in L Blom-Cooper, B Dickson and G Drewry (eds), *The Judicial House of Lords 1876–2009* (Oxford, OUP, 2009) 339.

[5] *Piro v W Foster & Co Ltd* (1943) 68 CLR 313 (HCA).

[6] ibid 320. See also 325–26 (Rich J), 326–27 (Starke J), 336 (McTiernan J), 341 (Williams J).

As regards Canada, it was in an Ontario case being appealed to the Privy Council, *Robins v National Trust Company*,[7] that Lord Dunedin giving the advice of the Board, famously said:

> [W]hen an appellate Court in a colony which is regulated by English law differs from an appellate Court in England, it is not right to assume that the Colonial Court is wrong. It is otherwise if the authority in England is that of the House of Lords. That is the supreme tribunal to settle English law, and that being settled, the Colonial Court, which is bound by English law, is bound to follow it. Equally, of course, the point of difference may be settled so far as the Colonial Court is concerned by a judgment of this Board.[8]

In Robert Sharpe's words, 'The imposition of the House of Lords as the infallible oracle for the entire empire was readily accepted in Canada'.[9]

The merits of this 'one common law' model were no doubt regarded as being certainty, consistency, coherence and comprehensiveness. In Justice Kirby's words, 'great weight was ... placed on maintaining uniformity within the English common law or "*the* Common Law" as it was usually described'.[10] No lesser a judge than Sir Owen Dixon commented, as late as 1946 in *Wright v Wright*,[11] that 'diversity in the development of the common law ... seems to me to be an evil'.

Of course, this 'one common law' model did not hold good across the whole of the Commonwealth because, even though appeals lay to the Privy Council, some jurisdictions, such as South Africa, were mixed rather than pure common law jurisdictions. The position of Scotland, albeit with appeals to the House of Lords, was also distinct and unique. Moreover, one should remember that there were common law jurisdictions—most obviously the United States of America—that were not part of the Commonwealth and where there were no appeals to the Privy Council. In all those jurisdictions, English law, the one common law, was not binding albeit that it might be persuasive.

Demise of the 'One Common Law'

It is only relatively recently that we have seen the erosion of the 'one common law' model. This is primarily the consequence of the recognition in Canada, Australia and New Zealand that decisions of the House of Lords are not binding. It is also linked to the abolition of the right of appeal to the Privy Council from those jurisdictions. English law may be persuasive in those jurisdictions but it is no longer binding.

In Canada,[12] civil appeals to the Privy Council were abolished by the Supreme Court Act 1949 (Can). But it was not until the 1960s that the Canadian Supreme Court broke free from subservience to English law. As late as 1959 it was being complained that Canadian decisions read as if they were written by 'English judges applying English law in Canada, rather than those of Canadian judges developing Canadian law to meet Canadian needs

[7] *Robins v National Trust Company* [1927] AC 515 (PC).

[8] ibid 519.

[9] R Sharpe, 'The Old Commonwealth: Canada' in L Blom-Cooper, B Dickson and G Drewry (eds), *The Judicial House of Lords 1876–2009* (Oxford, OUP, 2009) 351.

[10] Kirby, above n 4, 340.

[11] *Wright v Wright* (1948) 77 CLR 191 (HCA) 210.

[12] See generally Sharpe, above n 9, 351–59.

with guidance of English precedent'.[13] In the 1960s, the Canadian Supreme Court began to develop what Chief Justice Dickson described as 'a distinctively Canadian jurisprudence'.[14] Robert Sharpe has described this as a move from obedience to persuasion: 'English jurisprudence is no longer accorded automatic precedence, and its acceptance rests entirely upon its persuasiveness'.[15]

In Australia,[16] appeals to the Privy Council were legislatively abolished in stages: first, by the Privy Council (Limitation of Appeals) Act 1968 in Federal matters; secondly, by the Privy Council (Appeals from the High Court) Act 1975 from the High Court; and thirdly, and finally, by the Australia Act 1986 from State supreme courts. In 1963 in *Parker v R*,[17] the High Court of Australia for the first time decided that a recent House of Lords authority (on the *mens rea* for murder) would not be followed in Australia and this was confirmed in *Skelton v Collins*[18] which, contrary to the House of Lords' decision in *West (H) and Son Ltd v Shephard*,[19] rejected the awarding of a substantial sum of damages for loss of amenity to an unconscious seriously injured claimant. In similar vein, the Privy Council in *Australian Consolidated Press Ltd v Uren*[20] accepted that the High Court of Australia was entitled to reject the limitations on the availability of punitive damages set by the House of Lords in *Rookes v Barnard*.[21] In *Viro v R*,[22] the High Court held that it was no longer bound to follow decisions of the Privy Council, with minor possible exceptions. In 1986 in *Cook v Cook*,[23] the High Court stated that, while Australian courts would 'continue to obtain assistance and guidance from the learning and reasoning of United Kingdom courts'[24] their influence would depend on their quality: 'subject, perhaps, to the special position of decisions of the House of Lords given in the period in which appeals lay from this country to the Privy Council, the precedents of other legal systems are not binding and are useful only to the degree of persuasiveness of their reasoning'.[25]

The evolution was even slower in New Zealand.[26] It was not until the early 1970s in *Ross v McCarthy*[27] and *Bognuda v Upton & Shearer Ltd*[28] that the New Zealand Court of Appeal recognised that it was not bound by decisions of the House of Lords. In an article in 1987 entitled 'The New Zealand National Legal Identity'[29] Sir Robin Cooke declared that 'New Zealand Law … has now evolved into a truly distinctive body of principles and

[13] H Read, 'The Judicial Process in Common Law Canada' (1959) 37 *Canadian Bar Review* 265, 268.

[14] R Sharpe and K Roach, *Brian Dickson: A Judge's Journey* (Toronto, University of Toronto Press, 2003) 317–20.

[15] Sharpe, above n 9, 351, 355.

[16] See generally, Kirby, above n 4, 340–47, 349–50; Murray Gleeson, 'The Privy Council—an Australian Perspective' (lecture delivered in London in June 2008), available at www.hcourt.gov.au/assets/publications/speeches/former-justices/gleesoncj/cj_18jun08.pdf.

[17] *Parker v R* (1963) 111 CLR 610 (HCA).

[18] *Skelton v Collins* (1966) 115 CLR 94 (HCA).

[19] *West (H) and Son Ltd v Shephard* [1964] AC 326 (HL).

[20] *Australian Consolidated Press Ltd v Uren* [1969] 1 AC 590 (PC).

[21] *Rookes v Barnard* [1964] AC 1129 (HL).

[22] *Viro v R* (1978) 141 CLR 88 (HCA).

[23] *Cook v Cook* (1986) 162 CLR 376 (HCA).

[24] ibid 390.

[25] ibid.

[26] See generally K Keith, 'The Unity of the Common Law and the Ending of Appeals to the Privy Council' (2005) 54 *ICLQ* 197; Kirby, above n 4, 340, 347–50.

[27] *Ross v McCarthy* [1970] NZLR 449 (CA).

[28] *Bognuda v Upton & Shearer Ltd* [1972] NZLR 741 (CA).

[29] R Cooke 'The New Zealand National Legal Identity' (1987) 3 *Canterbury Law Review* 171, 182.

practices, reflecting a truly distinctive outlook'; and in 1996 in *Invercargill CC v Hamlin*,[30] in a case on the tort of negligence in the context of defective building, the Privy Council accepted that the New Zealand Court of Appeal was entitled to depart from English decisions not least because local conditions might differ from those in England. Finally, by the Supreme Court Act 2003 (NZ), the right of appeal to the Privy Council was abolished and the New Zealand Supreme Court was created as the final appellate body.[31]

Plainly the consequence of these developments is that one must now talk about Australian common law, Canadian common law and New Zealand common law, and elsewhere of Indian common law, Malaysian common law, Hong Kong common law, and so on. These are all distinctive common laws and may, and do, differ from the English common law.

It is of importance and interest to consider why the 'one common law' model—the harmonisation of the common law—has collapsed. Several reasons may be suggested.

1. Even though starting from essentially the same materials, different judges can reasonably take different doctrinal positions as to how the law should be developed. Even within one jurisdiction, dissenting judgments are accepted and are relatively common.[32] So, the judges of other jurisdictions might simply have taken the view that their own approach to a question on the common law was to be preferred to that taken by the House of Lords. For example, on punitive damages, *Rookes v Barnard*[33] has been widely criticised because the categories for which the House of Lords retained punitive damages lack any convincing rationale. It is not at all surprising therefore that in *Uren v John Fairfax & Sons Pty Ltd*[34] the High Court of Australia (upheld, as we have seen, by the Privy Council in *Australian Consolidated Press Ltd v Uren*)[35] did not wish to follow it.
2. The particular social conditions, values, culture and history of a country may mean that an appropriate development for England and Wales is not appropriate elsewhere. This was the point stressed by the Privy Council when it accepted that Australian and New Zealand courts could go their own way in cases such as *Uren* and *Invercargill*, although one may have considerable doubts as to whether there were such relevant differences on the facts of those cases.
3. The rest of the law in those countries, in particular statute law, may dictate that a different development of the common law is appropriate. Unless one believes that statute and common law can be entirely sealed off from each other, statutory law can affect common law in various ways. So, for example, the statutory no-fault accident compensation scheme in New Zealand may impact on the common law of tort in that country in ways that are irrelevant in England and Wales.
4. The judges of a country may have wished to develop the common law differently as an exercise in asserting the country's independence from Britain.

[30] *Invercargill CC v Hamlin* [1996] 1 NZLR 513 (PC).

[31] This followed Office of the Attorney General, *Discussion Paper: Reshaping New Zealand's Appeal Structure* (2000), available at www.crownlaw.govt.nz/uploads/PCDiscuss.pdf.

[32] Over the last 40 years, there were dissents in, on average, 18% of cases in the House of Lords/Supreme Court: see A Paterson, *Final Judgment: The Last Law Lords and the Supreme Court* (Oxford, Hart Publishing, 2013) 113.

[33] *Rookes v Barnard* [1964] AC 1129 (HL).

[34] *Uren v John Fairfax & Sons Pty Ltd* (1966) 117 CLR 118 (HCA).

[35] *Australian Consolidated Press Ltd v Uren* [1969] 1 AC 590 (PC).

5. The impracticability in terms of cost and time of having appeals heard by the Privy Council in London, often thousands of miles from the jurisdiction in question, may be thought to have been influential in inspiring countries to develop home-grown solutions administered by their home courts.

If diversity rather than uniformity has come to be regarded as a desirable development in common law jurisdictions, it may make one think very carefully about the present reverse academic movement to harmonise private law across the European Union. Lord Rodger in his article, '"Say not the Struggle Naught Availeth": The Costs and Benefits of Mixed Legal Systems', expressed his scepticism about statutory European harmonisation in typically forthright and colourful language:[36]

> [I]t is boring enough to find branches of McDonalds, the Body Shop, and Benneton in every major European city without finding exactly the same law too. To find ourselves tied into a monolithic codified system in which all final decisions are taken in the colourless prose of a court in Luxembourg—presumably increased to an even more enormous number of judges—is unattractive, to say the least.

He went on:

> Nor do I believe that the practical advantages would be so great as actually to justify the change, if politics are kept out of the picture. In the United Kingdom we have rubbed along very well for almost 300 years with two separate systems of private law [English and Scottish] which differ in many ways ... if the British experience shows anything, it is that having a unified form of contract law is not in fact necessary for developing a strong common market. Scots law has been able to exist quite satisfactorily over the last 200 years while trade has spread to create a single market throughout the United Kingdom. If businesses really want to work under one particular legal system rather than another, they can, and do, arrange it by inserting appropriate terms in their contracts.

There will be many English lawyers, one suspects the overwhelming majority, who would agree with Lord Rodger's scepticism.

But whether one agrees with Lord Rodger's preference for diversity or not, there is no doubt that the 'one common law' model no longer applies. The importance of this demise for the purposes of this chapter is that it has opened, or significantly widened, the way for comparative *common law*, as well as comparative civil law, to influence the English law of obligations.

III. English Supreme Court Judges as Foreign Lawyers

Before looking empirically at the influence of comparative law on the English law of obligations, it is worth digressing slightly to bring to light an often unacknowledged oddity about the role of our Supreme Court judges (and the Law Lords before them) which might be thought to make them particularly receptive to the influence of foreign law. The oddity is that our top judges are in two different contexts required to be foreign lawyers: that is, to decide and apply, without expert evidence, the law of a jurisdiction that is not English law.

[36] Lord Rodger, '"Say not the Struggle Naught Availeth": The Costs and Benefits of Mixed Legal Systems' (2003) 78 *Tulane Law Review* 419, 431.

The first is when they are sitting in the Privy Council. As we have seen, some very significant jurisdictions in the Commonwealth (eg Australia, New Zealand and Canada but also India, Pakistan, South Africa, Malaysia, Singapore, Hong Kong and Barbados) have abolished the right of appeal to the Privy Council. But the right of appeal remains for over 30 jurisdictions.[37] Although some judges (including some foreign judges) who are not members of the Supreme Court can sit in the Privy Council, the Privy Council normally comprises UK Supreme Court judges. It is a requirement of their position that, for a surprisingly substantial period of time (approximately 30 per cent to 40 per cent of their sitting time),[38] the UK Supreme Court judges sit (and before them the Law Lords sat) in the Privy Council to hear appeals from many Commonwealth countries. In that capacity the Supreme Court judges are (and before them the Law Lords were) applying the law of the country in question. It may be that, in most of them, English law in practice applies just as it previously did in, for example, Australia, Canada and New Zealand. Even if not, the variation from English law may be minor. However, that may not always be the case. Indeed, in relation to some jurisdictions the law in play is not even common law. So, just as in the past, there were, for example, appeals from Quebec which involved French civil law, so today if there were to be an appeal from Guernsey the Privy Council might be required to give a decision on Norman-French law, and there have been a number of recent appeals from Mauritius to the Privy Council on French civil law or a mix of French civil law and common law.[39] Lord Mance has referred to the 'linguistic relish'[40] with which judges like himself and the late Lord Rodger, a distinguished Roman law scholar, approached cases in the Privy Council, such as those on appeal from Mauritius, involving the need to engage with French and other foreign languages. The fact remains that it is extraordinary that, in cases not applying English law, UK Supreme Court judges have to be able to decide, and decide definitively at the apex of the jurisdiction in question, what the law of that foreign country requires.[41] An ability to understand other systems and reasoning would seem to be a necessary skill for a UK Supreme Court judge to have or to acquire, although it is to

[37] Anguilla, Antigua and Barbuda, Bahamas, Bermuda, British Antarctic Territory, British Indian Ocean Territory, British Virgin Islands, Cayman Islands, Cook Islands and Niue, Dominica, Falkland Islands, Gibraltar, Grenada, Guernsey, Isle of Man, Jamaica, Jersey, Kiribati, Mauritius, Montserrat, Pitcairn Islands, Saint Christopher and Nevis, St Helena and dependencies, St Lucia, St Vincent and the Grenadines, Sovereign Base of Akrotiri and Dhekelia, Trinidad and Tobago, Turks and Caicos Islands, Tuvalu, Brunei Civil Appeals from the Court of Appeal to the Sultan and Yang di-Pertuan for advice to the Sultan.

[38] *The Annual Report of the Supreme Court and Privy Council* (2012–13) records that the JCPC sat for 50 days whereas the Supreme Court sat for 118 days.

[39] See, eg, *Gujadhur v Gujadhur* [2007] UKPC 54; *Raphael Fishing Company Ltd v State of Mauritius* [2008] UKPC 43; *Société Alleck & Cie v Indian Ocean International Bank* [2008] UKPC 62.

[40] Lord Mance, 'Foreign Law and Languages' in A Burrows, D Johnston and R Zimmermann (eds), *Judge and Jurist: Essays in Memory of Lord Rodger of Earlsferry* (Oxford, OUP, 2013) 85, 90. He goes on to say, 'The Privy Council's resilient, and not infrequently, very significant jurisprudence often goes unnoticed in the United Kingdom': ibid 91.

[41] The following passage is from the *Annual Report of the Supreme Court and Privy Council* (2012–13): 'The JCPC is the Court of final appeal for the UK's Overseas Territories, the Crown Dependencies and for those Commonwealth Countries that have retained the appeal to Her Majesty in Council or, in the case of Republics, to the Judicial Committee. [There is then a reference to the list of the relevant countries set out in note 37 above.] 'Although the Judicial Committee was instituted by a United Kingdom Act, the substantive law which it applies is the law of the Country or Territory from which the appeal comes. The Judicial Committee therefore plays an important role in the development of law in the various constituent jurisdictions and the impact of its decisions extends far beyond the parties involved in any given case, and often involves questions arising out of the relevant Constitution and/or the fundamental rights and freedoms of the inhabitants of the Country or Territory.'

be doubted whether many have the additional linguistic skills of a Lord Rodger or a Lord Mance.

The second context is just as peculiar.[42] The UK Supreme Court (and the House of Lords before it) hears appeals, except on criminal law,[43] from Scotland.[44] Over the last 20 years of the House of Lords, it would appear that about 10 per cent of appeals to the House of Lords were from Scotland,[45] and in the first four years of the Supreme Court (2009 to March 2013) the figure was 17 per cent.[46] Scottish law is plainly different from English law. Scotland is a mixed system not a common law jurisdiction. It is no doubt for this reason that for 100 years,[47] by convention, two of the Law Lords and now UK Supreme Court judges have been Scottish lawyers, at least one of whom can be expected to sit on the Scottish appeals. A consequence of this is that, in appeals from Scotland, the 'English' Supreme Court judges are hearing and deciding on questions of Scottish law. Yet prior to being promoted to the Supreme Court it is very unlikely that any of them will have had any experience or knowledge of the law of that jurisdiction. It may be that in practice in modern times the 'English' judges tend to defer to the Scottish judges on matters of Scottish law. But that is not a requirement. Indeed in the past there was Scottish criticism of the Law Lords, including the Scottish Law Lords, for treating questions of Scottish law as if they were questions of English law thereby leading to an unwarranted 'Anglicisation of Scots law'.[48]

It should be noted that another consequence is that the two Scottish Supreme Court judges are required to sit in, and decide, cases on English law.[49] Indeed non-Scottish appeals form the majority of their work. There is, as far as I can tell, no practice or convention that they should defer to their colleagues when deciding an English law case: ie, there is no question of their having a lesser role to play than their colleagues.[50] Yet, until appointed, they are experts on Scottish law not English law, although it is no doubt correct to say that, given that it is a small and mixed jurisdiction, most top lawyers in Scotland know a great deal about English law too even where it does differ from Scottish law.

In considering the need for the top judges in the United Kingdom to be foreign lawyers, there is one other more recent phenomenon that is of interest. When the Hong Kong Court

[42] For an excellent modern analysis, see Paterson, above n 32, 233–46.

[43] Matters have been slightly muddied by appeals on devolution issues under the Scotland Act 1998 which go to the Supreme Court (and, before its creation, went to the Privy Council).

[44] The history of Scottish appeals to the House of Lords is examined by P Brodie, 'From Scotland and Ireland' in L Blom-Cooper, B Dickson and G Drewry (eds), *The Judicial House of Lords 1876–2009* (Oxford, OUP, 2009) 279–94. See also A Paterson, 'Scottish Lords of Appeal 1876–1988' [1988] *Juridical Review* 235. Brodie, commenting in relation to the House of Lords, said that it was largely because leave to appeal on civil matters has not been needed that that percentage represents 'a disproportionate Scottish element in the judicial business of the House': Brodie, above, 284.

[45] Brodie, above n 44, 279, 283–84.

[46] Paterson, above n 32, 233–46.

[47] Since the appointment of Lord Dunedin, as the second Scottish Law Lord, in 1913: see Brodie, above n 44, 279, 288.

[48] AD Gibb, 'Law from Over the Border' in L Blom-Cooper and G Drewry (eds), *Final Appeal: A Study of the House of Lords in its Judicial Capacity* (Oxford, Clarendon Press, 1972) 375–87; Brodie, above n 44, 279, 289–94.

[49] Blom-Cooper and Drewry, above n 48, 386, posed, without answering, the question whether this Scottish influence meant that English law may have become 'Scoticised'.

[50] Sometimes a Scottish Law Lord or Supreme Court judge explains what the law on Scotland is on the point in issue even though the case is on English law: see, eg, *Re Spectrum Plus Ltd* [2005] UKHL 41, [2005] 2 AC 680 [48]–[51]; *Miller v Miller* [2006] UKHL 24, [2006] 2 AC 618 [101]–[121]; *Marley v Rawlings* [2014] UKSC 2, [2014] 1 All ER 807 [87]–[93]. Typical is the approach of Lord Hodge in the last case who commenced his judgment with the following words: 'I agree and confine myself to some observations on how Scots Law might have dealt with the problem if it were the governing law': [87].

of Final Appeal was created in 1997 (and when, at the same time, appeals to the Privy Council from Hong Kong were abolished) it was decided that it would include, as non-permanent members of the court, some top judges from other common law jurisdictions such as the United Kingdom, Australia and New Zealand. So it is that, for example, Lords Hoffmann, Walker and Millett, while being Law Lords and indeed after their retirement from the Lords, have occasionally been out to sit in the Hong Kong court. In doing so, they have been required to apply Hong Kong law not English law.[51]

It is therefore clear, albeit commonly overlooked, that our top judges have to decide and apply foreign law. Of course, it does not necessarily follow from this that they will be in favour of using comparative law in developing English law. But one would have thought that it renders it more likely than would otherwise have been the case that they will be receptive to the merits of comparative law.

IV. Influence on the English Law of Obligations of Foreign Law: A 25-Year Survey

Introduction to the Survey

The survey carried out examines the use of comparative law by the House of Lords and the Supreme Court in cases on tort, unjust enrichment and contract in the last 25 years (1 April 1989–1 April 2014). In this respect, I have drawn on the pioneering work and methodology of Keith Stanton in his article 'Comparative Law in the House of Lords and Supreme Court'.[52] That work was confined to tort cases. I have expanded the survey to cover contract and unjust enrichment and have also slightly expanded the time period covered.

By focusing on the highest court one is of course missing out on the influence of comparative law on the lower courts. Clearly comparative law is used in the lower courts in England.[53] However, it is surely a fair assumption that its influence is greatest in the highest court so that the results of the survey can be taken as reflecting the maximum use of comparative law in the English courts.

I would make the following five methodological points about the survey:

1. Like Stanton,[54] I have taken out of the survey references to Scottish law. This is because of the role of the House of Lords and Supreme Court in being the highest court for

[51] See generally S Young and Y Ghai (eds), *Hong Kong's Court of Final Appeal: The Development of the Law in China's Hong Kong* (Cambridge, CUP, 2014), especially the chapter by A Mason 'The Common Law' 327, 336–47.

[52] K Stanton, 'Comparative Law in the House of Lords and Supreme Court' (2013) 42 *Common Law World Review* 269. For a different type of research on a similar theme, based on interviews with the Supreme Court judges, see E Mak, 'Why do Dutch and UK Judges Cite Foreign Law?' [2011] *CLJ* 420.

[53] An outstanding recent example was the judgment of Leggatt J in *Yam Seng Pte Ltd v International Trade Corporation Ltd* [2013] EWHC 111 (QB) in which, in deciding that there was an implied contractual term of good faith in performance, he relied not only on the civil law tradition but also the case law in Australia, Canada and New Zealand.

[54] Stanton, above n 52, 269, 273. Stanton writes, '[I]t would distort the results of this research to regard references to Scottish law as being to an overseas jurisdiction because the Scottish judges in the Supreme Court clearly see it as part of their function to incorporate Scottish law into the court's decision-making'. My reasoning for this exclusion, as set out in the text, is slightly different.

both systems. For similar reasons (in contrast to Stanton), I have also excluded from the survey appeals from Scotland to the House of Lords or Supreme Court.

2. Like Stanton,[55] I have taken out of the survey references to Privy Council decisions. Prior to the abolition of such appeals, the decisions of the Privy Council on appeals from, eg, Australia, Canada and New Zealand, were very influential on the English law of obligations. In contract, one thinks, for example, of appeals from New Zealand such as *Bisset v Wilkinson*[56] on misrepresentation and *The Eurymedon*[57] on exclusion clauses and privity; from Australia, *Barton v Armstrong*[58] on duress and *The New York Star*[59] on exclusion clauses; and from Canada, *The Strathcona*[60] on burdens being imposed on third parties, and *Maritime National Fish Ltd v Ocean Trawlers Ltd*[61] on self-induced frustration. In tort, one thinks almost immediately of the two appeals from Australia in *The Wagon Mound*[62] on remoteness. And in unjust enrichment there are the well-known appeals from New Zealand in *Auckland Harbour Board v R*[63] on restitution of money paid by a public authority and *Goss v Chilcott*[64] on failure of consideration and change of position. All these cases appear in the standard English textbooks and on English law school reading lists and they are well-known to English law students and practitioners. Indeed, most students would be surprised to realise that, as decisions of the Privy Council, they were and are technically not binding in England and Wales,[65] albeit binding in the relevant jurisdiction. The practical reality is that, because they are decisions of panels largely comprised of Law Lords, seeking to apply English law, they have been treated as if binding.

   The same goes for many other decisions of the Privy Council from jurisdictions in which it was assumed that English law was applicable. Prominent examples include from Hong Kong, *Pao On v Lau Yiu Long*[66] on consideration and economic duress, and *Philips Hong Kong Ltd v A-G of Hong Kong*[67] on penalty clauses; from Nigeria in *Ajayi v RT Briscoe (Nigeria) Ltd*[68] on promissory estoppel; from Jamaica in *Dextra Bank v Bank of Jamaica*[69] on mistake and change of position; from Eastern Africa in *Kiriri Cotton Co Ltd v Dewani*[70] on illegal contracts and mistake of law; from Belize in *A-G of Belize v*

[55] Stanton, above n 52, 269, 273.
[56] *Bisset v Wilkinson* [1927] AC 177 (PC).
[57] *New Zealand Shipping Co Ltd v Satterthwaite & Co Ltd (The Eurymedon)* [1975] AC 154 (PC).
[58] *Barton v Armstrong* [1976] AC 104 (PC).
[59] *Port Jackson Stevedoring Pty Ltd v Salmond & Spraggon (Aust) Pty Ltd (The New York Star)* [1981] 1 WLR 138 (PC).
[60] *Lord Strathcona Steamship Co Ltd v Dominion Coal Co Ltd (The Strathcona)* [1926] AC 108 (PC).
[61] *Maritime National Fish Ltd v Ocean Trawlers Ltd* [1935] AC 524 (PC).
[62] *Overseas Tankship (UK) Ltd v Morts Dock and Engineering Co Ltd* [1961] AC 388 (PC); *Overseas Tankship (UK) Ltd v Miller Steamship Co* [1967] 1 AC 617 (PC).
[63] *Auckland Harbour Board v R* [1924] AC 318 (PC).
[64] *Goss v Chilcott* [1996] AC 788 (PC).
[65] A recent exception to this has been recognised in *R v James and Karimi* [2006] EWCA Crim 14. The Court of Appeal here held that a Privy Council decision was binding and an earlier inconsistent House of Lords decision was not where the Privy Council was seeking deliberately to clarify English law, its members constituted half the members of the House of Lords and, as a result, the outcome of an appeal to the House of Lords was a foregone conclusion.
[66] *Pao On v Lau Yiu Long* [1980] AC 614 (PC).
[67] *Philips Hong Kong Ltd v A-G of Hong Kong* (1993) 61 BLR 41 (PC).
[68] *Ajayi v RT Briscoe (Nigeria) Ltd* [1964] 1 WLR 1326 (PC).
[69] *Dextra Bank v Bank of Jamaica* [2002] 1 All ER (Comm) 193 (PC).
[70] *Kiriri Cotton Co Ltd v Dewani* [1960] AC 192 (PC).

Belize Telecom Ltd[71] on implied terms; and from Jersey in *Pell Frischmann Engineering Co Ltd v Bow Valley Iran Ltd*[72] on contract damages.

It should be plain from this list that appeals to the Privy Council have greatly influenced and enriched the English law of obligations. However, it would be very misleading to describe this as the influence of comparative law. This is because, even if the 'one common law model' no longer held sway at the date of the case in question, the assumption in many of the cases was that the Privy Council was applying English law. For this reason, references to Privy Council decisions have been excluded from the survey.

3. I have not included references to EU law or to the European Convention on Human Rights (ECHR), including references from other jurisdictions to that law. English courts are bound to apply EU law as ultimately interpreted by the European Court of Justice in Luxembourg; and, since the Human Rights Act 1998, are bound to take account of the jurisprudence of the European Court of Human Rights in Strasbourg in interpreting the Convention rights incorporated into English law by that Act. Although one might describe references to decisions in Luxembourg or Strasbourg as involving the influence of 'foreign law' that would be misleading because, first, the foreign law in question is not the law of another country and because, secondly, that law is binding (or in the case of interpreting the ECHR virtually so) as a matter of English law. The now commonplace description of the Luxembourg and Strasbourg Courts as 'supranational' makes abundantly clear that they are part of the English legal framework. My concern in this chapter is not with that type of 'outside' influence. I have therefore excluded it from the survey.
4. It follows from what I said earlier about the demise of the one common law that, in order to consider the influence of comparative *common law*, the focus should essentially be on, eg, Australia, Canada and New Zealand *after* they have seen themselves as developing a distinctive common law. However, for the purposes of simplicity, I have included in the survey references to the laws in other common law jurisdictions at a time before, as well as after, the demise of the one common law model. Certainly the results of the survey do not suggest that there has been any drop in the number of references to the law in other common law courts since those courts stopped seeing themselves as applying English law.
5. The survey includes references to the case law of other jurisdictions however fleeting and including where the comparative law was rejected. For that reason alone, the survey must be viewed as, and is only intended to provide, a relatively crude snap-shot of the position.

Results of the Survey

Tort

As regards tort, of the 113 cases that were decided by the House of Lords or Supreme Court between 1 April 1989 and 1 April 2014, there were references to other common law

[71] *A-G of Belize v Belize Telecom Ltd* [2009] UKPC 10, [2009] 1 WLR 1988 (PC).
[72] *Pell Frischmann Engineering Co Ltd v Bow Valley Iran Ltd* [2009] UKPC 45, [2010] BLR 73.

jurisdictions in 72 cases (64 per cent) and to civil law in 11 cases (10 per cent).[73] Australia was the most cited jurisdiction with references in 56 cases. US law was cited in 42 cases, Canadian law in 36 cases, New Zealand law in 29 cases, German law in 11 cases, French law in nine cases, Irish in seven cases, South African in three cases, Dutch in three cases, Singaporean in one case, Hong Kong in one case, Israeli in one case and Norwegian in one case.

Many of the references to the law in other common law jurisdictions were in support of propositions about existing English law.[74] So, for example, in *Smoker v London Fire and Civil Defence Authority*,[75] Lord Templeman in setting out the law on when collateral benefits will, and will not, be deducted in assessing damages for personal injury included four Australian cases in his survey of the existing law.[76] In *Caparo Industries plc v Dickman*,[77] Lord Oliver illustrated when there is a duty of care in respect of pure economic loss under the principle in *Hedley Byrne & Co Ltd v Heller & Partners Ltd*[78] by referring to two earlier cases in the United States.[79]

In contrast, there have been other, and often more detailed, references to foreign law in support of significant developments in the law that the House of Lords or Supreme Court was undertaking.[80] In *White v Jones*,[81] in which it was held that the intended beneficiary under a will had a claim in the tort of negligence against the solicitor who failed to draw up the will properly, Lord Goff drew on the law in New Zealand, Canada, Australia, the United States, Germany, France and the Netherlands in support of the law being in favour of the claimant having a remedy. In *Williams v Natural Life Health Foods Ltd*,[82] the personal tortious liability of persons acting on behalf of a company was developed with reference to a case in New Zealand[83] and two cases in Canada.[84] In *Lister v Hesley Hall Ltd*,[85] the House of Lords relied heavily on Canadian case law[86] in developing the modern law of vicarious liability. In a particularly wide-ranging use of both civil law and other common law, Lord Bingham in *Fairchild v Glenhaven Funeral Services Ltd*,[87] in developing a novel

[73] Stanton's similar survey of tort cases over a slightly shorter timescale (and including references to ECHR law) produced very similar figures: ie, references to other common law jurisdictions in 66% of cases and references to civil law in 11% of cases.

[74] When used in this way, the law from another common law jurisdiction is essentially filling in gaps where there is no obvious English authority to which one can turn.

[75] *Smoker v London Fire and Civil Defence Authority* [1991] 2 AC 502 (HL).

[76] *National Insurance Co for New Zealand Ltd v Espagne* (1961) 105 CLR 569 (HCA); *Paff v Speed* (1961) 105 CLR 549 (HCA); *Graham v Baker* (1961) 106 CLR 340 (HCA); and *Jones v Gleeson* (1965) 39 ALJR 258 (HCA).

[77] *Caparo Industries plc v Dickman* [1990] AC 605 (HL), 638.

[78] *Hedley Byrne & Co Ltd v Heller & Partners Ltd* [1964] AC 465 (HL).

[79] *Glanzer v Shepard* 135 NE 275 (1922); *Ultramares Corp v Touche* 174 NE 441 (1931).

[80] Very occasionally, the approach in another common law jurisdiction has been *relied on* so as to *reject* a development being advocated. An example of this is *Derbyshire County Council v Times Newspapers Ltd* [1993] AC 534 (HL), where US cases, stressing the importance of free speech, were relied on in rejecting the argument that the English law should be developed so as to allow a local authority to sue for libel.

[81] *White v Jones* [1995] 2 AC 207 (HL).

[82] *Williams v Natural Life Health Foods Ltd* [1998] 1 WLR 830 (HL).

[83] *Trevor Ivory Ltd v Anderson* [1992] 2 NZLR 517 (CA).

[84] *London Drugs Ltd v Kuehne & Nagel International Ltd* (1992) 97 DLR (4th) 261 (SCC); *Edgeworth Construction Ltd v M D Lea & Associates Ltd* [1993] 3 SCR 206.

[85] *Lister v Hesley Hall Ltd* [2002] 1 AC 215 (HL). See also *Catholic Child Welfare Society v Various Claimants and Institute of the Brothers of the Christian Schools* [2012] UKSC 56, [2013] 2 AC 1.

[86] *Bazley v Currie* (1999) 174 DLR (4th) 45 (SCC); *Jacobi v Griffiths* (1999) 174 DLR (4th) 71 (SCC); *John Doe v Bennett* [2004] 1 SCR 436.

[87] *Fairchild v Glenhaven Funeral Services Ltd* [2003] 1 AC 32 (HL).

approach to causation, when dealing with an employee who had contracted mesothelioma after employment by more than one negligent employer, referred to the law in Australia, the United States and Canada, as well as French, German and Dutch law. In *Reynolds v Times Newpapers Ltd*,[88] in which the House of Lords developed the 'responsible journalism' qualified privilege in the law of defamation, cases from, for example, the United States, Australia and New Zealand[89] were carefully examined, albeit that the approach adopted was not identical to any of the solutions applied elsewhere. In *A v Hoare*,[90] in departing from the previous House of Lords decision in *Stubbings v Webb*[91] on the appropriate limitation period for an intentional trespass to the person, Lord Hoffmann accepted as compelling the reasoning of the High Court of Australia in *Stingel v Clark*[92] which had rejected *Stubbings*. In *Jones v Kaney*,[93] in which the Supreme Court (by a 5–2 majority) removed an expert witness's immunity from liability in the tort of negligence, Lord Collins relied on a number of decisions in the United States principally for their articulation of policy reasons for rejecting the immunity.[94] This was so even though the claimant was not seeking to rely on that material. His Lordship said: 'It is highly desirable that at this appellate level, in cases where issues of legal policy are concerned, the court should be informed about the position in other common law countries. This court is often helped by being referred to authorities from other common law systems, including the United States'.[95] Most recently in *Coventry v Lawrence*,[96] Lord Carnwath drew on cases in Australia, New Zealand, Ireland, Canada and the United States to support a more flexible approach to the use of damages, as opposed to injunctions, for the tort of private nuisance.

Sometimes the law in other common law jurisdictions has been examined, albeit to reject it as a way forward for English law. For example, in *Hunter v Canary Wharf Ltd*,[97] the House of Lords rejected US and Canadian authorities which had expanded the class of those who can sue in private nuisance beyond those with an interest in the land. In *Transco plc v Stockport Metropolitan BC*,[98] the High Court of Australia's decision in *Burnie Port Authority v General Jones Pty Ltd*,[99] abolishing the rule in *Rylands v Fletcher*[100] by absorbing it within the tort of negligence, was rejected; as was the High Court of Australia's decision in *Cattanach v Melchior*[101] in the wrongful life decision in *Rees v Darlington Memorial Hospital NHS Trust*.[102]

Turning to the use of civil law in tort cases, the great enthusiasts were, indisputably, Lord Goff and Lord Bingham. The former referred to civil law, especially German law, in

[88] *Reynolds v Times Newpapers Ltd* [2001] 2 AC 127 (HL).

[89] *New York Times Co v Sullivan* 376 US 254 (1964); *Lange v Australian Broadcasting Corp* (1997) 189 CLR 520 (HCA); *Lange v Atkinson* [1998] 3 NZLR 424 (CA) (subsequently [2000] 1 NZLR 257 (PC)).

[90] *A v Hoare* [2008] UKHL 6, [2008] 1 AC 844.

[91] *Stubbings v Webb* [1993] AC 498 (HL).

[92] *Stingel v Clark* [2006] HCA 37, (2006) 80 ALJR 1339.

[93] *Jones v Kaney* [2011] UKSC 13, [2011] 2 AC 398 [76]–[81].

[94] He also referred to a number of cases in Australia, New Zealand and Canada (and the United States), where the immunity had been upheld albeit that in general these did not involve, as this case did, a 'friendly expert' (ie, an expert retained by the client who now wishes to use that expert).

[95] ibid [76].

[96] *Coventry v Lawrence* [2014] UKSC 13, [2014] 2 WLR 433.

[97] *Hunter v Canary Wharf Ltd* [1997] AC 655 (HL).

[98] *Transco plc v Stockport Metropolitan BC* [2004] 2 AC 1 (HL).

[99] *Burnie Port Authority v General Jones Pty Ltd* (1994) 179 CLR 520 (HCA).

[100] *Rylands v Fletcher* (1868) LR 3 HL 330.

[101] *Cattanach v Melchior* [2003] HCA 38, (2003) 215 CLR 1.

[102] *Rees v Darlington Memorial Hospital NHS Trust* [2004] 1 AC 309 (HL).

Henderson v Merrett,[103] in which English law authoritatively accepted concurrent liability; in *White v Jones*,[104] in which, again as we have seen, it was held that the intended beneficiary under a will had a claim in the tort of negligence against the solicitor who failed to draw up the will properly; and in *Hunter v Canary Wharf Ltd*,[105] in which, again as we have seen, the argument was rejected that a person without an interest in land could sue in the tort of private nuisance. As we have also already seen, Lord Bingham made a particularly wide-ranging use of both civil and other common law in *Fairchild v Glenhaven Funeral Services Ltd*.[106] He also referred to German and French law in *Transco plc v Stockport Metropolitan BC*[107] on whether to retain liability under *Rylands v Fletcher*, and to German and Dutch law in the wrongful birth case of *Rees v Darlington Memorial Hospital NHS Trust*.[108]

Unjust Enrichment

As regards unjust enrichment, of the 24 cases that were decided by the House of Lords or Supreme Court between April 1 1989 and April 1 2014, there were references to other common law jurisdictions in 17 cases (71 per cent), and to civil law in two cases (8 per cent). Australia was by far the most cited jurisdiction with references in all the 17 cases where other common law was referred to. Canadian law was referred to in seven cases, New Zealand law in four cases, US law in four cases, South African in two cases, French law in two cases and German law in one case. Lord Goff alone made the references to civil law. The last occasion was in 1999 in *Kleinwort Benson Ltd v Lincoln CC*,[109] in which the mistake of law bar to mistaken payments was abolished.

Many of the references to the law in other common law jurisdictions were in support of propositions about existing English law. For example, Lord Walker in *Pitt v Holt*[110] referred to the Court of Appeal of Victoria in *Hookway v Racing Victoria Ltd*[111] and the New Zealand case of *University of Canterbury v Attorney-General*[112] for general propositions as to, respectively: ignorance triggering a mistake allowing restitution, albeit that the ignorance is not itself a mistake; and a mistake of the donor being as to a fact which is basic to the gift and sufficiently serious to allow restitution where the donee has encouraged or failed to correct that mistake. In *Foskett v McKeown*[113] (which, on one view, is best interpreted as a case on proprietary restitution for unjust enrichment), Lord Millett referred to a number

[103] *Henderson v Merrett* [1995] 2 AC 145 (HL).
[104] *White v Jones* [1995] 2 AC 207 (HL). But note that even Lord Goff in this case expressed the need for caution in using civil law. He said: 'Strongly though I support the study of comparative law, I hesitate to embark in an opinion such as this upon a comparison, however brief, with a civil law system; because experience has taught me how very difficult, and indeed potentially misleading, such an exercise can be. Exceptionally however, in the present case, thanks to material published in our language by distinguished comparativists, German as well as English, we have direct access to publications which should sufficiently dispel our ignorance of German law and so by comparison illuminate our understanding of our own': ibid 263.
[105] *Hunter v Canary Wharf Ltd* [1997] AC 655 (HL).
[106] *Fairchild v Glenhaven Funeral Services Ltd* [2003] 1 AC 32 (HL).
[107] *Transco plc v Stockport Metropolitan BC* [2004] 2 AC 1 (HL).
[108] *Rees v Darlington Memorial Hospital NHS Trust* [2004] 1 AC 309 (HL).
[109] *Kleinwort Benson Ltd v Lincoln City Council* [1999] 2 AC 349 (HL).
[110] *Pitt v Holt* [2013] UKSC 26, [2013] 2 WLR 1200 [105] and [121].
[111] *Hookway v Racing Victoria Ltd* [2005] VSCA 310.
[112] *University of Canterbury v Attorney-General* [1995] 1 NZLR 78 (HC).
[113] *Foskett v McKeown* [2001] 1 AC 102 (HL), 135.

of decisions in the United States[114] as illustrating the rules of tracing on the implicit assumption that they were the same as in English law. And in *Royal Bank of Scotland Plc v Etridge (No 2)*,[115] in which a contract of guarantee between a wife and a bank was rescinded (with consequent restitution) because of undue influence by a husband, the Australian case of *Yerkey v Jones*[116] was relied on for the proposition that, and for explaining why, a relationship of husband and wife is not a relationship of influence for the purposes of the law of undue influence.

In contrast, some of the most detailed references to foreign law have been in support of significant developments in the law that the House of Lords or Supreme Court was undertaking. So, for example, Lord Goff made extensive references to the law in other common law jurisdictions (Australia, Canada, New Zealand and the United States) in recognising for the first time the defence of change of position in *Lipkin Gorman v Karpnale Ltd*.[117] Similarly, in accepting that there is a right to restitution of unlawful tax exacted by a public authority in *Woolwich Equitable Building Society v IRC*,[118] his Lordship relied on the law in Australia, Canada and the United States. Again, in *Kleinwort Benson Ltd v Lincoln City Council*,[119] in removing the mistake of law bar to restitution of mistaken payments, Lord Goff extensively referred to the position in the 'common law world' (Canada, Australia, New Zealand and the United States, but also including within that description the mixed systems of Scotland and South Africa)[120] as well as in Germany and France.[121] In *Sempra Metals Ltd v IRC*,[122] the High Court of Australia's reasoning in *Hungerfords v Walker*[123] was referred to by Lords Hope, Nicholls and Walker[124] in favour of allowing compound interest

[114] Eg, *Baxter House Inc v Rosen* 278 NYS 2d 442 (1967); *Lohman v General American Life Insurance Co* 478 F 2d 719 (1973); *Vorlander v Keyes* 1 F 2d 67 (1924); *Holmes v Gilman* 138 NY 369 (1893); *Shaler v Trowbridge* 28 NJEq 595 (1877); *Truelsch v Northwestern Mutual Life Insurance Co* 202 NW 352 (1925); *Primeau v Granfield* 184 F 480 (1911). In the same context, he also referred to the Canadian case of *Jones v De Marchant* (1916) 28 DLR 561 and the Australian case of *Scott v Scott* (1963) 109 CLR 649 (HCA), although note that both those cases were decided at a time when the courts in Canada and Australia considered themselves to be applying English law.

[115] *Royal Bank of Scotland Plc v Etridge (No 2)* [2002] 2 AC 773 (HL) [19] (Lord Nicholls).

[116] *Yerkey v Jones* (1939) 63 CLR 649 (HCA). Note that this was decided at a time when the High Court of Australia considered itself to be applying English law.

[117] *Lipkin Gorman v Karpnale Ltd* [1991] 2 AC 548 (HL), 579. He referred to, eg, *Storthoaks Rural Municipality v Mobil Oil Canada Ltd* (1975) 55 DLR (3d) 1 (Supreme Court of Canada); *Australia and New Zealand Banking Group Ltd v Westpac Banking Corp* (1988) 164 CLR 662 (High Court of Australia); *Bank of New South Wales v Murphett* [1983] 1 VR 489 (Supreme Court of Victoria); New Zealand Judicature Act 1908, s 94B as amended by s 2 of the Judicature Amendment Act 1958; American Law Institute, *Restatement of the Law of Restitution, First* (1937) § 142.

[118] *Woolwich Equitable Building Society v IRC* [1993] AC 70. He referred to, eg, *Air Canada v British Columbia* (1989) 59 DLR (4th) 161 (Supreme Court of Canada, although note that he particularly relied on the dissenting judgment of Wilson J); *Atchison, Topeka and Santa Fe Rly Co v O'Connor* 223 US 280 (1912) (US Supreme Court); *Mason v New South Wales* (1959) 102 CLR 108 (High Court of Australia).

[119] *Kleinwort Benson Ltd v Lincoln City Council* [1999] 2 AC 349. He referred to, eg, *David Securities Pty Ltd v Commonwealth Bank of Australia* (1992) 175 CLR 353 (High Court of Australia); *Air Canada v British Columbia* (1989) 59 DLR (4th) 161 (Supreme Court of Canada); New Zealand Judicature Act 1908, s 94B (as amended by the Judicature Amendment Act 1958, s 2).

[120] ibid 373. He referred to *Morgan Guaranty Trust Co of New York v Lothian Regional Council* 1995 SLT 299 (Inner House of the Court of Session); *Willis Faber Enthoven (Pty) Ltd v Receiver of Revenue* 1992 (4) SA 202 (Appellate Division of the Supreme Court of South Africa).

[121] *Kleinwort Benson Ltd v Lincoln City Council* [1999] 2 AC 349 (HL), 374.

[122] *Sempra Metals Ltd v IRC* [2007] UKHL 34, [2008] 1 AC 561.

[123] *Hungerfords v Walker* (1989) 171 CLR 125 (HCA), 141–42.

[124] [2007] UKHL 34, [2008] 1 AC 561 [6], [87], [165]. Lord Walker also referred to a number of other Australian decisions and cited from Mason P in *Heydon v NRMA Ltd (No 2)* (2001) 53 NSWLR 600 (NSW Court of Appeal): ibid [179]; and Lord Nicholls said: 'The common law in Australia has developed in this way. The common law in England should do likewise': ibid [113].

to be awarded as damages or restitution. Most recently, in *Test Claimants in the FII Group Litigation v HMRC*,[125] Lords Walker and Sumption relied on the decision of the Supreme Court of Canada in *Kingstreet Investments Ltd v New Brunswick*,[126] and the dissent of Wilson J in that court in *Air Canada v British Columbia*,[127] to support the view that restitution under the *Woolwich* principle does not require a formal demand.

The heavy reference to Australian law is perhaps all the more remarkable because in recent years the High Court of Australia has taken the stance of rejecting the modern approach to the law of unjust enrichment.

Contract

Turning finally to contract, of the 49 cases that reached the House of Lords or Supreme Court in the last 25 years, there were references in 25 cases (51 per cent) to other common law jurisdictions and in five of them (10 per cent) there were also references to civil law. Australia was the most cited jurisdiction with references in 17 cases. Canadian law was referred to in nine cases, New Zealand law in eight cases, US law in six cases, South African law in two cases, Hong Kong law in one case, German law in four cases, French law in one case and Dutch law in one case.

Many of the references to the law in other common law jurisdictions were in support of propositions about existing English law. For example, in *Oceanbulk Shipping and Trading SA v TMT Asia Ltd*,[128] Lord Clarke referred to decisions in Canada and New Zealand as illustrating the 'self-evident' proposition that 'without prejudice' negotiations can be relied on in seeking rectification. In *Chartbrook Ltd v Persimmon Homes Ltd*,[129] Lord Hoffmann mentioned the decision of the Hong Kong Court of Final Appeal in *Jumbo King Ltd v Faithful Properties Ltd*[130] as a statement of the modern law of contractual construction that was consistent with the principles he had set out in the House of Lords in *Investors Compensation Scheme Ltd v West Bromwich Building Society*.[131] In *The Starsin*,[132] Australian and Canadian cases were relied on in support of the principles allowing Himalaya clauses to be enforced by those who, at first sight, are third parties despite the privity doctrine. Similarly, in *Bank of Credit and Commerce International SA v Ali*,[133] Lord Bingham, in setting out the existing English law on how one construes a contract releasing claims, referred to the

[125] *Test Claimants in the FII Group Litigation v HMRC* [2012] UKSC 19, [2012] 2 WLR 1149 [79], [173].

[126] *Kingstreet Investments Ltd v New Brunswick* 2007 SCC 1, [2007] 1 SCR 3.

[127] *Air Canada v British Columbia* [1989] 1 SCR 1161.

[128] *Oceanbulk Shipping and Trading SA v TMT Asia Ltd* [2010] UKSC 44, [2011] 1 AC 662 [33]. He referred to the first instance decisions in *Pearlman v National Life Assurance Co of Canada* (1917) 39 OLR 141 (Ontario) and *Butler v Countrywide Finance Ltd* (1992) 5 PRNZ 447 (New Zealand).

[129] *Chartbrook Ltd v Persimmon Homes Ltd* [2009] UKHL 38, [2009] 1 AC 1101.

[130] *Jumbo King Ltd v Faithful Properties Ltd* (1999) 2 HKCFAR 279, 296.

[131] *Investors Compensation Scheme Ltd v West Bromwich Building Soc* [1998] 1 WLR 896 (HL).

[132] *Homburg Houtimport BV v Agrosin Private Ltd (The Starsin)* [2003] UKHL 12, [2004] 1 AC 715. References were made to *J Gadsden Pty Ltd v Australian Coastal Shipping Commission* [1977] 1 NSWLR 575 (NSW Court of Appeal); *Sidney Cooke Ltd v Hapag-Lloyd Aktiengesellschaft* [1980] 2 NSWLR 587 (NSW Court of Appeal); *Chapman Marine Pty Ltd v Wihelmsen Lines* [1999] FCA 178 (Federal Court of Australia) [168]–[170] (Lord Hobhouse), [198] (Lord Millett); and to *ITO-International Terminal Operators v Mida Electronics Inc* (1986) 28 DLR (4th) 641 (Supreme Court of Canada) [56] (Lord Steyn), [154] (Lord Hobhouse).

[133] *Bank of Credit and Commerce International SA v Ali* [2001] UKHL 8, [2002] 1 AC 251 [9].

High Court of Australia's decision in *Grant v John Grant & Sons Pty Ltd*,[134] which had been 'frequently cited and relied upon'[135] in subsequent Australian case law.

In contrast, there have been other, and often more detailed, references to foreign law in support of significant developments in the law that the House of Lords or Supreme Court was undertaking. For example, in *Société Generale London Branch v Geys*,[136] Lord Wilson for the majority (Lord Sumption dissenting) referred to decisions in Australia, New Zealand and Canada in support of the view advocated by him that, as with the general law of contract, a repudiatory breach of an employment contract does not automatically terminate the contract but gives the employee an election whether to terminate or not. In *Fiona Trust Corp v Privalov*,[137] the law in the United States, Australia and Germany was cited by Lord Hope in support of moving English law forward by giving a wide interpretation to the scope of commercial arbitration clauses and to the separability principle. Lords Nicholls and Millett, dissenting in *Shogun Finance v Hudson*,[138] cited the US Uniform Commercial Code section 2-403 in favour of English law moving to the position that a mistake of identity does not render the contract void (although it may be voidable), and Lord Millett also referred to German law while pointing out that the relevant aspects of German law were part of the German law of property not contract.[139] In *Attorney-General v Blake*,[140] Lord Nicholls, giving the leading speech awarding an account of profits for breach of his undertaking to the Crown by the notorious spy George Blake, referred to the very similar outcome on very similar facts in the United States Supreme Court case of *Snepp v United States*.[141]

Occasionally the law elsewhere in the common law world has been referred to but rejected. This can be illustrated by two cases. In *Walford v Miles*,[142] Lord Ackner, giving the leading judgment laying down that in English law a 'lock-in agreement' framed as an obligation to negotiate in good faith is unenforceable, referred to, but so as to reject, the

[134] *Grant v John Grant & Sons Pty Ltd* (1954) 91 CLR 112 (HCA). He also referred by name to *Torrens Aloha Pty Ltd v Citibank NA* (1997) 144 ALR 89 (Federal Court of Australia).

[135] *Bank of Credit and Commerce International SA v Ali* [2001] UKHL 8, [2002] 1 AC 251 [15].

[136] *Société Generale London Branch v Geys* [2012] UKSC 63, [2013] 1 AC 523 [81], [83], [91] (where Lord Wilson referred to, eg, *Automatic Fire Sprinklers Proprietary Ltd v Watson* (1946) 72 CLR 435 and *Byrne v Australian Airlines Ltd* (1995) 131 ALR 422 (both High Court of Australia); *Paper Reclaim Ltd v Aotearoa International Ltd* [2007] 3 NZLR 169 (Supreme Court of New Zealand); and *Smart v Board of Governors of South Saskatchewan Hospital Centre* (1989) 60 DLR (4th) 8 (Saskatchewan Court of Appeal)); see also [100] (Lord Carnwath).

[137] *Fiona Trust Corp v Privalov* [2007] UKHL 40, [2007] 4 All ER 951 [31]–[32]. Lord Hope referred to *AT & T Technologies Inc v Communications Workers of America* 475 US 643 (1986) (US Supreme Court); *Threlkeld & Co Inc v Metallgesellschaft Ltd (London)* 923 F 2d 245 (2d Cir, 1991); *Prima Paint Corp v Flood & Conklin Mfg Co* 388 US 395 (1967) (US Supreme Court); *Comandate Marine Corp v Pan Australia Shipping Pty Ltd* [2006] FCAFC 192 (Full Court of the Federal Court of Australia). The German case relied on was the decision of 27 February 1970 of the Bundesgerichtshof which Lord Hoffmann appeared to have come across by reason of a reference to it by Schlosser in (1990) 6(1) *Arbitration International* 79: see [14].

[138] *Shogun Finance v Hudson* [2004] 1 AC 919 (HL) [35], [84].

[139] ibid [85]–[86]. He suggested that the clash with German law 'quite apart from anything else … would make the contemplated harmonisation of the general principles of European contract law very difficult to achieve'. In a sharp riposte to Lord Millett, Lord Hobhouse as one of the majority judges said: 'To cast doubt upon [the principles of English law] can only be a disservice to English law. Similarly, to attempt to use this appeal to advocate, on the basis of continental legal systems which are open to cogent criticism, the abandonment of the soundly based *nemo dat quod non habet* rule (statutorily adopted) would be not only improper but even more damaging': ibid [55].

[140] *Attorney-General v Blake* [2001] 1 AC 268 (HL), 287.

[141] *Snepp v United States* 444 US 50 (1980).

[142] *Walford v Miles* [1992] 2 AC 128.

contrary United States Court of Appeal decision in *Channel Home Centers, Division of Grace Retail Corp v Grossman*.[143] Similarly in *Johnson v Gore Wood*,[144] four of their Lordships (Lords Bingham, Cooke, Hutton and Millett)[145] referred to but, with the exception of Lord Cooke (who had been on the New Zealand Court of Appeal), largely rejected, the particular approach to damages for 'reflective loss' taken by the New Zealand Court of Appeal in *Christensen v Scott*.[146]

Conclusions from, and Comments on, the Survey

There are ten conclusions from, or comments on, the survey that should be stressed.

1. In the last 25 years, the House of Lords and Supreme Court have made reference to the law in other common law jurisdictions in 51 per cent of cases in contract, 64 per cent of cases in tort, and 71 per cent of cases in unjust enrichment. The main common law jurisdiction referred to in all three areas of the law of obligations has been Australia. In contract and unjust enrichment that is followed by Canada and then New Zealand and the United States; in tort, the United States is more relied on than Canada and New Zealand. I should confess that I was surprised at how high these figures are. It had somehow escaped my attention that so many references were being made by the House of Lords or Supreme Court to the law of other common law jurisdictions.
2. While it is true that some of the references to other common law jurisdictions are in support of propositions about existing English law[147]—and some of these date back to when there was perceived to be 'one common law' so that, strictly speaking, they are not comparative references at all—most of the detailed references to other common law jurisdictions have been in the context of developing,[148] or, more rarely, choosing not to develop,[149] English law. Within what one can overall describe as 'assisting the development of the law', the precise use of comparative common law has varied[150] from relying on the reasoning in a particular case or series of cases,[151] to seeing a range of possible solutions,[152] to reassurance that a particular solution is workable,[153] to the

[143] *Channel Home Centers, Division of Grace Retail Corp v Grossman* 795 F 2d 291 (1986).

[144] *Johnson v Gore Wood* [2002] 2 AC 1 (HL).

[145] ibid 35, 43–48, 52, 55, 65.

[146] *Christensen v Scott* [1996] 1 NZLR 273 (CA).

[147] See text to nn 74–79 above, referring to tort cases such as *Smoker v London Fire and Civil Defence Authority* [1991] 2 AC 502 (HL); text to nn 110–16 above, referring to unjust enrichment cases such as *Pitt v Holt* [2013] UKSC 26, [2013] 2 WLR 1200; and text to nn 128–35 above, referring to contract cases such as *Oceanbulk Shipping and Trading SA v TMT Asia Ltd* [2010] UKSC 44, [2011] 1 AC 662.

[148] See text to nn 80–96 above, referring to tort cases such as *White v Jones* [1995] 2 AC 207 (HL); text to nn 117–27 above, referring to unjust enrichment cases such as *Lipkin Gorman v Karpnale Ltd* [1991] 2 AC 548 (HL); and text to nn 136–41above, referring to contract cases such as *Société Générale London Branch v Geys* [2012] UKSC 63, [2013] 1 AC 523.

[149] See text to nn 97–102 above, referring to tort cases such as *Hunter v Canary Wharf Ltd* [1997] AC 655 (HL); and text to nn 142–46 above, referring to contract cases such as *Walford v Miles* [1992] 2 AC 128 (HL).

[150] For Stanton's analysis of the types of use in developing the law, see Stanton, above n 52, 269, 276–84.

[151] This is the commonest type of use: one example of many is *Stubbings v Webb* [1993] AC 498 (HL).

[152] As in, eg, *Reynolds v Times Newspapers Ltd* [2001] 2 AC 127 (HL).

[153] As in, eg, *Kleinwort Benson Ltd v Lincoln City Council* [1999] 2 AC 349 (HL).

articulation of policy reasons favouring a development,[154] to the recognition that a particular principle or approach has been widely accepted.[155]

3. The references to other common law jurisdictions have remained relatively consistent throughout the 25 years surveyed. While no doubt some Law Lords and Supreme Court Justices have been more willing to use comparative common law material than others,[156] that willingness has neither been confined to a few only of their Lordships nor has it been confined to any particular period within the last 25 years.
4. It follows from this survey that counsel bringing cases to the Supreme Court and arguing that the law of obligations should be developed in some way would be very well-advised to look carefully at the law in Australia,[157] Canada, New Zealand and the United States.[158] Indeed in *Commissioners of Customs and Excise v Barclays Bank*,[159] Lord Bingham went so far as to regard the lack of evidence from Commonwealth law as a reason for not developing the law so as to recognise a novel duty of care. His Lordship said: 'It is a notable feature of this appeal that the Commissioners adduce no comparative jurisprudence to support their argument. The House was referred to no material from any Commonwealth jurisdiction to show recognition of a duty such as that for which the Commissioners contend'.[160]
5. It also follows that in teaching and writing on the English law of obligations, we should strive to refer, at least where considering developments of English law, to the relevant law in at least Australia but also, depending on the subject matter, in Canada, New Zealand and the United States. In so far as we aspire to be teaching our students the sort of reasoning that will equip them to argue a case in the Supreme Court, we will be failing if we do not make them aware of, and expose them to, the thinking in the other major Commonwealth jurisdictions.[161] In other words, even blinkered English lawyers, purportedly interested only in the development of English law, must embrace comparative common law.

[154] As in, eg, *Jones v Kaney* [2011] UKSC 13, [2011] 2 AC 398.

[155] As in, eg, *Lipkin Gorman v Karpnale Ltd* [1991] 2 AC 548 (HL).

[156] See the rather sceptical view of Lord Hoffmann, '*Fairchild* and After' in A Burrows, D Johnston and R Zimmermann (eds), *Judge and Jurist: Essays in Memory of Lord Rodger of Earlsferry* (Oxford, OUP, 2013) 63, 64. After referring to the references to foreign law made by Lord Bingham in that case, Lord Hoffmann writes: 'The foreign authorities were cited in the way courts always use comparative law; as a rhetorical flourish, to lend support to a conclusion reached on independent grounds'. Even Lord Bingham did not suggest that reference to comparative law had a decisive influence: *Widening Horizons: The Influence of Comparative Law and International Law on Domestic Law*, Hamlyn Lectures 2009 (Cambridge, CUP, 2010) 1–28, esp 8.

[157] The point here being made is of course not undermined by the apparent fact that the reference to English cases by the High Court of Australia is even greater than vice versa. J Douglas, 'England as a Source of Australian Law: For How Long?' (2012) 86 *Australian Law Journal* 333, 337, writes: 'The High Court [of Australia] expects counsel to refer to the law of other common law jurisdictions, including the law of England, more than appears to be the case in the Supreme Court of the United Kingdom'.

[158] Vice versa, there has been considerable controversy about the use of foreign law, including it would seem English law, by the US Supreme Court. See, eg, the different opinions on the use of comparative law of Justice Kennedy (in favour) and Justice Scalia (against and dissenting) in deciding that a state's sodomy law was unconstitutional in *Lawrence v Texas* 539 US 588 (2003).

[159] [2007] 1 AC 181 (HL) [20].

[160] See similarly the comments of Lord Collins in *Jones v Kaney* [2011] 2 AC 398 (HL) [76], text to n 93.

[161] It is of interest that, while coverage of Commonwealth material is expressly referred to on the Sweet and Maxwell Common Law Library website in advertising *Clerk and Lindsell on Torts* (20th edn), there is no equivalent reference to Commonwealth material in the 'blurb' for *Chitty on Contracts* (31st edn) or *Goff and Jones on the Law of Unjust Enrichment* (8th edn).

6. In contrast to what has so far been said, the survey shows that the reference to civil law has been very much more limited. There have been references to civil law in only 10 per cent of contract cases, 10 per cent of tort cases, and 8 per cent of unjust enrichment cases. Moreover, those references were largely made by Lord Goff and Lord Bingham[162] and between 1994 and 2005. As Stanton concluded in his survey of tort law, 'It will be evident from this data that use of civilian law was actually a rarity even in the period between 1994 and 2005 and has virtually ceased since then'.[163] And later he said: 'The evidence from the cases surveyed is that in 2013 the English law of tort is more isolated from civilian influences than it was ten years ago'.[164]
7. It follows that it is a myth to think that the focus of attention in comparative law in our highest court has shifted, or is shifting, from common law jurisdictions to the civil law. Certainly English law cannot now be understood without the supranational law comprising European law and the law of the ECHR. Beyond that, the main focus of our highest court is on the law of obligations in Australia, Canada, New Zealand and the United States, not on Germany and France. In other words, the European focus of our supranational law has not led to comparative civil law being regarded as more important and useful than comparative common law.
8. The reasons for the relative lack of popularity of civil law as against other common laws are not difficult to pinpoint. The difficulties of language, the style of judgments, the very fact that at root one is not dealing with judge-made law, the lack of a shared legal heritage, let alone any differences in national culture and values, mean that it is much more difficult for our judges (and for counsel arguing before them) to feel confident and comfortable with civil law than with common law. Even if one or more of the judges have the linguistic ability, there is the problem that not all the judges sitting (or counsel) may have that ability. It surely cannot be satisfactory to use the material unless it is equally accessible to all. Professor Jane Stapleton, in a powerful and characteristically robust attack on the use of comparative civil law in tort cases,[165] also points to the difficulty in the selection of materials and the problems of superficiality. She concludes that, in contrast to comparative common law, 'foreign-language comparative tort law is fraught with danger: how to select resources, their degree of reliability and so on. It is rightly unpopular with courts and practitioners in English-speaking jurisdictions, which typically have sufficiently rich resources from within their own language pool'.[166] Admittedly, leading comparative civil lawyers, such as Walter Van Gerven, Sir Basil Markesinis[167] and Reinhard Zimmermann, have made great efforts to address these sorts of problems in the last 20 years by making the civil law cases more accessible to English lawyers not least through the publication in English of case

[162] For Lord Bingham's enthusiasm for comparative law, see Bingham, above n 156, esp 1–28.

[163] Stanton, above n 52, 269, 287.

[164] ibid 296.

[165] J Stapleton, 'Benefits of Comparative Tort Reasoning: Lost in Translation' in M Adenas and D Fairgrieve (eds), *Tom Bingham and the Transformation of the Law* (Oxford, OUP, 2009) 773–814.

[166] ibid 813.

[167] In B Markesinis, *Comparative Law in the Courtroom and Classroom* (Oxford, Hart Publishing, 2003) 212, the author argues, for example, that the best way forward is 'if the academic packages the foreign product in an attractive way'. Lord Phillips in his Foreword to the book neatly summarises Markesinis's central thesis that 'if comparative lawyers provide concrete, focused and detailed studies of the decisions of foreign courts, packaged to meet the need of practitioners, they have a valuable role to play in the development of the law': ibid iv.

books on the civil law of obligations. However, as yet, and with Lord Goff[168] and Lord Bingham no longer there to assist the cause, my survey shows that, in terms of influencing the UK Supreme Court, that work has largely fallen on deaf ears.

9. If one stands back from the detail of the survey, it perhaps ought to be more obvious than it is that our top judges may seek assistance and inspiration, especially in developing the law, from comparative law whether common law or civil.[169] No one is suggesting that foreign law should be anything other than persuasive. Rather it is a source that the judges should be entitled to take into account as potentially instructive. But as a persuasive source, and while there are some pitfalls to be avoided in terms of superficiality and misunderstanding, what could possibly be more helpful to an appellate judge than the experience of other jurisdictions in which the judges have had to deal with the same or similar issues? There are many of us in academia, engaged in practical legal scholarship, who seek to influence the judges by having our articles and books cited as a persuasive authority. If the argument for that is made out, as I fervently believe it is, how much more clear-cut is the argument that the actual decisions taken in other courts on similar facts should be persuasive. At the very least, foreign law should be no less persuasive than the writings of academics.
10. My final thought is that it follows from all that I have been saying that the Obligations Conference, bringing together every two years academic lawyers from across the world, especially from the common law world, is of invaluable importance even to those who are merely interested in English law.

[168] In *White v Jones* [1995] 2 AC 207 (HL) even Lord Goff expressed the need for caution: see above n 104. See also his short essay, 'Comparative Law: The Challenge to the Judges' in B Markesinis, *Law Making, Law Finding and Law Shaping* (Oxford, OUP, 1997) 37–41: 'I myself have attempted to exploit comparative law in my work as a judge. But I have to admit that this has opened my eyes to the very considerable difficulties involved in this exercise … In truth, *White v Jones* was a unique case … I have to admit that I have great difficulty in imagining when, in a future case of importance, a point will arise for decision on which authority from another legal system will be so directly relevant, and will be so readily available to us in the English language … Indeed, I am beginning to wonder whether it might be better if our judges concentrated more on comparative legal procedure than on comparative substantive law'.

[169] In rejecting the view of those who regard comparative law as irrelevant or misleading, Lord Bingham in *Widening Horizons*, above n 156, 6 has powerfully written: 'In no other field of intellectual endeavour—be it science, medicine, philosophy, literature, architecture, art, music, engineering or sociology—would ideas or insights be rejected simply because they were of foreign origin'.

3

Unity, Then Divergence: The Privy Council, the Common Law of England and the Common Laws of Canada, Australia and New Zealand

PAUL FINN

> I should have thought that the proposition that, subject only to special 'local considerations' (whatever that may mean), the common law today must necessarily be the same in all jurisdictions which started with it, is really hopelessly unreal.
>
> Sir Robin Cooke, 'The New Zealand National Legal Identity' (1987)[1]

For a judge in the United States, Cooke's observation would merely express a well-accepted reality wrought over two centuries ago by the American Revolution. Yet for a judge of the British Commonwealth or Empire, it would conjure up quite a different history and experience—a history of the 'hegemony of the English version of the common law' (to use Bora Laskin's memorable description)[2] and the experience of a 'distant tribunal',[3] the Judicial Committee of the Privy Council in London, as the final appellate body from decisions of colonial and Dominion courts.

A principal function of the Privy Council, as we well know, was to maintain uniformity with the common law of England.[4] Or, as a shrill Privy Council Office would have it in 1876 when faced with Canada's unsuccessful attempt to abolish Privy Council appeals:

> To abolish this controlling power … is obviously to destroy one of the most important ties which still connect all parts of the empire in common obedience to the source of law, and to renounce the last and most essential mode of exercising the authority of the Crown over its possessions abroad.[5]

[1] R Cooke, 'The New Zealand National Identity' (1987) 3 *Canterbury Law Review* 171, 177–78.

[2] B Laskin, *The British Tradition in Canadian Law*, Hamlyn Lecture Series (London, Stevens & Sons, 1969) 62.

[3] The description is A Inglis Clarke's in his *Studies in Australian Constitutional Law,* 1901 edn reprint (Sydney, Legal Books, 1997) 355.

[4] See generally, A Mason, 'The Break with the Privy Council and the Internationalisation of the Common Law' in P Cane (ed), *Centenary Essays for the High Court of Australia* (Sydney, LexisNexis Butterworths, 2004) ch 5.

[5] As quoted in MJ Herman, 'The Founding of the Supreme Court of Canada and the Abolition of the Appeal to the Privy Council' (1976) 8 *Ottawa Law Review* 7, 21–22.

There was no reticence in the Privy Council's espousal of the obligation this entailed. In *Robins v National Trust Co Ltd*,[6] a 1927 appeal from Canada, Viscount Dunedin stated what was then well understood:

> [T]he House of Lords … is the supreme tribunal to settle English law, and that being settled, the Colonial Court, which is bound by English law, is bound to follow it.

The consequences of both this Imperial tie and its abolition and disregard over time in country after country are my present concern. I will focus in the main on three countries: Canada, Australia and New Zealand. I do so both because of commonalities in each's story in relation, at least, to 'private law' (despite the considerable periods that separated their respective abolition of Privy Council appeals)[7] and because of the alchemy of sorts between the three, particularly in the 1980s and 1990s, which was itself a reflection of the emergence of each's own national version of the common law.

My justification for what I have to say is that there is matter here which can instruct, but which also is now passing from memory. This is the story of why various common law courts of the Commonwealth positively wished to, and did, develop the common law both to suit their own needs and circumstances and to express their own values and aspirations. That process began in earnest in Canada in the late 1970s and in Australia and New Zealand in the 1980s. There were, as will be seen, refreshing similarities in the ideas that animated, and the methodologies that were employed by, those judges who, in retrospect, gave direction to the evolutionary changes that were occurring in the common law of their own countries. These judges revealed their purposes, often provocatively, in extra-curial writings as well as in their judgments. I will allow them their own voices here. Particular reference will be made to the Canadians: Bora Laskin, Brian Dickson and Beverley McLachlin; the Australians: Owen Dixon, Anthony Mason and William Deane; and to the New Zealander: Robin Cooke.[8]

It was inevitable that difference and division between common law systems would result from liberation from Privy Council supervision. As Donovan Waters was to note in 1995 of the lack of significance to Canada of two then recent Privy Council appeals from New Zealand, they revealed 'how far the once doctrinally unified countries of the Commonwealth have gone in different directions'.[9]

The common laws of our respective countries now provide matter enough for contrast as well as for comparison—and this is obviously so in private law. Yet for all that, we need to remind ourselves that the general contours of the substantive common law have remained

[6] *Robins v National Trust Co Ltd* [1927] AC 515 (PC), 529.

[7] Canada abolished criminal appeals in 1935 and all appeals in 1949. Australia's abolition came in phases: 1968 (in appeals in matters of federal jurisdiction including those relating to the application and interpretation of the Constitution) Privy Council (Limitation of Appeals) Act 1968 (Cth); 1975 (appeals from the High Court in all matters) Privy Council (Appeals from the High Court) Act 1975 (Cth); and 1986 (remaining appeals from State Supreme Courts) Australia Act 1986 (Cth), s 11. New Zealand finally terminated appeals in 2003 after a long period of gestation, but by then New Zealand's Court of Appeal had plainly indicated that, while bound by Privy Council decisions, it was not bound to follow the House of Lords: see K Glover, 'Severing the Ties the Bind? The Development of a Distinctive New Zealand Jurisprudence' (2000) 8 *Waikato Law Review* 25.

[8] I mean no disrespect in not using titles and honorifics in referring to these eminent judges and in so doing I follow what appears to be an accepted Canadian convention.

[9] D Waters, 'Proprietary Relief: Two Privy Council Decisions—A Canadian Perspective' (1995) 25 *Canadian Business Law Journal* 60; see also, eg, P Finn, 'Common Law Divergences' (2013) 37 *Melbourne University Law Review* 509 on contrasts between equitable doctrines in Australian and English law.

relatively similar in common law jurisdictions (including the United States). Hence, when focusing on divergences, we need to be alert to the real significance of the particular subject of inquiry. Is our concern simply with methodological or doctrinal differences; or with policy differences and contrary outcomes; or with divergences which are products of the particular societal or statutory contexts which influence or contrive how the common law should be developed,[10] and so on.

I should preface what I have to say with two qualifications. In this setting, our concerns are with the law of obligations (or, essentially, private law).[11] What I wish to emphasise is that the judicial endeavour about which I will speak was by no means limited or confined to such a narrow setting. Private law was simply a part of what was addressed and not necessarily a particularly significant part. The Supreme Court of Canada, for example, was far more focused on federalism, the Privy Council's legacy and the Charter, as it developed its 'distinctively Canadian jurisprudence'.[12] In Australia, equity may have been the first to feel the wave of common law reform. But it was left in the wake of greater concerns in criminal procedure, public law and judicial review, a new order of constitutional issues and native title. This brings me to my second qualification. The concepts the judges invoked in justification of their endeavours were not unique to private law. In varying degrees they permeate common law systems.

In truth, I am only illustrating a small, but nonetheless important, part of much larger changes in the common law world within the British Commonwealth. I should emphasise this. If we view what I will say from the vantage point of the common law world at large, what I am really talking of is Canada, Australia and New Zealand taking their proper places in that world. In it I include, in particular, the United States in its rich diversity and India, the largest common law jurisdiction. On such a canvas we can see a system with a distinctive judicial method and with a commitment to the rule of law. But we can also see importantly, each country's commitment to its own people and their circumstances, history and values.

I. To the 1980s

> [T]he political and civil laws of each nation … should be so adapted in such a manner to the people for whom they are made, as to render it unlikely for those of one nation to be proper for another.
>
> Montesquieu, *The Spirit of Laws*[13]

I will not venture on the difficult comparative question of the value the Privy Council appeal gave to Canada, Australia and New Zealand save to make two brief comments. First,

[10] See, eg, *Commonwealth Bank of Australia v Barker* [2014] HCA 32, (2014) 312 ALR 356 on the significance of differing societal and statutory contexts for the implication of contractual terms.

[11] A description which, in my view, is rarely a helpful one for analytical purposes.

[12] B Dickson, 'The Development of a Distinctively Canadian Jurisprudence' 5, address to the Faculty of Law, Dalhousie University, 29 October 1983, Supreme Court Library, Speeches Delivered by the Right Hon Brian Dickson, typescript, vol 1, 464, as quoted in J Saywell, *The Lawmakers: Judicial Power and the Shaping of Canadian Federalism* (Toronto, University of Toronto Press, 2002) 277.

[13] A Cohler, B Miller and H Stone (eds), *Montesquieu: The Spirit of the Laws* (Cambridge, CUP, 1989) Bk 1, ch 3, 8.

the Privy Council record with local statutes (and especially with colonial Crown lands legislation in Australia),[14] with Canada's Constitution Act 1867 and Canadian federalism[15] and, with its foreshortened encounter with Australian federalism,[16] gave reason on occasion for pause if not for local exasperation[17] and protest.

A notable instance of such protest was made by the Chief Justice of New Zealand in 1903 at a special sitting of its Court of Appeal. This was convened in response to the Privy Council's decision in *Wallis v Solicitor-General for New Zealand*,[18] which was seen, locally, as casting doubt on the probity and independence of the Court. The Chief Justice noted that:

> Unfortunately this is not the only judgment of the Privy Council that has been pronounced under a misapprehension or an ignorance of our local laws ... At present we in New Zealand are, so far as the Privy Council is concerned, in an unfortunate position. It has shown that it knows not our own statutes, or our conveyancing terms, or our history.[19]

What made this 'altogether extraordinary' event the more surprising was that the editor of the *Law Quarterly Review* entered the lists in defence of the Privy Council.[20]

The second comment is that there is evidence enough that Privy Council decisions could themselves be the cause of 'divergences'[21] because of their lack of consistency over time,[22] or because they were not later followed in England. The relatively recent English Court of Appeal decision, *Sinclair Investments (UK) Ltd v Versailles Trade Finance Ltd*[23] is emblematic of the latter species of 'divergence'.[24]

Coincidentally, *Sinclair Investments* was overruled by the UK Supreme Court in *FHR European Ventures LLP v Cedar Capital LLP*[25] on the day that the original version of this chapter was presented at the Obligations Conference in Hong Kong. In so doing the Supreme Court more closely—but not completely—aligned English law with that prevailing in other common law countries in relation to the remedies available against a bribed fiduciary, though it did not do this for that reason.

[14] Which for the most part did not have English equivalents or analogues: see generally, P Finn, *Law and Government in Colonial Australia* (Melbourne, OUP, 1987) 2–6.

[15] There is a large literature on this subject: see, eg, PW Hogg and WK Albright, 'Canadian Federalism, the Privy Council and the Supreme Court of Canada: Reflections on the Debate about Canadian Federalism' (2005) 38 *University of British Columbia Law Review* 329, esp 339.

[16] See *Webb v Andrew* [1907] AC 81 (PC). For an account of the Privy Council's 'Joke' see L Zines, 'The Vision and the Reality' in P Cane (ed), *Centenary Essays for the High Court of Australia* (Sydney, LexisNexis Butterworths, 2004) 3–10.

[17] See, eg, the comments of Windeyer J in *Tooth v Power* (1889) 10 NSWR (Eq) 143, 156–58; see also *Jaques v Stafford* (1890) 11 NSWR (L) 127, 133. This said, the Privy Council did save local legislation from unwarranted emasculation by local courts as, eg, with Australia's revolutionary Claims Against the Government legislation; see *Farnell v Bowman* (1887) 12 App Cas 643 (PC) and Finn, above n 14, ch 6.

[18] *Wallis v Solicitor-General for New Zealand* [1903] AC 173 (PC).

[19] On this event, and on the later Maori petition to have Privy Council appeals abolished in relation to Maori land issues, see T Arnold 'Update on the Supreme Court' a paper given at the New Zealand Legal Research Foundation Annual General Meeting on 7 August 2003, available at www.crownlaw.govt.nz/uploads/UpdateSC.pdf.

[20] Note (1903) 19 *LQR* 249.

[21] As noted by Inglis Clarke, a critic of the retention of such appeals at the time of Australia's federation: see A Inglis Clarke, *Studies of Australian Constitutional Law* (Melbourne, Charles F Maxwell, 1905) 349–54.

[22] See, eg, *Borough of Bathurst v Mac Pherson* (1879) 4 App Cas 256 (PC) and *Bourke v Municipal Council of Sydney* [1895] AC 433 (PC); and see Finn, above n 14, 71–74 and 111–12.

[23] *Sinclair Investments (UK) Ltd v Versailles Trade Finance Ltd* [2012] Ch 453 (CA).

[24] As was indicated with no little directness by Etherton C in the subsequent Court of Appeal decision of *FHR European Ventures LLP v Mankarious* [2013] EWCA Civ 17.

[25] *FHR European Ventures LLP v Cedar Capital Partners LLC* [2014] UKSC 45, [2015] 1 AC 250.

Now to my immediate concern with the effects on local judiciaries of, first, adherence to, and then liberation from, the obligation to apply the common law of England.

Canada

A clause in Canada's proposed Supreme Court Act 1876 sought to make the Supreme Court of Canada's judgments and orders final and unappellable. It was faultily drafted. In any event, it could not have achieved its purpose. As its proponents were to discover, the Queen's prerogative to grant leave to appeal to the Privy Council could only be removed by an Imperial Statute.[26]

Importantly for the future, decisions on interpretation of the Constitution Act 1867, and in particular the provisions on division of powers between the Federal and provincial governments, remained exposed to Privy Council review. That became an abiding and escalating cause of dissatisfaction in Canada, the more so because in federalism cases the Privy Council inconveniently favoured the provinces, seemingly because of a preconceived, but ill informed, notion of the proper form of a federal system.[27]

Having to live with the consequences of decisions not of its own making,[28] the Supreme Court had to endure what has been called 'our arrested adolescence'[29] for over 70 years. Only from 1949 did Canada have, to use Laskin's description, 'a final court of and for Canadians'.

In his 1951 article, the title of which bears that phrase,[30] and almost two decades later, in his Hamlyn lecture series monograph, *The British Tradition in Canadian Law*,[31] Laskin acknowledged the overwhelming impact of English decisions both in the Canadian Supreme Court ('after becoming subjugated to the Privy Council') and in the court system more generally. This was reflected in the Supreme Court's practices of rarely citing 'other than English decisions'; of freely citing English texts and works such as *Halsbury*, as expositions of English decisions; and of treating local periodical literature with distaste.[32]

A leading Canadian scholar writing a decade after abolition could still observe:[33]

> A perusal of Canadian law reports not only verifies an absence of creative approach but conveys the impression that most of the opinions reported there are those of English judges applying English law in Canada, rather than those of Canadian judges developing Canadian law to meet Canadian needs with guidance of English precedent.

[26] This impediment was not removed until the passage of the Statute of Westminster 1931 (UK) but even then doubts were entertained in Canada as to whether comprehensive abolition was possible: see Herman, above n 5.

[27] See P Hogg and WK Wright, 'Canadian Federalism, the Privy Council and the Supreme Court: Reflections on the Debate About Canadian Federalism' (2005) 38 *University of British Columbia Law Review* 329, 339–40; and see generally Saywell, above n 12.

[28] *cf* B Laskin, 'The Supreme Court of Canada: A Final Court of and for Canadians' (1951) 29 *Canadian Bar Review* 1038, 1040; see also Laskin, above n 2, 1–2.

[29] See Herman, above n 5, 31.

[30] Laskin, above n 28, 1045, written as a law professor.

[31] Written as a judge of the Ontario Court of Appeal.

[32] Laskin, above n 28, 1045.

[33] HE Read, 'The Judicial Process in Common Law Canada' (1959) 37 *Canadian Bar Review* 265, 268.

A decade after this observation, Laskin could comment still: 'There has been no marked change since then'.[34] He did allow, though, that in the period since abolition: 'Canadian judicial creativity has not run dry, even if one could wish for less obvious dependency on the judicial work of another jurisdiction'.[35] And so he singled out for particular mention the Supreme Court's decision in *Fleming v Atkinson*,[36] which refused to accept that the House of Lords tort decision in *Searle v Wallbank*[37] stated what was the common law of Ontario.

In retrospect, one can add as well to this the 1954 Supreme Court's unjust enrichment decision of *Deglman v Guaranty Trust Co of Canada*[38] and the 1959 decision in *Roncarelli v Duplessis*[39] which, though having a Quebec provenance, applied common law concepts and was the clear precursor of the tort of misfeasance in public office in Canada.[40]

Laskin's frustration with the Canadian 'condition' was reflected in his early contrast of Australian and Canadian jurisprudence:[41]

> [Australia] can point to a body of legal doctrine which is much more its own than the legal doctrine expounded in this country. Of course, the High Court of Australia has been freer of Privy Council control [ie, in relation to federalism issues], but this is not a complete answer to the absence in Canada of an independent judicial tradition like that in Australia.

Others were to comment to like effect.[42] Laskin continued:

> Part of the answer lies in the conservative tradition of the Canadian legal profession reinforced by the awe and timidity of a colonial outlook, and in the late development of university law schools where free inquiry grounded in Canadian experience now gives promise of distinctively Canadian contributions to the common law system.

This last observation has proved to be prophetic.[43] As Saywell points out in his book, *The Lawmakers*,[44] of the 22 puisne judges who sat on the Supreme Court of Canada between 1980 and 2000, 11 were, or had been, full-time law professors at one stage of their careers and many of the others had lectured part-time.

If it was the case that English decisions (especially in private law) continued to be considered and often followed in the Supreme Court into the early 1970s, it is unsurprising that the years of Laskin (1970–84) and Brian Dickson (1973–90) 'witnessed the unmistakable fashioning of a distinct Canadian jurisprudence'.[45] Three factors facilitated this. The first was a change in the composition of the Court; the second was the elimination of the appeal as of right in favour of a special leave procedure; the third was the judicial relationship that developed between Laskin and Dickson after early disagreements. It had a like significance

[34] Laskin, above n 2, 49. See to like effect PS Atiyah, 'Book Review' (1969) 10 *Journal of the Society of Public Teachers of Law* 232: 'one is struck repeatedly by the paucity of fruitful and original ideas which have emerged from Canadian Courts in dealing with tort problems'.

[35] Laskin, above n 2, 5.

[36] *Fleming v Atkinson* (1959) 18 DLR (2d) 81 (SCC).

[37] *Searle v Wallbank* [1947] AC 341 (HL), a case of occupier's liability for injury caused to a motorist on a highway, by straying animals.

[38] *Deglman v Guaranty Trust Co of Canada* [1954] 3 DLR 785 (SCC).

[39] *Roncarelli v Duplessis* (1959) 16 DLR (2d) 689 (SCC).

[40] See G Fridman, *The Law of Torts in Canada*, 2nd edn (Toronto, Carswell, 2002) 879–84.

[41] B Laskin, 'The Supreme Court of Canada' (1951) 29 *Canadian Bar Review* 1046.

[42] See, eg, RJ Sharpe and K Roach, *Brian Dickson* (Toronto, University of Toronto Press, 2004) 145.

[43] Laskin, a former law professor, had studied both at Osgood Hall and at Harvard.

[44] Saywell, above n 12.

[45] Waters, above n 9, 90.

for Canadian legal development as did the relationship of Mason and Deane in the High Court of Australia after Deane's appointment in 1982.[46]

From his writings as a law professor, Laskin long espoused the view that, as the Supreme Court was now a 'free court',[47] it was reasonable to expect that 'it will explore the entire common law world and not only that part which is called Great Britain'. As a judge and then Chief Justice of Canada, he put this into practice—a practice which subsists to this day.[48] Perhaps the most internationally well known of his private law decisions, *Canadian Aero Service Ltd v O'Malley*[49] (a decision on the fiduciary obligations of corporate directors and officers), drew on authorities from the United States, England, Australia and New Zealand.

Both Laskin and Dickson appreciated the significance for the Court of the introduction of the special leave procedure. Laskin now considered the Court's 'paramount obligation' and 'main function [was] to oversee the development of the law ... to give guidance in articulate reasons ... and ... direction ... on issues of national concern'.[50] According to Dickson's biographers,[51] Dickson saw this development as 'of the highest importance' and was causing the Court to take a more policy-oriented approach. Parliament had given 'a clear mandate to shape and develop the law'.[52] And, this is what it did.

Not uncommonly for Canada in the 1970s, one of the most significant indicators of the private law 'divergences' that were to come had its genesis in a dissenting judgment. At issue in *Murdoch v Murdoch*[53] were the principles to govern the division of property between partners on the breakdown of a family relationship. The sole dissentient was Laskin.[54] Unlike the majority he considered the state of English law decisions followed by the majority, to be unsatisfactory. He turned to equity, to the constructive trust as it had evolved in the United States and to *Deglman* and its endorsement of unjust enrichment as providing bases for establishing an interest in property which it would be 'inequitable' to deny. This justified the award of relief to the wife who was not the legal owner of the ranch in question, who had not contributed to the purchase price, but who for 25 years had contributed to the ranch's development.

In 1978 in *Rathwell v Rathwell*[55] and then decisively in *Pettkus v Becker*,[56] in judgments in which Laskin concurred, Dickson enlarged on Laskin's dissent in *Murdoch*: the constructive trust was a flexible and ancient tool of equity that could 'accommodate the changing needs and mores of society in order to achieve justice'. In this setting, its invocation was sustained by the principle of preventing unjust enrichment.[57]

[46] See further discussion under 'Australia' below.

[47] Laskin, above n 41, 1046.

[48] One need only point to the exemplary comparative law methodology of the recent decision of the Court in *AI Enterprises Ltd v Bram Enterprises Ltd* 2014 SCC 12, [2014] 1 SCR 177, especially [50]–[73] (on the 'unlawful means' economic tort).

[49] *Canadian Aero Service Ltd v O'Malley* (1974) 40 DLR (3d) 371 (SCC).

[50] B Laskin, 'The Role and Function of Final Appellate Courts' (1975) 53 *Canadian Bar Review* 469, 479.

[51] Sharpe and Roach, above n 42, 146.

[52] ibid.

[53] *Murdoch v Murdoch* (1973) 41 DLR (3d) 367 (SCC).

[54] The recently appointed Dickson did not sit.

[55] *Rathwell v Rathwell* (1978) 83 DLR (3d) 289 (SCC).

[56] *Pettkus v Becker* (1980) 117 DLR (3d) 257 (SCC).

[57] This story is well described in Sharpe and Roach, above n 42, 179–92 (from which the above text is drawn) and in D Waters, *Law of Trusts in Canada*, 3rd edn (Toronto, Carswell, 2005) ch 10.

A like story could be told of the abandonment of the mistake of fact/mistake of law distinction for the recovery of money paid under mistake. Its genesis again was in a dissenting judgment, this time of Dickson (with Laskin concurring) and again resort was had to 'general principles of equity': 'would [it] be unjust to allow the recipient of the benefit to retain it?'[58] What is interesting to note in passing is that in the 1980s the High Court of Australia made similar innovations in relation, for example, to the use of the remedial constructive trust in relationship breakdowns[59] but by using different doctrinal (though nonetheless equitable) tools.

With the advent of the Charter of Rights and Freedoms in 1982, the future of a distinctively Canadian jurisprudence for the common law and otherwise was assured. As Dickson was to put it in 1983:[60]

> In my opinion the mandate of the Supreme Court of Canada is to oversee the development of a distinctive Canadian jurisprudence. Our ability to do this was sharply circumscribed in the days of appeals as of right and in an era predominated by a reflexive deference to British legal opinion. I think we have now emerged from that era. As I see it the challenge currently before our courts is to develop a jurisprudence that combines a respect for recognized rules and established principles with sufficient flexibility to meet the specific needs of an evolving Canadian reality. Change need not, and should not, take place at break-neck speed. Stare decisis is still alive and well, but blind obedience to the antiquity of disembodied precedence will no longer sway our court.

Australia

As in Canada, dissatisfaction with the Privy Council appeal from Australian colonial courts was significant. This was on a variety of scores but particularly on the hardship and inconvenience it entailed and on that body's lack of knowledge of local circumstances and conditions, and of local laws.[61] Nonetheless, it was the federation movement and the appellate jurisdiction to be given the High Court of Australia that sparked the abolition debate in earnest—first, in the Constitutional Conventions of the 1890s and, then, with the Imperial authorities in 1900 during negotiations for the enactment of Australia's Constitution. The shifting nature of what was proposed and the eleventh hour changes made in England, have little bearing on what needs to be said here. It should be said, though, given Canada's experience, that the Constitution supplemented by early Federal legislation secured the High Court exclusive jurisdiction to deal with federalism issues. There was no like acute irritant to match that visited upon the Canadians.[62]

[58] See Sharpe and Roach, above n 42, 198–200. And see *Nepean v Ontario Hydro* [1982] 1 SCR 347 and *Air Canada v British Columbia* [1989] 1 SCR 1161; and see generally Sharpe and Roach, above n 42, ch 9, on the extensive use Dickson made of academic writings.

[59] See, eg, *Muschinski v Dodds* (1985) 160 CLR 583 (HCA) and *Baumgartner v Baumgartner* (1987) 164 CLR 137 (HCA).

[60] B Dickson, 'Development of a Distinctively Canadian Jurisprudence' 5, quoted in Saywell, above n 12, 277.

[61] See, eg, the comments of Windeyer J in *Tooth v Power* (1889) 10 NSWR (Eq) 143, 156; see Deakin's comments on *Macleod v Attorney-General for New South Wales* [1891] AC 455 (PC) in Commonwealth Parliamentary Debates, House of Representative, 9 June 1903, 595; see W Harrison Moore, *The Constitution of the Commonwealth of Australia*, 2nd edn (Melbourne, Maxwell, 1910) 34 and 220 ff; and see generally, A Mason, 'The Evolving Role and Function of the High Court' in B Opeskin and F Wheeler (eds), *The Australian Federal Judicial System* (Melbourne, Melbourne University Press, 2000) 95, 95–97.

[62] See generally Zines, above n 16, ch 1.

Nonetheless, while the Constitution for practical purposes precluded the Privy Council from review of 'the limits inter se of the Constitutional powers of the Commonwealth and those of any State'[63] the Privy Council was otherwise able to deal with questions involving interpretation of the Constitution. This in time provided a source of dissatisfaction. From his early observations of the Privy Council, as counsel in 1924, Owen Dixon, later a Justice, and then Chief Justice, of the High Court, concluded that the Board 'did not go into [appeals] thoroughly'.[64] As his biographer observed, 'this would be a lifelong complaint of his in regard to Australian constitutional cases coming before the Board'.[65] Others shared that view. So, for example, Douglas Menzies (a future colleague of Dixon's on the High Court), considered that the Law Lords 'did no work behind the scenes' and 'treated it as bad form to do so' relying instead on 'facility of expression and finality of a decision'.[66]

By the mid-1950s, Dixon was importuning the Commonwealth government to terminate appeals from the High Court to the Privy Council, at least in constitutional cases, but to no avail. He finally turned to expressing his dissatisfaction in a judgment.[67] His object in so doing was 'to put [the Privy Council] on express notice of what we feel here'.[68] It was not until 1968 that appeals on constitutional and Federal matters generally were abolished.[69]

Importantly, given the particular concern of this chapter, though, common law decisions remained amenable to Privy Council appeals. This, in the event, came to matter to the High Court. Until the 1960s, it was accepted without question that the colonial common law inheritance was the common law of England. It was to be applied subject to its being capable of being applied given local conditions and circumstances. In short, the 'obligation' of *Robin*'s case was to be respected.[70] Though Dixon had on a number of occasions spoken against 'divergences',[71] it was he who, in 1963, with the concurrence of all other members of the Court, announced that the High Court would not follow the House of Lords decision in *DPP v Smith*[72] because it was considered fundamentally wrong.[73] The Court indicated that it would not adhere to its previous policy.

Three years later in *Skelton v Collins*,[74] the High Court reiterated what it said in *Parker*. Mr Justice Windeyer went on to observe:

> All judgments of the House of Lords are not equally persuasive and all statements in all speeches are not equally acceptable. This Court must consider the question for itself; and all the more so … if the decision in England was reached after reference to English decisions, not to the state of the law elsewhere, and seemingly to meet only economic and social conditions in England.[75]

So was exposed the real Achilles heel of the common law of England. It was its parochialism.

[63] See Constitution of the Commonwealth of Australia, s 74.

[64] As quoted in P Ayres, *Owen Dixon* (Melbourne, Miegunyah Press, 2003) 41.

[65] ibid 41–42.

[66] ibid 245.

[67] *O'Sullivan v Noarlunga Meat Ltd No 2* (1956) 94 CLR 367 (HCA), 375–76.

[68] Ayres, above n 64, 246.

[69] See Privy Council (Limitation of Appeals) Act 1968 (Cth).

[70] See Mason, above n 4, 69 and ch 5 generally.

[71] See, eg, O Dixon, 'Two Constitutions Compared' in O Dixon, *Jesting Pilate: And Other Papers and Addresses* (Sydney, Law Book Co, 1964) 104. This address was presented in August 1942.

[72] *DPP v Smith* [1961] AC 290 (HL).

[73] *Parker v R* (1963) 111 CLR 610 (HCA).

[74] *Skelton v Collins* (1966) 115 CLR 94 (HCA), a case on assessment of damages for personal injuries.

[75] ibid 135.

For some years prior to the Dixon statements in *Parker*, the High Court had developed a body of case law on occupier liability to trespassers. Put shortly, the position reached in *Commissioner for Railways (NSW) v Cardy*[76] was that an occupier owed a general duty of care to a trespasser to safeguard the trespasser from a grave danger of serious harm if the occupier had created or was responsible for its continued existence and was both aware of the likelihood of others encountering it and had the means of averting the danger or of warning of it. There being no direct guidance in House of Lords decisions, this was an ordered and creative development of the common law in Australia.[77] In 1964, a year after *Parker*, *Cardy* was overruled by the Privy Council in *Quinlan*'s case in what can only be described as an arrogant and patronising advice.[78] Australia now had its own difficulty. And, it was in private law.

To interpolate a personal note, I commenced studying law in 1964. *Quinlan* created another ardent abolitionist. It struck me then, as it does now, as preposterous that a foreign court could contrive the law in Australia on such a subject despite the considered views of our own High Court.

In 1966, the High Court again refused to follow another House of Lords decision.[79] This time it was *Rookes v Barnard*,[80] the exemplary damages decision. It narrowed the grounds for awarding such damages in England in a way that clearly departed from settled Australian law. Subsequently, in *Australian Consolidated Press Ltd v Uren*,[81] the Privy Council accepted the High Court's entitlement to decide as it did because '[i]n matters which may considerably be of domestic or internal significance the need for uniformity is not compelling'.[82]

Bora Laskin said at the time of this Privy Council decision:[83] '[It] suggests the end of the hegemony of the English version of the common law, of which other warnings have been given by the High Court of Australia itself'. The New Zealand courts as well were quick to see this implication in the *Uren* decision.

These developments from *Parker* onwards occurred, as Mason was to point out,[84] 'at a time when the process of dismantling the appeal to the Privy Council had begun in Australia'. By the time appeals from the High Court were abolished in 1975, the High Court's development of the common law was, for practical purposes, no longer constrained by binding English authority.[85]

In the 1980s, Australia reached a watershed in the history of what unequivocally was becoming its own common law to mould. Though the last link in Privy Council appeals[86] was not severed until the complex of Commonwealth, State and Imperial Australia Acts of 1986, the process of re-evaluation of significant parts of the common law had already begun.

1983 was a landmark year in High Court decisions. And it brought together for the first time Mason and Deane as members of the Court. In a Court of considerable talent, they

[76] *Commissioner for Railways (NSW) v Cardy* (1960) 104 CLR 274 (HCA).

[77] On *Cardy*, see Ayres, above n 64, 272.

[78] *Commissioner for Railways (NSW) v Quinlan* [1964] AC 1054 (PC); and see Fleming's withering comment on the Privy Council in his *The Law of Torts*, 3rd edn (Sydney, Law Book Co, 1965) 432–33.

[79] *Uren v John Fairfax & Sons Ltd* (1966) 117 CLR 118 (HCA).

[80] *Rookes v Barnard* [1964] AC 1129 (HL).

[81] *Australian Consolidated Press Ltd v Uren* [1969] 1 AC 590 (PC).

[82] ibid 641.

[83] In Laskin, above n 2, 62.

[84] Mason, above n 4, 70.

[85] ibid 72.

[86] ie, from State Supreme Courts in non-federal matters.

were to provide its intellectual leadership in private law, but by no means only in private law, for over a decade.

The process of legal renovation began predictably, given Australia's very distinctive preoccupation with equity jurisprudence,[87] with a significant number of equity cases concerned in the main with equitable intervention in contract and commercial dealings. Mason and Deane were gifted and creative equity lawyers and many of their early judgments were joint judgments. I described the dimensions of the change then wrought—and they were impressive—in an article I wrote in 1988.[88] I will not repeat here what I said there of the High Court's creativity in only a five-year period other than to note the following. First, this was a remarkable period in the transformation of Australia's private law, though this is often overlooked given the later decisions on constitutional law, criminal procedure, public law and native title. Secondly, the equity cases were concerned, in the main, with the imposition of standards of conduct in contractual and other relationships and dealings. There was a discernible moral dimension in the standards exacted, hence the Australian preoccupation with doctrines proscribing or precluding 'unconscionable conduct'.[89] Thirdly, as in Canada, the constructive trust as a remedy was acknowledged, and a reappraisal of equitable remedies and their availability was commenced.[90] However, unlike Canada, the constructive trust's imposition was not tied to, or founded upon, the concept of unjust enrichment.[91] Fourthly, in several cases the Court nonetheless recognised explicitly that 'the unifying concept of unjust enrichment was part of Australian law'.[92]

While, as in Canada, the adoption of a special leave requirement accentuated the role of the Court in the determination of questions of public importance, paradoxically, it spelt the decline of much commercial litigation outside of cases involving equity issues. Again, as with Canada's Supreme Court, it is still the case, for example, that the High Court has not determined the place and reach of a duty of good faith and fair dealing in Australian contract law notwithstanding that from the early 1990s the role, reach and provenance of such a duty has been debated in both State appellate courts and in the Federal Court.[93]

[87] The reasons for this are outlined at some length in Finn, above n 9, 515–18.

[88] See P Finn, 'Commerce, the Common Law and Morality' (1989) 17 *Melbourne University Law Review* 98.

[89] See, eg, the High Court decisions in *Legione v Hateley* (1983) 152 CLR 404 (promissory estoppel); *Commercial Bank of Australia v Amadio* (1983) 151 CLR 447 (unconscionable dealing); *Taylor v Johnson* (1983) 151 CLR 422 (unilateral mistake); *Hospital Products Ltd v United States Surgical Corp* (1984) 156 CLR 41 (fiduciary obligations); *United Dominions Corp Ltd v Brian Pty Ltd* (1985) 157 CLR 1 (joint ventures/fiduciary obligations); *Chan v Zacharia* (1984) 154 CLR 178 (fiduciary obligations); *Waltons Stores (Interstate) Ltd v Maher* (1988) 164 CLR 387 (equitable estoppel); *Moorgate Tobacco Co v Philip Morris Ltd (No 2)* (1984) 156 CLR 414 (breach of confidence).

[90] *Muschinski v Dodds* (1985) 160 CLR 583 (HCA) (constructive trust); *Baumgartner v Baumgartner* (1987) 164 CLR 137 (HCA) (property division and the constructive trust).

[91] See *Baumgartner v Baumgartner* (1987) 164 CLR 137 (HCA) 154; A Mason, 'Equity and Equitable Remedies in the Contemporary Common Law World' (1994) 110 *LQR* 238.

[92] Mason, above n 91, 251; *Pavey & Mathews Pty Ltd v Paul* (1987) 162 CLR 221 (HCA); *Australia and New Zealand Banking Group Ltd v Westpac Banking Corp Ltd* (1988) 164 CLR 662 (HCA); and see *Daly v Sydney Stock Exchange* (1986) 160 CLR 371 (HCA).

[93] See most recently the High Court's acknowledgement of this in *Commonwealth Bank of Australia v Barker* [2014] HCA 32, (2014) 312 ALR 356 [42], [107]; and see, eg, *Renard Constructions (ME) Pty Ltd v Minister for Public Works* (1992) 26 NSWLR 234 (CA); *Hughes Aircraft Systems International v Airservices Australia* (1997) 146 ALR 1 (FCA); *Burger King Corp v Hungry Jack's Pty Ltd* [2001] NSWCA 187, (2001) 69 NSWLR 558; *Esso Australia Resources Pty Ltd v Southern Pacific Petroleum NL* [2005] VSCA 228; and see generally, N Seddon, R Bigwood and M Ellinghaus, *Chesire and Fifoot's Law of Contract*, 10th Australian edn (Sydney, Butterworths, 2012) [10.41]–[10.47]; J Allsop, 'Good Faith and Australian Contract Law' (2011) 85 *Australian Law Journal* 341.

It is again noteworthy that the present state of the law in both countries is relatively similar and similarly unsettled.[94]

In 1987, in the year he became Chief Justice of Australia, Mason gave a speech on 'Future Directions in Australian Law'.[95] Relevantly for present purposes he said:[96]

> There is ... every reason why we should fashion a common law for Australia that is best suited to our conditions and circumstances ... The value of English judgments like Canadian, New Zealand and for that matter United States judgments, depends on the persuasive force of their reasoning.

We are back with Windeyer J in *Skelton v Collins*. Mason went on to acknowledge, first, the now available wealth of academic writings in Australia and overseas—there are obvious resonances with Laskin here; and, secondly, that an Australian common law was being developed.

An important consequence of that development was that it was necessary 'to part, in some respects at least, from the philosophy of ... legal formalism'. Put shortly, the courts had a responsibility to explain and to justify what they were doing: the policy considerations and the purposes pursued in legal developments ought not to be obscured by facades of doctrine and precedent.

By the time Mason ceased to be Chief Justice in 1995, there could be no doubting that there was a common law of Australia. Yet it was equally obvious by that time that there was a growing divergence in its common law (or such as continued to escape the legislative scythe) from England's and a closer alignment, at least with parts of its common law, with Canada, New Zealand and, more distantly, the United States. Importantly, though, the absence of a Charter or Bill of Rights imposed a limitation on what was acceptable in judicial law-making as compared with Canada and the United States in particular, as Mason was later to acknowledge.[97]

New Zealand

New Zealand[98] was the last settled and is much the smallest of the countries of present interest. By the end of the nineteenth century it had a legal system which, to an extent

[94] See, eg, *Bhasin v Hrynew* 2013 ABCA 98, (2013) 362 DLR (4th) 18 [29]–[32]; *Transamerica Life Canada Ltd v ING Canada Inc* (2003) 234 DLR (4th) 367(On CA) [41]–[64], a widely cited decision; see also J McCamus, 'The Future of the Canadian Common Law of Contract' (2014) 31 *Journal of Contract Law* 131; the comment of A Swan and J Adamski, *Canadian Contract Law*, 3rd edn (Ontario, Lexis-Nexis Canada, 2012) § 8.145, could be applied with equal justification to Australian courts: 'The idea that good faith permeates all contractual relations is one that Canadian courts have very curious problems in accepting'. But see now *Bhasin v Hrynew* 2014 SCC 71, [2014] SCR 495.

[95] See A Mason, 'Future Directions in Australian Law' (1987) 13 *Monash University Law Review* 149.

[96] ibid 154.

[97] A Mason, 'Forward' in P Rishworth (ed), *The Struggle for Simplicity in the Law* (Wellington, Butterworths, 1997) ix, x.

[98] In his chapter 'New Zealand Legal Method: Influences and Consequences' in a 2001 collection of essays on New Zealand legal method, Justice Robert Fisher explored the trajectory of New Zealand's legal method across two periods. The first was from English settlement until the 1970s/1980s; the second, until 2001. I am much indebted to his work. See R Bigwood (ed), *Legal Method in New Zealand* (Wellington, Butterworths, 2001) 27. It should be noted that Maori interests had been separated out by discreet legislation and by supplementary courts: ibid 26.

greater than in Canada and Australia, was English in character as Justice Robert Fisher noted in an essay entitled 'New Zealand Legal Method: Influences and Consequences':

> [M]ost of New Zealand's influential leaders and professionals were born or educated in England. The law was required to operate in an environment that was strongly oriented towards 'home'.[99]

Its jurisprudence was English; its legal method, formalist; and with a small population, judicial decisions were few and its own legal writings, very limited. The Privy Council was the final court of appeal. Such was its presence in the legal system that Fisher suggests that even in 2001, New Zealand lawyers were still required not only to refer to English authorities for their persuasive value but to predict the result if the matter at hand was taken to the Privy Council.[100] Unsurprisingly, to Fisher the hallmark of New Zealand's legal method betrayed a reverence for authoritative English pedigree as distinct from a focus on the consequence a new ruling was likely to produce in New Zealand—even when it was apparent that the English authority's reasoning was faulty or the results unsatisfactory.[101] And as both Fisher, and earlier, Robin Cooke indicated, the local determination to maintain consistency in the common law was pursued at the cost of the previous decisions of New Zealand's local courts.[102] Beyond all of this, and it became increasingly a difficulty for New Zealand in the latter decades of the twentieth century, it had to cope with the 'orthodoxy' of the Privy Council.[103]

Nonetheless, by the 1980s the tectonic plates of New Zealand law had been moving for some time. New Zealand, paradoxically, could make a virtue out of its small population and of the limited number of its decided cases. As Cooke put it, these provided it with:

> [t]he luxurious advantage of freedom to ransack the case law of the larger English speaking jurisdictions. And, we can be eclectic.[104]

Having learned from the *Uren* experience of Australia that departure from English common law was tolerable—that they were not 'bound' to follow House of Lords decisions[105]—increasing consideration was being given from 1970 to decisions of the High Court of Australia and the Supreme Court of Canada. While it took more than one judge to create for New Zealand its own legal identity, that change itself is associated with Robin Cooke's name.[106] He was not without his local and vocal critics.[107] To some, his decisions provided reason enough for retaining appeals to the Privy Council.[108]

[99] ibid 27.

[100] ibid.

[101] Fisher, above n 98, used the refusal in *Ross v McCarthy* [1970] NZLR 449 (CA) to reject the House of Lords decision in *Searle v Wallbank* [1947] AC 341 (HL) to illustrate this.

[102] R Cooke, 'Divergences: England, Australia and New Zealand' [1983] *New Zealand Law Journal* 297, 298 where illustrations of this are given; Fisher, above n 98, 36.

[103] See, eg, *Hart v O'Connor* [1985] 1 NZLR 159 (PC) 165, and the comments on it in R Cooke, 'The New Zealand National Legal Identity' (1987) 3 *Canterbury Law Review* 171, 177–78.

[104] See Cooke, above n 102, 297.

[105] See *Ross v McCarty* [1970] NZLR 449 (CA) 453, 455; *Bognuda v Upton and Shearer* [1972] NZLR 741 (CA); and generally K Glover, 'Severing the Ties that Bind? The Development of a Distinctive New Zealand Jurisprudence' (2000) 8 *Waikato Law Review* 25, 26–29.

[106] His many extra-curial writings have that change as a theme: see, eg, Cooke, 'Divergences', above n 102, 297; Cooke, 'The New Zealand Legal Identity', above n 103; R Cooke, 'Fundamentals' [1988] *New Zealand Law Journal* 158; R Cooke, 'Fairness' (1989) 19 *Victoria University of Wellington Law Rev* 421.

[107] See generally JA Farmer, 'Lord Cooke and Judicial Decisionmaking: A Prospective from the Commercial Bar' in P Rishworth (ed), *The Struggle for Simplicity in the Law* (Wellington, Butterworths, 1997) 53; J Smillie, 'Formalism, Fairness and Efficiency: Civil Adjudication in New Zealand' [1996] *New Zealand Law Review* 254.

[108] See Farmer, above n 107, 53.

While the Privy Council dealt unsympathetically with some number of New Zealand Court of Appeal decisions in the 1980s and early 1990s which could be said to have strategic significance in New Zealand's domestic law—and while it remained intolerant of local divergence, as, for example, in *Re Goldcorp Exchange Ltd*[109] (this decision attracted critics in Canada, New Zealand and Australia)[110]—in the end it had little choice but to concede it could not 'hold back the inevitable tide of disparity' (to use Robin Cooke's rejoinder).[111]

As the Privy Council said in *Lange v Atkinson*,[112] a case concerned with the defence of common law privilege in relation to the defamation of political figures:

> Their Lordships ... accept that there is a high content of judicial policy in the solution of the issue raised by this appeal; that different solutions may be reached in different jurisdictions without any faulty reasoning or misconception (see *Australian Consolidated Press Ltd v Uren* [1969] 1 AC 590 at 664); and that within a particular jurisdiction the necessary value judgment may be best made by the local Courts.

This retreat requires no comment other than to say that the sentiments expressed differ little from those expressed by Canada's emissary to London in 1876 in support of abolition of Privy Council appeals.[113] For 20 years and more previously, Commonwealth courts had been diverging sharply from England in doctrine, method and, often, in outcome when confronted with issues in which a national judgment, domestic policy or local concerns were properly to be expected to be given their rightful place. Emblematic of this were, first, the cases on property division on the breakdown of familial relationships[114] which in turn produced acceptance, outside of England and New Zealand, of the constructive trust as a remedy; and, secondly, the disparate decisions across the Commonwealth on a local authority's liability in tort for negligent inspection of houses under construction.[115]

Unlike Canada and Australia, New Zealand began the process of creating its own common law well before the abolition of the Privy Council appeal in 2003. The explanation of this was obvious enough. The common law world had moved on. So Robin Cooke would comment in 'Fundamentals' in 1988:[116]

> The stage has been reached in which virtually every major field of law in New Zealand law is radically, or at least very considerably different from English law. In many respects Australian and Canadian legal experience and ideas are now more relevant for us, as we work out our legal identity. The trend is evident in reciprocal legislative influence, but inevitably it has also come to be reflected in the approach of the appellate judges in particular to common law issues.

109 *Re Goldcorp Exchange Ltd (in rec)* [1995] 1 AC 74 (PC).

110 See Waters, above n 9, 90; R Sutton, 'Lord Cooke and the Academy: A View from the Law Schools' in P Rishwood (ed), *The Struggle for Simplicity in the Law* (Wellington, Butterworths, 1997) 13; P Finn, 'Equitable Doctrine and Discretion in Remedies' in W Cornish *et al* (eds), *Restitution: Past, Present and Future* (Oxford, Hart Publishing, 1998) 264.

111 See Cooke, above n 102, 297.

112 *Lange v Atkinson* [2000] 1 NZLR 257 (PC), 263.

113 '[C]ases are, by this appeal removed beyond the influence of local knowledge, of local experience, of local habits of thought and feeling, not strictly legal, which is yet essential to the formulation of sound judgment. These are unquestionably very great disadvantages.' As quoted in Herman, above n 5, 23; and see the similar comments of Dixon in *O'Sullivan v Noarlunga Meat Ltd (No 2)* (1956) 94 CLR 367 (HC), 375–76.

114 See, eg, *Pettkus v Becker* (1980) 117 DLR (3d) 257 (SCC); *Muschinski v Dodds* (1985) 160 CLR 583 (HCA); *Gillies v Keogh* [1989] 2 NZLR 327 (CA).

115 See, eg, *Invercargill City Council v Hamlin* [1996] 1 NZLR 513 (PC) and the cases referred to therein.

116 Cooke, 'Fundamentals', above n 106, 158.

From at least the 1980s until well into the 1990s, Canada, Australia and New Zealand shared self-consciously in the common pursuit of developing for the future their own versions of the common law which were suited, or adapted, to their respective needs and circumstances.

I would note in passing that this also was the time in which international conferences on private law subjects involving leading judges, practitioners and scholars from two or more Commonwealth countries (but mainly from Canada, Australia and New Zealand) began to be conducted with some regularity. They led often to the publication of collections of essays.[117] In their own way these publications fostered what, at the time, were a needed form of comparative private law studies and cross-jurisdictional understanding.[118]

II. Individualised Justice, Setting Standards of Conduct and Discretion in Remedy

> It has been said that judges write the values of the nation. No aspect of the law illustrates this more strikingly than does the recent growth of equitable remedies. In Canada, as elsewhere in the Commonwealth, courts have proved themselves ready and willing to use equitable concepts to supplement contract, tort and statute where the relief they provide is inadequate or where the standards they set fall short of perceived community standards of morality.
>
> Beverley McLachlin, 'Fairness and the Common Law: Using Equity to Achieve Justice'[119]

It is necessary to begin with a note on language. The Australian author, David Malouf, has reminded us 'that a shared language is not necessarily the same language'. This can rightly be said to be the case of the word 'equity' as used across the common law world or, for that matter, 'unconscionable conduct' with which the English in particular seem to have quite some difficulty[120]—though not at all the Australians, Canadians and Americans.[121]

'Equity' as used in England, New Zealand and Australia, refers to that body of doctrine developed originally in Chancery,[122] and which has continued to evolve as such in common law systems. In modern Canada it has a more diffuse meaning. It embraces traditional equitable doctrines and institutions (such as the trust and fiduciary relationships), but Canada has taken as well, a 'new, more liberal approach to equity',[123] often for reasons

[117] See, eg, in Canada T, Youdan (ed), *Equity, Fiduciaries and Trusts* (Toronto, Carswell, 1989); D Waters (ed), *Equity Fiduciaries and Trusts* (Toronto, Carswell, 1993); in New Zealand, the NZ Legal Research Foundation was (and is) particularly active in such activities; in Australia, the Law Book Co published six volumes of essays on various private law subjects in this period.

[118] See by way of illustration the volume edited by Waters referred to above n 117. Its first three chapters were devoted to 'The Place of Equity and Equitable Doctrines in the Contemporary Common Law World' and were written respectively by Anthony Mason ('An Australian Perspective'), Robin Cooke ('A New Zealand Perspective') and Beverley McLachlin ('A Canadian Perspective').

[119] In C Saunders (ed), *Courts of Final Jurisdiction: The Mason Court in Australia* (Sydney, Federation Press, 1996) 137.

[120] See Finn, above n 9, 518–19 and nn 54–58 therein.

[121] See, eg, the very lengthy chapter entitled 'Unconscionability' in S Waddams, *The Law of Contract*, 6th edn (Toronto, Canada Law Book Co, 2010) ch 14; and in the United States see Uniform Commercial Code, § 2-302 and, for the long understanding of it, *The Federalist*, vol 2, no LXXXI (New York, McLean, 1788) 309.

[122] And in the Exchequer Chamber.

[123] B McLachlin, 'Fairness and the Common Law: Using Equity to Achieve Justice' in C Saunders (ed), *Courts of Final Jurisdiction: The Mason Court in Australia* (Sydney, Federation Press, 1996) 119.

related to making equitable remedy (especially the constructive trust) available. Hence, Canada's law of unjust enrichment has 'equity' or 'equitable concepts' at its centre[124] (somewhat to the bemusement of English commentators).[125] Perhaps more importantly, Canada has permitted innovation and adaptation in remedies, blending common law and equitable remedies, concepts and defences to achieve desired outcomes.[126] So in *Rick v Brandsema*,[127] Abella J for the Supreme Court in an unconscionable dealings case endorsed Professor Waddams' view that:

> A rational legal system should surely permit the party complaining to receive a financial adjustment [i.e., compensation for loss] in lieu of rescission … The search for appropriate remedies, as for justice in other matters, requires a flexible and developing system.

Remedies could thus be moulded to secure 'practical justice'.[128] In Canada's 'equity' the osmotic influence of its southern neighbour is quite apparent.

Returning to my main concern, it was the case that some of the innovation engaged in by the Commonwealth courts was designed to do no more than secure greater consistency and coherence in principle and doctrine.[129] Such, for example, could be said to have been the intent of the ill-fated decision of the High Court of Australia in *Commissioner for Railways (NSW) v Cardy*.[130] Nonetheless, the twin impulses noted by Beverley McLachlin[131] were, in my view, the dominant forces which came into play in private law in Canada from the mid-1970s and in Australia and New Zealand in the 1980s. These were, first, to ameliorate the rigidities, the limitations and the inadequacies of contemporary common law doctrines which could be productive of injustices; and, secondly, to exact acceptable standards of conduct in relationships and dealings. The balances between certainty and fairness, between self-reliance and neighbourhood, between property law and remedial justice, were all shifting away from what hitherto had been their English settings.[132] Robin Cooke captured the dominant judicial mood in this: legal obligation was being asked to match 'the now pervasive concepts of duty to a neighbour and the linking of power and obligation'.[133]

[124] The pedigree for this appears to derive from Bora Laskin's dissenting judgment in *Murdoch v Murdoch* (1973) 41 DLR (3d) 367 (SCC), 385 and 388–89, and Dickson's judgment in *Pettkus v Becker* (1980) 117 DLR (3d) 257 (SCC), 270 ff.

[125] See, eg, J Beatson, 'Restitution in Canada: A Commentary' in W Cornish *et al* (eds), *Restitution: Past, Present and Future* (Oxford, Hart Publishing, 1998) 297 ff.

[126] As J Berryman observed in *The Law of Equitable Remedies*, 2nd edn (Toronto, Irwin Law, 2013) 6, 'Canadian courts have tended to eschew debates about the nature of fusion and have created a distinctive equity jurisprudence'.

[127] *Rick v Brandsema* (2009) 303 DLR (4th) 193 (SCC) [65].

[128] See generally, Berryman, above n 126. A like approach, led by Robin Cooke, has been taken to the fusion of common law and equitable remedies and defences in New Zealand: see *Aquaculture Corp v NZ Green Mussel Co Ltd* [1990] 3 NZLR 299 (CA), 301; *Day v Mead* [1987] 2 NZLR 443 (CA); and see generally A Butler (ed), *Equity and Trusts in New Zealand*, 2nd edn (Wellington, Thompson Reuters, 2009) [1.9] and [44.2]; contrast in Australia, *Pilmer v Duke Group Ltd (in liq)* (2001) 207 CLR 165 (HCA) [86]; but *cf* A Mason, 'The Place of Equity and Equitable Remedies in the Contemporary Common Law World' (1994) 110 *LQR* 238, 244.

[129] See Mason, above n 61, 117.

[130] *Commissioner for Railways (NSW) v Cardy* (1960) 104 CLR 274 (HCA).

[131] In the quotation heading this part, above n 119.

[132] Focusing primarily on Australia, I examined these changes in 'Commerce, the Common Law and Morality' (1989) 17 *Melbourne University Law Review* 87; 'Equitable Doctrine and Discretion' in Cornish *et al*, above n 110; and 'Modern Equity' in P Rishworth (ed), *The Struggle for Simplicity in the Law* (Wellington, Butterworths, 1997).

[133] *Nicholson v Permakraft (NZ) Ltd* (1985) 3 ACLC 453 (NZCA), 459.

That the three Commonwealth countries turned to 'equity' and 'equitable concepts' (howsoever understood) and to 'fairness' in this endeavour is unsurprising. That England did not is equally unsurprising. Prevailing legal policy in English law in relation (1) to the enforceability of voluntary promises[134] (then, and to a significant extent, now); (2) to the maintenance of certainty in contractual dealings and to immunisation of commercial contracts from fiduciary obligations and equitable estoppel;[135] and (3) to insistence on the primacy of property law in determining entitlements to interests in property and to a corresponding refusal to recognise the constructive trust as a remedy,[136] saw to that. A change of temper in England of the magnitude that occurred in the Commonwealth countries was unlikely in any event given the shackled state particularly of equitable doctrine in England.

The twentieth century was, for the most part, the century of the common law in England. A consequence of this was an increasingly petrified, if not forgotten, equity jurisprudence.[137] This was most notably so in doctrines concerned with 'fraud in equity' (or 'unconscionable conduct'). These in quite some measure were ignored or forgotten for decades until they were 'resuscitated' (or reimagined in a fashion) towards the end of the twentieth century.[138]

In contrast, Australia retained a much more robust and coherent equity jurisprudence, due in no small measure to the failure in New South Wales to implement a Judicature Act system until 1972.[139] This was reflected in legal education across the century.[140] Some number of practitioner-lecturers in equity were later to become High Court and State Supreme Court judges. Mason was among the former of these. From Australia's foundation in 1901 until the early 1980s there was an uncommonly large number of equity cases decided by the High Court. In aggregate these constituted the platform of principle and doctrine on which Mason and Deane in particular built thereafter. If Harvard-educated Bora Laskin had to

[134] Lord Cranworth's comments in *Jorden v Money* (1854) 5 HLC 185, 216; 10 ER 868, 882 remain the orthodoxy.

[135] *Cobbe v Yeoman's Row Management Ltd* [2008] 1 WLR 1752 (HL) [81]; see also D Neuberger, 'Thoughts on the Law of Equitable Estoppel' (2010) 84 *Australian Law Journal* 225, 231.

[136] *Sinclair Investments (UK) Ltd v Versailles Trade Finance Ltd* [2012] Ch 453 (CA) [37]; see also Lord Neuberger, 'The Remedial Constructive Trust: Fact or Fiction', Banking Services and Financial Law Conference, Queenstown, New Zealand, 10 August 2014; but contrast A Kull, 'Deconstructing the Constructive Trust' (2004) 40 *Canadian Business Law Journal* 358, 359: 'We see the constructive trust as a remedy for certain cases ... We do not spend any time worrying about the distinction between a "remedial constructive trust" and some other, because no US lawyer has ever heard that there is any other kind'; see also the observations of Deane J in *Muschinski v Dodds* (1985) 160 CLR 583 (CA), 614 to similar effect.

[137] Outside of the law of trusts, and of injunctions and specific performance.

[138] I refer, eg, to the unconscionable dealings doctrine: see *Cresswell v Potter* [1978] 1 WLR 255 (Ch) (but decided in 1968), and D Capper, 'The Unconscionable Bargain in the Common Law World' (2010) 126 *LQR* 403; undue influence: see *National Westminster Bank Plc v Morgan* [1985] 1 AC 686 (HL) and see R Bigwood, 'From *Morgan* to *Etridge*: Tracing the (Dis)Integration of Undue Influence in the United Kingdom' in J Neyers, R Bronaugh and S Pitel (eds), *Exploring Contract Law* (Oxford, Hart Publishing, 2009) ch 15; fiduciary obligations: *Bristol & West Building Society v Mothew* [1998] Ch 1 (CA); and equitable estoppel: see *Crabb v Arun District Council* [1976] Ch 179 (CA) (proprietary estoppel was first resuscitated in New Zealand, see *Thomas v Thomas* [1956] NZLR 785). Lord Denning's endeavours to create a 'new equity' (see *Re Vandervell's Trust (No 2)* [1974] Ch 269 (CA), 322) were for the most part still-born or short-lived: see, eg, the fate of *Solle v Butcher* [1950] 1 KB 671 (CA) in *Great Peace Shipping Ltd v Tsavliris (International) Ltd* [2003] QB 679 (CA).

[139] While Canada's story in this regard is varied, the move to a Judicature Act-like system occurred in some provinces on their creation of courts, and was virtually the norm in all common law provinces at the time of, or shortly after, the Judicature Acts in England: for the Canadian story see Laskin, above n 2, 10–21. New Zealand has never had a system of separate common law and equity courts: see Butler, above n 128, [1.7].

[140] Sir Frederick Jordan's *Chapters on Equity* ran to six editions and has its genesis in his lecture courses as Challis Lecturer in Equity at the University of Sydney: see W Gummow, 'The Equity of Sir Frederick Jordan' (1991) 13 *Sydney Law Review* 263.

turn to the United States equity jurisprudence for his inspiration,[141] the Australians had already built their own foundations.[142]

This is not the place to compare and contrast how Canada, Australia and New Zealand each developed and deployed equitable doctrines, concepts and remedies to their own ends. It would mislead, though, to suggest there was consistency, let alone uniformity, in what they did. National concerns, and acceptable national methodologies, had their own imperatives.

There are, though, a number of matters I should refer to by way of illustration of change and difference. First, doctrine. The unconscionable dealings doctrine remains all but moribund in England.[143] A line of High Court cases in Australia commencing in 1913[144] and leading up to the authoritative exposition of Fullagar J in *Blomley v Ryan*[145] paved the way for the landmark decision of *Commercial Bank of Australia v Amadio*.[146] Put shortly, the doctrine is now concerned with unconscionably taking advantage of a person in a position of serious disadvantage vis-à-vis the advantage taker in their relationship or dealing. These two decisions have given real vitality to the doctrine both in Australia (where the legislature has in any event now provided a more expansive statutory proscription of unconscionable dealing as is also the case in the United States)[147] and in New Zealand (where the New Zealanders have ignored what was heterodox in English and Privy Council decisions).[148]

What is notable about recent Australian law, though, is the apparent reluctance to countenance a place for this doctrine in commercial dealings.[149] The Canadians, rightly in my view, have no such reluctance.[150] Franchisees and small business tenants are quite often in asymmetric relationships of power with their franchisors and landlords. And they are often ruthlessly exploited. Canadian law in contrast with Australia's has been influenced by Lord Denning's 'principle of inequality of bargaining power'[151]—a principle later disavowed by the House of Lords.[152] While the Supreme Court of Canada has not dealt systematically with Canada's 'unconscionable bargains' doctrine, it has recognised it as part of Canadian law; has accepted that such bargains arose from situations of unequal bargaining power; and can be found (though not often) in dealings between commercial parties.[153]

[141] His dissent in *Murdoch v Murdoch* (1973) 41 DLR (3d) 367 (SCC), drew directly on Austen Scott's work on *Trusts* and on the famous observation of Cardozo that the 'constructive trust is the formula through which the consequences of equity finds expression'.

[142] See Finn, above n 9, 517.

[143] See, eg, *Boustany v Pigott* (1993) 69 P&CR 298 (PC); *Portman Building Society v Dusangh* [2002] 2 All ER (Comm) 221 (CA). References to it occupy little space in English texts: see, eg, J McGhee (ed), *Snell's Equity*, 32nd edn (London, Sweet and Maxwell, 2010) [8-034]; see also Capper, above n 138.

[144] *Dowsett v Reid* (1913) 15 CLR 695 (HCA).

[145] *Blomley v Ryan* (1956) 99 CLR 362 (HCA), 405.

[146] *Commercial Bank of Australia v Amadio* (1983) 151 CLR 447 (HCA).

[147] See Uniform Commercial Code, § 2-302.

[148] See, eg, the formulation of Richardson J in *Contractors Bonding Ltd v Smee* [1992] 2 NZLR 157 (CA), 174, and that of Tipping J in *Gustav v Macfield Ltd* [2008] 2 NZLR 735 (SC) [6]; see generally Butler, above n 128, ch 23. I would note that the English legacy of undue influence continues to destabilise New Zealand law: see ibid 690–91.

[149] See *Australian Competition and Consumer Commission v CG Berbatis Holdings Pty Ltd* (2003) 214 CLR 51 (HCA); *Kakavas v Crown Melbourne* [2013] HCA 24, (2013) 250 CLR 392.

[150] See, eg, *A&K Lick-a-Chick Franchises Ltd v Cordiv Enterprises Ltd* (1981) 119 DLR (3d) 440 (NSSC).

[151] *Lloyds Bank Ltd v Bundy* [1975] QB 326 (CA), 369.

[152] *National Westminster Bank Plc v Morgan* [1985] AC 686 (HL), 708.

[153] See *Tercon Contractors Ltd v British Columbia* (2010) 315 DLR (4th) 385 (SCC); see also *Hunter Engineering Co Ltd v Syncrude Canada Ltd* (1989) 57 DLR (4th) 321 (SCC). US law accepts this possibility as well. As was said in one case: 'generalisations are always subject to exceptions and categorisation is rarely an adequate substitute for

Turning, briefly, to equitable estoppel, Canadian law seems, somewhat surprisingly, to have maintained what in substance is English common law.[154] Proprietary and promissory estoppel, for the most part,[155] have been kept distinct,[156] the former being a cause of action limited to claims to, or relating to, property, and the latter, a defence to the enforcement of strict legal rights.[157] Australia and New Zealand in contrast have fused and enlarged the various forms of estoppel in equity (particularly promissory estoppel and proprietary estoppel) so as now to have a unified 'equitable estoppel' which can be used both offensively and defensively. It is informed by the principle that a person will not be permitted to falsify an assumption or understanding that they have caused or knowingly allowed another to rely upon where such falsification would be unconscionable.[158] Both countries now provide causes of action in circumstances where equitable relief would not be countenanced in English law.[159] To this extent they have moved much closer to United States law as represented in section 90 of the *Restatement of Contracts, Second*.[160] While New Zealand's courts have shown a willingness to incorporate common law estoppel by representation into 'a single overarching doctrine' (a course that Mason understandably favoured),[161] the Australian courts remain strangely reluctant to take this obvious step.[162]

It ought to be noted in passing that in the largest, but most ignored, common law jurisdiction, India, the country's Supreme Court accepted in 1978 that promissory estoppel could itself be a cause of action; its operation could not be shackled by the doctrine of consideration; and it could be applied, in appropriate circumstances, to governmental promises.[163] The decision is a commendable example of the creative use of comparative common law scholarship.[164]

The final doctrinal matter to be mentioned is fiduciary law. I simply note here that Canadian fiduciary law has a significantly different reach and content from Australian law, but not quite so New Zealand law. Canada has taken its law far beyond the mere protection of

analysis … even large business entities may have relatively little bargaining power, depending on the identity of the other contracting party and the commercial circumstances surrounding the agreement': see *A&M Produce Co v FMC Corp* 135 Cal App 3d 473, 489 (1982).

154 See *Ryan v Moore* [2005] 2 SCR 53 [50]–[52].

155 But see *Schwork v Cutting* [2010] ONCA 61 [34]: 'proprietary estoppel is a form of promissory estoppel'; *Wilson v Benson Estate* [2006] ABCA 287 [2].

156 *Belvedere v Brittain Estate* (2009) 306 DLR (4th) 754 (SCC); *Maracle v Travellers Indemnity Co of Canada* [1991] 2 SCR 50 [13]; *Ryan v Moore* [2005] 2 SCR 53.

157 But see the optimistic view of J McCamus, 'The Future of the Canadian Law of Contract' (2014) 31 *Journal of Contract Law* 131 who envisages Canada's adoption of the *Restatement of Contracts Second*, § 90.

158 See in Australia, *Waltons Stores (Interstate) Ltd v Maher* (1988) 164 CLR 387 (HCA), 404, and see also *Sidhu v Van Dyke* [2014] HCA 19, (2014) 251 CLR 505 [1]; in New Zealand, *National Westminster Finance NZ Ltd v National Bank of NZ Ltd* [1996] 1 NZLR 548, 549. See also, Butler, above n 128, ch 19; see also, Finn, above n 9, 526–31.

159 Contrast *EK Nominees Pty Ltd v Woolworths Ltd* [2006] NSWSC 1172 and *Cobbe v Yeoman's Row Management Ltd* [2008] 1 WLR 1752 (HL); see also *Baird Textile Holdings Ltd v Marks Spencer Plc* [2002] 1 All ER (Comm) 737 (CA) [91]–[95].

160 See, eg, *Hoffman v Red Owl Store Inc* 133 NW 2d 267 (1965) and *Drennan v Star Paving Co* 333 P 2d 757 (1958).

161 See *Commonwealth of Australia v Verwayen* (1990) 170 CLR 394 (HCA), 412; and see Butler, above n 128, 611–12.

162 UNIDROIT Principles of International Commercial Contracts, art 1-8 embodies such a doctrine. All of the examples given are derived from Australian case law.

163 See *Motilal Padampat Sugar Mills Co Ltd v State of Uttar Pradesh* 1979 (2) SCC 409.

164 References were made to English, American, Australian and Indian sources.

economic interests to encompass, for example, the parent–child relationship in sexual abuse cases,[165] patient access to a doctor's medical records,[166] and the Crown–Aboriginal people relationship.[167] The High Court in contrast, in its more recent mood of strict orthodoxy,[168] has refused to countenance such developments.[169] Seemingly, economic interests alone are what this body of law is designed to protect[170]—for the moment at least.[171]

Turning, secondly, to remedy: there were three developments in remedy that are deserving of mention, which partnered those in doctrine. These have been embraced or rejected to varying degrees by each of England, Canada, Australia and New Zealand. They are to this day the cause of discord as between these jurisdictions. I can only note them here, prefacing what I say with the observation that they betray strongly held views on legal policy and on appropriate methodology in each of the jurisdictions.

The first development was the open acceptance in Canada and Australia of the constructive trust as a remedy.[172] It was rejected forthrightly in England and then in New Zealand, albeit under the shadow of hostile House of Lords and Privy Council decisions.[173] Nonetheless, New Zealand of recent times has shown some propensity to flirt with the 'remedial constructive trust'[174] but its present status remains in doubt.[175] As in England, concerns about interference with property rights remain.

Secondly, the dramatic revival of the compensatory remedy,[176] and the range of demands being made on it, particularly in cases of breach of fiduciary duty and breach of confidence, have produced divergent, often contradictory responses to the assessment principles to be applied both generally and in relation to specific doctrines (given their individual purposes).[177] The absence of a jurisprudence developed over time has exposed a multiplicity of issues.[178]

[165] *KM v HM* (1992) 96 DLR (4th) 289 (SCC); see also in relation to doctor-patient and coerced sexual relations: *Norberg v Wynrib* [1992] 2 SCR 226 (L'Hereux-Dube and McLachlin JJ); and see in New Zealand, Butler, above n 128, 533–55 and 549–51.

[166] *McInerney v MacDonald* [1992] 2 SCR 138.

[167] *Guerin v R* (1984) 13 DLR (4th) 321 (SCC); and see also Sharpe and Roach, above n 42, 446–53; see also in New Zealand, Butler, above n 128, ch 43, 'Equity and Maori'.

[168] Both in doctrine and in methodology.

[169] See *Breen v Williams* (1996) 186 CLR 71 (HCA).

[170] *Paramasivam v Flynn* (1998) 160 ALR 203 (FCA).

[171] It should not be forgotten, for example, that the most fundamental of fiduciary relationships is that which exists between the state, its officers and agencies and the people: see PD Finn, 'The Forgotten Trust: The People and the State' in M Cope (ed), *Equity: Issues and Trends* (Sydney, Federation Press, 1995) ch 5; and see E Fox-Decent, *Sovereignty's Promise: The State as Fiduciary* (Oxford, OUP, 2011).

[172] While the remedial constructive trust has an unchallengeable place in Australian equity (see *Muschinski v Dodds* (1985) 160 CLR 583 (HCA), 614 (Deane J)), like all equitable remedies, it is discretionary and its award is limited by the consideration whether such would be appropriate to do what is 'practically just', having regard to the purpose or imperatives served by the individual doctrine giving rise to the constructive trust claim: see *Grimaldi v Chameleon Mining NL (No 2)* [2012] FCAFC 6, (2012) 200 FCR 296 [503]–[512] and [666]–[681].

[173] See in particular *Re Goldcorp Exchange Ltd (in rec)* [1994] 3 NZLR 385 (PC); and see Lord Neuberger, 'The Remedial Constructive Trust: Fact or Fiction', Supreme Court Speeches, 10 August 2014.

[174] See, eg, *Regal Castings Ltd v Lightbody* [2008] NZSC 87, [2009] 2 NZLR 433 (Tipping J); *Commonwealth Reserves I v Chodar* [2001] 2 NZLR 374 (HC).

[175] See *Strategic Finance Ltd v Bridgman* [2013] NZCA 357 [122]–[25].

[176] Beyond the law of trusts and directors' duties of care, skill and diligence; see Finn, above n 110, 260–61.

[177] See, eg, *Canson Enterprises Ltd v Boughton & Co* (1991) 85 DLR (4th) 129 (SCC); *Youyang Pty Ltd v Minter Ellison* (2003) 212 CLR 484 (HCA) [35]–[50]; K Barnett and S Harder, *Remedies in Australian Private Law* (Cambridge, CUP 2014) ch 9; for Canada, see Berryman, above n 126, 482–98; in New Zealand, Butler, above n 128, ch 32,

[178] (i) Are the principles governing assessment specific to each particular doctrine for which the remedy is an available one?—an issue of no little importance in Australia and Canada given the range and reach of the doctrines

What is clear is that we are far from a clear and coherent set of principles as between common law countries. This in quite some degree reflects how differently they each conceive of 'equity' and of 'fusion'.

Thirdly, and I need hardly comment on this, insofar as compensation is (or remains) an equitable remedy, its award is discretionary and, in a given instance, depends upon whether, in the circumstances, it is an appropriate remedy to do practical justice. The importance of this is that liability and remedy have been uncoupled. This, I would interpolate, reflects the 'basket' approach to remedy taken in modern statutes at least in Australia, as, for example, in the Corporations Act 2001 (Cth) and the inappropriately named Australian Consumer Law 2010 (Cth). I will refer below to the analogical use of such statutes.

Having spoken of applicable doctrine and remedy, I should add a note on recent doctrine and remedy in Australia—the more so, as I have said, because the developed state of Australian equity up to the 1980s paved the way for the Mason Court. By the mid-1990s, with Mason and Deane gone, Chief Justice Brennan saw the High Court's immediate future as one of 'consolidating the advances that had been made'.[179] At the same time Beverley McLachlin mused on whether, in Canada, 'the initial burst of creativity may be yielding to a period of consolidation, with the courts increasingly preoccupied with establishing appropriate doctrinal limits for the new equitable remedies'.[180]

In the event it has been Australia's fate for the High Court to revert to strictly doctrinal preoccupations and to forsake the 'creative art' of moulding the law 'to fulfill the needs of a changing social order'.[181] Lamentably, in fields as diverse as accessorial liability in equity,[182] penalties[183] and estoppel,[184] the trajectory of our own law has faltered, seemingly for fear of 'fusion' and because of reverence for nineteenth century (and earlier) jurisprudence—for

for which equitable compensation is now available if appropriate. In Australia the remedy is available, for any breach of an equitable obligation, be this for breach of trust, breach of confidence, breach of fiduciary duty, equitable estoppel, unconscionable dealing, undue influence, etc: see P Young *et al*, *On Equity* (Sydney, Law Book Co, 2009) [16.1160]. In Canada, the problem is compounded by the diversity of circumstances which can give rise to a breach of fiduciary duty, but Canada has also extended its use of the remedy beyond fiduciaries and trusts, see, eg, *Rick v Brandsema* (2009) 303 DLR (4th) 193 (SCC) [65] and *Dusik v Newton* (1985) 62 BCLR 1 (CA). (ii) In what circumstances should there be fusion of this equitable remedy and of a like common law one, for example, negligence; eg, *Bristol West Building Society v Mothew* [1998] Ch 1 (CA), 17; but contrast *Youyang Pty Ltd v Minter Ellison* (2003) 212 CLR 484 (HCA) [38]–[39]; and see *Downsview v First City Corp Ltd* [1993] AC 295 (PC); misappropriation of valuable confidential information or defamation?: see J Stuckey-Clarke, '"Damages" for Breaches of Purely Equitable Rights: The Breach of Confidence Example' in P Finn (ed), *Essays on Damages* (Sydney, Law Book Co, 1992) ch 4; and see *X v AG* [1977] 2 NZLR 623. (iii) When, and if so, to what extent do concepts such as mitigation, causation, foreseeability and remoteness have a role in assessment? (iv) What now is to be made of the contentious rule enunciated by the Privy Council in *Brickendon v London Loan and Savings Co* [1934] 3 DLR 465 (PC) 469? (v) And what of contributory negligence?: see *Day v Mead* [1987] 2 NZLR 443 (CA) or exemplary damages?: see *Acquaculture Corp v NZ Green Mussel Co Ltd* [1990] 3 NZLR 299 (CA), contrast *Bailey v Namol Pty Ltd* (1994) 53 FCR 102, 112–13; *Harris v Digital Pulse Pty Ltd* (2003) 56 NSWLR 298 (CA).

[179] FG Brennan, 'Looking to the Future' in C Saunders (ed), *Courts of Final Jurisdiction: The Mason Court in Australia* (Sydney, Federation Press, 1996) 265.

[180] B McLachlin, 'Fairness in the Common Law', in C Saunders (ed), *Courts of Final Jurisdiction: The Mason Court in Australia* (Sydney, Federation Press, 1996) 137.

[181] H Stone, 'Mr Justice Cardozo' (1939) 52 *Harvard Law Review* 353, 354.

[182] See *Farah Constructions Pty Ltd v Say-Dee Pty Ltd* (2007) 230 CLR 89 (HCA). I refer to the comments on *Barnes v Addy*.

[183] See *Andrews v Australian and New Zealand Banking Group Ltd* [2012] HCA 30, (2012) 247 CLR 205; and see J Carter *et al*, 'Contractual Penalties: Resurrecting the Equity Jurisdiction' (2013) 30 *Journal of Contract Law* 99.

[184] An overarching doctrine remains friendless as I have noted; see G Dal Pont, *Equity and Trusts*, 5th edn (Sydney, Law Books Co, 2011); see also *Sidhu v Van Dyke* [2014] HCA 19, (2014) 251 CLR 505.

what Brian Dickson called 'the antiquity of disembodied precedence'.[185] Principle, policy and ordered development all have been in flight in Australia's ultimate court of appeal.[186]

III. A Moral Endeavour and a Transparent Method

> The recent decade might be regarded as a period of legal transition in which we have been moving from an era of strict law to one which gives greater emphasis to equity and natural law. As Roscoe Pound said in *The Spirit of the Common Law*, the endeavour to make morals and law coincide will be an important future goal.
>
> Anthony Mason, 'The Place of Equity and Equitable Remedies in the Common Law World'[187]

There were important common threads in the private law jurisprudence[188] of the Supreme Court of Canada, the High Court of Australia and the Court of Appeal of New Zealand. Sometimes expressed in language of the common law, sometimes that of equity, they betrayed an accentuated concern for what I will describe simply as 'equity and justice' (to adapt the title of the Beverley McLachlin paper from which I quoted earlier). The particular emphasis in the language changed with the particular issue and matter of principle before each court and I note here a number of the refrains often used. In Australia, the most common were variants on 'unconscionability' and 'fairness'; in Canada, 'inequitable', 'unconscionable' or 'unjust'; in New Zealand, 'fairness' (or 'unfairness')'[189] and 'unreasonableness' and 'reasonable expectations'. Such concepts were, for the most part, not set up as tests of the respective rights and liabilities of parties—and the courts often enough disclaimed such was the case. However, they did acknowledge that the concepts were important touchstones, or organising (or informing) ideas for individual doctrines in which they were given more concrete and structured expression. Such should be apparent from what I have said so far.

The three courts, quite self-consciously, were changing the law. Principle and policy were important instruments in this and it was recognised in all three countries that no longer could they be hidden by what an Australian journalist described as 'thickets of legal theology', to justify their actions and to immunise themselves from public criticism. Hence, there was a change away from legal formalism to open explanation, to what Laskin described as 'articulate reasons'. Mason commented to the same effect in a number of articles,[190] as did Dickson who, after noting that it is obvious 'a person cannot write more clearly than he thinks' went on to comment that the 'identifying badge of a superior judgment is a focus on

[185] Saywell, above n 12, 277.

[186] The same affliction has befallen Australia's contract law: see, eg, *Western Export Services Inc v Jireh International Pty Ltd* [2011] HCA 45, 282 ALR 604 (refusing a special leave application); and see Carter *et al*, above n 183.

[187] A Mason, 'The Place of Equity and Equitable Remedies in the Common Law World' (1994) 110 *LQR* 238, 259.

[188] But by no means only private law.

[189] The New Zealand usage is particularly marked. 'Fairness' is the title of a Cooke article and is a recurrent formula in judicial decision: see, eg, *Elders Pastoral Ltd v Bank of New Zealand* [1989] 2 NZLR 180 (CA); *Gillies v Keogh* [1989] 2 NZLR 327 (CA), 331, 344; *Equiticorp Industries Group Ltd v Hawkins* [1991] 3 NZLR 700 (CA), 727; and *Liggett v Kensington* [1993] 1 NZLR 257 (CA), 293.

[190] See, eg, A Mason, 'Future Directions in Australian Law' (1987) 13 *Monash University Law Review* 149, 155–58.

principle and reason'.[191] And in describing the equity cases he participated in, Robin Cooke described the approach he adopted as involving 'a thorough analysis of the facts followed by the application of the broad principles of conscience, fairness and reason'.[192] What was espoused and practised in this period was transparent reasoning and reasons.

To a significant degree, as I have already indicated, the courts were concerned with prescribing standards of conduct and this led them to invoking 'community standards (or values)'. This is a contentious subject and has been recognised as such.[193] But it is important to appreciate its import if one is to understand what can occasion convergence and divergence both between jurisdictions and in the same jurisdiction over time.

In a well-known Canadian decision, *Harry v Kreutziger*,[194] a judge of the Court of Appeal of British Columbia, Lambert J-A, in asking whether a use of bargain power was 'unconscionable', said:

> The single question of whether the transaction, seen as a whole, is sufficiently divergent from community standards of commercial morality that it should be rescinded must be answered by an examination of the decided cases and a consideration, from those cases, of the fact patterns that require that the bargain be rescinded and those that do not. In that examination, Canadian cases are more relevant than those from other lands where different standards of commercial morality may apply, and recent cases are more germane than those from earlier times when standards were, in some respects, rougher and, in other respects, more fastidious. In my opinion, it is also appropriate to seek guidance as to community standards of commercial morality from legislation that embodies those standards in law.[195]

The burden of this is clear enough, but it is the final sentence of the quotation that I wish to emphasise. From at least the time of Roscoe Pound's article in the *Harvard Law Review* in 1908,[196] the symbiotic relationship of statute and the common law has been addressed regularly in scholarly writings in the United States. This phenomenon is of much more recent origin in Commonwealth countries generally.[197] As statute (at least outside the United Kingdom) entrenches significantly on what were previously the private law domains of the common law, the relationship is coming to assume no little importance for how the common law of a country develops.

Probably the principal catalyst to divergence between England and Australia, for example, is the very different legislative environments in which the private law of each country evolves and does its work. I have dealt with this recently, elsewhere.[198] And it is the subject

[191] As quoted in Sharpe and Roach, above n 42, 203.

[192] See R Cooke, 'A New Zealand Perspective' in D Waters (ed), *Equity Fiduciaries and Trusts* (Toronto, Carswell, 1993) 29.

[193] See Anthony Mason's views in 'Rights, Values and Legal Institutions: Reshaping Australian Institutions' in G Lindell (ed), *The Mason Papers* (Sydney, Federation Press, 2007) 80.

[194] *Harry v Kreutziger* (1978) 95 DLR (3d) 231 (BCCA).

[195] The inter-jurisdictional comparison suggested here might make one reflect on a relatively recent English decision where a Chancery judge observed: 'In a commercial context … a degree of self-dealing and ruthless behavior is expected and accepted to a degree': *Vercoe v Rutland Fund Management Ltd* [2010] EWHC 424 (Ch) [343].

[196] R Pound, 'Common Law and Legislation' (1908) 21 *Harvard Law Review* 383.

[197] I first wrote on the subject in 1992 where a deal of literature to that date is collected: see P Finn, 'Statutes and the Common Law' (1992) 22 *University of Western Australia Law Review* 7; see also A Burrows, 'The Relationship between Common Law and Statute in the Law of Obligations' (2012) 128 *LQR* 232; see also P Finn, 'Statutes and the Common Law: The Continuing Story' in S Corcoran and S Bottomley, *Interpreting Statutes* (Sydney, Federation Press, 2005).

[198] Finn, above n 9, 534–39.

of Sir Anthony Mason's chapter in this volume. All I wish to note here is that many of Australia's major developments in equity from the 1980s involved conduct that would have been actionable under generally cast statutes in any event. *Commercial Bank of Australia Ltd v Amadio*[199] (the unconscionable dealings case) and *Walton Stores (Interstate) Ltd v Maher*[200] (on equitable estoppel) are conspicuous examples.

In the age of statutes, the influence of statute upon the common law may often be no more than osmotic. Nonetheless, as statements of prevailing public policy and of appropriate standards to be adhered to in commercial and consumer dealings, they provide both a context in which judicial law-making will take place and a measure against which it may be judged. This is the significance of Lambert J-A's comment. And it points up what is a critically important matter of which account needs to be taken in understanding divergence—the statutory setting of the body of law in question, a factor recently emphasized by the High Court of Australia in declining to imply by law a term of mutual trust and confidence in all employment contracts.[201] Such a term has been accepted in England but in the context of a regulatory history of employment relationships and of industrial relations generally which, as the High Court recognised, differed from the Australian context.

IV. Conclusion

Canada, Australia and New Zealand are no longer required to accept ready-made solutions from England. Each is the master of its own destiny. To ignore this in any discussion of divergence, in particular, is radically to misunderstand the common law system itself—a system no longer artificially contrived by the Privy Council.

I have suggested already a number of obvious causes of divergence. There are many. But let me refer to two which are the two most often emphasised but the two most pointless on which to take cross-jurisdictional issue. The first is an aspect of judicial method. It fails to recognise that what is an acceptable form of judicial law-making in one country, may not be so in another. I recall a talk given in 1988 by the eminent Canadian scholar Donovan Waters who was comparing the Australian and Canadian law on 'unconscionable transactions'.[202] He delighted in commenting: 'Australia and Canada have reached Canaan—but the Canadians got there without a map'. However, Canadian judicial law-making can, on occasion, have designedly civil law, 'top down' or 'greenfield' characteristics which are less acceptable in Australia, or England even more so, where traditional common law methodology holds sway.[203]

The second are those disputes over doctrinal differences that produce little difference in case outcomes. Doctrinal differences, more often than not, are attributable to different intellectual histories and traditions. These need to be respected. One need only refer to Australia's long-standing equity tradition which has given it such prominence in Australian

[199] *Commercial Bank of Australia Ltd v Amadio* (1983) 151 CLR 447 (HCA).

[200] *Waltons Stores (Interstate) Ltd v Maher* (1988) 164 CLR 387 (HCA).

[201] *Commonwealth Bank of Australia v Barker* [2014] HCA 32, 312 ALR 356.

[202] See D Waters, 'New Directions in the Employment of Equitable Doctrines: The Canadian Experience' in TG Youdan (ed), *Equity, Fiduciaries and Trusts* (Toronto, Carswell, 1989) 411.

[203] See, eg, the comments of Beatson, above n 125, 298–99.

jurisprudence; to England's relatively recent but nonetheless enthusiastic embrace of the law of restitution;[204] or Canada's contemporary treatment of equity as a 'remedy'.[205] It would be unwise for critics in one country to expect the judges in another to abandon what has served them well. The Supreme Court of Canada, for example, recently found no compelling reason for abandoning its law on purchase money resulting trusts—it had provided 'certainty and predictability'—despite being importuned to do so in the cause of unjust enrichment.[206]

Beyond this, though, are those doctrinal differences which do produce significant differences in outcome, but do so because of the pervasive influence of generally worded statutes, the language and policy of which cast their shadow over common law doctrines. Such is the commonplace in the United States and Australia, as is exemplified by the 'unconscionable contracts' provision of the Uniform Commercial Code[207] and by the 'misleading or deceptive conduct' provision[208] of the Australian Consumer Law 2010 and its 1974 predecessor (which significantly, but with some variation, was modelled on United States Federal legislation).[209]

I have said little of the extent to which national common law courts now engage in what I might describe as comparative common law. It is used both to inform how a court might respond to a moral issue confronting it and as a justification for making or not making a departure from its existing law. What is important, though, is that it is a country's own final court of appeal which determines how its law will be shaped and developed irrespective of whether this results in divergence from, or similarity with, one or more other common law jurisdictions.

This is the fundamental change about which I have spoken. It brings to mind another quotation, which has a certain aptness as an end to my contribution to the conference for which it was prepared:

> There was a time when we came to such gatherings like poor relations to a table where the British played host, bringing with us, each one, a wariness of the rest that came from the reluctance of one poor relation to see his lowly status reflected in another's. Australians and Canadians, Australians and Scots, tended to ignore one another.
>
> Those days are gone. Britain no longer sits at the head of the table. The rest of us no longer use the British, or need them, in our dealings with one another. As often as not it is the British representatives at such gatherings now who feel marginalized and out of place.
>
> The fact is, there is no longer a 'centre' around which we circulate and dance. We have all shifted place.

The writer is the acclaimed Australian novelist and essayist, David Malouf; the gathering to which he referred was the annual judging of the Commonwealth Literary Prize for Fiction; and the work itself, written in 2002, had the title: *Made in England*.

[204] Or unjust enrichment.

[205] This is evident in the writings of Beverley McLachlin and in judicial decision: see, eg, *Garland v Consumers' Gas Co Ltd* [2004] 1 SCR 629, 237 DLR (4th) 384 [44] (Jacobucci J).

[206] See *Nishi v Rascal Trucking Ltd* 2013 SCC 31, [2013] 2 SCR 438 [28].

[207] § 2-302, said by its reputed author, Karl Llewellyn to be 'perhaps the most valuable section in the entire Code': see A Farnsworth, *Contracts*, 4th edn (New York, Aspen, 2004) § 4.28; see also Australian Consumer Law 2010 (Cth), ss 20 and 21.

[208] Australian Consumer Law 2010 (Cth), s 18, previously Trade Practices Act 1974 (Cth), s 52.

[209] See Federal Trade Commission Act 1914, s 5 (US), as amended in 1938 and *Hornsby Building Information Centre Pty Ltd v Sydney Building Information Centre Pty Ltd* (1978) 140 CLR 216 (HCA), 226–27.

4

A Conscious Effort to Develop a 'Different' Common Law of Obligations: A Possible Endeavour?

GOH YIHAN*

I. Introduction

More than two decades have passed since the Singapore Parliament passed the Application of English Law Act (AELA) in 1993. According to the then Minister for Law, one of the AELA's main purposes is to promote the development of an autochthonous Singapore common law, freed from its prior dependence on the English common law. Two decades later, and in the 50th year of Singapore's national independence, this chapter uses Singapore as a model jurisdiction to examine the extent to which it is possible to develop a 'different' common law of obligations[1] and to examine whether such a 'different' common law of obligations continues to have an influence in the greater common law world.

In order to achieve these broad objectives, this chapter draws on data from an empirical study of all reported Singapore court cases from 1965 to 2013. The data will be used in the following ways. First, it will be used to examine the extent to which, and explain the reasons why, the Singapore courts have developed a 'local' jurisprudence in certain areas of the common law of obligations. Secondly, the data will be used to examine and explain how the Singapore courts have relied on foreign cases in developing a 'different' common law of obligations. These two uses of the data will together shed light on just how 'different' Singapore's common law of obligations really is. Thirdly, the data will be used to ascertain how foreign courts are using this 'different' common law of obligations developed by the Singapore courts. Collectively, the data will be used to give a comprehensive study of the

* I would like to thank Yip Man for reading earlier versions of this chapter and providing valuable feedback, as well as Leung Liwen for able research assistance. All errors remain my own.

[1] For the purposes of this chapter, the common law of obligations includes the law of contract, the law of torts, the law of equity and the law of restitution. This study of Singapore's common law of obligations can be seen as a part of a larger empirical study of the Singapore legal system jointly undertaken by the same author: see Goh Yihan and Paul Tan (eds), *Singapore Law: 50 Years in the Making* (Academy Publishing, 2015) and Goh Yihan and Paul Tan, 'An Empirical Study on the Development of Singapore Law' (2011) 23 *Singapore Academy of Law Journal* 176. For an overview of the Singapore legal system, see Goh Yihan, *Singapore Chronicles: Law* (Institute of Policy Studies-Straits Times Press, forthcoming).

development of the Singapore common law of obligations since the passage of the AELA, and to explain whether it is ever possible to speak of a 'different' common law of obligations and, if so, whether it continues to have relevance in the greater common law world.

Ultimately, this chapter will show that while the desire to develop a 'different' common law of obligations is possible and still relevant in the greater common law world, such an ambition cannot be taken too far. Indeed, despite a conscious effort to develop a 'different' common law of obligations, the Singapore courts have continued to maintain commonality with other jurisdictions in certain areas of the common law of obligations. In the end, the Singapore experience shows that an attempt to develop a 'different' common law of obligations—within reasonable limits—will lead to the enrichment of the body of law that is the common law of obligations.

II. A Brief History of the Singapore Legal System

By way of background, it is to be noted that the Singapore legal system is based on and highly influenced by English law.[2] Indeed, while English law, including English common law, was never absolutely binding on the inhabitants of Singapore, it has been highly influential ever since Sir Thomas Stamford Raffles' founding of colonial Singapore in 1819. Its influence continued even after Singapore's independence in 1965. One reason for English law's continuing influence is its formal reception by the fledgling Singapore legal system. The mechanics of this reception are complex, but may be divided broadly into two distinct periods for present purposes: prior to the passage of the AELA in 1993, and the period after that.

Pre-1993: Reception of English Law

Before the AELA was passed in 1993, English law was received into Singapore by three means: general reception, specific reception[3] and Imperial legislation.[4] English common law was generally received in Singapore through the Second Charter of Justice of 1826 (Second Charter).[5] The effect of the Second Charter was to establish in colonial Singapore (and other British colonies in the Straits Settlements) a single legal system,[6] with laws and institutions that were able to provide 'Justice and Right'.[7] Sir Peter Benson Maxwell R in the landmark case of *Regina v Willans*[8] interpreted the expression 'Justice and Right' to mean

[2] See, eg, A Phang, 'Reception of English Law in Singapore: Problems and Proposed Solutions' (1990) 2 *Singapore Academy of Law Journal* 20, n 1 (for a sampling of the relevant literature on this topic).

[3] This concerns the situation where the local statute expressly provides for the reception of English law.

[4] This is simply legislation enacted at Westminster by the English Parliament and which has been expressly extended to Singapore.

[5] See generally A Phang Boon Leong, *From Foundation to Legacy: The Second Charter of Justice* (Singapore, Academy Publishing, 2006).

[6] ibid 7.

[7] ibid.

[8] *Regina v Willans* (1858) 3 Kyshe 16.

that the law of England, as it existed in 1826, was to be applied to the Straits Settlements, subject to modifications to suit the circumstances of the place and the customs, religions, usages and manners of the native inhabitants.[9] Therefore, while English common law as of 1826 was received into Singapore, it was not absolutely binding; at least, not without suitable modifications.

Yet, the reality was that English common law usually applied as though it were binding. Indeed, the transformative potential of the Second Charter was more discussed in the abstract than seriously tapped into to develop an autochthonous Singapore legal system.[10] Notwithstanding the statutory permission to take local conditions into consideration, the courts accepted English law almost uniformly. Modifications to English law to suit the local conditions were rarely exercised; this was especially so in land law and commercial law, where the greater commercial interests of the British Empire prevailed and which necessitated a common commercial jurisprudence.[11] Moreover, the continued vitality of English law was sustained even after Singapore's independence by section 5 of the Civil Law Act,[12] which provided for the specific and continued reception of English law in mercantile or commercial matters. This and the fact that cases from the Singapore Court of Appeal (or Court of Criminal Appeal prior to 1993) were subject to review by the Judicial Committee of the Privy Council were barriers to developing a fully fledged Singaporean jurisprudence.[13] This state of affairs generally continued until the passage of the AELA in 1993.

Application of English Law Act 1993 and Beyond

The influence of English common law on Singapore law diminished significantly after the AELA was passed in 1993. Indeed, the express purpose of the AELA, as set out in the first part of its Preamble, is 'to declare the extent to which English law is applicable in Singapore and for purposes connected therewith'.

The AELA achieved this effect by several sections, the key of which is section 3. This section provides that the common law of England, so far as it was part of the law of Singapore immediately before the commencement of the Act, shall continue to be the law of Singapore, subject to such modifications as applicable to the circumstances of Singapore and its inhabitants.[14] Although this largely repeated a similar position following the Second

[9] See, eg, A Phang, 'Cementing the Foundations: The Singapore Application of English Law Act 1993' (1994) 28 *University of British Columbia Law Review* 205, 208.

[10] An excellent example of such academic scholarship may be found in Phang, above n 5.

[11] Helena HM Chan, *An Introduction to the Singapore Legal System* (Singapore, Malayan Law Journal, 1986) 9–10.

[12] Cap 43, 1999 Rev Ed (Singapore).

[13] See R Beckman, 'Divergent Development of the Common Law in Jurisdictions which Retain Appeals to the Privy Council' (1987) 29 *Malaya Law Review* 254, which provides a detailed study of the difficulties that common law jurisdictions that retained appeals to the Privy Council faced in attempting to develop a jurisprudence different from that in England. *cf* J Koh, *The First Chief* (Singapore, Academy Publishing, 2010) 88 (recounting the Singapore government's pragmatic reasons for retaining appeals to the Privy Council until the 1990s, which largely concerned giving foreign investors the assurance of an established judicial system).

[14] For completeness, the Application of English Law Act (Cap 7A, 1993 Rev Ed) (Singapore), s 3 provides as follows: 'Application of common law and equity. 3.—(1) The common law of England (including the principles and rules of equity), so far as it was part of the law of Singapore immediately before 12th November 1993, shall

Charter, this was the first time such a position had been articulated in a local statute. Indeed, the specific practical effect of section 3 was that the Singapore courts retained, and did exercise, the power to depart from English law if the local conditions require such a departure. The broader effect of section 3 was therefore to encourage the development of an independent Singapore legal system in which the courts had both the power and confidence to reject or accept law originating from elsewhere, especially England.

The AELA was accompanied by other reforms that encouraged the development of an autochthonous Singapore legal system, all of which contributed to the development of a 'different' common law of obligations. In 1994, all appeals to the Privy Council from the Singapore Court of Appeal were abolished. Close to 30 years after its national independence, Singapore's judicial system was fully independent of external oversight. This was followed by the Court of Appeal's issuance of a Practice Statement in the same year, which stated that, as Singapore's highest court, it was free to depart from the decisions of the Privy Council.[15] Collectively, the major institutional barriers to the development of an autochthonous legal system were displaced. What remained was to change the mindset of a legal fraternity that might still be tied to the traditions of old.

Following these measures, the Singapore judiciary took the lead in changing that mindset and, along the way, in developing a unique body of Singapore law. These sentiments are reflected in a series of comments given and measures undertaken by members of the Bench. For example, in 1995, Yong Pung How CJ remarked that:[16]

> There has been a realisation over these years that Singapore has to develop its own responses to its own legal problems; Singapore has to develop a legal system that is autochthonous, that grows out of its own soil.

In 2008, Chan Sek Keong CJ, the first locally educated Chief Justice, issued a Practice Direction, which directed that 'where there are in existence local judgments which are directly relevant to the issue, such judgments should be cited in precedence to foreign judgments',[17] so that the courts are not 'unnecessarily burdened with judgments made in jurisdictions with differing legal, social or economic contexts'.[18] However, if foreign judgments are to be cited, counsel should ensure that they 'will be of assistance to the development of local jurisprudence on the particular issue in question'.[19] This Practice Direction came after a series of comments by Chan CJ that Singapore should develop the sophistication of its own jurisprudence and that this could only be done if Singapore lawyers and academics

continue to be part of the law of Singapore. (2) The common law shall continue to be in force in Singapore, as provided in subsection (1), so far as it is applicable to the circumstances of Singapore and its inhabitants and subject to such modifications as those circumstances may require'. It has been speculated that the probable source of s 3 is the New Zealand Imperial Laws Application Act 1988 (Act No 112 of 1988), s 5: see Phang, above n 9, 229.

[15] Practice Statement (Judicial Precedent) [1994] 2 SLR 689 (SGCA).

[16] See Hoo Sheau Peng *et al*, 'Speech delivered at the Singapore Academy of Law Second Annual Lecture, 12 September 1995' in *Speeches and Judgments of Chief Justice Yong Pung How* (Singapore, FT Law & Tax Asia Pacific, 1996) 193–94.

[17] Practice Direction No 1 of 2008: Citation of Judgments (in the Supreme Court of the Republic of Singapore), available at www.supremecourt.gov.sg/data/doc/ManagePage/548/Practice%20Direction%20No.%201.pdf.

[18] ibid.

[19] ibid.

'write [on] Singapore [law]'.[20] The practical effect of the Practice Direction, as well as the exhortation to write on Singapore law, was to further encourage the development of an independent Singapore legal system through the citation and creation of more local jurisprudence. It also discouraged the unnecessary citation of foreign cases, at least in the first instance, a move which emphasised the importance of developing and knowing about local cases as well.

A more recent development is that the Singapore courts have become more comparative in their jurisprudence. In part driven by the judiciary's effort to promote Singapore as a leading dispute resolution hub, there is a desire to maintain consistency with developments elsewhere, at least in commercial matters. Moreover, perhaps with the assurance that Singapore jurisprudence has developed sufficiently, the courts are also consulting cases from other jurisdictions so as to reach what they consider the best outcome for Singapore law.

This brief history of the Singapore legal system, from the Second Charter to the AELA, to the measures taken thereafter, and to the recent comparative outlook of the Singapore courts, sheds light on the events that led to the Singapore courts' development of a unique body of Singapore law and, with it, a 'different' common law of obligations which yet maintains broad similarities with other common law jurisdictions. With this background in mind, this chapter now explores, through the data from an empirical study of reported Singapore cases between 1965 and 2013, exactly how and why this development took place.

III. Growth of a Singaporean Jurisprudence and a 'Different' Common Law of Obligations

Nature of Singaporean Judicial Law-making

General Development of a Singaporean Jurisprudence

In order to assess the development of a Singaporean jurisprudence generally, the average number of Singapore cases cited per Singapore case, as well as the total number of Singapore cases cited per level of court, will be examined. The assumption behind using these metrics is that the more Singapore cases cited by the courts, the more indicative that there is, first, a body of Singaporean jurisprudence the courts can cite from, and that secondly, such jurisprudence is continually being developed by the courts. It must be emphasised that this charts the growth of a Singaporean jurisprudence *generally*, and is not confined to just the common law of obligations. That is something that will be looked at subsequently once the general picture is established.

[20] See Janice Heng, 'Cite local court rulings first: CJ urges lawyers; other cases can be used for comparison or criticism', *Business Times* (Singapore), 19 May 2007, 10; Melissa Sim and Tan Dawn Wei, 'Write on local law, CJ tells academics', *Sunday Times* (Singapore), 2 September 2007, 10; Chan Sek Keong, 'Welcome Reference for the Chief Justice: Response by The Honourable The Chief Justice Chan Sek Keong', Speech in Singapore, 22 April 2006, available at www.supremecourt.gov.sg/default.aspx?pgid=1001&printFriendly=true.

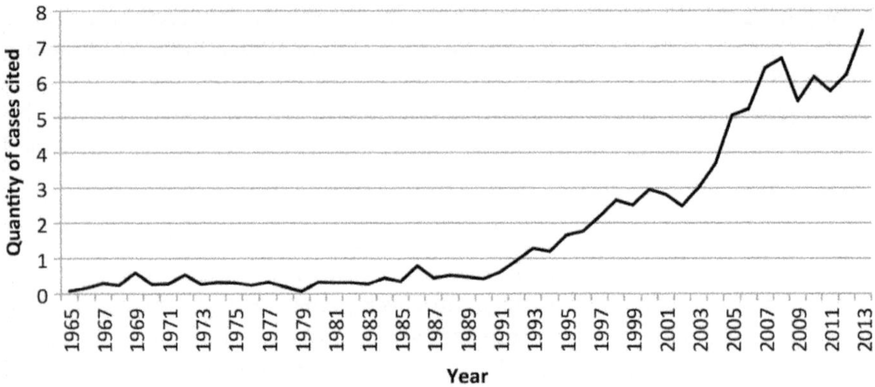

Figure 4.1: Average number of Singapore cases cited per Singapore case

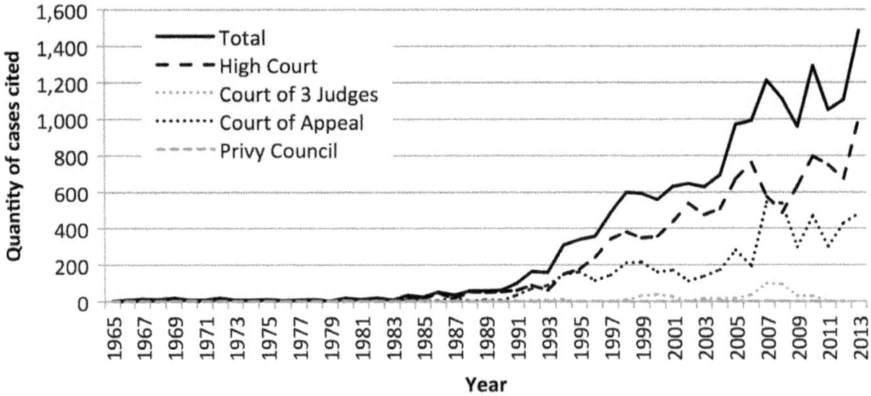

Figure 4.2: Total number of Singapore cases cited by level of court

Both Figure 4.1 and Figure 4.2 show that the average and total number of Singapore cases cited has seen a rapid increase since the early 1990s. Generally, this echoes local calls for the development of an independent body of Singapore law. For example, Yong CJ said in 1995 that Singapore 'must develop its own legal system, and where necessary, part company with the English'.[21] Indeed, the subsequent rise in the total number of Singapore cases cited by the Singapore courts, which can be taken as indicative of the growth of Singaporean jurisprudence, is not surprising for a number of historical reasons.

First, as recounted earlier, the AELA came into effect in 1993, followed by the Practice Statement in 1994. In between these two events, the government in February 1994 abolished all appeals to the Privy Council from the Singapore Court of Appeal. In fact, the Singapore Judiciary's ties to the Privy Council had already weakened starting from 1989,

[21] See 'S'pore must develop its own legal system', *Straits Times* (Singapore), 13 September 1995, 27; see also Diana Onn, 'Distinctively S'porean', *Business Times* (Singapore), 9 November 1995, 6; Karen Wong, 'Courts' role to develop the law', *Straits Times* (Singapore), 15 September 2000, 59.

when the government began passing a series of legislation to limit the right of appeal to the Privy Council, one result being that there was no right of appeal in civil cases unless parties agreed beforehand to such a right. The concerted judicial and legislative action undoubtedly led the Singapore courts to engage in the active development of a Singaporean jurisprudence. The Practice Direction of 2008 further encouraged these developments. Secondly, the increased availability and accessibility of Singapore cases through local law reports and electronic databases established in the early 1990s also had an effect on first increasing, and then sustaining, the citations of Singapore cases by the Singapore courts. The further publication of local law textbooks[22] and journals in the same period may also have contributed to the further dissemination (and hence citation) of Singapore cases.[23] Thirdly, the increase in the number of locally-trained judges and lawyers freed from the vestiges of English law in their legal education, and who had become sufficiently senior in the 1990s to shape the development of Singapore law, must also have played a part in the growth of a Singaporean jurisprudence.[24] Collectively, these historical reasons account for the rapid growth of a Singaporean jurisprudence *generally* starting from the early 1990s.

General Development of a 'Different' Common Law of Obligations

The rapid growth of a Singaporean jurisprudence generally is also particularly mirrored in the common law of obligations, as shown in Figure 4.3.

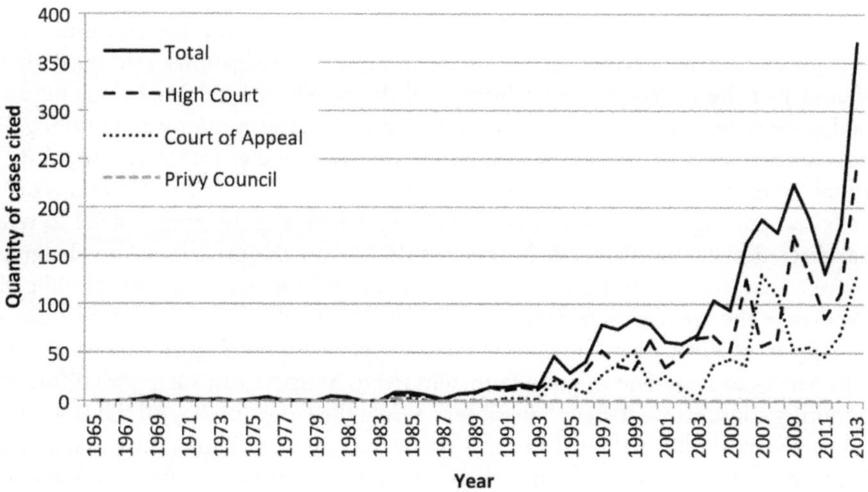

Figure 4.3: Total number of Singapore cases concerning the common law of obligations cited by level of court

[22] See 'Law Practice Series' (List of commissioned titles by Academy Publishing, Singapore Academy of Law), available at www.sal.org.sg/eBookshop/law_books_LawPracticeSeries.aspx?userId=.

[23] As Yong CJ put it, 'the rapid and significant development of our local legal system and jurisprudence has made it imperative for a parallel work dedicated to Singapore law and interpretation', in Audrey Lim, Koh Juat Jong and Chao Hick Tin (eds), *Speeches and Judgments of Chief Justice Yong Pung How* (Singapore, SNP, 2006) 121.

[24] See Lau Kok Keng *et al*, 'Legal Crossroads: Towards a Singaporean Jurisprudence' (1987) 8 *Singapore Law Review* 1, 7–8 (training of Singapore judges and lawyers affected the extent to which they were more familiar with English law, hence affecting the development of a local jurisprudence).

In fact, Figure 4.3 shows a more rapid development of a Singaporean jurisprudence in the common law of obligations in more recent years, compared with the general development of all areas of law in the same period (as reflected in Figure 4.2). In this regard, the rapid increase in the development of the common law of obligations may be explained by the constitution of a new, permanent, Singapore Court of Appeal around that time. Before 2008, Singapore had not had a permanent apex court since 1999. This new permanent court consisted of Chan CJ, Andrew Phang Boon Leong JA and VK Rajah JA. Chan CJ had been the Attorney-General for 16 years before being appointed Chief Justice. Phang JA had been an academic specialising in contract law for more than 20 years. Rajah JA had headed one of Singapore's largest law firms with a specialisation in commercial litigation. Each therefore brought to the apex court their individual expertise and enthusiasm in developing the common law of obligations in Singapore.

With these reasons in mind, it is necessary to turn to more substantial reasons to explain why the Singapore courts developed, and continue to develop, a 'different' common law of obligations.

When and Why do Singapore Courts Develop a 'Different' Common Law of Obligations?

Local Societal and Economic Conditions

First, local societal and economic conditions may have driven, and may continue to drive, the Singapore courts to develop a 'different' common law of obligations. This is a realisation of the ability of the courts to depart from English law where local conditions necessitate such a departure and can be found in several examples in the common law of obligations. Indeed, contract law, insofar as it affects family law, is a good example. In *TQ v TR*,[25] the Singapore Court of Appeal did not take the position adopted in other jurisdictions of automatically recognising the validity of prenuptial agreements, preferring instead to retain a judicial discretion to scrutinise such agreements, and in the process acknowledging the unique role that local circumstances, such as the prevailing views on marital obligations, have to play in the area. Also, in *HSBC Institutional Trust (Services) Ltd v Toshin Development Singapore Pte Ltd*,[26] the Singapore Court of Appeal, upholding an express agreement between parties to negotiate in good faith, alluded to Singaporean society's 'cultural value of promoting consensus whenever possible'.[27] While the Court of Appeal did not go so far as to depart from the English position that parties cannot be held to a duty to negotiate in good faith prior to contracting,[28] there is good reason to think that the court's reasoning, based as it is on a unique aspect of Singaporean society, could have led to a departure from the English position had the point been squarely before it.

But perhaps a more significant local societal and economic condition that has shaped the development of the common law of obligations in Singapore is its perennial land scarcity.[29]

[25] *TQ v TR* [2009] 2 SLR(R) 961 (SGCA).
[26] *HSBC Institutional Trust (Services) Ltd v Toshin Development Singapore Pte Ltd* [2012] 4 SLR 738 (SGCA).
[27] ibid [40].
[28] See *Walford v Miles* [1992] 2 AC 128 (HL).
[29] See generally Goh Yihan, 'Tort Law in the Face of Land Scarcity in Singapore' (2009) 26 *Arizona Journal of International and Comparative Law* 335.

By way of background, the total land area of Singapore is reported to be approximately 716.1 square kilometres.[30] This extremely small area comprises the mainland and other islands. This small total land area becomes a significant problem when Singapore's population is taken into account. With a population of 5.40 million people in June 2013,[31] Singapore's population density is very high, and was estimated at 7,540 persons per square kilometre at that time.[32] The population of Singapore is expected to grow even further because of governmental policies that encourage immigrants in the light of a declining birth rate. It follows that demand for the limited land becomes, and will continue to be, exceedingly high. Taken together, the spill-over societal and economic effects relevant to the development of a 'different' common law of obligations are threefold: a high cost of housing, a high building density and a high population density.

Insofar as the high cost of housing is concerned, notwithstanding the widespread access to public housing in Singapore,[33] the cost of public housing is still high relative to the average resident's income (with private housing naturally costing far higher). Public housing in Singapore is divided according to the number of rooms the unit concerned has. In this regard, in 2014, the heavily state subsidised cost of a build-to-order three-room unit was at least S$145,000 (about US$108,750).[34] A four-room unit cost about S$234,000 (about US$175,500)[35] and a five-room unit cost about S$393,000 (about US$294,750[36]). For those requiring public housing immediately, the resale prices are considerably higher, with the corresponding median prices at around (roughly) S$300,000, S$400,000 and S$450,000 for three-room, four-room and five-room units respectively.[37] By way of contrast, the median gross monthly income from work of full-time employed residents increased from S$2,927 (in 2009) to S$3,705 (in 2013), and the average monthly household income from work per household member among resident employed households increased from S$2,337 (in 2009) to S$3,204 (in 2013).[38] Thus, the average Singapore resident's outlay on housing is indeed a significant proportion of his or her lifetime earnings. This has, interestingly, led to the Singapore courts' robust protection of home-owners' economic interest in their properties even in the face of contrary English law.

The Singapore courts have expressly departed from the strict English position that excludes recovery for pure economic loss save in very limited circumstances.[39] The first

[30] See *Yearbook of Statistics Singapore, 2014* (Singapore, Department of Statistics Singapore, 2014) 9, 15. Even with land reclamation, the total land area of Singapore had only increased minutely, from 710.0 square kilometres in June 2009 to 716.1 square kilometres in June 2014.

[31] See ibid 9, for population data from 2009 to 2013.

[32] ibid. Singapore's population density is perennially very high in modern times.

[33] Over 80 per cent of Singapore's population lives in public housing. See *Yearbook*, above n 30, 14.

[34] See 'HDB's First BTO Launch for 2014', Press Release by the Housing and Development Board (HDB) of Singapore, available at www.hdb.gov.sg/fi10/fi10296p.nsf/PressReleases/28F24C0C184E131B48257C68000394ED?OpenDocument. A build-to-order flat is the cheapest public housing type in Singapore, but entails a long waiting time, as its name suggests. All costs stated here exclude grants. Note that grants are only available to first-timers as buyers of public housing.

[35] ibid.

[36] ibid.

[37] See 'Median Resale Prices by Town and Flat Type', HDB InfoWeb for Buying a Resale Flat, Latest Resale Cases Registered in 3rd Quarter 2014, www.hdb.gov.sg/fi10/fi10321p.nsf/w/BuyResaleFlatMedianResalePrices?OpenDocument.

[38] See *Yearbook*, above n 30, 11, 43, 51, 55, 68.

[39] Singapore law broadly follows English law in other areas of recoverability of pure economic loss.

departure from the exclusionary rule in respect of pure economic loss came in the Singapore High Court case of *Management Corp Strata Title Plan No 1272 v Ocean Front Pte Ltd*,[40] later upheld on appeal by the Singapore Court of Appeal. In that case, one of the issues raised was whether the plaintiff management corporation[41] could recover the cost of remedying defects caused by the developer of a condominium project when such expenses were pure economic loss. In the High Court, Warren Khoo J agreed with the House of Lords in *Murphy v Brentwood District Council*[42] that recovery was possible where there was a special relationship of proximity between builder and building owner that is sufficiently akin to contract to introduce the element of reliance, so that the scope of the duty of care owed by the builder to the owner is wide enough to cover pure economic loss.[43] Khoo J held that there was sufficient proximity akin to contract here since a developer of a condominium knows from the time of conceiving a plan to develop that the management corporation will come into existence.[44] He further held that to find a duty in these circumstances would not lead to indeterminate liability.[45] In doing so, Khoo J did not explicitly state that he was protecting what would be a significant housing outlay by the average Singapore resident, but the strong implication was that he was.

That policy consideration was more clearly stated in the resulting appeal in *RSP Architects Planners and Engineers v Ocean Front Pte Ltd*.[46] The Court of Appeal expressly departed from the English position with respect to the recovery of pure economic loss in cases of the present nature. The court acknowledged that on the basis of English law at that time, there was no duty of care owed by the developers to the management corporation.[47] However, it referred to authorities from other common law jurisdictions to find support that the exclusionary rule has been departed from.[48] In deciding to depart from the English position, the court stated that it was involved in a delicate balancing exercise in which consideration is to be given to all the conflicting claims of the plaintiffs and the defendants, viewed in a wider context of society.[49] The reference to the 'wider context of society' hinted at the high cost of housing in Singapore that must have influenced the court's decision. Without directly articulating this policy reason, the court found that there was sufficient legal proximity because the management corporation was an entity created by the developers, and the developers knew or ought to have known that if they were negligent in their construction of the common property, they would have to make compensation to the management

[40] See *Management Corp Strata Title Plan No 1272 v Ocean Front Pte Ltd* [1994] 3 SLR(R) 787 (SGHC).

[41] In Singapore, a management corporation is automatically formed when the strata title plan for development (in high rise projects) is lodged with the Chief Surveyor. Its main responsibility is to control and manage the common property.

[42] See *Murphy v Brentwood District Council* [1991] 1 AC 398 (HL), 398–99.

[43] ibid.

[44] See [1994] 3 SLR(R) 787 (SGHC) [56].

[45] ibid.

[46] *RSP Architects Planners and Engineers v Ocean Front Pte Ltd* [1995] 3 SLR(R) 653 (SGCA); see also DSL Ong, 'Defects in Property Causing Pure Economic Loss: The Resurrection of Junior Books and Anns' [1996] *Singapore Journal of Legal Studies* 257.

[47] See *RSP Architects Planners and Engineers v Ocean Front Pte Ltd* [1995] 3 SLR(R) 653 (SGCA) [47].

[48] See ibid [48]–[55] (citing the Australian cases of *Sutherland Shire Council v Heyman* (1985) 157 CLR 424 (HCA) and *Bryan v Maloney* (1995) 182 CLR 609 (HCA)). The court also referred to New Zealand and Canadian cases. See [1995] 3 SLR(R) 653 (SGCA) [56]–[62], citing *Winnipeg Condominium Corporation No 36 v Bird Construction Co Ltd* [1995] 1 SCR 85, *Invercargill City Council v Hamlin* [1994] 3 NZLR 513 (CA), and *Lester v White* [1992] 2 NZLR 483 (HC).

[49] See *RSP Architects Planners and Engineers v Ocean Front Pte Ltd* [1995] 3 SLR(R) 653 (SGCA) [68].

corporation.[50] It was only in the later and similar Court of Appeal decision of *RSP Architects Planners and Engineers v Management Corp Strata Title Plan No 1075*[51] that the court pointed out that 'the investment in real property is likely to represent a significant, if not the most significant, investment in an individual's lifetime (as opposed to the purchase of a mere chattel)', and is thus worthy of protection by the law. The land scarcity problem in Singapore was specifically highlighted as being the reason why there was no good reason to follow the exclusionary rule in respect of pure economic loss articulated in *Murphy*, at least with respect to building defects.

The high building density in Singapore means that buildings are close to each other and (except for those that are independent) depend on each other for support. While English law has not recognised the protection of a right of support, the Singapore courts have done so. For example, in *Xpress Print Pte Ltd v Monocrafts Pte Ltd*,[52] soil subsistence occurred on Xress Print's land due to Monocrafts' excavation of soil on its adjoining plot of land. Before the Singapore High Court, Xpress Print was faced with the old common law principle embodied in *Dalton v Angus*,[53] which was followed in Singapore by the Court of Appeal of the Straits Settlements[54] in *Lee Quee Siew v Lim Hock Siew*.[55] According to *Dalton*, a land-owner's right to support for his land extended only to the land in its natural state. Any right of support for buildings and other constructions on the land had to be acquired by easement. While suitable for an environment that is not densely populated, this was clearly untenable in the context of Singapore.

And so it was that the Singapore Court of Appeal rejected the principle in *Dalton* and held that a land-owner who sought to develop his property owed his neighbour an absolute duty not to interfere with the right of support for his building.[56] Xpress Print therefore succeeded in obtaining damages in the general tort measure.[57] In reaching this decision, the court reiterated the importance of its decision in Singapore in view of land use patterns, whereby all land available is used to a high density. It said that the damage that might be caused if land-owners were lackadaisical in their excavation works could be astronomical.[58] Here it can be seen how the land scarcity problem in Singapore again led to a 'different' development in the Singapore common law of obligations.

Finally, Singapore's high population density of approximately 7,540 persons per square kilometre[59] is especially evident in public housing, where residents typically live in

[50] See ibid [72]–[74].

[51] See *RSP Architects and Planners and Engineers v Management Corp Strata Title Plan No 1075* [1999] 2 SLR(R) 134 (SGCA); see also DSL Ong, 'The Test of Duty for Defects in Property Causing Pure Economic Loss' [1999] *Singapore Journal of Legal Studies* 667.

[52] *Xpress Print Pte Ltd v Monocrafts Pte Ltd* [2000] 2 SLR(R) 614 (SGCA); see also KS Teo, 'Land Law' in KS Teo (ed), *Singapore Academy of Law Annual Review of Singapore Cases 2000* (Singapore, Singapore Academy of Law, 2001); P Pillai, 'The Primacy of the Principle of Reciprocity in the Singapore Land Regime' (2001) 13 *Singapore Academy of Law Journal* 198; E Wong, 'Singapore Court of Appeal Takes Lead in Departing from Dalton v Angus' [2001] (May) *Singapore Law Gazette* 30.

[53] See *Dalton v Angus* (1881) 6 App Cas 740 (HL).

[54] Whose decisions, given the historical nexus with the Singapore court system, remain binding on all but the highest court in Singapore.

[55] *Lee Quee Siew v Lim Hock Siew* [1895–96] 3 SSLR 80, [1895–96] III SSLR 80, [1896] SSLR 10 (SSCA).

[56] See Pillai, above n 52, 200.

[57] *Xpress Print Pte Ltd v Monocrafts Pte Ltd* [2000] 2 SLR(R) 614 (SGCA) [52].

[58] ibid [48].

[59] As at the end of June 2013: see *Yearbook*, above n 30, 9.

30-storey blocks and there are even 50-storey blocks.[60] This highly urbanised environment led the courts to recognise the common law tort of harassment. In *Malcomson Nicholas Hugh Bertram v Mehta Naresh Kumar*,[61] Lee Seiu Kin JC acknowledged that English law provided no way of dealing with harassing conduct suffered by a person with no right to the land concerned through the property-related torts. He therefore created a new tort of harassment founded on a repeated course of conduct reasonably intended to cause worry, emotional distress or annoyance. In doing so, Lee JC pointed out that the last 200 years of improvements in technology had brought about three great changes in lifestyle, namely, urbanisation, widespread availability of leisure time and improved communication, all of which combined in Singapore to create a problem of harassment that did not and could not exist before.[62] There was thus a need for the common law to respond to this new problem by the creation of a tort not recognised in England. Subsequently, the High Court in *AXA Insurance Singapore Pte Ltd v Chandran s/o Natesan*[63] doubted Lee JC's authority to create such a tort, although this was not because the tort was not recognised in England but rather because the Singapore Parliament had legislated criminal sanctions for harassing conduct. As such, the court in *AXA Insurance* thought that it was not within the common law courts' province to provide a civil recourse for victims of harassment. Whether this view is correct has now been rendered irrelevant because the Singapore Parliament passed the Protection from Harassment Act 2014 to provide a statutory remedy.[64] Notwithstanding these developments, the creation of the tort of harassment in *Malcomson* is yet another example of how local societal and economic conditions in Singapore have led the courts to develop a 'different' common law of obligations.

Other Uniquely Local Developments

Another reason why the Singapore courts develop a 'different' common law of obligations is a desire to develop a Singaporean jurisprudence that gives the 'correct' answer to a legal issue, an answer that is not found in the established cases. The further development of such cases in subsequent case law promotes the growth of a 'different' Singaporean common law of obligations.

A well-known example in the common law of obligations, and specifically in the field of equity, is the Singapore High Court case of *Sumitomo Bank Ltd v Kartika Ratna Thahir*[65] ('*Sumitomo Bank*'). In that case, Lai Kew Chai J disagreed with the old English case of *Lister & Co v Stubbs*[66] and rejected the view that a fiduciary who accepted bribes was not a constructive trustee and was only liable to account. Lai J said that a Singapore court exercising its equitable jurisdiction must reflect the mores and sense of justice of the society that it served. Thus, he confined *Lister & Co v Stubbs* to its facts and declined to follow it.[67] While

[60] See 'Public Housing in Singapore', HDB InfoWeb, Housing and Development Board of Singapore, www.hdb.gov.sg/fi10/fi10320p.nsf/w/AboutUsPublicHousing?OpenDocument.

[61] *Malcomson Nicholas Hugh Bertram v Mehta Naresh Kumar* [2001] 3 SLR(R) 379 (SGHC).

[62] ibid.

[63] *AXA Insurance Singapore Pte Ltd v Chandran s/o Natesan* [2013] 4 SLR 545 (SGHC).

[64] Protection from Harassment Act 2014 (No 17 of 2014), ss 11, 14 (Singapore).

[65] *Sumitomo Bank Ltd v Kartika Ratna Thahir* [1992] 3 SLR(R) 638 (SGHC).

[66] *Lister & Co v Stubbs* (1890) 45 Ch D 1 (CA).

[67] *Sumitomo Bank Ltd v Kartika Ratna Thahir* [1992] 3 SLR(R) 638 (SGHC) [241]–[43].

Lai J referred to the mores and sense of justice of Singaporean society, the decision was perhaps not directly due to any particular local societal or economic condition but simply a judicial desire to reach the 'correct' result. In *Attorney-General for Hong Kong v Reid*,[68] the Privy Council, on appeal from the Court of Appeal of New Zealand, said that it was 'impressed' with the decision in *Sumitomo Bank*. More recently, the UK Supreme Court has also came to the same conclusion in *FHR European Ventures LLP v Cedar Capital Partners LLC*,[69] where it overturned *Lister & Co v Stubbs*.

More examples in the common law of obligations of the Singapore courts charting a path of their own can be found in the law of contract. In particular, the Singapore courts have steadfastly declined to follow the English approach, led by Lord Hoffmann, of reducing various doctrines of contract law to a broad interpretative approach. Thus, the Singapore Court of Appeal in *Sembcorp Marine Ltd v PPL Holdings Pte Ltd*[70] refused to follow the view taken in *Attorney-General of Belize v Belize Telecom Ltd*[71] that the implication of terms in fact was a facet of contractual interpretation. Similarly, the Singapore Court of Appeal has in a series of cases culminating in *Out of the Box Pte Ltd v Wanin Industries Pte Ltd*[72] declined to follow the 'assumption of responsibility' test for remoteness laid down in *The Achilleas*.[73] More recently, the Singapore Court of Appeal in *RBC Properties Pte Ltd v Defu Furniture Pte Ltd*[74] said that there is a strong case for reconsidering the prevailing English view that the measure of damages awardable under section 2(1) of the Misrepresentation Act[75] is that which would have been awarded in deceit. It thought instead that there was good reason why the measure of damages should be that awarded for negligent misrepresentation. However, because the issue was not directly before it, the court declined to express a determinative view of the matter.

The rapid growth in Singaporean jurisprudence, including the common law of obligations, starting from the 1990s, does not mean that local societal and economic conditions, and the judicial desire to develop a local jurisprudence, have led to the development of an *entirely* different common law of obligations. Indeed, as Singapore matures and develops its own jurisprudence, it is important to be sensitive to developing norms internationally. Thus, it might be more accurate to conceive of the Singapore common law of obligations as 'different', but also representing a by-product of both domestic and international influences. While internal or local reasons may account for the development of a 'different' common law of obligations, it is also true that Singapore law, including the common law of obligations, is still influenced by recourse to foreign cases. The difference between the present situation and the period following the Second Charter may be *how* foreign cases are being referred to.

[68] *Attorney-General for Hong Kong v Reid* [1994] 1 AC 324 (PC).
[69] *FHR European Ventures LLP v Cedar Capital Partners LLC* [2015] AC 250 (SC).
[70] *Sembcorp Marine Ltd v PPL Holdings Pte Ltd* [2013] 4 SLR 193 (SGCA).
[71] *Attorney-General of Belize v Belize Telecom Ltd* [2009] 1 WLR 1988 (PC).
[72] *Out of the Box Pte Ltd v Wanin Industries Pte Ltd* [2013] 2 SLR 363 (SGCA).
[73] *Transfield Shipping Inc v Mercator Shipping Inc (The Achilleas)* [2009] 1 AC 61 (HL).
[74] *RBC Properties Pte Ltd v Defu Furniture Pte Ltd* [2015] 1 SLR 997 (SGCA).
[75] This is materially similar to the English Misrepresentation Act 1967.

IV. Recourse to Foreign Cases

How and where do Singapore Courts Refer to Foreign Cases?

This chapter now examines another aspect of the development of a Singaporean jurisprudence (and more specifically, the development of a 'different' common law of obligations): the citation of foreign cases by the Singapore courts. The concern is with the identification of, first, the foreign jurisdictions the courts are citing, and, secondly, the subject matters in which the courts are citing the highest number of foreign cases. Together, they shed light on just how 'different' Singapore law generally, and the Singapore common law of obligations specifically, really are.

General Trend of Recourse to Foreign Judgments

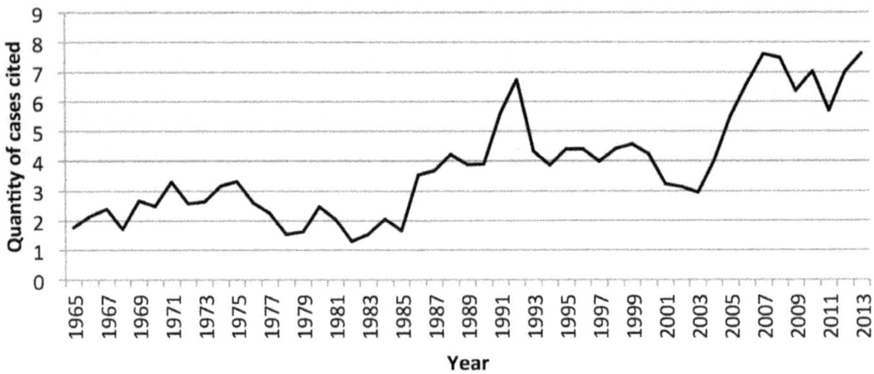

Figure 4.4: Average number of foreign cases cited per Singapore case

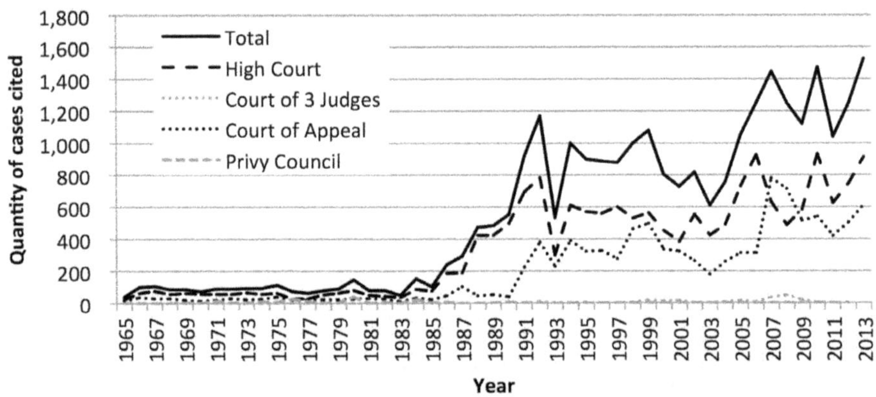

Figure 4.5: Number of foreign cases cited by level of court

Together, Figures 4.4 and 4.5 show an upward increase in the citation of foreign cases by the Singapore courts across all types of cases. A few more specific points may be noted.

The first point is that the citation of foreign cases generally increased between 1965 to about 1975, before declining. One possible reason for this is that it was only in 1969 that the Singapore courts finally became independent from the Malaysian system[76] (notwithstanding the fact that Singapore had become independent in 1965).[77] This was because the new government had more pressing social and economic problems to address, and regarded the judiciary as functioning satisfactorily although it was still tied to the Malaysian system. The ultimate separation from the Malaysian system could have prompted a renewed sense of judicial independence. By 1975, however, the caseload of the Singapore courts had increased so quickly with Singapore's rapid economic growth that the need to decide cases swiftly had taken precedence over the desire to develop a Singaporean jurisprudence. Furthermore, the Chief Justice of the time, Wee Chong Jin, did not like to develop the law in the abstract, preferring to decide cases before him narrowly. Thus, Singapore courts cited foreign cases, particularly English ones, mainly to follow them in order to aid in the fast disposal of cases. There was thus a clear increase in the number of foreign cases cited towards the end of the 1980s and continuing into the early 1990s.

The second point about the empirical data is that the citation of foreign cases largely declined after 1993. The primary reason for this is certainly the enactment of the AELA. There were also other developments around the time that may have accounted for a renewed desire for independence from foreign cases. There was a sense, perhaps shared by most in the legal profession for the first time in Singapore's history, of the need for a truly Singapore legal system. The sentiment is well captured by Andrew Phang Boon Leong JC (as he then was) in *Tang Kin Hwa v Traditional Chinese Medicine Practitioners Board*, where he said:[78]

> In one sense, this is to be welcomed, for English law, having been 'exported' to so very many colonies in the past, has now to be cultivated with an acute awareness of the soil in which it has been transplanted. It must also be closely scrutinised for appropriateness on a more general level—that of general persuasiveness in so far as logic and reasoning are concerned. This is the essence of the ideal of developing an autochthonous or indigenous legal system sensitive to the needs and mores of the society of which it is a part. Only thus can the society concerned develop and even flourish.

The judicial attitude had changed from a sense of respectful adherence to independent departure by the mid-1990s. It is significant that, even as the total number of reported cases increased in the 1990s, the overall number of foreign cases cited by the Singapore courts has declined generally ever since. This suggests that, on average, the number of foreign cases cited per reported Singapore case declined and corresponds with the drive to divorce Singapore from the *automatic* citation of foreign (and in particular, English) cases.

The third point about the empirical data is that there was an increase in the citation of foreign cases from 2002 to 2010. It will also be noted that the regularity with which the Singapore courts cited foreign cases again increased post-2005, reaching record levels in 2007 despite the years 2005 to 2007 not being record years in terms of the total number of reported cases. In 2008, the total number of foreign cases cited dropped slightly, corresponding to the overall decrease in the number of reported cases that year. This subsequent increase in the number of foreign cases cited may be explained by Singapore's ambition

[76] This had started in about 1968: see, eg, 'Singapore to have its own Court of Appeal', *Straits Times* (Singapore), 16 May 1968, 7; 'Singapore to have its own Supreme Court', *Straits Times* (Singapore), 13 June 1969, 6.

[77] See, eg, 'Independent S'pore Bill: full details', *Straits Times* (Singapore), 10 August 1965, 20, reporting that High Court cases will still go to the Federal Court of Malaysia and then to the Privy Council.

[78] *Tang Kin Hwa v Traditional Chinese Medicine Practitioners Board* [2005] 4 SLR(R) 604 (SGHC) [27].

to promote Singapore law, which requires a degree of coherence and consistency with international practice and jurisprudential norms.[79] This was articulated clearly by Andrew Phang Boon Leong JA in the Singapore Court of Appeal case of *Man Financial (S) Pte Ltd v Wong Bark Chuan David*,[80] when he said that 'in an increasingly interconnected world, local courts ought to eschew legal parochialism and look beyond their shores for relevant precedents—particularly where controversial or ... potentially outmoded legal doctrine are concerned'.[81] In a related vein, as disputes become more sophisticated and transnational in character, it is unrealistic to expect that reliance on prior local cases would be sufficient.[82] Finally, this increase in citation of foreign cases may also be accounted for by the emergence of a new generation of judges,[83] who while freed from the hold of the English legal tradition, are also confident to consult other jurisdictions to find the best approach. This translates therefore into a desire to develop a Singaporean jurisprudence with reference to, but not in complete compliance with, foreign cases.

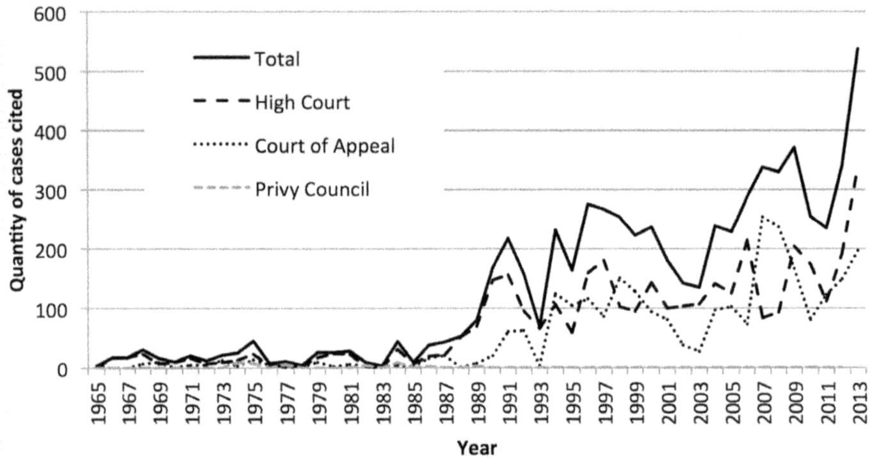

Figure 4.6: Total number of foreign cases cited in Singapore cases concerning the common law of obligations, by level of court

The reasons that explain the total number of foreign cases cited in Singapore cases generally apply equally to the Singapore cases concerning the common law of obligations specifically, as represented in Figure 4.6. Indeed, there is no reason to think that this should

[79] The relationship between a jurisdiction's ambition to be a hub for international arbitration work and the development of its jurisprudence has been noted by Chief Justice Chan: see Chan Sek Keong, 'Welcome Remarks by Chief Justice Chan Sek Keong', Speech for Conference on International Investment Arbitration, Supreme Court of Singapore, 20 January 2010 [10], available at cil.nus.edu.sg/wp/wp-content/uploads/2009/10/CJs-Welcome-Remarks-at-Conference-on-International-Investment-Arbitration-20-Jan-2010.pdf; see also Chan Sek Keong, 'Keynote Address by The Chief Justice of Singapore', Speech for XVI International Congress of Maritime Arbitrators 2007, Singapore, 26 February 2007 [11], available at www.siarb.org.sg/pdf/Seminar20070226-CJ.pdf.

[80] *Man Financial (S) Pte Ltd v Wong Bark Chuan David* [2008] 1 SLR(R) 663 (SGCA).

[81] ibid [132].

[82] This may be contrasted with times where there was resistance against foreign lawyers practising in Singapore and, by implication, the influx of foreign influence: Free Press Staff Reporter, 'Move backed: Government proposal to stop new foreign lawyers practising here', *Singapore Free Press* (Singapore), 16 September 1959, 1.

[83] As the permanent members of the Court of Appeal have received at least part of their education overseas, one would expect a deeper familiarity with foreign jurisprudence.

not be so. However, in order to better understand the Singapore courts' citation of foreign cases, even as they develop a 'different' common law of obligations, it is necessary to have regard to further aspects of such citation.

Which Foreign Jurisdictions are Cited in Singapore Cases?

The specific breakdown of the jurisdictions whose cases are cited in Singapore cases is represented in Figures 4.7 and 4.8.

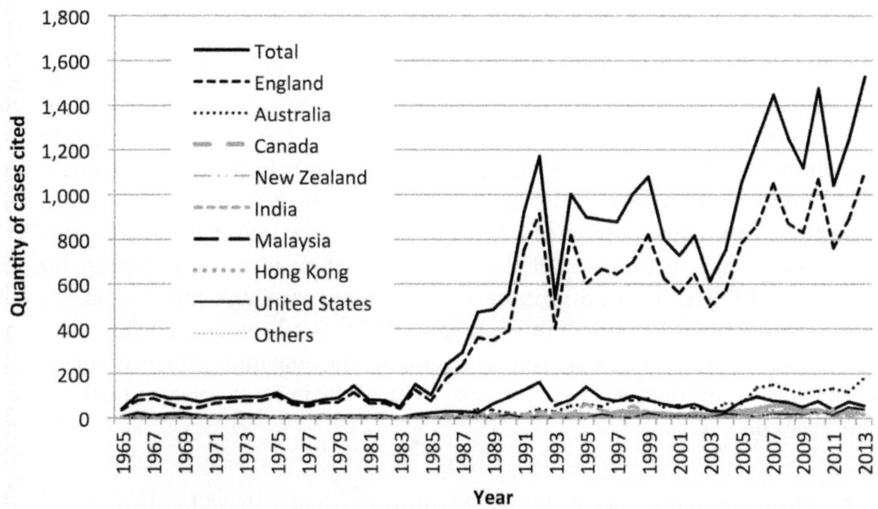

Figure 4.7: Total number of foreign cases cited in Singapore cases, by jurisdiction

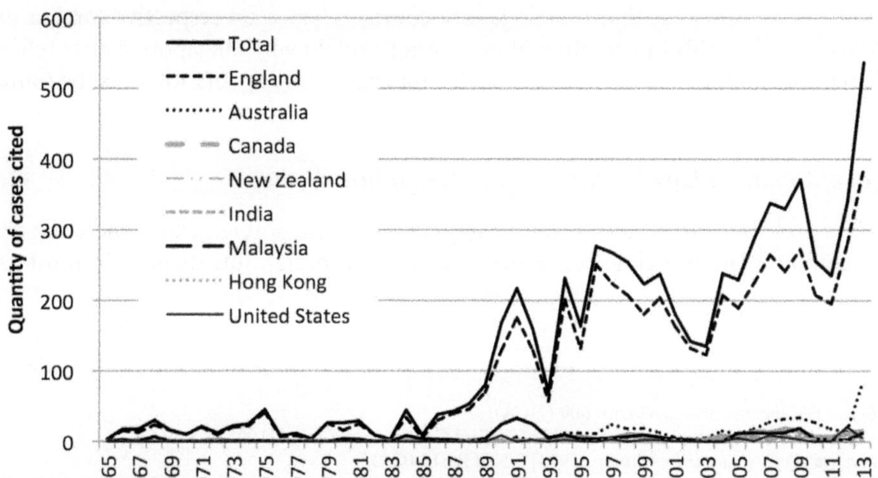

Figure 4.8: Total number of foreign cases cited in Singapore cases concerning the common law of obligations, by jurisdiction

Figure 4.7 confirms that English law is the dominant foreign influence across all areas of Singapore law even after the passage of the AELA. This is unsurprising given that Singapore's legal history is tied to English colonialism and given England's continued leadership of the common law world. Figure 4.8 shows that the same trend is also observed specifically in the common law of obligations.

There is also increasing reliance on cases from other jurisdictions. Where courts in these jurisdictions present judicial positions different from the English, Singapore courts have turned to these jurisdictions either as a source of reference or authority. This is especially true in the common law of obligations, which is still largely the domain of the common law and (largely) not statutorily regulated. There is thus fertile ground across common law jurisdictions for cross-references, and the Singapore courts have certainly taken advantage of this. Thus, as already noted, the Singapore courts have declined to follow the English courts' approach in refusing claims in negligence for pure economic loss from property defects, preferring to follow Australian,[84] Canadian[85] and New Zealand[86] cases that have departed from the English position. Also, as more decisions in the English courts become subject to distinctly European jurisprudence and legislation, it may be that there will be more citations of other common law jurisdictions such as Australia and Canada in the future.[87] Indeed, the assimilation of the United Kingdom into the European Economic Community in 1979 led to the Singapore government expressing concerns that the courts should not follow English courts blindly in light of that development. There is all the more reason for such a sentiment to take root now, and for the Singapore courts to increase their reference to other common law jurisdictions, particularly in cases concerning the common law of obligations.

Why do Singapore Courts Rely on Foreign Cases in Developing a 'Different' Common Law of Obligations?

While it can be observed that the Singapore courts' reliance on respective foreign jurisprudence is varied, this information alone cannot explain why Singapore courts rely on a particular foreign jurisdiction's cases in such a manner. That explanation must be found in other reasons.

Origin of Common Law Principle from Foreign Jurisdiction

First, it is probably correct to say that Singapore courts cite foreign cases where the origin of the common law principle concerned is from that foreign jurisdiction, in most cases,

[84] *Bryan v Maloney* (1995) 182 CLR 609 (HCA).

[85] *Winnipeg Condominium Corporation No 36 v Bird Construction Co Ltd* [1995] 1 SCR 85.

[86] *Invercargill City Council v Hamlin* [1994] 3 NZLR 513 (CA).

[87] See the observations of Teo Guan Siew, 'Choice of Law in *Foreign Non Conveniens* Analysis: *Puttick v Tenon Ltd* [2008] HCA 54' (2010) 22 *Singapore Academy of Law Journal* 440 (noting the restrictions of European legislation on the scope of the English courts' jurisdiction to stay proceedings on the grounds of *forum non conveniens*).

England. This is especially evident in the common law of obligations, and can be empirically illustrated by the Singapore courts' citation of English, Australian, Malaysian and Indian cases concerning contract law. Whereas English and Australian contract laws are similar to Singapore's, Malaysian and Indian contract laws, being based on a code, are less so. Figures 4.9 to 4.12 illustrate this particular point.

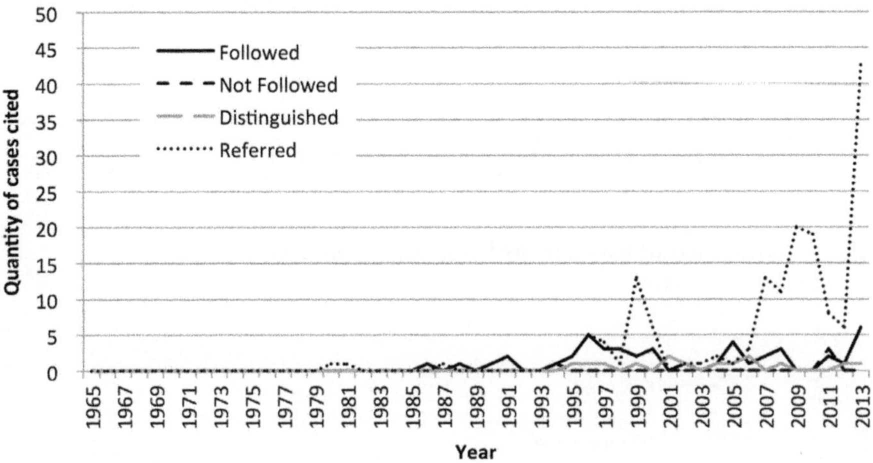

Figure 4.9: Australian contract law cases cited in Singapore contract law cases

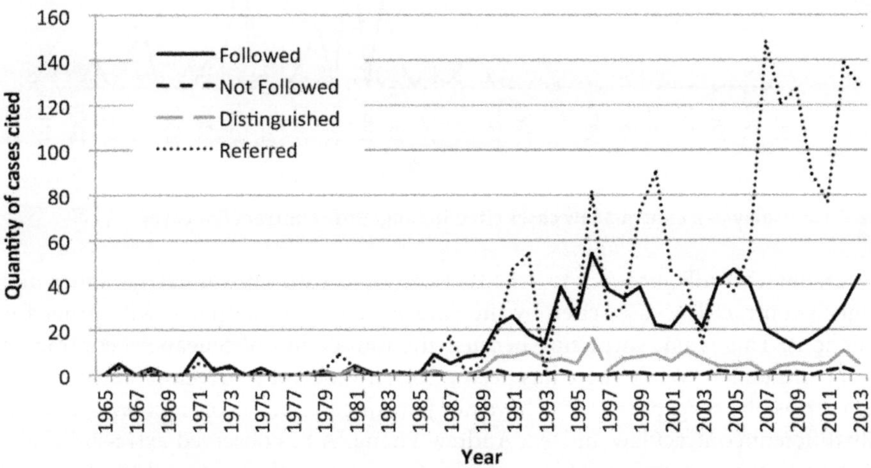

Figure 4.10: English contract law cases cited in Singapore contract law cases

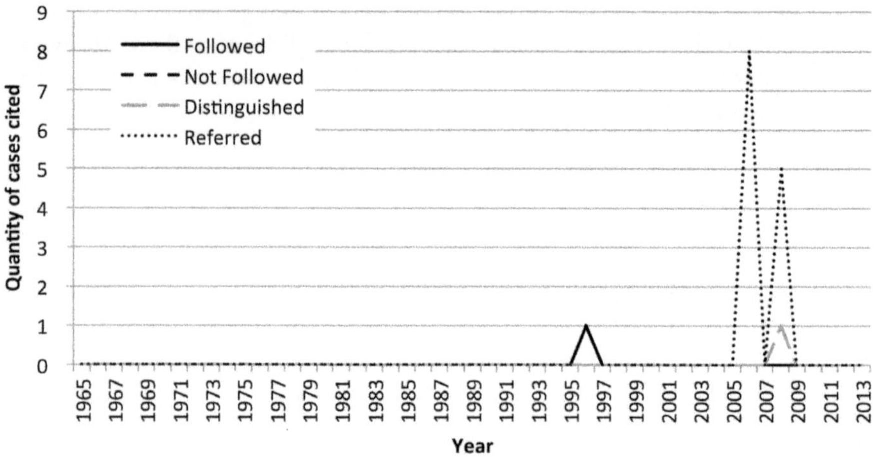

Figure 4.11: Indian contract law cases cited in Singapore contract law cases

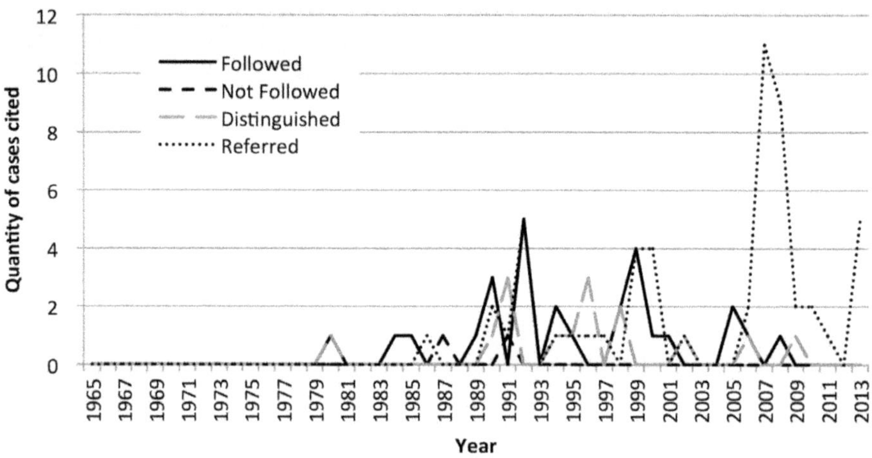

Figure 4.12: Malaysian contract law cases cited in Singapore contract law cases

It is evident from Figures 4.9 to 4.12 that there is a disproportionately higher number of English contract law cases cited by the Singapore courts compared with other foreign jurisdictions. This is not surprising because the foundation of Singapore contract law is English contract law. While there has been a concerted drive to develop Singapore law on its own terms, the Singapore courts have not jettisoned English contract law and crafted a wholly different contract law. Indeed, Andrew Phang JA has observed extra-judicially that 'English law is the foundation of Singapore law', a comment that was made in the context of a discussion on Singapore contract law.[88] That this is the case is further reflected by the fact

[88] Andrew Phang, 'Recent Developments in Singapore Contract Law: The Search for Principle' (2011) 28 *Journal of Contract Law* 3.

that the main academic texts relied on by practitioners and students have (until recently[89]) largely comprised English material. In contrast to the strong influence of English contract law, the numbers of Malaysian and Indian contract law cases that the Singapore courts cite are comparatively low. This may be because contract law in those jurisdictions is governed by a Contracts Act enacted in the nineteenth century,[90] which, while based on English law, has led to a very different development of contract law in those jurisdictions compared with English (and, consequently, Singapore) law. Malaysian and Indian contract law have thus become less relevant to Singapore contract law.

Another trend evident from the data is *how* the Singapore courts are citing the foreign contract law cases. Despite the broad acceptance of English contract cases, it can be seen that acceptance of those cases as being correct has decreased post-1990. This shows an increased willingness to disagree with English law, even though Singapore law originated from it. This is a trend that has become clearer in recent years. Thus, the fact of a similar common law heritage not only results in citation for the purpose of acceptance, but also engagement, inasmuch as Singapore now sees itself as part of a global legal network concerning the common law of obligations.

Resolution of Gap or Ambiguity in Local Law

At times, the Singapore courts rely on foreign cases to resolve a gap or ambiguity in Singapore law. This has happened especially in the common law of obligations. This ensures that there is a universal legal language unregulated by local statutes to which the Singapore courts can refer. In the past, Singapore courts have inevitably referred to English cases to resolve such gaps. Recently, however, a more comparative mindset has affected the Singapore courts. There appears to be an increased willingness to look at jurisdictions other than England where there is a gap or ambiguity in the local law. The relevant examples in the common law of obligations are many. One example, which we have already seen, is the Singapore Court of Appeal's reference to non-English jurisdictions in addressing the duty of care in negligence cases concerning pure economic loss. In the realm of contract law, the Singapore Court of Appeal in *Sembcorp Marine Ltd v PPL Holdings Pte Ltd*[91] referred to a host of cases not only from England, but other jurisdictions, in resolving a perceived gap in the local law relating to the interpretation of contracts.

These two reasons show why the Singapore courts continue to rely on foreign cases, albeit not as a matter of strict adherence. The implication, so far as the common law of obligations is concerned, is that while the Singapore courts have actively tried to develop a 'different' common law of obligations, that attempt is also constrained by continued reference to foreign cases, which ensures some degree of consistency with the greater common law world. The foundation of Singapore's common law of obligations has remained largely similar to other common law jurisdictions.

[89] See eg, ABL Phang (ed), *The Law of Contract in Singapore* (Singapore, Academy Publishing, 2012).

[90] Namely, the Malaysian Contracts Act 1950 (Act 136) and the Indian Contracts Act 1872.

[91] *Sembcorp Marine Ltd v PPL Holdings Pte Ltd* [2013] 4 SLR 193 (SGCA).

When do Singapore Courts Resist Reliance on Foreign Judgments in Developing a 'Different' Common Law of Obligations?

Just as Singapore courts rely on foreign cases in their judgments, they also reject foreign cases, and this applies equally to the common law of obligations, where the judicial assessment is that the foreign cases are wrong. In particular, the recent willingness of the courts to depart from English cases in the common law of obligations is quite apparent—evidenced by the decline in the number of English cases followed and the increase in the number of English cases not followed. A recent example of the courts' willingness to depart from the English position is the Singapore Court of Appeal's decision in *MFM Restaurants Pte Ltd v Fish & Co Restaurants Pte Ltd*,[92] which declined to follow the 'assumption of responsibility' test for remoteness. This, as already mentioned, evinces the Singapore courts' steadfast rejection of attempts elsewhere to reduce contractual principles to a core doctrine of contractual interpretation. In other instances where the courts took a position different from the English, such as in torts, other common law jurisdictions were widely consulted.[93]

The conclusion that emerges is that while English cases are being cited as a point of first reference, this is done mainly for the reason that the common law of obligations in Singapore is still founded on English law. However, beyond this starting point, Singapore courts do not necessarily follow English law, at least not without also consulting other jurisdictions. Moreover, even when Singapore courts cite cases from other jurisdictions, this certainly does not amount to blindly following the approach of any one particular foreign jurisdiction. The approach, instead, is more consultative. What is happening is that Singapore courts are building a Singaporean jurisprudence through the careful selection and amalgamation of the best practices and norms from a wide range of jurisdictions.

The net result from the above discussion is that the Singapore common law of obligations retains a core that is similar to English law, but increasingly supplemented by local refinements and departures, which sometimes lend a different perspective or viewpoint. The question is how relevant this 'different' common law of obligations is in the greater common law world.

V. Influence of a 'Different' Common Law of Obligations

To examine the relevance of Singapore's 'different' common law of obligations in the greater common law world, the citation of Singapore cases by foreign courts will be studied.

[92] *MFM Restaurants Pte Ltd v Fish & Co Restaurants Pte Ltd* [2011] 1 SLR 150 (SGCA).

[93] See the following tort cases, some of which have been discussed above: *RSP Architects Planners and Engineers v Ocean Front Pte Ltd* [1995] 3 SLR(R) 653 (SGCA) (departing from *Murphy v Brentwood District Council* [1991] 1 AC 398 (HL) and *D & F Estates Ltd v Church Commissioners of England* [1989] AC 177 (HL)) as well as *Malcomson Nicholas Hugh Bertram v Naresh Kumar Metha* [2001] 3 SLR(R) 379 (SGHC) (which came to a different conclusion on the actionability of harassing actions than the English Court of Appeal in *Wong v Parkside Health NHS Trust* [2001] EWCA Civ 1721). See now, also, *Spandeck Engineering v Defence Science and Technology Agency* [2007] 4 SLR(R) 100 (SGCA).

This will shed some light on the extent to which Singapore cases are being cited in foreign jurisdictions, and the reasons why. Secondly, how different aspects of Singapore law (ie, different subject matters, including aspects of the common law of obligations) are being cited in foreign jurisdictions will be examined.

Overview

A brief overview of the citation data can be seen in Figure 4.13, which shows the total number of Singapore cases (across all areas of law and not limited to the common law of obligations) cited in foreign cases from selected jurisdictions,[94] excluding Malaysia.[95]

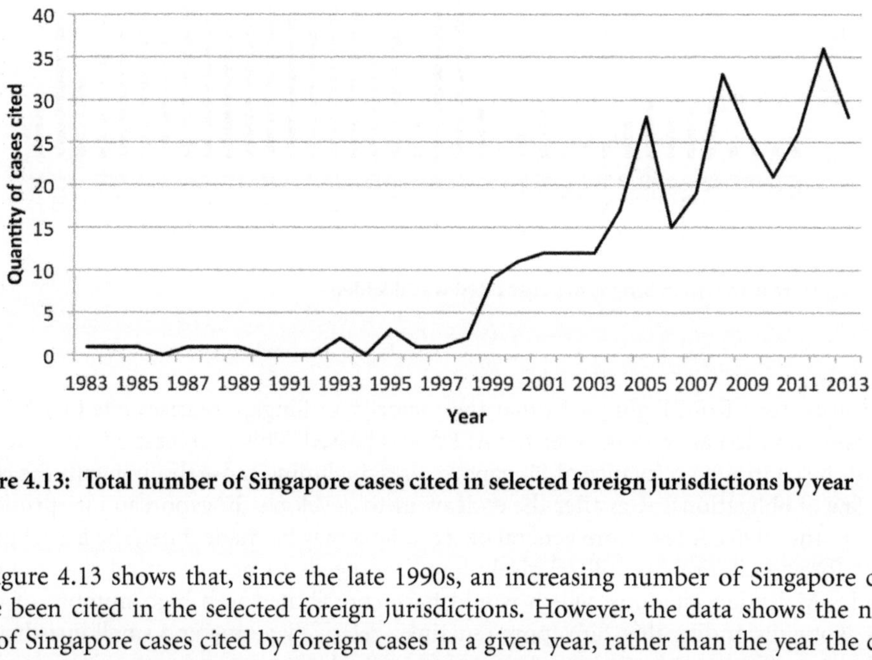

Figure 4.13: Total number of Singapore cases cited in selected foreign jurisdictions by year

Figure 4.13 shows that, since the late 1990s, an increasing number of Singapore cases have been cited in the selected foreign jurisdictions. However, the data shows the number of Singapore cases cited by foreign cases in a given year, rather than the year the cited Singapore case was decided. Therefore, while the data may reflect the increasingly comparative approach taken by foreign courts, it may not fully explain why Singapore cases have been

[94] These are Australia, Canada, China (including Hong Kong), India, New Zealand, the United Kingdom, the United States and a small number of other jurisdictions.

[95] Although closely related to Singapore both politically and legally, Malaysian cases are excluded because Singapore cases were once also reported in the Malaysian law reports. The result is that it is difficult to distinguish Singaporean from Malaysian cases in the relevant period, and to ascertain the actual number of Malaysian cases in which Singapore cases have been cited.

so cited. In order to do that, Figure 4.14 shows the year in which the Singapore case cited by foreign cases was decided.

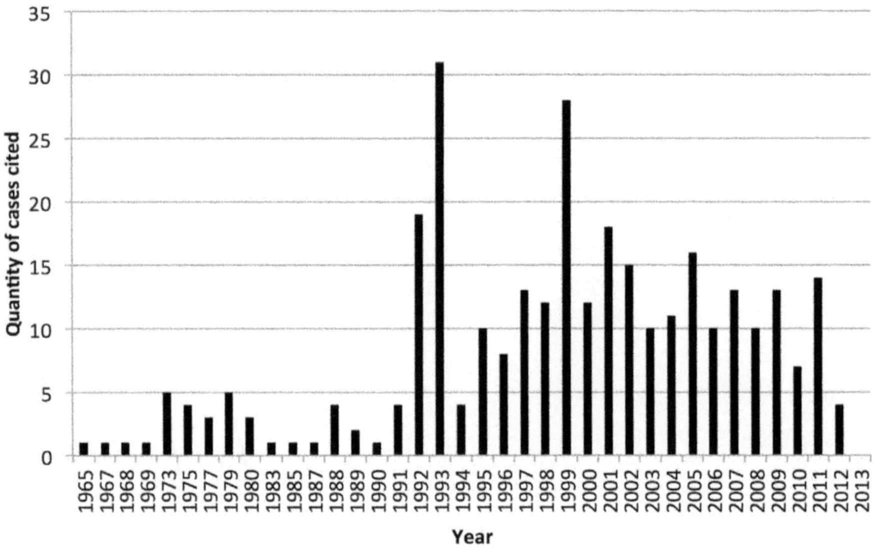

Figure 4.14: Year in which Singapore case cited was decided

It can be seen from Figure 4.14 that the majority of Singapore cases cited by foreign cases were decided after 1994, after the ALEA was passed. This is at least a limited reflection of the continued relevance of Singapore cases, including those dealing with the common law of obligations, even after the endeavour to develop a Singaporean jurisprudence began in the 1990s. A few more general observations may be made. First, the actual number of foreign citations is still relatively low. One needs to bear in mind that the data excludes Malaysian citations, which would have contributed to a high number of citations. Notwithstanding this, Singapore remains a relatively young and small jurisdiction. While recent Singapore cases have departed from English law, thereby constituting a new point of view that may be of interest to foreign jurisdictions, the majority of cases from Singapore's independence have followed English law. There is therefore not a large body of uniquely Singaporean case law that foreign cases may cite for reference. Furthermore, as has been seen above, some Singapore departures from English law are a result of internal societal and economic conditions within Singapore. These departures may therefore not be as relevant to a foreign jurisdiction as a novel perspective on a universally applicable legal principle.

In the following sections, it will be considered where Singapore cases are being cited as well as how they are being cited. An attempt will then be made to explain the data before concluding what the future may possibly hold for the spread of Singapore cases, including the relevance of a 'different' common law of obligations.

Jurisdictions Citing Singapore Law

General Observations

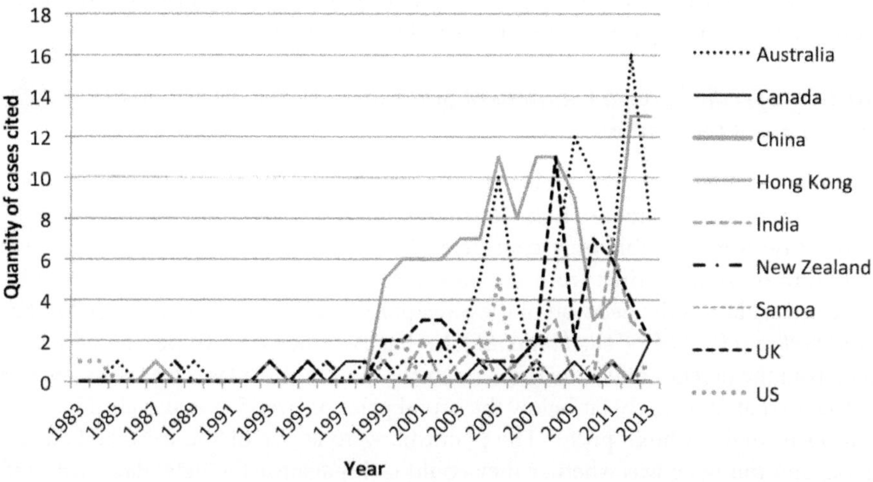

Figure 4.15: Total number of Singapore cases cited in selected foreign jurisdictions

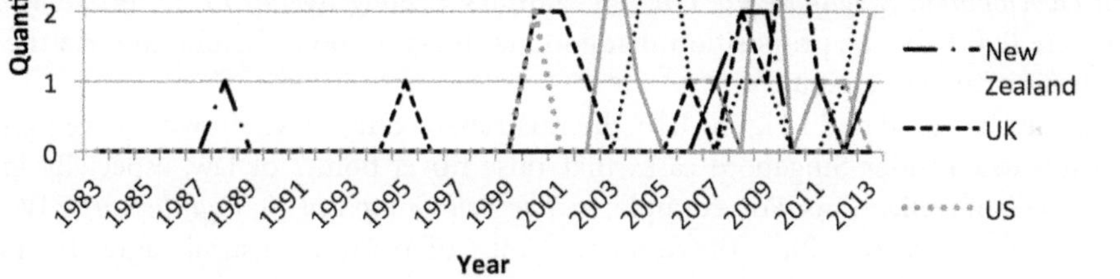

Figure 4.16: Total number of Singapore cases cited in selected foreign jurisdictions, for the common law of obligations only

Figure 4.15 summarises the foreign jurisdictions that have cited Singapore cases across all areas of law. It is clear from the citation data that Australia, England and Hong Kong are the three jurisdictions that have cited Singapore cases the most. In contrast, Canada, the United States and other jurisdictions rarely cite Singapore cases.

This is not surprising. Australia, England and Hong Kong share a common legal heritage with Singapore that facilitates the transfer of legal views and ideas. However, there may be more jurisdiction-specific reasons to explain why these jurisdictions are among those that cite Singapore cases the most. For example, it can be seen in Figure 4.16 that Australian and English courts have shown an increased willingness to consider Singapore cases, especially in the common law of obligations. Thus, while the data establishes that foreign jurisdictions have cited Singapore cases concerning the common law of obligations, it remains to be examined more closely on a jurisdiction-by-jurisdiction basis.

Jurisdiction-Specific Foreign Citations of Singapore Cases Concerning the Common Law of Obligations

Turning first to the English courts' citation of Singapore cases, a first example, already mentioned above, is the Singapore High Court case of *Sumitomo Bank*. In this example, the Singapore case was probably only considered by the Privy Council because it presented a novel point of view, distinct from the prevailing English law. Yet another example, this time in contract law, is the decision of the Singapore Court of Appeal in *Chwee Kin Keong v Digilandmall.com Pte Ltd*[96] ('*Digilandmall*'). In that case, the plaintiffs purchased 1,606 laser printers from the defendant via the latter's website. However, the laser printers were mistakenly advertised at S$66 each, far below the actual price of over S$3,000 each. The plaintiffs thus stood to make a huge profit. The plaintiffs were aware of the mistake before their purchase, and the issue was whether they could claim against the defendant, who refused to carry out the contract. The case raised issues of contractual formation and unilateral mistake. More importantly for our present purposes, the fact pattern was unique, and this was sufficient to prompt foreign judicial interest. For example, in the English High Court case of *Statoil ASA v Louis Dreyfus Energy Services LP*,[97] Aikens J was referred by counsel to *Digilandmall*. Aikens J accepted that the case stood for the classic rule that a contract can be set aside for unilateral mistake where the purchasers knew that a mistake had been made by the sellers: in such a case, the parties were not agreed on the most fundamental term of the contract, that is, the price.[98] A final, more recent, example is the English High Court's citation of the Singapore Court of Appeal case of *HSBC Institutional Trust (Services) Ltd v Toshin Development Singapore Pte Ltd*[99] in *Emirates Trading Agency LLC v Prime Mineral Exports Pte Ltd*[100] for the proposition that good faith is not too indefinite to form the sufficient basis of an agreement.

From the citation data in Figure 4.16, the Australian courts have shown an even greater propensity to consider Singapore cases that raise novel points of law, especially in the common law of obligations. For example, in *The Bell Group Ltd (in liquidation) v Westpac Banking Corporation (No 9)*,[101] the Supreme Court of Western Australia agreed with the

[96] *Chwee Kin Keong v Digilandmall.com Pte Ltd* [2005] 1 SLR(R) 502 (SGCA), on appeal from *Chwee Kin Keong v Digilandmall.com Pte Ltd* [2004] 2 SLR(R) 594 (SGHC).
[97] *Statoil ASA v Louis Dreyfus Energy Services LP* [2008] EWHC 2257 (Comm), [2009] 1 All ER (Comm) 1035 (QB).
[98] [2009] 1 All ER (Comm) 1035 (QB) [94].
[99] *HSBC Institutional Trust (Services) Ltd v Toshin Development Singapore Pte Ltd* [2012] 4 SLR 738 (SGCA).
[100] *Emirates Trading Agency LLC v Prime Mineral Exports Pte Ltd* [2014] EWHC 2104 (Comm).
[101] *The Bell Group Ltd (in liquidation) v Westpac Banking Corporation (No 9)* [2008] WASC 239, (2008) 39 WAR 1.

Singapore Court of Appeal in *Chan Kern Miang v Kea Resources Pte Ltd*[102] that, in relation to a *Barnes v Addy*[103] claim, it is not necessary to join the person who is said to have breached a fiduciary duty in order to succeed against a third party. Furthermore, the Federal Court of Australia in *Grimaldi v Chameleon Mining NL (No 2)*[104] cited *Sumitomo Bank* as 'preordain[ing]' its rejection of *Lister & Co v Stubbs.*[105] Another example is the citation of the Singapore Court of Appeal case of *Xpress Print Pte Ltd v Monocrafts Pte Ltd* by the New South Wales Supreme Court in *Piling v Prynew Nemeth*,[106] in connection with the proposition that there is a right of support from the adjoining soil. With reference to *Xpress Print*, the New South Wales Supreme Court noted that the rule in *Dalton v Angus* has been criticised and was 'clearly inappropriate', although the court regarded itself as bound by it.[107]

The above instances show that Australian courts cite Singapore cases concerning the common law of obligations when they advance a different point of view from English law, thereby lending support to the Australian court's departure from English law. Australian courts also cite Singapore cases where there has been an agreement to resolve a question in accordance with Singapore law. For example, in *Limit (No 3) Ltd v ACE Insurance Ltd*,[108] the New South Wales Supreme Court cited seven Singapore cases to decide an issue concerned with the law of nuisance in Singapore. These cases do not, of course, show an independent interest in Singapore law. However, more broadly, the Australian courts' interest in Singapore cases can be explained by other reasons. For example, an increasing number of lawyers in Singapore are now educated in Australia.[109] Moreover, as French CJ, the Chief Justice of Australia, said, Singapore and Australia share a common legal heritage as a legacy of colonial histories.[110]

The similar societal and economic conditions of Hong Kong and Singapore help explain why Hong Kong courts cite Singapore cases concerning the common law of obligations. For example, in the Hong Kong case of *Lau Tat Wai v Yip Lai Kuen Joey*,[111] the Singapore case of *Malcomson Nicholas Hugh Bertram v Naresh Kumar Mehta*[112] was cited to support the application of the Singapore law on harassment to Hong Kong on the basis of the similar conditions in both jurisdictions. Chan J in the Hong Kong Court of First Instance noted that the social conditions in Singapore 'are not very different to those of Hong Kong'[113] and that *Malcomson* 'serves to demonstrate that the time must have come for Hong Kong to recognise this tort [of harassment]'.[114] Moreover, both Singapore and

[102] *Chan Kern Miang v Kea Resources Pte Ltd* [1998] 2 SLR(R) 85 (SGCA).
[103] *Barnes v Addy* (1874) LR 9 Ch App 244.
[104] *Grimaldi v Chameleon Mining NL (No 2)* [2012] FCAFC 6, (2012) 200 FCR 296, (2012) 287 ALR 22 (FCA).
[105] ibid [582].
[106] *Piling v Prynew Nemeth* [2008] NSWSC 118.
[107] ibid [42].
[108] *Limit (No 3) Ltd v ACE Insurance Ltd* [2009] NSWSC 514.
[109] See 'Common links and old ties', *Straits Times* (Singapore), 24 January 1971, 16; and 'CJ tells Aussie Bar Convention: common law tradition has not been violated', *Straits Times* (Singapore), 2 July 1974, 7 (assertion of 'numerous common identities' between Western Australia and Singapore, both having a common law heritage).
[110] R French, 'Singapore Academy of Law Annual Lecture 2013: "The Rule of Law as a Many Coloured Dreamcoat"' (2014) 26 *Singapore Academy of Law Journal* 1, 5.
[111] *Lau Tat Wai v Yip Lai Kuen Joey* [2013] HKCFI 639, [2013] 3 HKC 361, [2013] 2 HKLRD 1197 (HKCFI).
[112] [2001] 3 SLR(R) 379.
[113] [2013] 2 HKLRD 1197 [60].
[114] ibid [61].

Hong Kong also share a common law heritage with similar motivations to develop the law locally, a fact alluded to in 2009 by Chief Justice Andrew Li of Hong Kong.[115]

How Foreign Jurisdictions are Citing Singapore Cases

The preceding discussion has shown the total number of Singapore cases cited by foreign jurisdictions. Figure 4.17 shows *how* foreign cases have cited Singapore cases, ie, whether they were followed, not followed, distinguished or merely referred to.

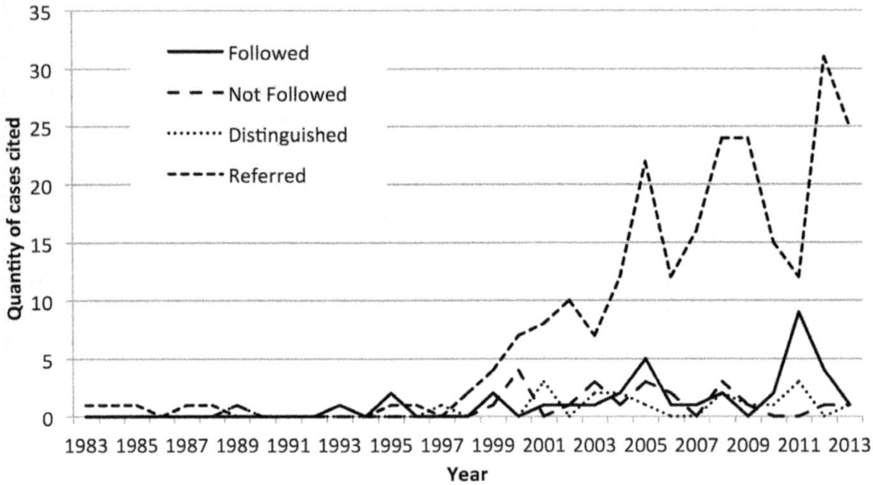

Figure 4.17: Total number of Singapore cases cited in foreign jurisdictions, by manner of citation

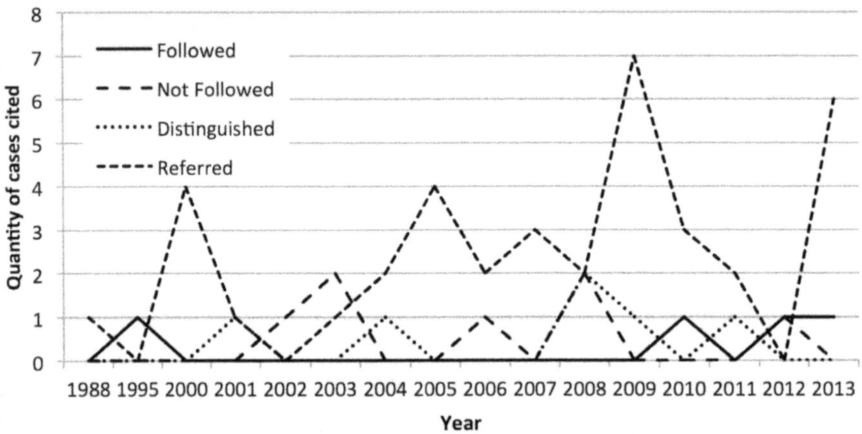

Figure 4.18: Total number of Singapore common law of obligations cases cited in foreign jurisdictions, by manner of citation

[115] A Li, 'Singapore Academy of Law Annual Lecture 2009: The Development of the Common Law in Hong Kong under "One Country, Two Systems"' (2009) 21 *Singapore Academy of Law Journal* 375 [5]. See also [18], where Li CJ said that Singapore cases are frequently cited before the Hong Kong courts, presumably because of the similarities between the two jurisdictions.

It can be seen from Figure 4.17 that, very generally, when Singapore cases are cited by foreign courts, they are very often just 'referred' to. Less often are they 'followed', and rarely are they 'distinguished' or 'not followed'. There is a more in-depth engagement with Singapore law by the top three foreign jurisdictions in which Singapore cases are cited greatly in number compared to other jurisdictions. While the majority of Singapore cases are merely 'referred' to in these three jurisdictions, there is also a greater proportion of Singapore cases being actively engaged with, that is, 'followed', 'distinguished' and 'not followed'. This is largely replicated in Figure 4.18, which shows the total number of Singapore common law of obligations cases cited in foreign jurisdictions.

Figures 4.17 and 4.18 are supplemented by Figures 4.19 to 4.24, which show more specifically how the English, Australian and Hong Kong courts are citing Singapore cases, first generally, then followed by specific citation of Singapore common law of obligations cases.

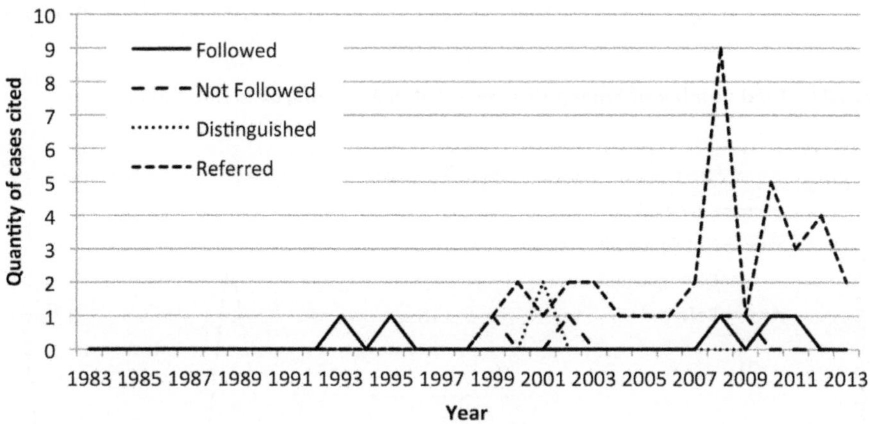

Figure 4.19: Total number of Singapore cases cited in England, by manner of citation

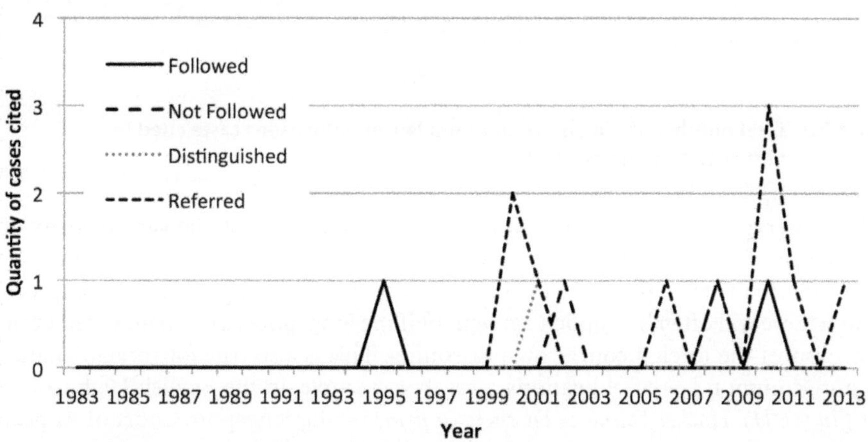

Figure 4.20: Total number of Singapore common law of obligations cases cited in England, by manner of citation

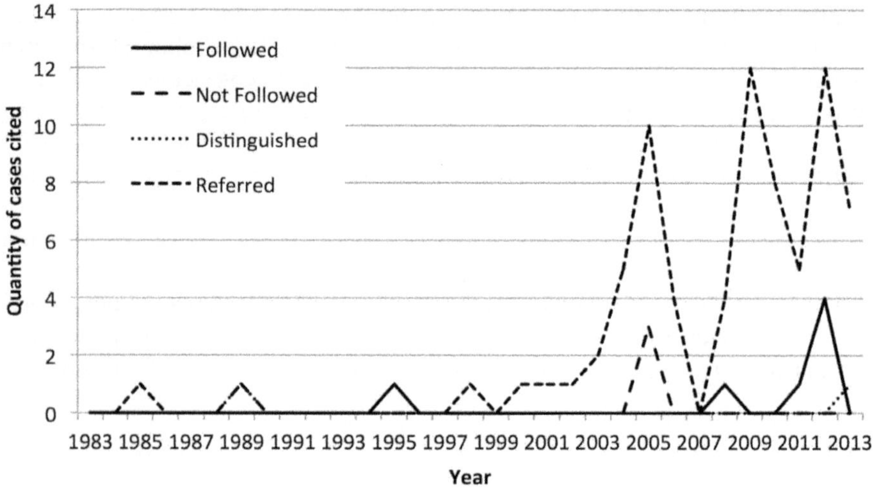

Figure 4.21: Total number of Singapore cases cited in Australia, by manner of citation

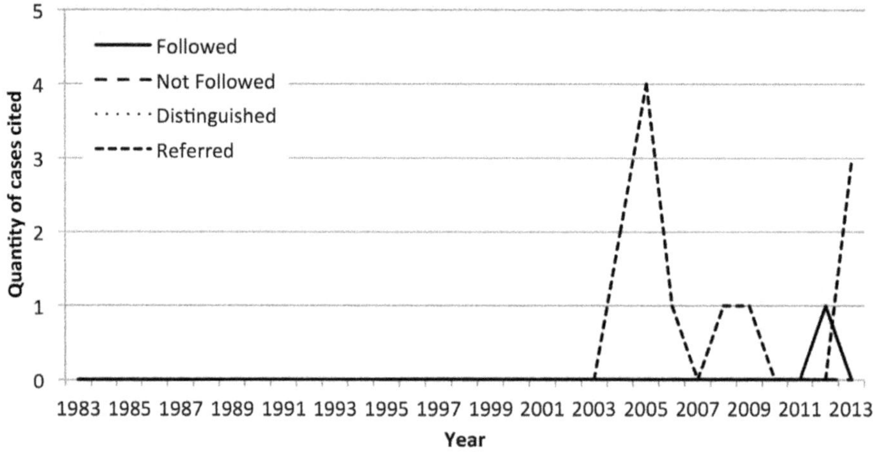

Figure 4.22: Total number of Singapore common law of obligations cases cited in Australia, by manner of citation

A few observations may be made about this citation data. First, the vast majority of foreign citations of Singapore cases are mere 'referrals', which means that the court concerned simply refers to the Singapore case in question, without explicit agreement or disagreement, although there will often be implicit agreement if the Singapore case is being used peripherally to support the foreign courts' own reasoning. This is also true for foreign citations of Singapore common law of obligations cases. For example, in the English High Court case of *Griffin v UHY Hacker Young & Partners (a firm)*,[116] the Singapore Court of Appeal case

[116] *Griffin v UHY Hacker Young & Partners (a firm)* [2010] EWHC 146 (Ch), [2010] All ER (D) 109.

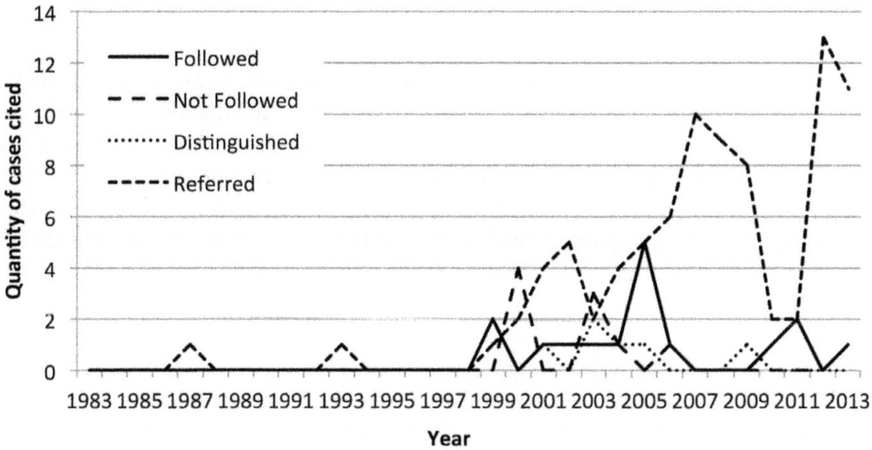

Figure 4.23: Total number of Singapore cases cited in Hong Kong, by manner of citation

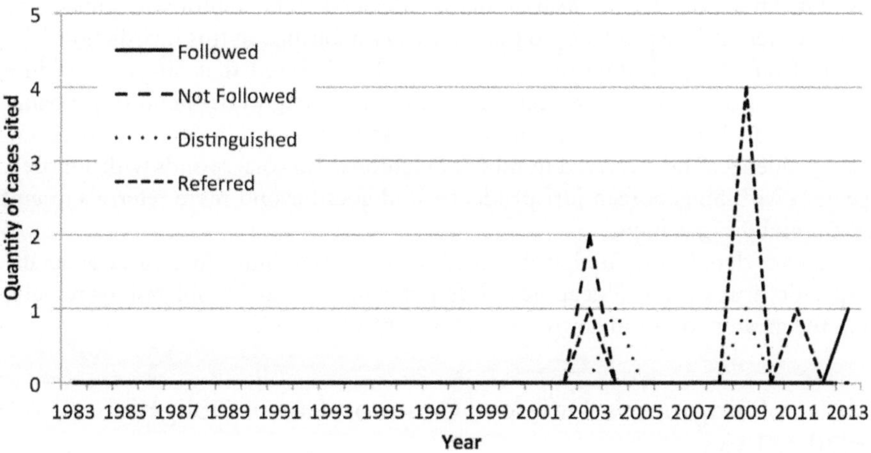

Figure 4.24: Total number of Singapore common law of obligations cases cited in Hong Kong, by manner of citation

of *United Project Consultants Pte Ltd v Leong Kwok Onn (trading as Leong Kwok Onn & Co)* ('*United Project Consultants*')[117] was cited along with other cases in the court's discussion of the *ex turpi causa* principle. Although the English High Court noted the House of Lord's disagreement with an aspect of *United Project Consultants*, it did not appear to doubt (or agree) with the main thrust of the Singapore case. In that light, the Singapore case was cited only as a point of reference.

Secondly, apart from mere 'referrals', there are some examples of foreign cases explicitly not following Singapore cases, including those concerning the common law of obligations.

[117] *United Project Consultants Pte Ltd v Leong Kwok Onn (trading as Leong Kwok Onn & Co)* [2005] 4 SLR(R) 214 (SGCA).

For example, in *Stone v Rolls Ltd (in liquidation) v Moore Stephens (a firm)*,[118] various members of the House of Lords referred to the Singapore Court of Appeal case of *United Project Consultants* when dealing with the *ex turpi causa* defence. Lord Phillips of Worth Matravers agreed that *United Project Consultants* showed that for the defence to operate, the illegality concerned must involve turpitude in certain situations.[119] However, Lord Walker of Gestingthorpe was less accepting of the Singapore case when considering the 'very thing' argument, holding that the reasoning 'shows confusion of thought'.[120] However, he did not seem to disagree with the more general principle that Lord Phillips had agreed with.[121] Disagreement notwithstanding, the English courts in this situation showed a willingness to engage with the Singapore court's reasoning.

Singapore cases were also 'not followed' where their reasoning proceeded on a basis that did not appeal to the court in the foreign jurisdiction. This has occurred in cases concerning the common law of obligations. For example, in the English High Court case of *Walters v North Glamorgan NHS Trust*[122] ('*Walters*'), Thomas J declined to follow the Singapore High Court case of *Pang Koi Far v Lim Djoe Phing*[123] on an issue of whether damages could be claimed for psychiatric harm. While holding eventually that the plaintiff could claim in the case before him, Thomas J stated that he did not find the Singapore case 'of any assistance' because it had been decided on the basis of cases decided in the Californian Supreme Court, which 'is a different jurisprudence to that that was established in this jurisdiction'.[124]

Overall, from the preceding two parts, it can be observed that Singapore's 'different' common law of obligations continues to be cited by foreign jurisdictions, probably at a rate greater than it was before Singapore embarked on a conscious effort to develop its own jurisprudence. The increased number of citations also corresponds with a more active engagement with Singaporean jurisprudence, and goes beyond mere referrals to embody agreement and disagreement.

Having considered how foreign jurisdictions are citing Singapore cases generally, the more specific issue of how Singapore's 'different' common law of obligations remains relevant in the greater common law world will now be discussed.

Relevance of Singapore's 'Different' Common Law of Obligations Over Other Laws

Overview

In order to discuss the relevance of Singapore's 'different' common law of obligations, it is necessary to break down the Singapore cases cited by foreign jurisdictions into their respective subject matters. This is done in Figure 4.25.

[118] *Stone v Rolls Ltd (in liquidation) v Moore Stephens (a firm)* [2009] UKHL 39, [2009] 1 AC 1391.
[119] ibid [24].
[120] ibid [180].
[121] ibid [180].
[122] *Walters v North Glamorgan NHS Trust* [2002] EWHC 321, [2002] Lloyd's Med Rep 227 [2003] PIQR P2.
[123] *Pang Koi Far v Lim Djoe Phing* [1993] 2 SLR(R) 366 (SGHC).
[124] Above n 122 [41].

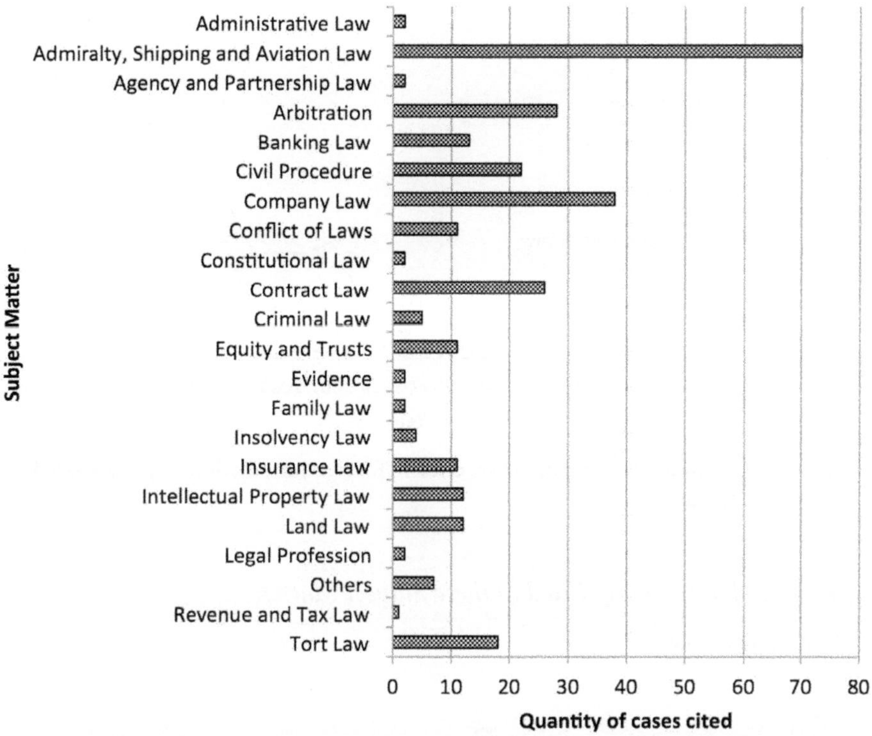

Figure 4.25: Total number of Singapore cases cited in foreign jurisdictions, by subject matter

Figure 4.26 groups these Singapore cases into more general categories: 'Law of Obligations', 'Other Commercial Law', 'Personal Law', 'Procedural Law', 'Public Law' and 'Others'. 'Law of Obligations' comprises contract, tort, equity and restitution cases. 'Personal Law' comprises family law cases; 'Procedural Law' comprises civil procedure, conflict of laws and evidence law cases; 'Public Law' comprises administrative law, constitutional law, criminal law and legal profession cases; and finally 'Other Commercial Law', the largest category, comprises the remaining subject matters, save for those already in the 'Law of Obligations' category. This covers areas such as banking law, which are of course concerned with aspects of the common law of obligations but not predominantly so.

Figure 4.26 shows that the vast majority—by far—of Singapore cases cited in foreign cases concerned the 'Other Commercial Law' category, followed by the 'Law of Obligations' category, both categories being within the more general field of commercial law. This is not surprising since commercial law permeates much of law and is perhaps the main area that the courts deal with. Procedural law is a distant third: this may be explained by the similar, if limited, civil procedure laws Singapore shares with certain jurisdictions. Finally, both personal and public law Singapore cases are not often cited by foreign courts.

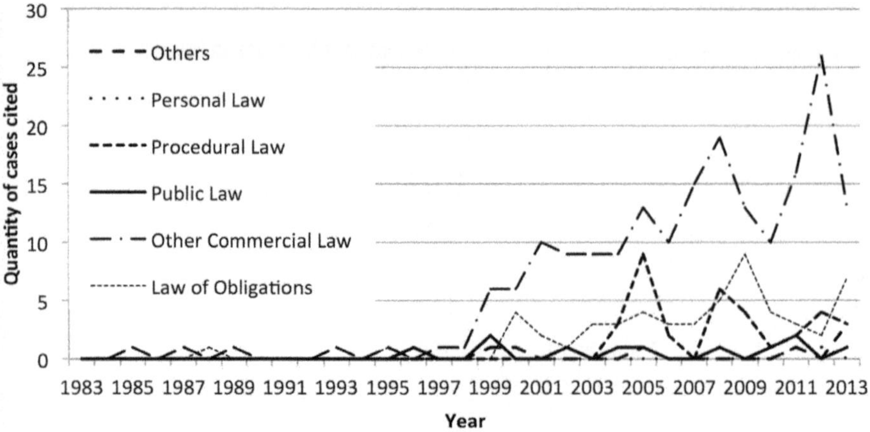

Figure 4.26: Total number of Singapore cases cited in foreign jurisdictions, by aggregated subject matter

How Singapore Law is Being Cited in these Subject Matters

Other Commercial Law

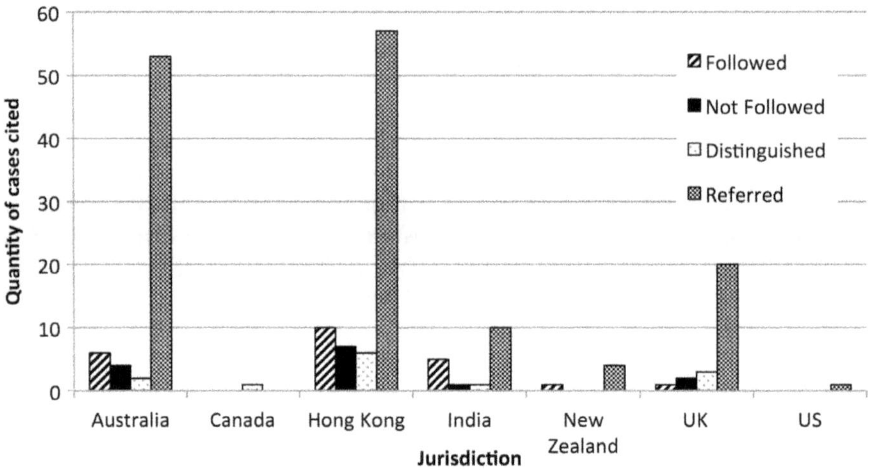

Figure 4.27: Number of Singapore other commercial law cases cited in foreign jurisdictions

From Figure 4.27, Singapore commercial law cases, excluding common law of obligations cases, are being similarly cited in selected foreign jurisdictions. In all jurisdictions, the vast majority of references were 'referrals', in which the Singapore case is cited without explicit agreement or disagreement. This perhaps shows that commercial laws are, by and large, uniform around the world.

Personal Laws

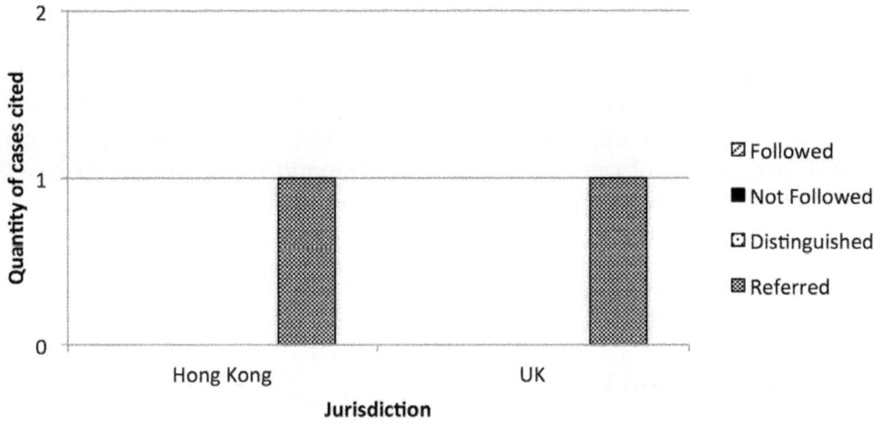

Figure 4.28: Number of Singapore personal law cases cited in foreign jurisdictions

As expected, personal laws were not really cited much in the selected jurisdictions (see Figure 4.28). Where they were, the majority were referrals. In fact, because tort law cases are categorised outside this category, there were few instances of active engagement (beyond mere 'referral'). This is perhaps attributable to the fact that these areas of law are predominantly domestic and developed in accordance with Singapore's unique set of societal conditions.

Common Law of Obligations

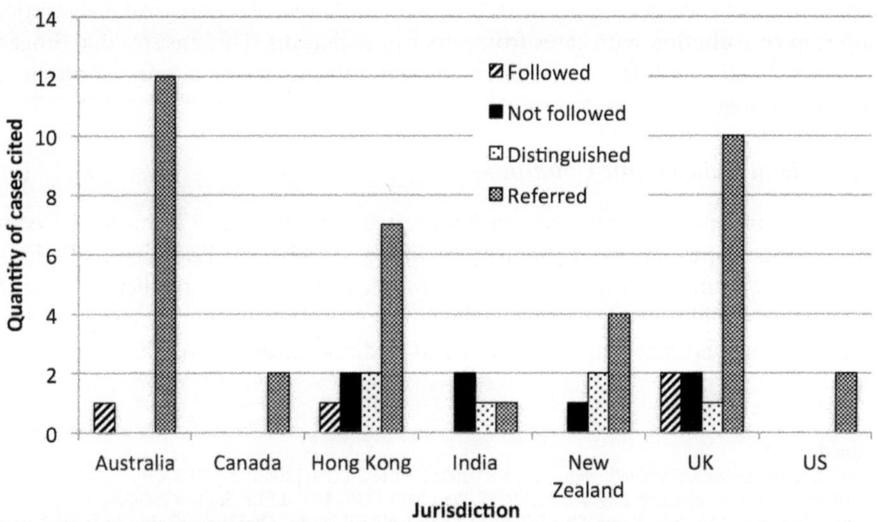

Figure 4.29: Number of Singapore common law of obligations cases cited in foreign jurisdictions

There appears to be greater foreign engagement with the Singapore common law of obligations cases (see Figure 4.29). Compared with other commercial cases, this may be explained by the fact that the common law of obligations does not generally concern jurisdiction-specific statutes, and thus lends itself to more ready discussion. There have been instances of disagreement. In England, the one instance of disagreement was found in *Walters*, a torts case discussed above.[125] And the New Zealand High Court, in *Body Corporate 188529 v North Shore Council*,[126] distinguished the Singapore Court of Appeal's analysis of the existence of duty of care to a management committee (which finds its New Zealand equivalent in the body corporate) in *RSP Architects Planners and Engineers v MCST Plan No 1075*.[127] While the New Zealand court found the analysis of the Singapore case 'of interest',[128] it eventually distinguished the Singapore case because the relevant New Zealand statutory provisions were different.

Explaining the Citation Data

In the light of the citation data presented above, it is suggested that there are four main reasons why Singapore cases, especially those concerning the common law of obligations, are being cited by foreign cases.

Shared Legal Heritage

The first reason, and this is a rather obvious one, is that foreign jurisdictions cite Singapore cases because of a shared legal heritage. This is easily observable by the fact that civil law jurisdictions very rarely cite Singapore cases, if at all. Instead, almost all of the foreign citations of Singapore cases have come from common law jurisdictions. This is especially the case for Singapore cases concerning the common law of obligations. Furthermore, given that this area of law is not subject to as many statutory regulations (and even if so, these remain quite consistent worldwide), the courts therefore retain greater discretion to develop it in consultation with cases from other jurisdictions. This ensures that Singapore cases, even if developed differently, will remain relevant since they are founded on the same shared legal heritage.

Shared Societal or Economic Conditions

A second reason why Singapore cases are being cited in foreign cases is due to shared societal or economic conditions. This is illustrated in the case of Hong Kong, a jurisdiction that Singapore shares much in common with. As smaller common law jurisdictions mature, it may be that they will become similar to Singapore socially and economically. And when that occurs, it may be that Singapore cases will find relevance in those jurisdictions. This

[125] Above n 122.

[126] *Body Corporate 188529 v North Shore Council* [2008] NZHC 1179, [2008] 3 NZLR 479.

[127] *RSP Architects Planners and Engineers v MCST Plan No 1075* [1999] 2 SLR(R) 134 (SGCA).

[128] *Body Corporate 188529 v North Shore Council* [2008] NZHC 1179, [2008] 3 NZLR 479 [55]. This paragraph (along with [29]–[57] of the judgment) was not reported in the New Zealand Law Reports. However, the Singapore case was cited as having been 'referred to' in the headnotes, see [2008] 3 NZLR 479, lines 41–43.

reason probably applies more strongly to the common law of obligations, which govern aspects of commercial and personal law that are not fundamentally jurisdictional, in contrast to criminal or constitutional law.

Point of Reference

A third reason why Singapore cases are being cited in foreign cases is that the maturity of Singapore legal reasoning provides a useful point of reference. Insofar as the common law of obligations is concerned, this may be explained by the fact that this area of law does not generally concern jurisdiction-specific statutes, and thus lends itself to more ready discussion. Indeed, there have been examples above of foreign jurisdictions, especially Australia, which have referred to Singapore cases as support for departing from the prevailing English position. This is where Singapore's 'different' common law of obligations is being cited precisely because of its difference from English law.

More broadly, this may be one of the many lasting legacies of the AELA. Singapore law and its reputation has matured to the point that foreign jurisdictions are interested to find out what the Singaporean approach is. However, given the small size of Singapore's jurisdiction, the number of any such citations will likely be low.

VI. Conclusion

The ambition to develop Singapore's own jurisprudence generally and its common law of obligations specifically is an ongoing enterprise. Serious efforts towards this end began only in the 1990s with the introduction of both institutional and other changes designed to reduce its dependence and reliance on foreign (in particular, English) law and jurisprudence. The data collected confirms that during this period, local jurisprudence grew (evidenced by the increased number of reported cases as well as the length of judgments); the number of local cases cited in subsequent cases increased; the gap between citations of local cases relative to foreign cases correspondingly narrowed; and there was a greater willingness to depart from case law across various subject areas. The desire to develop a 'different' common law seems to be successful insofar as a unique brand of the common law of obligations in Singapore is developing.

Yet, this Singapore brand of the common law of obligations cannot be entirely unique. As Singapore entered the twenty-first century, the priority has been to promote Singapore law as part of an overall strategy to position Singapore as a hub for legal activity and services in the region. Cases have no doubt become more complex, just as commercial transactions have become more sophisticated and transnational in character. As a consequence, the data also shows that while the number of local cases cited relative to foreign cases remains high, it is clear that Singaporean jurisprudence is developing in a more cosmopolitan fashion—more foreign cases are being cited than ever before, and cases from jurisdictions other than England are being cited more regularly than before. At the same time, Singapore courts are careful to distinguish or not follow foreign cases where necessary. The Singapore legal system is certainly more complex—neither totally reliant on foreign law nor completely local—than it has ever been in its (relatively) short history.

The mix of uniqueness and orthodoxy in the Singapore common law of obligations can be said to have had some influence. While the desire to develop a 'different' common law of obligations is possible and, indeed, mandated at times by local circumstances, such an ambition cannot be taken too far. Thus, despite a conscious effort to do so, the Singapore courts have in fact restrained themselves in certain areas and continued to adopt the more common perspective. Finally, the Singapore experience shows us that an attempt to develop a 'different' common law of obligations, within reasonable limits, will lead to the enrichment of the body of law that is the common law of obligations.

5

A Common Law of Tort: Is there a European Rift in the Common Law Family?

PAULA GILIKER

> It is highly desirable that at this appellate level, in cases where issues of legal policy are concerned, the court should be informed about the position in other common law countries. This court is often helped by being referred to authorities from other common law systems, including the United States.
>
> Lord Collins of Mapesbury JSC in *Jones v Kaney* (2011)[1]

Lord Collins expresses a view shared by many English judges of the benefits to be gained from a broader common law perspective in determining questions of legal policy: in this instance, whether expert witnesses retained by a party in litigation can be sued for professional negligence. More recently, Lord Neuberger in *Crawford Adjusters (Cayman) Ltd v Sagicor General Insurance (Cayman) Ltd*[2] has commented on the 'extraordinary rich seam of learning and thought' which could be mined from other common law jurisdictions.[3] His Lordship noted, in particular, the assistance gained from surveying legal developments in larger jurisdictions such as the United States which provided the wisdom of 'almost infinitely more judges than here'.[4] This chapter will examine the nature of common law ties and, in particular, the extent to which political changes in the twentieth century and beyond have put the ongoing relationship between these jurisdictions to the test. The law of tort provides a particularly good basis for this review. Primarily a judicial creation with limited statutory intervention, it is a law of *civil* wrongs, with an immediate connection with the society within which it operates, its values and its practices. The courts, in determining which conduct will be judged wrongful in a particular society, will therefore, by their judgments, give an insight into the culture and practice of the system within which law is applied. As Cotterrell has observed, law is not only the rules of the system, but the ways of 'doing' law, practising, invoking and developing it.[5] This chapter will therefore examine

[1] *Jones v Kaney* [2011] UKSC 13, [2011] 2 AC 398, [76].

[2] *Crawford Adjusters (Caymnan) Ltd v Sagicor General Insurance (Cayman) Ltd* [2013] UKPC 17, [2014] 1 AC 366 (Privy Council decision examining whether the tort of malicious prosecution should be extended to civil proceedings).

[3] ibid [197].

[4] ibid [193].

[5] R Cotterrell, 'Culture, Comparison and Community' (2006) 2 *International Journal of Law in Context* 1, 2.

how the common law courts 'do' tort law and, in particular, the impact of the decision of the United Kingdom to join the European Union (then European Economic Community) on 1 January 1973 and of the introduction of the Human Rights Act 1998 in October 2000 (which permits UK citizens to bring claims for breach of the European Convention on Human Rights in the UK courts). Have these events created a rift in the common law family as the 'parent' joins a new European family leaving its 'children' to fend for themselves, or have the ties which have bound the common law family over centuries proven harder to break?

I. The Common Law Legal Family

Samuel defines the common law family[6] or legal tradition as one based on the Anglo-American legal system.[7] What unites these jurisdictions are shared values, practices and beliefs. In particular, a common history, based on colonialism which imported a dominant parent legal system into each jurisdiction, has led to similarities in terms of legal structure, analysis and procedure.[8] Leading comparative lawyers Zweigert and Kötz identify five factors as indicative of a particular 'style' of legal system:

> The following factors seem to us to be those which are crucial for the style of a legal system or legal family: (1) its historical background and development, (2) its predominant and characteristic mode of thought in legal matters, (3) especially distinctive institutions, (4) the kind of legal sources it acknowledges and the way it handles them, and (5) its ideology.[9]

Overall, the common law legal family satisfies these requirements, although it is worth noting that they presume a shared ideology and mode of thought in legal (to which we must add broader notions of social, economic and political) matters. Zweigert and Kötz juxtapose the common law focus on case law and preference for experience over theory with the systematic approach of the civil law, marked by a tendency to use abstract legal norms.[10] A common history, methodology (be it rules of statutory construction or the doctrine of precedent), legal training and institutional framework all therefore serve to unite the common law legal family and distinguish it from 'rival' families such as those based on

[6] There is a wealth of literature discussing the meaning of 'legal family' and whether it is better described as a 'legal tradition' or 'culture' or even '*mentalité*' to use the phrase of Pierre Legrand (see, eg, his 'European Legal Systems are Not Converging' (1996) 45 *ICLQ* 52; and *Fragments on Law as Culture* (Deventer, Willink, 1999)).

[7] 'Common Law' in JM Smits (ed), *Elgar Encyclopedia of Comparative Law*, 2nd edn (Cheltenham, Edward Elgar, 2012).

[8] R Goff, 'The Future of the Common Law' (1997) 46 *ICLQ* 745.

[9] K Zweigert and H Kötz, *An Introduction to Comparative Law*, 3rd edn (Oxford, Clarendon Press, 1998) 68. There are, of course, numerous other classificatory systems which have been advocated, far too numerous to mention and which often reflect the values of their time, eg, P Esmein, 'Le droit comparé et enseignement du droit' (1905) *Congrès international du droit comparé—Actes*, vol I, 451. Husa identifies a number of factors as relevant, including history; ideology; legal style; legal argumentation and thinking; the codification level of law; judicial reasoning; the structural system of law; the structure of the court system; the spirit and mentality of legal actors; training of lawyers; law's relation to religion and to politics; the economic basis of law; the background philosophy of legal thinking and sources of law: J Husa, 'Legal Families' in JM Smits (ed), *Elgar Encyclopedia of Comparative Law*, 2nd edn (Cheltenham, Edward Elgar, 2012) 492–93.

[10] Zweigert and Kötz, above n 9, 69–70.

the civil law, Islamic, Hindu or indigenous legal traditions. It is the law of practice, not of universities, with the judge playing a particularly significant role.[11]

We can also identify a sense of security which derives from membership of a legal family. Few jurisdictions, particularly in our globalised world, will wish to isolate themselves from the wider legal community. Families give us a sense of shared values and rules by which we can measure our own behaviour, even if we choose to rebel on occasion. Indeed, the comfort and convenience of a dominant legal tradition is often difficult to shake. Watson has commented that belonging to a particular legal tradition or family will play an important role in shaping legal change in a number of ways: 'borrowing from other systems, the form taken by most legal change, is by no means always the result of a systematic search for the best solution'.[12] Law reform, he notes, will have a bias for the familiar. It will not therefore simply be a question of objectively assessing the most appropriate transplants. Law-makers will be drawn to particular systems by virtue of factors such as the prestige given to the system, their accessibility and linguistic tradition.[13] He notes, in particular, among lawyers and layman alike the mythology of the common law as somehow superior to other legal systems.[14] The result, as Kahn-Freund has also observed, is that legal development and change will not necessarily rest on an objective survey of 'best solutions', but will reflect political factors, notably the receptivity of those in power to external change.[15] From the common law perspective, there is an undeniable sense of safety and reassurance in sticking to the familiar: the language is that of English; the legal terminology (both substantive and procedural) that of the same legal dictionary; the actors, institutions and the mechanisms for change are all immediately recognisable. We know how the hierarchy of different sources of law interact, what it means for a court to 'distinguish' an earlier decision, how to identify the *ratio decidendi* of the case without the need to refer to a single textbook for guidance. The implicit language of the (common) law is shared within the legal family and serves both to reassure and to make the application of the law easier. This is taught in our Law Schools and instilled into our identity as lawyers.

In contrast, to understand law outside the legal family, a learning process will be needed to comprehend fully the different rules of substantive and procedural law, new legal terminology, and to overcome linguistic barriers. Stapleton has argued that practitioners and judges in an English-speaking jurisdiction should exercise extreme caution in using comparative materials from foreign language systems and that sufficiently rich resources exist within their own language pool.[16] Mak, in her study of the UK and Dutch Supreme Courts' use of foreign law, finds also that UK judges are often hampered by their lack

[11] RC Van Caenegem, *Judges, Legislators and Professors* (Cambridge, CUP, 1987). See also D Howarth, *Law as Engineering: Thinking about What Lawyers Do* (Cheltenham, Edward Elgar, 2014) 148: 'The world of the law, especially in common law countries, is … self consciously practical, [it] distains the merely theoretical and cares less about whether lawyers have well stocked minds than about whether they know what they are doing'.

[12] A Watson, 'Legal Change: Sources of Law and Legal Culture' (1983) 131 *University of Pennsylvania Law Review* 1121, 1157.

[13] A Watson, 'Comparative Law and Legal Change' [1978] *CLJ* 313, 317.

[14] ibid 331. Equally, for a French lawyer, the *Code civil* has iconic status, rendering comparisons outside the civil law world unlikely: see Collectif Paris II, *1804–2004. Le Code civil: un passé, un présent, un avenir* (Paris, Dalloz, 2004).

[15] O Kahn-Freund, 'On Uses and Misuses of Comparative Law' (1974) 37 *MLR* 1, 18.

[16] J Stapleton, 'Benefits of Comparative Tort Reasoning: Lost in Translation' (2007) 1(3) *Journal of Tort Law* Art 6.

of languages, noting that judges with a background in academia seemed more open to consultation of academic writings on foreign legal systems.[17] For Bobek, judicial willingness to make use of comparative inspiration can be summed up in three words: time, access and understanding.[18] Principled and practical considerations, therefore, indicate that systems with a common foundation and language should remain close. Örücü notes that between 1972 and 1993 almost 75 per cent of references to foreign law in the British courts were made to other common law jurisdictions.[19]

II. Divergence in the Common Law Family

The law is not, however, static: 'law is a living thing and it evolves and changes constantly, even while some culturally and deeply rooted basic features do change at a remarkably slow pace'.[20] The Commonwealth of nations has developed into a political association of states. While the common law may still exist as a legacy of colonialism, it cannot be assumed to have the same legal content in every common law jurisdiction. If we, for example, consider Canada, Australia and New Zealand which remain (excluding the private law of Québec) common law systems, time has brought forth changes. These states abolished the right of appeal to the Judicial Committee of the Privy Council in London[21] in 1949,[22] 1986[23] and 2003,[24] respectively. English law is no longer binding and is merely persuasive.[25] Commentators have noted the creation of 'local' versions of the common law, adapted to that country's own characteristics and the customs of its people.[26] In the context of tort law, the judges

[17] E Mak, 'Why Do Dutch and UK Judges Cite Foreign Law?' [2011] *CLJ* 420, 448.

[18] M Bobek, *Comparative Reasoning in European Supreme Courts* (Oxford, OUP, 2013) 36, but see more generally ch 3.

[19] E Örücü, 'Comparative Law in British Courts' in U Drobnig and S Van Erp (eds), *The Use of Comparative Law by Courts* (The Hague, Kluwer, 1999) 263–65.

[20] Husa, above n 9, 492.

[21] In the 1930s the Judicial Committee of the Privy Council was said to be the final court of appeal for more than a quarter of the world.

[22] Criminal appeals to the Privy Council were ended in 1933. Civil appeals ended in 1949, when an amendment to the Supreme Court Act transferred ultimate appellant jurisdiction to Canada.

[23] Culminating in the Australia Act 1986 (Cth). Appeals to the Privy Council from decisions of the High Court of Australia were effectively ended by the combined effects of the Privy Council (Limitation of Appeals) Act 1968 (Cth) and the Privy Council (Appeals from the High Court) Act 1975 (Cth). However, a right of appeal to the Privy Council remained from State courts, in matters governed by State law, until the passage of the Australia Acts, both State and Federal.

[24] Supreme Court Act 2003 (NZ). The Act came into force on 1 January 2004, officially establishing the New Zealand Supreme Court, and at the same time ending appeals to the Privy Council in relation to all decisions of New Zealand courts made after 31 December 2003. This New Zealand legislation does not, however, affect rights of appeal from the Cook Islands and Niue.

[25] See, eg, the contributions of Justices Kirby (High Court of Australia) and Sharpe (Court of Appeal for Ontario) in 'The Old Commonwealth' in L Blom-Cooper QC, B Dickson and G Drewry (eds), *The Judicial House of Lords 1876–2009* (Oxford, OUP, 2009) ch 19. See also Paul Finn, Chapter 3, 'Unity, then Divergence: The Privy Council, the Common Law of England and the Common Laws of Canada, Australia and New Zealand'.

[26] Consider, for example, M Vranken, 'Australia' in JM Smits (ed), *Elgar Encyclopedia of Comparative Law*, 2nd edn (Cheltenham, Edward Elgar, 2012); J Toohey, 'Towards an Australian Common Law' (1990) 6 *Australian Bar Review* 185; R Cooke, 'The New Zealand National Legal Identity' (1987) 3 *Canterbury Law Review* 171; K Glover, 'Severing the Ties that Bind? The Development of a Distinctive New Zealand Jurisprudence' (2000) 8 *Waikato Law Review* 25.

in these jurisdictions on a number of occasions have chosen not to follow House of Lords' authority in favour of legal rules more suited to their own society. Stevens, for example, has noted policy divergence between the highest courts of the United Kingdom, Canada, Australia and New Zealand which, in his view, is demonstrative of a more conservative and pro-defendant stance in the highest UK court, reflecting a desire to resist an expansion of liability.[27] On this basis, the Supreme Court of Canada in *Canadian National Railway Co v Norsk Pacific Steamship Co*[28] in 1992 was quite willing to declare that the UK House of Lords' decision in '*Murphy v Brentwood District Council* [1991] 1 AC 398 does not represent the law in Canada'.[29] Justice of the High Court of Australia, Sir Anthony Mason, was equally happy to state that 'There is … every reason why we should fashion a common law for Australia that is best suited to our conditions and circumstances … The value of English judgments, like Canadian, New Zealand and for that matter United States judgments, depends on the persuasive force of their reasoning'.[30] On this basis, in relation to claims relating to pure economic loss arising from defective buildings, a distinct line of authority may be seen in Canada,[31] Australia,[32] New Zealand[33] and beyond.[34] Indeed, Martin has commented that the Privy Council in *Invercargill*, by recognising the importance of divergence in the common law, with each jurisdiction developing law appropriate to its own social setting, effectively talked itself out of a job.[35] In effect, the Privy Council acknowledged that its role could no longer be to unify Commonwealth law. As Lord Lloyd stated in that case:

> [t]he ability of the common law to adapt itself to the differing circumstances of the countries in which it has taken root, is not a weakness, but one of its great strengths. Were it not so, the common law would not have flourished as it has, with all the common law countries learning from each other.[36]

[27] R Stevens, 'Torts' in L Blom-Cooper QC, B Dickson and G Drewry (eds), *The Judicial House of Lords 1876–2009* (Oxford, OUP, 2009) 630–31. He also notes that cases such as *Rookes v Barnard* [1964] AC 1129 (HL), *BRB v Herrington* [1972] AC 877 (HL) and *Alcock v Chief Constable of South Yorkshire* [1992] 1 AC 310 (HL) have found little favour in Australia.

[28] *Canadian National Railway Co v Norsk Pacific Steamship Co* [1992] 1 SCR 1021, (1992) 91 DLR (4th) 289.

[29] ibid 303 (DLR) (La Forest J).

[30] A Mason, 'Future Directions in Australian Law' (1987) 13 *Monash University Law Review* 149, 154. See also P Finn, 'Common Law Divergences' (2013) 37 *Melbourne University Law Review* 509, 511 ('Today, it is abundantly clear that there are separate bodies of English and Australian common law').

[31] *Winnipeg Condominium Corp No 36 v Bird Construction Co* (1995) 121 DLR (4th) 193 (SCC).

[32] *Bryan v Moloney* (1995) 182 CLR 609 (HCA).

[33] The New Zealand Court of Appeal in *Invercargill v Hamlin* [1994] 3 NZLR 513 justified this in the light of the different social and political conditions in New Zealand, notably in relation to the role of councils. This argument was accepted by the Privy Council: [1996] AC 624. See also, more recently, R Tobin, 'Local Authority Liability in Tort to Owners of Defective Buildings: The New Zealand Position' (2013) 42 *Common Law World Review* 151, and A Gunawansa, 'Pure Economic Loss Relating to Construction Defects: A Comparative Analysis' (2010) *Construction Law Journal* 439.

[34] See, eg, Singapore: *RSP Architects Planners and Engineers v Ocean Front Pte Ltd* [1996] 1 SLR 113; *RSP Architects Planners and Engineers (Raglan Squire & Partners FE) v Management Corp Strata Title Plan No 1075* [1999] 2 SLR 449. Appeals to the Privy Council were abolished in Singapore in 1993. See also M Chen-Wishart, 'Legal Transplant and Undue Influence: Lost in Translation or a Working Misunderstanding?' (2013) 62 *ICLQ* 1, who notes, in particular, the distinction between Western and South-East Asian cultures which influences the interpretation of even 'common' legal principles.

[35] R Martin, 'Tortious Liability for Defective Premises in English Law after *Murphy v Brentwood*: Learning from the Commonwealth' (1997) 2 *Newcastle Law Review* 82, 89. See also R Martin, 'Diverging Common Law: *Invercargill* goes to the Privy Council' (1997) 60 *MLR* 94.

[36] *Invercargill v Hamlin* [1996] AC 624 (PC), 64.

Divergence, therefore, exists. Indeed, it is difficult to deny in the face of the New Zealand Accident Compensation Scheme, which, for over 40 years, has replaced tort provisions relating to personal injury and death with a no-fault compensation scheme.[37] Equally, from 2002, there has been significant legislative reform of civil liability in Australia following its 'insurance crisis', triggered by the rise of public liability premiums and the collapse of the insurance company, HIH.[38] Post-2002, legislative reform has appeared in all Australian jurisdictions (including the Commonwealth) and has led to divergences across Australia despite recommendations that change should be uniform.[39] Barnett and Harder report, for example, that no two jurisdictions in Australia have exactly the same rules on contributory negligence nor for the assessment of compensation for personal injury.[40]

Tort law will therefore continue to evolve and will change in response to national initiatives which will make the 'higher level' policy choices which are not within the power of the judiciary. The limitations of private litigation make this inevitable. While hardly surprising, it does lead to fragmentation of the common law world. On this basis, statutory intervention and judicial activism at a domestic level will lead to divergence and it is unavoidable that this will lead to a loosening of ties.

III. New Influences: Supra-national Law and Europeanisation

While such divergence is inevitable, new influences also threaten the traditional relationship of common law states. Supranational law encourages fresh alliances and new groupings of states. As Glenn has observed, national legal systems can no longer be assumed to be autonomous and static, but are subject to new forms of non-state law which render the idea of a fixed legal family hopelessly out-of-date.[41] Further, globalisation[42] and the growth of international jurisdictions such as the International Court of Justice render it difficult for nation states to think solely in terms of national policy initiatives and this will be as applicable to

[37] Information can be gathered from the website of the Accident Compensation Corporation which administers the scheme, www.acc.co.nz. See, further, K Oliphant, 'Beyond Misadventure: Compensation for Medical Injuries in New Zealand' (2007) 15 *Medical Law Review* 357; P Blake, 'Medical Mishap: No Fault Compensation as an Alternative to Civil Litigation—a Review of 30 Years' Experience with the New Zealand Accident Compensation Corporation System' (2010) 78 *Medico-Legal Journal* 126; and S Todd, 'Forty Years of Accident Compensation in New Zealand' (2012) 28 *Thomas M Cooley Law Review* 190.

[38] In May 2002, a Ministerial Meeting on Public Liability comprising Ministers from the Commonwealth, States and Territory governments jointly agreed to appoint a Panel to examine and review the law of negligence including its interaction with the Trade Practices Act 1974. This led to the Ipp Report: Commonwealth of Australia, *Review of the Law of Negligence: Final Report* (Canberra, Canprint Communications Pty Ltd, 2002) chaired by Justice David Ipp.

[39] For the impact of the reforms on the tort of negligence see, eg, B McDonald, 'The Impact of the Civil Liability Legislation on Fundamental Policies and Principles of the Common Law of Negligence' (2006) 14 *Torts Law Journal* 268; J Dietrich, 'Duty of Care under the "Civil Liability Acts"' (2005) 13 *Torts Law Journal* 17.

[40] K Barnett and S Harder, *Remedies in Australian Private Law* (New York, CUP, 2014) 164.

[41] HP Glenn, 'Comparative Legal Families and Comparative Legal Traditions' in R Zimmermann and M Reimann (eds), *The Oxford Handbook of Comparative Law* (Oxford, OUP, 2006).

[42] W Twining, *Globalisation and Legal Theory* (Cambridge, CUP, 2000); W Twining, 'Globalisation and Comparative Law' in E Örücü and D Nelken (eds), *Comparative Law: A Handbook* (Oxford, Hart Publishing, 2007) 69–75.

the law of tort as any other area of law.[43] Consider, for example, global litigation arising from the use of asbestos and against the tobacco industry and it is clear that states will be drawn together by transnational litigation.[44] Lord Cooke correctly observed in 2004 that, 'the common law of England is becoming gradually less English. International influences—from Europe, the Commonwealth and even the United States, sometimes themselves pulling in different directions—are gradually acquiring more and more strength'.[45]

The influence of supra-national law, that is, a form of international law which operates at a level above the nation state, is of particular interest in this context. In private law, the United Nations Convention on Contracts for the International Sale of Goods (CISG)[46] is perhaps the best known example.[47] To date, 80 states have ratified the CISG,[48] including Australia, Canada, New Zealand and the United States. These states share a uniform international sales law—a 'common law' if you will—and are united, not by history, but a common interest in international trade on a global scale. Yet, supra-national law can also be divisive. If you are not a participating state (for example, the United Kingdom remains unwilling to ratify the CISG on the basis that it is too broadly formulated to give the certainty which English contract lawyers expect)[49] then you will be excluded from this developing area of law. Whatever the merits (or otherwise) of CISG, it serves to divorce the United Kingdom from its common law brethren.

The most obvious supra-national law affecting English tort law is that of EU law. Despite having no formal basis in the Treaty of Rome, the European Court of Justice (Court of Justice of the European Union, CJEU) has found that the EEC Treaty created its own legal order for the benefit of which states have limited their sovereign rights.[50] This renders the CJEU superior to national courts and, under the doctrine of direct effect, national courts are expected to provide a remedial response to breaches of EU legal provisions which are sufficiently clear, precise and unconditional to be considered justiciable.[51] Further, the doctrine of indirect effect states that national courts now have duties to interpret existing legislation in line with EU law.[52] Article 19 of the Treaty on European Union (TEU) re-iterates

[43] R Michaels and N Jansen, 'Private Law Beyond the State? Europeanization, Globalisation, Privatization' (2006) 54 *American Journal of Comparative Law* 843, 861–64.

[44] See A-M Slaughter, 'A Global Community of Courts' (2003) 44 *Harvard International Law Journal* 191, 204.

[45] R Cooke, 'The Road Ahead for the Common Law' (2004) 53 *ICLQ* 273, 274.

[46] See www.cisg.law.pace.edu/cisg/text/treaty.html.

[47] See P Huber, 'Comparative Sales Law' in R Zimmermann and M Reimann (eds), *The Oxford Handbook of Comparative Law* (Oxford, OUP, 2006). Consider, also, UNIDROIT (International Institute for the Unification of Private Law) which produces principles for international commercial contracts. UNIDROIT's 63 member states are drawn from the five continents and represent a variety of different legal, economic and political systems as well as different cultural backgrounds.

[48] See www.cisg.law.pace.edu/cisg/countries/cntries.html.

[49] S Moss, 'Why the UK has Not Yet Ratified the CISG' (2005) 25 *Journal of Law and Commerce* 483; J Beatson, A Burrows and J Cartwright, *Anson's Law of Contract*, 29th edn (Oxford, OUP, 2010) 20; JS Hobhouse, 'International Conventions and Commercial Law: The Pursuit of Uniformity' (1990) 106 *LQR* 530.

[50] Case 6/64 *Costa v ENEL* [1964] ECR 585, 593. See, generally, P Craig and G de Búrca, *EU Law: Text, Cases and Materials*, 6th edn (Oxford, OUP, 2015) ch 9.

[51] Case 26/62 *Van Gend en Loos v Nederlandse Administratie der Belastungen* [1963] ECR 1 and Case 41/74 *Van Duyn v Home Office* [1974] ECR 1337. Note that the rule remains that the direct effect of a Directive may only be pleaded against the state and not against an individual (vertical not horizontal effect): Case 152/84 *Marshall v Southampton and South-West Hampshire Area Health Authority (Teaching)* [1986] ECR 723.

[52] Case 14/83 *Von Colson v Land Nordrhein-Westfalen* [1984] ECR 1891; Case C-106/89 *Marleasing SA v La Comercial Internacional de Alimentacion SA* [1990] ECR I-4135; Cases C-397–403/01 *Pfeiffer v Deutsches Rotes Kreuz, Kreisverband Waldshut eV* [2004] ECR I-8835.

that 'Member States shall provide remedies sufficient to ensure effective legal protection in the fields covered by Union law'.[53] On this basis, Jaremba remarks, 'all national judges, regardless of their specialization and position in the national judicial architecture, are EU law judges'.[54]

In the United Kingdom, the European Communities Act 1972 makes provision for the incorporation of EU law into the domestic system,[55] although there is evidence that UK politicians did not fully appreciate the consequences of EU membership and its potential impact on parliamentary sovereignty at the time.[56] Article 288 of the Treaty on the Functioning of the European Union (TFEU) provides that to exercise the Union's competences, EU institutions may adopt regulations, directives, decisions, recommendations and opinions. A number of EU Directives have brought changes to UK private law. In tort law, Council Directive 85/374/EEC, commonly known as the Product Liability Directive,[57] is perhaps the best known of these examples. The Directive imposes strict liability on manufacturers for defective products and, in so doing, strikes at the very heart of *Donoghue v Stevenson*[58] fault-based liability.[59] EU law has also introduced a new form of tort law: state liability for breach of EU law (the so-called *Francovich* liability).[60] While, as yet, there have been few successful claims under this head, it creates a new area of tort law, albeit one which the tort community has generally struggled to understand and correctly conceptualise.[61]

EU law therefore creates a divide in the common law legal community.[62] Only two Member States (the United Kingdom and Ireland) are common law jurisdictions[63] and these two states find themselves now in the curious position of being minority systems in a Union of states dominated by civil law jurisdictions. Unsurprisingly, EU law is primarily influenced by the civil law legal tradition, although the common law has had some impact over the years. This is most clearly seen in the style of legislation and judgments—judgments which, of course, bind Member States. More recently, there have been a number of ambitious projects which have sought to harmonise some or all aspects of the private law of European Member States. In the last ten years, the European Commission has commissioned a Draft

[53] See also Charter of Fundamental Rights, Art 47: '[e]veryone whose rights and freedoms guaranteed by the law of the union are violated has the right to an effective remedy before a tribunal in compliance with the conditions laid down in this Article'.

[54] U Jaremba, 'At the Crossroads of National and European Union Law: Experiences of National Judges in a Multi-level Legal Order' (2013) 6 *Erasmus Law Review* 190, 196.

[55] As a dualist state, unlike many continental European countries, this was a necessary step. Until incorporating legislation is enacted, the national courts have no power to enforce treaty rights and obligations either on behalf of the government or a private individual.

[56] D Nicol, *EC Membership and the Judicialization of British Politics* (Oxford, OUP, 2001).

[57] Council Directive 85/374/EEC of 25 July 1985 on the approximation of the laws, regulations and administrative provisions of the Member States concerning liability for defective products [1985] OJ L210/29.

[58] *Donoghue v Stevenson* [1932] AC 562.

[59] Further changes to domestic tort law from EU Directives are discussed in P Giliker, *The Europeanisation of English Tort Law* (Oxford, Hart Publishing, 2014) ch 3.

[60] So named after the leading case of C-6/90 *Francovich v Italian Republic* [1991] ECR I-5357.

[61] Labelling it unhelpfully a form of breach of statutory duty. For criticism, see K Stanton, 'New Forms of the Tort of Breach of Statutory Duty' (2004) 120 *LQR* 324; P Giliker, 'English Tort Law and the Challenge of *Francovich* Liability: 20 Years On' (2012) 128 *LQR* 541.

[62] See J Beatson, 'Has the Common Law a Future?' (1997) 56 *CLJ* 291, 292–95, who speculates that England and Wales will become the Québec of Europe!

[63] Cyprus and Malta are mixed jurisdictions.

Common Frame of Reference,[64] providing a model for a European Civil Code,[65] and has engaged in a public consultation on the future of European Contract Law in which one option was again the introduction of a European Civil Code.[66] Its 2011 proposal for a regulation on a Common European Sales Law,[67] which would have introduced into every Member State a common sales law for cross-border contracts for the sale of goods and digital content, has only recently been withdrawn due to lack of support. Further, research groups, such as the European Centre of Tort and Insurance Law in Vienna, continue to engage in studies to identify common principles of tort law across Member States.

Such activities inevitably lead to divergences between the United Kingdom and Ireland and the rest of the common law legal family, both in substantive law, but also in tort policy. For example, in seeking to protect consumers, EU law may introduce strict liability provisions or insist that the Directive is one of maximum harmonisation which sets an absolute standard in the domestic law of the Member State from which no divergence is permitted. This is, in fact, the case with the Product Liability Directive and France, therefore, found itself in violation of EU law in retaining domestic legal provisions which provided *greater* protection for consumers than that stated in the Directive.[68] Loss of tort law dominium, therefore, removes the possibility of the national courts looking further overseas—it is from the CJEU, not the High Court of Australia or Supreme Court of Canada, where guidance must now be sought.

From 2000, however, UK tort law has faced a further challenge to its domestic 'sovereignty' and this comes from the introduction of the Human Rights Act (HRA) 1998. The European Court of Human Rights may be considered as having 'supra-national aspects' in that as a signatory to the European Convention on Human Rights (ECHR), the United Kingdom is bound in international law by decisions in which it is involved.[69] However, it is the introduction of the HRA 1998 which has made a significant difference.[70] Section 2(1) of the Act requires the court, in determining a question which has arisen in connection with a Convention right, to 'take into account' judgments of the European Court of Human Rights. Equally, so far as it is possible to do so, primary legislation and subordinate legislation must be read and given effect in a way which is compatible with the Convention rights.[71] This gives the UK courts a 'constitutional' role in examining the Convention-compatibility of legislation, but also requires the courts to use the case law of the European Court of Human Rights (ECtHR) to inform its interpretation of these rights.

[64] C von Bar and E Clive (eds), *Principles, Definitions and Model Rules of European Private Law: Draft Common Frame of Reference* (Munich, Sellier, 2009 and Oxford, OUP, 2010) vols I–VI.

[65] N Jansen and R Zimmermann, 'A European Civil Code in All but Name' [2010] *CLJ* 98.

[66] *Green Paper from the Commission on Policy Options for Progress towards a European Contract Law for Consumers and Businesses*, COM(2010)348 final.

[67] COM(2011)635 final. Withdrawn in December 2014. The Commission currently supports a modified proposal which will simplify the rules relating to online purchases of goods and digital content by consumers.

[68] Case C-52/00 *Commission v France* [2002] ECR I-3827.

[69] ECHR, Art 46 (binding force and execution of judgments).

[70] Feldman reports that between 2002–08, 37.5 per cent of the House of Lords caseload came from claims under the HRA 1998: 'Human Rights' in L Blom-Cooper QC, B Dickson and G Drewry (eds), *The Judicial House of Lords 1876–2009* (Oxford, OUP, 2009) 546.

[71] HRA 1998, 3(1). HRA 1998, s 4 provides that if the court is satisfied that a legislative provision is incompatible with a Convention right, it may make a declaration of incompatibility.

Three further provisions are of particular importance from a tort law perspective. Section 6(1) provides that '[i]t is unlawful for a public authority to act in a way which is incompatible with a Convention right', to which section 6(3) adds that the term 'public authority' includes the court or tribunal itself. Sections 7 and 8 establish a cause of action for victims against a public authority which has acted (or proposes to act) in a way which is made unlawful by section 6(1). These provisions give claimants a distinct cause of action against public authorities which have violated one or more of the Convention rights contained in Schedule 1 to the Act, but section 6 also, it has been argued, places an obligation on, or at least encourages, the court (as a public authority) to interpret the law more generally in a Convention-compliant manner.[72] From the perspective of this chapter, it is clearly the latter point which is of importance. If the English courts take seriously their obligation to develop the law of tort in this way, then this will lead to a fundamental review of the nature of existing tort law. To what extent, for example, should torts protecting against personal injury or death be revised to reflect the values contained in Articles 2 (right to life) or 3 (prohibition of torture)? How should torts protecting against reputational damage such as defamation and malicious falsehood respond to Article 10 (freedom of expression)? The European Court of Human Rights' ruling in *Osman v United Kingdom*[73] in 2000 indicated that Convention rights (here Article 6: the right to a fair trial) could strike at the heart of concepts as fundamental as the 'duty of care' doctrine in negligence. Although this ruling was subsequently corrected by the ECtHR,[74] it did lead to a number of House of Lords and Court of Appeal decisions in which the court adopted a far more generous approach to the imposition of a duty of care on public authorities than seen previously.[75] Further, the courts have demonstrated a greater willingness to re-examine established immunities against negligence liability, for example, the immunity of a barrister for negligence in court.[76] Additional examples of the influence of Convention rights on tort reasoning may be found in private nuisance[77] and defamation.[78] Moreover, in *D v East Berkshire Community NHS Trust*,[79] the court was even prepared to accept that an established House of Lords decision such as *X v Bedfordshire County Council*[80] could, post-HRA, be subject to review by the Court of Appeal, despite its overt reference to policy in a British, rather than European, context. In her 2001 work *Tort Law and Human Rights*,[81] Wright predicted that the HRA 1998 would present a far greater challenge to the courts than the European Communities Act 1972.

It is European influences therefore—EU law but also European human rights law—which threaten an irreversible split in the common law legal family. As European Directives

[72] Known as strong or weak indirect horizontal effect: see M Hunt, 'The Horizontal Effect of the Human Rights Act' [1998] *PL* 423; G Phillipson, 'The Human Rights Act, "Horizontal Effect" and the Common Law: A Bang or a Whimper?' (1999) 62 *MLR* 824.

[73] *Osman v United Kingdom* (23452/94) (2000) 29 EHRR 245.

[74] *Z v United Kingdom* (29392/95) (2002) 34 EHRR 97.

[75] See, eg, *Barrett v Enfield LBC* [2001] 2 AC 550 (HL) (refusal to strike out negligence actions by children in care); *L (A Child) v Reading BC* [2001] EWCA Civ 346, [2001] 1 WLR 1575 (refusal to strike out negligence claim against police); *W v Essex CC* [2001] 2 AC 592 (HL) (refusal to strike out parents' claim for psychiatric injury).

[76] *Arthur JS Hall & Co v Simons* [2002] 1 AC 615 (HL).

[77] *McKenna v British Aluminium Ltd* [2002] Env LR 30 (QB).

[78] *O'Shea v MGN Ltd* [2001] EMLR 40 (QB).

[79] *D v East Berkshire Community NHS Trust* [2003] EWCA Civ 1151, [2004] QB 558 (also known as *JD*).

[80] *X v Bedfordshire CC* [1995] 2 AC 633 (HL).

[81] J Wright, *Tort Law and Human Rights* (Oxford, Hart Publishing, 2001).

harmonise tort law in all 28 Member States, it will be the CJEU which supervises the application of the law, and EU policy which determines its content. Further, the European Convention on Human Rights has the potential to reshape tort law, tearing out the historical roots of the causes of action and creating a rights-based framework for liability. Are we hearing, therefore, the death knell for a 'common law of tort'? Will the days of Supreme Court justices referring to Commonwealth case law soon be a distant memory?

IV. Is there a European Rift in the Common Law Legal Family?

To misquote Mark Twain: 'Reports of the death of the common law of tort are greatly exaggerated'. It is clear that such a rift has not materialised. The judicial statements at the commencement of this chapter indicate an ongoing belief that comparisons within the common law world remain relevant and useful. Stanton, in a survey of the use of comparative law in tort cases between 1990 and 2013,[82] observes that the UK Supreme Court continues to draw on the work of a small number of other common law jurisdictions, notably Australia, Canada and the United States, but also South Africa, Hong Kong, India and Singapore. He finds that the use of civil law in tort cases such as *White v Jones*[83] and *Fairchild v Glenhaven Funeral Services Ltd*[84]—much celebrated by comparative lawyers such as Markesinis[85]—in reality owe more to the enthusiasm and linguistic ability of judges such as Lords Bingham and Goff than any sea-change in court practice.[86] The key question, therefore, is, bearing in mind the changes outlined above: *why* have EU and ECtHR law made so little difference to English private law?

Three key factors may be identified which have combined to minimise the impact of Europeanisation on English tort law with the result that, despite membership of the European Union for 40 years and almost 15 years of the HRA 1998 being in force, English judges still feel a greater affinity with common law sources. These three factors will be examined below.

Nature of EU Intervention at National Level

A reader would look in vain in any UK tort textbook for a chapter on EU tort law. In reality, the focus of the European Union has been on matters relating to inter-state trade and consumer protection. Given the European Commission's aim of improving the internal market and the economic goals of the EU generally, this is hardly surprising, but it does signify that there has been limited EU intervention into tort law. Yet, even where intervention has

[82] K Stanton, 'Comparative Law in the House of Lords and Supreme Court' (2013) 42 *Common Law World Review* 269.

[83] *White v Jones* [1995] 2 AC 207 (HL).

[84] *Fairchild v Glenhaven Funeral Services Ltd* [2003] 1 AC 32 (HL).

[85] See, eg, BS Markesinis and J Fedtke, *Engaging with Foreign Law* (Oxford, Hart Publishing, 2009).

[86] See Stanton, above n 82, 295–96. See also Mak, above n 17.

occurred, for example, in the 1985 EEC Directive on Product Liability,[87] the very nature of EU law has led to it having limited impact at a domestic level. This is due to a number of reasons. First, the main vehicle for introducing EU law into national tort law has been through Directives. Article 288(3) TFEU provides that: 'A directive shall be binding, as to the result to be achieved, upon each Member State to which it is addressed, *but shall leave to the national authorities the choice of form and methods*' (emphasis added). This means that, in practice, states have considerable discretion how to transpose Directives into national law and the United Kingdom has generally favoured use of secondary legislation, rendering any such changes of low visibility, frequently placed in statutory instruments with no reference to the EU origin of the measure in the title.[88] Even where primary legislation is used (for example, the Product Liability Directive was implemented in Part 1 of the Consumer Protection Act 1987), the measures are introduced as part of a national initiative, in this case, to legislate on a number of different regulatory matters concerning consumers. There is therefore a distinct danger that the new law is treated simply as a domestic statute, merging into national law with limited recognition of its EU origins.[89]

Secondly, the CJEU has shown itself on a number of occasions willing to defer to national courts, permitting divergence at a national level. In *Veedfald*,[90] for example, the European Court of Justice avoided ruling on the question whether flushing a kidney with a defective fluid which rendered it unusable for transplant was personal injury or property damage under the Product Liability Directive. This issue (of considerable importance in applying the Directive) was left for the national court to resolve. Equally, where cases have been brought by the Commission challenging the manner in which the Directive has been transposed into national law, the response of the CJEU has often been generous. Indeed, the United Kingdom benefitted from such generosity in *European Commission v United Kingdom*[91] in relation to its transposition of Article 7(e) of the 1985 Directive.

Finally, the success of the Article 267 TFEU preliminary reference mechanism, which seeks to ensure the consistent application of EU law across Member States, is contingent on the willingness of the national courts to make references to the CJEU asking for interpretative guidance. Evidence to date indicates that many national courts (including the United Kingdom) are reluctant to do so and may in any event rely on the '*acte clair*' doctrine whereby no reference is required when the correct application of EU law is so obvious that there is no scope for any reasonable doubt how the matter in question should be resolved.[92] In *Three Rivers District Council v Bank of England (No 3)*,[93] for example, the House of Lords made no preliminary reference on the basis of the *acte clair* doctrine, despite a strong dissenting judgment by Auld LJ in the Court of Appeal in that case.

[87] See above n 57.

[88] K Syrett, *The Foundations of Public Law*, 2nd edn (Basingstoke, Palgrave, 2014) 255.

[89] Compare, eg, the treatment of the 1987 Act in *A v National Blood Authority* [2001] 3 All ER 289 (QB) and *Tesco Stores Ltd v Pollard* [2006] EWCA Civ 393.

[90] Case C-203/99 *Veedfald v Arhus Amtskommune* [2001] ECR 1-3569. See G Howells in (2002) 10 *European Review of Private Law* 847; P Rott, 'What is the Role of the ECJ in EC Private Law?' (2005) 1 *Hanse Law Review* 6.

[91] *European Commission v United Kingdom* [1997] ECR I-2649.

[92] Case 283/81 *CILFIT and Lanificio di Gavardo SPA v Ministry of Health* [1982] ECR 3415; Craig and de Búrca, above n 50, 479–482.

[93] *Three Rivers District Council v Bank of England (No 3)* [2000] UKHL 33, [2003] AC 1.

Separation of Human Rights Claims from Ordinary Tort Law Actions

While EU law has had limited impact on English tort law, the HRA 1998 has arguably had a more marked effect. This is domestic legislation and, as indicated earlier, has the potential by virtue of the doctrine of indirect horizontal effect to bring changes even in private law. In the privacy case of *Campbell v MGN Ltd*,[94] the House of Lords accepted that, following the Act, the Article 8 right to respect for private and family life would receive greater protection in English law by means of developing the existing action for breach of confidence; Lord Nicholls commenting that the nature of the action would in future be better encapsulated as a tort protecting against misuse of private information.[95] More recently, Dingemans J in *Weller v Associated Newspapers Ltd*[96] traced the history of this new action, noting a move towards full recognition of its status as a distinct tort.[97]

Elsewhere in tort law, however, initial concerns that the HRA 1998 would result in fundamental changes to tort law principle have proven unfounded. A significant step in the 'containment' of the HRA in this field has been the courts' decision that once actions could be brought against public authorities under sections 7 and 8 of the Act, 'it is quite simply unnecessary now to develop the common law to provide a parallel cause of action'.[98] In other words, the actions under the HRA 1998 and tort law would exist side-by-side, but would remain distinct from each other. The decision of the House of Lords in the conjoined cases of *Van Colle v Chief Constable of Hertfordshire; Smith v Chief Constable of Sussex Police*[99] provides a good illustration of how this operates in practice. In the first case (Van Colle), a claim had been made under the HRA 1998, alleging that police negligence had led to the murder of a prosecution witness by the person against whom he was due to give evidence. Applying ECtHR case law on Article 2 ECHR (the right to life), the House of Lords unanimously rejected the claim. In *Osman v United Kingdom*,[100] the ECtHR had found that Article 2 would only be violated if 'the authorities knew or ought to have known at the time of the existence of a real and imminent risk to the life of an identified individual or individuals from the criminal acts of a third party and that they failed to take measures within the scope of their powers which, judged reasonably, might have been expected to avoid that risk'.[101] On the facts, Van Colle had been giving evidence in relation to a minor offence, where the defendant had no record of violence and no explicit death threats had been reported to the police. Their Lordships found that, in the circumstances, the police could not have reasonably anticipated that there was a real and immediate risk to Van Colle's life.

[94] *Campbell v MGN Ltd* [2004] UKHL 22, [2004] 2 AC 457.
[95] ibid [14].
[96] *Weller v Associated Newspapers Ltd* [2014] EWHC 1163 (QB) [20]–[25].
[97] The Court of Appeal in *Vidal-Hall v Google Inc* [2015] EWCA Civ 311, [2015] 3 WLR 409 recently accepted that, for the purposes of service out of jurisdiction, this action should be classified as a tort.
[98] *Van Colle v Chief Constable of the Hertfordshire Police* [2008] UKHL 50, [2009] 1 AC 225 [136] (Lord Brown). See also *Jain v Trent Strategic Health Authority* [2009] UKHL 4, [2009] 1 AC 853 [39] (Lord Scott).
[99] *Van Colle v Chief Constable of Hertfordshire; Smith v Chief Constable of Sussex Police* [2008] UKHL 50, [2009] 1 AC 225.
[100] *Osman v United Kingdom* (App no 23452/94) (1998) 29 EHRR 245.
[101] ibid [116]. Contrast *DSD v Commissioner of Police for the Metropolis* [2015] EWCA Civ 646 (HRA 1998 claim successful against the police for breach of ECHR, Art 3 due to systematic failings in investigating a series of rapes and sexual assaults) and *Michael v Chief Constable of South Wales Police* [2015] UKSC 2, [2015] 2 WLR 343 (claim based on ECHR, Art 2 allowed to proceed to trial).

The second case of Smith, however, was brought in negligence, the claimant having missed the one-year deadline for claims under the HRA 1998. He too had been subject to an attack which he argued could have been prevented by the police and submitted that, in the light of the HRA, the House of Lords decision in *Hill v Chief Constable of West Yorkshire*[102] (that the police did not owe a duty of care to individual members of the public for the conduct of criminal investigations) should be revisited. The majority of the Lords (Lord Bingham dissenting) rejected this argument and found that the policy rationales set out in *Hill* were still valid. This meant that 'the interests of the wider community must prevail over those of the individual'.[103] Significantly, Lord Hope explained that claims under the common law and the HRA 1998 should, in future, develop independently:

> the common law, with its own system of limitation periods and remedies, should be allowed to stand on its own feet side by side with the alternative remedy. Indeed the case for preserving it may be thought to be supported by the fact that any perceived shortfall in the way that it deals with cases that fall within the threshold for the application of the *Osman* principle can now be dealt with in domestic law under the 1998 Act.[104]

Such a view is supported by Nolan, who argues that convergence of the tort of negligence and human rights liability would undermine the former's coherence, weakening its structural underpinnings and cutting across its core principles.[105] While recent cases such as *Rabone v Pennine Care NHS Foundation Trust*[106] and *Smith v Ministry of Defence*[107] suggest that this division may not be watertight and that, in particular, Article 2 remains an area where tort and human rights law are likely to overlap,[108] these cases indicate a strong desire by the UK courts to retain control over tort policy. Indeed, there has been a recent flurry of judicial lectures in which distinguished judges have questioned the relationship between the ECtHR and the UK courts and asserted the ability of the English courts to interpret the content of Convention rights.[109] It seems clear that the UK courts are far from willing to pass control of tort law development to an external court.

UK Judges as 'Global' Rather than 'European' Judges

The final limiting factor is one of identity, namely, the degree to which judges in England and Wales see themselves as 'European' rather than 'common law' judges. In a sense this

[102] *Hill v Chief Constable of West Yorkshire* [1988] QB 60.

[103] See *Van Colle*, above n 98, [75] (Lord Hope).

[104] ibid [82]. See also *Michael v Chief Constable of South Wales Police* [2015] UKSC 2, [2015] 2 WLR 343 [125]–[27] (Lord Toulson).

[105] D Nolan, 'Negligence and Human Rights Law: The Case for Separate Development' (2013) 76 *MLR* 286, distinguishing between public law/human rights norms and those of private law. See also J Wright, 'A Damp Squib? The Impact of Section 6 HRA on the Common Law: Horizontal Effect and Beyond' [2014] *PL* 289.

[106] *Rabone v Pennine Care NHS Foundation Trust* [2012] UKSC 2, [2012] 2 AC 72.

[107] *Smith v Ministry of Defence* [2013] UKSC 41, [2014] 1 AC 52 (although, in this case, the negligence case was allowed to proceed to trial).

[108] See, eg, Lord Mance in ibid [142]. Note also his comments in *Rabone*: *Rabone v Pennine Care NHS Foundation Trust* [2012] UKSC 2, [2012] 2 AC 72 [121].

[109] See, eg, Lord Sumption, 'The Limits of Law', 27th Sultan Azlan Shah Lecture, Kuala Lumpur, 20 November 2013; and Lord Judge, 'Constitutional Change: Unfinished Business', Speech given at University College London, 4 December 2013. For a riposte from an ECtHR judge, see P Mahoney, 'The Relationship Between the Strasbourg Court and the National Courts' (2014) 130 *LQR* 568.

chapter has gone a full circle. It started by examining the nature of the common law legal family and its impact on its members. It noted the part this played in shaping the identity of lawyers, the culture within which its members are trained and the ties which give rise to common terminology, similar institutions and easily recognisable substantive and procedural rules.[110] These characteristics, of course, serve to distinguish England and Wales (and Ireland) from the rest of continental Europe.[111] It is something which is not necessarily articulated but nevertheless implicitly accepted by all participating in the legal process. Therefore, while judges in England and Wales are familiar with EU law and have indeed received training prior to the implementation of the HRA 1998 on human rights law, their background is in the vast majority of cases that of a common law practitioner, trained in a similar manner to that found in common law jurisdictions across the world. In this light, it would be surprising *if* these judges did not feel more comfortable and secure in an English-speaking common law environment.[112]

For Bobek, the relationship between UK and EU/ECtHR judges may be described as a 'marriage of convenience', entered out of necessity as a result of the decisions of politicians rather than based on love or affection.[113] In this light, it is to be expected that while attachment to overseas dominions and former colonies will be diminished, a residual level of affection and trust will survive. Bell argues that in choosing comparisons to add 'luster' to their judgments, common law judges will be drawn to courts which are considered by the legal community to be the most prestigious and 'proximate', that is similar in nature.[114] This signifies that a court will be more likely to refer to a system seen as sufficiently cognate than to a less familiar system, even if it has a strong reputation in other ways, for example, the German Constitutional Court. 'Some legal systems', Bell comments, 'are naturally more proximate than others. Usually this is because they belong to the same so-called legal family'.[115]

Recent decisions of the UK Supreme Court in the tort field ably illustrate this continued attachment to authority from other common law jurisdictions. In the 2014 private nuisance case of *Coventry v Lawrence*,[116] Lord Carnwath made reference both to academic authority[117] and comparative case law, using sources from Australia, New Zealand, Ireland, Canada and the United States.[118] These are systems with which his Lordship was clearly comfortable

[110] Commentators have also noted the extent to which the education and experiences of individual judges influence how they use 'foreign' law: BS Markesinis, 'Judicial Mentality: Mental Disposition or Outlook as a Factor Impeding Recourse to Foreign Law' (2006) 80 *Tulane Law Review* 1325; M Kirby, 'The Common Law and International Law: A Dynamic Contemporary Dialogue' (2010) 30 *Legal Studies* 30, 59.

[111] See S Glanert, 'Speaking Language to Law: The Case of Europe' (2008) 28 *Legal Studies* 161, who notes the obstacles that such factors place in the way of projects to harmonise European private law.

[112] A recent survey has also indicated the extent to which lower court judges in continental Europe prefer their own legal culture to that of what they perceive to be the abstract and remote rules of EU law: see T Nowak *et al*, *National Judges as European Union Judges: Knowledge, Experience and Attitudes of Lower Court Judges in Germany and the Netherlands* (2011), discussed in Jaremba, above n 54.

[113] Bobek, above n 18, 41.

[114] J Bell, 'The Relevance of Foreign Examples to Legal Development' (2011) 21 *Duke Journal of Comparative and International Law* 433. See also Watson who argues that inertia, a bias for the familiar and accessible, and the dominance of case law over legislation has led law-makers to opt for common law rules regardless of whether the rule in question is the 'best' rule for the society in question: A Watson, 'Comparative Law and Legal Change' [1978] *CLJ* 313.

[115] Bell, above n 114, 453.

[116] *Coventry v Lawrence* [2014] UKSC 13, [2014] 1 AC 822.

[117] See, eg, Ben Pontin's 'valuable recent book', *Nuisance Law and Environmental Protection* (Lawtext Publishing, 2013) and A Beever, *The Law of Nuisance* (Oxford, Hart Publishing, 2013), cited at [176] and [179], respectively.

[118] *Coventry v Lawrence* [2014] UKSC 13, [2014] 1 AC 822 [241] ff.

and was able to seek guidance in a case which sought to determine, inter alia, when a court should exercise its discretion to award damages in lieu of an injunction. Equally, in the 2012 vicarious liability case of *Various Claimants v Catholic Child Welfare Society*,[119] the Supreme Court found considerable assistance in the Supreme Court of Canada's decision in *Bazley v Curry*[120] and, indeed, traced its influence on the development of vicarious liability in English law:[121]

> Starting with the Canadian authorities a common theme can be traced through most of the cases to which I have referred. Vicarious liability is imposed where a defendant, whose relationship with the abuser put it in a position to use the abuser to carry on its business or to further its own interests, has done so in a manner which has created or significantly enhanced the risk that the victim or victims would suffer the relevant abuse. The essential closeness of connection between the relationship between the defendant and the tortfeasor and the acts of abuse thus involves a strong causative link.[122]

Such cases demonstrate that far from moving away from common law comparisons, the UK Supreme Court is prepared to be guided by them and that the old hierarchical view of the parent influencing the legal development of its offspring has long been rejected. Lord Neuberger, in a recent lecture on the relationship between Britain and Europe, reiterated this point. His Lordship argued that, despite the European influences discussed in this chapter, Britain has been unable unequivocally to identify itself with the rest of Europe. He attributed the ongoing connection between the United Kingdom, United States and the Commonwealth to a combination of geography, history, politics, culture and language:

> The Commonwealth … provides us with an alternative international organisation or club to the EU. To many people countries such as Australia, Canada, New Zealand, India and South Africa, as well as smaller places such as Hong Kong and Singapore, represent political and cultural traditions which are much closer to ours than mainland European countries … As a UK judge, I can and do sit, and feel at home, in the Hong Kong Court of Final Appeal, that could not be said about any European court, other than Ireland.[123]

V. Conclusion

A number of conclusions may be drawn from this study. First, we live in a changing world and the common law legal family should not be seen as static, but evolving over time. This is not a bad thing—it is progress. Secondly, common law jurisdictions will continue to make their own political decisions about the development of tort law, whether it is to replace fault with 'no fault' liability or reduce civil liability to a statutory framework. Thirdly, while new influences arise (globalisation, Directives harmonising sections of European private law, increased political attention relating to the protection of human rights on a local, European

[119] *Various Claimants v Catholic Child Welfare Society* [2012] UKSC 56, [2013] 2 AC 1.

[120] *Bazley v Curry* (1999) 174 DLR (4th) 45 (SCC).

[121] In *Lister v Hesley Hall Ltd* [2001] UKHL 22, [2002] 1 AC 215, the House of Lords had also found *Bazley* and *Jacobi v Griffiths* (1999) 174 DLR (4th) 71 (SCC) to be 'luminous and illuminating' judgments which would henceforth be the starting point for consideration of similar cases: [27] (Lord Steyn).

[122] *Various Claimants v Catholic Child Welfare Society* [2012] UKSC 56, [2013] 2 AC 1 [86] (Lord Phillips (on behalf of the Court)).

[123] Lord Neuberger, 'Cambridge Freshfields Annual Law Lecture 2014: The British and Europe', 12 February 2014, [37]–[38].

or international scale), similar questions of tort law arise across the developed world. In such a legal environment, it would be most unwise to ignore the wisdom of others. As Lord Bingham stated, 'there is a world elsewhere'.[124] Despite EU membership, the introduction of the HRA 1998, the wealth of literature on European private law (much of it in English) and even the development of European tort law principles (for example, under Article 340(2) TFEU),[125] English tort law remains close practically, but also conceptually, to its common law family, despite the loosening of ties indicated in this chapter. There remains, in the words of Australian judge, Kirby, a relationship which has evolved 'from one of dutiful obligation to one of friendship, shared interests, and mutual regard'.[126]

It is important, however, to ensure that familiarity does not affect the quality of future legal development. Concerns, for example, have been raised by the tendency to restrict comparisons to a limited club of the 'old' Commonwealth jurisdictions rather than monitoring global legal developments.[127] Watson, for example, has identified a tendency to choose comparators from convenience rather than seeking the 'best solution'.[128] In a world where electronic resources give us access to materials from across the world, it is vital, therefore, not to think simply in terms of family loyalty but consider which systems can provide the analytical keys we seek in terms of legal development. Ease of access is not necessarily a synonym for quality. That said, the common law legal family has much to offer, as shown in this chapter. Nevertheless, it would be wrong to assume that every issue will be treated in the same way regardless of socio-economic or political divergences at a local level. Ultimately, therefore, this chapter argues for discernment. The merits of the common law family must be balanced against the issue at hand. If, for example, the question relates to the scope of Article 10 ECHR, then clearly Convention jurisprudence is more relevant than that under the Canadian Charter of Rights and Freedoms. Equally, in interpreting Part 1 of the Consumer Protection Act 1987, the court is likely to find case law on the Product Liability Directive more helpful than that on the US *Restatement (3d) of Torts: Products Liability*. If, as in *Coventry v Lawrence*, the court is seeking to understand the relationship between law and equity, then common law authority is likely to prove more useful. In today's world, we exist in different circles (family, work, social, virtual) and the same applies to legal systems. To limit ourselves to one circle would be to diminish our well-being and social development. Equally, for common law systems to confine themselves to the common law family would be unduly restrictive. This does not mean, however, that engagement with new friends should lead to the neglect of familial bonds. The common law legal family remains a relevant source of law which will continue to assist both legislators and judges, but it will only be by well-chosen comparisons, which give the courts relevant material providing an insight into the legal issue in question, that we will enrich our understanding and critical appreciation of the law.

[124] TH Bingham, 'There is a World Elsewhere: The Changing Perspectives of English Law' (1992) 41 *ICLQ* 513.

[125] 'In the case of non-contractual liability, the Union shall, in accordance with the general principles common to the laws of the Member States, make good any damage caused by its institutions or by its servants in the performance of their duties.' See H Koziol and R Schulze (eds), *Tort Law of the European Community* (Vienna/New York, Springer, 2008).

[126] 'The Old Commonwealth' in Blom-Cooper, Dickson, and Drewry, above n 25, 347.

[127] Douglas, however, argues that one reason for the Australian courts to monitor English developments is to ensure it keeps in touch with the world generally: J Douglas, 'England as a Source of Australian Law: For How Long?' (2012) 86 *Australian Law Journal* 333, 349.

[128] Watson, above n 114.

6

A Judicial Perspective on the Development of Common Law Doctrine in the Light of Statute Law

ANTHONY MASON

I. Introduction

The purpose of this chapter is to examine the judicial development of the common law, mainly in Australia, by reference to statute law and to explain why this development of the common law has not been as extensive as one might have expected. In approaching this question I proceed on the footing that judicial elaboration of the common law by reference to statute consists mainly in development by reference to statutory policy and reasoning by analogy from statute.

Much has been written on the subject of the use that can or should be made of statutes in the development of the common law (in which I include equity). For my purposes, it is necessary only to refer to the four well-known ways in which, according to Roscoe Pound, the courts might make use of statutory provisions in elaborating the common law.[1] They were: (1) the statutory development might be received fully into the law as both a rule and a principle to be treated as superior to judge-made rules and as a basis for reasoning by analogy or preference to judge-made rules; (2) the development might be received fully into the law as a basis for reasoning by analogy and as being of equal and co-ordinate authority in this respect as judge-made rules upon some general subject; (3) the development might not be received into the body of the law and might be given effect directly only by means of a liberal interpretation so as to cover the whole field the statute was intended to cover, but not to be treated as a basis for reasoning by analogy; and (4) the development might be treated as being unsuited to reasoning by analogy and applied directly only but with a narrow application so that the statute is confined to situations which it covers expressly.

The formulation of the four categories indicates that Pound's conception of reasoning by analogy from statute, included reasoning by reference to policy considerations.

Pound himself favoured categories (1) and (2) above but considered that (4) above represented the then conventional common law attitude. He considered, however, that the evolutionary trend would lead to the approach in category (2) and, eventually, the approach in category (1).

[1] R Pound, 'Common Law and Legislation' (1908) 21 *Harvard Law Review* 383, 385.

It is now evident that Pound's expectations have not been fully realised. The Australian, New Zealand and English experience provides some support for the approach in category (1). While the earlier authorities fell into categories (3) and (4), the more recent cases provide stronger support for category (2).

What do We Mean by Policy in this Context?

As Neil McCormick once said 'Policy has become a hideously inexact word in legal discourse'.[2] In its strictest and narrowest sense 'policy' in the context of law generally designates factors or considerations of a non-ethical kind as in the expression 'policy considerations'. In this narrowest sense, policy excludes 'values' which is often used to denote ethical values, though its use is by no means always so confined. But from time to time each term is used in an all-embracing sense so as to include the other. In the title of this chapter and in the chapter generally, I employ the term 'policy' to denote both non-ethical and ethical values, notwithstanding the difference between them.

The courts are concerned to make value judgments and to consider policy questions in a variety of situations. They include formulation of legal principles and rules, the exercise of discretions, the application of standards such as reasonableness, notably in tort cases involving the existence of a duty of care and breach of duty.

Reasoning by Analogy

Reasoning by analogy is an important aspect of judicial decision-making. Reasoning by analogy involves a comparison of two things or, more relevantly, an established rule and a proposed rule and then inferring, based on similarities in the situations to which they are addressed, that the proposed rule should mirror the established rule in the situation to which it is addressed. Considerable caution is required in analogical reasoning because 'analysis by analogy is problematic and the issues are never exactly the same'.[3] Moreover, an analogy may be 'strained' (because the apparent similarities lack relevance or are too distant) or 'false' (because the dissimilarities outweigh the similarities), or 'weak' or 'overbroad' (when the similarities are inadequate to support the logical inference proposed).[4]

Reasoning by analogy 'should be conducive to coherence in the development of the law'.[5] In *Sullivan v Moody*,[6] the High Court of Australia said that the problems in determining the duty of care 'may [sometimes] concern the need to preserve the coherence of other legal principles or of a statutory scheme which governs certain conduct or relationships'.[7]

There is no reason in principle why analogical reasoning from statute is less appropriate than analogical reasoning from established common law rules. As Cooke J said in

[2] N McCormick, *Legal Reasoning and Legal Theory* (Oxford, Clarendon Press, 1978) 263.
[3] *Cantwell v Sinclair* [2011] NSWSC 1244 [115].
[4] See D Lind, 'Basic Categories of Argumentation in Legal Reasoning' (2014) 11 *Judicial Review* 429, 438.
[5] *Brookfield Multiplex Ltd v Owners Corporation Strata Plan 61288* [2014] HCA 36, (2014) 313 ALR 408 [25].
[6] *Sullivan v Moody* (2001) 207 CLR 562 (HCA).
[7] ibid [50].

South Pacific Manufacturing Co Ltd v NZ Security Consultants and Investigations Ltd,[8] 'the analogy of a statute may properly influence the development of the common law'. This statement has been accepted as correct;[9] though, in Australia, Callinan J left the question open.[10]

Overall, there have been fewer instances of the courts drawing upon statutory policy in order to develop the common law than might have been expected. Sometimes, courts have found that there is no true analogy with a statutory rule because a different or divergent policy appropriately applies to the situation. One striking example is *Ralston v Capper*,[11] where the US Federal District Court refused to draw an analogy between Federal antitrust law and the Racketeer Influenced and Corrupt Organisations Act 1970 (RICO). The Court regarded the analogy as 'strained' because the two statutory schemes were more dissimilar than similar, the purpose of the antitrust statute being to promote competition in the marketplace, whereas RICO had the opposite purpose.[12]

Statutory Interpretation

The rules of statutory interpretation reveal how we view the relationship between common law and statute. Our approach to statutory interpretation shows that we regard common law and statute as two different bodies of law, even if Gleeson CJ was able to say that they:

> are not separate and independent sources of law; the one the concern of parliaments, and the other the concern of the courts. They exist in a symbiotic relationship.[13]

The symbiotic relationship to which Gleeson CJ referred certainly means that, on the one hand, statutes can alter, displace or influence the development of the common law. On the other hand, the relationship also acknowledges that statutes, like the Australian Constitution, operate in a common law world[14] and that the common law rules of interpretation, supplemented by statutory rules of interpretation, govern the meaning of statutes. In this search for meaning, the High Court of Australia has said, rather controversially, that legislative intention is a fiction which serves no useful purpose.[15] Ascertainment of legislative intention, it is said, is no more than the outcome of the application of the rules of interpretation, which have been applied to reach the preferred result and which are known to parliamentary counsel and the courts.[16] The meaning which the legislature is taken to have intended is called the 'legal meaning' of the statutory provision under consideration.[17]

[8] *South Pacific Manufacturing Co Ltd v NZ Security Consultants & Investigations Ltd* [1992] 2 NZLR 282 (CA), 298.

[9] See A Burrows, 'The Relationship between Common Law and Statute in the Law of Obligations' (2012) 128 *LQR* 232, 254.

[10] *Esso Australia Resources Ltd v Federal Commissioner of Taxation* [1999] HCA 67, (1999) 201 CLR 49 [144].

[11] *Ralston v Capper* 569 F Supp 1575 (ED Mich, 1983).

[12] ibid 1580.

[13] *Brodie v Singleton Shire Council* (2001) 206 CLR 512 (HCA) [31].

[14] See *Lange v Australian Broadcasting Corporation* [1997] 189 CLR 520 (HCA), 563–64.

[15] See *Zheng v Cai* [2009] HCA 52, (2009) 239 CLR 446 [28]; *Dickson v The Queen* [2010] HCA 30, (2010) 241 CLR 493 [32]; *Lacey v Attorney-General (Queensland)* [2011] HCA 10, (2011) 242 CLR 573 [43]–[44]; but see also J Goldsworthy, 'Legislative Intention Vindicated' (2013) 33 *OJLS* 82; R Elkins and J Goldsworthy, 'The Reality and Indispensability of Legislative Intentions' (2014) 36 *Sydney Law Review* 39.

[16] *Lacey v Attorney-General (Queensland)* [2011] HCA 10, (2011) 242 CLR 573 [43]–[44].

[17] *Project Blue Sky Inc v Australian Broadcasting Authority* [1998] HCA 28, (1998) 194 CLR 355 [78].

The rules of statutory interpretation, for the most part created by the courts but supplemented by statutory provisions, are designed to reflect and to implement the division of functions between the legislative and judicial branches of government. Respect for that division is reflected in the principle that the process of interpretation of a statute by the courts must not cross the boundary between interpretation, on the one hand, and legislation or amendment, on the other.

The boundary between interpretation and legislation or amendment, though often invoked, is by no means clearly visible, as the cases dealing with the interpretive provisions of statutory human rights regimes in the United Kingdom, New Zealand and Australia strikingly demonstrate.[18] The location of the boundary largely depends on the scope and content of judicial power. Australia takes a narrow view of judicial power compared with the United Kingdom, where relatively little attention has been devoted to the topic. Although the courts are not authorised to develop statute law by trespassing beyond the interpretation of statutory provisions, it is recognised that courts can develop the common law not only by reference to analogical reasoning from statutes but also by reference to policy and values expressed in statutes.

There have been a plenitude of cases which generate the question whether a statute should be interpreted strictly so as to preserve the pre-existing common law or whether it should be interpreted broadly so as to override or displace the pre-existing common law regime. The interpretation adopted in the many cases has not been uniform. Sometimes the courts have read the statute in the light of the pre-existing law and construed the statute narrowly, though more recently the courts have favoured a liberal interpretation which results in the statute covering the field it was intended to cover.[19]

According to the common law principle of legality, a statute will not be construed so as to interfere with fundamental (or established) common law rights, freedoms, immunities or principles in the absence of an unmistakable and unambiguous expression of intention so to do; in this respect general words will rarely be enough.[20] The Supreme Court of New Zealand has affirmed[21] Bennion's statement that 'the courts should be slow to impute to Parliament an intention to override established rights and principles where that is not clearly spelt out'.[22]

It seems that this principle does not extend to general common law principles which cannot be characterised as 'fundamental' or 'established'. In relation to the general common law there is no requirement for unmistakable clarity of expression to interfere with general common law principles.[23] In such cases, it is said that there is nevertheless a weak presumption

[18] See, eg, *Ghaidan v Godin-Mendoza* [2004] UKHL 30, [2004] 2 AC 557; *Sheldrake v DPP* [2004] UKHL 43, [2005] 1 AC 264; *R (Wilkinson) v IRC* [2005] UKHL 30, [2005] 1 WLR 1718 [17]; *Ahmed v HM Treasury* [2010] UKSC 5, [2010] 2 AC 534 [112]–[117]; *R v Hansen* [2007] 3 NZLR 1; *Momcilovic v The Queen* [2011] HCA 34, [2011] 245 CLR 1.

[19] See *Concrete Constructions (NSW) Pty Ltd v Nelson* (1990) 169 CLR 594 (HCA).

[20] See *Coco v The Queen* (1994) 179 CLR 427 (HCA), 437; *Saaed v Minister for Immigration and Citizenship* [2010] HCA 23, (2010) 241 CLR 252 [58]; *Electrolux Products Howe Products Pty Ltd v Australian Workers' Union* [2004] HCA 40, (2004) 221 CLR 309 [21]. The principle has given rise to questions which remain to be resolved; see Brendan Lim, 'The Normativity of the Principle of Legality' (2013) 37 *Melbourne University Law Review* 372.

[21] *Gopp v Judicial Committee* [2008] 3 NZLR 774 (SC) [26].

[22] FAR Bennion, *Bennion on Statutory Interpretation: A Code*, 5th edn (London, LexisNexis, 2008) 823.

[23] *Malika Holdings Pty Ltd v Stratton* (2001) 204 CLR 290 [27]–[31] (HCA); *Gifford v Strang Patrick Stevedoring Pty Ltd* [2003] HCA 33, (2003) 214 CLR 269 [36]–[37].

that the statute does not intend to alter the common law.[24] In England, the presumption has been applied to changes in statutory law, while in Australia, Finn J applied the principle of legality to abrogation of a statutory right.[25] The well-established presumption that statutes do not contradict one another would operate to produce the same outcome.[26]

Unless applied to statutory rights and principles, the common law principle of legality and the presumption just discussed would appear to privilege common law over statutory law. In principle, however, this privilege cannot be supported and almost certainly will give way to equal treatment of common law and statutory rights and principles.

The existence of a weak presumption that a statute does not intend to alter the common law may assist a court in reaching a conclusion that, notwithstanding that intention, the statute should nevertheless be read as not prohibiting development of the common law, so long as the development is consistent with the statute and with its purpose. As we shall see, the Australian cases do not always recognise this distinction.

II. Development of the Common Law by Analogy from Statute: England

Recognition that statutes may be used in order to develop the law analogically is by no means a recent advance in England. As Professor Andrew Burrows has demonstrated in his illuminating article 'The Relationship of Common Law and Statute in the Law of Obligations',[27] the development of the common law in England by the analogical use of statutes can be traced back beyond 1940. The judgments in the cases cited by Professor Burrows proceed on the basis that the common law (including equity) should be developed to take account of the statutory advance. There are, of course, cases in which it is not altogether clear whether or not the decision turns on statutory interpretation or statutory analogy. The Australian decision in *Miller v Miller*,[28] to be discussed later, is a striking example of a case which turned on an ascertainment by construction of the statutory purpose and an analogy with the doctrine of illegality as applied in trust and contract situations.

One case identified by Professor Burrows in which reasoning by analogy from statute was applied in developing common law concepts and principles was *Samuels v Davis*.[29] If the contract between dentist and patient for the provision of a denture amounted to a sale of goods, there was implied under the Sale of Goods Act 1893 (UK) a term that the goods should be reasonably fit for their purpose. The Court of Appeal held that it was unnecessary to decide whether the contract was one for the sale of goods or for work and materials because, even if it were a contract for work and materials, the common law would apply a term similar to the one implied by the statute.

[24] *Gifford v Strang Patrick Stevedoring Pty Ltd* [2003] HCA 33, (2003) 214 CLR 269.
[25] *Buck v Comcare* (1996) 66 FCR 39.
[26] *Saraswati v The Queen* (1991) 172 CLR 1 (HCA), 17.
[27] Burrows, above n 9, 231.
[28] *Miller v Miller* [2011] HCA 9, (2011) 242 CLR 446 [99]–[102].
[29] *Samuels v Davis* [1943] KB 526 (CA).

Another example was *Universe Tankships Inc of Moravia v International Transport Workers Federation (The Universe Sentinel)*,[30] where the House of Lords by majority decided that a statutory trade dispute defence under the Trade Union and Labour Relations Act 1974 (UK) could protect the defendants in an action for restitution of an unjust enrichment based on duress, notwithstanding that the statute provided for the defence to apply to torts. Their Lordships extended by analogy the defence to the claim in question. And in *Interfoto Ltd v Stiletto*,[31] Bingham LJ held that English contract law protects parties to a contract from 'unfairness' in contract terms. In doing so, he drew on examples in the general law and statute.

Another English instance of resort to analogy from statute in common law development is *Malik v Bank of Credit and Commerce International SA*.[32] There are also cases on the development of common law causes of action, such as the cause of action for breach of privacy to protect privacy in the light of the provisions of the Human Rights Act 1998.[33] I put these cases to one side because they comprise a special category of cases arising from the impact of the European Convention on Human Rights and Fundamental Freedoms ('the Convention'), through the medium of the statutory provisions, on common law development.

III. Development of the Common Law by Analogy from Statute: Australia

In Australia, the legitimacy of analogical reasoning from statute to develop the common law is not quite as firmly established as it is in England. In *Lamb v Cotogno*,[34] there was a challenge to the award of exemplary damages against the defendant who had so driven a car that the plaintiff, who was on the bonnet of the car, was thrown to the ground and seriously injured. The driver held compulsory cover in respect of the vehicle pursuant to the Motor Vehicles (Third Party) Insurance Act 1942 (NSW) which indemnified him against liability for damage arising out of the use of the vehicle. The High Court rejected the challenge unanimously, holding that it was appropriate to award exemplary damages in the circumstances of the case and that the effect of the statute was not to abrogate the availability of such damages. In the course of its judgment the Court said:

> Even if it were possible for a court to go beyond what a statute actually enacts and to draw from it some principle to be applied by way of analogy in fashioning the common law, it would not assist the defendant's argument in this case.[35]

[30] *Moravia v International Transport Workers Federation (The Universe Sentinel)* [1983] 1 AC 366 (HL), 385, 391, 401.

[31] *Interfoto Ltd v Stiletto* [1989] QB 433 (CA), 439.

[32] *Malik v Bank of Credit and Commerce International SA* [1998] AC 20 (HL).

[33] See, eg, *Campbell v Mirror Group Newspapers Ltd* [2004] 2 AC 457 (HL); *Douglas v Hello Ltd (No 2)* [2006] QB 125 (CA).

[34] *Lamb v Cotogno* (1987) 164 CLR 1 (HCA).

[35] ibid 11.

The Court went on to say:

> there is no principle or trend to be discerned in the ... Act or any other legislation concerning the measure of damages to be applied in cases of compulsory insurance. Clearly the Act is drafted against a background of the common law and if any inference is to be drawn from it ... it is that there was no intention to disturb the existing situation.[36]

It should be said that the last sentence does not fully answer the critical question, that is, whether the statute prohibited the courts from developing the existing common law.

The same comment must be made about the statement made in the unanimous judgment of the High Court in *Toll (FGCT) Pty Ltd v Alphafarm Pty Ltd*:[37]

> In most common law jurisdictions, and throughout Australia, legislation has been enacted in recent years to confer on courts a capacity to ameliorate in individual cases hardship caused by the strict application of legal principle to contractual relations. As a result, there is no reason to depart from principle, and every reason to adhere to it, in cases where such legislation does not apply, or is not invoked.[38]

Lamb v Cotogno notwithstanding, there are cases in which Australian judges have advanced the common law by means of analogical reasoning from statutes. In an article entitled 'Unconscionability as a Restriction on the Exercise of Contractual Rights', published as long ago as 1986,[39] Justice Priestley referred to two cases decided by the New South Wales Court of Appeal, one dealing with the enforceability of cohabitation agreements and the other dealing with the choice between the implication of joint tenancy as against tenancy in common.

In the first case, *Seidler v Schallhefer*,[40] the question was whether the old public policy according to which agreements tending to encourage sexual immorality were void should be reconsidered. The Court concluded that it should be modified at least to the extent of recognising the validity of an agreement to continue an existing illicit relationship for a specified period in order to bring it to an end by marriage or separation. In reaching this conclusion, after noting that there had been a change in community views about extramarital cohabitations, the Court relied on Commonwealth and State legislation recognising de facto relationships. As Hutley JA said:

> it was from that legislation that the principles of public policy have to be distilled. It tends to treat those living in stable relationships, though not married, in the same way as the married.[41]

In the second case, *Carmody v Delehunt*,[42] the question was whether a house property purchased by two people with equal contributions but registered in the name of one, though it was agreed that they should own it in equal shares and to transfer it into both names, was to be held as equitable joint tenants or tenants in common. The old presumption was that, where two parties pay the purchase price in equal proportions, they intend to held as joint

[36] ibid 12.

[37] *Toll (FGCT) Pty Ltd v Alphafarm Pty Ltd* [2004] HCA 52, (2004) 219 CLR 165.

[38] ibid [48].

[39] See JW Carter (ed), *Rights and Remedies for Breach of Contract* (Sydney, Committee for Postgraduate Studies in the Department of Law, Sydney University, 1986) 57, 74.

[40] *Seidler v Schallhefer* [1982] 2 NSWLR 80 (CA).

[41] ibid 101.

[42] *Carmody v Delehunt* [1984] 1 NSWLR 667, 670 (CA).

tenants. Section 26 of the Conveyancing Act 1919 (NSW) provided that in the construction of written instruments a disposition of the beneficial interest in property for two or more persons together beneficially should be deemed to be tenants in common. But the section applied only to instruments and did not cover the instant case. Nevertheless, the Court held that the policy manifested in the statutory provision was inconsistent with the policy underlying the old presumption, with the consequence that the old presumption should be discarded.

In his article, Priestley regarded these cases as standing for the proposition:

> that courts are, if not required then at the very least entitled to revise their conception of a particular public policy when a course of legislation (in this case both State and Commonwealth) clearly indicates a different approach deliberately adopted for remedial purposes from that taken by the unregulated common law.[43]

I emphasise the opening words of the passage quoted because I shall suggest later that the courts may be under an obligation, though not an absolute obligation, to modify the unregulated common law in the circumstances mentioned. I also note that the proposition quoted is just one element in the judge's discussion of factors which influenced the attitude of the NSW Court of Appeal in developing the common law.

There are a number of instances of remedial statutes in Australia whose purpose is to provide relief in the case of contracts which have historically exposed the weaker party to oppression or unfairness. Specific statutes have addressed money lending contracts, hire-purchase agreements and credit sale agreements and have provided for relief not available at common law, by means of remedies based on broader grounds than those recognised by the common law. These statutes might have been used to reformulate equitable doctrines based on 'unconscionability' to embrace cases of inequality of bargaining power resulting in unfairness, but that has not been the case. The courts have proceeded on the view that these statutes are specifically limited in their operation to the situations which they address, perhaps because parties have been content to pursue the statutory remedy. Whatever the reason, these statutes have not resulted in broader development of the common law.

Other statutes having a more general application have provided remedies which are not dissimilar. The Contracts Review Act 1980 (NSW) was such a statute. It provided for relief in circumstances where a contract is 'unjust' or its terms are 'unjust' and required the court to have regard to a number of factors, including whether or not there was any material inequality in bargaining power between the parties to the contract.[44] The relief provided for is much wider than at common law. The Australian Consumer Law[45] provides for relief in the case of unconscionable conduct and also in the case of unfair terms in consumer contracts. It might have been expected that its provisions would have led to some development of general law doctrines, more particularly because 'unjust' is a less demanding standard than unconscionable and because statutory relief in relation to unfair terms might have generated an initiative similar to that evidenced in *Interfoto*.[46] But that seems not to have been the case, possibly because parties seeking relief look to the statutory provisions

[43] See Carter, above n 39, 57, 74.
[44] Contracts Review Act 1980 (NSW), s 9.
[45] Competition and Consumer Act 2010 (Cth), Sch 2 (which sets out the Australian Consumer Law).
[46] *Interfoto Ltd v Stiletto* [1989] QB 433 (CA), 439. See above n 31.

because they provide broader grounds of relief and remedies. That statement is subject to the qualification that in *ACCC v Lux Distributors Pty Ltd*,[47] it was recognised that statutory standards of honesty and fairness may provide a foundation for common law development of concepts such as unconscionable conduct.[48]

In 1984 in *Moorgate Tobacco Co Ltd v Philip Morris Ltd (No 2)*,[49] the High Court of Australia adopted an approach similar to that adopted by the NSW Court of Appeal in the two cases to which I referred earlier. In *Moorgate*, Deane J (with whose judgment the other members of the Court agreed) addressed the interrelation between the common law and the provisions of Part V of the Trade Practices Act 1974 (Cth), especially section 52. His Honour indicated that in deciding what development, if any, there should be of the common law on a particular subject, the court should have regard to what the Parliament had determined to be 'the appropriate balance between competing claims and policies'.[50]

In *R v L*,[51] the High Court held that, if it was ever the common law that by marriage a wife gave her irrevocable consent to sexual intercourse with her husband, it was no longer the common law. In rejecting the argument that marriage gave rise to such a consent, Mason CJ, Deane and Toohey JJ said that the Court was justified:

> in refusing to accept a notion that is so out of keeping with the view that society now takes of the relationship between the parties to a marriage. The notion is out of keeping also with recent changes in the criminal law of this country made by statute, which draw no distinction between a wife and other women in defining the offence of rape.[52]

The judgment then cited the relevant legislative provisions in five of the Australian States.

In *Peters (WA) Ltd v Petersville Ltd*,[53] the High Court of Australia applied the approach stated by Deane J in *Moorgate*. The Court was there concerned with the operation of the common law doctrine of restraint of trade and section 45 of the Trade Practices Act 1974 (Cth) as amended. In their joint judgment, Gleeson CJ, Gummow, Kirby and Hayne JJ pointed out that section 45 in its original form used the expression 'restraint of trade' in its common law sense but did not do so by looking to the 'static content' of the doctrine at the time of the enactment of the provision.[54] Instead, the statute incorporated 'the changing standards of the common law'.[55]

Their Honours went on to consider section 4M, an amendment to the Trade Practices Act introduced in 1977. The section provided that the Trade Practices Act 'does not affect the operation of the law relating to restraint of trade in so far as that law is capable of operating concurrently with the Act … but nothing in [that] law … affects the interpretation of this Act'. This provision, their Honours said, applied according to its terms, while the common law was free to develop independently of the statute, provided it operated consistently with the statute.[56]

[47] *Australian Competition and Consumer Commission v Lux Distributors Pty Ltd* [2013] FCAFC 90 [23].
[48] See also *Director of Consumer Affairs Victoria v Scully* [2013] VSCA 292, (2013) 303 ALR 168 [56].
[49] *Moorgate Tobacco Co Ltd v Philip Morris Ltd (No 2)* (1984) 156 CLR 414 (HL).
[50] ibid 445.
[51] *R v L* (1991) 174 CLR 379 (HCA); see also *PGA v The Queen* [2012] HCA 21, (2012) 245 CLR 355.
[52] *R v L* (1991) 174 CLR 379 (HCA), 390.
[53] *Peters (WA) Ltd v Petersville Ltd* (2001) 205 CLR 126 (HCA).
[54] ibid [30].
[55] *United States v Associated Press* 52 F Supp 362, 370 (SDNY, 1943).
[56] *Peters (WA) Ltd v Petersville Ltd* (2001) 205 CLR 126 (HCA) [32].

Picking up the point made by Deane J in *Moorgate*, the joint judgment pointed out that, while section 4M left the common law free to develop in the fashion identified in section 4M, it did not deny that in such development the courts could have regard to the statute. That, their Honours observed, was a point of significance in *Peters (WA) Ltd v Petersville Ltd*, where the question was whether the restraint imposed could be reconciled with the public interest, and Part IVA of the Trade Practices Act established a detailed regime with particular stated exceptions.[57]

In *Adelaide Steamship Co Ltd v Spalvins*,[58] a subpoena had been issued to the Australian Securities and Investment Commission (ASIC) seeking legal advice received by ASIC. One issue was whether or not ASIC had waived privilege. The question for the Court was whether matters relating to the loss of legal privilege ought to be determined by applying principles derived from the common law or from the Evidence Act 1995 (Cth). The Evidence Act provisions were directed to privilege in the context of the giving of evidence and not to processes that were ancillary to a proceeding in which evidence was sought to be given, such as discovery. So the question arose whether the statutory provisions should be applied to the ancillary processes.

Although the Court accepted that in ancillary proceedings, it was the common law that determines the availability of a client privilege claim, the Court concluded that the relevant common law principles must adapt to the new statutory setting.[59] The Court offered three reasons for this conclusion. First, the Court considered that the claims to legal professional privilege are most commonly made in civil litigation in ancillary processes, and that the privilege itself evolved as an exception to testimonial compulsion at trial and was then applied derivatively in ancillary processes, so that changes in principles applied at trial provide the paradigm and should be rationally reflected in the derivatives.[60]

Secondly, the Court could see no reason for ascribing different policies and purposes, and hence differing attributes, to the privilege depending upon whether or not evidence is being adduced at trial. Absent such a reason, the legislatively prescribed attributes of the privilege ought to be reflected as those of the common law in jurisdictions where the two operate in tandem.[61] The third reason was that impractical consequences could ensue if differing principles were to be applied by the Act and the common law.[62]

Esso Australia Resources Ltd v Federal Commissioner of Taxation[63] concerned two different provisions in the Evidence Act 1995 (Cth), sections 118 and 119. They provided that evidence was not to be adduced if, on objection by a client, a court found that adducing the evidence would result in disclosure of certain confidential communications or the contents of certain confidential documents made or prepared for the dominant purpose of a lawyer providing to a client legal advice or professional legal services relating to certain proceedings or anticipated or pending proceedings. The Court held that sections 118 and 119 concerned the adducing of evidence and did not apply to a request for the making available of documents for inspection.

57 ibid [33].
58 *Adelaide Steamship Co Ltd v Spalvins* (1997) 152 ALR 418 (FCA).
59 ibid 428.
60 ibid.
61 ibid.
62 ibid 429.
63 *Esso Australia Resources Ltd v Federal Commissioner of Taxation* [1999] HCA 67, (1999) 201 CLR 49.

The important aspect of the decision for present purposes is the High Court's conclusion that sections 118 and 119 could not form a basis for modification, by analogy or derivation, of the common law. This was because the Evidence Act did not apply throughout Australia. The Act then applied only in Federal courts, the State of New South Wales and the Australian Capital Territory. Gleeson CJ, Gaudron and Gummow J pointed out that 'there is but one common law in Australia which is declared by this Court as a final court of appeal'.[64] Elsewhere in Australia there were different statutory regimes governing privilege with residual common law principles. So there was 'no consistent pattern of legislative policy to which the common law in Australia can adapt itself'.[65] A modification of the common law of the kind under consideration, if implemented only in the jurisdictions in which the Evidence Act applied, would lead to a fragmentation of the Australian common law contrary to the 'one common law' in Australia recognised by the High Court authorities.

The Court then went on to invoke the well-known remarks of Lord Diplock in *Warnink v J Townshend & Sons (Hull) Ltd*,[66] namely:

> Where over a period of years there can be discerned a steady trend in legislation which reflects the view of successive Parliaments as to what the public interest demands in a particular field of law, development of the common law as that part of the same field which has been left to it ought to proceed upon a parallel rather than a divergent course.

In *Warnink*, Lord Diplock used the increasing recognition by Parliament of the need for more rigorous standards of commercial honesty as a factor to support an extension of the common law concept of passing off by analogy from previous cases. Here statute was used to support the common law analogy because statute provided a statutory policy to reinforce that extension. It was not a case in which the analogy was taken from statute. *Warnink* was comparable with *R v L*[67] except in so far as *R v L* may be regarded as analogy from statute.

It would, however, be a mistake to draw from Lord Diplock's positive remarks a negative implication that, absent a consistent pattern of legislation in one jurisdiction manifesting a particular policy, it is then not legitimate to modify the common law. For example, where, in a non-federal jurisdiction, a statute clearly expresses a general policy and applies it in a particular field of law, why is that not an appropriate basis on which to modify the common law in that or a related field so that it is consistent with the statutory policy?

The basis for the 'one common law for Australia' proposition was the Australian Constitution's establishment of the High Court of Australia as a final court of appeal for Australia. It is a doubtful constitutional foundation for the proposition[68] and a frail foundation for the extension of the proposition to a restriction on the autonomy of the States by denying to a State court the capacity to mould the common law in that jurisdiction so as to reflect statutory policy in that jurisdiction. If a statute in a particular jurisdiction has clearly manifested a general policy, why should the courts of that jurisdiction not take account of it, even if other State legislatures have not adopted the same policy?

[64] ibid [23], citing *Lange v Australian Broadcasting Corporation* (1997) 189 CLR 520 (HCA), 563; see also *Lipohar v The Queen* (1999) 200 CLR 485 (HCA), 505–10; *PGA v The Queen* [2012] HCA 21, (2012) 245 CLR 355 [25].

[65] *Esso Australia Resources Ltd v Federal Commissioner of Taxation* [1999] HCA 67, (1999) 201 CLR 49 [23].

[66] *Warnink v J Townshend & Sons (Hull) Ltd* [1979] AC 731 (HL), 743.

[67] *R v L* (1991) 174 CLR 379 (HCA).

[68] See James Stellios, 'The Centralisation of Judicial Power Within the Australian Federal System' (2014) 42 *Federal Law Review* 357, 375.

Presumably the 'one common law' theory means that, in so far as there is left in each particular jurisdiction a common law residue after statutory alteration or modification of the common law, the part of that residue that is common to all jurisdictions must remain uniform. It is obvious that the residue will differ from jurisdiction to jurisdiction. In an 'Age of Statutes', is there much point in insisting on the uniformity of a nation-wide common law when the content of the common law varies considerably across the relevant Australian jurisdictions as a result of statutory modifications which themselves vary across those jurisdictions? Take, for example, the wide-ranging amendments made to the common law of tortious liability by the Civil Liability Act 2002 (NSW) which have been replicated in other Australian jurisdictions, but with significant variations.

The extension of the 'one common law' theory in *Esso Resources* presents an obstacle to development of the common law from statute in Australia, albeit not an insurmountable obstacle.

Impact of the Australian Constitution on Common Law Development

Analogical development of the common law by reference to statute invites attention to the impact of the Australian Constitution on development of the common law. In *Lange v Australian Broadcasting Corporation*,[69] the High Court was called upon to consider what effect the constitutional implication of freedom of communication as to government had on the common law of defamation. The Court answered this question by saying:

> Of necessity the common law must conform with the Constitution. The development of the common law in Australia cannot run counter to constitutional imperatives. The common law and the requirements of the Constitution cannot be at odds. The common law of libel and slander could not be developed inconsistently with the Constitution for the common law's protection of personal reputation must admit, as an exception, that qualified freedom to discuss government and politics which is required by the Constitution.[70]

The effect of the judgment was that both statute and common law may provide for a greater degree of protection of political discourse but they cannot provide for less. In a case of this kind, the impact of the Constitution on the development of the common law by the High Court generally resembles the impact of the Human Rights Act 1998 (UK) and European Convention on the development of the common law, subject of course to appropriate qualification arising from the difference between Constitution and statute. I should mention that in an earlier case where the impact of the constitutional implication on the law of defamation arose for consideration, I favoured the view that the implication generated a constitutional defence to an action in defamation.[71] *Lange* overruled that view so that we now have a species of common law that has the backing of the Constitution and cannot be altered by the legislature.

Here the Constitution, like the Human Rights Act 1998, mandates a requirement to be complied with in the development of the common law (and the enactment of statutes) whereas, with analogical development of the common law from statute, the statute does not

[69] *Lange v Australian Broadcasting Corporation* (1997) 189 CLR 520 (HCA).
[70] ibid 566.
[71] *Theophanous v Herald & Weekly Times Ltd* (1994) 182 CLR 104 (HCA).

directly mandate that development, even if a court is bound to consider and make its own judgment on the possible development.

IV. Relevance and Complications of Judicial Resort to Policy Considerations Generally

Courts resort to policy considerations when the rules, principles and standards of the settled common law do not provide a clear determination of the question, or where existing principles, rules or standards are up for re-consideration as a result of statutory advance or otherwise. Resort to policy considerations will often reveal conflicting considerations and values, in which event a court will be compelled to make a choice between them or arrive at a balance between them. In either event the court will enunciate a rule, principle or standard according to which the question for decision and other like questions may be resolved.

Courts also resort to policy considerations in areas of judicial discretion, particularly statutory discretions when the ambit of the discretion is relatively undefined. The Court is then required to identify factors relevant to the exercise of the discretion, factors which will involve policy considerations and values.

A major problem that confronts courts in assessing policy considerations is the relative absence of authoritative materials on which policy arguments can be constructed. All too often it emerges that the judicial examination of policy arguments consists of identifying and evaluating policy considerations discussed in previous cases or in articles in academic journals and in textbooks. Sometimes judicial discussion will take account of authoritative surveys or reports by expert panels or committees. At other times judicial discussion will take account of changes in social behaviour and attitudes of which judges are aware, as in the NSW case, *Seidler v Schallhefer* to which I referred earlier, though in that case observable change in social attitudes was reinforced by legislative provisions. *R v L* was a similar example.

In these circumstances, statutes as a source of established or recognised policy have an important part to play in the development of the common law, particularly when they resolve competing claims and policy considerations, as in *Moorgate*. In matters of social policy statutes often manifest a policy that has steadily evolved as a result of a change in community behaviour or attitudes as, for example, in the matter of what was described in earlier days as sexual immorality. In these cases, legislation follows and gives effect to changes in community behaviour and attitudes. On the other hand, in relation to economic policy considerations, legislation is often enacted in advance of community opinion.

Despite the attraction and importance of statute as a source of common law development, the courts have not availed themselves of it in many cases. There are some obvious reasons for this state of affairs.

1. It is only in recent times, as a result of the work of commentators, that lawyers have cast aside their old view that common law and statute are distinct and separate bodies of law so that the common law develops independently of statute.
2. Lawyers have been accustomed to thinking about the law as existing in separate and insulated compartments. It is easier to understand principles of law in this way without

undertaking the challenging task of trying to work out how these principles might interact with each other. Statute and common law are a particular example of this compartmentalised approach.

3. Statutory provisions often take the form of remedying a particular defect in the common law. The statute then has a limited operation and, apart from its effect in modifying the common law, it may have little utility as a source of common law development. And sometimes statutes exhibit an intention to replace the common law and cover the field exhaustively.
4. The capacity of the courts to draw on statutory policy is not infrequently thwarted by the limited way in which parties present their cases, even when statutes provide new and expanded remedies in particular fields, the parties simply avail themselves of the statutory remedies, without arguing in favour of judicial reformulation of the common law.
5. When statute replaces the common law with a detailed regulatory regime, it may be difficult to deduce a legislative intention that the courts are free to develop the common law. Even if a particular development is consistent with the statute, that development may only serve to complicate rather than simplify the law and that is an undesirable development.

There are, in addition, other factors that have inhibited judicial resort to statute as a resource for common law development. One such factor is that because it has been thought that, unlike the common law, statutory law is incapable of development, it has been suggested that any alteration of the common law proceeding from statute is unalterable. It is, however, an inherent characteristic of the common law that it is capable of continuing development. In the light of that inherent characteristic, in the absence of clear provision to the contrary, a statute should not be interpreted as freezing the common law as it exists at a given point of time. *Peters (WA) Ltd v Petersville Ltd*,[72] mentioned earlier, is a case in point. Absent such a clear provision, the way is open for appropriate common law development unless it is inconsistent with the statute or impairs the coherence of the law.

The High Court of Australia has identified the coherence or congruity of the law as an important policy consideration which can be central in the development of the common law, as it was in *Miller v Miller*.[73] The Court there pointed out, 'the principles applied in the tort of negligence must be congruent with those applied in other areas of the civil law (most notably contracts and trusts)'.[74] The particular question in *Miller v Miller* was: Would it be incongruous for the law to proscribe the plaintiff's conduct and yet allow recovery in negligence for damage suffered in the course of, or as a result of, that unlawful conduct?[75] The Court held that the statutory purpose of proscribing dangerous or reckless driving was not consistent with one offender (the driver) owing a co-offender, albeit a passenger, a duty to take reasonable care. The driver and the co-offender were complicit in the offence

[72] *Peters (WA) Ltd v Petersville Ltd* (2001) 205 CLR 126 (HCA) [30]; see also *British Railways Board v Herrington* [1972] AC 877 (HL), 921.

[73] *Miller v Miller* [2011] HCA 9, (2011) 242 CLR 446 [15]; see also *Sullivan v Moody* (2001) 207 CLR 562 (HCA) [42], [53]–[55]; *Agricultural & Rural Finance Pty Ltd v Gardiner* [2008] HCA 57, (2008) 238 CLR 570 [100]; *CAL No 14 Pty Ltd v Motor Accidents Insurance Board* [2009] HCA 47, (2009) 239 CLR 390 [39]–[42].

[74] *Miller v Miller* [2011] HCA 9, (2011) 242 CLR 446 [11].

[75] ibid [16].

of illegally using the vehicle, the statutory purpose of section 371A of the Criminal Code (WA) being inconsistent with one offender owing a co-offender a duty to take reasonable care. The incongruity arose from recognising that the purpose of the statute was to deter and punish the use of a vehicle in circumstances that often lead to dangerous and reckless driving.[76]

It is not my purpose to evaluate the reasoning in *Miller*. It is extremely complex. My purpose is simply to draw attention to this doctrine of 'incongruity', 'incoherence' or 'contrariety' and make two points. The first is that these words are imprecise and give little guidance. Presumably they convey something more than 'inconsistency'. That said, the cases in which the relevant question arises are situation-specific and precise guidance may well be an elusive goal. The second point is that the doctrine presents another difficulty in the use of statute as a source of common law development.

Leaving Questions to be Resolved by the Legislature

In Australia, there has been at times a strong tendency on the part of courts to refuse to engage in development of the common law and leave the question to be resolved by legislatures. Although the examples are not cases involving statutory policy, the judicial mindset revealed is applicable to cases involving development of the common law from statute. Two well-known examples are both High Court of Australia decisions. The first was *State Government Insurance Commission v Trigwell*[77] (a decision to which I was a party), where the Court considered that the controversial policy question whether the common law immunity of the owner of land from liability for injury to persons using the adjacent highway from the owner's straying stock should be left to the legislature for resolution. This was because the policy question was controversial and the Court was ill-equipped to assess it.

Likewise, in *Breen v Williams*,[78] the Court considered that the patient had no right to access his doctor's medical records at common law or in equity, despite Canadian and United States authorities to the contrary. The question whether the law should be altered was, the Court held, a matter for the legislature. The reasons for this conclusion advanced by the members of the Court are not altogether clear. It seems that the Court considered that the case was not appropriate for development of the common law. In this respect, Gaudron and McHugh JJ, however, said, 'Any changes in legal doctrine, brought about by judicial creativity, must "fit" within the body of accepted rules and principles'.[79] This statement is a precursor to the doctrine of 'incoherence'. Their Honours also said: 'In a democratic society, changes in the law that cannot logically or analogically be related to existing common law rules and principles are the province of the legislature'.[80]

The first of these statements, if not the second, asserts that any change in legal doctrine must be consistent with accepted rules and principles, a proposition that cannot be satisfied when the change, for whatever reason, involves the necessary rejection or contradiction of

[76] ibid [101]. It should be noted that the plaintiff succeeded on the basis that, on the evidence, she had sought to withdraw from the criminal enterprise before the accident occurred.

[77] *State Government Insurance Commission v Trigwell* (1979) 142 CLR 617.

[78] *Breen v Williams* (1996) 186 CLR 71 (HCA).

[79] ibid 115.

[80] ibid.

a settled rule or principle. The doctrine, however, cannot justify a court's refusal to decide a question of developing the common law when statute clearly manifests a policy opposed to that underlying settled rule or principle. The actual recognition of indigenous title in *Mabo v Queensland (No 2)*[81] stands in contrast with the later statement made in *Breen v Williams*, notwithstanding what was said in the leading judgment in *Mabo (No 2)*.[82]

True it is that these days the judicial mindset has changed. It is now generally recognised that legislatures no longer give continuing attention to the state of the law, particularly the civil law of obligations. Judges are more willing to scrutinise the sufficiency of existing rules and principles and to re-formulate them when appropriate, whether the reconsideration is on a purely doctrinal basis or otherwise. So much so that Professor Burrows, in the article to which I referred earlier, has expressed the view that:

> it is an abdication of judicial responsibility for judges, at least in the law of obligations, to decline to develop the common law on the grounds that legislation is more appropriate. Even if a statutory solution would be better, no-one can predict whether legislation will, or will not be passed.[83]

My Assessment of the Burrows View

While there is much to be said for the Burrows view, it is too absolute. There are cases where a court would be justified in awaiting a legislative response. One example is where there is a political controversy about a possible change in the law to reflect changes in social or economic conditions and a change in the law is recommended by a Law Reform Commission but the executive government decides that it will not implement the recommendation. Other examples may be given where the court is not equipped to undertake the inquiries and assessments required to arrive at a conclusion that there should be judicial development of the common law. As I said in *Trigwell*, a court is neither a legislature nor a law reform agency and it lacks a capacity to engage in the processes which enable such bodies to inform themselves about policy issues.[84] True it is, as Professor Burrows argues, that by staying its hand, a party is, or may be, denied the relief it would otherwise be entitled to. On the other hand, the other party then succeeds on the basis of the law as it has been declared at that time.

It may also be necessary to take account of differing views across jurisdictions about the relationship between the legislature and the judiciary. In Australia, for instance, which for the most part lacks a judicially enforceable statutory Bill of Rights, a more favourable view might perhaps be taken than in the United Kingdom of the desirability of a court leaving a matter for legislative resolution, eg, where a policy issue attracts different statutory responses in two or more jurisdictions. The narrow view of the scope of judicial power in Australia contributes to the judiciary's cautious view of its law-making role.

If a court should decide that a question of law should be left to the legislature for resolution, the court should state fully and precisely the reasons for taking that course. The court needs to justify its decision not to decide the question itself.

[81] *Mabo v Queensland (No 2)* (1992) 175 CLR 1 (HCA).
[82] ibid 43.
[83] Burrows, above n 9, 232.
[84] *State Government Insurance Commission v Trigwell* (1979) 142 CLR 617 (HCA), 633.

7

Public Actors and Private Obligations: A Judicial Perspective

SIAN ELIAS

This chapter is a judicial perspective shaped by a small jurisdiction that has always been happy to borrow and learn from others. Our inclination is ever towards convergence, but local conditions and preferences have in some things pushed us to diverge. Because of our circumstances we have always relied heavily on statute law. And, as a result, I think we may have had a less suspicious view of statutes than the older common law jurisdictions and have been willing from earliest times to see statutes and common law as forming one legal order. We have never found it difficult to reason by analogy with statutes and look to statutes for help in identifying the values of our society, when it is necessary to take them into account in shaping the common law. Because of the circumstances of a new country, much that in other countries is undertaken locally or by private parties has in New Zealand been undertaken by the state. Public and private have not diverged as starkly as may have been the case in other jurisdictions.

How the law of obligations treats public actors is therefore something that has been an important focus of our law. Addressing it offers an opportunity to consider divergence and convergence in different jurisdictions of the common law, but it also invites reflection on how we treat the public dimension in private law.

I. The State as Litigant

Under the rule of law described by Dicey, governments are subject to ordinary law and accountable in the ordinary courts.[1] Doing justice between the individual and the state is, as Lord Denning recognised, every bit as important as doing justice between individuals.

In the statutes common to many common law jurisdictions which remove procedural and jurisdictional impediments to suing the Crown,[2] equivalence is usually 'as nearly as

[1] AV Dicey, *Introduction to the Study of the Law of the Constitution* 10th edn (London, MacMillan, 1961) 193.

[2] Crown Proceedings Act 1950 (NZ), s 3; Crown Proceedings Act 1947 (UK), s 1; Crown Liability and Proceedings Act, RSC (1985) (Can); Judiciary Act 1903 (Cth), s 64. In Australia and Canada there are in addition statutes governing non-federal cases. The New Zealand Act is modelled on the UK Crown Proceedings Act 1947 but it replaced earlier legislation which had removed Crown immunity. The Limitation Act 1950 arguably narrowed the scope of the pre-existing immunities.

possible'.[3] In New Zealand, however, the right to bring civil proceedings against and to defend those brought by the Crown is recognised without qualification in legislation as a human right.[4] The right is 'to have those proceedings heard, according to law, in the same way as civil proceedings between individuals'. The provision was explained in the White Paper which preceded enactment of the Bill of Rights Act 1990 as being:[5]

> designed to give constitutional status to the core principle recognised in the Crown Proceedings Act 1950: that the individual should be able to bring legal proceedings against the Government, and more generally to engage in civil litigation with it, without the Government enjoying any procedural or jurisdictional privileges. This is central to the rule of law.

In *Darker v Chief Constable of West Midlands Police*,[6] other members of the House of Lords affirmed that the public policy that those who suffer wrongs should have a remedy required existing immunities to be strictly confined. Lord Cooke of Thorndon simply said flatly that immunities of the Crown were in principle inconsistent with the rule of law.[7] The New Zealand courts have yet to consider whether the enactment of section 27 of the Bill of Rights Act affects the interpretation of the Crown Proceedings Act or the development of the common law concerning the liabilities of the Crown. Some reconsideration of existing authority may be necessary.

On the other hand, the law also imposes liabilities on public actors which either have no equivalence for private individuals or corporations or in respect of which officials are particularly exposed because of their functions. The exposure of public actors arising out of their exercise of public functions is something the law has been particularly sensitive to.

The reach of the state means that liability of the Crown and public bodies may be indeterminate. It may seem unfair if the 'deep pockets' of public actors set them up as defendants of last recourse when intermediate actors are principally culpable. Public actors may be more constrained in their freedom to contract or held to higher standards of fairness and rationality under doctrines of common law and equity than individuals and private corporations. They may also be exposed to public law liabilities, including for breach of rights, which overlap with private law liabilities and which have not always been satisfactorily reconciled with them in the case law.

Because wide discretions are conferred on officials and public bodies to act in the public interest (a responsibility not shared by those acting in their own interests), their failure to use powers that might have protected others from harm raises in acute form questions of liability based on omission, which the common law has always found more difficult than liability based on positive action. Because choices have to be made by those acting in the public interest, the courts are often uncomfortable about the standards to be applied in judging fault and nervous about trespassing into matters of policy for which political accountability is more appropriate. Some of the remedies in private law may seem inappropriate or inconsistent with the discretionary relief available in judicial review. It is necessary sometimes to confront conflicting duties, as in the cases of harm suffered by both children and parents falsely accused of their abuse. And those exercising powers of a public nature

[3] *Graham Barclay Oysters Pty Ltd v Ryan* [2002] HCA 54, (2002) 211 CLR 540 [12] (Gleeson CJ).

[4] Under the New Zealand Bill of Rights Act 1990, s 27(3).

[5] Geoffrey Palmer, 'A Bill of Rights for New Zealand: A White Paper' [1984–1985] I *AJHR* A6, 111–12.

[6] *Darker v Chief Constable of West Midlands Police* [2001] 1 AC 435 (HL).

[7] ibid 453.

are accountable also under the judicial review jurisdiction. So public actors are more equal for some purposes and less equal for others.

Although these challenges for the law must be acknowledged, they are not always confined to public actors and are more general issues for the law of obligations. They do not explain the incoherence and uncertainty of so much of the law and the confusion in application of public law concepts in cases where the courts are concerned with the correction of legal wrongs to individuals. Although the tort of negligence has been the main embarrassment, other areas of the law of obligations and the remedies available to meet their breach present challenges in the task of doing justice between the individual and the state in the twenty-first century.

There are a number of factors which bear on this. One may be the success of modern administrative law, including that developed by regulatory agencies other than courts. It has come at a time when statutory restatement and reform of much of the heartland of the law of obligations may have led to a narrowing focus on the ends and values of private law. The analogies provided by these statutes and the values they adopt did not galvanise the development of the common law, as they should have done. The development of other forms of accountability for the use of public power may have led to a view that accountability through the law of obligations is largely an irrelevance.

The courts have sometime not helped. In negligence, for example, too many novel cases (and not simply those involving the exercise of public powers) have been entertained on summary applications to strike out proceedings on grounds of law, meaning that questions of breach and causation have received insufficient attention. It may not have helped that in a number of these cases judges have succumbed to two traps described by Lord Goff: the 'temptation of elegance' (the expression of a solution so beautifully that it carries too much authority) and the 'fallacy of the instant, complete solution'.[8]

There are no instant solutions and I certainly do not attempt elegance. The common law needs constant attention. It is a process, as Benjamin Cardozo rightly described it.[9] And in that process, in part one of continuing convergence and divergence, it is important to have a sense of the direction and values of the whole law, of which the largely judge-made law of obligations is part only.

II. Public and Private Obligations

Since *Entick v Carrington*,[10] liability in tort has been the principal method of vindication of the rule of law when its violation by public authorities affects the legal rights and interests of individuals. It is important to the rule of law that the servants of the Crown, except where immunity is specifically conferred, are liable for trespass, nuisance and negligence, as citizens are to each other. As with other citizens, they are also liable for exemplary damages for behaviour which warrants it, as was established in the *North Briton* litigation.[11]

[8] Lord Goff, 'The Search for Principle' (1983) 69 *Proceedings of the British Academy* 169, 172–73.

[9] Benjamin Cardozo, *The Growth of the Law* (New Haven, CT, Yale University Press, 1924) 73.

[10] *Entick v Carrington* (1765) 19 StTr 1029.

[11] *Wilkes v Wood* (1763) 98 ER 489.

What we call public law is itself not isolated from the general body of common law from which it diverged in part in the latter half of the twentieth century with judicial development of modern judicial review.[12] The principles of administrative law were developed in tort, contract, company law, labour law, criminal law and equity.[13] As Sir Anthony Mason has pointed out, modern administrative law is founded on equitable principles and has its roots in private law.[14]

In New Zealand, an appellate judge recently complained in a claim concerning fair treatment in tendering about being asked, in judicial review proceedings, to entertain a private law action in 'public law drag'.[15] In that case, concerning tendering, all parties accepted that the public body which had called for the tenders was amenable to judicial review.[16] It is not obvious why there were concerns that judicial review was not appropriate, particularly since under New Zealand legislation the procedure may be invoked in respect of the powers exercised 'under the instrument of incorporation, rules or bylaws of any body corporate'.[17] But, more importantly, the comment that the case was being dressed up in public law costume raises questions about why implication of a term to achieve equivalent fairness was not equally available in a private law suit for breach of contract.[18]

The outcome in the actual case may well not have been different if more equivalence between what the Court saw as private and public law principles had been adopted. But there is something wrong with the law if there is a risk of a legal black hole here.[19]

Conversely, in an appeal from New Zealand in negligence the Privy Council expressed the view that a factor pointing against liability in negligence was that the decision of the Minister there in issue could have been judicially reviewed.[20] (Sir Robin Cooke, writing extra judicially in 2004, has said of this decision that 'the case seems to belong to a

[12] As scholars such as Dawn Oliver and Peter Cane have been at the forefront in pointing out: D Oliver, *Common Values and the Public-Private Divide* (London, Butterworths, 1999); P Cane, 'Accountability and the Public-Private Divide' in N Bamforth and P Leyfeld (eds), *Public Law in a Multi-Layered Constitution* (Oxford, Hart Publishing, 2003) 247.

[13] A point made in 1987 by DGT Williams, 'Criminal Law and Administrative Law: Problems of Procedure and Reasonableness' in P Smith (ed), *Criminal Law: Essays in Honour of JC Smith* (London, Butterworths, 1987) 170, 171.

[14] A Mason, 'The Place of Equity and Equitable Remedies in the Contemporary Common Law World' (1994) 110 *LQR* 238, 238.

[15] *Lab Tests Auckland Ltd v Auckland District Health Board* [2008] NZCA 385, [2009] 1 NZLR 776 [405].

[16] Although Hammond J expressed the concern that he would not want counsel in other cases automatically to assume reviewability, on the basis of what had happened in that case: ibid [360].

[17] Judicature Amendment Act 1972 (NZ). And see D Mullan 'The State of Judicial Scrutiny of Public Contracting in New Zealand and Canada' (2012) 43 *Victoria University of Wellington Law Review* 173, 194.

[18] The judgment of the Court of Appeal noted that there was nothing amounting to fraud, corruption or bad faith in the decision of the Board and pointed to the indications of the Privy Council in an appeal from New Zealand that 'public law notions' were not to be imported into a 'contractual framework': *Lab Tests Auckland Ltd v Auckland District Health Board* [2008] NZCA 385, [2009] 1 NZLR 776 [60]. In *Pratt Contractors Ltd v Transit New Zealand* [2003] UKPC 83, [2005] 2 NZLR 433, the Privy Council had been willing to imply a duty of good faith and fair dealing but only if it met the test for implication of contractual terms and, as well, such implied term was held not to be equivalent to public law standards. And in *Royal Australasian College of Surgeons v Phipps* [1999] 2 NZLR 1 (CA), the view was taken in the Court of Appeal that judicial review is not available for commercial operations or to question commercial judgments.

[19] As may have been the case in the Australian decision of *Griffith University v Tang* [2005] HCA 7, (2005) 221 CLR 99.

[20] *Takaro Properties Ltd v Rowling* [1987] 2 NZLR 700 (PC), 709–10. See also *Watkins v Secretary of State for the Home Department* [2006] UKHL 17, [2006] 2 AC 395, 409.

bygone era and must be of limited help as a precedent'.[21]) Something similar was said more recently by the House of Lords in *Watkins*. In such cases, the private/public divide is used, in Carol Harlow's words as 'a boilerplate answer, a formalist brush off'.[22]

Insistence on observance of legality, reasonableness and fairness in the conduct of public functions may be sought in judicial review by anyone with standing. The ends are vindication of law and just administration. Remedies are discretionary and procedural requirements may properly be imposed on such claims, including for reasons of good administration. High policy content may in some cases set limits to judicial supervision.

Those who have claims of legal right which are personal to them are in a different position. Subject to limitation and other defences, they are entitled to the relief available under law (which may include discretionary equitable remedies). In such cases separation of powers deference has little, if any, scope except perhaps in the policy choices where the courts are asked to respond to novel wrongs.

Public law litigation is concerned with public good. Private litigation is not so limited. The two bodies of doctrine are, as I have suggested, closely linked by shared principles and often the same end serves both purposes. But the responses of law to wrongs to the public good and wrongs to individuals may properly vary. When public law actions are also private law wrongs, conflation or deference may erode private rights and disempower those who are wronged from seeking correction.

In the United Kingdom and in Australia it has been suggested that public bodies with statutory duties will be liable in negligence for their failure to exercise the powers only if not to do so was irrational or compellable by mandamus.[23] The better view seems to me that whether public bodies are liable for the negligent exercise of statutory powers does not turn on whether their use is lawful, for the reasons given by Gaudron J in *Crimmins v Stevedoring Industry Finance Committee*:[24]

> Liability will arise in negligence only if there is in the circumstances a duty to act. What is in question is not a statutory duty of the kind enforceable by public law remedy. Rather, it is a duty called into existence by the common law by reason that the relationship between the statutory body and some member or members of the public is such as to give rise to a duty to take some positive step or steps to avoid a foreseeable risk of harm to the person or persons concerned. In the case of discretionary powers vested in a statutory body, it is not strictly accurate to speak, as is sometimes done, of a common law superimposed upon statutory powers. Rather the statute pursuant to which the body is created and its powers conferred operate 'in the milieu of the common law'. And the common law applies to that body unless excluded. Clearly common law duties are excluded if the performance by the statutory body of its functions would involve some breach of statutory duty or the exercise of powers which the statutory body does not possess.

In *R (Lumba) v Secretary of State for the Home Department*,[25] some of the Judges of the UK Supreme Court suggested that where a statutory power to detain had been wrongly exercised, as opposed to having been made without available authority at all, there would

[21] R Cooke, 'The Road Ahead for the Common Law' (2004) 53 *ICLQ* 273.

[22] C Harlow, *State Liability: Tort Law and Beyond* (Oxford, OUP, 2004) 39.

[23] *Stovin v Wise* [1996] AC 923, 952 (Lord Hoffmann), slightly modified in *Gorringe v Calderdale Metropolitan Borough Council* [2004] 1 WLR 1057 (HL). See also *Sutherland Shire Council v Heyman* (1985) 157 CLR 424 (HCA).

[24] *Crimmins v Stevedoring Industry Finance Committee* [1999] HCA 59, (1999) 200 CLR 1 [25]–[26].

[25] *R (Lumba) v Secretary of State for the Home Department* [2011] UKSC 12, [2012] 1 AC 245.

be 'a private law claim only if the misuse amounted to an abuse of power (including but not limited to cases of misfeasance or other conscious misuse of power)'.[26] The majority rejected this 'causation defence' and took the view that unlawful exercise of a power meant that there was no justification for the detention. They considered, however, that since the detention could have been lawfully imposed, the plaintiff was entitled to nominal damages only. But the minority suggestion carries the persistent view that invalidity must be established in judicial review and that the private law action is 'collateral'.[27]

III. Supervisory Jurisdiction

It is worth considering the extent to which the function of the courts is constant in what we treat as private law and what we treat as public law. I start with a case that is very familiar. It has been a favourite of mine since law school days when it and I were very young and the law was almost exclusively male.

In *Nagle v Fielden*, a woman trainer was denied a licence by the Jockey Club except through the subterfuge of her 'head lad'.[28] She had no contract with the Club. Nevertheless, the Court of Appeal considered that the courts have jurisdiction to make a declaration of right wherever justified. The rule under which the Jockey Club acted was arguably contrary to public policy and the right to work of the plaintiff was affected. Lord Denning held that when an association exercised 'a predominant power over the exercise of a trade or profession, the courts may have jurisdiction to see that this power is not abused'.[29] Danckwerts LJ considered that the courts 'have the right to protect the right of a person to work when it is being prevented by the dictatorial exercise of powers by a body which holds a monopoly'.[30] And, referring to the argument that the courts have no power to intervene, Salmond LJ said, witheringly:[31]

> This is a familiar argument on behalf of anyone seeking to exercise arbitrary power free from any control by the courts. One of the principal functions of our courts is, whenever possible, to protect the individual from injustice and oppression.

The supervisory jurisdiction of the courts is most familiar today in public law. And today we would probably classify *Nagle v Fielden* as a public law case. But before *Ridge v Baldwin* and the development of modern administrative law, things were not so categorical. Indeed, many of the principles and values drawn on by Lord Reid in *Ridge v Baldwin*[32] were taken from cases we would treat as private law cases.

[26] ibid [193] (Lord Walker), and see [170] (Lord Scott).

[27] *Boddington v British Transport Police* [1999] 2 AC 143 (HL). In New Zealand, challenge in criminal proceedings to the validity of bylaws and other delegated legislation has been well established but there are suggestions that such challenges may be coming to be regarded as 'collateral', with judicial review seen as the correct route: *Siemer v Solicitor-General* [2013] NZSC 68, [2013] 3 NZLR 441, n 255.

[28] *Nagle v Feilden* [1966] 2 QB 633 (CA).

[29] ibid 647.

[30] ibid 650.

[31] ibid 654.

[32] *Ridge v Baldwin* [1964] AC 40 (HL).

The common law has always paid close attention to power and its abuse wherever it is found and modern administrative law simply throws up new aspects of familiar conflicts earlier dealt with in tort and equity and in exercise of a supervisory jurisdiction not confined to public law. (The amenability of non-statutory bodies to judicial review remains a work in progress in some jurisdictions,[33] but not in Scotland, where the supervisory jurisdiction of the court is available irrespective whether the powers checked are in statute, contract or other instrument,[34] and in New Zealand, where broader jurisdiction has been exercised.)[35]

The supervisory jurisdiction is concerned with discretion—with the choices legitimately available to those whose conduct may affect the rights of others. When reasonableness or other standards are preconditions for liability under statute or common law, the court is undertaking essentially the same supervisory function as in the case where it holds those exercising public powers within bounds that are reasonable. These essentially supervisory standards are applied throughout the private law actions with which the law of obligations is concerned. They are behind terms implied into contracts, the business judgment rule applied to directors, the scope permitted to trustees, the imposition of fiduciary obligations, and the recognition of duties of care and what amounts to their breach. And, in turn, the doctrine applied in exercising supervision in these areas of law is helpful across the categories and in public law supervision also.

The measures used in supervision according to the interests engaged are most commonly the standards of reasonableness, fairness or unconscionability. What is unreasonable or unfair or unconscionable depends on context.[36] In matters of very great moment affecting rights, it may be that even a supervisory jurisdiction requires something close to a standard of correctness, as the Canadians have recognised.[37] In others, where choices are entirely open it may require little more than a check to exclude bad faith or unconscionable conduct. This range is encountered in private law as in public law.

The nature and responsibilities of government and public bodies are inevitably important context in considering their liabilities to private law suits. A sense of what is public is therefore important in private law. But so is a sense of what is private right.

IV. Private Law Actions

Unless they have immunities, public authorities are liable in private law suits for breach of contract, tort and other obligations. I want to touch briefly on some straws in the wind in relation to some of these sources of enforceable obligations. In addition, I add a few points about duty of care and all that.

[33] *R v Panel on Take-overs and Mergers, ex parte Datafin plc* [1987] QB 815 (CA) remains an outlier in the United Kingdom and Australia.

[34] *West v Secretary of State for Scotland* [1992] SLT 636 (Inner House).

[35] *Finnigan v New Zealand Rugby Football Union* [1985] 2 NZLR 159 (CA).

[36] *Minister for Immigration and Citizenship v Li* [2013] HCA 18, (2013) 249 CLR 332.

[37] *Dunsmuir v New Brunswick* 2008 SCC 9, [2008] 1 SCR 190.

Contract

The extent to which the modern state relies on contracting poses significant challenges for administrative law. It also throws up the importance of the private remedies available both to those who contract with public agencies and those who are the recipients of entitlements under service contracts between public bodies and providers under a relaxed privity doctrine. Beatson pointed out some years ago that the issues raised by good faith and fairness in precontractual duties and long-term or relational contracts can usefully be illuminated by public law principles.[38] That has added urgency given the contracting out of many of the functions of public bodies.

The need to address the contracting state seems likely to advance the long-term project of bringing law and equity properly together. If so, it will offer opportunities to build on Australian experience with fiduciary doctrine and estoppel and New Zealand experience with the full range of remedies derived from common law, equity or statute to fit the needs of the case and do practical justice.[39]

The adaptation of contract in matters such as the implication of terms to secure values of fairness and reasonableness, as well as good faith, remains a work in progress in the United Kingdom, Australia and New Zealand. Analogies with statutes protective of the vulnerable or concerned with fair treatment are likely to be increasingly used to provide content to such terms, for the reasons given by Lord Diplock,[40] Cooke P[41] and Lord Steyn:[42] because they are helpful in bringing the law into line with community expectations.

Liability for Breach of Fiduciary Obligations

In restating the principles on which relief for breach of fiduciary obligations will arise in *Alberta v Elder Advocates of Alberta Society*, the Supreme Court of Canada accepted that liability may attach to governments as well as to private actors.[43] It considered, however, that the special characteristics of governmental responsibilities and functions meant that fiduciary obligations would arise only in limited and special circumstances.[44] In *Alberta* itself, the Supreme Court held that there was no duty in relation to increases in charges for residents of nursing homes. The duty was to fulfil the statutory care obligations, which had not been breached. The setting of the accommodation charge in that case was a regulatory function the Court acknowledged it would be slow to interfere with. How to fund healthcare required the balancing of competing interests; the Crown could not meet its wider obligations if a fiduciary obligation were imposed.

[38] J Beatson, 'Judicial Review in Contract' in J Beatson and D Friedmann (eds), *Good Faith and Fault in Contract Law* (Oxford, OUP, 1995) 263.

[39] *Mouat v Clark Boyce* [1992] 2 NZLR 559 (CA), 565–66; *Aquaculture Corp v New Zealand Green Mussel Co Ltd* [1990] 3 NZLR 299 (CA); *Day v Mead* [1987] 2 NZLR 443 (CA). And see Mason, above n 14, 241–42.

[40] *Erven Warnink BV v J Townsend & Sons (Hull) Ltd* [1979] AC 731 (HL), 743.

[41] *South Pacific Manufacturing Co Ltd* [1992] 2 NZLR 282 (CA), 298.

[42] *Malik v Bank of Credit and Commerce International SA* [1998] AC 20 (HL), 52–53.

[43] *Alberta v Elder Advocates of Alberta Society* 2011 SCC 24, [2011] 2 SCR 261.

[44] ibid [37].

Other jurisdictions have yet to follow the Canadian example in applying the fiduciary principle outside the area of economic interests,[45] although Kirby J in the High Court of Australia was prepared to accept that child abuse could amount to a breach of fiduciary duty,[46] and the New Zealand Court of Appeal has been prepared to proceed on that assumption, without deciding the point.[47] Of particular interest to us in New Zealand are the Canadian decisions holding that the Crown is under fiduciary obligations to Indian bands, the latest being *Tsilhqot'in Nation v British Columbia*.[48] That approach has produced some sympathetic dicta in New Zealand cases concerning claims by Maori, but has not yet been further developed, although a case is pending in the Supreme Court in which such claims are made.[49]

Misfeasance in Public Office, Breach of Statutory Duty, False Imprisonment and Breaches of Rights

The ancient tort of misfeasance in public office has been given new life in major decisions in Australia,[50] New Zealand,[51] England[52] and Canada.[53] In its most recent restatement by the Canadian Supreme Court, it has been defined as 'deliberate disregard of official duty coupled with knowledge that the misconduct is likely to injure the plaintiff'.[54]

In jurisdictions with remedies for breaches of rights, the basis of reconciliation of the tort with remedies for breach of the right remains uncertain. New Zealand breaches of the Bill of Rights Act have been treated as a category of public law compensation. A path not taken was to build on the tort. If so, the remedy would not have been discretionary. An open question is whether in cases of misfeasance in public office which also entail breaches of the Bill of Rights Act the Bill of Rights Act breach can be taken into account in the damages awarded and, if so, whether proof of damage will remain necessary irrespective of the breach of the right, as the House of Lords has affirmed for England and Wales in *Watkins v Secretary of State for the Home Department*.[55] At present, it seems that Bill of Rights compensation stands apart.

Although breach of statutory duty is often said to be simply a matter of statutory interpretation, its status as a tort empowers those who are wronged by non-observance of a duty the statute confers upon them. Wade and Forsyth have suggested that human rights damages which are available under the UK Human Rights Act 1998 can be seen as a species of

[45] *Breen v Williams* (1996) 186 CLR 71 (HCA).

[46] *Williams v Minister, Aboriginal Land Rights Act* (1994) 35 NSWLR 497 (CA), where Kirby P (at 510) and Priestley JA (at 510–11) held that child abuse could be actionable as breach of fiduciary duty.

[47] The Court of Appeal proceeded on the basis that the abuse suffered by a child placed in foster care was in breach of a fiduciary obligation assumed by the Superintendent and Director of Child Youth and Family, but found that the claim had been rightly rejected by the High Court because there was no disloyalty or bad faith on the part of the officials: *S v Attorney-General* [2003] 3 NZLR 450 (CA).

[48] *Tsilhqot'in Nation v British Columbia* 2014 SCC 44, [2014] 2 SCR 256.

[49] *Paki v Attorney-General* [2010] NZSC 88 (leave).

[50] *Mengel v Northern Territory* (1995) 185 CLR 307 (HCA).

[51] *Garrett v Attorney General* [1997] 2 NZLR 332 (CA).

[52] *Three Rivers District Council v Bank of England (No 3)* [2003] 2 AC 1 (HL).

[53] *Odhavji Estate v Woodhouse* 2003 SCC 69, [2003] 3 SCR 263.

[54] ibid [23].

[55] *Watkins v Secretary of State for the Home Department* [2006] UKHL 17, [2006] 2 AC 395.

breach of statutory duty.[56] That path was also not taken in New Zealand, where the statute was silent on the provision of such a remedy and the legislative history indicated that had been a deliberate decision.[57] Nor has the idea been picked up in England and Wales.

False imprisonment is committed when someone is detained or imprisoned without lawful justification.[58] The tort is one of strict liability so is not excused by belief that the detention is lawful.[59] Although not confined to public office holders, officials are those principally exposed to liability under the tort. Wrong calculation of release dates[60] or undue delay in bringing a prisoner before the court[61] will trigger false imprisonment.

Some cases in England have considered whether mistreatment or more stringent confinement than is authorised by law constitutes false imprisonment. To date, the view has been taken that these do not constitute false imprisonment on the basis that there is no entitlement to release and no residual liberty interests in those circumstances.[62]

Whether the reluctance to extend liability in tort will ease under the influence of the Human Rights Act is not clear. That may depend on whether remedies under the Act are considered to be sufficient. That was the view tentatively expressed by the New Zealand Court of Appeal in a claim for negligence as well as Bill of Rights compensation.[63] On the other hand, in *Baigent*'s case, Gault J (who dissented from the decision of the courts to grant a remedy in damages for breach of the Bill of Rights Act) thought that the tort of false imprisonment might well have to develop under the influence of the Bill of Rights Act to deal with cases of failure to charge promptly, or provide access to counsel, or other breaches of rights.[64] So far, that suggestion has not been taken up.

In both Australia and New Zealand the character of the plaintiff has had a significant effect on the damages awarded for the torts of false imprisonment or misfeasance in public office.[65] On the other hand, exemplary damages may be appropriate where the conduct of the defendant has been high-handed or abusive. Reluctance to give undeserving plaintiffs windfalls and fears of indeterminate liability when many have been affected by the same policy characterised as high-handed are likely to curb the availability of such damages. And if, as in New Zealand, exemplary damages are confined to cases of conscious wrongdoing, their role may shrink even further.[66]

It must be expected that in many cases where officials are liable in tort there will be associated Bill of Rights Act breaches. The compensation awarded in New Zealand under the

[56] HWR Wade and CF Forsyth *Administrative Law*, 10th edn (Oxford, OUP, 2009) 639.

[57] Nevertheless, in *Simpson v Attorney-General (Baigent*'s case*)* [1994] 3 NZLR 667 (CA), the Court of Appeal awarded public law damages for breach of the New Zealand Bill of Rights Act 1990. But such damages are discretionary and available only where other remedies are not sufficient to mark the breach of rights.

[58] *Willis v Attorney-General* [1989] 3 NZLR 574 (CA), 579.

[59] *R v Governor of Brockhill Prison, ex parte Evans* [2001] 2 AC 19 (HL).

[60] ibid.

[61] *Whithair v Attorney-General* [1996] 2 NZLR 45 (CA).

[62] *R v Deputy Governor of Parkhurst Prison, ex parte Hague*; *Weldon v Home Office* [1992] 1 AC 58 (HL). The New Zealand Court of Appeal indicated some support for the decision in *Hague* in *Zaoui v Attorney-General* [2004] NZCA 573, [2005] 1 NZLR 577 (CA) [101].

[63] *Garrett v Attorney-General* [1997] 2 NZLR 332 (CA), 350.

[64] *Simpson v Attorney-General (Baigent*'s case*)* [1994] 3 NZLR 667 (CA), 711.

[65] *Manga v Attorney-General* [2000] 2 NZLR 65 (HC); *Spautz v Butterworth* (1996) 41 NSWLR 1 (CA).

[66] *Couch v Attorney-General (No 2)* [2010] NZSC 27, [2010] 3 NZLR 149.

Bill of Rights Act is discretionary and available only where other remedies (declarations, exclusion of evidence and so on) are not sufficient to mark the breach of rights.

In *Taunoa*,[67] a case where prisoners were subjected to a strict regime held to be unlawful and in breach of rights, the only claim made was for Bill of Rights compensation. The New Zealand Supreme Court emphasised the public law nature of the compensation remedy adopted in *Baigent*'s case. Three of the judges thought that compensation might be appropriate to mark the public interest in vindication of rights even if full compensation had been provided in tort to the person wronged. A majority of the Judges considered that compensation for Bill of Rights breach should be 'moderate' and should not 'generally approach the level of damages in tort'.[68] Where there has been failure to comply with the minimum standards of criminal procedure in the Bill of Rights Act there has been some disagreement in first instance decisions in New Zealand about whether the measure of damages for breach may differ according to whether there was, for example, no power to arrest or whether an arrest failed to follow the correct procedure,[69] echoing the debate that exercised the UK Supreme Court in *Lumba*.

Under the Canadian Charter of Rights and Freedoms, too, remedies for breach of the Charter rights are those the court considers 'just and appropriate in the circumstances'.[70] The Supreme Court of Canada has made it clear that the existence of a claim in tort does not bar a claimant from obtaining damages under the Charter. But such damages must not lead to a doubling up of compensation and seem also to be modest.[71] The remedy is positioned in public law. The Supreme Court has described damages awarded under section 24(1) of the Charter as serving the objectives of '(1) compensating the claimant for loss and suffering caused by the breach; (2) vindicating the right by emphasizing its importance and the gravity of the breach; and (3) deterring state agents from committing future breaches'.[72] The Chief Justice explained that vindication underlines the seriousness of the harm to the claimant, but also marks 'the harm the Charter breach causes to the state and to society'.[73]

In *Lumba*, the UK Supreme Court divided on the question whether breach of the Human Rights Act 1988 should be marked by an award of 'vindicatory damages' in addition to the nominal damages award made in respect of the claimant's false imprisonment.[74] The Judges in the minority would have made a modest conventional award of £1,000. Despite rejection of the 'causation defence' to liability for false imprisonment, a majority in the Supreme Court considered that the fact that the detention would inevitably have been lawfully imposed meant that the plaintiff was entitled to nominal damages only. The Judges in the majority were of the view that there was no occasion to introduce a new category of 'vindicatory damages' to the established categories of compensatory damages (including nominal damages for a trespassory tort where no loss could be shown) and exemplary

[67] *Taunoa v Attorney-General* [2007] NZSC 70; [2008] 1 NZLR 429.

[68] ibid [265] and [258] (Blanchard J).

[69] *Attorney-General v Niania* [1994] 3 NZLR 106 and *Caie v Attorney General* [2005] NZAR 703 (HC).

[70] Canadian Charter of Rights and Freedoms, s 24(1).

[71] See *Vancouver (City) v Ward* 2010 SCC 27, [2010] 2 SCR 28, where the award of CAN$5,000 to mark the Bill of Rights breach in respect of a strip search was upheld in addition to the CAN$5,000 in general damages for false imprisonment.

[72] ibid [31].

[73] ibid [28].

[74] *R (Lumba) v Secretary of State for the Home Department* [2011] UKSC 12, [2012] 1 AC 245.

damages. Lord Dyson explained that the 'unruly horse' of 'vindicatory damages' was not one to be set loose on 'our law':[75]

> It is one thing to say that the award of compensatory damages, whether substantial or nominal, serves a vindicatory purpose: in addition to compensating a claimant's loss, it vindicates the right that has been infringed. It is another to award a claimant an additional award, not in order to punish the wrongdoer, but to reflect the special nature of the wrong. As Lord Nicholls made clear in *Ramanoop*, discretionary vindicatory damages may be awarded for breach of the Constitution of Trinidad and Tobago in order to reflect the sense of public outrage … It is a big leap to apply this reasoning to any private claim against the executive. …
>
> In my view, the purpose of vindicating a claimant's common law rights is sufficiently met by (i) an award of compensatory damages, including (in the case of strict liability torts) nominal damages where no substantial loss is proved; (ii) where appropriate, a declaration in suitable terms; and (iii) again, where appropriate, an award of exemplary damages. There is no justification for awarding vindicatory damages for false imprisonment to any of the [plaintiffs].

Whether over time the view that tort damages and Bill of Rights responses are different will remain is open to question; as is the evolution of the private law torts to better reflect the private human right.

Non-delegable Duties of Care

The important decision of the UK Supreme Court in *Woodland v Essex County Council*[76] builds on Australian authority[77] in holding that non-delegable duties of care are owed, outside the hazard cases, where the defendant has a pre-existing relationship under which it owes a vulnerable or dependent claimant placed in its care a duty of protection and a third party to whom it delegates the care causes harm through the performance of the very function delegated to him. A non-delegable duty of this nature can only arise where it is fair, just and reasonable to impute it: 'the courts should be sensitive about imposing unreasonable financial burdens on those providing critical public services'.[78] Significantly Lord Sumption, who delivered the principal decision, pointed out that it was 'important to bear in mind that until relatively recently, most of the functions now routinely delegated by schools to independent contractors would have been performed by staff for whom the authority would have been vicariously liable'.[79]

In *State of New South Wales v Lepore*,[80] cited by Lord Sumption, Gaudron J had adverted to categories of those especially vulnerable, in respect of whom a non-delegable positive duty to protect was appropriate. They involved institutions for the young or vulnerable, such as 'schools, prisons, nursing homes, old peoples' homes and geriatric wards'.[81]

[75] ibid [100]–[101].

[76] *Woodland v Essex County Council* [2013] UKSC 66, [2014] 1 AC 557.

[77] *Commonwealth v Introvigne* (1982) 150 CLR 258 (HCA); *Kondis v State Transport Authority* (1984) 154 CLR 672 (HCA); *New South Wales v Lepore* [2003] HCA 4, (2003) 212 CLR 511 (HCA).

[78] *Woodland v Essex County Council* [2013] UKSC 66, [2014] 1 AC 557 [25].

[79] ibid [25].

[80] *New South Wales v Lepore* [2003] HCA 4, (2003) 212 CLR 511 (HCA).

[81] ibid [123], quoting *Lister v Hesley Hall Ltd* [2002] 1 AC 215 (HL), 250 (Lord Millett).

In New Zealand, the Supreme Court has yet to consider non-delegable duties of care. Liability for harm suffered by children placed in foster homes was imposed on the Crown in extension of vicarious liability.[82] The non-delegable duty of care may provide a more principled basis for further development.

Duty of Care and its Breach

Whether there is a duty of care not to cause harm to the plaintiff is inevitably a judgment. Much comfort, better predictability, and some efficiency is to be gained from proceeding by analogy with cases previously decided. That is common law methodology after all, and is good policy. In novel cases, the only sure method is close attention to the features of the case from which the judgment is made: in other words, as the Australians would have it, the 'salient features'.[83] Sooner, rather than later, it is better to focus on the facts because, as Peter Birks said 'no right can be understood without understanding the events which bring it into being':[84]

> You owe me five farthings! The immediate response is 'why?', meaning because of what facts. This is the very heart of the law of obligations. Upon what facts do obligations arise? Or, synonymously, what are their causative events?

Further control for floodgates concerns than is provided by a test of foreseeability alone in establishing whether a duty of care exists is necessary to meet the 'untidy complexity of life' and considerations of 'practical justice'.[85] But now that a little distance has been achieved from *Anns* and *Murphy*, perhaps it may be said that it is hard to see what all the fuss was really about. In New Zealand it was never thought that Lord Wilberforce's formulation of a two-step test had omitted considerations of proximity.[86]

While duty of care remains an important filter, greater focus on breach was overdue. Some considerations may equally be relevant to duty of care or breach. While it may not matter greatly in cases that go to trial whether a policy factor is considered in connection with duty of care or its breach, on strike-out on a threshold question of duty of care it may matter a great deal.[87]

Questions such as the defendant's knowledge of risk (which, as is illustrated by *Pyrenees Shire Council v Day*,[88] may be critical to liability) may well be unsuitable for determination on summary consideration. Similarly, whether budgetary constraints which make it necessary to prioritise expenditure and effort (and which apply equally to private defendants) counter the existence of a duty of care is often better taken into account in determining

[82] *S v Attorney-General* [2003] 3 NZLR 450 (CA).

[83] *Perre v Apand Pty Ltd* [1999] HCA 36, (1999) 198 CLR 180, 253 (Gummow J); and *Graham Barclay Oysters Pty Ltd v Ryan* [2002] HCA 54, (2002) 211 CLR 540, 597–98 (Gummow and Hayne JJ).

[84] P Birks 'Definition and Division: a Meditation on Institutes 3.13' in P Birks (ed), *The Classification of Obligations* (Oxford, Clarendon Press, 1997) 17.

[85] *Smith v Littlewoods Organisation Ltd* [1987] AC 241, 511 (Lord Goff).

[86] *South Pacific Manufacturing Co Ltd v New Zealand Security Consultants & Investigations Ltd* [1992] 2 NZLR 282, 294–95 (Cooke P).

[87] *Barrett v Enfield London Borough Council* [2001] 2 AC 550 (HL), 587 (Lord Hutton); *Lonrho v Fayed* [1992] 1 AC 448 (HL), 470 (Lord Bridge).

[88] *Pyrenees Shire Council v Day* [1998] HCA 3, (1998) 192 CLR 330.

breach rather than duty of care, as Cory J suggested in *Just v British Columbia*.[89] The categorical responses given in cases where public authorities owe duties which may conflict (as in the care of children cases), may have been decided on a more principled basis if the obligations had been addressed in the context of breach. If, as has been suggested, the High Court of Australia has moved to place greater emphasis on breach, such a move seems to me one to be welcomed.[90]

In New Zealand, as in Canada and Australia, the fact that loss is economic only is relevant to, but does not control, the question whether it is sufficiently proximate to found a duty of care. Sir Robin Cooke, speaking of Lord Denning's 'impossible distinction', said of pure economic loss that '[e]xemplary and nominal damages aside, a plaintiff awarded monetary redress for damage to his property is essentially being compensated for economic loss. It is in his pocket, not in his person, that he has suffered'. That is the approach we have taken. Duties of care to successive owners of property have not prompted us to consider the sort of 'transference' proposed by Lord Goff.[91] We have preferred a more direct approach to questions of proximity, as the Supreme Court has confirmed, but as was explained years before by Sir Robin Cooke:[92]

> The point is simply that, prima facie, he who puts into the community an apparently sound and durable structure, intended for use in all probability by a succession of persons, should be expected to take reasonable care that it is reasonably fit for that use and does not mislead. He is not merely exercising his freedom as a citizen to pursue his own ends. He is constructing, exploiting or sanctioning something for the use of others. Unless compelling grounds to the contrary can be made out, and subject to reasonable limitations as to time or otherwise, the natural consequences of failure to take due care should be accepted.

In New Zealand, as in other jurisdictions, consequential financial loss is a question for application of remoteness principles.[93] Relational financial loss (claims based on damage to the property of others) has been allowed in New Zealand,[94] as in Canada[95] and Australia.[96] In New Zealand we have followed the more open Australian approach in *Perre v Apand*,[97] formerly followed in Canada,[98] rather than the more recent classification adopted in Canada in *Bow Valley Husky*.[99]

[89] *Just v British Columbia* [1989] 2 SCR 1228.

[90] See *Brodie v Singleton Shire Council* [2001] HCA 29, (2001) 206 CLR 512, 577–78 (Gaudron, McHugh and Gummow JJ), 601 (Kirby J).

[91] *Leigh and Sillavan Ltd v Aliakmon Shipping Co Ltd (The Aliakmon)* [1986] AC 785 (HL).

[92] R Cooke, 'An Impossible Distinction' (1991) 107 *LQR* 46, 70.

[93] In *Taupo Borough Council v Birnie* [1978] 2 NZLR 397 (CA) it extended to loss of profits.

[94] *Williams v Attorney-General* [1990] 1 NZLR 646 (CA); *Riddell v Porteous* [1999] 1 NZLR 1 (CA).

[95] *Canada National Railway Co v Norsk Pacific Steamship Co Ltd* [1992] 1 SCR 1021.

[96] *Caltex Oil (Australia) Pty Ltd v The Dredge 'Willemstad'* (1976) 136 CLR 529 (HCA).

[97] *Perre v Apand Pty Ltd* [1999] HCA 36, (1999) 198 CLR 180 (sale of infected potato seed, as a result of which the plaintiffs were unable to export potatoes to Western Australia), declining to depart from *Caltex Oil (Australia) Pty Ltd v The Dredge 'Willemstad'* (1976) 136 CLR 529 (HCA). And see *Barclay v Penberthy* [2012] HCA 40, (2012) 246 CLR 258 (loss suffered by a business as a result of injury to employees in plane provided for business purposes by defendant).

[98] *Canada National Railway Co v Norsk Pacific Steamship Co Ltd* [1992] 1 SCR 1021.

[99] In *Bow Valley Husky (Bermuda) Ltd v Saint John Shipbuilding Ltd* [1997] 3 SCR 1210, it was held that relational economic loss could be recovered in special cases. The three recognised categories were cases of 'transferred' loss; cases where there was a common adventure between the claimant and the party suffering direct physical loss; and shipping cases involving the law of general average. While other categories were not ruled out if policy pointed in favour of recognition of a duty, in that case any duty based on proximity was cancelled out by the fact that recognition of a duty on those facts would set up potentially indeterminate liability.

Public Duties and Powers

In *Stovin v Wise* Lord Nicholls found proximity in the functions of the authority conferred by legislation.[100] 'Parliament', he said, 'confers powers on public authorities for a purpose':[101]

> An authority is entrusted and charged with responsibilities, for the public good. The powers are intended to be exercised in a suitable case. Compelling the public authority to act does not represent an intrusion into private affairs in the same way as when a private individual is compelled to act.

And that was the conclusion also reached earlier by Mason J in *Sutherland Shire Council*:[102]

> It scarcely needs to be mentioned that the reasons which lie behind the common law's general reluctance to require an individual to take positive action for the benefit of others have no application to a public authority with power to take positive action for the protection of others by avoiding a risk of injury to them.

Liability in tort where public bodies fail to use such powers has variously been put on the basis of a duty to act in the circumstances and the general reliance that members of the community are entitled to place on performance of the functions. In Australia and in the United Kingdom, there has been a retreat from a concept of general reliance in finding a duty of care in the context of statutory responsibilities.[103] But how statutory responsibilities are treated by a community is inevitably highly material to questions of proximity. While the fiction may not be necessary, the metaphor (as Kirby J described it) is surely useful. Where there is no real choice but to rely on those with statutory responsibilities to perform their obligations with reasonable care, imputing indirect reliance is a commonsense approach 'at least if the factors point otherwise to a duty of care', as Cooke P was careful to point out.[104]

The statute may, of course, be inconsistent with a duty of care. And close attention to the statutory scheme is important. Where the statutory scheme does not exclude liability, however, the legislative response to perceived vulnerability may well be a strong argument in favour of liability in tort. I do not think it is right to criticise this approach as imposing 'leapfrog liability',[105] for the reasons given by Wilson J in Canada in *Kamloops*:[106] those with duties to check were set up to protect against the very risk that in these cases has eventuated.

In *Invercargill City Council v Hamlin*, the Privy Council referred to the fact that new building legislation in New Zealand had not sought to change the approach taken to liability in the case law.[107] It treated that circumstance as justifying departure from *Murphy v Brentwood District Council*[108] in New Zealand conditions. If anything, the Privy Council understated the effect of the new legislation, which replaced the earlier and more open-ended

[100] *Stovin v Wise* [1996] 1 AC 923 (HL).
[101] ibid 935.
[102] *Sutherland Shire Council v Heyman* (1985) 157 CLR 424, 468.
[103] *Pyrenees Shire Council v Day* [1998] HCA 3, (1998) 192 CLR 330; and *Gorringe v Calderdale Metropolitan Borough Council* [2004] 1 WLR 1057 (HL).
[104] *South Pacific Manufacturing Co Ltd* [1992] 2 NZLR 282 (CA), 297.
[105] Harlow, above n 22, 16–17.
[106] *Kamloops v Nielsen* [1984] 2 SCR 2, 33.
[107] *Invercargill City Council v Hamlin* [1996] 1 NZLR 513 (PC), 522.
[108] *Murphy v Brentwood District Council* [1991] 1 AC 398 (HL).

responsibilities of local authorities to regulate the construction of buildings with a system of assurance of building code compliance which included as an element recognition of tortious liability. The legislature seems to agree that liability of local authorities suits New Zealand conditions.

Despite *Hamlin*, the extensive widespread failure in New Zealand of buildings to meet weather-tightness standards and further legislative changes have meant that the Supreme Court has had occasion to revisit *Hamlin* and to consider its limits on a number of occasions since 2008. We have confirmed the approach followed in New Zealand for 30 years,[109] declined to confine it to modest homes (which would have set up asymmetry between the liability of local authorities and the liability of private certifiers),[110] and have applied it to buildings with mixed residential and commercial purposes.[111] We have, by majority, declined to recognise a duty of care on the part of the regulatory authority which supervised local authorities in their functions and set building standards.[112]

Different jurisdictions will not always reach the same outcomes in cases of tortious liability of public actions, as is illustrated in relation to the liability of public bodies in building cases. They turn in part on the values preferred in different societies. And New Zealand divergence in such cases is partly explained by local legislation. But I do not think the latest destination each of us has arrived at turns on the path followed: two-step, three-step, incrementalist or atomist. Since negligence is a relational wrong, proximity is a good enough label for connection (as long as not limited to spatial and temporal connections). And what is 'fair, just, and reasonable' is inevitably a judgment of policy. Justice Gummow is surely right that the search for some overall principle to serve as a test is a mirage.[113]

V. Concluding Thoughts

Divergence between private and public in law needs to be justified. The law of obligations, which attaches to public officials and public bodies, serves the rule of law. A sense of what is public is necessary in the law of obligations. So too, however, is the private interest in correction of wrongs or the fulfilment of promises or the redress of what is unfair or unreasonable or unconscionable. The law of obligations should not cede the ground to public law. The common law needs to be kept fit for purpose to respond to claims of private right and the needs of the societies we live in. That will not be done by shining a more powerful light on a diminishing body of doctrine. It is necessary to engage with the values of legislation and the scope changes in enacted law leave for the common law.

[109] *North Shore City Council v Body Corporate 188529* [2010] NZSC 158, [2011] 2 NZLR 289.

[110] *McNamara v Auckland City Council* [2012] NZSC 34, [2012] 3 NZLR 701. Private certifiers could not under the legislation contract out of liability for negligence.

[111] *Body Corporate No 207624 v North Shore City Council [Spencer on Byron]* [2012] NZSC 83, [2013] 2 NZLR 297.

[112] *North Shore City Council v Attorney-General* [2012] NZSC 49, [2012] 3 NZLR 341.

[113] *Vairy v Wyong Shire Council* (2005) 223 CLR 422 (HCA), 445.

It was a great privilege to attend the conference. The work of scholars of the calibre assembled is of the greatest help to judges in all jurisdictions. Judges dealing with the press of cases, responding to actual controversies, need such help in understanding the architecture of the law, so that they do not get lost in the thicket of the single instances. And for final courts of appeal, the critiques of judgments and the windows provided into comparative legal reasoning, is essential. It was good to be able to put faces to so many whose work I have found immensely valuable and to say to your faces how much it is appreciated.

8

The Tort Liability of Public Authorities: A Comparative Analysis

PETER CANE*

I. Introduction

The aim of this chapter is to explore, and offer an explanation of, a striking difference between US law, on the one hand, and English and Australian law, on the other, in relation to the tort liability of public authorities, namely, the central role of the concept of 'sovereign immunity' in US law as compared with English and Australian law. The proffered explanation is in terms of a distinction between two models of the tort liability of public authorities, namely, a private law model and a public law model. To explain this distinction it is necessary, first, to contrast pure and hybrid versions of these two models.

In a *pure* private law model, private tort law, ie, tort law as it applies to relations between private individuals, would apply unmodified to relations between private individuals and public authorities. In a *pure* public law model, there would be a categorical distinction between private tort law applicable to relations between private individuals and public tort law applicable to relations between private individuals and public authorities. This is not to say that in a pure public law model, private tort law and public tort law would not share common features. However, in this model, unlike the pure private law model, public tort law would be understood as a legal category distinct from and autonomous of private tort law rather than as an application of private tort law to relations between private individuals and public functionaries.

The distinction I will use in this chapter is not between a pure private law model and a pure public law model but between impure or hybrid versions of these two models. From this point onwards, the terms 'private law model' and the 'public law model' should be read as references to the hybrid versions of these models. In the (hybrid) private law model, private tort law applies not only to relations between private individuals but also to relations between private individuals and public authorities. However, in this model the substantive law of tort as it applies between private individuals may be modified in its application to relations between private individuals and public authorities to take account of the difference between a private individual pursuing personal projects and purposes, and a public

* Research for this chapter was partly funded by the Australian Research Council. Thanks to Zsofia Korosy for research support and to Anthony Sebok for helpful discussion.

authority pursuing public projects and purposes. In the private law model, tort law as it applies to relations between private individuals and public authorities is understood as an extension, to relations between private individuals and public authorities, of tort law as it applies to relations between private individuals.

In the (hybrid) public law model, by contrast, not only may the difference between a private individual and a public authority affect the substantive law; it is also reflected in different understandings of the basic function(s) of tort law as it applies to relations between private individuals, on the one hand, and relations between private individuals and public authorities, on the other. In the private law model, the functions of tort law as it applies to relations between private individuals—whatever they might be—are also functions of tort law as it applies to relations between private individuals and public authorities. By contrast, in the hybrid public law model, the functions of tort law as it applies to relations between private individuals and public authorities are understood not in terms of the functions of private tort law but in terms of the functions of other mechanisms for controlling the exercise of public power, such as judicial review. Put differently, in the public law model, tort law as it applies to relations between private individuals and public authorities is understood as an analogue of other public law controls on the exercise of public power.

My main argument (and the explanation I offer in relation to sovereign immunity) is that US law rests on a public law model of public authority tort liability, whereas English and Australian law rest on a private law model. In this chapter, I will also suggest, by way of conclusion, that the distinction between the private law and public law models of tort law is associated with a distinction between two different understandings of the nature and functions of law: non-instrumentalist and instrumentalist, respectively.

In what follows, the term 'tort' will be used in a broad sense. In this sense, a tort is a wrong, and tort liability is wrong-based. Tortious wrongs are distinguished from contractual wrongs, on the one hand, and equitable wrongs, on the other. In principle, a monetary remedy is always available to satisfy a tort claim, even if the remedy is limited to nominal damages. A tort is not necessarily a private law wrong. In particular, there may be torts that only public authorities (as opposed to private individuals) can commit. An example in Anglo-Australian law is the tort of misfeasance in public office. An example in US law is the liability for breach of the Constitution recognised in *Bivens v Six Unknown Named Agents of the Federal Bureau of Narcotics*.[1] There are three possible sources of tort liability, broadly understood: common law (ie, judge-made law), statute and the Constitution. Thus, we can refer respectively to common law torts, statutory torts and constitutional torts.

II. Development of the Law

The first step in the analysis is to trace the history of the development of the law governing tort liability of public officials and agencies in our three jurisdictions. The relevant law in

[1] *Bivens v Six Unknown Named Agents of the Federal Bureau of Narcotics* 403 US 388 (1971). Rules that create torts that only public functionaries can commit impose obligations on them but give them no rights. By contrast, rules that create torts that may be committed by private individuals as well as public functionaries impose obligations on both groups but also give both rights.

all three systems is extremely complex and unsettled. Fortunately, for our purposes, much of the complexity can be ignored and reasonably brief accounts will suffice.

England

It is anachronistic to talk about 'torts' and 'tort liability' in their modern senses in respect of the period before the nineteenth century.[2] In relation to that earlier period, these terms should be understood as referring to wrongs and liabilities that we would today conceptualise as tortious. By the thirteenth century it was accepted that the monarch was subject to, not above, the law. However, in the feudal scheme of things a lord could not be sued in his own court; and it followed that the monarch, sitting at the top of the feudal ladder, could not be sued in the monarch's courts. Anyway, no-one would have thought of suing the monarch personally.[3] On the other hand, it also came to be accepted that the monarch ought, in justice, to provide some redress for citizens harmed by legal wrongs committed by royal officials. The petition of right was the first mechanism developed to provide such redress. Petitions of right were distinguished from petitions of grace. A petition of right was based on an assertion that a legal wrong had been done. In answer to a petition of right the monarch could consent to the submission of the petitioner's complaint to a court for resolution.

Because the petition of right was procedurally complex, various alternative mechanisms were developed to enable citizens to obtain judicial redress for wrongs committed by royal officials. As a result, the petition of right fell out of use from the fifteenth century. It was revived in the nineteenth century in response to the acquisition by central government of many new functions to address social and economic problems generated by the industrial revolution. The expansion of government activity made it much more likely that conduct by central government officials and agencies (as opposed to local government entities) would cause harm to individual citizens for which legal redress was expected. The petition of right procedure was streamlined by the Petitions of Right Act 1860. However, it was held that the petition of right was not available in relation to government torts.[4] The reason given was that 'the King can do no wrong', by which was meant that conduct that would be tortious if it were that of a private individual would not be tortious if it were that of the Crown. Because the petition of right procedure assumed that a wrong had been done and only had the effect of waiving the Crown's immunity from suit for that wrong, the fact that Crown conduct could not amount to a tort prevented use of the petition of right procedure in relation to torts. Even if the Crown waived its immunity from being sued in tort, it could not be held liable.

This holding was of great practical significance. By this time, most of the executive power and functions that had resided, both before and after the English Revolution, in

[2] Useful accounts include: WS Holdsworth, 'The History of Remedies Against the Crown' (1922) 38 *LQR* 141 and 280; EM Borchard, 'Government Liability in Tort' (1924) 34 *Yale Law Journal* 1 and 130; (1926) 36 *Yale Law Journal* 1, 757 and 1039; RD Watkins, *The State as a Party Litigant* (Baltimore, MD, Johns Hopkins Press, 1927); LL Jaffe, 'Suits Against Governments and Officers: Sovereign Immunity' (1963) 27 *Harvard Law Review* 1.

[3] The monarch personally is still immune from suit: Crown Proceedings Act 1947, s 40(1).

[4] *Viscount Canterbury v Attorney-General* (1843) 12 LJ Ch 281; *Tobin v R* (1864) 12 CBNS 310, 143 ER 1148; *Feather v R* (1865) 6 B&S 257, 122 ER 1191.

the monarch had shifted to ministers and departments. Although the monarch's immunity from non-consensual suit in the royal courts had originally been based on feudal ideas, it survived the demise of feudalism and shifted, with other royal prerogatives and immunities, from the monarch to the 'government'. Central government came to be understood as 'the Crown' (as opposed to the monarch personally); and the monarch's immunity from suit (except in relation to the monarch's own personal conduct) was re-conceptualised as Crown immunity attaching to central government. Therefore, the effect of the decision that the petition of right was not available in relation to torts was to immunise central government from tort liability.

The scope of Crown immunity depends on the definition of 'the Crown'. The term covers ministers of state and central government departments[5] but also extends somewhat further to include certain non-departmental agencies.[6] Leaving aside the monarch in her personal capacity, the Crown, being a metaphysical entity, necessarily acts through a legal entity, whether an individual or a corporation.[7] Probably by the end of the fifteenth century it was accepted that Crown immunity did not protect what are normally referred to as 'officials'—a term that can be taken to include individuals and agencies that act on behalf of the Crown and are, in this sense, part of the Crown. The underlying reasoning is important. The petition of right procedure assumed that a legal wrong had been done. Just as the monarch could not be sued personally, so also the monarch could not be sued vicariously for wrongs done by royal officials in their capacities as such.[8] However, in order to satisfy the general principle that legal wrongs ought to be remedied, the responsible official could be sued personally. Actions for damages against local officials were a common form of redress in the fifteenth and sixteenth centuries; and the prerogative writs were developed in the seventeenth century in order to address some of the perceived shortcomings of actions for damages.[9] By the end of the nineteenth century, Dicey was able to make a virtue of necessity by placing the personal liability of public officials at the very centre of his concept of the rule of law.[10] Moreover, it was firmly established by the middle of the nineteenth century that public agencies that were not part of the Crown could be sued in tort in the same way as a private individual.[11]

Crown immunity from tort liability (and, by implication, from being sued in tort) was selectively modified by the Crown Proceedings Act (CPA) 1947. The Act imposes on the Crown, as 'if it were a private person of full age and capacity',[12] vicarious liability for the torts of its servants and agents (and independent contractors), and direct (personal) liability

[5] *Town Investments Ltd v Department of the Environment* [1978] AC 359, 381 (Lord Diplock).

[6] P Cane, *Administrative Law*, 5th edn (Oxford, OUP, 2011) 340–44.

[7] Of course, a corporation, being a metaphysical entity, also necessarily acts through a natural person.

[8] Nor could a superior officer of the Crown be held vicariously liable for the torts of a subordinate officer: T Cornford, 'Legal Remedies Against the Crown and its Officers Before and After *M*' in M Sunkin and S Payne (eds), *The Nature of the Crown: A Legal and Political Analysis* (Oxford, OUP, 1999) 239–40. In modern law, vicarious liability rests not on authorisation or control of the superior by the subordinate but on the nature of the relationship between them and the connection between that relationship and the tortious conduct.

[9] EG Henderson, *Foundations of English Administrative Law: Certiorari and Mandamus in the Seventeenth Century* (Cambridge, MA, Harvard University Press, 1963) 34–35; JH Baker, *Introduction to English Legal History*, 4th edn (London, Butterworths LexisNexis, 2002) 144.

[10] AV Dicey, *An Introduction to the Study of the Law of the Constitution*, 10th edn (ECS Wade) (first published in 1885, London, Macmillan, 1959) 193–95.

[11] See, eg, *Mersey Docks and Harbour Board Trustees v Gibbs* (1866) LR 1 HL 93. Some protection was provided by the Public Authorities Protection Act 1893: Watkins, above n 2, 47–49.

[12] Crown Proceedings Act 1947, s 2(1).

for breach of duties owed by an employer to employees and duties attaching to the occupation of land. The Act also imposes liability for breach of statutory duties that are 'binding also upon persons other than the Crown'.[13] Immunity is expressly conferred in relation to torts committed in exercising judicial functions. Gaps in the Act's coverage may be of practical significance, as in a recent case in which it was held that the Crown cannot be held directly liable to prisoners in its capacity as gaoler because such liability is not mentioned in the CPA 1947.[14] There are also special provisions in the CPA 1947 limiting the Crown's tort liability for death and injuries suffered by members of the armed forces while on duty.[15] Moreover, even where immunity has been removed, it does not follow from the fact that the Crown is amenable to suit that the relevant substantive law of tort will be applied against the Crown in the same way that it would apply against a private individual. Courts have developed various principles the effect of which is to protect the Crown and other public authorities from tort liability in relation to certain types of activities or decisions.[16] The tort liability of the Crown depends partly on the nature and scope of the statutory exceptions to the background principle of immunity, and partly on the way tort law is applied to the Crown in cases where the immunity has been removed.

State liability has been very significantly expanded as a result, first, of Britain's accession to the European Union and, secondly, of the enactment of the Human Rights Act (HRA) 1998. Under EU law, Member States can be held liable in damages for serious breaches of EU law.[17] Under section 8 of the HRA 1998, 'just satisfaction' may be awarded to remedy infringements of rights conferred by the European Convention on Human Rights (ECHR) by public authorities (including courts). Just satisfaction may take the form of a monetary award. In both cases, the public authority can be sued in English courts and the liability rests on the government ('the state') as such. Both EU law and ECHR law contain rules determining whether particular conduct can be attributed to the state, but neither regime imposes liability on government officials as such. In all cases, the state's liability is direct rather than vicarious, and is tort-like in nature.

United States

In the United States,[18] 'Crown immunity' was translated into 'sovereign immunity'. In the *Federalist Papers*, Alexander Hamilton wrote that 'it is inherent in the nature of sovereignty

13 Crown Proceedings Act 1947, s 2(2).

14 *Morgan v Ministry of Justice* [2010] EWHC 2248(QB). See also PW Hogg, 'Victoria's Crown Proceedings Act' (1970) 7 *Melbourne ULR* 342, 345–47. Concerning remedies see Cornford, above n 8, 245–50, 263.

15 Crown Proceedings Act 1947, s 10.

16 Cane, above n 6, ch 8.

17 ibid 314–15; P Cane, 'The Constitutional Basis of Judicial Remedies in Public Law' in P Leyland and T Woods (eds), *Administrative Law Facing the Future: Old Constraints and New Horizons* (London, Blackstone Press, 1997) 258–60. Such damages may be available for breaches of EU law by the legislature and the judiciary as well as the executive.

18 Useful accounts include: PH Schuck, *Suing Government: Citizen Remedies for Official Wrongs* (New Haven, CT, Yale University Press, 1983) ch 2; RA Cass, 'Official Liability in America: Actors and Incentives' in J Bell and AW Bradley (eds), *Governmental Liability: A Comparative Study* (London, UK National Committee of Comparative Law, 1991); RH Fallon, DJ Meltzer and DL Shapiro, *Hart and Wechsler's The Federal Courts and the Federal System* (Westbury, NY, Foundation Press, 1996) ch 9; HM Goldberg, 'Tort Liability for Federal Government Actions in the United States: An Overview' in D Fairgrieve, M Andenas and J Bell, *Tort Liability of Public Authorities in Comparative Perspective* (London, BIICL, 2002); PL Strauss, *Administrative Justice in the United States*, 2nd edn (Durham, NC, Carolina Academic Press, 2002) ch 9; DB Dobbs, PT Hayden and EM Bublick, *The Law of Torts*, 2nd edn (West, 2011).

not to be amenable to the suit of an individual *without its consent*'.[19] However, according to Erwin Chemerinsky, '[a]t the very least, the framers' intent is completely ambiguous as to sovereign immunity'.[20] The Constitution is silent on the matter. Nevertheless, in 1793 the US Supreme Court decided that a State government could be sued for breach of contract in the original jurisdiction of the Supreme Court by a citizen of another State.[21] The decision provoked a strong and quick reaction from the debt-ridden States and was reversed by the Eleventh Amendment, ratified in 1795. By the end of the nineteenth century, the implications of the amendment had been extended to an acceptance that the Federal government, as well as the governments of the States, was 'sovereign' and in that capacity not liable to be sued without its consent, even for breaches of the Constitution. Initially, Congress was the prime forum for dealing with monetary claims against the United States.[22] This procedure was never uncontroversial or entirely satisfactory; and in response to the press of other business, immunity was first waived in 1855 with the creation of the Court of Claims to deal with contract disputes, initially as advisor to Congress and subsequently with the power of final decision, subject to review by the Supreme Court. Other selective waivers followed, but Congress continued to be involved in dealing with monetary claims against the United States in respect of which immunity had not been waived.

In a message to Congress in 1942, President Roosevelt complained about the amount of time Congress and the President were spending on dealing with individual complaints against the government. The eventual result was the Federal Tort Claims Act 1946. The Act provides that '[t]he United States shall be liable … relating to tort claims, in the same manner and to the same extent as a private individual under like circumstances'.[23] However, this provision is subject to various exceptions. For instance, the United States cannot be held liable for pre-judgment interest or punitive damages. Immunity attaches to the performance of judicial and legislative functions.[24] The United States cannot be sued in tort for assault, battery, malicious prosecution or abuse of process unless the claim arises out of 'acts or omissions of investigative or law enforcement officers'.[25] Nor can it be sued in tort for libel, slander, misrepresentation, deceit or interference with contract rights. Perhaps most significantly of all, the United States cannot be sued in respect of 'the exercise or performance or the failure to exercise or perform a discretionary function or duty … whether or not the discretion involved be abused'.[26] In addition, the Supreme Court has held that strict tort liability cannot be imposed on the government[27] and that it cannot be held liable for torts of military personnel committed in the course of duty.[28]

[19] A Hamilton, J Madison and J Jay, *The Federalist Papers* (with an Introduction by L Goldman) (Oxford, OUP, 2008) 399 (*Federalist* 81) (original emphasis).

[20] E Chemerinsky, 'Against Sovereign Immunity' (2001) 53 *Stanford Law Review* 1201, 1206.

[21] *Chisholm v Georgia* 2 US (2 Dall 1793) 419.

[22] See generally FD Shimomura, 'The History of Claims Against the United States: The Evolution from a Legislative Toward a Judicial Model of Payment' (1985) 45 *Louisiana Law Review* 625. There were colonial antecedents: CA Desan, 'The Constitutional Commitment to Legislative Adjudication in the Early American Tradition' (1998) 111 *Harvard Law Review* 1381.

[23] 28 USC § 2674.

[24] The President is also absolutely immune from suit and liability in tort in respect of official acts: *Clinton v Jones* 520 US 681 (1997).

[25] 28 USC § 2680(h).

[26] 28 USC § 2680(a).

[27] *Laird v Nelms* 406 US 797 (1972).

[28] *Feres v United States* 340 US 135 (1950).

Whereas under English law the vicarious liability of the Crown for the torts of its servants and agents does not exclude the personal liability of the servant or agent, the remedy against the United States under the Federal Tort Claims Act is exclusive of any claim against the official who committed the tort,[29] even in cases where one of the statutory exceptions protects the government as such from liability.[30] On the other hand, under certain conditions Federal officials can be sued, effectively in tort, for breach of the Constitution despite the fact that the United States is not subject to such liability because it has not waived immunity in relation to such claims.[31] The value of such official liability as a substitute for government liability is conditioned by the fact that officials performing certain functions (notably judicial and legislative functions) enjoy absolute immunity from suit, and that officials generally enjoy qualified immunity, which effectively means that they can be held liable only for negligent conduct, even if the relevant cause of action has no, or a lesser, fault element so that a non-official defendant could be held liable regardless of negligence.[32] Whereas official liability may be understood as a mechanism for ameliorating the harshness of sovereign immunity, the rules about absolute and qualified immunity may be understood, in part, as ameliorating the harshness of imposing liability on individual officials in respect of the performance of their public functions.[33]

Despite the various statutory waivers of immunity from tort liability, the Supreme Court has repeatedly reasserted the basic rule of sovereign immunity in relation to the Federal government.[34] Furthermore, it adheres to a principle that waivers are to be interpreted strictly in favour of the government. In recent years, the Supreme Court has also contracted rather than expanded the constitutional liability of Federal officials.[35]

Australia

The basic rule of Crown immunity from tort liability and the petition of right procedure were both received, along with the generality of English law, into the law of the

[29] 28 USC § 2676. This provision was introduced in 1988 by what is known as the 'Westfall Act'. In 1941 a government inquiry stated that 'a private action for damages' against an official was 'the basic judicial remedy for the protection of individual rights against illegal official action': Fallon, Meltzer and Shapiro, above n 18, at 995–96.

[30] Goldberg, above n 18, at 527.

[31] *Bivens v Six Unknown Named Agents of the Federal Bureau of Narcotics* 403 US 388 (1971).

[32] YS Lee, 'The Judicial Theory of a Reasonable Public Servant' (2004) 64 *Public Administration Review* 425. On the early development of official immunity see A Woolhandler, 'Patterns of Official Immunity and Accountability' (1987) 37 *Case Western Reserve Law Review* 396; S Kian, 'The Path of the Constitution: The Original System of Remedies, How it Changed, and How the Court Responded' (2012) 87 *New York University Law Review* 132, 132–58. For empirical data supporting the claim that qualified immunity rarely affects the outcome of a claim under *Bivens v Six Unknown Named Agents of Federal Bureau of Narcotics* see AA Reinert, 'Measuring the Success of *Bivens* Litigation and its Consequences for the Individual Liability Model' (2010) 62 *Stanford Law Review* 809.

[33] There are, of course, additional justifications for absolute judicial and legislative immunity, for instance.

[34] In about 30 States, sovereign immunity has been generally waived subject to exceptions. In others, the basic rule is retained subject to specific waivers. In a few, broad immunity is retained: Dobbs, Hayden and Bublick, above n 18, 362. Nevertheless, '[v]ery substantial areas of immunity remain even under the most liberal statutes': ibid 365.

[35] VC Jackson, 'Suing the Federal Government: Sovereignty, Immunity, and Judicial Independence' (2003) 35 *George Washington International Law Journal* 521, 565–66; A Bernstein, 'Congressional Will and the Role of the Executive in *Bivens* Actions: What is Special about Special Factors?' (2011) 45 *Indiana Law Review* 719.

various Australian colonies.[36] The first local development was the enactment, from the 1850s onwards, of statutory provisions that replaced the petition of right with a similar procedure that did not, however, require the consent of the government. In 1887, the Privy Council held that such provisions were effective to impose tort liability.[37] By the time of Federation, all but one of the colonies had gone further by enacting general provisions to the effect that in claims against the government, the rights of the parties would be 'the same' or 'as nearly as possible be the same' as in a case between citizen and citizen. A corollary of this general rule was the vicarious liability of governments for the torts of their officials. The full force of vicarious liability was lessened by a judge-made rule that the government would not be liable for torts committed by an official exercising 'independent discretion'.[38] Importantly, this limitation on vicarious liability applied to police officers not only in Australia but also in England, but has now been reversed by statute in both places.

The Australian Constitution gives the Parliament power to 'make laws conferring rights to proceed against the Commonwealth or a state in respect of matters within the limits of the judicial power' (section 78). In exercise of this power, section 64 of the Judiciary Act 1903 provides that 'in any suit to which the Commonwealth or a State is a party, the rights of parties shall as nearly as possible be the same, and judgment may be given and costs awarded on either side, as in a suit between subject and subject'. Section 56 confers on the High Court and State courts jurisdiction to hear claims against the Commonwealth 'whether in contract or in tort'. The effect of these various provisions is understood to be that the Commonwealth government has never enjoyed any immunity from suit. To the extent that immunity is considered to serve legitimate public purposes, those purposes can be promoted by reference to the phrase (or concept) 'as nearly as possible' to justify treating a government defendant differently from the way a private individual would be treated in similar circumstances (whether more or less favourably).

Perhaps because the Australian Constitution is concerned almost entirely with distribution of power between the Commonwealth and the States and between the various organs of the federal government, and contains very few express or implied protections for individual rights, Australian law recognises no category of constitutional torts.[39] In other words, under Australian law there is no liability for breach of the Constitution as such. Only if a breach of the Constitution also amounts to a common law or statutory wrong will it be actionable in damages.

Comparative Analysis

Amongst our three jurisdictions, the starkest contrast is between US law and Australian law. The starting point of US law is sovereign immunity: the principle that the

[36] Useful accounts include: M Aronson and H Whitmore, *Public Torts and Contracts* (Sydney, Law Book Company, 1982) ch 1; P Finn, *Law and Government in Colonial Australia* (Melbourne, OUP, 1987) ch 6; PD Finn, 'Claims Against the Government' in *Essays on Law and Government*, vol 2, *The Citizen and the State in the Courts* (North Ryde, NSW, LBC Information Services, 1996); P Cane and L McDonald, *Principles of Administrative Law: Legal Regulation of Governance*, 2nd edn (Melbourne, OUP, 2012) 282–90; M Leeming, *Authority to Decide: The Law of Jurisdiction in Australia* (Sydney, Federation Press, 2013) ch 8.

[37] *Farnell v Bowman* (1887) 12 App Cas 643.

[38] For a modern account of the rule see K Barker, P Cane, M Lunney and F Trindade, *The Law of Torts in Australia*, 5th edn (Melbourne, OUP, 2012) 757–59.

[39] *Lange v Australian Broadcasting Corporation* (1997) 189 CLR 520, 563; M Leeming, 'Common Law Within Three Federations' (2007) 18 *Public Law Review* 186, 198.

United States cannot be sued without its consent. By contrast, the starting point of Australian law is that the Commonwealth government can be sued and held liable as if it were a citizen, subject to such modifications as may be appropriate, in the application of substantive law, to take account of the identity and role of the defendant as a public authority. A corollary of the US starting point of sovereign immunity is an emphasis on the distinction between the liability of the sovereign and the liability of officials of the sovereign. To the extent that the sovereign is immune from liability, the principle of legality demands that officials who act on behalf of the sovereign should be amenable to suit and liability. By contrast, the amenability of officials to liability is much less important where the government can be held vicariously liable for the torts of its officials. Nevertheless, even in that case the government may escape liability where no responsible official for which the government is vicariously liable can be identified and the government is not subject to direct liability.

Leaving aside liability under EU law and the HRA 1998, the English position falls somewhere between that in the United States and that in Australia. Technically, the starting point is Crown immunity. In practice, however, the effect of the waiver in respect of vicarious liability has been to embed a general principle of government liability. Cases in which the Crown can potentially be held liable neither directly nor vicariously are quite rare. As a result, the standard technique for protecting the government from tort liability in circumstances where this is considered appropriate is to modify the substantive rules of liability in their application to public authorities rather than to rely on the background principle of immunity. In the United States, by contrast, although manipulation of substantive rules of liability plays a part in protecting the government, the basic principle of sovereign immunity is still extremely important both in principle and practice.

III. Explaining the Law

These patterns of similarity and difference present various puzzles that it is the aim of this chapter to unravel and explain. In relation to the United States, the biggest puzzles are why sovereign immunity became embedded in the law in the nineteenth century and why it has persisted so strongly to the present day. In relation to Australia, by contrast, the most obvious question is how and why the historical legacy of Crown immunity was so soon and so comprehensively renounced. Concerning England, the phenomenon perhaps most requiring explanation is how the practice of extensive state liability can co-exist with the continued adherence, in theory anyway, to a foundational principle of Crown immunity.

United States

The acceptance and persistence of sovereign immunity in US law are puzzling for various reasons. Indeed, they have often been considered a mystery[40] and attributed (somewhat implausibly) to no more than judicial misunderstanding of English law by US judges in

[40] Cass, above n 18, 113–14.

the nineteenth century.[41] In the first place, how is sovereign immunity, in the sense of the immunity of the government from suit without its consent, to be reconciled with the founding myth of the US Constitution and system of government, namely, that sovereignty resides in the people and that all organs of government are delegates of the people—in other words, that none is sovereign in the sense that the English monarch was sovereign or the English Parliament is sovereign? Secondly, what is the source of the rule of sovereign immunity? As we have seen, the Constitution is silent on the issue and no statute has ever enacted the doctrine. The Eleventh Amendment, in its terms, deals only with the liability of state governments and only in relation to actions by citizens of other states brought in federal courts. The standard explanation is that the 'common law' is the source of the rule. However, given the limited role of common law as a source of federal law,[42] it is surprising that so fundamental and important a doctrine as sovereign immunity is attributed to the judges rather than to the Constitution. Thirdly, it has been strongly argued that sovereign immunity is not only absent from the Constitution but is actually inconsistent with it.[43] It also seems to be in conflict or, at least, in tension with the spirit if not the letter of the foundational decision in *Marbury v Madison*.[44]

A fourth and different type of puzzle arises from the contrast between the ethos of sovereign immunity and the extremely active role that US courts play in protecting constitutional rights from government infringement and encroachment. Not only does US law recognise damages liability for breaches of constitutional rights but also, by creative use of the remedy of injunction, US courts have become deeply involved in reform and even management of public administration not only by making policy but also by overseeing its execution. By entertaining large-scale, public interest and structural reform litigation in relation, for instance, to conditions in prisons and racial segregation in schools, US courts have expanded the judicial function far beyond what is considered constitutionally appropriate or acceptable in England and Australia.[45]

In the face of these various puzzles, describing acceptance and persistence of sovereign immunity as mysteries based on misunderstanding is weak and unsatisfying, even if perhaps explicable as a reflection of a common normative judgement that the doctrine is unjustifiable, ought never to have been adopted, and ought to be abandoned. I suggest that a more illuminating and plausible explanation may be available.

In eighteenth-century colonial America a strong tradition had become established that claims against the government would be dealt with by petition to the legislature rather

[41] The latter view was that of EM Borchard, 'Government Liability in Tort' (1924) 34 *Yale Law Journal* 1.

[42] Federal courts have very little power to make law outside the context of interpreting and applying the Constitution and statutes. See, eg, TW Merrill, 'The Common Law Powers of Federal Courts' (1985) 52 *University of Chicago Law Review* 1; J Tidmarch and BJ Murray, 'A Theory of Federal Common Law' (2006) 100 *Northwestern University Law Review* 585.

[43] E Chemerinsky, 'Against Sovereign Immunity' (2001) 53 *Stanford Law Review* 1201. But contrast A Hill, 'In Defense of Our Law of Sovereign Immunity' (2001) 42 *Boston College Law Review* 485.

[44] *Marbury v Madison* 5 US 137 (1 Cranch 1803). In fact, although the Court held that it had no jurisdiction to make an order of mandamus against the Secretary of State, it made clear that in principle such an order could be made. The Court subsequently held that the Federal Court for the District of Columbia had jurisdiction to make such an order. This was the only Federal Court with such jurisdiction until 1962!

[45] JC Yoo, 'Who Measures the Chancellors Foot? The Inherent and Remedial Authority of the Federal Courts' (1996) 84 *California Law Review* 1121.

than by suit in a court.[46] When it came to drafting a federal constitution, one of the fears of the anti-federalists was that the new Federal courts would entertain suits against the States. The statement by Alexander Hamilton quoted earlier addressed this concern. It is not surprising, therefore, that the decision in *Chisholm v Georgia* attracted such a strong and quick reaction, manifested in the Eleventh Amendment. At the Federal level, amongst the first actions of the new Congress was the establishment of an administrative procedure for handling claims against the United States. However, this procedure was not intended to be exclusive, and Congress enacted its first private claims Bill in September 1789. For the next 150 years, Congress would continue to be directly involved in the handling of claims against the United States.[47]

Relevant to understanding the role of Congress in handling claims is an important difference between the US system of government, on the one hand, and the English and Australian systems, on the other, in respect of taxation and appropriation. In the English and Australian systems, the executive makes proposals to the legislature for the raising and expenditure of revenue, and the legislature reacts to those proposals. This arrangement has deep historical roots. English monarchs had two sources of revenue. One was income generated by royal assets and the exercise of prerogative powers, for instance, powers to impose customs duties. The monarch did not need Parliament's consent or co-operation to secure and exploit this source of revenue. The monarch needed to go to Parliament to request resources only when the monarch's personal and prerogative assets were inadequate to generate sufficient income, typically to meet the costs of war. Traditionally, too, the spending of revenue, once raised, was at the discretion of the monarch. An important result of the English Revolution was to give Parliament more control over public spending. Nevertheless, even now the role of Parliament is largely reactive and such control as it has over public spending is exercised after the event.

By contrast, in the US system the constitutional power of raising and spending revenue and of paying debts[48] belongs to Congress, not the executive.[49] As a result, Congress has much more initiative and control over taxation and public spending than the English or the Australian Parliament. This was certainly true in the nineteenth century and remains true today even though, in the course of the twentieth century, Congress ceded considerable power over the federal budget and federal spending to the President. As a result of its constitutional primacy in this area, the handling of monetary claims against the government was considered an important aspect of Congress's financial responsibilities. In this light we

46 This historical account is drawn mainly from Shimomura, above n 22.

47 For a helpful account as at 1942 see A Holtzoff, 'The Handling of Claims Against the Federal Government' (1942) 9 *Law and Contemporary Problems* 311.

48 US Constitution, art I, § 8, cl 1. In *United States v Realty Co* 163 US 467 (1896), the Court found the constitutional basis of Congressional handling of claims against the government in this provision, rather than in the appropriations power: Shimomura, above n 22, 669–70.

49 K Bradshaw and D Pring, *Parliament and Congress* (London, Quartet Books, 1973) ch 7. It has also been argued that the constitutional power of Congress to create Federal courts and to regulate their jurisdiction supports sovereign immunity: Jackson, above n 35, 535–36. JE Pfander, 'Sovereign Immunity and the Right to Petition: Toward a First Amendment Right to Pursue Judicial Claims Against the Government' (1997) 91 *Northwestern University Law Review* 899, argues that the Petition Clause of the First Amendment, which guarantees the 'right of the people ... to petition the Government for a redress of grievances' creates a right of judicial redress for government wrongdoing.

may reinterpret the doctrine of sovereign immunity[50] along the following lines. For practical purposes, sovereign immunity is concerned primarily with the liability of the executive branch of government. The immunities of legislators from liability for the exercise of legislative power,[51] and of judges for the exercise of judicial power, are generally uncontroversial, at least in their core applications. Historically in the United States (as opposed to England), the effect of sovereign immunity was to channel claims against the executive to Congress rather than the courts. The effect of the rule that sovereign immunity could be waived was that Congress could legislate to allow claimants access to courts for resolution of their claims. The other option was to channel claims to the executive itself, subject to scrutiny and control by Congress. As noted above, this was done in 1789 and it remains an element of current arrangements. Under the Federal Tort Claims Act, for instance, heads of Federal agencies are expressly empowered to 'consider, ascertain, adjust, determine, compromise, and settle' claims for damages against the United States, and such settlements are declared to have final and conclusive effect.[52] Moreover, under the Act claims must first be presented to the head of the appropriate agency, who has six months to deal with the claim.[53]

Against this background, waiver of sovereign immunity can be understood in terms of what David Rosenbloom calls 'load-shedding'[54] by Congress to enable it to devote more of its resources to other activities rather than in terms of providing citizens with recourse against the government that would not otherwise be available.[55] In other words, the issue was not whether citizens would have a remedy against the government but only how that remedy would be provided, whether by administrative process, legislative enactment or judicial decision.[56] Relevant to addressing this issue was the constitutional position of Congress as the organ primarily responsible for public expenditure.

By the middle of the twentieth century, Congress had ceased to play a direct role in handling claims against the government. Claims are now handled either by the executive itself or by a court. There is a continuing, unlimited appropriation to meet judgments against the government and control by Congress is effectively limited to regulating the claims process and the incidence of claims. One result is that Congress has ceded to the courts significant power to make policy and law concerning the liability of the government. Because sovereign immunity is understood to be a common law doctrine, albeit, apparently, one of constitutional or quasi-constitutional status,[57] it would theoretically be open to the

[50] At the Federal level, anyway. Concerning the State level see Jackson, above n 35, 537–39.

[51] HJ Krent, 'Reconceptualizing Sovereign Immunity' (1992) 45 *Vanderbilt Law Review* 1529, 1541–42.

[52] 28 USC § 2672.

[53] 28 USC § 2675.

[54] DH Rosenbloom, *Building a Legislative-Centered Public Administration: Congress and the Administrative State, 1946–99* (Tuscaloosa, AL, University of Alabama Press, 2000) 110–12.

[55] Jackson, above n 35, suggests that sovereign immunity may also be understood as providing protection for the independence of the judiciary by enabling judges to avoid controversial interference with executive functions.

[56] Whether Congress has provided an alternative means of redress also played a part in the reasoning in *Bivens v Six Unknown Named Agents of Federal Bureau of Narcotics*: AA Reinert and LN Mulligan, 'Asking the First Question: Reframing *Bivens* after *Minneci*' (2013) 90 *Washington University Law Review* 1471.

[57] Notoriously, the term 'common law' is used in many different senses. Indeed, Cass, above n 18, 110, 112, suggests that it is 'loosely indicative of the body of law inherited from English common law courts, whether now codified in statute form or not and however modified from its English origins'. As used here, three connotations of the term deserve to be mentioned. First, common law is law made by judges; secondly, common law can be 'corrected' or 'changed' by judges; and thirdly, common law can be overridden by statute. To say that a common law rule such as sovereign immunity is 'constitutional' is to say that (1) it is made by judges; but (2) it cannot be 'changed' by

US Supreme Court to curtail, although perhaps not to abolish, the principle. On the contrary, however, the Supreme Court has maintained and even strengthened the rule. A possible explanation for this initially surprising state of affairs may be that the Supreme Court understands the doctrine of sovereign immunity not primarily in terms of the relationship between citizens and the government but as being concerned with the relationship between the branches of government.[58] Strong arguments have often been made against sovereign immunity understood in terms of the relationship between citizens and the government. On the other hand, perhaps there is not such a clear case against the doctrine understood in terms of inter-branch relations. Its abolition would significantly change the relationship between the legislature and the executive, on the one hand, and the judiciary and the executive, on the other. It would deprive the legislature and the judiciary of an important tool for regulating public spending. The legislature's role in regulating public spending derives from the Constitution, and the effect of legislation waiving sovereign immunity may be understood as a delegation of one aspect of this role, perhaps only temporarily or conditionally, to the judiciary.

Understood in such structural and institutional terms, the fact that the Constitution says nothing expressly about claims against the government would have no more significance than the fact that it says nothing explicitly about judicial review of legislation and executive action. On the contrary, just as judicial review of legislation and executive action are considered to be either implicit in the constitutional text or, at least, an outworking of the constitutional scheme, so the doctrine of sovereign immunity might similarly be understood as a corollary of the system of separate institutions and shared powers that the Constitution creates.[59] The puzzle would then be how the Constitution could be read to require judicial review of legislation and executive action but to deny judicial determination of monetary claims against the government. The answer, it seems, would have to turn on the fact that monetary claims have a direct impact on public spending, the primary responsibility for which is allocated by the Constitution to Congress, not the courts.

judges although it may be 'reinterpreted' or 'corrected' by them; and (3) it cannot be overridden by statute. To say that a common law rule such as sovereign immunity is 'quasi-constitutional' is to say that (1) it is made by judges; (2) it can be changed or corrected or reinterpreted by judges; and (3) it can be changed or overridden by statute only by the use of clear, unequivocal and explicit language. The rule of sovereign immunity is that the government cannot be sued unless consent to suit is given by legislation. The Supreme Court requires such legislative waivers to be clear, unequivocal and explicit and it interprets any ambiguity against the government. It seems that the rule itself, namely, that statutory consent is required for suits against the government, could not be changed by statute. The common law is important in this context not only because it is said to be the source of the rule of sovereign immunity but also because '[f]rom the earliest days, the availability of relief against federal officials resulted from a mixture of judge-made ['common law'] remedies and legislatively organised judicial jurisdiction': Jackson, above n 35, 569.

58 Remember that in the English version of the immunity rule, it was the consent of the Crown (ie, the defendant) that was required, not that of Parliament, whereas in the US version it is the consent of the legislature, not of the executive (the defendant) that is needed.

59 Krent, above n 51. According to Shimomura, the doctrine of no state liability without Congressional consent was developed in response to the creation of the Court of Claims, which ushered in a period during which the power to deal with claims against the government was shared between Congress and a court: Shimomura, above n 22, 666–70. However, the Court of Claims was understood to be an art I 'legislative court' (ie, part of the legislative branch) not an art III court (ie, part of the judicial branch) until 1953, when Congress 'declared' it to be an art III court: Shimomura, ibid 686–87. In 1982, the Court of Claims was reconstituted as the (art I) United States Claims Court, decisions of which are reviewable by the Court of Appeals for the Federal District: Shimomura, ibid 697–98.

However, this explanation creates another puzzle because in US law, the doctrine of sovereign immunity is understood to be relevant not only to claims for monetary remedies but also to claims for non-monetary remedies, notably mandatory and prohibitory orders (injunctions). Thus, in 1976 Congress amended the Administrative Procedure Act by inserting a comprehensive waiver of the immunity of the United States from claims for non-monetary relief.[60] The fact that sovereign immunity applies to non-monetary as well as monetary remedies weakens the reconciliation, suggested in the previous paragraph, between sovereign immunity from tort liability and *Marbury v Madison*. It is not clear how, if at all, the apparent tension between sovereign immunity from non-monetary remedies and the decision in *Marbury v Madison* can be resolved. Fortunately, this is not the topic here.

We have seen that in the case of monetary remedies the doctrine of sovereign immunity encouraged claims against government officials as opposed to the government itself. The doctrine had the same effect in relation to non-monetary remedies, and the enactment of the 1976 provision significantly reduced the need for, as well as the willingness of, courts to entertain claims against officials for non-monetary remedies.[61] The understanding of sovereign immunity, ie, the rule that the government cannot be sued without its consent, as being relevant equally to non-monetary as to monetary remedies underpins the claim in this chapter that the United States embodies a public law model of tort liability of public authorities. In this model, monetary remedies are understood as one possible response to a claim against the government, appropriate in certain circumstances but not in others; and like claims for non-monetary remedies, claims for monetary remedies are understood as much in terms of controlling the exercise of public power as in terms of vindicating the rights of individuals and redressing harm.

Yet another puzzle in US law is the combination of a strong doctrine of sovereign immunity with heavy judicial involvement in the reform of public administration at both the policy-making and policy execution levels. At this point in the analysis it will be helpful to introduce a distinction between two types of diffusion of public power, horizontal and vertical. Power is diffused horizontally when it is divided or shared between organs at the same level of government. Power is diffused vertically when it is divided or shared between organs at different levels of government. The analysis so far has referred to both forms of diffusion. On the one hand, the Eleventh Amendment was ratified to protect State governments from suits in federal courts brought by citizens of other States. On the other hand, I have suggested that the adoption and persistence of a strong doctrine of sovereign immunity at the Federal level can be explained in terms of diffusion of power between the various organs of the Federal government.

I now want to suggest that we can resolve the paradox, of the combination of a strong doctrine of sovereign immunity at both the Federal and State levels of US government with heavy judicial involvement in the reform of public administration, by reference to vertical diffusion of powers between Federal, State and local organs of government. In the US system, public power is highly diffused horizontally and vertically. For instance, many public services that are delivered in Australia by the Federal government or State governments are

[60] 5 USC § 702.

[61] KE Kovacs, 'Revealing Redundancy: The Tension Between Sovereign Immunity and Nonstatutory Review' (2005) 54 *Drake Law Review* 77.

delivered in the United States by local, sub-state governmental authorities. The Eleventh Amendment does not protect such entities. Moreover, in *Ex parte Young*[62] the Supreme Court held that an injunction could be issued against a state official to restrain a breach of the Constitution and that such a remedy was not barred by the Eleventh Amendment.[63] A provision of the Civil Rights Act 1871 (now referred to as 'section 1983'),[64] imposes liability on any 'person' who, 'under color of' state law, infringes another's rights under the Constitution or a Federal law. Although States are not 'persons' for the purposes of section 1983, state officials and sub-state governmental units are.[65] The amenability of state officials and sub-state agencies to suit under section 1983 has facilitated the use of courts to achieve social and institutional change, and led to their heavy involvement in reform of public administration at the levels of policy-making and execution, despite the system's commitment to a strong concept of sovereign immunity.[66] On the other hand, the strong ethos of sovereign immunity may have provided governments with political, if not legal, resources to resist judicial interference in public administration.

The remedial bases of structural reform litigation are non-monetary remedies, particularly the injunction. So far as concerns monetary remedies for governmental torts, the opinion of one leading commentator is that:

> while the US approach generates a great deal of cost in the process of evaluating claims, that process yields virtually no substantial compensation to the claimants. Studies of litigation over official harm, especially suits against officers, uniformly find that the quite considerable amount of such litigation includes a trivial number of settlements, a large number of dismissals, and numerous cases that pass the summary judgement hurdle only to fail at trial.[67]

To summarise the argument of this section: sovereign immunity from tort liability was adopted and survives in the United States because it is understood not primarily in terms of the rights of the citizen against government but rather in terms of the relationship between the various institutions of government. Similarly, damages in tort are understood not primarily as a remedy for wrongs against citizens but rather as one in a box of tools for controlling and constraining the exercise of public power.

Australia

As we have seen, reform of the doctrine of Crown immunity began in Australia at about the same time as the unavailability of the petition of right procedure in relation to tort claims was being established in England. As we have also noted, change in Australia took place in two steps: first, reform of the petition of right mechanism to remove the requirement of consent and, apparently, to give it general application; and secondly, the express application

[62] *Ex parte Young* 209 US 123 (1908).

[63] Schuck, above n 18, 46.

[64] 42 USC § 1983.

[65] Cass, above n 18, 129–30; JC Jeffries 'The Liability Rule for Constitutional Torts (2013) 99 *Virginia Law Review* 207, 232–41.

[66] See, eg, Schuck, above n 18, 47–51; CR Epp, *Making Rights Real: Activists, Bureaucrats, and the Creation of the Legalistic State* (Chicago, IL, University of Chicago Press, 2009).

[67] Cass, above n 18, 142–43.

of tort law to the Crown (ie, the government) on the same, or as nearly as possible the same, terms as it would apply to private individuals. The second step was complete in all Australian jurisdictions except Victoria by the turn of the twentieth century.

The accepted explanation for the early and complete abolition of Crown immunity in Australia was well summarised by the Privy Council in *Farnell v Bowman*,[68] in which it was held that the first phase of reform had been effective to make the Crown amenable to tort liability:

> It must be borne in mind that the local Governments in the Colonies, as pioneers of improvements, are frequently obliged to embark on undertakings which in other countries are left to private enterprise, such, for instance, as the construction of railways, canals, and other works for the construction of which it is necessary to employ many inferior officers and workmen. If, therefore, the maxim that 'the king can do no wrong' were applied to Colonial Governments in the way now contended for by the appellants [ie, to deny the amenability of the Crown to liability in tort], it would work much greater hardship than it does in England.

Because Australia was founded as a penal colony, the establishment of effective government preceded the development of a vibrant civil society. Because Australia's population, even today, is very small relative to its geographical size, and its climatic conditions are often very challenging, both large-scale private enterprise and government below the level of the colonial authorities were slow to develop. The result was that levels of government which, it was assumed, would benefit from the protection of Crown immunity and which, in the United States, would have benefited from the protection of sovereign immunity, were much more frequently and significantly in direct contact with the citizenry than their counterparts in either England or the United States, where many of the services that were provided by colonial governments in Australia were the business of private enterprise or non-sovereign governmental units. For this reason, Australian citizens were more likely to suffer injury and harm at the hands of 'sovereign' governments than their counterparts in England and the United States.

Furthermore, in Australia in the late nineteenth century, unlike America in the late eighteenth, there was no significant anti-federalist movement. As a result, the conditions that were the immediate trigger of the ratification of the Eleventh Amendment in the United States did not exist in Australia. Moreover, except in Victoria, Crown immunity had been effectively abolished in all the States by the time of federation. It has also been pointed out that whereas the Australian Constitution vests legislative power in the Queen-in-Parliament and executive power in the Queen, it vests judicial power directly in the High Court and other courts. The implication is that Federal courts are not the sovereign's, thus undermining one of the historical premises of Crown immunity.[69] There has been considerable debate in recent years about whether, at the federal level, Crown immunity was abolished by the Constitution (section 78) or by statute (sections 56 and 64 of the Judiciary Act 1903).[70] The currently accepted view is that the immunity from suit was abolished by the Constitution but that the Crown's amenability to tort liability is the result of statute.

[68] *Farnell v Bowman* (1887) 12 App Cas 643, 649.

[69] *The Commonwealth v Mewett* (1997) 191 CLR 471, 547 (Gummow and Kirby JJ).

[70] B Selway, 'The Source and Nature of the Liability in Tort of Australian Governments' [2002] *Tort Law Review* 14; G Hill, 'Private Law Actions Against the Government (Part 1): Removing the Government's Immunity from Suit in Federal Cases' (2006) 30 *Melbourne University Law Review* 716.

This means that Parliament cannot reintroduce immunity from suit but it can determine the incidence, nature and extent of the Commonwealth government's liability in tort. As in the United States, the law applicable to a tort claim against the federal government is the law of the state or territory in which the tort was committed. However, because Australia (unlike the United States) has a national common law and because the High Court (unlike the US Supreme Court) is a general court of appeal on issues of State (and Territory) law as well as issues of Federal law, the High Court has more control over the law governing the tort liability of the Federal government than the US Supreme Court has over the law governing the tort liability of the US Federal government.

Despite the fact that in all Australian jurisdictions statutory provisions establish the amenability of the top tier of government to tort liability, these provisions are almost never referred to in court decisions about government tort liability.[71] It is generally acknowledged that rules of tort law may require some modification or qualification when applied against a defendant who is a government agency or official rather than a private individual. Relevant legislative provisions address this issue through the formula that the liability of the government should be 'the same' or 'as nearly as possible the same' as that of a private individual. However, in working out the implications of the difference between private individuals, on the one hand, and government officials and agencies, on the other, courts do not refer to the statutory formula but rather treat the issue as one to be dealt with as a matter of common law (or interpretation of the statute under which the allegedly tortious action was undertaken). This perhaps indicates how completely the English heritage of Crown immunity has been repudiated in Australia. Indeed, on one view (which may be the legally correct view) the Crown in Australia was always amenable to tort liability and the English rule to the contrary was never part of Australian law.[72] This may help to explain why Australian courts in recent years have been more willing to impose liability on public authorities than their English counterparts.[73] The basic issue in Australian law is not whether, and the extent to which, government immunity from tort liability has been removed but rather the extent to which government officials and agencies require or deserve treatment different from that due to private individuals in tort law. In a significant sense, the starting point of Australian law is government liability not government immunity, and the onus of persuasion rests on the government to argue that it should be accorded special treatment.

It is certainly worthy of note that despite the much greater continuity between English and Australian law (at least for the first 200 years of European occupation of Australia) than between English and US law, Australian law has so effectively jettisoned the idea of government immunity from tort liability whereas US law has honed and refined that concept much more than English law ever did, and has given it a continuing existence that, as we shall see, it no longer has even in English law. On the other hand, the tort liability of Australian government officials and agencies, and public authorities, is of less political and social significance than the tort liability of US governmental officials and agencies because

[71] Selway, above n 70. But see G Hill, 'Private Law Actions Against the Government (Part 2): Two Unresolved Questions about Section 64 of the Judiciary Act' (2006) 29(3) *University of New South Wales Law Journal* 1.

[72] *Commonwealth v Mewett* (1997) 191 CLR 471, 542–45 (Gummow and Kirby JJ).

[73] See generally Barker *et al*, above n 38, 583–98. For a political analysis of retrenchment of public authority tort liability in the 1980s in England see D Priel, 'The Indirect Influence of Politics on Tort Liability of Public Authorities in English Law' (2013) 47 *Law and Society Review* 169.

the Australian Constitution contains few provisions protective of individual rights and Australian law does not recognise the category of constitutional torts.

England

It was argued above that the constitutional power of Congress over taxation and spending helps to explain the development of sovereign immunity in the United States. There was some English precedent for the involvement of Congress in handling claims against the government. In the medieval period, Parliament had very little control over royal spending. The monarch was, of course, entirely free to decide how to spend prerogative revenues. Originally, money granted by Parliament took the form of new sources of revenue that the monarch could exploit rather than grants of public funds; and Parliament exercised little or no control over how this 'extraordinary' revenue was spent. Things began to change in the seventeenth century as Parliament increasingly provided revenue in the form of grants and specified the purposes for which such grants were to be spent.[74] When grants made to the monarch for specific purposes were not fully spent, the surplus became available to Parliament for disbursement:

> Having no executive responsibility, the Commons could only use it to satisfy the claims of individuals. In these circumstances ... petitions for pecuniary relief multiplied vastly and members of the House were tempted to promote petitions on behalf of their friends.[75]

In order to end this practice, in 1706 the House of Commons passed a resolution to the effect that public expenditure could be approved only on the basis of a proposal by the executive. In this way, the House disabled itself from entertaining petitions for monetary relief and handed to the government complete control over money claims against the Crown. At the same time, the control over appropriation acquired by the Commons as a result of the English Revolution also put an additional hurdle in the way of claimants against the Crown. In the medieval period, the monarch was able to satisfy claims without seeking parliamentary approval. Now, claimants needed not only the Attorney-General's consent for the claim to be adjudicated but also parliamentary approval for the payment of any damages awarded by a court.[76]

As we have seen, to this day the rules that the Crown is immune from suit and not amenable to tort liability formally underpin English law as they underpin US law. However, although Crown immunity from tort liability has not been as completely removed as in Australia, for all practical purposes the starting point of English law, as of Australian law, is that tort law applies to the government as nearly as possible in the same way as it applies to private individuals. Any idea that government immunity from liability remains the law's starting point was further undermined when the European Court of Justice introduced Member State liability for serious breaches of EU law. Furthermore, the provisions of the

[74] By the end of the century, 'the authority of the House of Commons in financial matters had become fully established': PDG Thomas, *The House of Commons in the Eighteenth Century* (Oxford, Clarendon Press, 1971) 71.

[75] Bradshaw and Pring, above n 49, 310.

[76] *The Commonwealth v Mewett* (1997) 191 CLR 471, 545.

HRA 1998 that create monetary remedies for infringement of rights conferred by the European Convention of Human Rights contain no suggestion that they operate to waive state immunity from liability, and they are not understood as having that effect.

Initially, some argued that the HRA 1998 had created a new species of tort liability which, because of the quasi-constitutional status of the HRA, could meaningfully be classified as a constitutional tort. However, the UK Supreme Court has rejected this classification of liability under the HRA. It has stressed that the measure of liability under the HRA 1998, namely, just satisfaction, is significantly different from tort damages. Providing just satisfaction may not require monetary relief; and even if it does, the measure of that relief may be different from the analogous measure of tort damages. The Court has also made it clear that the purpose of liability under the HRA, namely, to address infringements of Convention rights by public authorities, is different from the role of tort law, which is to establish and enforce a regime of mutual rights and obligations. In other words, we might say that liability under the HRA 1998 is conceived as being a part of public law, not an aspect of private law.[77]

In this respect, it is also noteworthy that in English law (and also in Australian law), unlike US law, the doctrine of Crown immunity has never been understood as relevant to the availability of non-monetary public law remedies. When such remedies were originally developed in the seventeenth century they were conceptualised as 'prerogative' exercises of royal power over inferior organs of government. The prerogative writs were facilities provided by the monarch to citizens for their protection against abuse and excess of power by officials at local government level. They were not available against the Crown because the Crown was, in theory, their provider, not because the Crown was immune. By the end of the nineteenth century, when most executive power had shifted from the monarch to the elected executive, the issue of whether the prerogative writs were available against ministers inevitably arose. That they were so available was not finally settled until the end of the twentieth century in a case that also decided that the injunction is available against ministers.[78] However, the unavailability of coercive, non-monetary remedies against the government was not understood in terms of the lack of consent by the government to be amenable to these remedies. Rather, just as the prerogative writs had originally been created by the judges, so their availability against particular organs of government was understood to be a question for the judges to decide; and judicial unwillingness to award such remedies against ministers is commonly explained in terms of separation of (executive and judicial) powers.

[77] Cane, above n 6, 219–23; D Nolan, 'Negligence and Human Rights Law: The Case for Separate Development' (2013) 76 *MLR* 286.

[78] *M v Home Office* [1994] 1 AC 377. However, it seems to have been assumed since at least the middle of the nineteenth century that the prerogative writs would lie against ministers, and in practice they were frequently awarded against ministers in the twentieth century without comment. The modern counterparts of the prerogative writs (which are called 'orders') are either statutory or common law in origin and bear their prerogative heritage only in the title of the claim: *R (A) v B*, where 'R' stands for 'Regina/Rex'. By contrast, the injunction is a private law remedy and so, in principle, within the scope of Crown immunity. The Crown Proceedings Act 1947 provides that injunctions are not available in 'civil proceedings' (including tort actions) against the Crown (s 21(1)(a)), or against an officer of the Crown 'if the effect of granting the injunction … would be to give any relief against the Crown which could not have been obtained in proceedings against the Crown' (s 21(2)), but gives the court power to award a declaration *in lieu*. See further Cane, above n 17, 248–55.

We may speculate that one reason why English courts no longer think about the tort liability of government in terms of its consent to being sued is that the approach to, and understanding of, the availability of non-monetary remedies against the government has been extended to the law concerning the availability of monetary remedies against the government. In English law today, specifying the scope of the government's liability, like that of public authorities generally, is understood to be within the power of the courts, subject to the overriding force of statute. In the English and Australian way of thinking, the role of the courts in deciding the scope of the liability of public authorities and their amenability to monetary and non-monetary remedies is an important aspect of the rule of law. In the English context, despite the fact that the executive typically controls the legislature, the implication is that gaps in the coverage of the Crown Proceedings Act are better understood not as withholdings of consent to submit to judicial judgment but as legislative limits on judicial power; not as exercises of prerogative but as limitations on the role and power of the judiciary vis-à-vis the executive. Such limitations are commonly understood in terms of separation of executive and judicial power, and the relationship between government and the courts.

In US law, thinking about the amenability of the government to both monetary and non-monetary remedies is framed by the concept of sovereign immunity. In neither Australian law nor, I have argued, in English law, is thinking about government liability, whether to non-monetary or to monetary remedies, now framed by the concept of sovereign immunity but rather by understandings of separation of judicial power and the rule of law. The question in both English and Australian law is not whether the government has consented to liability but, quite directly, about the appropriate nature, incidence and scope of government liability. Put differently, the question concerns the extent to which tort law as it governs relations between private individuals should govern relations between private individuals and public authorities. This is what I mean by saying that English and Australian law adopt a private law model of public authority tort liability whereas US law adopts a public law model of public authority tort liability. In the public law model, tort law is understood as merely one of a set of possible government liabilities that are all subject to the same principle of no liability without consent. By contrast, in English and Australian law, government tort liability is understood as an application or extension of the very same species of liability that applies between private individuals. This understanding was embedded in Australian law by the turn of the twentieth century and in English law by the turn of the twenty-first century. This explains why liability under the HRA 1998 is not conceptualised as (quasi-constitutional) tort liability: it is not an application or extension of private law but a species of public law liability for a public law wrong, not a private law wrong. In English law (as in Australian law) damages are not normally available as a remedy for public law wrongs. From this perspective, the significance of section 8 of the HRA 1998 is not that it creates a new species of (quasi-constitutional) tort liability but rather that it potentially imposes monetary liability for breach of a public law wrong.

IV. Conclusion

Whatever the basis and merits of arguments for the abolition of sovereign immunity, in this chapter I have suggested that its establishment and continuance in US law may be explicable by constitutional and institutional features of the US system of government, just as its abandonment in Australia and its effective demise in England may be explicable by constitutional and institutional features of those systems of government.

Finally, I want to suggest, without much elaboration, that the distinction between the private law and public law models of the tort liability of public authorities may be associated with a contrast between two different conceptions of the nature and functions of law: non-instrumentalist and instrumentalist, respectively. Non-instrumentalism stresses the normative character of law as an embodiment of concepts such as right and wrong, and reciprocal rights and obligations. Instrumentalism, by contrast, stresses law's capacity and adaptability as means to ends. The public law model conceptualises remedies against the state as a toolkit that citizens can use both offensively and defensively, to protect their rights and interests against, and to control, abuse and excess of public power. It conceptualises immunity as a weapon of self-defence[79] that the government can deploy against citizens and the courts. By contrast, the private law model conceptualises tort remedies against the state as justified responses to wrongs done to the citizen by the state in the same way as it conceptualises remedies against citizens as justified responses to wrongs done to other citizens (or the state). For the non-instrumentalist, remedying torts, whether committed by citizens or public authorities, is about repairing and redressing wrongs, not controlling (public) power. Even more abstractly, we may associate the public law model with broad movements of intellectual thought, such as legal realism, and economic and critical analysis of law, which focus on the effects of law rather than its normativity. By contrast, we may associate the private law model with an understanding of law as a highly institutionalised analogue of interpersonal morality, focusing on what law prohibits, requires and allows rather than on what it does.

Very crudely, I think it is reasonable to say that the US approach to law is more instrumental than either the English or the Australian approaches. If that is right, it should come as no surprise that US law embodies a public law understanding of the tort liability of public authorities while English and Australian law embody a private law understanding.

[79] NW Barber, 'Self-Defence for Institutions' (2013) 72 *CLJ* 558.

9

We'll Meet Again: Convergence in the Private Law Treatment of Public Bodies

NIAMH CONNOLLY

I. Introduction

> Genes are not blueprints specifying the structure of a person; they are better thought of as *recipes* for producing a person over many years.[1]

Stories of twins brought up apart who turn out to be remarkably similar have demonstrated the unexpected power of genetic predispositions. Likewise, the story of the rejection of the doctrine of Crown immunity across the common law world reveals a clear picture of parallel development. Like separated twins, almost all our jurisdictions have steadily and increasingly embraced the principle of governmental liability in private law. The outlier is the United States, which remains committed to governmental immunities. Certainly, there were temporary divergences, as some countries moved sooner or pushed further. Nonetheless, we have all struck out determinedly in the same direction.

This pattern calls for explanation. The doctrine of Crown immunity was a firmly established feature of the common law for centuries before our tale begins in the late nineteenth century. The most evident limits on the liability of the government were the requirement for litigants to obtain permission to sue and the exclusion of tort claims. We all started from this inherited rule of immunity before our legal systems parted ways. Is it not remarkable that so many common law countries independently turned their backs on this legacy?

The explanation, I believe, lies in our shared genes. The seeds of this dramatic and sustained move away from immunities were embedded in the common law all along: they were just as much part of our legal heritage as the immunity rule itself. The liberal values of the common law inform our conceptions of private law and public law at a fundamental level. Legal culture in most common law countries has a non-instrumentalist view of private law, which emphasises the ideal of interpersonal justice in bilateral relationships. In public law, we share a commitment to the rule of law. Transplanted to the changing conditions of the twentieth and twenty-first centuries, these seeds naturally blossomed into the ideal of governmental liability.

[1] J Haidt, *The Happiness Hypothesis* (London, Arrow, 2006) 32.

In Dicey's time, other aspects of legal culture held these challenges to governmental immunity in check. The common law quietly accepted the latent contradiction between the rule of law and Crown immunity. Austin's theory of legal sovereignty was taken to militate against governmental liability. A formalist legal culture muted the objection that governmental immunity denies interpersonal justice. A strongly individualistic mindset presumed that there was always a human actor responsible for actions done on behalf of a collective entity. This view was reinforced in relation to public power because common lawyers did not view the state as a legal person. In the twentieth century, as our legal cultures evolved in broadly similar ways, these attitudes which had led us to tolerate Crown immunity in earlier times faded away. And so, it became clear that governmental immunity conflicts with our common legal culture.

We have not yet reached the end of our journey. However, the fact that we are already walking the same road because of our shared legal culture and values indicates that we can continue this process together. Some jurisdictions, which still condition governmental liability in tort on vicarious liability, should introduce direct institutional liability. The other challenges that we all face spring from the need occasionally to modify the substantive liability rules in order appropriately to apply them to governmental bodies. One reason for this is that constitutional principles reach out into bilateral private law relationships between public bodies and other people. Private law is not hermetically sealed off from public law. The final part of this chapter proposes an outline roadmap which is compatible with the legal values which have brought us this far. The rule of law does not mean that we should never vary the rules for public bodies. However, we must always be guided by the common law's commitment to defending the interests of the individual.

II. Sovereign Immunity and Its Decline in the Common Law World

Crown Immunity in the English Common Law

Our starting point is the doctrine of Crown immunity, which had been part of English law for centuries before the nineteenth century. While it was always understood that the English King was not above the law, there were significant obstacles to the idea that he could be judged by the courts.[2] How could he issue a writ or enforce an order against himself?[3] The practical solution was that the King would, without being subject to legal judgment, offer redress to aggrieved subjects.[4] The petition of right was the procedure whereby a subject asked the King to recognise a claim which would exist as a matter of right as against any

[2] WS Holdsworth, 'The History of Remedies Against the Crown' (1922) 38 *LQR* 141, 144; LL Jaffe, 'Suits Against Governments and Officers: Sovereign Immunity' (1963) 77 *Harvard Law Review* 1, 3; RFV Heuston, *Essays in Constitutional Law*, 2nd edn (London, Stevens & Sons, 1964) 33.

[3] *R v Powell* [1841] 1 QB 352, 361, 113 ER 1166; W Blackstone, *Commentaries*, 9th edn (London, 1783) vol 1, 242.

[4] Holdsworth, above n 2, 142.

other person.[5] Of course, this required a judicial enquiry to determine if the right existed on the facts. So the procedure necessarily allowed the courts to adjudicate on claims, applying the common law, after the King consented.[6] The petition of right was recognised in property, equity and contract claims.[7] Despite its discretionary origins, it came to be seen as a matter of right and was systematically granted.[8] Consequently, it was always effectively possible to sue the government, albeit with prior consent.[9] Statutes were occasionally enacted to streamline the procedure.[10] The growth in petitions of right in the nineteenth century prompted the Petitions of Right Act 1860.[11]

The other significant obstacle to suing the state was the Crown's substantive immunity from tort actions.[12] This only hardened into a firm rule in the nineteenth century.[13] The idea that the King's acts could not be characterised as wrongful even extended to exclude claims against the Crown based on vicarious liability, as the King could not be thought to have commanded his servants to commit a wrong. People who suffered harm through unlawful official actions could, however, sue the individual official responsible.[14] This device provided compensation for the victim of harm, as well as deterring wrongful infringements: each public servant was responsible to make sure he did not exceed his lawful authority.[15] Indeed, the use of private law to protect subjects' freedoms against infringement by the state was seen as central to the implementation of the rule of law in England.[16] However, this system limited recourse to those cases where harm could be attributed to a single identifiable individual.[17] It did not provide redress for systemic failures.

Administrative practices frequently softened the effect of these harsh legal rules. Sometimes the state offered people *ex gratia* compensation payments.[18] Until *Adams v Naylor*, English government departments would designate a nominal defendant to facilitate legal

[5] ibid 148.

[6] ibid 142, 151.

[7] *Pawlett v Attorney General* (1667) Hardres Rep 465, 145 ER 550; *Thomas v R* (1874) 10 LR QB 31; Holdsworth, above n 2, 143, 152; WS Holdsworth, 'The History of Remedies Against the Crown' (1922) 38 *LQR* 280.

[8] EM Borchard, 'Government Liability in Tort' (1924) 34 *Yale Law Journal* 1, 7; Holdsworth, above n 7, 291; HL Deb 4 March 1947, vol 146, cols 63, 73.

[9] Jaffe, above n 2, 3.

[10] ibid 6.

[11] Petition of Right Act 1860 (23 & 24 Vict c 34); *Davidson v Scottish Ministers* [2005] UKHL 74 [8]; G McLay, 'The Problem with Suing Sovereigns' (2010) 41 *Victoria University of Wellington Law Review* 403, 407.

[12] *Feather v R* (1865) 6 B&S 257, 122 ER 1191.

[13] PD Finn, 'Claims Against the Government Legislation' in PD Finn (ed), *Essays on Law and Government* (Sydney, Law Book Company, 1996) vol 2, 25, 26; Holdsworth, above n 7, 289; Jaffe, above n 2, 8, 19.

[14] F Blachly and M Oatman, 'Approaches to Governmental Liability in Tort: A Comparative Survey' (1942) 9 *Law and Contemporary Problems* 181, 184 ff.

[15] *Sand v Child* (1693) 3 Lev 352, 83 ER 725; *Davidson v Scottish Ministers*, above n 11, [73]; AV Dicey, *Introduction to the Study of the Law of the Constitution*, 8th edn (London, Macmillan, 1924) 33; C Harlow, 'Fault Liability in French and English Public Law' (1976) 39 *MLR* 516, 527; JCP Goldberg, 'The Constitutional Status of Tort Law: Due Process and the Right to a Law for the Redress of Wrongs' (2005) 115 *Yale Law Journal* 524, 535.

[16] *Entick v Carrington* (1765) 2 Wils KB 275, 95 ER 807; *AB v Lord Advocate* (1916) 2 SLT 200, 327; *Davidson v Scottish Ministers*, above n 11, [73]; WE Rumble (ed), *Austin: The Province of Jurisprudence Determined* (Cambridge, CUP, 1995) 221; Dicey, above n 15, 189, 382; AV Dicey, 'The Development of Administrative Law in England' (1915) 31 *LQR* 148, 152; Goldberg, above n 15, 535.

[17] *Raleigh v Goschen* (1898) 1 Ch 73; TT Arvind, 'Restraining the State Through Tort? The Crown Proceedings Act in Retrospect' in TT Arvind and J Steele (eds), *Tort Law and the Legislature: Common Law, Statute and the Dynamics of Legal Change* (Oxford, Hart, 2013) 405, 409.

[18] McLay, above n 11, 419; Australian Law Reform Commission, *The Judicial Power of the Commonwealth: A Review of the Judiciary Act 1903 and Related Legislation* (ALRC No 92, 2001) [25.14].

actions.[19] The government frequently defended and indemnified individual functionaries.[20] These mechanisms ensured that victims of harm would obtain compensation and that the cost would be borne by the state, even without legal liability. Consequently, from a pragmatic point of view, state immunity was not considered a source of great injustice.

If Crown immunity were a relic of ancient feudal principles or the divine right of kings, then it would be easy to dismiss as a glaring anachronism in any modern democracy. However, the common law doctrine was accepted in late nineteenth century thought. The question of subjecting the Sovereign to the law and to judgment had exercised political theorists throughout Europe for centuries, even after ideas of republican government emerged.[21] Like the common law rule, Grotius reasoned that the Sovereign must be above the law, not as a matter of right, but because no higher authority can judge him.[22] British legal philosophers and constitutional theorists adapted these ideas to their domestic constitutional context.[23] The views of Austin and Dicey are particularly relevant and influential. Austin believed that sovereign power is logically incapable of legal limitation.[24] He accepted that the legal Sovereign itself might submit to appear before its own courts, but if the Sovereign were sued on a positive law which it created itself, then it could always abrogate that law.[25] Given the connection between legal sovereignty and immunity, the United Kingdom's adherence to parliamentary sovereignty offered, on its face, a hospitable environment for sovereign immunity.

However, both Austin and Dicey already provided challenges to the doctrine of Crown immunity. Austin's challenge was explicit: he argued clearly that, in a system where several organs collectively constitute the Sovereign, each constituent part must be subject to the rule of the whole Sovereign. Individually, they are not sovereign but subordinate.[26] The King, like individual members of Parliament, is subject to the law.[27] So, for Austin, the common law's doctrine of immunity might be 'useful or expedient', but was certainly not an inevitable consequence of sharing in the aggregated sovereign power.[28] Dicey, on the other hand, did not himself perceive the challenge which his work posed to Crown immunity. One of his core themes was his commitment to the equality of all before the law as a core component of the rule of law.[29] He strenuously rejected the idea of administrative tribunals, so as not to exempt public officials from the ordinary law.[30] He enthusiastically endorsed the fact that the common law held individual officials liable in private law for their conduct when

[19] *Adams v Naylor* [1946] AC 543 (HL); *Royster v Cavey* [1947] 1 KB 204 (CA).

[20] HL Deb 4 March 1947, vol 146, col 63; PW Hogg, *Liability of the Crown*, 2nd edn (Sydney, Law Book Company, 1989) 82–83.

[21] JN Figgis, *Political Thought from Gerson to Grotius: 1414–1625: Seven Studies* (Kitchener, Ontario, Batoche Books, 1999).

[22] P Borschberg, *Grotius, the Social Contract and Political Resistance: A Study of the Unpublished Theses LVI*, New York University Institute for International Law and Justice Working Paper 2006/2007 (2007) 59, available at www.ssrn.com/abstract=969250.

[23] See DEC Yale, 'Hobbes and Hale on Law, Legislation and the Sovereign' (1972) 31 *CLJ* 121.

[24] Rumble, *Austin*, above n 16, 212.

[25] ibid 239.

[26] ibid 198, 218.

[27] ibid 188, 198, 218.

[28] ibid 220.

[29] Dicey, above n 15, 189.

[30] ibid 198.

serving the state. However, Dicey simultaneously accepted, without critical examination, the positive law doctrine that the King cannot be prosecuted for wrongs.[31]

This unquestioning acceptance would not last. The dramatically changing role and scale of government set the scene for people to look at governmental immunity in a new light.[32] Especially in the colonies, the state conducted large-scale development activities, which led to an increase in accidents involving governmental entities.[33] This prompted a sense that the law should respond.[34] Besides, against the background of the growth of government, people began to perceive the administration as separate from the King. This separation strained fictions like the notion that the King could do no wrong. It raised questions about the relationship between the monarch, state and government.[35] It was unclear which organs of government should benefit from Crown immunity.[36] The government's expansion also increased the appetite for judicial oversight of its conduct. Under Dicey's influence, most common lawyers resisted the notion of a special administrative law in the early twentieth century. This meant that private law was the available instrument of control, but immunities hindered its effectiveness.[37] How would the ancient doctrine of Crown immunity fare in these new conditions?

Decline of Crown Immunity

The fate of Crown immunity is clear and striking. At the beginning of the period which interests us, our common law systems shared the doctrine and the legal values which accommodated it. Yet, beginning in the late nineteenth century, jurisdictions scattered around the world began to abolish governmental immunities. First Australia and New Zealand, and later England, Canada and Ireland, repudiated the doctrine of Crown immunity. India's judiciary has embraced public law compensation claims against the state, though Parliament has not yet excised the remaining limits on liability in tort. The United States is the sole exception to this almost universal trend away from sovereign immunity.

Sub-group One: Abolition of State Immunity

Australia was the first mover to legislate to abolish governmental immunity, beginning with Queensland in 1866.[38] By the time of federation, almost all the Australian colonies

[31] ibid 24.

[32] AV Dicey 'Droit Administratif in Modern French Law' (1901) 17 *LQR* 302, 304–5.

[33] *Farnell v Bowman* (1887) 12 App Cas 643; Finn, above n 13, 31.

[34] See M Lobban, 'Common Law Reasoning and the Foundations of Modern Private Law' (2007) 32 *Australian Journal of Legal Philosophy* 39, 53–54; Australian Law Reform Commission, above n 18, [22.39].

[35] WH Moore, 'Liability for Acts of Public Servants' (1907) 23 *LQR* 12.

[36] *Gilbert v Corporation of Trinity House* (1886) 17 QBD 795, 801; *Dunbar v Guardians of Ardee Union* [1897] 2 IR 76, 88 (CA).

[37] *R v Legislative Committee of the Church Assembly, ex parte Haynes-Smith* [1928] 1 KB 411; see *City of Enfield v Development Assessment Commission* (2000) 199 CLR 135, 143–44; Heuston, above n 2, 194; RJ Tresolini, 'The Development of Administrative Law' (1951) 12 *University of Pittsburgh Law Review* 362, 370; T Bingham, *The Business of Judging* (Oxford, OUP, 2000) 207; AE Cassimatis, 'Judicial Attitudes to Judicial Review: A Comparative Examination of Justifications Offered for Restricting the Scope of Judicial Review in Australia, Canada and England' (2010) 34 *Melbourne University Law Review* 1, 11; Arvind, above n 17.

[38] Finn, above n 13, 25; Claims Against the Government Act 1866 (29 Vic No 23) (Qld).

already allowed people to sue public bodies.[39] Both the Constitution and the Judiciary Act 1903 took this line and endorse the principle of governmental liability.[40] *Commonwealth v Mewett* affirms that the Constitution itself removes the doctrine of Crown immunity.[41] The Judiciary Act 1903 attributes jurisdiction for actions in contract or tort against the Commonwealth to specific courts, and provides that the rights of the parties in cases involving the Commonwealth or a State should mirror as closely as possible the rights which exist between private parties.[42] This leaves scope for the necessary modification of substantive law to allow for the specificities of the State. Since Australia carved its own path in abolishing governmental immunity, it was mostly uninfluenced by England's Crown Proceedings Act 1947 and retains a more expansive general principle of governmental liability.[43]

Ireland also abolished Crown immunity completely. It did so, not through legislation, but through judicial interpretation of its Constitution, which did not expressly refer to the issue. The landmark 1972 Irish Supreme Court decision of *Byrne v Ireland*[44] established that people can sue the state in private law without restriction. The Supreme Court reasoned that popular sovereignty is inconsistent with state immunity.[45] All common law royal prerogatives ceased to be part of Irish law in 1922. Thereafter the King only enjoyed the powers granted to him by the people through the Constitution.[46] The Constitution gave the legislative power to Parliament and the judicial power to the courts; there was no reason why this would make the state itself above the law.[47] Far from creating governmental immunity, the whole logic of the Constitution is that the state and all its organs are subject to the law, which is inconsistent with granting it special privileges.[48] The state's constitutional duty to defend the rights of the citizen bolsters the argument: it must offer justice even against itself.[49] The Irish approach has had the most sweeping effect in removing all vestiges of governmental immunities.

In other countries, also, the Constitution has removed Crown immunity. Whereas in Ireland, the Constitution defeated a common law rule, elsewhere specific constitutional provisions invalidated pre-existing statutes. Nigeria is a case in point. After independence in 1963, Nigeria restored by statute the rule of governmental immunity in tort.[50] When a group

[39] N Seddon, 'Case Comment: *The Commonwealth v Mewett* (1997) 191 CLR 471: Common Law Actions, Commonwealth Immunity and Federal Jurisdiction' (1999) 27 *Federal Law Review* 165; Australian Law Reform Commission, above n 18, [22.14].

[40] Constitution of the Commonwealth of Australia, s 78; *Baume v Commonwealth* (1906) 4 CLR 97; G Hill, 'Private Law Actions Against the Government (Part 1): Removing the Government's Immunity from Suit in Federal Cases' (2006) 30 *Melbourne University Law Review* 716, 719.

[41] Seddon, above n 39, 169.

[42] Judiciary Act 1903 (Cth), ss 56, 58, 64; Finn, above n 13, 28, 33; Australian Law Reform Commission, above n 18, [22.35].

[43] Crown Proceedings Act 1958 (Vic), s 25; Crown Proceedings Act 1980 (Qld), s 9(2); Crown Proceedings Act 1988 (NSW), s 5; Crown Proceedings Act 1992 (ACT), s 5(1); Crown Proceedings Act 1992 (SA), s 5(1); Crown Proceedings Act 1993 (NT), s 5(1); Crown Proceedings Act 1993 (Tas), s 5(1); cf Crown Suits Act 1947 (WA), as amended by Limitation Legislation Amendment and Repeal Act 2005 (WA); see Law Reform Commission of New South Wales, Report on Proceedings By and Against the Crown (Sydney, 1976) 20–21.

[44] *Byrne v Ireland* [1972] IR 241 (IESC).

[45] ibid 262.

[46] ibid 274–75.

[47] ibid 267.

[48] ibid 299.

[49] Constitution of Ireland 1937, art 40.3; *Byrne v Ireland*, above n 44, 281, 303.

[50] Petition of Right Act 1958 (as amended by Legal Notice No 112 of 1964) (Nigeria).

of soldiers went on the rampage against citizens, the courts were unable to offer redress.[51] Then the 1979 Constitution introduced an express provision that the judicial power is competent, for all matters between government and any person, to determine their civil rights and obligations.[52] This invalidated the statute which allowed for immunity.[53] Similarly, the 1991 Constitution of Sierra Leone provides that claims may be brought against the government as of right, without prior authorisation.[54] The Sierra Leone Supreme Court held that this invalidated incompatible provisions in the Petitions of Right Act 1960.[55] Lastly, the New Zealand Bill of Rights, enacted in 1990, confers an expansive right to sue the government.

These examples, from Australia to Ireland to Sierra Leone, show that the most complete abolition of governmental immunity has usually been effected through a written constitution, though there is no reason legislation cannot achieve the same goal. In addition, constitutional assertions of the right to sue the state have become more common in the last part of the twentieth century, suggesting that the tide has completely ebbed for state immunity in recent decades.

Sub-group Two: Legislative Exceptions Substantially Erode Governmental Immunity

The second family of countries are those in which a very moth-eaten principle of Crown immunity remains on the books, but in reality has no substance. England is the prime example. England was much slower to legislate to expand the state's liability to suit than Australia or New Zealand. The Crown Proceedings Act was not introduced until 1947. This delay partly reflects a sense that no great injustice was being done, given the administrative practices which accompanied the legal doctrine of immunity. Reforms were considered from the 1920s on, at the instigation of legal and commercial groups. An important committee recommended that the Crown should in general be in the same position as other persons to sue and be sued.[56] This included liability in tort law and equal treatment concerning costs. However, opposition from some government departments led to stalemate.[57] It was only when the House of Lords condemned the practice of naming nominal defendants that the balance shifted in favour of reform.[58]

The Crown Proceedings Act 1947 does not completely abrogate the rule that the state is not liable in tort; instead it creates large exceptions.[59] This means that, in theory, the

[51] *Ransome-Kuti v Attorney-General* 1985 NWLR (Pt 6) 211; H Ogunniran, 'The Successive Demise of the Doctrine of State Immunity from Tort Liability: A Comparative Appraisal with Emphasis on the Nigerian Experience' (1992) 4 *African Journal of International and Comparative Law* 369.

[52] Constitution of 1979 (Nigeria), s 6(6)(b); Constitution of 1999 (Nigeria), s 6(6)(b).

[53] *Alhaji Chief AB Bakare v Attorney-General of the Federation* [1990] 5 NWLR 516.

[54] Constitution of Sierra Leone 1991 (Act No 6 of 1992, Sierra Leone), s 133.

[55] *All People's Congress v Nasmos* [1999] SLSC 2.

[56] Crown Proceedings Committee Report (Cmd 2842, 1927); HL Deb, 4 March 1947, vol 146, col 65; see also *Report of the Committee on Ministers' Powers* (Cmd 4060, 1932) 112.

[57] HL Deb 4 March 1947, vol 146, col 66; *Matthews v Minister of Defence* [2003] 1 AC 1163, 1185 (HL); JM Jacob, 'The Debates Behind an Act: Crown Proceedings Reform, 1920–1947' (1992) *PL* 452; Arvind, above n 17, at 406.

[58] *Adams v Naylor*, above n 19; *Royster v Cavey*, above n 19.

[59] New Zealand Law Commission Issues Paper, *A New Crown Civil Procedure Act for New Zealand* (NZLC IP35, 2014) [3.15].

principle of sovereign immunity still exists in English law.[60] However, the number of exceptions has increased over time, so that Crown immunity is greatly attenuated.[61] There are so many holes that there is no cheese left. Despite the form of the Act, England belongs among the jurisdictions which rejected governmental immunity.

New Zealand was, like Australia, a remarkably early mover against immunities but there have been many twists and turns since. From 1871, New Zealand allowed contract claims to be brought in the ordinary courts, at first with the Governor's consent.[62] By 1877, the need for prior consent and the restriction to contract were removed.[63] This provided very expansive scope for governmental liability. However, the next reform restricted liability to public works.[64] Then New Zealand enacted a statute modelled on the English Act, which excludes the direct institutional liability of public bodies.[65] Now, the New Zealand Bill of Rights unequivocally recognises a right to bring civil actions against the Crown just as against other defendants.[66] The tension between the statute and the Bill of Rights has not yet been addressed.[67] The courts also award public law damages against the government for breaches of the Bill of Rights.[68] In a legal culture which appears highly receptive to governmental liability, the 1950 Act looks anachronistic. The New Zealand Law Commission recommends reform, particularly to introduce direct liability in tort.[69]

Canada made incremental, minor reforms to governmental immunity rather than wholesale reform. From the late nineteenth century, people could sue the Crown through the petition of right procedure.[70] From 1887, they could sue the federal government for claims arising from public works.[71] In 1938, the public works restriction was replaced by vicarious liability for the negligence of public servants.[72] The only province in which governmental immunities were removed early was Quebec, whose relevant statute was interpreted to allow tort actions.[73] In the absence of significant home-grown reforms, most provinces and the federal government adopted solutions modelled closely on the English Act.[74] The requirement for permission to sue was removed and the federal government's liability in

[60] Finn, above n 13, 25; H Street, 'Tort Liability of the State: The Federal Tort Claims Act and the Crown Proceedings Act' (1949) 47 *Michigan Law Review* 341, 347, 365; Hogg, above n 20, 84.

[61] See Peter Cane, 'The Tort Liabilities of Public Authorities: A Comparative Analysis', ch 8 of this volume.

[62] Crown Redress Act 1871 (New Zealand).

[63] Crown Redress Act 1877 (New Zealand).

[64] Crown Suits Act 1881 (New Zealand); Crown Suits Act 1908 (New Zealand); Crown Suits Amendment Act 1910 (New Zealand); S Anderson, '"Grave Injustice", "Despotic Privilege": The Insecure Foundations of Crown Liability for Torts in New Zealand' (2009) 12 *Otago Law Review* 1, 14 ff.

[65] Crown Proceedings Act 1950 (New Zealand); Anderson, above n 64, 18.

[66] Bill of Rights Act 1990 (New Zealand), s 27(3); see Sian Elias, 'Public Actors and Private Obligations: A Judicial Perspective', ch 7 of this volume, text accompanying nn 4–5.

[67] See Sian Elias, ch 7 of this volume, text after n 7.

[68] *Simpson v Attorney General* [1994] 3 NZLR 667 (NZCA).

[69] New Zealand Law Commission, above n 59, [1.2].

[70] Petition of Right Act 1875 (Canada); Petition of Right Act 1876 (Canada); *Rudolph Wolff & Co v Canada* [1990] 1 SCR 695.

[71] Exchequer Court Act 1887 (Canada).

[72] Hogg, above n 20, 82; GS Lester, 'Suing the Federal Crown in Tort: Some Practical Points to Remember' (2000) 23 *Advocates' Quarterly* 444, 448.

[73] *R v Cliche* (1935) SCR 561.

[74] Uniform Model Act 1950 'An Act respecting Proceedings against the Crown' in Conference of Commissioners on Uniformity of Legislation in Canada, *Proceedings of 1950*, 76.

tort was extended to vicarious and occupier's liability.[75] This approach has left residual immunities and practical obstacles.[76]

Despite the incompleteness of Canada's statutory abolition of governmental immunity, there seems to have been a subsequent shift in favour of increased governmental liability. From the 1980s, Canadian courts expanded the circumstances in which governmental bodies were held liable in tort.[77] Interestingly, British Columbia, which waited until 1974 to reform the law, chose not to follow the English model. Instead, it provided for the full liability of the state as if it were a person.[78] The Law Reform Commission of Canada recommended in 1985 that Crown liability in tort be reformed to introduce direct institutional liability.[79] Likewise, citing the 'philosophical backdrop' of the Canadian Charter of Rights and Freedoms, Ontario's Law Reform Commission recommended that the government be open to suit in the same way as others, including direct institutional liability.[80]

Sub-group Three: Waiting for Legislative Reform

India is in a category of its own: it is very clear that governmental immunity does not fit in Indian legal culture, but Parliament has not yet abolished it. There never was a requirement to obtain a petition of right, and the Constitution provides that the national and state governments may sue and be sued directly.[81] Government contracts have certain formality requirements, but otherwise are subject to ordinary contract law.[82] The difficulties exist in relation to tort claims against the state. The Union and individual States can be liable through vicarious liability for the acts of their servants.[83] However, the Indian Supreme Court has excluded that liability when the harm arises in performance of a 'sovereign' function.[84] More recent decisions criticise this distinction between sovereign and non-sovereign powers, suggesting, as an alternative, excluding tort liability for policy decisions.[85] Commentators say that the 'sovereign functions' rule has been diluted but not overruled.[86]

[75] Crown Liability Act SC 1952–53 (Canada).

[76] PW Hogg, 'Government Liability: Assimilating Crown and Subject' (1994) 16 *Advocates' Quarterly* 366, 368; see Public Authorities Protection Act RSO 1990, c P-38 (Ontario), s 7(1); Lester, above n 72, 459; *Rudolph Wolff & Co v Canada* [1990] 1 SCR 695.

[77] Hogg, above n 76, 373; *Tock v St John's Metropolitan Area Board* (1989) 64 DLR (4th) 620; *Kamloops (City) v Neilson* (1984) 10 DLR (4th) 641; *Laurentide Motels v Beauport (City)* [1989] 1 SCR 705; *Just v British Columbia* (1989) 64 DLR (4th) 689.

[78] Crown Proceedings Act SBC 1974, c. 24 (British Columbia), s 2(c).

[79] Law Reform Commission of Canada, *The Legal Status of the Federal Administration,* Working Paper 40 (Ottawa, Law Reform Commission of Canada, 1985) 69–71.

[80] Canadian Charter of Rights and Freedoms, s 2, Part 1 of the Constitution Act 1982 (Canada); Ontario Law Reform Commission, *Report on the Liability of the Crown* (OLRC, 1989) 1, 3, 17.

[81] Constitution of India, art 300.

[82] Constitution of India, art 299; Indian Contract Act, 1872; *Bhikaraj Jaipuria v Union of India* AIR 1962 SC 113.

[83] *Secretary of State v Sheoramjee,* AIR 1952 Nag 213; *State of Rajasthan v Vidyawati* AIR 1962 SC 933; *Achut Rao Hari Bhau Kodwa v State of Maharashtra* (1996) 2 SCC 634; National Commission to Review the Working of the Constitution, Consultation Paper on Liability of the State in Tort (New Delhi, 2001) [4.3].

[84] *P & O Steam Navigation Co v Secretary of State* 5 BHCR App P 1 (Supreme Court, Calcutta); *Secretary of State v Hari Bhanji* (1882) ILR 5 Mad 273 (High Court, Madras); *Rao v Advani* AIR 1949 Bom 277, 51 Bom LR 342; *Kasturi Lal v State of Uttar Pradesh* AIR 1965 SC 1039; National Commission to Review the Working of the Constitution, above n 83, ch 3.

[85] *Nagendra Rao v State of Andhra Pradesh* AIR 1994 SC 2663, (1994) 6 SCC 205.

[86] VK Sircar, 'Compensation for Violation of Fundamental Rights: A New Remedy in Public Law Distinct from Relief of Damages in Tort' (1995) 1 *Judicial Training Research Institute Journal* 1, 3; UC Srivastava, 'Tortious Liability of State under the Constitution' (1997) *Judicial Training Research Institute Journal* 1, 3; *State of Gujarat v Memon Mohamed* AIR 1967 SC 1885; National Commission to Review the Working of the Constitution, above n 83, [1.3], [5.3], [6.4].

Parliament will have to legislate before the last vestiges of Crown immunity in private law disappear. The first report of the Law Commission in 1956 began attempts to reform the law on governmental liability. A Bill was introduced in 1967, but was defeated due to State resistance.

The remaining limitations are particularly striking given India's constitutional order. Like Ireland, India possesses a written Constitution, subscribes to popular sovereignty and permits judges to invalidate unconstitutional laws.[87] The courts award compensatory damages in public law for the infliction of harm through breaches of the Constitution.[88] This sits uneasily alongside the exemption from private law liability for actions related to 'sovereign functions'. The Supreme Court has emphasised that the lingering private law immunity cannot impede actions seeking damages under the Constitution.[89] It is quite clear that the Indian judiciary believes that the government can be liable to individual citizens whom it injures. It has been suggested that citizens can avoid the immunity problem by formulating a claim as a breach of their fundamental rights instead of a tort.[90] The overall picture seems to be that Indian law has rejected the principle of governmental immunity, even though Parliament still has not legislated on it.

Sub-group Four: Vitality of Government Immunity in the United States

When it comes to governmental immunity, the United States contrasts dramatically with other common law jurisdictions.[91] The Constitution, legislation and judicial attitudes have all been oriented towards limiting exposure to suit. Early US decisions seem to have accepted the dogma of immunity as an attribute of sovereignty without critical examination.[92] Not only do the Union and the States continue to enjoy significant immunities, but the States' immunities expanded around the turn of the millennium. The apparent willingness in the United States to continue to accept immunities is a puzzle.[93] One would have expected the United States, as a constitutionalist legal order which had broken free of monarchy, to jettison the doctrine of Crown immunity.[94]

The immunity of the States and of the United States are distinct. In *Chisholm v Georgia*, the US Supreme Court allowed a litigant to sue Georgia.[95] In response, the Eleventh Amendment to the Constitution was passed to prevent people from suing individual States without their consent.[96] Recent Supreme Court decisions have expanded States' immunity

[87] Constitution of India, art 13(2).

[88] *Nilabati Behera v State of Orissa* (1993) 2 SCC 746, AIR 1960, 1993 SCR (2) 581; *Rudul Sah v State of Bihar* 1983 AIR 1086, 1983 SCR (3) 508.

[89] *Nilabati Behera v State of Orissa*, above n 88; *Challa Ramkonda Reddy v State of Andhra Pradesh* AIR 1989 AP 235; *State of Andhra Pradesh v Chella Ramakrishna Reddy* AIR 2000 SC 2083; National Commission to Review the Working of the Constitution, above n 83, [7.1]; Sircar, above n 86.

[90] Srivastava, above n 86, 4.

[91] See Peter Cane, 'The Tort Liabilities of Public Authorities: A Comparative Analysis', ch 8 of this volume.

[92] Blachly and Oatman, above n 14, 187; Borchard, above n 8, 4, 24; *Railroad Company v Tennessee* 101 US 337, 339 (1879); *Cunningham v Macon and Brunswick Railroad* 109 US 446, 451 (1883); *Kawananakoa v Polyblank* 205 US 349, 353 (1907); *United States v Thompson* 257 US 419 (1922).

[93] Street, above n 60, 342.

[94] E Chemerinsky, 'Against Sovereign Immunity' (2001) 53 *Stanford Law Review* 1201, 1202; Jaffe, above n 2, 2.

[95] *Chisholm v Georgia* 2 US 419 (2 Dall 1793).

[96] *Hans v Louisiana* 134 US 1 (1890).

to become 'effectively absolute'.[97] The Constitution is silent concerning the Federal government but the courts extended the requirement for consent to these cases too.[98] Only Congress and State legislatures can authorise suits.[99] Commentators propose many alternative justifications for the mysterious immunity of the federal government. The Supreme Court considers sovereign immunity a background principle of constitutional law.[100] The rules on when individual officials can be sued are complex; many senior officials who exercise discretion in carrying out their functions also enjoy immunities.[101]

The Federal Tort Claims Act 1946 waived sovereign immunity for tort claims based on the negligence of employees, where other employers would be vicariously liable.[102] However, this statute has been described as 'deceptive', because there are so many exclusions.[103] It does not assist if the tort is an intentional or strict liability tort.[104] It excludes liability for discretionary functions, which is interpreted to cover all policy decisions.[105] Six hundred people died in the Texas City disaster of 1947, when fertiliser manufactured and transported by the government exploded. In *Dalehite v United States*, the Supreme Court refused a claim for compensation under the 'discretion' exception because the plaintiff was alleging defects in planning.[106] State statutes authorising suits are frequently interpreted restrictively, in particular so as to exclude claims in tort.[107] There was some movement to abolish the immunities of lower-level public entities in the 1950s and 1960s.[108] However, US law remains far more protective of public bodies than that of other common law jurisdictions.[109] The courts' enthusiasm for governmental immunity has even affected the overlap with public law compensation claims. The courts interpreted the law granting jurisdiction over claims for breach of constitutional rights restrictively to exclude jurisdiction if the constitutional claim was also a tort.[110] The liability of the individual state agent is used to sanction breaches of constitutional rights, though even here, they may enjoy qualified immunity.[111] It is clear that the United States still embraces governmental immunities.

[97] *Seminole Tribe v Florida* 517 US 44 (1996); *Alden v Maine* 527 US 706 (1999); MD Falkoff, 'Abrogating State Sovereign Immunity in Legislative Courts' (2001) 101 *Columbia Law Review* 853, 854; JR Siegel, 'Waivers of State Sovereign Immunity and the Ideology of the Eleventh Amendment' (2003) 52 *Duke Law Journal* 1167, 1170, 1183; Chemerinsky, above n 94, 1202.

[98] PF Figley and J Tidmarsh, 'The Appropriations Power and Sovereign Immunity' (2009) 107 *Michigan Law Review* 1207, 1209; Chemerinsky, above n 94, 1205.

[99] *Chisholm v Georgia* 2 US 419, 446 (2 Dall 1793); *Cohens v Virginia* 19 US 264, 411 (1821); Borchard, above n 8, 5.

[100] *Alden v Maine* 527 US 706 (1999).

[101] *Land v Dollar* 330 US 731 (1947); *Larson v Domestic and Foreign Commerce Corp* 337 US 682 (1949); *Gregoire v Biddle* 177 F 2d 579 (1949), 339 US 949 (1950); *Barr v Matteo* 360 US 564, 572–74 (1959); *Schneider v Smith* 390 US 17 (1968).

[102] Federal Tort Claims Act 1946, s 1346(b); see Street, above n 60, 350.

[103] VG Setser, 'The Immunities of the State and Government Economic Activities' (1959) 24 *Law and Contemporary Problems* 291, 302.

[104] PF Figley, 'Understanding the Federal Tort Claims Act: A Different Metaphor' (2009) 44 *Tort Trial and Insurance Practice Law Journal* 1105.

[105] Ogunniran, above n 51, 379; Street, above n 60, 352.

[106] *Dalehite v United States* 346 US 15, 42 (1953).

[107] Borchard, above n 8, 6, 9.

[108] ML Rustad, 'Twenty-First Century Tort Theories: The Internalist/Externalist Debate' (2013) 88 *Indiana Law Journal* 419, 429.

[109] Setser, above n 103, 301.

[110] *United States v North American Transportation Co* 253 US 330, 335 (1920); Street, above n 60, 344; see Fifth Amendment to the Constitution of the United States.

[111] *Bivens v Six Unknown Named Agents of the Federal Bureau of Narcotics* 403 US 388 (1971).

The Pattern Emerges: A Family Group

Widespread Rejection of Crown Immunity

Look beyond the relatively minor differences and these four categories of response resolve into just two. The United States remains committed to the doctrine of sovereign immunity. All other common law jurisdictions have resiled from it. They have universally dispensed with the need for prior consent and permitted tort actions against the state. The striking pattern which calls for explanation is the similarity of the evolution which has happened in every country except the United States.

As we have seen, the reform of governmental immunities has not been identical in every country. Some jurisdictions abolished governmental immunities in their Constitutions; others through legislation. Yet the mechanism used does not furnish an important dividing line between jurisdictions. Nor is it significant whether or not the law introduced a positive affirmation of the state's liability to civil suit, if the functional effect of the scheme is that the government is usually liable to suit. The essential unity of all these countries' rejection of immunities outweighs these differences. Along the way, differences in the timing of reform allowed significant but temporary divergence. Some differences still remain in the extent of governmental liability. Yet, all of these countries are on the same journey. The process resembles those mechanical horse-racing game machines in amusement arcades, which have a row of plastic race horses lined up on a short track. The horses jolt and shudder spasmodically along the track and it is hard to predict which will reach the finish first. Sometimes one horse advances; sometimes another. Yet they are all on exactly parallel tracks.

The United States is a case apart. It clearly falls outside the pattern which unites all of the other common law countries. Unique constitutional considerations dictate its distinctive approach to immunities. Sovereign immunity is part of a complex constitutional balance in American federalism and the separation of powers. States are sovereign within the United States, with the State legislatures representing the people.[112] The Eleventh Amendment restrains Federal judicial power.[113] In this context, upholding the principle of state immunity aims to defend the autonomy of the States.[114] In addition, at both State and Federal level, it is seen as a usurpation of the legislative power for judges to impose a financial burden on the state.[115] The citizen-litigant becomes invisible in this constitutional calculus. Since the United States has unique reasons for choosing the opposite approach to every other common law country, the anomaly of it retaining governmental immunity does not undermine the mission of seeking an explanation for the pattern which unites everyone else.

Temporary Divergence Due to Timing

Each jurisdiction reformed the law on governmental immunity at a time of its choosing. This created temporary periods of divergence. For example, in the early twentieth

[112] T Jefferson, 'Jefferson's Draft' in BB Oberg (ed), *The Papers of Thomas Jefferson* (Princeton, NJ, Princeton University Press, 2003) 30:536; J Walker, 'Interprovincial Sovereign Immunity Revisited' (1997) 35 *Osgoode Hall Law Journal* 379, 381; Figley and Tidmarsh, above n 98, 1247.

[113] Siegel, above n 97, 1219.

[114] ibid 1209.

[115] Falkoff, above n 97, 865.

century, Australia had already abolished Crown immunity, but the English courts applied the doctrine faithfully, even expansively.[116] India is still waiting for statutory reform of governmental immunity. Some countries may have reformed the law later than others, but this does not necessarily mean that their legal culture or values were very different at the time. A societal or judicial desire to remove immunities is insufficient to effect change. Nothing will happen until the competent law-makers act, and in most systems, that has been Parliament. There can be a time lag. The legislative and executive powers in a parliamentary system sometimes take longer than judges to come round to the merits of facilitating civil suits against the government.[117] Consider India: the values which support governmental liability are demonstrably present, most clearly in the award of public law damages against the state. The judges have done as much as they feel they can, but Parliament will have to take the final steps.

Besides, even while some countries steamed faster ahead, there were also elements of commonality in how legislatures responded to changing conditions and the risk of harm through public activities. In Britain,[118] the United States[119] and Canada,[120] governments legislated for compensation when the state caused harm in specific contexts: transportation, public works, workers' injuries and damage by merchant vessels. Later too, mutual influences favoured partial convergence, especially the influence of the English Act after 1947. When Canada and New Zealand adopted a model based on the English statute, this created a sub-group of countries with similar laws, even though, for New Zealand, this meant pulling back from a more liberal position.

Although all the jurisdictions concerned have now converged on a general principle of governmental liability, the differences in the timing of reform leave their marks on present law. There is a rough correlation between the timing of reform and its extent. The first wave, in the Antipodes in the nineteenth century, was an extensive abolition of immunity. The second wave, following the Crown Proceedings Act 1947, was more limited. From about the 1970s onwards, reforms and recommendations for reform have all been more complete.[121] Some of us are further along the path than others—and those who reformed later are among those who have progressed furthest.

Substantive Differences Today

A number of differences still remain between jurisdictions. In many cases, the legislation which abolished the petition of right left in place other, ancillary, privileges and immunities.[122] In Canada, for example, the reforming legislation left undisturbed privileges

[116] Arvind, above n 17, 420.

[117] Setser, above n 103, 294.

[118] Ministry of Transport Act 1919 (United Kingdom).

[119] Borchard, above n 8, 35.

[120] Exchequer Court Act 1887 (Canada).

[121] *Byrne v Ireland*, above n 44 (IESC); Crown Proceedings Act SBC 1974 (British Columbia), s 2(c); Constitution of 1979 (Nigeria), s 6(6)(b); Bill of Rights Act 1990 (New Zealand), s 27(3); Constitution of Sierra Leone 1991 (Act No 6 of 1992, Sierra Leone), s133; Law Reform Commission of Canada, above n 79; Ontario Law Reform Commission, above n 80; National Commission to Review the Working of the Constitution, above n 83; New Zealand Law Commission, above n 59.

[122] P Lagassé, 'Parliamentary and Judicial Ambivalence toward Executive Prerogative Powers in Canada' (2012) 55 *Canadian Public Administration* 157.

concerning remedies, discovery, limitation and the effect of statutes.[123] The contours of the law can be complex, and vary across jurisdictions for no particular substantive reason.

The most significant divergence which still exists lies between those countries which followed the English model and those which did not. The English model has not fully eradicated governmental immunities because it conditions governmental liability on a wrong attributable to an individual public servant. Section 2 of the Crown Proceedings Act 1947 refers only to vicarious, employer's and occupier's liability. This excludes the possibility of a public body as a corporate entity being directly responsible for a tort.[124] This interpretation was confirmed by the rejection of the claims based on unlawful exile and misfeasance in public office in *Chagos Islanders v Attorney-General*.[125] The situation is the same in Canada and New Zealand.[126] This vicarious liability model leaves gaps in compensation where loss is due to systemic failures.[127]

While we have not yet all arrived at the same point, the process of law reform to eradicate procedural barriers to governmental liability continues. The United Kingdom has removed instances of Crown immunity during the years since the passage of the Crown Proceedings Act 1947.[128] The Australian Law Reform Commission recommended in 2001 that legislation should be enacted to remove the last vestiges of privilege for the Commonwealth and States in private law matters.[129] In particular, the gap relating to direct institutional liability seems to be closing. British Columbia and the Australian States already have direct liability.[130] The current recommendations in New Zealand are for full exposure to liability, and the introduction of the direct liability of governmental bodies in tort.[131] These continuing reforms hold out the prospect that all our paths may again meet in the future.

III. Explaining Convergence: Common Legal Values

If state liability were merely the updated application of a rule which we shared before our legal systems diverged, then it would be unsurprising that this rule evolved in the same way after we drifted apart. However, none of us inherited the principle of Crown liability. We all started with the doctrine of Crown immunity and chose, independently, to reverse it. Why did all these countries, diverse in so many ways, abandon the doctrine of immunity? It is no coincidence. The reasons for repudiating immunity lie deep in our common legal culture. The normative values of the common law, as it has developed over the twentieth century,

[123] Hogg, above n 76, 369; Lester, above n 72, 444; Ontario Law Reform Commission, above n 80.

[124] Arvind, above n 17, 431; *Chagos Islanders v Attorney-General* [2004] EWCA Civ 997 [20].

[125] *Chagos Islanders v Attorney-General*, above n 124; see also *Trawnik v Lennox* (1985) 1 WLR 552 (Ch D), [1985] 2 All ER 368 (CA); *Morgan v Ministry of Justice* [2010] EWHC 2248 (QB) [25]–[26].

[126] Crown Liability and Proceedings Act, RSC 1985, c C-50, s 3(b); Lester, above n 72, 458.

[127] Hogg, above n 20, 102; see *Warwick Shipping v Canada* [1984] 1 FC 998 (CSA).

[128] Post Office Act 1969; Merchant Shipping Act 1995 (UK).

[129] Australian Law Reform Commission, above n 18, [23.1]–[23.4].

[130] Crown Proceeding Act, RSBC 1996, c 89, s 2(c); Crown Proceedings Act 1958 (Vic); Crown Proceedings Act 1980 (Qld); Crown Proceedings Act 1988 (NSW); Crown Proceedings Act 1992 (ACT); Crown Proceedings Act 1992 (SA); Crown Proceedings Act 1993 (NT); Crown Proceedings Act 1993 (Tas); Crown Suits Act 1947 (WA); see *Bowman v Farnell* (1886) 7 LR (NSW) 1.

[131] New Zealand Law Commission, above n 59.

are thoroughly incompatible with according the state a privileged position in private law. Ours is a legal culture in which both public and private law share the objective of protecting individual freedom.[132]

Private Law Reasons for Governmental Liability

Non-Instrumentalist Values of Private Law

Many jurists throughout the common law world subscribe to an essentially moral, non-instrumentalist conception of private law, related to notions of rights and corrective justice.[133] Within those countries where it prevails, this is frequently simply assumed as 'an implicit but fundamental feature of legal thought'.[134] We can contrast this mentality with the more consequentialist approaches to private law which have dominated twentieth century American private law scholarship. These have had limited influence in other common law jurisdictions.[135] There is a clear boundary between these two views of private law, which mirrors the systems' tolerance of governmental immunities. Immunities are repugnant to private law culture in most common law jurisdictions in a way in which they are not in the United States.

The value of individual liberty is deeply embedded in the common law. Contract law institutionalises the freedom of the individual to decide his own commitments.[136] Tort law protects his liberty from attack.[137] Equality is also fundamental.[138] We construct private law obligations in a spirit of equal respect for the autonomy of each party.[139] Honoré articulates this logic: neither person is more deserving than the other, so neither is entitled to harm the other.[140] These foundations of freedom and equality inform our conception of justice in bilateral relations. Each person is a self-determining agent, whose conduct in consenting to an obligation or committing a wrong may justify imposing legal obligations. To protect the autonomy of potential defendants, we usually require moral responsibility in order to fix them with legal liability.

132 See Dicey, above n 15, 199; J Charvet and E Kaczynska-Nay, *The Liberal Project and Human Rights* (Cambridge, CUP, 2008); G Samuel, 'Governmental Liability in Tort and the Public and Private Law Division' (1988) 8 *Legal Studies* 277, 288.

133 See D Nolan and A Robertson, 'Rights and Private Law' in D Nolan and A Robertson (eds), *Rights and Private Law* (Oxford, Hart Publishing, 2012) 1; JL Coleman, 'The Practice of Corrective Justice' in DG Owen (ed), *Philosophical Foundations of Tort Law* (Oxford, Clarendon, 1995) 53, 66.

134 P Cane, 'Searching for United States Tort Law in the Antipodes' (2011) 38 *Pepperdine Law Review* 257, 280.

135 ibid.

136 T Gutmann, 'Some Preliminary Remarks on a Liberal Theory of Contract' (2013) 76 *Law and Contemporary Problems* 39, 49; JS Kraus, 'Philosophy of Contract Law' in JL Coleman, KE Himma and SJ Shapiro (eds), *Oxford Handbook of Jurisprudence and Philosophy of Law* (Oxford, OUP, 2004) 687, 688; *Town Investments Ltd v Department of the Environment* [1978] AC 359, 393 (HL).

137 Heuston, above n 2, 103; Goldberg, above n 15, 606; JCP Goldberg, 'Tort Law for Federalists (and the Rest of Us): Private Law in Disguise' (2005) 28 *Harvard Journal of Law and Public Policy* 3, 4.

138 DG Owen, 'Why Philosophy Matters to Tort Law' in DG Owen (ed), *Philosophical Foundations of Tort Law* (Oxford, Clarendon, 1995) 1, 9; JDB Mitchell, 'The Causes and Effects of the Absence of a System of Public Law in the United Kingdom' (1965) *PL* 95, 102.

139 F Roedl, 'Contractual Freedom, Contractual Justice, and Contract Law (Theory)' (2013) 76 *Law and Contemporary Problems* 57, 70.

140 T Honoré, 'The Morality of Tort Law: Questions and Answers' in DG Owen (ed), *Philosophical Foundations of Tort Law* (Oxford, Clarendon, 1995) 73, 79.

The purpose of the private law of obligations is to attain interpersonal justice in the bilateral relationship between two people.[141] When some interaction between the parties creates an imbalance between them, the law can intervene to rectify it. The law is specifically concerned with the connection between the parties rather than extrinsic factors. For Weinrib, the correlativity which is at the heart of corrective justice requires that we take account of considerations which are unifying, bipolar and reflect transactional equality.[142] On this understanding, private law is not about distributing burdens according to the common good or socially desirable goals.[143] The 'rights and liabilities of the parties before the court are of the essence'.[144] The connection between the defendant's duties and the claimant's rights is taut, like the rope in a tug of war. We can only dispense one party from liability at the expense of the other.

The primary objection to immunities within this conception of private law is that they frustrate the objective of ensuring interpersonal justice.[145] This simultaneously offends the ideals of autonomy and equality, by subordinating the other person's interests to those of the privileged person.[146] This concern is nothing new. The nineteenth century decisions which establish that statutory corporations set up by the state are liable in private law clearly invoke the sentiment of justice.[147] Likewise, early twentieth century commentators, such as Holdsworth, were concerned with injustice.[148] Immunities rob Peter to pay Paul.

By restoring a disturbed balance between two people, the law protects each person's legal rights. In the common law tradition, private law defines our fundamental rights to personal security and freedom. It would compromise the mission to protect these interests if our laws surrendered them to attack by public actors. Locke concluded that a man's property must be protected against the supreme power just as it is against other men if it is to be protected at all.[149] As well as a primary right to have others respect our interests, we also have a secondary right to redress in the event of infringements. Lord Clyde said that immunity, 'runs counter to the policy that no wrong should be without a remedy'.[150] Defenders of the doctrine of Crown immunity used to argue that administrative practices ensured that victims obtained redress. However, the victims of tortious conduct should not depend on 'the whims and caprices of the government'—an interested party—to obtain compensation for the infringement of legal rights.[151]

One recurrent argument in favour of governmental immunity is that it serves the common good by protecting the public finances from unwanted liabilities. However, if we try to justify an immunity by reference to the common good, that makes the individual claimant who has the misfortune to have come into contact with the defendant pay the price

141 Coleman, above n 133, 67; Gutmann, above n 136, 51.

142 EJ Weinrib, *The Idea of Private Law* (Oxford, OUP, 2012) 120.

143 Charles Fried, *Contract as Promise* (Cambridge, MA, Harvard University Press, 1981) 85; P Cane, 'Fault and Strict Liability for Harm in Tort Law' in G Jones and W Swadling (eds), *The Search for Principle: Essays in Honour of Lord Goff of Chieveley* (Oxford, OUP, 1999) 171, 199.

144 *Credit Suisse v Allerdale BC* [1997] QB 306, 356 (CA).

145 Blachly and Oatman, above n 14, 211, 213.

146 Setser, above n 103, 291.

147 *Ruck v Williams* (1858) 3 H&N 308, 320, 157 ER 488.

148 *Macgregor v Lord Advocate* 1921 SC 847, 852; Holdsworth, above n 7, 292; Arvind, above n 17, 406.

149 J Locke, *The Second Treatise of Civil Government* (London, 1690) s 138.

150 *Darker v Chief Constable of West Midlands Police* [2001] 1 AC 435, 456 (HL); see Goldberg, above n 15, 535.

151 Ogunniran, above n 51, 377; Hogg, above n 20, 96.

for whatever socially desirable objective motivates the exemption.[152] That is objectionable. A non-instrumentalist tort law does not mandate sacrificing the interests of the individual to wider societal goals because that fails to respect his freedom.[153] Corrective justice focuses on the bilateral connection between the parties, and disregards extrinsic concerns. If the community needs to make demands of citizens for the common good, these demands must be defined by law, and should be principled and proportionate, not arbitrary.

The doctrine of Crown immunity was also unjust from the perspective of public servants. It held them liable for infringements while exonerating the entity which commanded them. Individual officers of the state bore the onus of proving lawful authority for their actions.[154] Many commentators seem to have been content that this provided the claimant with redress and kept the state in check. However, blaming the wrong defendant is unjust. If we believe that the collective body itself is the entity which is morally responsible for the conduct in question, then it is unjust to hold the individual official liable in its place. Laski memorably describes the public officials who bore the brunt of Crown immunity as 'vicarious victims'.[155] A morally blameless functionary could not exculpate himself. The law drew no distinction between cases where a public servant knowingly exceeds his authority and those where he reasonably believes his conduct to be lawful and proper.[156] This traditional solution depends for its legitimacy on the premise that the burden of liability rightfully belongs to the official in the first place.

The exception proves the rule. The United States retains governmental immunities for constitutional reasons. However, it is also clear that American private law thinking provides a more receptive space for immunities than the rest of the common law world. Tort law is widely viewed in the United States as a form of public, regulatory law rather than private law designed to protect the interests of individual litigants.[157] Despite a resurgence of American scholarship engaging with the theory of tort law, consequentialist law and economics approaches remain the dominant orthodoxy.[158] The idea of immunities is not necessarily inconsistent with an idea of tort law as regulatory and designed to serve the common good rather than the interests of specific individuals.

Evolution of Our Private Law Culture in the Twentieth Century

The widespread idea that private law should do justice between two parties, based on their equal autonomy, makes immunities unpalatable. This presents us with a little puzzle: why did our nineteenth century predecessors accept Crown immunity, while we, heirs to their legal system and values, reject it? The key to understanding why their values, transmitted to today's world, can no longer tolerate immunities lies in the evolution of private law and legal culture over the twentieth century.

152 *Matthews v Minister of Defence*, above n 57, 1203.

153 See Nolan and Robertson, above n 133, 22; Goldberg, above n 137, 11; F Du Bois, 'Human Rights and the Tort Liability of Public Authorities' (2011) *LQR* 589, 599; Weinrib, above n 142, 110.

154 Heuston, above n 2, 101.

155 HJ Laski, 'The Responsibility of the State in England' (1919) 32 *Harvard Law Review* 447, 451.

156 Borchard, above n 8, 8, 21.

157 L Green, 'Tort Law Public Law in Disguise' (1959) *Texas Law Review* 1; see Goldberg, above n 137; Rustad above n 108; Goldberg, above n 15, 581; Owen, above n 138, 2; Coleman, above n 133, 57.

158 Owen, above n 138, 9; Kraus, above n 136.

Today's legal culture emphasises striving to offer justice in each case.[159] This was not the mentality of judges at the end of the nineteenth century. They were formalist, in that they applied the internal logic of the law, without requiring the outcome to correspond to an external standard of justice. The job of the courts was to administer exactly the justice which the law delimited.[160] Austin disparaged the idea of refusing to apply the law in order to do the 'justice of the case'.[161] The legal system greatly valued predictability and certainty, which outweighed the risk of occasional injustices.[162] A utilitarian outlook justified taking account of longer-term outcomes. Atiyah explains that the goal of encouraging desired behaviours in society also frequently trumped doing justice in the circumstances of each individual case.[163] At the start of the twentieth century, this began to change, when prominent writers asserted that the job of the courts was to offer justice, which might sometimes require developing the law.[164]

Lawyers in the previous century accepted that those cases which fell outside the established causes of action should not get a legal remedy.[165] In the mid-nineteenth century, judges in tort cases stuck closely to traditional causes of action and resisted the over-expansion of liability.[166] From the early twentieth century, judges tended to extend tort liability through cases such as *Donoghue v Stevenson*.[167] Furthermore, there is now a societal expectation in favour of seeking legal redress whenever a person is injured.[168] Lacey explains that our attitudes have changed, so that we now tend to attribute responsibility for misfortune to those who cause it, rather than simply accepting events as part of the vicissitudes of life.[169] We speak the language of rights in private law, in a way which our predecessors did not.

These cultural shifts have gone hand in hand with the extension of redress in areas which bear upon governmental liability. In the nineteenth century, vicarious liability was much more restrictive and many jurists were hostile to it.[170] Liability was based on control, and perceived as imputing the employee's fault to the employer.[171] Reluctance to impute the employee's fault to the employer circumscribed vicarious liability, for example, where the

[159] PS Atiyah, 'From Principles to Pragmatism: Changes in the Function of the Judicial Process and the Law' (1980) 65 *Iowa Law Review* 1249, 1255.

[160] Rumble, *Austin*, above n 16, 157.

[161] ibid 162.

[162] WE Rumble, 'John Austin, Judicial Legislation and Legal Positivism' (1977) 13 *Western Australian Law Review* 77, 96; J Skelly Wright, 'Law and the Logic of Experience: Reflections on Denning, Devlin, and Judicial Innovation in the British Context' (1980) 33 *Stanford Law Review* 179, 182; PS Atiyah, 'Justice and Predictability in the Common Law' (1992) 15 *University of New South Wales Law Journal* 448, 452, 458.

[163] Atiyah, above n 159, 1250–51.

[164] JW Salmond, 'The Theory of Judicial Precedents' (1900) 16 *LQR* 376, 389.

[165] See JW Salmond, *The Law of Torts*, 4th edn (London, Stevens and Haynes, 1916) 9.

[166] Lobban, above n 34, 45, 57.

[167] *Donoghue v Stevenson* [1932] AC 562, 583 (HL); GL Williams, 'The Foundations of Tortious Liability' (1939) 7 *CLJ* 111, 132; AES Tay, 'The Sense of Justice in the Common Law' (1979) *Bulletin of the Australian Society of Legal Philosophy* 1, 19.

[168] PS Atiyah, 'The Legacy of Holmes Through English Eyes' (1983) 63 *Boston University Law Review* 341, 360, 376–77.

[169] N Lacey, '"Philosophical Foundations of the Common Law": Social not Metaphysical' in J Horder (ed), *Oxford Essays in Jurisprudence*, 4th Series (Oxford, OUP, 2000) 17, 34.

[170] Atiyah, above n 168, 360–61.

[171] F Pollock, 'Liability for the Torts of Agents and Servants' (1885) 1 *LQR* 207, 218; Hogg, above n 20, 86; see *Enever v R* (1906) 3 CLR 969.

employee committed fraud. In addition, the doctrine of common employment hindered claims against private employers as well as public ones.[172] In modern times, vicarious liability continues to expand.[173] It is seen as a means of protecting the employee from the burden of liability.[174] It is justified not because the employer is at fault in any way, but because the enterprise has put someone in the position to harm others through performing the functions it entrusts to him.[175] This rationale translates readily to public bodies.[176] All the constraints which militated against vicarious immunity in the case of public bodies have disappeared.[177]

Another legal development which reinforces the arguments against governmental immunity is the rejection of the immunity in tort of charitable institutions.[178] The House of Lords repudiated this doctrine as early as 1866; it has left a longer legacy in the United States.[179] A rationale in late nineteenth century US decisions is that it would be an improper use of funds donated for charitable purposes to use them to pay tortious liabilities.[180] Some argued too that if vicarious liability is justified by profit-making, it cannot apply to charities. Each of these arguments could apply to the state. Charitable immunity is a close relation of governmental immunity; a legal system that rejects charitable immunity is less likely to endorse state immunity.

When it comes to the liability of public bodies, the evolution of our attitudes to corporations is another crucial change. Perhaps it is even the most important transformation. Over the past century, we have come to view artificial legal persons as proper targets for liability. Both criminal and civil liability are constructed on the paradigm of a responsible human person.[181] Over time, our societies became accustomed to corporations in the commercial world and came to view them as independent actors who should be held accountable for their actions.[182] We have moved from an individualist to a communitarian view of the entities to which we can attach responsibility.[183] This entices us to side-step concerns about how we can translate models of responsibility designed for human beings to artificial entities, in the interests of ensuring that the collective entity will be held liable and the victim will not be deprived of a remedy.

[172] *Priestly v Fowler* (1837) 3 M&W 1, 150 ER 1030; *Dunbar v Guardians of Ardee Union* [1897] 2 IR 76, 91 (CA); see *Matthews v Minister of Defence*, above n 57, [81], [82] (HL); AM Linden, 'Public Law and Private Law: The Frontier from the Perspective of a Tort Lawyer' (1976) 17 *Cahiers de droit* 831, 837.

[173] *Bazley v Curry* [1999] 2 SCR 534; *Jacobi v Griffiths* [1999] 2 SCR 570; *Lister v Hesley Hall Ltd* [2001] UKHL 22, [2002] 1 AC 215.

[174] P Morgan, 'Recasting Vicarious Liability' (2012) 71 *CLJ* 625; N McBride, *Private Law at the Crossroads: Is There a Right Way Forward?*, University of Cambridge Faculty of Law Research Paper 56/2014 (2014) 13, available at www.ssrn.com/abstract=2483725.

[175] *Byrne v Ireland*, above n 44, 280; Cane, above n 143, 187; J Bell, 'The Basis of Vicarious Liability' (2013) 72 *CLJ* 17, 20.

[176] Finn, above n 13, 36.

[177] Bell, above n 175, 20.

[178] *Holliday v St Leonard* (1861) 11 CB (NS) 192, 142 ER 769.

[179] *Mersey Docks and Harbour Board Trustees v Gibbs* (1866) 11 HLC 686, 11 ER 1500; *Gilbert v Corporation of Trinity House* (1886) LR 17 QBD 795; *Donaldson v Commissioners of the General Public Hospital in Saint John* (1890) 30 New Brunswick 279.

[180] *Perry v House of Refuge* 63 Md 20, 1885 WL 3235 (Md), 52 Am Rep 495.

[181] *R v Cory Brothers* [1927] 1 KB 810.

[182] Lacey, above n 169, 34.

[183] See MS Moore, *Placing Blame* (Oxford, OUP, 1997) 37.

It looks very odd to modern eyes that legal commentators once doubted whether companies could be liable for torts committed outside their corporate capacity.[184] Why should the corporation be let off the hook because it ordered the employee to do something which the company could not lawfully do? However, a corporation could only act at all through actions of duly authorised agents.[185] Without sufficient, lawful authorisation, employees' actions could not be attributed to the company. This is perfectly logical and reflects a mentality in which the actions of metaphysical entities are always, first, the actions of a human being. However, once our cultural perceptions change so that the collective entity becomes 'real' to us, then it instead resembles the unjust evasion of responsibility by the body which is truly responsible. Sometimes the difficulty in suing parts of the government has been their lack of legal personality.[186] The change in how people perceive collective entities means that even unincorporated associations can appear to be proper targets for responsibility. The extension of vicarious liability to unincorporated associations embodies this shift in perception.[187]

The fact that we are today willing to regard corporate entities as the subjects of legal liability gives us a choice between attributing responsibility for an act done by a public servant either to him or to the agency which he represents. This is a choice that our nineteenth century predecessors did not perceive. It is open to us to characterise the harmful act as the act of the individual officer or of the collective body. There is a logic to the French distinction between the personal fault of the agent and the fault of the service.[188] Perceiving the governmental body as a potential responsible party changes everything: it is no longer satisfactory that the governmental official is always liable, and the omission of institutional liability takes on the appearance of a gap.

Public Law Reasons for Governmental Liability

The common law family does not just share a common understanding of private law. We also possess a set of constitutional values, 'grounded in a broadly liberal conception of legitimate governance'.[189] This is why our jurisdictions' approaches to governmental immunity did not fracture along a dividing line according to whether they are explicitly constitutionalist. Our unifying constitutional values outweigh differences such as whether or not countries have a written constitution.[190] And just as in private law, the evolution of our legal culture since the nineteenth century has made governmental immunity harder to justify.

[184] AL Goodhart, 'Corporate Liability in Tort' (1926) 2 *CLJ* 350; DIC Ashton-Cross, 'Suggestions regarding the Liability of Corporations for the Torts of Their Servants' (1950) 10 *CLJ* 419; J Getzler, *Disciplining the Corporation through Tort Liability and Disability*, Oxford Law and Finance Workshop (2010), available at www.law.tau.ac.il/Eng/_upload/dbsattachedfiles/Getzler-paper.pdf.

[185] Goodhart, above n 184, 353–54, 359.

[186] *Trawnik v Lennox*, above n 125; New Zealand Law Commission, above n 59, [3.10]; Anderson, above n 64, 17.

[187] *Various Claimants v Institute of the Brothers of the Christian Schools* [2010] EWCA Civ 1106; Morgan, above n 174, 630.

[188] Blachly and Oatman, above n 14, 209.

[189] TRS Allan, *Constitutional Justice* (Oxford, OUP, 2001) 5.

[190] ibid 4.

As a matter of pure logic, our constitutional convictions in the nineteenth century were already incompatible with Crown immunity. The rule of law favours liability and Austin himself explained that legal sovereignty did not justify the doctrine of Crown immunity. However, his idea of a legal Sovereign, unlimited by law, strongly influenced mindsets. In addition, for much of the twentieth century, judges became more communitarian and deferential to government. The rise of human rights culture and related phenomena such as common law constitutionalism have since restored the liberal emphasis on protecting the rights of the individual from government.

The Rule of Law

The core public law argument against governmental immunities is that they are incompatible with the constitutional principle of the rule of law, which is so deeply engrained in all our constitutions.[191] The rule of law requires that every legal person, including governmental agencies, be subject to law. The organs of state have no legal right to infringe the liberty of citizens outside the scope of the powers granted to them.[192] For Dicey, the principle necessarily entailed that every legal actor's rights must be judged by the ordinary courts.[193] This may not be necessary, but there must certainly be an independent judiciary and fair legal procedures.[194] The underlying objective of the rule of law is to protect individual freedom against government oppression.[195] It 'embodies the liberal and individualistic bias of the common law in favour of the citizen'.[196]

There is an inherent logical tension between the constitutional principles of the rule of law and parliamentary sovereignty.[197] Yet, this seems not to affect the strength of our commitment to the rule of law in a significant way. Both parliamentary sovereignty and the rule of law are foundational constitutional principles in the United Kingdom, New Zealand and Canada.[198] In the eyes of common law constitutionalists, England is not out of step with more obviously constitutionalist countries, because the common law itself is the birthplace and repository of constitutionalism.[199] With the exception of Parliament, all other public

[191] *Darker v Chief Constable of West Midlands Police*, above n 150, 448, 453; Heuston, above n 2, 48; House of Lords Select Committee on the Constitution, *Report: The Process of Constitutional Change*, 15th Report of Session 2010–12, [10]; see also New Zealand Supreme Court Act 2003 (NZ), s 3(2); Preamble, Canadian Charter of Rights and Freedoms, s 2, Part 1 of the Constitution Act 1982 (Canada).

[192] NS Marsh, 'The Rule of Law as a Supra-National Concept' in AG Guest (ed), *Oxford Essays in Jurisprudence* (Oxford, OUP, 1961) 223, 248; Allan, above n 189, 10.

[193] Dicey, above n 15, xxxvii.

[194] Marsh, above n 192, 252.

[195] Dicey, above n 15, 389.

[196] TRS Allan, 'Legislative Supremacy and the Rule of Law: Democracy and Constitutionalism' (1985) 44 *CLJ* 111, 119.

[197] RFV Heuston, 'Sovereignty' in AG Guest (ed), *Oxford Essays in Jurisprudence* (Oxford, OUP, 1961) 198, 199; Marsh, above n 192, 241–42; TRS Allan, *Law, Liberty and Justice: The Legal Foundations of British Constitutionalism* (Oxford, Clarendon, 1993) 16; see Allan, above n 189, 13, 201 ff; T Bingham, 'The Rule of Law and the Sovereignty of Parliament' (2008) 19 *King's Law Journal* 223, 224; JEK Murkens, 'The Quest for Constitutionalism in UK Public Law Discourse' (2009) *OJLS* 1, 9.

[198] *Rothmans of Pall Mall (NZ) Ltd v Attorney-General* [1991] 2 NZLR 323, 330 (HCNZ); Supreme Court Act 2003 (NZ), s 3(2); House of Lords Select Committee on the Constitution Report, above n 191, [10]; see also New Zealand Supreme Court Act 2003 (NZ), s 3(2); Preamble, Canadian Charter of Rights and Freedoms, s 2, Part 1 of the Constitution Act 1982 (Canada).

[199] T Poole, 'Back to the Future? Unearthing the Theory of Common Law Constitutionalism' (2003) 23 *OJLS* 435; Dicey, above n 15, 161.

bodies are legally required to abide by the legal limits of their powers and functions.[200] The rule of law is the basis of judicial review in administrative law.[201] The state is liable to people whom it detains without lawful authority.[202] Likewise, it must return taxes which have been levied without proper authority.[203] New Zealand unequivocally demonstrates that a strong commitment to the right to sue the state fits comfortably alongside parliamentary sovereignty. The New Zealand Bill of Rights Act 1990 declares the right to sue the Crown and the courts award public law damages.[204] The current Law Commission consultation document affirms that the right to obtain civil redress from the government is inherent in the rule of law.[205] All this confirms that the public law values which favour removing governmental immunities are deeply embedded in those countries which combine parliamentary sovereignty and the rule of law.

The rule of law may be an ancient constitutional principle, but it is also a work in progress.[206] Dicey overlooked the contradiction between Crown immunity and the rule of law, but if everyone is to be equal before the law, that must include the organs of the state as collective entities. Commentators and law reformers have highlighted this dichotomy since the early twentieth century: Crown immunity prevents the full realisation of the rule of law.[207] It exposes citizens to the substantive risk of abuse of power.[208] The rule of law was already an important shared value in the nineteenth century; recent constitutionalist tendencies accord it increased weight.[209] In modern times, removing governmental immunities is a further step towards more complete implementation of the principle.

The key to understanding why Dicey ignored the conflict between Crown immunities and the rule of law is that, for him, the liability of the individual official was logically prior to the immunity of the state.[210] If we imagine ourselves operating within the legal culture of the late nineteenth century, several assumptions would shape our reasoning about liability for damage done by those acting for public bodies. First, we would not see collective entities as real and substantial in the same way that people do today.[211] In Dicey's world, every act done is first attributable to a human being, and might then be attributed indirectly to a corporation. The state in particular is not viewed as a legal entity.[212] Since the act is that of a human being, he is morally and legally responsible for it, even where he acts on behalf of

200 *Credit Suisse v Allerdale BC*, above n 144; J Laws, 'Law and Democracy' (1995) *PL* 72, 75.

201 Laws, above n 200, 79.

202 *R (Lumba) v Secretary of State for the Home Department* [2011] UKSC 12 (UKSC).

203 *Woolwich Equitable Building Society v Inland Revenue Commissioners* [1993] AC 70 (HL); J Beatson, 'Finessing Substantive "Public Law" Principles into "Private Law" Relations' (1997) *Acta Juridica* 1, 17.

204 New Zealand Bill of Rights Act 1990, s 27(3); *Simpson v Attorney General*, above n 68.

205 New Zealand Law Commission, above n 59, [1.3], [2.2].

206 Allan, above n 196, 113.

207 Moore, above n 35, 12; Laski, above n 155, 463; G Hewart, *The New Despotism* (London, Benn, 1929) 162–64; G Hill, 'Private Law Actions Against the Government (Part 2): Two Unresolved Questions about Section 64 of the Judiciary Act' (2006) 29 *University of New South Wales Law Journal* 1, 30; *Report of the Committee on Ministers' Powers* (Cmd 4060, 1932) 112; Australian Law Reform Commission, above n 18, [22.44]; New Zealand Law Commission, above n 59, [1.3], [2.2].

208 *Davidson v Scottish Ministers*, above n 11, 73; Ogunniran, above n 51, 370.

209 Allan, above n 196.

210 HW Arthurs, 'Rethinking Administrative Law' (1979) 17 *Osgoode Hall Law Journal* 1, 6; RA Cosgrove, *The Rule of Law: Albert Venn Dicey, Victorian Jurist* (Chapel Hill, NC, University of North Carolina Press, 1980) 95.

211 HJ Laski, 'The Basis of Vicarious Liability' (1916) 26 *Yale Law Journal* 105, 123.

212 P Cane, 'Public Law and Private Law: A Study of the Analysis and Use of a Legal Concept' in J Eekelaar and J Bell (eds), *Oxford Essays in Jurisprudence*, 3rd Series (Oxford, Clarendon Press, 1987) 57, 61.

his employer.[213] Therefore, every wrong done by a government agent is properly that agent's responsibility. There is a presumption against shifting that responsibility to any collective entity. For Dicey, of course, the personal responsibility of the government official also takes on a constitutional significance: 'obedience to administrative orders is no defence to an action or prosecution for acts done in excess of legal authority'.[214] These parts fit neatly together: the act is not the act of the public body, but of the individual, and since the individual is liable in private law, all is well. The availability of redress from the official is not just a palliative for an unfortunate lack of governmental liability, but the correct solution.[215] Examined against the background of modern assumptions, this reasoning fails to convince. We accept the public body as a proper subject of liability and are willing to attribute the agent's actions to the body he represents. It is no evasion of liability by the individual if we determine that the proper party to hold responsible is the state.

Public Law and the Control of Governmental Power

Contemporary understandings of public law support the argument that the state must be liable for harm it inflicts on citizens. In a liberal democracy, public law, both constitutional and administrative, is about the legal control of governmental power.[216] The government is not of a superior status to others.[217] The state has power over us, but power is accountable, and tied to specific purposes.[218] This view of public law is protective of the individual liberty of the citizen, just as private law is.[219] Public bodies can act in ways which impinge on our interests and rights, not because they are more important than we are, or generally entitled to disregard our interests, but only because and in so far as those specific harmful acts are justified by law.[220] In *R v Somerset County Council, ex parte Fewings*, Laws J underlined the fundamental distinction that ordinary legal persons should be free to do anything that the law does not prohibit, whereas for public bodies, 'any action to be taken must be justified by positive law'.[221] A culture like this has no place for the maxim that the state can do no wrong. Nor do we assume that individual interests must be sacrificed to the public good, unless such sacrifice is authorised by Parliament. This view of public law is receptive to the possibility of suing the government in private law. Indeed, removing immunities reaffirms our democratic ideals.[222]

213 Pollock, above n 171, 207.

214 Dicey, above n 15, 33.

215 ibid 25.

216 H Woolf, 'Public Law—Private Law: Why the Divide?' (1986) *PL* 220, 221; H Woolf, 'Droit Public—English Style' (1995) *PL* 57, 61; Laws, above n 200, 81.

217 D Kinley, 'Crown Immunity: A Lesson from Australia?' (1990) 53 *MLR* 819, 824; Finn, above n 13, 31; Hogg, above n 76, 370–71.

218 E Fox-Decent, 'Democratizing Common Law Constitutionalism' (2010) 55 *McGill Law Journal* 511, 518.

219 *R v Somerset County Council, ex parte Fewings* [1995] 1 All ER 513, 524 (EWHC); J Laws, 'The Constitution: Morals and Rights' (1996) *PL* 622.

220 *Nagendra Rao v State of Andhra Pradesh*, above n 85; JF Stephen, *History of the Criminal Law of England* (London, Macmillan, 1883) vol 2, 63.

221 *R v Somerset County Council, ex parte Fewings*, above n 219, 524; *Eshugbayi Eleko v Officer Administering the Government of Nigeria* [1931] AC 662.

222 New Zealand Law Commission, above n 59; National Commission to Review the Working of the Constitution, above n 83, [6.1].

Some of the traditional hostility to public law in common law culture reflected a preconception that public law was inevitably permissive in orientation. When the term 'public law' entered our predecessors' vocabulary, they understood it differently to today.[223] Common lawyers adopted Dicey's distinction, originally derived from Ulpian, which differentiated between public good and private interests.[224] If public law is concerned with the public interest, it might seem to follow naturally that it is not designed to protect the interests of the individual.[225]

Kennedy tracks three phases of legal 'consciousness' between the nineteenth century and today, which map exactly to common law attitudes to public law.[226] It began with the familiar nineteenth century model of classical liberalism, which emphasised private law's protection of individual rights. Despite this liberal orientation in private law, other values such as positivism, legal sovereignty and Dicey's opposition to administrative law limited the legal system's commitment to control state power. The second phase, which lasted from the beginning of the twentieth century to the 1960s, was the social period, in which law was conceived as a means to attain social goals and individual rights faded from view.[227] Canada's Law Reform Commission noted retrospectively the influence of the outdated 'idea that the State is intrinsically superior to the individual'.[228] The communitarian perspective which accompanied the rise of the welfare state shaped common lawyers' assumptions about the proper function of public law. Liberalism went out of fashion.[229] The purpose of government was to promote the public interest, to which the interests of individuals must yield.[230] Judges should not second-guess the decisions of experts. Administrative law was highly circumspect and judges carefully avoided interfering with any administrative discretion.[231]

The third phase, beginning after the Second World War, has been the global rise of the human rights model, which requires judges to uphold the rights of the individual and the rule of law.[232] Since the 1960s, a civil liberties perspective pushed back against the idea that expert administrators should be trusted to make decisions which affected individuals in pursuit of the public good.[233] Contrary to assumptions in the first part of the twentieth century, the human rights mentality does not require adherence to any particular political

223 F Pollock, 'The Contact of Public and Private Law' (1923) 1 *CLJ* 255, 256.

224 Pollock, above n 223, 255; see D Johnston, 'The General Influence of Roman Institutions of State and Public Law' in DL Carey Miller and R Zimmermann (eds), *The Civilian Tradition and Scots Law* (Berlin, Duncker & Humblot, 1997) 87.

225 Beatson, above n 203, 2.

226 D Kennedy, 'Two Globalizations of Law and Legal Thought' (2003) 36 *Suffolk University Law Review* 631.

227 See also HF Jolowicz, 'Political Implications of Roman Law' (1948) 22 *Tulane Law Review* 62, 81; JDB Mitchell, 'The Constitutional Implications of Judicial Control of the Administration in the United Kingdom' (1967) 25 *CLJ* 46, 58.

228 Law Reform Commission of Canada, above n 79, 33, 53.

229 SL Guterman, 'Social Democracy and the Tradition of Western Constitutionalism' (1960) 6 *New York Law Forum* 119, 131.

230 AW Bradley, 'The Redress of Grievances' (1962) 20 *CLJ* 82, 89; see also Cane, above n 212, 64.

231 Mitchell, above n 138, 110; J McBride, 'Damages as a Remedy for Unlawful Administrative Action' (1979) 38 *CLJ* 323, 325, 330.

232 Kennedy, above n 226, 632, 672–74; MJ Horwitz, 'The History of The Public/Private Distinction' (1982) 130 *University of Pennsylvania Law Review* 1423, 1427.

233 Kennedy, above n 226, 672–73.

ideology.[234] Its 'passive individualism' is open to government policies of all political shades; the judge's role is to make sure that government respects the bounds imposed by law.[235]

In recent decades, almost all common law jurisdictions have enacted Bills of Rights.[236] This restores the place of the individual in public law and demonstrates also that our governments subscribe to this set of values. Human rights instruments specifically target state power and envisage the award of remedies against the state.[237] Courts in Ireland, India, New Zealand, Canada, the United States and the United Kingdom can award damages for the breach of public law rights.[238] The existence of public law damages could act as a palliative, reducing the pressure to abolish immunities, as in India. More likely, though, this express commitment to governmental liability in public law habituates citizens to governmental liability and makes civil law immunities stand out as anomalous.[239]

This dramatic cultural shift towards greater legal constraint of government entailed the development of a more vigorous administrative law from the 1960s.[240] We can see it in the landmark vindication of the rule of law in *Roncarelli v Duplessis*.[241] In *Burmah Oil*, the House of Lords held that the Crown prerogative to destroy the plaintiff's property in the public interest was conditional on granting compensation.[242] We see it also in the trend towards common law constitutionalism and the recalibration of the balance between parliamentary sovereignty and the rule of law. This important evolution has shaped the widespread contemporary understanding that public law defends the rights of the individual against those who wield governmental power.[243]

At various times, in various places, people have argued that governmental liability should be restricted in the public interest because it imposes a burden on public funds.[244] A related concern is that imposing private law obligations on state bodies hinders the business of government.[245] The public interest argument may have had some purchase in the communitarian mentality of the first part of the twentieth century, but it is inconsistent with current views, which defend the individual against the collective interest. It is unjust arbitrarily to sacrifice one individual to the community.[246] Refusing a legal right purely to save the exchequer money is not justifiable as a matter of distributive justice any more than corrective justice. In a democracy, the costs of citizenship should be distributed in a principled

234 ibid 634.

235 Cane, above n 212, 60–61; Allan, above n 196, 134, 140; P Craig, *Political Constitutionalism and Judicial Review* (2009) 58–59, available at www.ssrn.com/abstract=1503505.

236 New Zealand Bill of Rights Act 1990 (NZ); Human Rights Act 1998 (UK).

237 Article 13, European Convention for the Protection of Human Rights and Fundamental Freedoms, 4 November 1950, ETS 5 (Council of Europe).

238 *Vancouver v Ward* 2010 SCC 27, [2010] 2 SCR 28 (Canada); Human Rights Act 1998 (U), s 8.

239 *Nilabati Behera v State of Orissa*, above n 88; *Simpson v Attorney General*, above n 68; *Choudry v Attorney-General* [1999] 2 NZLR 582, 595 (NZCA).

240 DCM Yardley, 'The Abuse of Powers and its Control in English Administrative Law' (1970) 18 *American Journal of Comparative Law* 565; HWR Wade, *Constitutional Fundamentals* (London, Stevens, 1980) 42, 61–63, 71–73.

241 *Roncarelli v Duplessis* [1959] SCR 121, 16 DLR (2d) 689 (SCC); see RA MacDonald, 'Was Duplessis Right?' (2010) 55 *McGill Law Journal* 401.

242 *Burmah Oil Company (Burma Trading) Ltd v Lord Advocate* [1964] 2 WLR 1231, [1965] AC 75 (HL).

243 *DK Basu v State of West Bengal* AIR 1997 SC 610 [44].

244 See Heuston, above n 2, 193; E Campbell, 'The Citizen and the State in the Courts' in PD Finn (ed), *Essays on Law and Government* (Sydney, Law Book Company, 1996) vol 2, 1, 19; Arvind, above n 17, 416–17.

245 Borchard, above n 8, 32; Setser, above n 103, 294; *Enever v R* (1906) 3 CLR 969 (HCA).

246 T Bingham, 'The Uses of Tort' (2010) *Journal of European Tort Law* 3, 15; Principle II, Recommendation No R(84)15, Council of Europe, *Recommendations to Member States 1984* (Strasbourg, 1985).

manner, as decided by Parliament.[247] The community should bear the cost of government failures, rather than unlucky individuals. It is appropriate to view compensation claims as 'an ordinary expense of government'; part of the cost of carrying out its functions.[248]

Modern ideas about fundamental rights and the rule of law militate against there being any 'no-go' areas or general immunities.[249] The changing interpretation of the act of state doctrine exemplifies this. This long-established common law doctrine grants the government immunity from liability for acts done against foreigners abroad. The traditional justification was that the law regards protection as correlative to allegiance.[250] This has feudal overtones and feels outdated today.[251] We began to see liberal criticism of the doctrine in the 1960s.[252] The defence has recently been re-examined in the English courts, in cases arising out of harm done through military operations overseas.[253] These decisions affirm that the doctrine is part of the law, but their whole tenor is restrictive. The defence is exceptionally narrow: it only applies to authorised and deliberate acts done abroad to further the government's foreign policy, and its effect is merely to stop the English court deciding a claim based on the tort law of the country in which the conduct happened.[254] It does not impede either public law actions or claims under the Human Rights Act 1998. These limits make it proportionate and compatible with the European Convention on Human Rights' right of access to the courts.[255] The rule cannot be justified by non-justiciability, considering that administrative law no longer exempts certain areas from judicial review.[256] The reason it exists is that British judges should not undercut the executive on matters of foreign policy.[257] Although the rule still exists, it has been severely curtailed in order to meet current expectations about the availability of redress and the protection of individual rights.

Sovereignty does not Require Governmental Immunity

Another issue which can colour attitudes to governmental liability from a public law perspective is sovereignty. In the nineteenth century, common law thinkers were fully committed to Austin's view that the legal system has a legal Sovereign which is necessarily unrestricted by law.[258] This worldview is an obstacle to the legal liability of the Crown.

[247] *Attorney-General v De Keyser's Royal Hotel Ltd* [1920] AC 508, 553 (HL).

[248] GA Bermann, 'Integrating Governmental and Officer Tort Liability' (1977) 77 *Columbia Law Review* 1175, 1176; Ogunniran, above n 51, 370; Arvind, above n 17, 410; Jacob, above n 57, 458.

[249] D McGoldrick, 'The Boundaries of Justiciability' (2010) 59 *ICLQ* 981, 1018.

[250] GL Williams, 'The Correlation of Allegiance and Protection' (1950) 10 *CLJ* 54; JG Collier, 'Act of State as a Defence Against a British Subject' (1968) 26 *CLJ* 102.

[251] See C Tran, 'Revisiting Allegiance and Diplomatic Protection' (2012) *PL* 197, 203; *Al-Jedda v Secretary of State for Defence (No 2)* [2010] EWCA Civ 758, [2011] QB 773 (CA); McGoldrick, above n 249, 1010.

[252] *Attorney-General v Nissan* [1969] 2 WLR 926, [1970] AC 179, 220 (HL).

[253] *Al-Jedda v Secretary of State for Defence (No 2)*, above n 251; *Mohammed v Ministry of Defence* [2014] EWHC 1369 (QB); *Belhaj v Straw* [2014] EWCA Civ 1394; *Rahmatullah v Ministry of Defence* [2014] EWHC 3846 (QB).

[254] *Mohammed v Ministry of Defence*, above n 253, [396]–[97].

[255] European Convention for the Protection of Human Rights and Fundamental Freedoms, 4 November 1950, ETS 5 (Council of Europe), art 6; *Al-Jedda v Secretary of State for Defence (No 2)*, above n 251, [2011] QB 773 [216]; *Al-Jedda v United Kingdom* (2011) 35 EHRR 23 (ECtHR).

[256] *Mohammed v Ministry of Defence*, above n 253; *Rahmatullah v Ministry of Defence*, above n 253; see McGoldrick, above n 249, 1015.

[257] *Mohammed v Ministry of Defence*, above n 253, [394], [408].

[258] WJ Brown, 'The Jurisprudence of M Duguit' (1916) 32 *LQR* 168, 181–82.

Duguit identified the problem in stark terms: the argument that sovereignty is unlimited is logically compelling, but permits the destruction of the individual by the state.[259]

The first answer to this (which should suffice) is that Austin himself emphasised that his view of sovereignty did not justify Crown immunity in the British system. The principle that the legal sovereign cannot be subject to law can only apply when a state's sovereign power is a single unitary entity.[260] Austin expressly distinguishes between a person's membership of the composite sovereign body—in which capacity he is sovereign—and his separate existence as an individual apart from that body—in which capacity he is subject to law. There is no justification for either the King or individual members of Parliament to be immune from civil liability. In addition, since sovereignty relates to the law-making power, it never justified the immunity of the executive.[261]

In any case, modern scholarship queries the Austinian proposition that a legal system must have a legal Sovereign with unlimited law-making power.[262] McCormick makes this argument, based on Dicey.[263] If it is the common law which has determined that Parliament is sovereign, then you can construct a legal system in which there is no Sovereign.[264] Sovereignty was a political fact, which could change.[265] There is no normative reason why there must be some body endowed with near-absolute legislative powers. Laski argued that the unlimited legal Sovereign is incompatible with democracy, which is based on responsibility.[266]

The trend has been to move away from unlimited law-making power. Most clearly, those countries with a written Constitution founded on popular sovereignty have no legal Sovereign in Austin's sense. The powers of the state and all its organs, including the legislature, are subject to the Constitution. This is the rationale for Irish Supreme Court's decisive rejection of state immunity.[267] The people collectively are politically sovereign, but individually they are subject to the law and the courts. In many Commonwealth countries, the concept of the Crown must accommodate devolved or Federal government. Once the power of government is divided among distinct organs, it is no longer logically necessary (if ever it was) that any of these entities be above the law. Even in the United Kingdom, the absolute character of parliamentary sovereignty is beginning to erode.[268] The supremacy of European Union law is a specific challenge.[269] The rise of common law constitutionalism may also limit the power of Parliament. Once you accept that there are certain fundamental

[259] L Duguit, *Traité de droit constitutionnel*, 3rd edn (Paris, Ancienne Librairie Fontemoing, 1927) vol 1, 631.

[260] Jaffe, above n 2, 4.

[261] *Re M* [1994] 1 AC 377, 395 (HL).

[262] N McCormick, 'Beyond the Sovereign State' (1993) 56 *MLR* 1, 12; see also J Goldsworthy, 'Is Parliament Sovereign? Recent Challenges to the Doctrine of Parliamentary Sovereignty' (2005) 3 *New Zealand Journal of Public and International Law* 7, 10.

[263] McCormick, above n 262, 12; see Dicey, above n 15, 70.

[264] McCormick, above n 262, 12; PP Craig, 'Public Law, Political Theory and Legal Theory' (2000) *PL* 211, 225.

[265] HWR Wade, 'The Basis of Legal Sovereignty' (1955) 13 *CLJ* 172, 196.

[266] Laski, above n 155, 466.

[267] *Byrne v Ireland*, above n 44, 297.

[268] *R (Jackson) v Attorney-General* [2005] UKHL 56, [2006] 1 AC 262; *AXA General Insurance v Lord Advocate* (2011) UKSC 46, [51]; M Gordon, 'The Conceptual Foundations of Parliamentary Sovereignty: Reconsidering Jennings and Wade' (2009) *PL* 519; cf Goldsworthy, above n 262.

[269] M Elliott, 'United Kingdom: Parliamentary Sovereignty Under Pressure' (2004) 2 *International Journal of Constitutional Law* 545.

constitutional rules which even Parliament cannot change, then it follows that there is no legal Sovereign in the absolute sense used by Austin.

Convergence on Governmental Liability

The common law family shares constitutional commitments to the rule of law and judicial protection of the individual against the misuse of public power. The evolution of our public law culture in the latter part of the twentieth century has removed all justification for governmental immunity. Since we now perceive public bodies, and not just their servants, as appropriate targets for legal responsibility, it follows that these bodies must be subject to the courts. Today, the fundamental orientation of public law is to control the use of state power. We have abandoned the view that the individual is subordinate to the public good. We no longer believe in absolute legal sovereignty—and even if we did, it would not justify immunity for constituent parts of the Sovereign. These values unite us and explain why so many common law countries have rejected governmental immunity.

Let us not gloss over the differences between our constitutional orders. They may set limits to our complete convergence concerning state liability. Constitutional monarchies which subscribe to parliamentary sovereignty are likely to make exceptions to the general principle of liability for Parliament and for the Queen. Logically, parliamentary sovereignty only means that Parliament can enact laws as it pleases through the proper forms; Austin told us that it does not follow that it should not be liable for civil wrongs. However, most common law countries which are enculturated to parliamentary sovereignty would most likely have objections rooted in the separation of powers to judges judging Parliament, even in civil matters. Similarly, the New Zealand Law Commission is happy to retain personal immunity for the Queen herself, noting that this is not likely to arise.[270] This is not strictly necessary but may reflect public sensibilities in a monarchy.

On the other hand, the future could bring further convergence in the public law values of the main family of common law countries. The rise of the culture of human rights has been an international phenomenon, which is nudging diverse legal orders towards greater legal control of government. Constitutionalist attitudes, in the form of common law constitutionalism, seem increasingly to be gaining traction in the United Kingdom.[271] Many now believe that parliamentary sovereignty is not prior to the law or superior to the rule of law.[272] There are indications that the common law may even contain substantive limits on legislative power.[273] At this point, predicting the future course of such trends remains purely speculative.

270 New Zealand Law Commission, above n 59, [8.9].

271 *AXA General Insurance v Lord Advocate*, above n 268, [51]; Poole, above n 199, 436; Murkens, above n 197, 10–11.

272 Wade, above n 265, 187; H Woolf 'Droit Public—English Style' (1995) *PL* 57, 68.

273 MD Walters, 'The Common Law Constitution in Canada: Return of Lex Non Scripta as Fundamental Law' (2001) 51 *University of Toronto Law Journal* 91; V Kazmierski, 'Draconian but Not Despotic: The "Unwritten" Limits of Parliamentary Sovereignty in Canada' (2009) 41 *Ottawa Law Review* 245.

IV. The Onward Journey

Our shared legal values explain why we have collectively turned our backs on governmental immunity over the past century. This kinship opens up the prospect that we can reach towards a common solution to the difficulties which governmental liability can raise.

The immediate next step is to remove all remaining traces of immunities and privileges, as our normative commitments in private law and public law require.[274] The New Zealand Law Commission's current recommendation is for the straightforward removal of all vestigial immunities, so that 'the Crown can sue and be sued as another person can be'.[275] Similar reforms in the United Kingdom, Canada and India would be consonant with those countries' legal values and make the law more straightforward. The key change required in those jurisdictions which modelled their law on the English Act is to introduce direct institutional liability, not predicated on the liability of individual civil servants. This is the New Zealand Law Commission's principal recommendation.[276] Vicarious liability is an incomplete answer to the need to hold the state accountable.[277] Governmental bodies should be liable in private law for their organisational deficiencies even when no single, identifiable individual is to blame.[278] If necessary, national Parliaments could still create specific statutory immunities, as an exception to the general rule.[279] However, exceptions must be granted 'grudgingly': they must be narrow and fully justified.[280] Instead of immunities, the better way to address any differences in how the state should be treated in private law is to remove procedural barriers and then take account of the relevant policy-type concerns within substantive law.

This prospect of future convergence on a fully animated principle of governmental liability necessarily excludes the United States. There is no sign of them following the other common law jurisdictions down the path of abolishing immunities. Despite the United States' commitment to the rule of law, the delicate constitutional balance between the judicial and legislative powers and between the States and the Union includes governmental immunity. Besides, the dominant American understanding of the purpose of private law mutes the argument for governmental liability rooted in private law values.

Removing all governmental immunities is not the end of the story. It merely sets the stage for the next challenge: how exactly to apply the rules of private law to the state. Our starting point is the positive affirmation that public bodies are subject to the ordinary private law, but we must feel free to modify the ordinary rules where this is required. A public body exists at the intersection of a chain of commitments, imposed on it by both public law

[274] Hogg, above n 20, 104.

[275] New Zealand Law Commission, above n 59, [3.17]; Clause 6 of the Draft Crown Civil Proceedings Bill (NZLC IP35, 2014).

[276] New Zealand Law Commission, above n 59, [2.6]; Anderson, above n 64.

[277] New Zealand Law Commission, above n 59, [1.6]; Law Reform Commission of Canada, above n 79, 69–71.

[278] New Zealand Law Commission, above n 59, [3.7]; Sieur Auxerre, Rec Conseil d'État, 17 February 1905, 165 (French Conseil d'État); *Adams v Naylor*, above n 19; *Ransome-Kuti v Attorney-General*, above n 51; *Matthews v Minister of Defence*, above n 57; *Couch v Attorney-General* [2008] NZSC 45, [2008] 3 NZLR 725; *Couch v Attorney-General (No 2)* [2010] NZSC 27, [2010] 3 NZLR 149; HL Deb 4 March 1947, vol 146, col 64; Anderson, above n 64; Ogunniran, above n 51, 393; Australian Law Reform Commission, above n 18, [25.22].

[279] New Zealand Law Commission, above n 59, [2.4]; Kinley, above n 217, 824.

[280] *Darker v Chief Constable of West Midlands Police*, above n 150, 453.

and private law.[281] If we applied the exact same rules of private law to it, sometimes they would contradict the constraints which emanate from constitutional law. If, on the other hand, we accept that effects of constitutional principle reach out even into a public entity's private law relationships, this forces us sometimes to vary the private law rules. Besides, people can legitimately be reluctant to hold the state liable in certain specific circumstances. It is uncontroversial to suggest that limited duties of care might arise on a battlefield.[282] We should carefully articulate and critically examine our intuitions and concerns about liability in specific circumstances. These objections must withstand scrutiny before they can justify varying the rules which bind governmental bodies. However, the cautious and principled modulation of substantive rules is much more rational, sensitive and responsive to the demands of justice than immunities could ever be.

Our commitment to subjecting the public body to private law provides the directional thrust of this approach. We must insist on always giving due weight to interests of corrective justice in the bilateral relationship. The individual who comes in contact with the state must not be lightly sacrificed to the common good. These cornerstones will ensure that we choose solutions that uphold the normative values which have led us to forswear immunity.

Corrective Justice and the State

The value of corrective justice is usually viewed as an archetypal private law value. This is the ideal which requires a person to remedy a wrong which he directly causes another person or to return an unjustified gain. It is orthodox to assume that it applies in bilateral relationships between a person and a governmental body when those relationships fall to be judged by private law. I would go further: the ideal of corrective justice is relevant to bilateral relationships between a person and state organs, regardless of whether we designate the relationship or the claim for redress as private law or public law. There are two preconditions necessary for corrective justice logic to apply: the relationship must be directly bipolar and one party must not be authorised by law to make the specific intrusion on the interests of the other.

Even in relationships between the state and its citizens which reflect the state's right to command obedience, the law only recognises the state's superior authority to make those specific demands which are authorised by law. The relationship between the revenue authorities and a taxpayer is a relationship of unequal power: provided the authorities comply with the law, they may limit the individual's freedom in the interest of distributive justice. However, if the interference with his rights is not authorised by the law, then neither the identity of the public body nor the fact that the intrusion might serve distributive justice gives the authorities the right to do as they choose. On the contrary, if the specific interaction which occurs is not permitted by law, the concept of interpersonal justice, which reflects underlying values of equality and autonomy, is fully relevant. The state, no less than another person, must give you back your property unless it is lawfully entitled to seize it. It should compensate your losses when it wrongfully causes you harm. These principles do not apply only in those scenarios where you have interacted with the state as an equal, but

[281] *Credit Suisse v Allerdale BC*, above n 144, 343.

[282] *Groves v Commonwealth* (1982) 150 CLR 113 (HCA).

also in those cases where it exercised its public power over you. Interpersonal justice may not always be determinative, but is certainly relevant.

The defining feature of this value of corrective justice is that it arises to address disturbances in bilateral relationships. A bilateral relationship can exist between a citizen and a representative of the state, whether their dealings are consensual or arise through the exercise of state power. Every citizen has a right to a fair trial and the state has a corresponding duty to every citizen to ensure that trials are fair. If the state fails to fulfil this obligation to one accused person, the connection that the unfair trial forges between them is direct and bilateral. So, while private law is defined as the law of bilateral relationships, bilateral relationships arise in public law too.[283] The nexus connecting the parties does not have to have existed prior to the interaction which justifies the creation of the obligation. Nor does the connection between the parties have to be unique. Even in normal private law, the rights and duties which exist before the event generally do not tie just two specific people together.[284] The bilateral connection between two identified individuals crystallises when they interact in some way. There is no fundamental difference between the bipolar character of relationships which arise between two ordinary people and those which arise between a person and the public authorities.

In addition to a direct bilateral connection, corrective justice is predicated on equality.[285] The basic premise of private law is that each person must respect the equal autonomy of the other. This reciprocity necessarily exists when we consider relationships between two human beings, who inevitably have an equal entitlement to self-determination. At first glance, it might seem that the public body and the citizen are not equal; that the state is superior because it has legal power to compel the unwilling citizen. However, our liberal political model categorically rejects this assertion of superiority. It is not a general power of compulsion. The state may imprison me, but only if I am convicted of a crime. Outside the delimited boundaries of the lawful use of coercive power, the state must engage with other legal persons as their equal. It does not matter whether the interaction is one which appears on its face to be one of equality or one premised on domination and subordination: whenever it falls outside the parameters of what the law actually permits, the state is obliged to respect the other person's freedom.

The proposition that governmental bodies are equal to other people can be challenged from another angle. We assume that each party's duty to respect the other's autonomy must be reciprocal and equal because all humans have the same entitlement to self-determination. In contrast, public bodies are quintessentially means to an end, not free, self-determining agents.[286] They do not have any rights which they enjoy for their own sake.[287] Accordingly, the Kantian argument for everyone to respect the equal autonomy of his partner does not apply for the benefit of public bodies. We choose nonetheless to allow the public body to avail of the protections of private law, as if it were a self-determining person. We do the same

[283] Weinrib, above n 142.

[284] GC Keating, 'Is the Role of Tort to Repair Wrongful Losses?' in D Nolan and A Robertson (eds), *Rights and Private Law* (Oxford, Hart Publishing, 2012) 367, 383, 396.

[285] Weinrib, above n 142, 120.

[286] D Oliver, 'The Frontiers of the State: Public Authorities and Public Functions under the Human Rights Act' (2000) *PL* 476, 483.

[287] *R v Somerset County Council, ex parte Fewings*, above n 219, 524; see Du Bois, above n 153, 604.

for all artificial legal persons.[288] One reason is that it would indirectly harm the interests of stakeholders in corporate entities if the law deprived them of the protection which private law confers. Nor could collective entities achieve the purposes for which they are created if they were deprived of the protection which private law affords. So there are good reasons why we normally assume that other people must treat the freedom of corporations or governmental bodies with equal respect to that which they themselves deserve—but we are not philosophically committed to this proposition. This distinction offers the key to solving some tricky problems which arise in adjudicating relations between the state and other people. It is not immoral to curtail the private law rights of public bodies. Other people are entitled to corrective justice from governmental bodies, but the force of the governmental body's reciprocal claim against them is weaker.

Another possible objection to applying the logic of corrective justice to the state's liability concerns the second, parallel, objective of such liability: controlling the use of governmental power.[289] Trespass, false imprisonment and misfeasance in public office exemplify the dual function of the private law liability of government agents.[290] Is this aim to curb the abuse of power fair, and compatible with corrective justice? First, the reason for the defendant's liability is located in its own conduct. The law sanctions it when it fails to comply with the rules which govern its powers. This means that the state defendant is not simply arbitrarily sacrificed to an extraneous public interest. The primary goal is to require the individual defendant to obey the legal rules which bind it; this only incidentally promotes the responsible use of public power. Besides, if we are concerned with a public body as opposed to a human being, its lack of autonomy indicates that it is justifiable for us to take a consequentialist approach. Secondly, we might worry that a reason for imposing liability, such as controlling public power, which only applies to one party is incompatible with corrective justice.[291] However, the idea that the reason for intervening must concern both parties to the bilateral relationship does not necessarily require that the wrong must be one which either party could commit. The duty connects the two parties, and therefore the breach of that duty provides a reason for intervention from both perspectives. With public bodies, these are duties which are defined elsewhere in the law. Yet it is not so different from forcing a trustee to account for breach of his fiduciary duties. The private law liability of public bodies has traditionally been pluralistic but this is not objectionable. The two functions of the government's liability in private law cohere. This account, by which two parties to a bilateral relationship can have unequal entitlements to corrective justice, which will be triggered by the breach of constraints which bind only one of the parties, does not conform exactly to Weinrib's model. It is justified by reference to external normative values, specifically the defence of the liberty of the individual. We do not require the concept of corrective justice itself to do all the heavy lifting. Instead it acts as an intermediate stage in our reasoning: when we observe that a transgression by a public body causes an imbalance in a bilateral relationship, the language of corrective justice encapsulates the proposition that the other person should receive redress from it.

[288] See N Oman, 'Corporations and Autonomy Theories of Contract: A Critique of the New Lex Mercatoria' (2006) 83 *Denver University Law Review* 101, 113–22.

[289] Linden, above n 172, 856.

[290] Harlow, above n 15, 527; J Murphy, 'Misfeasance in Public Office: A Tort Law Misfit?' (2012) 32 *OJLS* 51, 63.

[291] Weinrib, above n 142, 120.

Corrective justice grounds claims against public bodies, provided the parties are in a bilateral relationship and the interaction between them has not been ordained by law. The cases which permit citizens to recover unjustified tax demands from the state demonstrate this. Levying taxes is an archetypal relationship of authority, yet when the taxes are not lawfully due, the state must treat the taxpayer as an equal and restore the payment.[292] Corrective justice explains why the state is not merely sanctioned for exceeding its powers or stripped of its improper receipts, but must restore them to the individual taxpayer. This logic of interpersonal justice applies against the state, regardless of whether we might view the case as a private law case or a public law case.[293] It applies even when the wrong, which leads us to characterise the transfer between the parties as a disturbance of the proper order, is a breach of public law norms. Of course, from a procedural point of view we care about defining the case as a private law case or a public law one. However, from a substantive point of view, classifying it in this way does not help us to identify and balance the relevant principles.

It follows that bilateral relationships between the state and another person are likely simultaneously to evoke both constitutional principle and the ideal of interpersonal justice. The policy rationale for the *Woolwich* claim is the constitutional principle of legality.[294] This sits comfortably alongside the commutative justice argument for restitution. Call it private or public, these two distinct principles must affect the outcome. Sometimes these different values may point to conflicting responses. Crucially, however, the way to reconcile them in case of conflict is not to focus on whether the relationship or legal action is properly private law or public law. That is a red herring: either way, the state owes a duty to respect the person's private law rights and the person has a claim to redress for an unjustified disturbance in the bipolar relationship.

Modifying Substantive Private Law Rules

The rule of law firmly requires that public bodies be subject to private law claims. However, the picture is more complex than this. I have already argued that the values of private law—principally commutative justice—can apply to the government even when the claim arises outside of private law. Equally, when the legal action is situated within private law, other principles still interlope and it can be perfectly legitimate to modify the rules applied to the state. Our commitment to the rule of law does not require us unthinkingly to parrot Dicey's conviction that public bodies must invariably be governed by the 'ordinary law'. A strong general principle of subjection to ordinary civil law accommodates a more nuanced application.[295] We can have specific rules for public bodies without elevating them above ordinary citizens.[296] Some changes may favour public bodies and others disadvantage them. So long as judges and law-makers are sensitive to the central importance of protecting the interests of the individual, they can tailor appropriate and just solutions to real conundrums.

292 *Woolwich Equitable Building Society v Inland Revenue Commissioners*, above n 203.

293 *Murphy v Attorney General* [1982] IR 241 (IESC); *Woolwich Equitable Building Society v Inland Revenue Commissioners*, above n 203.

294 R Williams, *Unjust Enrichment and Public Law* (Oxford, Hart Publishing, 2010).

295 Finn, above n 13, 40.

296 Hogg, above n 76, 367; Finn, above n 13, 35; JWF Allison, 'Variation of View on English Legal Distinctions Between Public and Private' (2007) 66 *CLJ* 698, 709.

The state is different from other people, in ways that can matter for certain causes of action.[297] There may be one criterion which it is difficult to establish when the defendant is a governmental entity.[298] For example, if a taxpayer wanted to recover unlawfully levied taxes using the ground of duress, he would face the obstacle that the compulsion to pay his taxes was not illegitimate. If the state wanted to plead the private law restitution defence of change of position, should it be debarred as a 'wrongdoer' because making an illegal demand is wrong in public law?[299] If we accept the proposition that sometimes the rules designed for private parties do not fit the state, we will have to examine closely the law in each context to identify any required modifications.

Private law's traditional function of controlling the misuse of public power provides an important reason for varying the rules. There are limits to how effectively ordinary private law can do the work of protecting the individual from state power. Private law is blind to the inequality which exists between the state and law-abiding citizens, as exemplified in the unlawful taxation scenario.[300] In addition, assuming that the state must be subject to the 'ordinary' private law leads us to apply traditional common law principles designed to capture moral responsibility, such as requiring fault and excluding liability for omissions. The presumption that there must usually be a recognised private law cause of action, which would be available against any defendant, unduly restricts the scope of state liability. Thus, where there is no recognised tort covering an activity, as in the case of tapping telephones, the common law is powerless to restrict state action.[301] Private law's central assumption that legal actors have the liberty to do whatever is not prohibited constitutes the wrong starting point for governmental bodies. Protecting our freedom means only allowing state bodies to exercise powers which the law confers on them. In order effectively to prevent the misuse of public power, there need to be both special causes of action and modified tests for liability in relevant cases against the state. The *Woolwich* principle responds to this need for special causes of action in the context of the restitution of overpaid taxes. In order to uphold the principle of legality, the common law endorses a unique criterion for liability: the state must simply reimburse taxes levied without valid legal basis.[302] Unlike ordinary unjust enrichment claims, there is no need to establish an unjust factor which indicates that the claimant's consent to the enrichment was impaired. Instead, the courts have properly shaped a rule which serves the dual goals of interpersonal justice and control of illegal governmental action.[303]

The fact that public bodies are merely instruments, which exist to serve society, licenses us to adopt unusually strict control of their conduct. The importance of upholding constitutional principle, coupled with such bodies' imperfect claim to autonomy, places the options of strict liability or liability for omissions squarely on the table.[304] All the private

[297] P Cane, *Administrative Law*, 5th edn (Oxford, OUP, 2011) 200.

[298] *Smith v Chief Constable of Sussex* [2008] UKHL 50.

[299] *Test Claimants in the FII Group Litigation v Commissioners for Revenue and Customs* [2008] EWHC 2893 (Ch) [339].

[300] Finn, above n 13, 36.

[301] *Malone v Commissioner of Police of the Metropolis (No 2)* [1979] Ch 344.

[302] *Woolwich Equitable Building Society v Inland Revenue Commissioners*, above n 203; Williams, above n 294.

[303] *Woolwich Equitable Building Society v Inland Revenue Commissioners*, above n 203; *Kingstreet Investments Ltd v New Brunswick (Finance)* 2007 SCC 1, [2007] 1 SCR 3 (SCC); *Murphy v Attorney General*, above n 293.

[304] Du Bois, above n 153, 592.

law rules that we have carefully designed to balance two equal, competing autonomies can legitimately be revisited when private law engages in the task of defending the individual against the state. It may be appropriate, for example, to adopt a wider conception of duty of care in cases of breach of statutory duty brought against public bodies than that applied to private citizens.[305]

Judicial respect for the separation of powers provides a different reason to modify ordinary private law rules when judging governmental bodies.[306] The courts are traditionally very reluctant to hold the state liable where people perform statutory duties, exercise discretion or make policy decisions.[307] The separation of powers is understood to require a lenient approach towards the careless exercise of executive power. Perhaps this has been taken too far: it is perfectly possible to hold somebody liable for negligently exercising a statutory discretion without expressing a view as to the decision he should have reached.[308]

Even when the relationship between a public body and another person is indubitably a private law one, public law considerations may still intrude. Questions of capacity or authority affecting governmental contracts will be decided by public law rules.[309] *Churchward v R* decided that the government would not be liable on contracts unless and until Parliament voted the necessary allocation of funds.[310] The common law provides for restitution of money paid out by the state without legal authorisation, as well as of taxes unlawfully claimed.[311] The rationale for these causes of action is to uphold constitutional rules: the *Auckland* precedent ensures the lawful disbursement of public money. In these cases, it seems correct to vindicate constitutional principle by modifying the usual private law tests, circumventing private law's usual rationale that the claimant did not consent to the payment. Yet, whenever we change the ordinary rules to reflect constitutional imperatives, this necessarily affects the interests of the person who finds himself, even involuntarily, in a bilateral relationship with the state.

Resolving a Conflict of Constitutional Principle and Private Law Logic

Sometimes the public law and private law reasoning will align. This happens in the overpaid taxes scenario. The public law imperative that the state return the money which it was not legally entitled to accept and the private law ideal of corrective justice both point to the same solution. At other times, however, the two sets of values can conflict. When this happens, giving effect to the constitutional principle will deprive a party of his normal legal rights, and upholding his private law rights will undermine the constitutional principle.

Such conflicts of the two sets of principles can arise in relation to defences as well as causes of action. Take the defence of change of position in restitution claims. Change of

[305] G McLay, 'The New Zealand Supreme Court, the Couch Case and the Future of Governmental Liability' (2009) 17 *Torts Law Journal* 77.

[306] Arvind, above n 17, 432.

[307] *Enever v R* (1906) 3 CLR 969.

[308] *Barrett v Enfield London Borough Council* [2001] 2 AC 550, 586; see P Craig, *Administrative Law*, 4th edn (London, Sweet & Maxwell, 2003) 898.

[309] *Credit Suisse v Allerdale BC*, above n 144.

[310] *Churchward v R* (1865) 6 B&S 807, 122 ER 1391; cf *New South Wales v Bardolph* (1934) 52 CLR 455.

[311] *Auckland Harbour Board v R* [1924] AC 318 (PC).

position is a private law defence, designed to protect the reliance interest of a person who relies in good faith on the validity of a payment. The idea that a defendant will not be left in a worse position than if he was never enriched helps legitimise unjust enrichment law's intrusion on the innocent defendant's autonomy. English law assumes that this defence cannot apply against a *Woolwich* claim for the restitution of overpaid taxes.[312] It is intuitively compelling that that the state should not be able to invoke the defence of change of position in order to refuse to return to the taxpayer receipts which were never due.[313] Like the cause of action itself, denying the state this defence simultaneously preserves constitutional principle and protects the individual.[314] Bant identifies the reason for denying the ordinary private law defence as 'stultification'.[315] It is important not to undermine the constitutional principle in regulating the relationship between the parties.

Consider now the contrasting scenario: should the innocent outsider who receives public funds which are not lawfully disbursed be able to invoke change of position if he has, indeed, spent the money in good faith? Australian authorities suggest that he cannot.[316] This does not seem right. Even though the constitutional principle is important, it is unjust to prioritise it at the expense of an innocent individual. Certainly, we should recognise the state's right to recover unjustified payments, even though this puts outsiders at a relative disadvantage, but the backstop must be the protection that the change of position defence offers the innocent recipient.[317] There must be a limit to the extent to which we are willing to intrude on the liberty of any one person in order to achieve public law goals for the collective good.

Resolving the conflict which exists when the two orders of values collide requires a more complicated approach than simply choosing one set of values that must systematically prevail. Public law logic does not necessarily trump the private law logic, if that would penalise the innocent outsider. The risk of contradicting or stultifying the constitutional constraint on power justifies denying the state the change of position defence, but we should disapply this stultification logic when it would sacrifice the rights of private parties.[318] If this answer to the dilemma is correct, it means treating the state differently to other legal actors. This inequality of treatment is acceptable because the state is not a human being, whose autonomy we need to protect.

We have precedents in company law for favouring the interests of innocent third parties over upholding the public-interest regulation of corporations. The rule in *Turquand*'s case protects the outsider who deals in good faith with a company.[319] Similarly, many jurisdictions legislated to insulate outsiders from the consequences of companies exceeding limits

[312] *Test Claimants in the FII Group Litigation v Commissioners for Revenue and Customs*, above n 299, [339]; E Bant, 'Restitution from the Revenue and Change of Position' [2009] *Lloyd's Maritime and Commercial Law Quarterly* 166.

[313] *Test Claimants in the FII Group Litigation v Commissioners for Revenue and Customs*, above n 299, [340].

[314] C Mitchell, P Mitchell and S Watterson, *Goff and Jones: The Law of Unjust Enrichment*, 8th edn (London, Sweet & Maxwell, 2011) [27.51].

[315] Bant, above n 312, 172.

[316] *Commonwealth v Burns* [1971] VR 825 (VICSC); *Attorney-General v Gray* [1977] 1 NSWLR 406 (NSWCA); *Commonwealth v Davis Samuel Pty Ltd (No 7)* [2013] ACTSC 146 (ACTSC).

[317] *Auckland Harbour Board v R*, above n 311.

[318] *Test Claimants in the FII Group Litigation v Commissioners for Revenue Customs* [2014] EWHC 4302 (Ch) [315].

[319] *Royal British Bank v Turquand* (1856) 6 E&B 327.

on their capacity.[320] We uphold the private law rights of the outsider, even though that effectively means that the corporate entity can avoid legal restrictions on its powers.

So we must do our best to uphold both the public and private principle. When they conflict, we can legitimately put constitutional principle first at the expense of the public body. It is permissible to deprive governmental bodies of the benefit of rules which are designed to protect human autonomy.[321] In contrast, we must resist the temptation to put constitutional principle first when it would prejudice the other party. Our guiding principle should be a presumption against sacrificing the individual to the state or to the public interest. This is explicitly an ethical commitment which reflects the liberal values which shape both public and private law. Admittedly, the price of prioritising the interests of the individual will sometimes be that we fail to control or cure the breach of public law norms. This is made more tolerable because the cost of that failure will be spread among us all rather than imposed on one person.

We should not lightly disregard the private law rights of the public body. The autonomy point does not support placing public bodies in a disadvantaged position across the board. If the cause of action gives effect to private law logic, then the state should benefit from private law defences, because there is no conflict with constitutional imperatives.[322] Corporations would be useless tools if they did not have private law rights. Likewise, public bodies, which exist to serve the interests of the community, should not be at the mercy of others, unprotected by law. It is only in those difficult cases where public law logic would be thwarted by a defence whose purpose is to protect a defendant's liberty that we might fashion an appropriate solution by bearing in mind that the public body is merely a means to an end and has no freedom to vindicate. Sometimes the public interest in preserving the freedom of all citizens is best served by insisting on compliance with public law rules. At other times, it is more important to require the public body to respect the freedom of the specific person with whom it finds itself in a bilateral relationship.

The thrust of this argument clearly favours protecting the private law rights of individuals when they collide with the constitutional rules which bind public bodies. It is unjust arbitrarily to sacrifice individual rights to the common good. However, perhaps we should not go so far as to rule out ever tempering this commitment to protect the individual. There could conceivably be exceptional situations in which the state should be excused from its private law liabilities on public policy grounds.[323] The dormant contract law doctrine of 'executive necessity' purports to allow the executive to disown contractual obligations which would impede the government's performance of its functions.[324] If the doctrine does allow the state to avoid its private law obligations, it should be vanishingly rare and entail compensation.[325] A related debate has taken place in the law of restitution.

[320] Companies Act 1985 (UK), s 35, amended by Companies Act 1989, s 108; Corporations Act 2001 (Australia), s 125; Companies Act 1993 (NZ), s 17; Canada Business Corporations Act 1985 (Canada), s 16(3).

[321] See *Test Claimants in the FII Group Litigation v Commissioners for Revenue Customs* [2014] EWHC 4302 (Ch) [323].

[322] See ibid [337].

[323] National Commission to Review the Working of the Constitution, above n 83, [6.1].

[324] SK O'Byrne, 'Public Power and Private Obligation: An Analysis of the Government Contract' (1992) 14 *Dalhousie Law Journal* 485, 519–20.

[325] *Ansett Transport Industries (Operations) v Commonwealth* (1977) 139 CLR 54; N Seddon, 'The Interaction of Contract and Executive Power' (2003) 31 *Federal Law Review* 541, 547; JM Evans, 'Governmental Factors in Contracts of Public Authorities' (1972) 35 *MLR* 88, 93; Cane, above n 297, 234–38.

Canadian law ultimately rejected a proposed 'fiscal chaos' defence to claims for overpaid taxes.[326] In contrast, the Irish Supreme Court endorsed a policy defence based on 'transcendent considerations'.[327] It is hard to overstate how exceedingly rare that defence could be: the case involved a decade's worth of income tax paid by all the married taxpayers in the country under statutes which turned out to be unconstitutional. We accept that defences such as prescription extinguish claimants' rights to demand corrective justice in private law regardless of the merits of their claims; it is not inconceivable that the state could have access to similar defences that other parties cannot raise. We can best engage with these difficult questions about the contours of state liability by bearing in mind the bedrock of legal values and assumptions which motivated the abolition of immunities. Our ethical ideal should remain to vindicate the private law rights of individuals in all their dealings with the state.[328]

V. Conclusion

The history of the reform of Crown immunity around the common law world is predominantly a story of convergence. A large family of common law jurisdictions has uniformly repudiated the idea of governmental immunity in private law. We may have set out at different moments, or taken slightly different routes, but all these countries have affirmedly chosen the same path. This common journey beautifully illustrates our shared legal heritage. The evolution of our legal culture throughout the twentieth century meant that the ingredients that were firmly embedded in all our legal systems at the outset ripened into full incompatibility with the notion of governmental immunity.

At the heart of our shared values is the respect for the liberty of individuals which animates both public and private law. A non-instrumentalist understanding of private law emphasises the need to offer corrective justice to each person. It does not support sacrificing the rights of one individual to serve a collective interest. In public law, the rule of law demands that governmental agencies be subject to legal control. Those who exercise public power may not encroach on anybody's private law rights unless the law authorises them to do so. The logic of both sets of values converges on the proposition that the state should be legally liable for violating peoples' private law rights.

The evolution of our legal culture over the past century undercut the likelihood that people would tolerate immunities. People in our societies increasingly expect that wrongs ought to lead to legal redress. We have gradually come to view collective entities as proper targets for direct legal responsibility. This altered perspective has upturned the logic of Crown immunity, whereby the human agent was the self-evident locus of responsibility. Likewise, in the late twentieth century, we abandoned assumptions about public law which previously held in check the force of the constitutional argument against immunities. Once these disappeared, the arguments for governmental liability were irresistible.

[326] *Kingstreet Investments Ltd v New Brunswick*, above n 303; cf *Air Canada v British Columbia* [1989] 1 SCR 1161.

[327] *Murphy v Attorney General*, above n 293.

[328] *X (Minors) v Bedfordshire County Council* [1995] 2 AC 633 (HL).

Since the legal values that bear upon governmental liability are so closely aligned among this family of jurisdictions, we can continue our onward journey together. Accepting the principle of liability is just a staging-post. We face difficult questions about how to apply private law to public bodies, and the legal values which defeated governmental immunities should inform our search for answers. Our guiding imperatives are to protect individual freedom and to ensure that those who wield state power obey the law. Consequently, we are deeply committed to the principle that governmental bodies are subject to private law rules and adjudication. However, our normative commitments do not require that public bodies must always be subject to the exact same rules as everyone else. Sometimes, the ordinary rules do not fit, or fail sufficiently to restrict government actions. Sometimes, even in private law interactions between a government agency and another person, constitutional rules should be taken into account. The values of private law occasionally collide with constitutional principle. We will be called to resolve such conflicts by varying the ordinary private law rules. The underlying common law values which justify the principle of governmental liability should be our touchstone. These values call us to defend the principle that each person is entitled to interpersonal justice in his bilateral dealings with the state.

10

How to have a Common Private Law: The Presuppositions of Legal Conversation

ALLAN BEEVER*

I. Introduction

In *Smith v Leech Brain & Co Ltd*, Lord Parker CJ maintained that:

> it is important that the common law, and the development of the common law, should be homogeneous in the various sections of the Commonwealth. I think it would be lamentable if a court sitting here had to say that while the common law in the Commonwealth and Scotland has been developed in a particular way, yet we in this country, and sitting in these courts, are going to proceed in a different way.[1]

The context for this remark was that the Lord Chief Justice seemed forced to choose between the approach to remoteness set out by the English Court of Appeal in *In Re Polemis and Furness*[2] and that advanced by the Privy Council in *The Wagon Mound (No 1)*.[3] According to strict interpretations of the doctrine of precedent, the former was binding on him. Nevertheless, Lord Parker declared himself ready to abandon it in favour of the latter.[4]

Given the special, not always easy to define, place of the Privy Council in English law, this was not unexpected. However, Lord Parker was not motivated merely by deference to the Privy Council or its judges. His firm position was that the common law throughout the Commonwealth ought to be 'homogenous'. He described the alternative as 'lamentable'.

Compare this with the position taken by the New Zealand Court of Appeal in *Invercargill City Council v Hamlin*.[5] The question for this Court was whether New Zealand law ought to be brought into line with the English, as represented by the decision of the House of Lords in *Murphy v Brentwood District Council*.[6] The judges answered with a unanimous

* Thanks to Charles Rickett.

[1] *Smith v Leech Brain & Co Ltd* [1962] 2 QB 405 (QBD), 415–16.

[2] *In Re Polemis and Furness* [1921] 3 KB 560 (CA).

[3] *Overseas Tankship (UK) Ltd v Morts Dock & Engineering Co Ltd (The Wagon Mound, No 1)* [1961] AC 388 (PC).

[4] However, Lord Parker also thought that, in the end, it was not necessary to choose between these views.

[5] *Invercargill City Council v Hamlin* [1994] 3 NZLR 513 (CA).

[6] *Murphy v Brentwood District Council* [1991] 1 AC 398 (HL).

and resounding 'No'. No doubt aware that an appeal to the Privy Council was inevitable and that the chance of convincing that body effectively to rule that *Murphy* was wrongly decided infinitesimal, the judges determined on a strategy of arguing that, while appropriate for England and Wales, *Murphy* would be wrong for New Zealand. This was because, in the words of McKay J, the 'scene in New Zealand ... is so very different from that in the United Kingdom'.[7] As Richardson J explained, 'the common law of New Zealand should reflect the kind of society we are and meet the needs of our society',[8] the implication being that, as New Zealand society is not like English society, New Zealand law should not be like English law.

Cooke P went further, working these ideas up into a declaration of independence, albeit one that called also for mutual respect:

> One need hardly labour that Judges in different common law countries may legitimately differ in their conclusions in such a field ... While the disharmony may be regrettable, it is inevitable now that the Commonwealth jurisdictions have gone on their own paths without taking English decisions as the invariable starting point. The ideal of a uniform common law has proved as unattainable as any ideal of a uniform civil law. It could not survive the independence of the United States; constitutional evolution in the Commonwealth has done the rest. What of course is both desirable and feasible, within the limits of judicial and professional time, is to take into account and learn from decisions in other jurisdictions. It behoves us in New Zealand to be assiduous in that respect.[9]

This rhetoric is hard to defy. The Privy Council certainly failed to do so when it heard the appeal.[10] But what is to be made of this, not as rhetoric, but as argument?

First, it is of course true that the various common law jurisdictions 'may' differ in their conclusions in the sense that the courts in London do not have the authority they once had.[11] The common law no longer emanates from England alone. And it is of course also true that the political independence of the United States, Australia, Canada and New Zealand made some division inevitable. But that alone does not argue for the position Cooke P needs in order to justify his stance in *Hamlin*: that divergence can be not merely legitimate but desirable. It is one thing to say that the New Zealand courts are permitted to deviate from English law and that they will inevitably do so; it is another to say that it can be a good thing when they do. To put this another way, as far as Cooke P's argument has taken us, it remained entirely possible for the Privy Council to have agreed that the New Zealand courts have the authority to depart from English law but to have held also that New Zealand law ought to be brought into line with *Murphy*, not because English law has authority over New Zealand law, but because the position adopted in *Murphy* is right and that advanced in *Hamlin* wrong.

We have already seen the New Zealand Court's response to this: that the law must respond to local conditions and that conditions in New Zealand are different to those in England. The problem with this answer is that it is in tension with other claims Cooke P makes, claims that have equal rhetorical force to those already examined.

[7] *Invercargill City Council v Hamlin*, above n 5, 546.

[8] ibid 524.

[9] ibid 523.

[10] *Invercargill City Council v Hamlin* [1996] AC 624 (PC).

[11] However, it is worth remembering that at the time the Privy Council remained New Zealand's final court of appeal. It is very difficult to make sense of the New Zealand Court of Appeal's position given this fact. However, I generally overlook that difficulty in the following.

If the law rightly responds to local conditions and thus jurisdictions can appropriately diverge, then why is this described as resulting in regrettable disharmony? Why is it regrettable and why is it disharmony? Is it not better described as justified variation? Moreover, though Cooke P accepts what perhaps all accept, that the common law jurisdictions can and should learn from each other, how exactly is this possible? If the law responds to local conditions, conditions that are said to be 'so very different' in New Zealand from those in England, then how can the New Zealand courts learn anything from English law or vice versa? Is it not rather that, according to this view, the only thing to be learnt is how different Brits and Kiwis are?

This chapter holds that the positions advanced in *Leech Brain* and *Hamlin* are half right and half wrong. It maintains that Lord Parker was wrong to claim that the common law jurisdictions must be homogenous and that divergence is lamentable. Nevertheless, his Lordship was right to insist that homogeneity is an ideal at which the jurisdictions must aim, a view that entails that divergence is problematic in the sense to be defined below. On the other hand, the New Zealand Court of Appeal was wrong to claim that the law responds to local conditions—at least wrong to say that the common law, the judge made law, characteristically does so—and that divergence is unremarkable. But the Court was right to maintain that it is legitimate for the jurisdictions to diverge and that this is to be celebrated rather than regretted. And Cooke P was also right to insist that the jurisdictions must learn from each other and that divergence is to be viewed, in some way, as regrettable and as disharmony.

The difficulty is that this looks paradoxical. If homogeneity is an ideal, then how can it not be lamentable when the law fails to achieve it? And how can divergence be legitimate if it is not local conditions to which the law responds? Finally, if divergence is legitimate, then how can it properly be regarded as regrettable disharmony and how can the jurisdictions learn from each other? The aim of this chapter is to answer these questions. In order to do so, it is first necessary to distinguish between three ways of learning.

II. Learning as Observation, Application and Engagement

There are many ways in which one can learn from other cultures. For the purposes of our investigation, it is useful to distinguish between three. Most basically, one learns from other cultures simply by witnessing them. One learns, for instance, that business cards are much more important in China than they are in Australia; that while touching a child's head can be appropriate in Canada it is not in Thailand; and that Westerners eat with knives and forks, Thais with forks and spoons and Chinese with chopsticks. These cultural differences are interesting in their own right and, naturally, one learns something when one notices them. We can call this *learning as observation*.

Compare that form of learning with the following example. Imagine that a clothing entrepreneur discovers that a foreign people use a certain type of fibre in the production of their clothing and realises that the fibre could be utilised for clothing manufacture in her own country. This begins as observation but it goes beyond that. There is not merely learning-that here but also learning-from. The entrepreneur learns that the foreign culture utilises the fibre and learns from this that the fibre can be used at home. The knowledge acquired from the observation is applied, hence the label *learning as application*.

Importantly, this form of learning does not require the learner strongly to connect with the culture from which she learns. For instance, it might be that the fibre is used in the foreign culture for religious reasons only, but that may have no effect on the decision to employ it at home. In fact, the entrepreneur may be entirely ignorant of this or dismiss the belief out of hand as superstition.

That form of learning needs to be compared to a third, labelled *learning as engagement*. This learning is engaged because it takes the reasons offered in the foreign culture for the cultural practice to be reasons that apply directly to the home culture. Imagine, for instance, a heart surgeon based in Australia who, on a tour of hospitals in the United States, discovers that American heart surgeons utilise a technique for conducting angioplasties with which our surgeon is unfamiliar. The Australian surgeon asks why this technique is used and is told that it reduces the risk of morbidity by 20 per cent. It would be very odd if our surgeon were to respond to this by thinking: 'How interesting these Americans are. I wonder if there is anything we can do with this information back home in Australia?' Learning as application is strange in this context. The normal response is rather immediately to take the reasons for using the procedure in the United States as reasons for adopting it in Australia. This is learning as engagement.

These reasons need not be decisive. It may be that they are discovered to be outweighed by countervailing reasons. Perhaps the surgeon later learns that the procedure also increases the risk of mortality by 20 per cent. It might also be discovered that the reasons are bad ones. Perhaps the new procedure actually increases the risk of morbidity. Nevertheless, it remains the case that the reasons that apply in the United States directly apply to Australia. More fully, it is accepted that if the reasons given are good in the United States, then they are good (though not necessarily decisive) in Australia. Conversely, if the reasons given are bad in the United States, then they are bad in Australia. Likewise, if the reasons are found to be bad in Australia, then this shows that they must also be bad in the United States and, if the reasons are confirmed to be good in Australia, then this gives more evidence to show that they are also good in the United States. The learning involved here is not learning by application but by engagement.[12] The clothing entrepreneur can be entirely indifferent to the fact that the fibre is used for religious reasons in the observed culture, but the surgeon cannot be likewise indifferent to the risk of morbidity.

The distinction between learning as application and as engagement can be a fine one. Moreover, I do not claim that the distinction possesses any special significance beyond its ability to clarify issues for the purposes of the following analysis. But it is important to stress the way in which it is employed here. Most significantly, the distinction does not turn on whether the learner is concerned with the reasons given in the foreign culture. Again, an example should help to clarify this point.

Imagine that a ministerial study group leaves Canada to examine recent education reforms in the United Kingdom. One task of this group is to examine the reasons for reform given in the United Kingdom. The group decides that these reasons are compelling and advises that the reforms be adopted in Canada. The point to be made here is that, if the approach

[12] I do not mean to suggest that learning by application cannot be appropriate in this context. Imagine, for instance, that Americans and Australians had different heart structures, such that the procedure was advantageous for Americans but deleterious for Australians. In those circumstances, learning by engagement would be inappropriate and learning by application desirable. But that is not standard with respect to medical procedures.

of the study group is to consider whether the reasons given in the United Kingdom apply in Canada (as it will almost certainly be), then the learning is by application rather than by engagement. The clothing entrepreneur took a *practice* found in a foreign culture and applied it to her home environment. The study group learns from *reasons* given by a foreign culture and applies this learning to its home environment. But the study group does not take these reasons as immediately applying to Canada. This can be revealed by noticing the following possibilities. The study group may conclude that the reasons are (1) good in the United Kingdom and good in Canada; (2) good in the United Kingdom but bad in Canada; (3) bad in the United Kingdom and bad in Canada; or (4) bad in the United Kingdom but good in Canada. Options (2) and (4) would not be possible if the form of learning were learning as engagement as this approach takes the reasons given in the foreign culture as reasons that apply directly to the home culture.

It is an extremely important feature of the common law that, traditionally at least, Commonwealth courts learn from each other by engagement rather than by application. A paradigm instance of this learning is found in *Caparo Industries v Dickman*,[13] in their Lordships' examination of the decision of the New Zealand Court of Appeal in *Scott Group Ltd v McFarlane*.[14]

Lord Bridge quoted the key section of Richmond P's judgment in *Scott Group* and then simply stated that he agreed with Richmond P's reasoning.[15] Lord Oliver also quoted from Richmond P's judgment and concluded that the appropriate position was 'correctly and admirably stated in the passages from the judgment of Richmond P. in the *Scott Group* case to which I have already referred'.[16] These are not examples of observing what was done in New Zealand and seeking an application for these ideas in England. On the contrary, the reasons given in the judgment of the New Zealand Court of Appeal were taken as reasons that applied directly to English law. This is learning as engagement.

The relationship between *Caparo* and *Scott Group* is particularly useful for our purposes because, on the issue relevant to *Caparo*, Richmond P was in the minority in *Scott Group*. On this matter, he was opposed by Woodhouse and Cooke JJ. The treatment of their Honours' judgments in *Caparo* is also instructive. Lord Oliver said:

> Now, of course, any decision of the Court of Appeal of New Zealand is entitled to the very greatest respect, but it has to be observed that the majority view was based upon an interpretation of Lord Wilberforce's observations in the *Anns* case [1978] A.C. 728, 751–752 which has since been severely qualified by subsequent decisions of this House.[17]

Moreover, as his Lordship later explained, this qualification arose because the original interpretation of the judgment in *Anns* was mistaken.[18] Lord Oliver was not saying, as it were, 'I have considered the majority's position in *Scott Group*, but I cannot find any useful application for it in England'. He was saying that the argument presented by the majority is unsound. It was important for Lord Oliver to do this, because he took those reasons to have direct application to English law. Our clothing entrepreneur can be indifferent to the

[13] *Caparo Industries v Dickman* [1990] 2 AC 605 (HL).
[14] *Scott Group Ltd v McFarlane* [1978] 1 NZLR 553 (CA).
[15] *Caparo*, above n 13, 624.
[16] ibid 650.
[17] ibid 647.
[18] ibid 648.

reasons for the use of the fibre in the foreign culture. It matters not one iota to her whether they are good or bad. But because Lord Oliver was engaged with New Zealand law, because he took the reasons given in that law to be of direct application to English law, it was important for him to show that those given by Woodhouse and Cooke JJ were mistaken—mistaken in New Zealand and mistaken in England. Again, this is learning as engagement, in this case learning from mistakes.

III. The Position

The purpose of this chapter is not to argue in favour of any position, at least not directly. It is to uncover what must be true about law if this form of learning between jurisdictions is possible. It is, in this way, an investigation into the transcendental presuppositions of this element of legal practice. It is also an attempt to bring together, as far as possible, the positions advanced in *Leech Brain* and *Hamlin*, both of which seem to be getting at something important. Because of this focus, a position is formally outlined now and investigated in the remainder of the chapter. It is assumed that the position represents the (or at least a) standard view of the relationship between common law jurisdictions. It is the view found in the vast majority of the case law, for instance. The question is whether we can make sense of it, whether it is really possible. It is this.

First, it is legitimate for common law jurisdictions to differ. By legitimate, I mean that divergence does not involve the violation of authority. The New Zealand Court of Appeal was right to assert in *Hamlin* that English law does not have authority over New Zealand law, for instance. Secondly, this is not merely the political reality; the independence of the jurisdictions is desirable from the perspective of the common law itself.[19] That law would be weaker, not stronger, if it were controlled by a Supreme Court in, say, London. The ability of common law jurisdictions to reach divergent positions is to be celebrated. Thirdly, the common law jurisdictions can learn from each other in the sense of learning as engagement. The position advanced here supports the traditional legal practice. In general, at least, reasons that apply to one jurisdiction apply directly to another.[20] Finally, despite the fact that divergence is legitimate and that the possibility of divergence is desirable and to be protected, divergence is always problematic. By this I mean that, at least in the vast majority of cases, divergence is to be regarded as disagreement.

This last notion is usefully compared with the position taken in *Hamlin*. The judges in that case did not say that *Murphy* was wrongly decided and should not be applied in New Zealand (or in England). Their claim was that, though *Murphy* might be fine for English conditions, it did not suit New Zealand's. This is divergence without disagreement. It is contended that this is illusory. *Hamlin* and *Murphy* are not appropriately different responses

[19] I do not mean to suggest that this is necessarily the case. It is possible, for instance, that the decision-making in a particular jurisdiction is so poor that it would be better were it to lose its independence. I make no comment as to whether any such jurisdictions exist.

[20] Naturally, there are exceptions. The most notable, and perhaps the only, is when legislation varies between the jurisdictions. This is an investigation of the common law and of common law reasoning and is not designed to take legislation into account.

to different circumstances; they are irreconcilable. The decision in *Hamlin* is in conflict with that of the House of Lords in *Murphy*.[21] It is notable that, despite the New Zealand Court of Appeal's official position, this is the way in which the case is normally understood. Few take *Hamlin* to be compatible with *Murphy* or believe that the judges in that case really thought it was.

It is also important to stress that the fourth element of the position underlies the third. If divergence were not problematic in the relevant sense, then it would be hard to see how anything relevant to lawyering could be learnt from it.[22] If New Zealand and English societies are so different that their common laws ought to diverge, then what has New Zealand law to learn from English law or vice versa? It is rather that, because the laws in principle ought not to diverge that divergence can be learnt from. How that is possible needs to be explained.

As already noted, this position appears to be paradoxical. But we can remove this appearance via a brief examination of the structure of meta-ethics.

IV. Topography of Meta-Ethics

In this area as in many others, terminology can be problematic. We need to distinguish between positions that are here labelled cognitivism and non-cognitivism, relativism and objectivism, subjectivism and cultural relativism. Different theorists employ these terms differently and there can be no guarantee that my use of them corresponds to their use elsewhere. But terminology is not important in itself. The conceptual distinctions between the positions examined ought to be clear and the logic of the position advanced should be transparent. Terminology is a mere tool to this end. Moreover, it should be said that the following investigation is of course far from exhaustive. It merely draws the most basic of maps. This is sufficient for the points that need to be made here. In part, this is because, though the following discussion suggests that various positions ought to be rejected, its aim is not to prove this but rather to reveal the possibilities inherent in the view that it supports. It may well be that sophisticated versions of other views are able to reach similar conclusions.[23]

Meta-ethics is in part the study of the meaning of moral statements. A meta-ethicist asks, for example, not whether abortion is morally permissible, but what it means to say that abortion is morally permissible. She is concerned to understand the logical structure of moral claims. Understood in this way, a fundamental distinction in meta-ethics is between cognitivism and non-cognitivism. Cognitivism is the view that moral utterances express propositions and thus have truth values. We return to that view shortly. Non-cognitivism holds that moral statements do not express propositions and so do not have truth values. We examine this view first.

[21] Which is why the acceptance of *Invercargill City Council v Hamlin* [1994] 3 NZLR 513 (CA) in *Invercargill City Council v Hamlin* [1996] AC 624 (PC) must strike one as craven, even given the political circumstances and even if one prefers the New Zealand position. See also *Lange v Atkinson* [2000] 1 NZLR 257 (PC).

[22] As opposed to, say, anything relevant to sociology.

[23] I am thinking especially of the quasi-realism advanced by Simon Blackburn. See, eg, S Blackburn, *Essays in Quasi-Realism* (Oxford, OUP, 1993).

An initial difficulty with non-cognitivism is that the theory clashes with the grammatical form of moral statements. 'Murder is wrong', for instance, resembles 'Snow is white' in form, both appearing to be statements of fact, utterances in the indicative. But the non-cognitivist responds that, in the moral realm, form disguises content. Though moral utterances are voiced in the indicative mood, they are in fact expressions of some kind. That begs the question: What kind? At this point, non-cognitivism divides into various sub-theories. Emotivists maintain that moral utterances are expressions of emotion. 'Murder is wrong' means something like 'Murder, yuck' and 'Charity is good' means something like 'Charity, yay'. Similarly, prescriptivists hold that moral statements are commands, so 'Murder is wrong' means 'Don't murder!' while 'Charity is good' means 'Be charitable!'. The key point here is that, on these views, the utterances are not in reality statements and so do not possess truth values. While 'Murder is wrong' appears to be a statement assessable for truth, if it in fact means 'Murder, boo' or 'Don't murder!' then no truth claim is being made by the utterance. No proposition is expressed. The utterance cannot be true or false.

A similar question can be posed for cognitivism. If moral utterances have truth values, what kind of truth is in question? Again, there are various answers. The main divide at this point is between relativism and objectivism.[24] Relativists hold that the truth of a moral utterance is relative to something, objectivists hold that the truth holds universally. It is particularly important to stress that relativism is a cognitivist theory, as will become clearer in the following. (If relativism were not cognitivist, then what exactly would be relative to what?)

In principle relativism could come in infinite forms, but there are two most popular flavours. The first is subjectivism. This favourite view of undergraduate students maintains that the truth of a moral claim is relative to the beliefs of the person uttering it. So, for instance, if I believe that abortion is morally permissible and I say 'Abortion is morally permissible', then my claim is true. This is because the statement means 'abortion is morally permissible in my opinion'. The utterance is, as they say, true for me. Conversely, if I believe that abortion is morally permissible and I say 'Abortion is morally impermissible' then my claim is false, because the utterance means 'abortion is morally impermissible in my opinion' and that is not my opinion. The utterance is, as we might say, false for me.

Despite its adolescent attractiveness, subjectivism has at least two serious problems. The first is that it is very difficult to accept that all moral claims are merely a matter of opinion. There can be no doubt that Himmler believed the extermination of the Jews to be a moral imperative, but few will happily conclude that he was correct to believe this, even if only correct for him. And it would be difficult to maintain one's subjectivism while being shipped to some modern Auschwitz on the grounds that one's persecutors sincerely believed in what they are doing and so must be right … for them.

The second problem is that the theory has a deeply puzzling consequence. If I believe that abortion is morally permissible and say 'Abortion is morally permissible' and you believe that abortion is morally impermissible and say 'Abortion is morally impermissible', then on the face of it we are having a disagreement. In some parts of the world, this disagreement might result in one of us being shot. But subjectivism makes this impossible to understand. If my statement means that abortion is morally permissible in my opinion and if

24 Strictly, the contrary of relativism is absolutism, but that term has such unfortunate connotations that I have thought it best to avoid it here.

your statement means that abortion is morally impermissible in your opinion, then both statements are true. Moreover, as I know that your opinion is that abortion is impermissible, it seems that I ought to recognise immediately that your statement is true. Likewise, as you know that my opinion is that abortion is permissible, you ought to recognise that my statement is true. So why do we argue then? According to subjectivism, it seems that we are agreeing with each other and realise this, without somehow realising that we realise it.

Note that this difficulty has nothing to do with tolerance. The point is not that, according to subjectivism, we ought to tolerate our differences, to agree to disagree or the like.[25] The point is that, if subjectivism is right, there is no disagreement to tolerate. Most philosophers have found this conclusion so counter-intuitive that they have searched for another theory.[26]

A second form of relativism holds that moral claims are true relative to the values of the culture in which they are uttered: cultural relativism.[27] So, for instance, if I utter 'Sexual discrimination is wrong', that claim is true as it is accepted by the culture in which I live.[28] In other parts of the world and at other times of my culture's history, however, the utterance would be false, reflecting the different cultural values in play.

Assuming that you are from my culture, this theory can explain how moral disagreement is possible. When I utter 'Sexual discrimination is wrong', I make a claim that is true. It is true because it accurately reflects the relevant cultural values. Thus, if you reject my claim, you are wrong to do so—your rejection is the utterance of a false claim—because your statement does not reflect the values of our culture.

That is an improvement on subjectivism, but it seems that serious problems remain. First, though cultural relativism can explain the existence of our disagreement, it locates that disagreement in an odd place. Against the theory, it does not seem that our disagreement is about the values of our culture. For instance, you are unlikely to feel defeated if I present the results of an opinion poll showing that 95 per cent of people in our society share my view of the matter. It seems that our disagreement is about sexual discrimination and not about our culture's attitude towards sexual discrimination. Secondly, while cultural relativism can at least partially account for the existence of interpersonal moral disagreement, it faces the same difficulties as subjectivism when applied interculturally. For instance, most of us want to be able to say that Western culture was wrong to accept sexual discrimination in the past and that the culture has improved in this regard through time. But it is impossible to make quite that claim according to cultural relativism. Given that theory, we can say that, according to our contemporary cultural values, our past culture was wrong and society has improved, but we must also recognise that, according to the cultural values of our past, it is we who are wrong, they who are right, and there has

[25] We see in the following that this claim is false, but the point here is that it is not relevant.

[26] The trend historically was to move from subjectivism to non-cognitivism.

[27] Note that this term is also used to refer to quite different notions not under consideration here. For instance, anthropologists might use 'cultural relativism' to refer to the quite clearly correct idea that different cultures have different moral values in fact. That use of the term is not employed here.

[28] In fact, this is not entirely clear. It is arguable that sexual discrimination is accepted in fact, though not in principle, and so is accepted in the values that the culture really has. It is also difficult to determine the relevant culture. Is it the culture in which I was born or in which I live now? If it is the latter, is it the culture of the Auckland University of Technology, of Auckland, of New Zealand, of the Western world? I leave these and other important questions unanswered here.

been deterioration rather than improvement. In short, then, we cannot say that there has been improvement (or decline) in any area *simpliciter*. As these claims are themselves moral claims, we can only make them relative to a set of cultural values.

This feature of meta-ethical cultural relativism has led many to think that the theory demands intercultural tolerance. The idea is that, as there is no standpoint that can be adopted that permits one culture to criticise another, a demand for tolerance necessarily results. It is important for our purposes to see that this is not the case. Let us take an example.

The decision of the New Zealand Court of Appeal in *Awa v Independent News Auckland Ltd*[29] involved a dispute between the immediate and extended families of the entertainer, Billy T James.[30] When James died, his body was forcibly taken from his home by members of his Maori extended family against the wishes of his Pakeha (ie, European) immediate family so that he could lie on the local *marae*, the Maori public home of James' extended family, so that he could be buried in accordance with the custom of his Iwi (tribe) on Taupiri mountain. As one might imagine, this case generated considerable controversy. In part, this was because a clash of cultural values was involved. On one side stood Pakeha culture, according to which a person's funeral ought to be organised in accordance with the wishes of his immediate family (James' expressed intentions were conflicting). On the other stood Maori culture with its emphasis on established protocol and the extended family.[31] If one imagines that I am a member of the Pakeha culture, how ought I react to a case of this kind according to cultural relativism?

It is tempting to think that, as cultural relativism holds that there is no overarching truth of the matter as to what ought to have been done in such a case, I ought to advise tolerance and understanding of both points of view. But that is quite mistaken. According to cultural relativism, there is a truth of the matter, it is just that the truth is relative. As I am a member of the Pakeha culture, the right thing for me to do is what my cultural values tell me to do: to deplore the actions of James' extended family and their values (given the assumptions that we are making). It is true that, were I Maori, the same actions would be immoral, but that is not to the point. Meta-ethical cultural relativism tells me that moral truth is relative to culture, it does not tell me that I ought to inhabit or even consider the cultural views of others—unless, coincidentally, these happen to be my culture's values.

The claim that one should be tolerant of other cultures is a normative, not a meta-ethical, claim. According to cultural relativism, then, it follows that the claim is true if and only if it is uttered by a person in a culture that values intercultural tolerance.

Because this point is of much importance for the discussion that follows, it is worth clarifying it by means of an imaginary discussion between a cultural relativist and an imperialist. In this discussion, the imperialist accepts without question the meta-ethical claims made by the philosopher.

Imperialist: I am proud of the way that our great nation has civilised the savage peoples of this world. It is a great privilege for them to learn to live, even in

[29] *Awa v Independent News Auckland Ltd* [1997] 3 NZLR 590 (CA).

[30] That is a slight simplification, as James' family circumstances were complex, but the simplification is of no moment here.

[31] Of course, we are once again simplifying. This is necessary in order to uncover the relevant theoretical points.

small part, as we do and to be taught to adopt our superior values. I trust that they are grateful.

Philosopher: You say that, but in fact there are no culturally independent moral truths. Your moral values are true only because and to the extent to which they are reflected in the values of your culture. These people who you deem to be savages have their own culture with its own values. According to those values, what you call savagery is good and right. And it is good and right, for them.

Imperialist: Yes, it is good and right for them. So what?

Philosopher: Well, as those values are good and right for them, you should respect those values.

Imperialist: Why on earth should I do that? The values you point to are good and right for them, but, thankfully, I am not one of them. I am me. We are talking about what I should do. According to your theory, the moral thing for me to do is to obey the values of my own culture and they quite rightly tell me that I must civilise these savages.

Philosopher: But in order to call them savages, you must think that there is some standpoint from which you can compare the two cultures and show that yours is the best. But I tell you that there is no such standpoint.

Imperialist: Yes there is. There is the standpoint of my culture. According to that standpoint, we are civilised and they are savages. What more need be said?

Philosopher: But, objectively speaking, that standpoint is no better than the standpoint of the cultures you describe as savage. From their standpoint, it is your culture that is defective.

Imperialist: I thought you told me that there was no objective standpoint. And I don't care what my culture looks like from their perspective. Why should I be concerned with that?

Philosopher: I guess that the point I am trying to make is that, as there is no way of comparing these cultures objectively, you have to accept that your culture is no better than any other and thus you should learn to tolerate cultural differences.

Imperialist: Oh, I am happy to accept as a matter of meta-ethics that there is no way of comparing cultures as if from some view from nowhere. But I'm not bothered about that. I am not theorising, I am doing. And what I am doing you can give me no reasons for not doing. As you have told me, moral truth is relative to cultural values and my cultural values tell me that I have a duty to civilise these savages, so stand aside.

Philosopher: [Now desperate] But you cannot justify imposing your views on the people of another culture unless, at least in principle, you can show *them*, or some neutral person, that your values are superior.

Imperialist: Ah, now you have changed your mind. What you have just said reflects no value in my culture. It seems to me that you are appealing to a value you think to be true regardless of the values of any culture. Aren't you really an objectivist?

It is wrong to think that meta-ethical cultural relativism necessarily supports tolerance. This is evident from the structure of the claim that tolerance is a moral requirement. A person who insists on intercultural tolerance does not intend to make an assertion relative to any particular culture; she means to state something intended to hold for all cultures. She is saying that you ought to be tolerant regardless of your culture's beliefs.

Moreover, even when cultural relativism promotes tolerance, it does so in a particular fashion. If the values of my culture entail that I ought to be tolerant of the cultures of others, then cultural relativism tells me that I ought to be tolerant. This is because the truth of a moral claim, for me, is determined by the values of my culture. As it were, it is my culture that tells me to be tolerant of other cultures. According to this view, then, moral investigation is carried out by examining the beliefs of one's own culture. This position entirely rules out learning from other cultures by engagement. Learning as observation is possible as is learning by application—for instance, one might observe another culture and see that their practice reveals a better way of realising one's own cultural values—but as learning as engagement treats the reasons given in another culture as a reason that applies directly in one's own, it runs entirely against the spirit of cultural relativism. Thus, cultural relativism can be said to promote intercultural separation rather than association.

We turn now to meta-ethical objectivism. Naturally, this theory has its own difficulties. It is not necessary for our purposes to explore them. We need to examine only the relationship between objectivism, tolerance and learning.

As many have thought that cultural relativism leads to tolerance, it is also widely believed that objectivism tends to intolerance. The idea is that, if moral truth is universal, then this justifies one culture imposing its moral beliefs on another on the basis that the second culture's beliefs are false. Some objectivist theories may promote this form of imperialism, but objectivism need not do so. In order to see this, it is necessary to separate ontology and epistemology. Some examples will help to clarify this distinction and its application in this context.

I have no idea how many planets there are in the Andromeda galaxy. If two astronomers were to produce different numbers, I would be unable to choose between them.[32] Nevertheless, I am sure that there is a certain number of planets in that galaxy. The important point is this. My inability to determine the fact of the matter does not incline me to think that there is no fact of the matter. Epistemological uncertainty does not undermine ontological objectivity. Here, I am sure that there is a truth, it is just that I do not know what it is. Similarly, I do not know how language evolved. Though I am aware of different theories, I am in no position to say which is right. Nevertheless, I am sure that there is some reason language evolved. Some story, perhaps one not yet told, is right. Again, that I do not know the fact of the matter does not make me think that there is no fact of the matter. I am sure there is a truth, though I do not know what it is.

The general point to be made here is that objectivism is compatible with *fallibilism*. Objectivism is an ontological, fallibilism an epistemological, position. We can think that there is a truth of the matter without thinking that it is easy to discover what that truth is or that one can ever be sure that one is in possession of it. This is important in the moral realm because, if there are moral truths, they are notoriously difficult to be certain of. Thus, fallibilism seems the appropriate position to adopt in this context.

[32] This assumes, of course, that the numbers are remotely plausible. 'Four' would not do it.

The combination of objectivism and fallibilism promotes tolerance. According to objectivism there is a universal moral truth, but according to fallibilism we cannot be sure what it is. For that reason, interference with other cultures can be justified only in exceptional circumstances. In general, for all we know, they may be right and we may be mistaken. Moreover, not only should differences between cultures generally be tolerated, they can often be learnt from. On this view, for instance, it may be that the values of another culture are superior to our own, though, as always, it is difficult to be sure. Thus the combination of objectivism and fallibilism permits learning as engagement.[33]

Most significantly, this picture suggests that cultures can be understood, as it were, as experiments in morality, where each culture, through its own development, attempts to deepen its connection with the good life. On this view, cultures are to be viewed in part as learning resources for each other. All cultures are engaged in a common endeavour, an attempt to uncover the good life, and so each can learn from the others. This presents another argument for tolerance. Damaging others' experiments into the good life undermines the ability of all cultures, including one's own, to learn from those experiments.

V. Possibility of Inter-Jurisdictional Conversation

This discussion of meta-ethics, rudimentary though it necessarily was, helps us to understand how the position advanced above is possible. Later, we will also see that it helps to diagnose difficulties with opposing views. Let us now return to the theory advanced in section III. Recall that this possessed four features. The aim now is to show how each of these features is supported by a legal analogue of meta-ethical objectivism coupled with fallibility.

First, the position holds that divergence between the common law jurisdictions is legitimate. This is justified because, though there is an objective truth at which the law of the various jurisdictions aims, that truth can be very difficult to discover and one can never be sure whether a particular jurisdiction is in possession of it. In areas where the jurisdictions diverge, therefore, it is very often not clear which position is to be supported, if any. Even if all jurisdictions bar one adopt a particular view, it is possible that the aberrant jurisdiction has matters right, or at least more right than the others. Thus, the epistemological fallibilism of the position undermines the justification for inter-jurisdictional authority. And even if, say, the judges in London were better than the judges in Wellington, the latter may, on any particular matter, have a preferable view.

It has been claimed that there is an objective truth at which the law aims. At this point, we can be entirely neutral about the nature of this truth. However, as it will be convenient to have a term to refer to this notion, we will call it *legal justice*. As defined here, then, legal justice is the truth or good at which the law aims, whatever that is.

[33] To take one example, imagine that I ask an inhabitant of a traditional Samoan village why as an adult he continues to live along with his parents. He responds that his parents need to be looked after, they help in raising the children, and so on. These are themselves reasons for me to reintegrate my parents into my life, despite my culture's antagonistic attitude towards the integration of the extended family.

Secondly, the legitimacy of jurisdictional divergence is no mere matter of *Realpolitik*, it is desirable and strengthens the common law. This is because the different common law jurisdictions are to be regarded, as it were, as experiments in legal justice. They are engaged in an attempt to obtain an often elusive truth and divergence can aid in that search. Were divergence to be eliminated, the variety of these attempts would be also, making the common law less able to determine, in part by trial and error, what succeeds and what fails.

Thirdly, the common law jurisdictions are able to learn from each other. This is an immediate consequence of what has been said above. Because all jurisdictions are aimed at the realisation of legal justice, it is possible for courts to learn from the attempts of courts in other lands. What is more, this learning can take the form of learning as engagement, a point revisited in section VI below.

Finally, divergence is nevertheless problematic in the sense that it must be regarded as disagreement. This also follows from the above. Because all jurisdictions aim at the same thing, when two diverge, one at least must be wrong.[34]

Let us apply these ideas to the positions with which we began. In *Leech Brain*, Lord Parker was right to insist that divergence in the common law is problematic. However, it is at best an exaggeration to maintain that it is 'lamentable'[35] and, while homogeneity is an ideal, it is not realisable. The common law is a common endeavour, but that endeavour is conducted in an imperfect world by imperfect people and so not only does not require uniformity, it demands tolerance of nonconformity. In these respects the position taken by the New Zealand Court of Appeal in *Invercargill City Council v Hamlin* is to be preferred, recognising as it does that divergence is legitimate and inevitable. However, this Court mislocates the justification for this position. It is not that the law responds to local conditions that differ between jurisdictions. If that were so, then it would not be possible to make sense of Cooke P's claims that divergence is to be regarded as regrettable disharmony and that the jurisdictions can learn from each other. The relativism advanced by the Court undermines these possibilities. The better position is not to see the courts as trying to do different things, trying to respond to different conditions, but trying to do the same thing where reasonable people can often reasonably disagree as to what ought to be done. This is a tolerance that permits and encourages engagement.

On this interpretation, the message that ought to have been sent by the New Zealand Court of Appeal to the Privy Council in *Hamlin* was not that New Zealand law must respond to local New Zealand conditions, but that New Zealand law ought to be allowed to develop independently so that New Zealand lawyers can properly conduct the New Zealand experiment into realising legal justice in that jurisdiction,[36] a position that would advance the law of both jurisdictions in the long term, even if the position taken in *Hamlin* is wrong.

[34] See section VI below for clarification, however.

[35] *Smith v Leech Brain & Co Ltd* [1962] 2 QB 405 (QBD), 415–16.

[36] In effect, the plea was for the Privy Council to abolish itself as New Zealand's highest court, at least in these areas. Again, I think that this aligns with how the judgment, and the Privy Council's response to it, is generally understood. It is also to be noted that, in the end, the New Zealand Court of Appeal succeeded in this regard. See also *Lange v Atkinson* [2000] 1 NZLR 257 (PC), where the Privy Council effectively constituted the New Zealand Court of Appeal as, on some issues, a higher court of appeal than the Privy Council, meaning that the Court of Appeal was two appellate courts sitting at two different levels in the judicial hierarchy, and where appeals from the Court could be heard (even possibly by an identical bench) in that same Court. At that point, there was nothing left to do but to abolish appeals to the Privy Council, which was accomplished in 2003.

VI. Some Implications

This chapter has focused on the common law. But the analysis also applies to non-common law jurisdictions. Very frequently, their courts are attempting to do what ours are. For this reason, they too can be learnt from. Thus, comparative law is important because it enables us to learn, not only by observation and application, but by engagement. That said, however, the last is less frequent in this context because of the difficulty involved in translating ideas between legal families. Though the jurisdictions are frequently trying to get at the same thing, they have different traditions of getting there. To a lesser extent, this is also true of the division between the law of the Commonwealth and that of the United States. Here, then, in order to understand what the law is trying to achieve and how the law is trying to achieve it, it is necessary to uncover these traditions. Despite these difficulties, this can make comparative law even more important in terms of engagement. The traditions are at once both enabling and obscuring. For instance, the tradition of the common law as a whole may obscure problems with that law which, once one comes to terms with the tradition of civilian law that would otherwise be obscuring, German and Italian law can reveal.[37] Comparative law, therefore, is both valuable in its own right and as a form of engagement.

On the other hand, the position advanced here does not sit well with certain conceptions of the nature of law, as will be evident from the discussion of *Hamlin* above. It is here that we must confront the content of what we have been calling legal justice.

It is a widely held view that the law is at base a response to social conditions motivated by what we call policy concerns. These concerns, it is thought, are not different in kind to those considered by legislatures and the like. The point to be made here is that, if this were true, then this calls for a form of relativism that undermines the notion that the different jurisdictions could be engaged with each other. Rather, on this view, the learning that can occur between jurisdictions is that of observation and application but not engagement, just as it is in the political realm.

I will not argue against this view here, but it is significant to note that it is inconsistent with our ordinary view of the inter-jurisdictional operation of the common law, as involving engagement. That view makes sense only if the law is aiming at something far more definite and universal, ie, *common*, than policy or like notions. Elsewhere, I have presented a theory of law that can accommodate this vision, and others have done likewise. This is not the place to explore those views, but the following reflections are in order.

If positions of the kind advanced in *Hamlin* continue to find favour, then the common law is doomed to disintegration. If the law is based on policy, then why would we expect, or even want, greater uniformity in law than we find in our legislatures and executives? But that disintegration would be a very significant loss for the law and for our societies. It would mean that, instead of being involved in a common endeavour and instead of being able to

[37] Such as the doctrine of consideration, for example? See, eg, AT von Mehren, 'Civil Law Analogous to Consideration: An Exercise in Comparative Analysis' (1959) 72 *Harvard Law Review* 1009 and SA Smith, *Contract Theory* (Oxford, Clarendon Press, 2004) 215–22. Both authors are experts in civilian contract law.

learn from each other, each jurisdiction would be on its own. A very important resource would be lost, perhaps the most important resource that the common law possesses.[38]

This issue can also be approached from the other side. As has been noted, the fact is that our courts regard themselves as being engaged with other jurisdictions. They do not treat the common law of other countries as our legislatures treat others' statute law. This suggests that the mainstream understanding of law is in need of revision. In that light, let us turn to *Hamlin* one last time.

Recall McKay J's claim that the 'scene in New Zealand … is so very different from that in the United Kingdom'.[39] What were these differences said to be? Richardson J's arguments were that New Zealand has a high proportion of owner-occupier housing; that there has been considerable government support for private housing in New Zealand; that New Zealand experienced a large housing boom in the 1950s and 1960s; and that it was not common practice in New Zealand for those purchasing new houses to have those houses inspected by engineers or architects. It is surely clear that none of these considerations support the Court's claims that the New Zealand scene is different from that in the United Kingdom. After all, the position in the United Kingdom was not even considered.

Hamlin involved a plaintiff who had purchased a house that had not been built to an acceptable standard and as a result developed defects such as cracking walls and stuck doors. His claim was that the building inspector of the defendant council had negligently approved the building's foundations and thus the council was responsible for his loss. This case had nothing to do with the proportion of owner-occupier housing, the level of government support for housing, the existence of housing booms or common housing inspection practices. What matters is much more general: that people live in houses, that they need to be able to move between rooms, that they use doors to do so, that they find cracks in walls problematic, that they rely on inspectors, that (crucially in my view) inspectors do not provide guarantees to future purchasers,[40] and so on. There is no divide here between the United Kingdom and New Zealand. The division is entirely in terms of the decisions of the courts.

Similarly, *Hercules Managements v Ernst & Young*[41] involved a defendant firm of accountants who performed an audit of a third party company's financial statements for the company's AGM. The plaintiff shareholders of the company relied on this audit in choosing to invest in the company. It was alleged that the audit was conducted negligently and the plaintiffs detrimentally relied on the audit reports. It was accepted, however, that the defendant did not prepare the reports to facilitate investment decisions of this kind. The Supreme Court of Canada found for the defendant, an outcome that mirrors the decisions of Richmond P in *Scott Group* and the House of Lords in *Caparo*. However, the Canadian court supported its view on the basis that an alternative result would have a deleterious impact on the supply

[38] In my view, the common law's two most important resources are its history and its interjurisdictionality. But if law is based on policy, these cannot be strengths, as policy varies radically both between jurisdictions and in a jurisdiction over time. The common law has already lost most of its connection to its history—witness, for instance, the decline in the importance placed on legal history in law schools—and it will soon lose its interjurisdictionality. We can agree with Lord Parker that this is to be lamented.

[39] *Invercargill City Council v Hamlin* [1994] 3 NZLR 513 (CA), 546.

[40] A Beever, *Rediscovering the Law of Negligence* (Oxford, Hart Publishing, 2007) 250–51, 254–56.

[41] *Hercules Managements v Ernst & Young* [1997] 2 SCR 165.

and cost of accounting services in Canada. That concern was irrelevant. The issue was not the impact on accounting services or the like, but the relationship, or lack thereof, between the defendant and the plaintiff as Richmond P and the House of Lords explained.

These shifts to relativism are unmotivated and destructive. The general conception of law that demands them should be abandoned.

VII. Conclusion

The common law jurisdictions are engaged with each other in the sense explained above. They are involved in a common endeavour. This chapter has sought to describe the nature of this endeavour. It has sought to explain how homogeneity can be an ideal and how it can yet be valuable to permit divergence. It presents a theory that accords with the practice of the common law in this regard. The issue for the future is whether this practice will be retained or abandoned by our courts. If it is to be the latter, much of value will be lost.

11

The Philosophies of the Common Law and their Implications: Common Law Divergences, Public Authority Liability and the Future of a Common Law World

DAN PRIEL

Prologue

Following the economic crisis of the last few years, John Maynard Keynes has once again assumed centre-stage.[1] In this chapter I am not going to speak about Keynes's economic ideas, but will attempt to say something about the significance he accorded to ideas. In the concluding paragraphs of his *General Theory of Employment, Interest, and Money*, Keynes famously wrote that:

> the ideas of economists and political philosophers, both when they are right and when they are wrong, are more powerful than is commonly understood. Indeed the world is ruled by little else. Practical men, who believe themselves to be quite exempt from any intellectual influences, are usually the slaves of some defunct economist … I am sure that the power of vested interests is vastly exaggerated compared with the gradual encroachment of ideas.[2]

Keynes alludes in these brief remarks to a longstanding debate among historians and philosophers of history on the relative significance of ideas and interests.[3] In this chapter I will explore the influence of ideas on the common law. I will attempt to show that different answers to a philosophical question on the authority of the common law have very practical implications for the question of the relevance of convergence and divergence between different legal systems. Even more contentiously, I will argue that these philosophical debates have implications for substantive questions of tort law. In both domains, we cannot make

[1] For a comprehensive survey see '2008–09 Keynesian Resurgence' in Wikipedia, available at http://en.wikipedia.org/wiki/2008%E2%80%9309_Keynesian_resurgence.

[2] JM Keynes, *A General Theory of Employment, Interest, and Money* (London, Macmillan, 1936) 383.

[3] See, eg, Q Skinner, *Liberty Before Liberalism* (Cambridge, CUP, 1998) 101–8.

complete sense of the debate and have no basis for choosing one answer over another without attending to underlying ideologies. Even lawyers who believe themselves to be engaged in 'practical' scholarship, seeking to account for the law as found in the cases and basing whatever normative suggestions they make on nothing more than the idea that like cases be treated alike,[4] should not ignore the significance of these ideas.

I. The Puzzle of the Authority of the Common Law

For all the talk about the decline of the state, the rise of supranational legal regimes, and the growing significance of foreign, transnational and international law, much law is still tethered to nation states. And many who have thought about the matter have argued that within limits, states have legitimate authority to make laws that apply to the people who live within their boundaries. These days such accounts typically connect the authority to make laws to democracy. How exactly this link is to be drawn is, of course, a contested question, but no matter how one wishes to fill in the details, they do not seem to fit the common law particularly well. First, the principal law-makers in the common law are judges, who are typically unelected and unrepresentative. If the authority of law depends on its democratic credentials, then the common law seems to flout this requirement. Second and related, the common law seems to transcend state or other political boundaries, while tying together legal systems that sometimes have no political links to each other, and are geographically (and perhaps in other ways) far apart.

This puzzle can be presented in the following, very rough, syllogism:

(1) The (legitimate) authority of law derives from the authority of the state.
(2) The (legitimate) authority of the state derives from having democratic institutions.
(3) The common law is undemocratic.

Hence, (4) the authority of the common law looks suspect.

As presented, this syllogism is not meant to be an air-tight deductive argument, as its premises are very vaguely phrased. Nonetheless, it is helpful for presenting the problem of what I will call the puzzle of the authority of the common law, as well as for outlining possible answers to it. I will distinguish between three positions that can be placed on a spectrum that has complete legal localism at one end and legal universalism at the other. The first approach I will consider answers the puzzle by rejecting premise (3). Thus, this approach solves the puzzle of the common law's authority by explaining it away. It seeks to subsume the authority of the common law within a broader account of democratic authority. The second approach rejects premise (1). This view asserts, in effect, that the error in this argument is the thought that the authority of law derives from the state. On this view,

[4] See, eg, A Burrows, *Understanding the Law of Obligations: Essays on Contract, Tort and Restitution* (Oxford, Hart Publishing, 1998) 108, 118–19, 127; Andrew Burrows, 'The Influence of Comparative Law on the English Law of Obligations', ch 2 of this volume. On the question-begging nature of treating like cases alike see D Priel, 'Review of L Weinreb, *Legal Reason: The Use of Analogy in Legal Argument*' (2008) 57 *Journal of Legal Education* 579, 580–82; C Webb, 'Treating Like Cases Alike: Principle and Classification in Private Law' in A Robertson and HW Tang (eds), *The Goals of Private Law* (Oxford, Hart Publishing, 2009) 215, 227–28.

the authority of law derives from its content, from the correspondence of laws to an external standard—say, morality or natural law. So understood, even if the authority of the state is derived from maintaining democratic institutions, the authority of law (or at least the authority of the common law) is independent of those institutions. In fact, even the authority of democratic institutions on this view is derived from deeper moral principles that are not themselves majoritarian. The third approach focuses on premise (2). At its strongest, this view seeks the authority of the state in the idea of a political tradition, which it sees as more foundational than democracy. Though this view can be stated generally, in its legal incarnation, its proponents do not deny that the authority of *some* law is derived from the authority of the state, but they reject the idea that this is true of the authority of *all* law. Specifically, proponents of this view typically draw a sharp distinction between statute law, for which they think something like the syllogism is true, and common law, whose authority, they argue, is grounded in tradition.

What do these debates in political philosophy have to do with the concern of 'practical lawyers' about divergences in the common law? As I will try to demonstrate, quite a lot. The first view lends itself to the idea that convergence among common law countries is, if it happens, an interesting empirical finding, but it rejects outright the view that sees convergence as a normative ideal. The second view also rejects the ideal of common law convergence, but it does so in a very different way. The second view implies an ideal of *universal* convergence, one in which divergences among common law jurisdictions are no more problematic than divergence between common law and non-common law jurisdictions. It is only the third approach that fits the view (quite popular in certain circles) that common law jurisdictions, *and only* common law jurisdictions, ought to aim for convergence. To many who study the laws of contract, tort, property, trusts, and so on (those areas of law sometimes simply called 'the common law') talk of English, Canadian or Australian common law is in some sense misleading. Ultimately, they say, there really is just one common law. More than a description of reality, this is thought to be a normative claim: Divergences between (say) English and Australian law are a cause for concern, while divergences between (say) English and French law are not.[5]

In what follows I attempt to further explain the theoretical presuppositions of these competing approaches. I will first try to substantiate my claim that the different attitudes to the question of authority relate to different conceptions of authority. I will then argue that these differences also manifest themselves in different answers to substantive questions within private law. I will demonstrate this claim by looking at a few of the last decisions of the House of Lords and argue that we can make better sense of some divergences among the Law Lords if we understand them to hold different views on the authority of (common) law. Finally, I will argue that even assuming the view of authority that is most sympathetic to common law convergence, there are practical constraints that make such a convergence difficult to maintain. This explains why we see growing divergences among common law jurisdictions, a trend that I predict will continue.

[5] For example, contrast Robert Stevens's claim that divergences within the common law are 'disturbing', which he makes in 'Torts' in L Blom-Cooper *et al* (eds), *The Judicial House of Lords: 1876–2009* (Oxford, OUP, 2009) 629, 630, with his affirmation of divergences between common law and civil law jurisdictions in *Torts and Rights* (Oxford, OUP, 2007) 341, 347.

II. Three Views on the Authority of (Common) Law

In this section I will present three views about the authority of the common law. I will first present these views as ideal-types. As will become clearer towards the end of this section, reality is typically more complex; nevertheless, I believe the ideal-types approach helps to bring to light the issues that are at stake.[6]

Ideal-Type 1: Legal Localism

No-one finds it odd that Britain's constitutional law is different from Germany's or that France's copyright laws are different from those of the United States. No-one finds it odd that these differences are not confined to details, that they reflect a different 'philosophy' about separation of powers or democracy, about what these areas of law seek to achieve, or what values a legal system should strive to protect or promote through them. Why should tort or contract law be any different? Presenting the question in this way helps articulate a view. On this view, whether law deals with the regulation of air travel, the definition of and punishment for theft, the formation of contracts, or the legal response to cartels, it is the product of state authorities. True, some of the laws are created by the legislature, other laws by other public bodies (administrative tribunals, government bureaucrats, courts), but this fact does not show that the source of authority of laws of the second kind is any different from that of laws of the first kind. The fact that judges make law is thus *in itself* not more problematic than the fact that civil servants make law. (Even legislation, officially enacted by a democratically-elected legislature, is rarely exclusively, or even primarily, the work of the people's democratically-elected representatives; but that is a separate matter.) In short, this view subsumes the common law under the general law-making power of the state. The way to solve the puzzle of the authority of the common law is not to present the common law as unique—the common law on this view is law just like any other—but rather by explaining how the way it is promulgated can be made to fit our ideas of democratic authority. In the modern state where much law is not created by elected representatives, that does not look like an insurmountable challenge.

If the mere fact that judges make law in those areas we call 'common law' is not a challenge to democratic authority (any more than any other delegated law-making is), it does, however, affect the specific contours of its institutions. For in a place in which this is the dominant conception of the authority of the common law we can expect to see its institutions shaped and understood in a way that fits these democratic credentials. Within the common law world, the country whose legal institutions reflect this view more purely than any other is the United States. And indeed, there are certain features unique to US common law that make sense only if one assumes the view that the authority of law derives from its being made by state institutions. I will mention three. Much more than in other common

[6] The ideas in this section are developed in greater detail in D Priel, 'Conceptions of Authority, Common Law Divergences, and the Future of a Common Law World' (unpublished manuscript). Unlike the three-fold typology found in this chapter, there I present a related, but somewhat different, four-fold typology.

law countries the 'common law' of the United States is nowadays codified. If the common law is not unique, if this area of law is not somehow a unique domain of the judiciary, then like all other law it should be found in statute. A second feature in which US common law now differs from most of the rest of the common law world is its continued commitment to a jury trial in both criminal and civil matters. Part of the justification offered for maintaining the jury trial is that it is a popular law-making institution, a means for 'the people' to have a say in, or control over, what the law is.[7] Finally, there is the method of appointing judges. What strikes outsiders as one of the oddest features of US law is the prevalence of elected judiciary in State courts. Even with Federal judges, who are not elected, their nomination process is openly political in a manner that has no parallel in other common law countries. This practice looks much less odd against the view that the law-making activity of judges must satisfy democratic constraints. All this fits a view much more dominant in US politics than elsewhere, which is that the executive and the judiciary (and not just the legislature) are representative of the people.[8]

The answer to the puzzle of the authority of the common law, then, is that there is no puzzle. Judge-made common law is not undemocratic if, first, it is conceived of as a form of democratic law-making power; and, second, when there are various institutional mechanisms in place as well as an underlying democratic ethos, that turn this idea into a reality. When this approach is applied to the question of common law convergence, it implies a relatively unsympathetic view of convergence. Different legal systems will, of course, sometimes converge, but this is, more or less, a happenstance. It is not at all something to aim for. While not universally accepted, this view about common law convergence is very popular in the United States.

Ideal-Type 2: Legal Universalism

At the other end of the spectrum we find the universalist view according to which underlying the law there are some general principles applicable to all the world. This position has a long and distinguished history under various names, but it is probably best known as 'natural law'. Stated abstractly, the idea that law should match some pre-existing, universal, standards is very familiar. It is held not just by self-styled natural lawyers, but also by their supposed intellectual opposites, legal positivists.[9] It is also held across the political spectrum, although those on the right tend to call those principles 'natural rights' whereas those on the left usually prefer to speak of 'human rights'.

Here, however, I prefer to talk about a more specific idea, the view that law *has authority* because, and to the extent that, it matches pre-existing universal morality. Understood as a view about authority, legal universalism is not embarrassed by the obvious reality of divergence between the laws of different countries. A proponent of this view needs to accept

[7] See JE Carroll, 'Nullification as Law' (2014) 102 *Georgetown Law Journal* 579.

[8] See RJ Pushaw, 'Justiciability and Separation of Powers: A Neo-Federalist Approach' (1996) 81 *Cornell Law Review* 393, 420–25.

[9] Even the more specific claim, that law is authoritative to the extent that it matches morality, is nowadays a familiar positivist idea. This is achieved by the fact that most legal positivists these days think of it as a thesis about legal validity rather than a thesis about authority. For more on this see D Priel, 'Toward Classical Legal Positivism' (2015) 101 *Virginia Law Review* 987, 995–96, 1019–20.

two propositions: first, that there are universal moral principles that underlie the law; and second, that the authority of positive law derives from its correspondence with natural law.

This view thus attempts to answer the puzzle of the authority of the common law by denying that the authority of law derives from its democratic credentials. If this is so, then the fact that the common law is undemocratic is not, by itself, a reason to question its authority any more than the authority of any other law. Thus, in pure form, this view rejects the uniqueness of the common law, but it does that in the opposite way to legal localism: no law is authoritative because of its democratic credentials. Both common (judge-made) law and statutes ultimately derive their authority from their correspondence to pre-existing moral norms. This view also rejects the uniqueness of the common law in another sense. It denies that there is anything special to common law *jurisdictions*, and therefore it denies that legal convergence should be limited just to these jurisdictions. If the underlying authority of all law is its correspondence with universal morality, it follows that the ideal of convergence of law extends to the whole world.[10]

Thus, in one sense, this view endorses a very strong version of convergence. In another sense, however, this view sees no value in convergence per se. There is on this view little or no value in convergence if different legal systems converge on the wrong rules or principles. Even when legal systems converge on the right principles, the fact of convergence does not add to the goodness of the situation. Of course, it is better if more jurisdictions identify the right answers to what the content of their laws should be, but the fact of convergence *itself* is of little value.

A seemingly intractable challenge to this view is the fact that in the modern state much law-making is done by democratic institutions and does not pay particular heed to universal morality and is premised on the unique needs of a particular time and place. Even if one accepts that the common law reflects some universal values, the fairly insignificant amount of law-making done by judges these days, when compared to the vast amount of law-making in the modern regulatory state, would seem to render this position completely untenable as an argument for the authority of all law.

A proponent of legal universalism may respond in three ways. The most radical response asserts that only universal laws—laws that avoid the promotion of particular policies—do not violate the rule of law, and only these laws can ultimately be justified. This was, for example, Hayek's answer in *The Road to Serfdom*. In the chapter on the rule of law Hayek argued that only general rules that similarly apply to all (all over the world) are consistent with the rule of law.[11] Closer to contemporary debates, this is also the answer offered by Allan Beever. Though he constructs his view somewhat differently, Beever believes that 'there is an objective truth at which the law of the various jurisdictions aims'. He therefore rejects the idea that divergence between jurisdictions is to be explained by different 'respons[es] to local conditions that differ between jurisdictions'; rather, he thinks that what explains

[10] For an example of this view see Allan Beever, 'How to Have a Common Private Law: The Presuppositions of Legal Conversation', ch 10 of this volume. Though at one point he says that 'divergence [between common law jurisdictions] is always problematic' (ibid, text following n 20) he is clear that the ideal of convergence he aims for is not limited to the common law world (ibid, section V).

[11] FA Hayek, *The Road to Serfdom* (London, Routledge, 2001 [1944]) 76, 79. Hayek contrasts there a 'permanent framework of laws', which consists of 'rules applying to general types of situations' with 'the direction of economic activity by a central authority'. (In later writings he may have been closer to the universal common law approach I will discuss below.)

those divergences is that different courts are 'trying to do the same thing where reasonable people can often reasonably disagree as to what ought to be done'.[12] As presented, this argument is fallacious. It is clearly not true that as a general matter laws cannot differ on the basis of local conditions: if one thinks that laws can be used to promote overall welfare, it is plain that local conditions will matter a great deal for determining the appropriate content for laws. Beever's argument can only go through with the addition of a missing premise, namely, that local conditions are *irrelevant* in law-making, and this view, in turn, can only be sustained if he assumes (like Hayek) that laws ought not be used to promote welfare.[13]

Others, of less libertarian leanings, have adopted more accommodating strategies. One such approach recognises the legitimacy of democratic law-making but considers it secondary (logically and normatively) to the universal principles enshrined in the common law. Consequently, democratically-adopted laws that conflict with the fundamental principles of the common law lack legitimate authority and may be declared legally invalid by a court, regardless of an enabling constitutional provision.[14] As this accommodating approach is more commonly adopted by Commonwealth public law scholars, I will set it aside here.

The last response to the challenge from democracy is more often found in the work of Commonwealth private law scholars. Rather than prioritising between the common law and statute, it sees the two as distinct and largely independent domains. This approach seeks further support for the normative significance of the distinction between common law and statute by tying it to a series of additional, partially overlapping, distinctions, as shown in Table 11.1.

Table 11.1: The common law–statute divide

Common law	**Statute**
Courts	Legislatures
Private law	Public law
Morality (and moral philosophy)	Politics (and political philosophy)
Principle	Policy
Corrective justice	Distributive justice
Individual rights	General welfare
Expertise (about morals)	Democracy

[12] Allan Beever, 'How to Have a Common Private Law: The Presuppositions of Legal Conversation', ch 10 in this volume, text following n 35.

[13] Elsewhere Beever claims that policy should have no place in *any* law (and not just in 'private law'). See A Beever, *Rediscovering the Law of Negligence* (Oxford, Hart Publishing, 2007) 71. It is this view, as well as views he expresses elsewhere, that warrant treating his position as very close to Hayek. See D Priel, 'Private Law: Commutative or Distributive?' (2014) 77 *MLR* 308, 328–29. However, in some places Beever accepts something like the distinctions found in Table 11.1. See Beever, *Rediscovering*, ibid 13–14, 52–53. In these places Beever accepts the weaker thesis only that the common law should not be used to promote welfare.

[14] See, eg, John Laws, *The Common Law Constitution* (Cambridge, CUP, 2014) 3 ('The common law is the interpreter of our statutes, and is the crucible which gives them life … [S]tatute law and government policy alike are delivered to the people through the prism of [common law] principles [such as reason, fairness, and the presumption of liberty]. This is the gift of the common law, the unifying principle of our constitution. It is the means by which legislature and government are allowed efficacy but forbidden oppression'); J Laws, 'Law and Democracy' [1995] *Public Law* 72.

The authority of the common law on this view is still derived from its correspondence to moral truth; by contrast, the authority of statute derives from different societies' adoption of different policies on the basis of their political preferences, as revealed by democratic processes. This view thus abandons common law universalism with regard to subject matter, but maintains it with regard to geographic scope. The ideal convergence of private law on this view is not limited to common law jurisdictions: reflecting universal morality, the content of private law should ideally be more or less the same throughout the world; public law, however, is for each political community to develop in accordance with its own values.

It is well beyond the scope of this chapter to carefully examine the merits of this view, but I will make three brief critical remarks about it. Beginning with an empirical observation, a fundamental problem with this approach is that it simply does not correspond to reality. The areas of law that are typically classified as 'private law' (contract, tort, and property) are shot through with statutes, which are often clearly motivated by distributive concerns. The divide also breaks down on the other side, since judges quite constantly invoke policy and distributive considerations in their determination and justification of common law rules.

I turn now to more theoretical concerns. Defenders of the view that private law should be free from policy often argue that this should be so, because the introduction of policy considerations into private law will necessarily render that area of law incoherent.[15] But the strategy represented in Table 11.1 does not avoid the problem of incoherence (assuming it is a problem), it only shoves it out of the private lawyer's sight. So long as private law and public law come into contact, the clashes between principle and policy, between rights and general welfare, between corrective and distributive justice are not avoided, they are moved somewhere else. If anything, the strategy that insists on somehow not talking about these interactions, on engaging in private law as if public law does not exist (and vice versa), only makes the problem worse.

Finally, for this view to be plausible there has to be something about judges that explains *why* they should decide certain questions and not democratic institutions. The typical answer democracies give to this question is that they allocate law-making power to non-democratic bodies when these bodies have special expertise on certain matters. Following this rationale, it makes sense to give this power to judges if there is something about them that lends credence to the idea that they are experts on identifying true, universal morality. Though such claims are sometimes made, it is entirely unclear what they are based on. Despite the veneration still accorded to appellate judges, most judges have not left a mark on history as particularly original or insightful thinkers, and very few of them would make it onto any list of history's greatest moral thinkers. To even make sense, we should believe that there is something in the training or occupation of judges that makes them moral experts, but there is little reason to think that. For myself, I am not sure what would count as moral expertise, but if repeated engagement with moral questions had been shown to sharpen one's moral sensibilities, moral philosophers would have made better candidates for the judiciary than lawyers. At the very least, then, for this claim to make sense, we would have expected judges to immerse themselves in the writings of moral philosophers (rather than those of lawyers) as a precondition for getting the job.

[15] See EJ Weinrib, *The Idea of Private Law*, rev edn (Oxford, OUP, 2012) 32–44.

Ideal-Type 3: Common Law Universalism

The two positions just outlined correspond, at least roughly, to one understanding of the divide between two familiar legal philosophies: legal positivism and natural law. These two approaches dominate jurisprudential discussions to such an extent that they seem to exhaust the theoretical space. These two views, however, neglect a third position, one that is in fact the most popular within the common law world (outside the United States). This approach sees a special unity among all common law jurisdictions but not between common law and non-common law jurisdictions. In other words, proponents of this view take a midway position between the two views considered earlier. To many common lawyers this view comes so naturally that they hardly bother to think about the fact that if they write on the law of contract, they may take particular interest in the judicial pronouncements of their own jurisdiction, but they will also closely follow developments in other common law jurisdictions. On the other hand, they will make much less of an effort to keep track with developments in the law of contract of non-common law jurisdictions, even when those non-common law jurisdictions (as is the case in Canada or Britain) belong to their own country! This view is not meant as a mere description of reality: as mentioned, many think that this view implies that common law systems *ought* to converge.

Can we make sense of this view? From the perspective of universalist natural law, this view seems odd. It asks us to assume, in effect, that all legal (or moral) wisdom descended on certain parts of the world and not on others. From the perspective of the localist view, this view is odd in asserting that its laws should aim to be similar to those of several completely independent countries. The key to understanding the common law convergence view is that it presupposes a distinct view of authority, one that sees the authority of law (or at least the authority of the common law) as grounded in history. On this mode of authority, we *ought* to do certain things in a particular way today, because of the *fact* that we did certain things in a similar way in the past.

This view thus asks us to derive an ought from an is. Could such a view ever be justified? Several arguments have been proposed in defence of this view, but here I will only consider one. This view maintains that we can make sense of our duties to others only by assuming our membership in a community; they further argue that the content of those obligations is neither a product of some social contract nor derived from reason. Rather, it derives from the history of that community. It is this history that shapes our normative realities and it implies that it is only through an engagement with the community's political past that we can identify our present-day obligations to other members of the community.

A key element to this view is the idea of tradition, not merely as a description of a certain set of ideas, but as a normative concept.[16] By 'tradition' I mean an amalgamation of prevailing ideas and concepts in a particular community combined with a more-or-less conscious sense of participation in a joint endeavour with past members of that community. Whatever the normative merits of this view may be, there are many reasons to think that the

[16] For a very strong version of this view, especially in relation to precedent, see AT Kronman, 'Precedent and Tradition' (1990) 99 *Yale Law Journal* 1029; *cf* I Hampsher-Monk, 'Political Languages in Time: The Work of J.G.A. Pocock' (1984) 14 *British Journal of Political Science* 89, 105 ('The notion of tradition which is so essential to an understanding of precedent-based behaviours pervades … [Pocock's] work, and plays a key role in his notion of explanation of history in the history of ideas').

common law *tradition* embraces something like this view. Legal rules are often developed by careful attention to past practice rather than by direct appeal to reason.

This idea is in plain sight with the doctrine of precedent. Within a broadly Hartian version of legal positivism precedents create rules (or at least parts of rules). Precedent on this view is simply a different technique of promulgating legal rules. Within the natural law view precedents are understood as an ongoing enterprise seeking to find out what the law is. Different decisions reflect the ongoing enterprise of discovering moral truth, but by themselves precedents have no significance: like the rest of the law, their authority derives from their content, if it corresponds to morality. From this perspective past decisions are merely a repository of attempts at discovering moral truths whose existence and content is entirely independent of legal practice. This is the background that explains why both views find it a real puzzle why we should follow a 'wrong' precedent, a precedent that we now judge to be inconsistent with the requirements of morality. But this problem is entirely the product of the assumption that what we ought to do is fixed outside of our practices. If this assumption is rejected—as it is within this understanding of the authority of the common law—the problem does not arise, or rather arises in a much more attenuated form. So long as we can show that the precedent itself followed on the tradition, it makes little sense to claim that the precedent is 'wrong'. On this view precedents can only be seen as wrong when they can be shown to be wrong 'the day they were decided', ie, when they can be shown to be themselves departures from the requirements *of the tradition*, not of some universal moral standard.[17]

The greatest strength of this account for our purposes is that it provides a ready explanation for the view that finds divergences among common law jurisdictions problematic but is indifferent to divergences between common law systems and other legal systems. To see this, contrast the tradition view with a different view that was once used to explain common law convergence. Around the turn of the twentieth century one finds Anglophone legal scholars speaking of a 'national character' shared by the English-speaking world. Whether such a thing as a national character exists is suspect,[18] but even if it did, on this view the *fact* of common law convergence (and common law–non-common law divergence) would be explained by the tendency of nations having laws that match their national 'traits'.[19] This view thus strongly suggests that common law convergence would emerge naturally and without conscious attempt at maintaining convergence.

[17] For a clear example see *R v R* [1992] 1 AC 599, where the House of Lords repudiated the doctrine that a man cannot rape his wife. Most of the decision was focused on the weak precedential force of the doctrine, with a short discussion on changing moral and social standards with little or no discussion about the timeless wrongness of this view. In fact, the decision stated that it 'reflected the state of affairs in these respects at the time it was enunciated': ibid 616.

[18] For reasons to doubt see A Terracciano *et al*, 'National Character Does Not Reflect Mean Personality Trait Levels in 49 Cultures' (2005) 310 *Science* 96.

[19] See eg, AV Dicey, 'A Common Citizenship for the English Race' (1897) 71 *Contemporary Review* 457, 468–69; J Bryce, 'The Influence of National Character and Historical Environment on the Development of the Common Law' (1907) 8 *Journal of the Society of Comparative Legislation* 203, 203–4, 206–8. I do not address here the question of the scope of convergence, but it is interesting to note in this context that those who talk of the importance of convergence in the common law almost always talk of convergence between England, Australia, Canada, New Zealand and to a lesser extent the United States. Much less is said of the importance of convergence with India, by far the most populous common law country; or, for that matter, with the 30-odd jurisdictions for which the Privy Council in London is still the court of final appeal.

Though not without difficulties, the tradition view can provide a less mysterious basis for explaining the fact of common law convergence. Since different common law countries share a history, we have an explanation for the fact of convergence. Unlike the national character explanation, the tradition view also provides an argument for maintaining convergence. A tradition, in the way I use it here, involves participation in a joint endeavour and implies that those jurisdictions that belong to a single tradition will have reason to uphold the tradition, not because it is a tradition and not simply out of respect for the past, but because of their present commitment to the continued existence *of the community* constituted and epitomised by the tradition. To the extent that the tradition is (seen to be) made up of all jurisdictions that derive from the common law of England, all of them should be committed to maintaining their convergence. Since there is no similar tradition tying common law jurisdictions with civil law jurisdictions, there is no normative requirement for maintaining convergence with them.

In this respect the common law universalism view is the mirror image of legal universalism (this is important to highlight, since both views are sometimes called 'natural law'): the tradition view limits the scope of convergence, and in one sense subscribes to a weaker ideal of convergence; but in another sense it endorses a much stronger version of it. Unlike legal universalism (as well as, of course, legal localism) this view sees convergence *by itself*, ie, convergence regardless of what legal systems converge on, as valuable. Once a tradition settles on a path, then straying from that path is wrong; this is the sense in which a tradition has normative force. That path may not be inherently better than other paths, but it has normative force because it is the one taken.[20]

The tradition view of the common law also has an answer to the puzzle of the authority of the common law. The common law is not democratic in the majoritarian sense, nor is it derived from the authority of the state. The common law is justified for its ability to maintain the deep currents of thought of a particular community, one that in the case of the common law (so the argument would go) extends beyond state boundaries. This last point also helps us identify another explanatory advantage of this view over legal universalism, namely, that it better fits legal practice and the role judges have in it. To justify the allocation of decision-making power to judges the legal universalist must hold that judges are moral experts, that they are better than others in finding moral truths. The proponent of the common law tradition view maintains the far more plausible view that judges are experts in the common law tradition. It is exactly for this reason that a large part of their training and working life is dedicated to mastering past legal materials (and not the work of moral philosophers). That is also why in writing their decisions they consult and cite past cases: not just, perhaps not even primarily, in order to economise on their time and effort by not having to think from scratch on legal questions presented to them. From the common law tradition view, the act of consulting past cases and trying to find the answer in them (or perhaps through them) reflects the ongoing commitments derived from being part of a non-universal tradition. This perspective also provides the means for understanding and explaining how the common law can change, as it is influenced by changing ideas, as well as

[20] Stevens says so explicitly: 'Legal systems have their own internal logic. Saying that the common law of torts is rights-based, while other legal systems are not, is not intended to be an implicit reprimand of other ways of doing things'. Stevens, *Torts and Rights*, above n 5, 347.

why it changes so slowly. Unlike universalism which assumes that moral constants remain largely unchanged, the common law tradition view can explain how two legal decisions from different eras can be different from each other, without having to hold that either decision was wrong.

Yet another explanatory advantage of this view is that it can account for how the common law can be political in one sense—it reflects certain political commitments (for instance, a certain conception of liberty)—while remaining apolitical in another, as its political commitments are distinct from the everyday politics of majoritarian democracy. Against this background we can make sense of why this view of the authority of the common law is also unsympathetic to policy. It is not because policy reflects an intrusion of politics per se into the domain of law; it is rather the intrusion of the *wrong kind* of politics, the kind of everyday politics which is the proper domain of government and majoritarian democracy. This explains why many defenders of 'blackletter law' insist on the autonomy of law and legal scholarship: though the law will be influenced by popular views, those can only be relevant to the law to the extent that they are manifested in, or translated into, 'internal' legal categories. It is only by insisting on the relative closure of law, by avoiding the 'intrusion' of ideas from other disciplines (either directly or through legislation, where such ideas are more likely to have an impact) that the common law tradition can be maintained.

Even though this view provides a more convincing account of certain familiar features of the common law than either localism or universalism, it is surprisingly absent from jurisprudential discussions.[21] This is probably because in present-day moral discourse the usual assumption is that our moral obligations are fixed constants, true regardless of our acceptance or recognition of them. Most jurisprudential debates, and both legal positivists and natural lawyers, assume that the law is on the lookout for those fixed constants, which it aims to match. Much of what one sees in actual common law practice amounts to a rejection of this view.

This view is, of course, not without its difficulties. One set of concerns (at least for some) is that this view tends to be conservative. A different set of concerns has to do with the fuzzy concept of 'tradition'. Much historical work has been dedicated to showing how traditions are invented or manufactured.[22] The common law tradition is no exception. English common law is originally in fact the law of the Norman (French) conquerors. In the centuries that followed, English lawyers continued to draw unselfconsciously on Roman law and their civilian contemporaries. As recently as the late nineteenth century, when English (and American) lawyers had to construct a theory for the case law after the collapse of the writ system, they relied heavily on legal treatises written by civil lawyers.

In a way, these historical facts are *on their own* of relatively little significance, because traditions depend on a continued commitment to the perpetuation of a myth. So long as the myth is believed, it can provide sufficient normative foundation for its continued existence. Of course, traditions can be (and often have been) challenged for their inaccuracy, but it is

[21] The most systematic attempt to develop such ideas in the context of the common law has been provided by Postema. See eg, GJ Postema, *Bentham and the Common Law Tradition* (Oxford, Clarendon Press, 1986) 63–77. The work of Ronald Dworkin (perhaps unconsciously) bears important similarities (as well as important dissimilarities) with this view, but it is rare to see his work discussed outside the legal positivism/natural law dichotomy. The matter is discussed at length in D Priel, 'Making Some Sense of Nonsense Jurisprudence' (unpublished manuscript).

[22] See E Hobsbawm and T Ranger (eds), *The Invention of Tradition* (Cambridge, CUP, 1983).

typically not historians alone that topple a tradition. Still, it is interesting to note that those who wish to create greater convergence among all European legal systems have worked hard on creating an opposite narrative, one that emphasises the historical links among all those legal systems that are together said to have contributed to (surprise!) a single 'Western' or 'European legal tradition'.[23]

Complicating the Picture

As stated at the beginning of this section, the account provided so far in this section is somewhat simplified. This is because it does not adequately cover all possible answers to the question of the authority of the common law. This simplification was attained by distinguishing between the view that *all* law derives its authority from the state, *all* law derives its authority from correspondence with external moral standards, and the view that draws a sharp divide between the common law and statute with regard to their authority. These three views can thus be presented as shown in Tables 11.2–11.4.[24]

Table 11.2: The state law conception of authority

	Universal	Common law	Local
Statutes			✓
Common law			✓

Table 11.3: The natural law conception of authority

	Universal	Common law	Local
Statutes	✓		
Common law	✓		

Table 11.4: The common law conception of authority

	Universal	Common law	Local
Statutes		✓	
Common law		✓	

Tables 11.2–11.4 present three distinct and non-overlapping models of authority. The tables are useful also for highlighting other possible configurations of the authority of law. Some of these may not be adopted by anyone, but others are live possibilities. As we

[23] See, eg, R Zimmermann, 'Roman Law and European Culture' [2007] *New Zealand Law Review* 341, 365–72.

[24] The scholars I focus on tend to write on private law and their views on the authority of statute are not always clear. Many, it seems, favour the kind of division of authority represented by Table 11.5. If there are adherents to the view represented by Table 11.4, perhaps they are best represented by some of the proponents of common law constitutionalism. I cannot discuss their views here.

have seen, however, proponents of both the natural law and the common law models have attempted to address the shortcomings of their approach, both positive and normative, by defending a weaker position that typically looks more like that shown in Table 11.5.

Table 11.5: Mixed conceptions of authority

	Universal	Common law	Local
Statutes			✓
Common law	(✓)	(✓)	

There are possibly other ways in which the different basic approaches may intersect. A longer essay might have attempted a more elaborate taxonomy. But since legal taxonomies only serve as useful models of reality, there is a point at which an over-elaborate model obscures more than it illuminates.

There is another important way in which the picture presented so far may seem to be a simplification of reality. I indicated that the view summarised in Table 11.2 corresponds with US common law, the view summarised in Table 11.3 is more commonly an academic view, and the view summarised in Table 11.4 reflects English common law. Of course, reality is more complicated than that. One can find examples of people or courts in the United States who express views that are closer to the second or third approach, just as one can find outside the United States people who express views quite similar to the first.[25] Once one goes beyond, models more subtle differences arise. For example, even when tradition-based positions are defended in the context of US law, three facts are notable. First, such arguments are more commonly directed at explaining and justifying the common law that engulfs the United States Constitution as well as courts' power of judicial review, rather than the common law of contract and tort. This reflects the fact that at least among legal academics, it is the Constitution, rather than the common law, that is more commonly seen these days as the source of Americans' communal commitments.[26] Traditional common law, decided by State courts by (usually) elected judges and often on the basis of legislation, has less significance in the US polity. Second and related, even Americans sympathetic to the idea of law as a tradition now see the 'American way of law'[27] as a distinct tradition,

[25] Even this might be challenged. US law, much more than other common law jurisdictions, is committed to the 'natural law' idea that sees no clear distinction between law and morality and that is willing to infuse moral ideas into the law whether or not they have been formally incorporated by a legislative statement. See PS Atiyah and RS Summers, *Form and Substance in Anglo-American Law: A Comparative Study of Legal Reasoning, Legal Theory, and Legal Institutions* (Oxford, Clarendon Press, 1987) 43–46. It is notable, however, that when moral norms are being incorporated, what is often said to be incorporated are norms accepted by the American public, not universal moral criteria.

[26] For a tradition-based justification of judge-made constitutional law see DA Strauss, 'Common Law Constitutional Interpretation' (1996) 63 *University of Chicago Law Review* 877, 891–94, 900–3, 929–30. For a similar answer to the countermajoritarian difficulty of judicial review of legislation see A Bickel, *The Least Dangerous Branch: The Supreme Court at the Bar of Politics*, 2nd edn (New Haven, CT, Yale University Press, 1986) 23–33.

[27] I borrow this phrase from RA Kagan, *Adversarial Legalism: The American Way of Law* (Cambridge, MA, Harvard University Press, 2001). See also the series of 12 articles exploring 'commonplace aspects of the American justice system that are virtually unique in the world', available at http://topics.nytimes.com/top/news/us/series/american_exception/. For a more partisan argument that US law and society were created in conscious opposition to the legal systems and ideas of the Old World see SG Calabresi, '"A Shining City on a Hill": American Exceptionalism and the Supreme Court's Practice of Relying on Foreign Law' (2006) 86 *Boston University Law Review* 1335.

one that despite its historical roots in English common law, has long since charted its own distinct path founded on distinctly US values. Finally, it seems to me that the US approach is more open to the influence of *contemporary* prevailing values *from without*, rather than to the reasoned elaboration of *past* legal materials in order to derive certain normative commitments *from within*. This, again, is a reflection of the greater role for ideas of self-government in the US version of the common law, rather than the elitist enterprise which is more characteristic of the common law approach elsewhere.[28]

III. Implications

The last section has already explored some ways in which 'philosophical' differences manifest themselves in differences in legal practice, for instance by providing an explanation for the unique US practice of elected judiciary. I have also attempted to show that these different ways of thinking about the common law also lead to different attitudes on the question of the significance of convergence. In this section I explore this matter further by looking more concretely into one manifestation of the question of common law convergence, namely, the attitude toward reliance on foreign legal materials. Perhaps more intriguingly, I then turn to a substantive question, the scope of negligence liability of public authorities. I will try to show that the divergence in views in recent House of Lords decisions on the matter can be explained, at least in part, by drawing on the ideas canvassed in this chapter.

Use of Comparative Law in Private Law

Basil Markesinis has been an indefatigable champion of the value of reliance on foreign law, and while he has been able to find many adherents to the cause in Europe (including England), he has been frustrated and puzzled by most Americans' lack of interest in foreign law and outright resistance to relying on it in developing their law.[29] His attempts at explaining this failure have focused mostly on what he perceived to be tactical errors made by US proponents of the use of foreign law. He admonished them for failing to answer questions such as whether foreign law can be used to restrict or enlarge constitutional rights, or their use of 'strong and emotive language'.[30] These are unconvincing explanations.[31] There is no

[28] For more on the US case see Priel, above n 6, section II(b)–(c). See also D Priel, 'The Law and Politics of Unjust Enrichment' (2013) 63 *University of Toronto Law Journal* 533. In the latter essay I exploited these different understandings of law as the basis for explaining Americans' lack of interest in unjust enrichment. Without using the terminology used in this chapter, I argued there that the thriving of unjust enrichment is the product of a need to solve problems with areas of law *within* a tradition-based conception of authority of the common law, which does not allow for radical changes in those areas of law. When those concerns are absent, there is less need for a distinct area of law of unjust enrichment.

[29] See B Markesinis, 'National Self-Sufficiency or Intellectual Arrogance: The Current Attitude of American Courts Towards Foreign Law' (2006) 65 *CLJ* 301.

[30] ibid 311.

[31] For an illuminating exploration of the strengths and limitations of reliance on foreign law, as well as a valuable critique of Markesinis (albeit rather different from mine) see J Stapleton, 'Benefits of Comparative Tort Reasoning: Lost in Translation' in M Andenas and D Fairgrieve (eds), *Tom Bingham and the Transformation of the Law: A Liber Amicorum* (Oxford, OUP, 2009) 773.

recognition in any of the opponents' writing on the matter that it is the incompleteness of the proponents' arguments that is the basis of their opposition. The language used is also a poor explanation. Opponents of same-sex marriage in the United States have also used strong and emotive language, and yet on that matter their opponents are losing ground fast. What is completely absent from Markesinis's writings on the matter is any serious attempt to consider the significance of *ideas*.[32]

Though Markesinis's remarks are general, he expressed particular dismay at Americans' unwillingness to look at foreign law in the 'the domains of contract or tort',[33] stating also that 'the introvertedness or self-sufficiency of Americans is now spreading to, should I say *infecting*, private law as well as public law where, at least, one can make with greater cogency the argument about democracy being trumped by unelected officials, namely judges'.[34] These remarks reveal Markesinis's own normative commitments, and his unwillingness to recognise that the source of the resistance is ideological. Markesinis assumes that public law and private law have different sources of authority, which explains why he thinks private law is more readily appropriate for comparative law. This is not a description of what things are in the world; it follows from a particular political position, one that itself sees public law as the product of local politics, but private law as something else. My anecdotal experience is that the idea that there is a fundamental distinction between private and public law is one that many US lawyers reject, and if my explanation above is correct, we can see why.

When the political presuppositions that underlie Markesinis's views are brought to the fore, what he takes to be obvious—that examining foreign law is conducive to the 'search for truth and justice'[35]—appears much less obvious than he presents it. Markesinis fails to understand that what *counts* as 'justice' (or at least 'justice according to law') and what *counts* as 'truth' with regard to a proposition of law, depends on an underlying political philosophy. In a political community that sees its legal justice and legal truth as derived from the will of *its* people, the use of foreign law is a subversion of truth and justice, whether or not the law in question is a common law jurisdiction.[36] Of course, not all Americans accept this view, and there are many who see value in reference to foreign law. But if we seek to understand their views, these are often best explained by the presupposition that at least part of the law is grounded in different notions of authority.

[32] Markesinis is sceptical to the idea of 'legal culture' as having much explanatory power in B Markesinis, 'Judicial Mentality: Mental Disposition or Outlook as a Factor Impeding Recourse to Foreign Law' (2006) 80 *Tulane Law Review* 1325, 1356 n 89.

[33] Markesinis, above n 29, 324.

[34] B Markesinis, 'Understanding American Law by Looking at It through Foreign Eyes: Towards a Wider Theory for the Study and Use of Foreign Law' (2006) 81 *Tulane Law Review* 123, 171. See also his remark that 'it does not take much ingenuity but only a minimum amount of disingenuousness to claim that, for instance, even ordinary contract and tort rules can be linked to "values" held dear by some societies in order to preserve the status quo'. Markesinis, above n 29, 317.

[35] Markesinis, above n 34, 170.

[36] See *Roper v Simmons* 543 US 551, 626–27 (2005) (Scalia J, dissenting) ('The [majority's] special reliance on the laws of the United Kingdom is perhaps the most indefensible part of its opinion … It is beyond comprehension why we should look … to a country that has developed, in the century since the Revolutionary War—and with increasing speed since the United Kingdom's recent submission to the jurisprudence of European courts dominated by continental jurists—a legal, political, and social culture quite different from our own'). On the proliferation of statutes across the United States that prohibit judicial reliance on *any* foreign law see A Elliott, 'The Man Behind the Anti-Sharia Movement', *New York Times*, 30 July 2011, available at www.nytimes.com/2011/07/31/us/31shariah.html.

Implications for Substantive Private Law

In this section, I turn to a more speculative suggestion. I will attempt to show that different views about the authority of the common law and the value of common law convergence correspond in a non-coincidental way to different attitudes to the question of negligence liability of public authorities. To demonstrate this point, I will compare the views of Lord Bingham and Lord Hoffmann, probably Britain's most influential judges of the last two decades.

Bingham and Hoffmann have expressed rather different views on the value of comparative law, especially when it came from European, civil law countries. Bingham was a lifelong champion of 'widening the horizons' of English law.[37] Hoffmann, by contrast, has always been more sceptical of European influences on indigenous English law.[38] Where Bingham thought the European Convention on Human Rights was a document of surpassing significance for its affirmation of universal human rights,[39] Hoffmann thought the very idea of universal human rights close to incoherent, and has defended instead 'the essentially national character of rights'.[40] While Bingham wrote that 'our law has been enriched by the injection of international jurisprudence, emanating from [the European Court of Human Rights in] Strasbourg, and binding on the UK in international law',[41] Hoffmann expressed doubts about the very legitimacy of that court.[42]

This difference also played itself out in Bingham's and Hoffmann's respective judicial opinions. In a case dealing with the legality of indefinite detention of foreign nationals in British prisons, Bingham, relying on extensive analysis of European legal materials, rejected the government's position and declared some legislation incompatible with the European Convention. Hoffmann reached the same conclusion, but on wholly different grounds. He thought that it is the affirmation of 'a quintessentially British liberty' that supports the petitioners' case, not any European jurisprudence. His speech reads as a textbook statement of the view that sees the common law as a unique political tradition:

> I would not like anyone to think that we are concerned with some special doctrine of European law. Freedom from arbitrary arrest and detention is a quintessentially British liberty, enjoyed by the inhabitants of this country when most of the population of Europe could be thrown into prison at the whim of their rulers. It was incorporated into the European Convention in order to entrench the same liberty in countries which had recently been under Nazi occupation.

[37] See T Bingham, *Widening Horizons: The Influence of Comparative Law and International Law on Domestic Law* (Cambridge, CUP, 2010); T Bingham, '"There Is a World Elsewhere": The Changing Perspectives of English Law' in *The Business of Judging: Selected Essays and Speeches 1985–1999* (Oxford, OUP, 2000) 87. See also his remark in *Fairchild v Glenhaven* [2002] 1 AC 32 [32]: 'In a shrinking world … there must be some virtue to uniformity in outcome whatever the diversity of approach in reaching that outcome'.

[38] See Lord Hoffmann, 'Human Rights and the House of Lords' (1999) 62 *MLR* 159; Lord Hoffmann, 'The Universality of Human Rights' (2009) 125 *LQR* 416.

[39] Bingham, *Widening Horizons*, above n 37, 83.

[40] Hoffmann, 'Universality', above n 38, 417; Lord Hoffmann, 'Bentham and Human Rights' (2001) 54 *Current Legal Problems* 61, 74–76. Curiously, in both these essays Hoffmann invoked the authority of Bentham in support of his views, even though Bentham was a cosmopolitan if there ever was one. See P Schofield, 'The Legal and Political Legacy of Jeremy Bentham' (2013) 13 *Annual Review of Law and Social Science* 51, 61–62, and sources cited therein.

[41] Bingham, *Widening Horizons*, above n 37, 82.

[42] Hoffmann, 'Universality', above n 38, 429–30.

> The United Kingdom subscribed to the Convention because it set out the rights which British subjects enjoyed under the common law ...[43]

> The 'nation' is a social organism, living in its territory (in this case, the United Kingdom) under its own form of government and subject to a system of laws which expresses its own political and moral values. When one speaks of a threat to the 'life' of the nation, the word life is being used in a metaphorical sense. The life of the nation is not coterminous with the lives of its people. The nation, its institutions and values, endure through generations. In many important respects, England is the same nation as it was at the time of the first Elizabeth or the Glorious Revolution. The Armada threatened to destroy the life of the nation, not by loss of life in battle, but by subjecting English institutions to the rule of Spain and the Inquisition. The same was true of the threat posed to the United Kingdom by Nazi Germany in the Second World War. This country, more than any other in the world, has an unbroken history of living for centuries under institutions and in accordance with values which show a recognisable continuity.[44]

So far, Bingham and Hoffmann's respective views seem to reflect two competing conceptions of authority. I would like to tie these differences now to a substantive question of law on which they expressed widely divergent views, namely, the scope of negligence liability of public authority. In an essay entitled 'The Uses of Tort' Bingham criticised the majority's view in *Smith v Chief Constable of Sussex Police*,[45] a case in which a majority of the House of Lords (against Bingham's sole dissent) held that police forces owe no duty of care to individuals for failure to prevent them from being attacked, even when the individual provides the police with specific information about the prospect of being subject to a violent attack by a particular, identified individual. Bingham concluded his essay with these words:

> If the virtual immunity now extended by English law to large areas of police activity were removed, there would no doubt be a cost falling, directly or indirectly, on the community who fund the service. If economy were all, the present law has its virtue. But if a member of the public *whom a public service exists to serve* suffers significant injury or loss through the culpable fault or reprehensible failure of that service to act as it should, is it not consistent with ethical and, perhaps, democratic principle that the many, responsible for funding the service, should bear the cost of compensating the victim? I shall leave that as a rhetorical question, confident that my own answer to it is clear.[46]

[43] *A v Secretary of State for the Home Department* [2004] UKHL 56, [2005] 2 AC 68 [88]; *cf* Bryce, above n 19, 204–5; K Minogue, 'The Elusive Oakeshott', *The American Conservative* (Oct 2009) 24, 25 ('The idea of human rights [Oakeshott] thought a rather second-rate caricature of the inherited Common Law freedoms of English-speaking peoples'). Contrary to Hoffmann (see above n 40), Oakeshott recognised Bentham as an enemy of tradition. See M Oakeshott, 'The New Bentham' in *Rationalism in Politics and Other Essays*, expanded edn (Indianapolis, IN, LibertyPress, 1991) 132, 139. As indeed he was. See J Bentham, 'The Book of Fallacies' in J Bowring (ed), *The Works of Jeremy Bentham* (Edinburgh, William Tait, 1843) vol II, 375, 398–400.

[44] *A v Secretary of State*, above n 43, [91]. The Human Rights Act 1998, Hoffmann said, allows courts to declare that a statute 'is incompatible with the human rights of persons *in this country* ... The declaration of the court enables Parliament to choose with full knowledge that the law does not accord with *our* constitutional traditions': ibid [90] (emphasis added).

[45] *Smith v Chief Constable of Sussex Police* [2008] UKHL 50, [2009] AC 225. The case was decided together with *Van Colle v Chief Constable of Hertfordshire Police*, by which name the joint case is known.

[46] Lord Bingham, 'The Uses of Tort' (2010) 1 *Journal of European Tort Law* 3, 15 (emphasis added). See also T Bingham, 'Who Then in the Law Is My Neighbour?' in *The Business of Judging: Selected Essays and Speeches 1985–1999* (Oxford, OUP, 2000) 363, 372–73.

At almost the same time, Lord Hoffmann delivered the Bar Council Law Reform Lecture, which dealt with the question of negligence liability of public authorities. In his lecture Hoffmann stated:

> Some people said that it was illogical that highway authorities should have what they called an immunity from liability for non-repair. But that immunity was exactly the same as everyone else had. No one owed a private law duty to repair the highway. The highway authority owed a public law duty to repair, but that, as a matter of ancient policy, was not enforceable in private law.[47]

There is no way the difference between these two statements can be reconciled by appeal to context or nuance. What Bingham called 'virtual immunity' enjoyed by the police, Hoffmann disparaged as 'what [some people] called an immunity'. These two statements reflect two divergent philosophies. Bingham's claim is grounded in a particular view on the obligations a democratic state owes its citizens. By contrast, Hoffmann adopts the libertarian view that treats the state and police officers acting on its behalf as a kind of private actors. It is true that Hoffmann's concession with regard to the existence of a public law duty complicates the picture, but not by much. By drawing the distinction Hoffmann affirms that members of the public do not have a standing, as citizens, to demand that a public authority perform its duties and then seek compensation when their failure leads to their injury. In this way he keeps the two branches of law (and their underlying authorities) separate. This implies a fundamentally different view of the relationship between individuals and the state than Bingham's.

Hoffmann's suggestion that the state is treated just like any other person has a semblance of neutrality: in the eyes of private law we are all equal. Except that, of course, tort law does not treat us all as equal. Parents are treated differently from others with regard to their children; employers are treated differently from others with regard to their employees; doctors are treated differently from others with regard to their patients. By treating the state in this context as a stranger, Hoffmann equates (for the purposes of tort law) public bodies' provision of services to a stranger's act of charity.[48]

Do the differences on the proper place of European and comparative law in English law and their different views on the question of the scope of tort liability of public authorities have anything in common? Though it is difficult to answer this question with certitude, I believe the answer is 'yes'. At one level, Bingham's legal cosmopolitanism may have been influenced by the fact that the outcome he favoured was available in other jurisdictions. This is not much of a speculation since Bingham surveyed the law regarding tort liability of public authorities in several common law and civil law jurisdictions and stated that *Van*

[47] Lord Hoffmann, 'Reforming the Law of Public Authority Negligence', Bar Council Law Reform Lecture, 17 November 2009, 3, available at www.barcouncil.org.uk/media/100362/lord_hoffmann_s_transcript_171109.pdf. Hoffmann expressed similar views in his judicial capacity in, among other places, *Stovin v Wise* [1996] AC 923; *Gorringe v Calderdale Metropolitan Borough Council* [2004] UKHL 15, [2004] 1 WLR 1057. However, it is interesting that Hoffmann adopted the exact opposite view when it served *restricting* tort liability against the state. In a nuisance case against public authorities, Hoffmann stated that the question of evaluating the defendant's reasonableness 'becomes very different when one is dealing with the capital expenditure of a statutory undertaking providing public utilities on a large scale'. *Marcic v Thames Water Utilities Ltd* [2003] UKHL 66, [2004] 2 AC 42, [63].

[48] Howarth has pointedly summarised Hoffmann's view as 'affirm[ing] the extraordinary rule ... that the public rescue services have no duty to rescue anyone'. D Howarth, 'Public Authority Non-Liability: Spinning Out of Control?' (2004) 63 *CLJ* 546, 547.

Colle would have been decided differently 'in most of the world's leading jurisdictions'.[49] Such a finding can influence a judge in two ways. Factually, showing that liability has been imposed on the police in other jurisdictions in similar circumstances provides some assurance that the legal rule he proposed is not crazy and that it is unlikely to have seriously detrimental effects if adopted. This may have been particularly important in the context of liability of public authorities, as a familiar argument for restricting public authority liability is its potentially deleterious effects.[50] In this respect, legal decisions from other jurisdictions can serve as a source of empirical data that may be more readily accessible to judges than more rigorous empirical studies. Normatively, Bingham's openness to European law has led him to embrace the view that common law duties should aim to correspond to human rights principles derived from European jurisprudence, thereby promoting greater convergence between English and European law.[51]

I think, however, that the link between Bingham's views on legal convergence and his views on the scope of negligence liability of public authorities runs deeper than that. Bingham's basis for the imposition of liability in *Smith* rests on his conception of what the state owes individuals and his views on European convergence stem from a single intellectual source: universal human rights. In the context of liability of public authorities, it has led him to formulate a liability principle without which, he thought, the law 'fails to perform the basic function for which such a law exists'.[52] And a fundamental function of that law—tort law—is to protect human rights.[53] As he put it, a democratic state that cares for human rights is obligated to the 'democratic principle that the many, responsible for funding the service, should bear the cost of compensating the victim'. This duty is very different from the duties of other individuals, and failure to maintain it can amount to commission of a tort.

Hoffmann's opposing substantive view is not simply based on the claim that the state is treated the same as individuals. That, as we have seen, is clearly an unsatisfactory argument. Once we acknowledge the significance he accords to the common law tradition, we can see a more plausible explanation for his view. The deep thread Hoffmann finds in the common law tradition—what he calls 'the quintessentially British liberty'—is the negative liberty concerned primarily with protection against unlawful arrest. What Hoffmann could not find in that tradition is the kind of relationship between the state and its citizens (he calls them 'subjects') that underlies Bingham's view. What about the possible objection that the existence of an ancient British liberty does not preclude the possibility of creating new duties derived from public law? To this Hoffmann replies, once again appealing to tradition, that it is 'ancient wisdom' that public law rights cannot be the basis for private law remedies.

[49] Bingham, above n 46, 13.

[50] See *Hill v Chief Constable of West Yorkshire Police* [1988] AC 53, 63; *Van Colle*, above n 45, [74]–[77], [108], [132]–[133].

[51] ibid [58]. This suggestion was rejected by some of the other judges on the panel: ibid [82], [136].

[52] ibid [57]. Bingham reiterated these words in Bingham, 'The Uses of Tort Law', above n 46, 270.

[53] ibid 269; Tom Bingham, 'Tort and Human Rights' in *The Business of Judging: Selected Essays and Speeches 1985–1999* (Oxford, OUP, 2000) 169, 170. Also ibid 179 ('the law of tort has the fertility and flexibility to protect nearly all of the most basic human rights').

IV. Future of a Common Law World

Earlier in this chapter I attributed to the common law tradition view the idea that common law jurisdictions ought to converge because of the normative force of commitment to a shared tradition. A crucial word here is 'commitment': a tradition requires a certain normative attitude that seeks its own perpetuation. When this commitment is gone, a tradition can disintegrate fairly quickly. Unlike the United States, which broke its ties with Britain from its inception, the Commonwealth nations maintained close political and legal links with Britain, and they also inherited the British political system of parliamentary supremacy and a more modest role for popular sovereignty. In line with that political tradition, the tradition view of the common law remained dominant, a fact that helps explain the continued commitment in these countries to maintaining common law convergence. And yet, in recent years we witness declining convergence even there.[54] In this section I try to explain why this process is taking place and why it is likely to continue apace.

Contrary to Stevens's view that 'as common lawyers we are part of the same family whether we like it or not',[55] my view is that within the tradition view convergence is the product of more-or-less conscious decisions on the part of legal practitioners to maintain commonality. When this effort disappears, two formerly close legal systems will tend *naturally* to drift apart. This point is crucial for understanding the tradition view and for highlighting another important contrast between it and the universalist view. Apart from the differences mentioned earlier, these two views are likely to see the process of convergence as proceeding according to a wholly different pattern. On the universal view convergence can emerge 'naturally' as a result of two different jurisdictions identifying (possibly completely independently of each other) the requirements of universal morality. After all, according to this view the requirements of morality are accessible to all rational creatures, and so a process of trial and error should eventually lead all legal systems to converge. An imperfect analogy is the biological concept of convergent evolution, where two species develop similar traits independently of each other because of similar evolutionary pressures. This view can see reason as imposing similar pressures on all humans, pressures that ultimately should lead their laws to converge. (That this does not happen in reality is reason to doubt the veracity of this picture.)

This process is very different from the tradition view, where history and path dependence are crucial for what counts as a right answer today, and therefore convergence is extremely unlikely to emerge naturally. I will elaborate on this point with the aid of a simple model. This model can be loosely analogised, once again borrowing from evolutionary biology, to speciation, the process (or rather set of processes) by which a single species splits into two. On the tradition view, maintaining convergence requires an effort to master the legal materials of more than one jurisdiction and guaranteeing that they proceed relatively in

[54] For statements of the growing legal independence of, respectively, Australia, New Zealand and Canada, see P Finn, 'Common Law Divergences' (2013) 37 *Melbourne University Law Review* 509, 510–11, 536; R Cooke, 'The New Zealand National Legal Identity' (1987) 3 *Canterbury Law Review* 171; GV La Forest, 'Who is Listening to Whom? The Discourse Between the Canadian Judiciary and Academics' in BS Markesinis (ed), *Law Making, Law Finding, and Law Shaping: The Diverse Influences* (Oxford, OUP, 1997) 69, 70–75, 81–82.

[55] R Stevens, 'The Divergence of the Australian and English Law of Torts' in S Degeling *et al* (eds), *Torts in Commercial Law* (Sydney, Thomson Reuters, 2011) 37, 40.

tandem. This is because on this view there are no right answers in the abstract; rather, right answers to outstanding or novel legal questions emerge from past decisions. It follows that maintaining convergence between jurisdictions has costs, the most obvious being that doing so requires attaining and mastering more legal materials that are less accessible. Historically, part of the difficulty may have been simply physical: it was more difficult to have access to all the law reports and academic commentary from another country. These days, when access to legal materials from all over the world is much easier, the problem may be the opposite: the ease of access to legal materials from all over the world results in an overwhelming glut that discourages straying too far beyond one's own jurisdiction. Either way, this cost is enough that without effort small differences will tend to emerge between two formerly close jurisdictions, and these differences can fairly quickly become larger and therefore increasingly difficult to overcome. Once paths begin to diverge, the costs of using legal materials from another jurisdiction increase, as that jurisdiction begins to use different concepts, use similar words with somewhat different meanings, as well as develop its common law against a different statutory background. In this way small differences grow bigger until use of materials from that jurisdiction becomes too costly to bother.

At least when differences are small, the costs of maintaining convergence may not be overwhelming and will be worth incurring as they would be outweighed by the benefits of maintaining convergence. There are two typical types of cases for which this is likely to be the case: first, when one legal system is young or small and as such lacking in sufficient case law, which is the central building block for the common law tradition; and second, when another legal system is considered superior in terms of its law-makers' (perceived) expertise. (Obviously, these two scenarios are often, although not always, related.) But as legal systems mature, the benefits of convergence decline while the costs increase. Judges in the formerly 'expert' legal system will no longer seem necessarily superior to the local judiciary, especially when it comes to local conditions, in terms of both facts and values. And with a thicket of local legal materials increasing, keeping up with the materials of another jurisdiction will become more onerous and seem less necessary. (Arguably, there is an optimal amount of cases to master and rationalise, beyond which any effort to articulate a more-or-less coherent single tradition from the cases becomes unwieldy and the tradition approach begins to break down. This may be one reason for the decline of doctrinal scholarship in the United States.) A different cost to convergence is an inevitable result of the fact that the common law exists in an environment increasingly more saturated with statute, and the common law must often be understood and interpreted in relation to that legislation. Since legislators are much less concerned about maintaining convergence, legislation is more likely to move in different directions in different countries, based on the local needs and political forces. This will push the common law in different jurisdictions in different directions, making maintaining common law convergence more difficult. Insisting on the importance of convergence may appear an elitist concern against the need to come up with legal solutions deemed to better fit the values of the particular community. Even from a more legal point of view, caring for common law convergence may look like an 'academic' self-indulgence compared with maintaining internal coherence within each legal system between its judge-made and statutory law.

Another possible cost of maintaining convergence is that with growing maturity and expertise, the relationship between the two legal systems has to change from largely unidirectional (where one legal system is primarily a law-maker and another is primarily a law-taker) to a reciprocal one. But lawyers in the formerly 'superior' legal system may not acquiesce in their new lower status. This creates a problem, since without *them* agreeing to that, lawyers of the formerly 'receiving' legal system will not see the situation as one of convergence, but rather as one in which they must accept and follow what is imposed from above (or outside). And this will be perceived as an additional, possibly prohibitively hefty, cost. (Could this be the reason why it is mostly English scholars who lament the decline of common law convergence while those from, say, Australia or Canada seem much less concerned about going their own way?)

For these reasons, even within the tradition view, common law convergence will tend to *naturally* decline with time unless it is vigilantly pursued. In fact, the tradition view may actually call for *less* convergence once two legal systems have begun charting their separate ways. Once two legal systems have begun taking two different paths, the tradition view with the premium it places on path dependence may call for keeping them to these paths rather than attempting a precipitous shift toward another approach just for the sake of getting closer to a solution adopted in another jurisdiction. As a result, the tradition view that in some cases supports convergence, beyond a certain point can actually encourage divergence.

At a deeper level, there is, I think, a decline in the appeal of the tradition view itself. This is a crucial point, because maintaining convergence is valuable *only if one accepts the tradition view of the authority of the common law*. With different degrees of intensity, one finds the question 'Why *should* our common law be grounded on the tradition model of authority?' being asked. Of course, the question is rarely asked in quite this way, but in different formulations, it is asked at increasing frequency. As mentioned earlier, the tradition view of the common law depends on a perception of law as an autonomous discipline, of law as the generator of normative requirements on the basis of careful elaboration of its own past materials, where expertise consists of mastering the contents of countless court decisions. Though not completely obsolete, this idea is on the wane.

One reason for that is that the tradition view is premised on the idea that the authority of the common law derives from judges' ability to discover in legal materials certain values that run deep in a particular community. This view thus could avoid the puzzle of the authority of the common law by assuming both that judges are experts and that their expertise is of value for determining the content of legal rules for a particular community. These days, both assumptions look suspect. The first assumption has been affected by the many detailed studies which have suggested that the seemingly neutral, equal, common law has (perhaps completely innocuously) shown greater concern for the interests of certain groups rather than others, unsurprisingly the groups of those who belong to the elite that on the tradition view shape the common law. As a result, even someone sympathetic to tradition as a source of authority might not like the way the common law implements it. In response, the common law has changed in various ways to address this problem, although the extent of its success is, of course, a controversial matter. The second concern is, I think, even more serious, as it touches on the *nature of lawyers', especially judges', alleged expertise*. For the tradition-based approach not only accepts but actually celebrates the common law's separation from external standards. The common law expert is someone who does not know much about the way the law actually works in practice, and who has little ability to assess the potential effects of different rules. Even more simply, the common law expert has relatively little knowledge of the extent to which the common law adequately addresses actual concerns and needs of the population. It is, for example, notable that the idea that sexual harassment or stalking should be treated as a tort (a matter that in terms of numbers it is potentially relevant to the lives of millions) did not originate from doctrinal tort scholars, but exactly from those who adopted an 'external' or critical perspective on the law. For what the common law considers expertise—great knowledge of a mass of cases and the ability to work them out to a more-or-less coherent account of 'the law'—can hardly help with addressing developing needs of society. (Could it be that such considerations are considered 'external' to the evaluation of the common law because they are external to what the common law experts know?) Instead, the tradition-based approach suggests that the question of how certain areas of life should be structured is ideally to be decided on nothing more than the primitive tools of the Talmudic scholar and the scholastic student: mastery of past pronouncements made by people who are ignorant of the law's effects, and who focus their attention on the articulation of verbal formulae and 'tests' for identifying whether a new decision adequately follows past decisions or is properly 'distinguishable' from them. When stripped of its mysticism the tradition view can thus be seen as a little more than seventeenth-century policy analysis.

It is this reality that has led to the narrowing down of the scope of decision-making given to this kind of expertise, as is evident from the decreasing significance of the common law. In areas still governed by the common law, there have been various attempts to change the common law in various ways that will give its decision-makers the tools to make better-informed decisions. This process further weakens the hold of the appeal to the normative force of a historical tradition. Instead, judges are increasingly attempting to make decisions based more on an assessment of the contemporary needs of their particular society, taking also into account local cultural, social, political circumstances. And these, needless to say, are not exactly the same across the common law world.

To be sure, England, Canada, Australia and New Zealand are all democratic, developed countries; but then so are Denmark and Japan. There might have been a time in the past when, perhaps, one could speak of similarity in values between England and its former colonies (although I suspect that even then this was more an elite concern than something that preoccupied the whole population), but with much immigration from non-English speaking countries and the slow development of more uniquely local ways, it makes little sense to maintain that Australian, Canadian, English (or is it British?) and New Zealand cultures are all the same. These differences, even if not huge, can (and do) have an effect on the outcomes of cases, especially contentious ones. Differences between common law countries are then seen not as a cause for concern, but as a sign of independence.

Against all this, we can return to the questions posed at the beginning of this chapter: Why do some lawyers consider it more important that the tort law of England and Australia or the contract law of Canada and New Zealand be similar than their constitutional law, their company law or their labour law? Why, even though criminal law is (or used to be) part of the 'common law', are there no concerned voices about the fact that the criminal laws of different common law countries may be different? I believe the way I set up the question helps identify the answer. As far as I can see, maintaining common law convergence is important for those who seek to maintain the tradition view of the common law itself (and along the way, validate their own kind of expertise). What better proof could there be for the idea that the common law is a matter of non-political expertise than the fact that politically independent states share the same common law? Common law convergence is thus valued for proponents of the tradition view both for demonstrating the truth of this view and for perpetuating it.

Common law convergence, however, is a rather weak reed for maintaining a view that is independently unattractive. As we have seen, the common law convergence view is deeply connected to the idea of law as an autonomous discipline, and this is a view held these days by a shrinking minority. We know too much about the world to think that the path to improving the law exclusively, or even primarily, depends on analysing judges' pronouncements. As a result, the decline in commonality is both indicative of, and itself a contributor to, the decline of the theory of authority that values common law convergence and the autonomy of law, a process which in turn weakens the hold of convergence even further.

V. Concluding Remarks

The last section should not be misunderstood. My claim is not that common lawyers should not consider what happens in other countries; and if they do, it is more likely that they will do so with courts from the rest of the English-speaking world. That is why what I said in this chapter should not be understood to mean that in 50 years' time common law judges will no longer be able to understand each other's judgments. If nothing else, there is no language barrier to overcome, and there are other non-legal links that keep common law jurisdictions closer to each other than others. And in law, perhaps more than elsewhere, old habits die hard. It is notable, however, that common lawyers care much less than they used to whether their own legal system adopts the same solutions as other common law countries,[56] and my claim is that this trend will continue and probably intensify. My prediction is thus that most Commonwealth lawyers will care about Commonwealth convergence the same way they feel about maintaining convergence with US law, which means, not much.

More generally, this chapter was motivated by an underlying normative claim. It is important to note that those who would like to maintain convergence in the common law are really making a very narrow claim in two senses. They intend common law convergence to be limited to a small list of legal areas, namely, contract, tort and restitution (even property law, let alone criminal law or family law, no longer look like obvious candidates for convergence); and they intend it to be limited to a small subsection of common law countries, namely, England, Canada, Australia and New Zealand. This convergence is presented as required by nothing more than the *fact* of a shared history (recall Stevens's words: 'as common lawyers we are part of the same family whether we like it or not') and it delivers precisely the kind of convergence that fits the tradition view of common law authority and its supposedly non-political nature. What I have sought to show is that this call for convergence is not free from politics. Indeed, Stevens himself has alluded to a more positive reason for maintaining common law convergence when he said that '[t]he shape and nature of the common law has been determined by its method of creation. Civil codes are the products of the choices of legislators, under the influence of legal scholars, and it is unsurprising that the choices made differ in many respects from those of judges, whose role and concerns are

[56] For many examples see Stapleton, above n 31, 786–90.

not the same'.[57] This is partly true, but Stevens's mistake, like that of many other proponents of the tradition view, is to think that once a legal system belongs to the common law, it must be understood and justified in terms of the tradition view of authority. As I have attempted to show, this is not the case. If the common law does not interact with politics anywhere else, its underlying theory of authority is not politically neutral, but one that has real-world, practical implications.

The concluding section has made what may be understood as another prediction (or perhaps just a bit of wishful thinking), and that is that the decline in convergence is part of a decline of the tradition view itself, and that its decline may bring with it not just the dissolution of the idea of a common law *world*, but also the decline of the idea of the *common law* as a decision procedure. If this is to happen, we will witness a decline in the view that mere mastery of past court decisions, together with some facility with language and informal logic, are a good basis for adequately regulating any aspect of human behaviour. In medieval times this was the method used because this was the only method available; it is no longer the case.

That is why, even though the common law is still with us, it is far less important than it used to be. Its marginalisation is proof of the mistrust in this method of regulation and its experts. Even where the common law governs a question, it is rarely left to its own devices and is virtually everywhere accompanied by extensive legislative regulation. With regard to those decisions still given to judges, there is growing awareness on the part of the judges that they should base their decisions on the scope of the legal rules they adopt on better information on the social effects of their choices. Many proponents of the common law method resist this move, making the point that judges do not have the necessary knowledge or ability to assess questions of social policy. But since such considerations are clearly relevant for deciding such questions, if it is indeed the case that judges cannot evaluate them, the sensible solution is not to remove the *considerations* for the decision-making process, but to remove the *judges* from it. The prevalence of regulation is proof that this is in fact the solution that has been adopted in countless contexts. One implication of the argument in this chapter is that this process cannot be separated from the decline in common law convergence.

[57] Stevens, *Torts and Rights*, above n 5, 342.

12

Obligations, Governance and Society: Bringing the State Back In

TT ARVIND

I. The Retreat of Obligations

'The owl of Minerva begins its flight only with the onset of dusk', so Hegel said in one of his more famous aphorisms.[1] By this, he meant that it is in a philosophical tradition's dying light that its particular, distinctive features come into clearest focus. So, it would seem, it is with the law of obligations. The past 30 years have seen an explosion in obligations theory, shedding new light on the nature and significance of a vast range of its peculiar features. Yet this comes at a time when the law of obligations is less relevant in the common law world than it has ever been in modern times—and in ways that show a striking, and surprising, convergence in different common law jurisdictions, whilst at the same time representing a dramatic divergence with the past of the common law.

Two trends in the recent history of the law of obligations illustrate the extent of this convergence and divergence. The first is its retreat in the face of other, more recently formed areas of law. Take, for example, the rise of public law. The place that is today occupied by public law was once seen as part of the province of the law of obligations. As late as 1949, Lord Denning forcefully expressed the view in his Hamlyn Lectures that it was private law—tort, estoppel and the equitable remedies of declaration and injunction—that would accomplish the great task of bringing the administrative state under the rule of law. The prerogative writs—mandamus, certiorari, prohibition—were, in his view, unsuited to play this broader role.[2] Views similar to Denning's were once broadly held,[3] but few today would assert a similar view in any common law jurisdiction. The signs of the demise of this approach can already be seen in the case which is widely taken to mark the revival of the tort of negligence, the decision of the House of Lords in *Home Office v Dorset Yacht*.[4] Lord Diplock, in a little remarked-on passage in his concurring speech in that case, held that it was not generally the province of the law of tort to define the standards of conduct

[1] GWF Hegel, *Elements of the Philosophy of Right* (HB Nisbet trans, Cambridge, CUP, 1991) 23.

[2] A Denning, *Freedom Under the Law* (London, Stevens, 1949) 126.

[3] TT Arvind, 'Restraining the State through Tort? The Crown Proceedings Act in Retrospect' in TT Arvind and J Steele (eds), *Tort Law and the Legislature: Common Law, Statute and the Dynamics of Legal Change* (Oxford, Hart Publishing, 2012).

[4] *Home Office v Dorset Yacht Co Ltd* [1970] AC 1004 (HL).

to which public authorities are held. That task was appropriately left to public law, and recovery in *Dorset Yacht* itself was only permissible because the actions of the Home Office were in breach of a public law standard. This restricted vision of the role of tort law, whilst not conventionally seen as part of that case's ratio, underlay his later decision in *O'Reilly v Mackman*,[5] and also closely parallels more recent jurisprudence in England,[6] Ireland[7] and Australia[8] on the liability of public authorities in tort—and, in particular, the concerns about the effects of the imposition of private law standards upon the functioning of public bodies that underlies this jurisprudence.[9]

This trend is not universal, with Canada[10] and New Zealand,[11] in particular, being more willing to grant a role to the law of obligations in relation to public bodies. Far more widespread, however, is the second, and not unrelated, trend, namely, the growing displacement of the law of obligations by new forms of administrative redress which are provided not by the courts but by the regulatory and administrative bodies that characterise the modern state. Financial services, where regulation has replaced the common law for all practical purposes, are the most obvious example, but the trend is far broader, encompassing disputes ranging from noisy neighbours to the industrial exploitation of sub-soil resources. This displacement is to some extent legislative, reflected in statutes such as the UK's Infrastructure Act 2015, which replaces trespass and nuisance[12] with a new, discretionary statutory scheme of compensation[13] in relation to harm caused by the exploitation of petroleum or geothermal energy. But it is not just a statutory phenomenon. The courts, too, have contributed in significant ways to the displacement of the law of obligations by regulation. The decision of the UK House of Lords in *Marcic v Thames Water*[14] is a clear example. But so, too, are the police liability cases in the various commonwealth jurisdictions that have refused to find a duty of care. The effect of these cases, and particularly the English[15] and Irish[16] authorities, has been to create a new form of non-justiciable duty previously unknown to the common law, with the courts in effect withdrawing from the task of determining whether the police discharged their legal obligations in a given case.

Cumulatively, these trends point to a diminution of the role of the law of obligations in setting standards of conduct in relation to the type of questions that arise in modern social life, with that task being increasingly left to statute, regulation and private frameworks. This diminution is seen in a wide variety of decisions in the past four decades,

[5] *O'Reilly v Mackman* [1983] 2 AC 237 (HL).

[6] See J Steele, '(Dis)owning the Convention in the Law of Tort' in J Lee (ed), *From House of Lords to Supreme Court: Judges, Jurists and the Process of Judging* (Oxford, Hart Publishing, 2010).

[7] *LM v Commissioner of An Garda Siochana* [2011] IEHC 14.

[8] *Sullivan v Moody* [2001] HCA 59, (2001) 207 CLR 562.

[9] This parallels the trend in certain sections of obligations theory, where the relationship between private law wrongs and public law wrongs is seen as requiring the removal of obligations involving public bodies (such as the tort of misfeasance in public office, or duties of care involving the exercise of statutory powers by public authorities) from the law of obligations. See, eg, E Descheemaeker, *The Division of Wrongs: A Historical Comparative Study* (Oxford, OUP, 2009) 37–38.

[10] *Hill v Hamilton-Wentworth Regional Services Board* 2007 SCC 41, [2007] 3 SCR 129.

[11] *Couch v Attorney-General* [2008] 3 NZLR 725.

[12] Infrastructure Act 2015, ss 43–44. See in particular s 44(1) and (3), which confer rights to use land and to leave it in a different condition after use.

[13] Infrastructure Act 2015, s 45.

[14] *Marcic v Thames Water* [2003] UKHL 66, [2004] 2 AC 42.

[15] *Michael v Chief Constable of South Wales Police* [2015] UKSC 2, [2015] 2 WLR 343.

[16] *AG v JK, Minister for Justice Equality and Law Reform* [2011] IEHC 65.

ranging from *Photo Productions v Securicor*,[17] which ended the role of the common law in determining the limits of freedom of contract in favour of leaving it to statutory regulation, to the peculiar direction taken by the *ex turpi causa* defence in the recent English cases of *Gray v Thames Trains*[18] and *Twigger v Safeway*.[19] The reasoning in both cases rested on the view that it was not appropriate for the law of obligations to intervene in an attribution of responsibility made by some other branch of law, nor to take any action that might seem to dilute or interfere with it. In *Caparo Industries plc v Dickman*[20] itself, as in its counterparts elsewhere,[21] it was ultimately a regulatory framework—the role of the statutory audit under the Companies Act 1948—that proved decisive.

Equally, they also correlate with a diminution in the perceived public importance of the law of obligations. Across the common law world, governments have been amending procedural and substantive rules to eliminate entire areas of the law of obligations, or to ration access to the courts. The Ipp Reforms in Australia, the reforms to costs and legal aid in England and Wales, and the abolition of the civil action for breach of health and safety law in England and Wales[22] illustrate the breadth and range of the types of measures that have been taken with the express purpose of reducing the public role of the law of obligations. And, as the last of these examples demonstrates, the object of these changes is *only* to reduce the role of the law of obligations—not regulation. The reforms to health and safety law did not diminish the powers of the Health and Safety Executive, or reduce its prosecutorial powers. It was only the law of obligations that was their target. Likewise, the fact that the majority of common law courts, in cases like *Caparo*,[23] *Esanda*[24] and *Hercules Management*,[25] have held auditors not liable to third parties for negligently approving false accounts does not mean that auditors are thereby off the hook. It simply means that responsibility for dealing with this particular issue has passed into the domain of regulatory action, through instruments such as the EU Audit Directive[26] and Regulation.[27]

These trends become even starker when we put them in the context of the role played by the law of obligations in responding to matters of current social concern. A central feature of the legal response to the nineteenth century banking crises was the role played in it of concepts and frameworks taken from private law, with notions of 'fraud', 'trust' and 'fiduciary conduct' playing a leading role not just in the actual legal proceedings brought against those held responsible for bank failures, but also in the laws that were enacted in the wake of the failures.[28] Against this backdrop, the absence of these legal ideas in the response

[17] *Photo Productions v Securicor* [1980] AC 827 (HL).

[18] *Gray v Thames Trains Ltd* [2009] UKHL 33, [2009] 1 AC 1339.

[19] *Twigger v Safeway* [2010] EWCA Civ 1472, [2011] 2 All ER 84.

[20] *Caparo Industries plc v Dickman* [1990] 2 AC 605 (HL).

[21] See, eg, the decision of the Supreme Court of Victoria in *R Lowe Lippmann Figdor and Franck v AGC (Advances) Ltd* [1992] 2 VR 671.

[22] Enterprise and Regulatory Reform Act 2013, s 69.

[23] *Caparo Industries plc v Dickman*, above n 20.

[24] *Esanda Finance Corporation Ltd v Peat Marwick Hungerfords* (1997) 188 CLR 241.

[25] *Hercules Managements Ltd v Ernst & Young* [1997] 2 SCR 165.

[26] Directive 2014/56/EU of the European Parliament and of the Council of 16 April 2014 amending Directive 2006/43/EC on statutory audits of annual accounts and consolidated accounts [2014] OJ L158/196.

[27] Regulation (EU) 537/2014 of the European Parliament and of the Council of 16 April 2014 on specific requirements regarding statutory audit of public-interest entities [2014] OJ L158/77.

[28] S Wilson, *The Origins of Modern Financial Crime: Historical Foundations and Current Problems in Britain* (Abingdon, Routledge, 2014).

to the ongoing banking crisis is striking, and points to a very significant shift in the legal understanding of the role private law ideas can and should play within the broader legal system.[29]

What we see, therefore, is a clear trend towards the subordination of the law of obligations to other areas of law, and a corresponding reduction in the role it plays in the modern state, which mark not just a limited convergence within the common law world, but also a divergence with the historical role of the law of obligations. Is this trend, then, a matter of concern, and should it be reversed? These questions are the subject of this chapter. The central argument it makes is that whilst regulation has an important role to play within the legal system, the trend of letting it displace the law of obligations is misconceived because there are reasons to return to a broader role for the law of obligations. Explaining why this is so and what that broader role is, however, requires us to significantly alter our understanding of what the law of obligations is, and why it matters. It requires us to move from looking at the *convergences* in the law of obligations to *divergences* present and past—the emergence, in the present, of approaches in some jurisdictions that challenge the trend of the retreat of obligations; and the presence, in the past, of a radically different conception of the role of the law of obligations in the polity. This, in turn, requires us to start by bringing the state back into private law;[30] in other words, putting the law of obligations back in its social and political context, and viewing it as a key part of the constitutional institutions of a common law polity.

II. Bringing the State Back In

To suggest bringing the state into private law is controversial, given that private law theory has for the past 30 years striven to get the state out of obligations theory. Theorists calling for a 'private' understanding of the law of obligations have consistently rejected the idea that obligations are rooted in public goals, or that it is connected with the state. This reluctance to link the law of obligations with the state appears to have its roots in the idea that doing so robs the law of its principled basis and makes it instead the product of an arbitrary will, turning the judge into a figure akin to a Hobbesian sovereign.[31] Whilst such a view reflects, arguably, the influence of positivism on common law theory and of the Hobbesian idea of the state on legal positivism, it represents a very narrow understanding both of the state and of obligations. Neither parliamentary legislators, nor judges, nor administrators,

[29] TT Arvind, J Gray and S Wilson, 'From the Mid-Nineteenth Century Bank Failures in the UK to the 21st Century Financial Policy Committee: Changing Views of Responsibility for Systemic Stability' in M Hollow *et al* (eds), *Complexity, Crisis and the Evolution of the Financial System: Critical Perspectives on American and British Banking* (Cheltenham, Edward Elgar, 2015).

[30] The idea of 'bringing the state back in' draws on a strand of thought within political science, which starting in the 1980s began to point to the importance of studying the organisational structures of governance, and the relationships they have both as between themselves and with the polity, in order to better understand how the operation of government shapes social and political processes. See P Evans *et al* (eds), *Bringing the State Back In* (Cambridge, CUP, 1985).

[31] See, eg, A Beever, 'Policy in Private Law: An Admission of Failure' (2006) 25 *University of Queensland Law Journal* 287.

nor any other officials, are despots in modern legal systems, nor do they act capriciously.[32] To link the law of obligations with the state is, instead, to suggest that it forms part of the constitutional arrangements of a polity.

On every understanding, the law of obligations is a fundamental part of the political life of a community. It forms part not only of the community's public life, but of that portion of its life by which standards of behaviour and acceptable conduct are created, elaborated, modified, refined and upheld. Any claim in relation to the nature and structure of the law of obligations is, therefore, a claim about the systems and structures its constitution embodies. This is true regardless of whether that claim is a characteristically realist one about the law's social basis or goals, or a characteristically idealist one about the inner reason or principle immanent in the law. To claim that the private law of England or Ireland or Australia is a device for efficiently allocating losses, or a reflection of Kantian ethics, is to claim that there is something about the principles on which English or Irish or Australian society is constituted that legitimises this mode of governance.

Every such claim has two components. First, it entails a claim in relation to the institutional structure of the country's system of governance, positing that in the current institutional set-up, the role assigned to the courts is to do a certain thing (eg, reverse unjust enrichment) but not another (eg, ensure that resources in society are justly distributed). Secondly, it entails a claim in relation to the nature of the principles that determine how a particular institution of governance should do that certain thing (eg, that courts should determine whether someone has been unjustly enriched with reference to Kantian conceptions of right, rather than considerations of community welfare).

The focus of past work, from theorists as diverse as Ronald Dworkin[33] and Richard Posner,[34] has almost exclusively been on the normative implications of the second of these claims. In the few cases where institutional issues have been considered, the consideration has begun with a certain constitutional ideal and proceeded to explore the implications of that ideal for the content of the law of obligations. Theorists therefore begin with the idea of liberal democracy, as Goldberg and Zipursky did, and move from there to exploring what types of civil recourse such a system might require.[35] Others begin with the idea of a society of moral actors, and proceed from there to construct a system of rights that such a society would recognise. Yet others begin with the idea of political morality and work from there to the rights and policies that a legal system must embody.

Whilst this is an entirely logical way to proceed if the aim is to present a purely philosophical vision of the law of obligations which a hypothetical legal system might devise, it is entirely inadequate if the aim is to present an account of the shape of the existing law of obligations. Common law constitutional documents do not set out a self-evident theory of the judicial role in private disputes, nor do they discuss the role of private law adjudication in governance. The constitutional role of these institutions can, therefore, only be gathered from an examination of practice across the common law world, combined with an analysis

[32] On this point more broadly, see TT Arvind, 'Vilhelm Lundstedt and the Social Function of Legislation' (2013) 1 *Theory and Practice of Legislation* 33.

[33] R Dworkin, *Justice for Hedgehogs* (Cambridge, MA, Belknap Press, 2011).

[34] R Posner, *The Problematics of Moral and Legal Theory* (Cambridge, MA, Belknap Press, 1999).

[35] JCP Goldberg and BC Zipursky, 'Rights and Responsibility in the Law of Torts' in D Nolan and A Robertson (eds), *Rights and Private Law* (Oxford, Hart Publishing, 2012).

of what these practices tell us about the role of obligations within the state. The question is not what factors might, in the abstract, justify endowing legal officials with the very significant powers that they currently have to choose between conflicting social expectations and to uphold the preferences of one group over the preferences of another. It is, rather, what it is about common law constitutions that accounts for their being given this role, and how that relates to the roles assigned to other bodies embedded within the state.

This is a task that must begin, as Anne Orford has recently pointed out in relation to international law, with description, analysing the operation of the body in question without preconceptions as to its role or operation.[36] Put thus, the question becomes: What form of governance does the law of obligations represent, and what makes it a useful instrument of governance, given the range of other instruments of governance available to a society? This question demands an answer that is not merely normative but also descriptive—an answer, in other words, which is concerned not just with delineating the institutions an ideal community would have, but with understanding and evaluating the institutions which common law jurisdictions have, and the place of the law of obligations within these. The answer to this question must begin by analysing the relationship between the law of obligations and regulatory frameworks.

III. Obligations and Regulation: Describing the Relationship

The period that has seen the retreat of the law of obligations has also seen a convergence in the direction in which the state has evolved in most common law jurisdictions. This evolution has been marked, in particular, by three trends: the rise of the administrative state, the entrenchment of the idea that the state should provide a certain level of social welfare, and the increased use of direct regulation by executive agencies. Each of these has brought the law of obligations into contact with other agencies of the state in ways with which obligations theory has not fully grappled.

The rise of regulation, for example, has created new rights and duties that have radically altered the character of the legal relations that subsist between persons in society. Securities law, the law pertaining to public utilities, and the law governing financial institutions are the most obvious examples, but there are others. Many of these new regulations lie close to the law of obligations, in the sense that they deal with issues with which the law of obligations can also deal, but are nevertheless remedied through a complaint to a regulatory authority rather than through a civil action. Simultaneously, the growth of the welfare state, and the consequent assumption of more and more responsibilities towards the public by administrative and regulatory bodies, inserted the state into areas of interaction that would otherwise have been occupied entirely by private bodies. These developments raise the question of what distinguishes the law of obligations from the operation of these agencies and aspects of the legal system. Contemporary obligations theory has tended to deal with this question by assuming that regulation and obligations are oriented

36 A Orford, 'In Praise of Description' (2012) 25 *Leiden Journal of International Law* 609.

around achieving fundamentally different things—achieving fair distributions as opposed to corrective justice, or advancing state goals as opposed to defending individual rights. But if we turn to description and, as Orford suggests, examine the *actual* functioning of regulatory bodies rather than philosophical theories as to how they *should* function, the situation can be seen to be a lot more complex, in that regulatory bodies frequently respond in ways that are ordinarily taken to be characteristic of the law of obligations.

Financial regulation, once again, serves as a good example. Consider, for instance, the mis-selling of financial products, such as the mis-selling of payment protection insurance in the United Kingdom or the Commonwealth Bank financial planning scandal in Australia. A central element of the regulatory response in each case, by the FSA in the United Kingdom[37] and the ASIC in Australia, was the creation of a formula for compensation that all lenders were required to follow, as well as a process and tests to identify individuals who were victims of mis-selling. In terms of the factors identified by obligations theory, the regulators' action was triggered by a causative event that is substantially similar to causative events that are the subject of the law of obligations, namely, wrongs. The character of the response, equally, vindicated a right conferred by the law, and reflected the correlativity of the relations between the parties. The response in both cases would thus appear to reflect corrective justice, rights and other matters traditionally considered to be characteristic, and distinguishing, features of the law of obligations. Nor is this an outlier. *Sturges v Bridgman*[38] would today, were it to arise, be a matter for an administrative body in much of the common law world. In England, it would be a case for the local authority exercising statutory powers under the Environmental Protection Act 1990, even though the action in nuisance survives. In New Zealand, the situation would in all probability have been dealt with before it arose through the resource consent procedure under the Resource Management Act 1991, with an outcome that might have differed significantly from that actually produced by the operation of the tort of negligence.

Here, then, is the problem. The features that obligations theory claims to be the distinguishing features of the law of obligations—its constitutive essence—do not distinguish it from regulation. The administrative state is as capable of vindicating rights as the law of obligations, and regulatory bodies can dispense corrective justice with as much efficacy. The result of the neglect of the relationship between obligations and regulation, and between obligations and the state, is that the law of obligations is withdrawing from having any role in defining the bounds of acceptable conduct in an ever-growing set of areas. Remedying this requires us to put the focus back on the relationship of the common law with the state, and on the question of the contribution of the law of obligations to governance.

IV. Obligations in the Polity

Outside obligations theory, the law of obligations and the institutions that deal with the law of obligations are widely seen as being part of the infrastructure of governance.

[37] Specifically, through imposing an enforceable obligation upon financial institutions to follow a particular process and employ specified criteria in responding to complaints of mis-selling. See Policy Statement 10/12 'The Assessment and Redress of Payment Protection Insurance Complaints'.

[38] *Sturges v Bridgman* (1879) LR 11 Ch D 852.

The World Bank's Governance Indicators, for example, include aspects of the law of obligations (specifically, contract enforcement) within the factors that indicate how good the quality of governance in a country is.[39] The point is also not alien to obligations theory, particularly amongst theorists who write from contextualist or realist perspectives.[40] The reason why it is appropriate and accurate to describe the law of obligations in these terms lies in the nature and character of the relationship between legal and social institutions.

Institutions are created in response to uncertainty, and, specifically, the varieties of uncertainty that arise out of human interaction.[41] Human interaction is uncertain, first, in relation to the impact others' actions may have on a person and, secondly, in relation to the impact of future events (including events not within human control) on a person's dealings with others. At the heart of this uncertainty is the problem of conflicting expectations; or, to put it differently, the problem that others will act in the furtherance of goals or expectations that are in conflict with, or not in harmony with, mine. Much of the law of obligations is devoted to dealing with precisely such conflicts, for example, dealing with the conflict between an individual's expectation that he can use his property as he chooses, including for the purpose of making chocolate, against his neighbour's expectation that he should be able to use his property for purposes that require a degree of stillness, such as running a doctor's consulting room;[42] or a customer's expectations of support from an insurance company in the event of a loss caused by insured events, against the company's corporate goals that may lead them to seek to minimise payments they make.

Institutions, as cultural anthropologists have long pointed out,[43] deal with the problems of conflicting expectations by creating rules, shared conceptual structures and entrenched patterns of thought.[44] These operate by encouraging particular ways of viewing problems,[45] by defining certain types of conduct as permissible and others as impermissible, and thus influencing the manner in which people behave.[46] Institutions also uphold these structures by creating a mechanism or system to respond to violations of these norms—or, at least, a belief in the existence of such mechanisms or systems.[47] It was this phenomenon that the Scandinavian realists referred to as 'legal consciousness',[48] anticipating by half a century the empirical work of the 1980s.[49] Legal consciousness ends the uncertainty associated with

[39] World Bank and IBRD, *A Decade of Measuring the Quality of Governance* (World Bank, 2006).

[40] Hugh Collins, for example, has argued that the term 'regulation' encompasses any system of rules intended to govern the behaviour of its subjects: H Collins, *Regulating Contracts* (Oxford, OUP, 1999) 9.

[41] J Knight, *Institutions and Social Conflict* (Cambridge, CUP, 1992) 1–3.

[42] *Sturges v Bridgman* (1879) LR 11 Ch D 852.

[43] See especially M Douglas, *Risk and Blame* (Abingdon, Routledge, 1990); M Douglas, *How Institutions Think* (Syracuse, Syracuse University Press, 1986).

[44] In early modern common law, these were seen as a source of law, under the head of 'comen erudition' (common learning). See JH Baker, 'Why the History of English Law Has Not Been Finished' (2000) 59 *CLJ* 62.

[45] See, eg, LM Lopucki, 'Legal Culture, Legal Strategy, and the Law in Lawyers' Heads' (1996) 90 *Northwestern University Law Review* 1498.

[46] D North, *Institutions, Institutional Change and Economic Performance* (Cambridge, CUP, 1990) 3.

[47] A classic example is the use of the idea of formulae implicating divine retribution in legal forms in antiquity. See, eg, the formulae set out in MN Tod, *International Arbitration Amongst the Greeks* (Oxford, Clarendon Press, 1913) 115–16.

[48] See esp AV Lundstedt, *Obligationsbegreppet* (Uppsala, L Norblads Bokhandel, 1930).

[49] SE Merry, *Getting Justice and Getting Even: Legal Consciousness among Working-Class Americans* (Chicago, IL, University of Chicago Press, 1990); P Ewick and S Silbey, *The Common Place of Law: Stories from Everyday Life* (Chicago, IL, University of Chicago Press, 1998).

not knowing how others will behave by engendering a feeling of protection, arising from the consciousness that the legal system will 'make whole' those harmed by actions which transgress the bounds it sets and, through entrenching a feeling that these outcomes are in some sense apposite to that society.

Viewing the law of obligations in this light helps us make sense of otherwise puzzling features of the law, which do not quite fit with what obligations theory tells us the law should look like. The idea of correlativity between the plaintiff and defendant, for example, is foundational to the literature on corrective justice, yet it fits at best uneasily with the law. In particular, the remedial aspect of obligation, which, in corrective justice theories, constitutes the actual corrective step, does not in the real world display correlativity. The advent of mandatory liability insurance has deliberately and purposefully moved the law of obligations away from remedial correlativity in the course of the twentieth century.[50] The majority of claims in areas such as personal injury, but also in relation to damage to commercial property, are today defended and paid by insurance companies. This is not just a simple matter of an indemnity: the result of these arrangements is that the nominal plaintiffs and defendants frequently have little or no influence over, or involvement in, the steps that in theory constitute the actual correction of the wrong.[51] This trend poses a challenge not just for corrective justice theory, but also for the variants of deterrence theory that characterise the law and economics literature. If, however, the institutional logic underlying the law of obligations is the problem of dealing with the uncertainty that others' actions in pursuit of their own interests may harm your interests, encouraging a system of 'making whole' is both rational and defensible, even if it reflects neither proper correlativity nor deterrence. So, too, is an institutional framework which sets and upholds expectations in relation to the conduct of others, as regulation does. A law of obligations motivated by such a logic thus has much in common with the worlds of regulation and the welfare state, making it easy to see how and why matters can slide from the one to the other as readily as they do in the modern legal system.

Viewing the law of obligations in the light of governance has, however, one further feature whose implications run even deeper. An institution of governance must not just deal with expectations, but with *conflicting* expectations. The role of the law of obligations arises not primarily in cases where there is broad agreement on what the standards are, or whose resolution can be grounded in unchanging moral rights which 'rational people can recognise'.[52] Its role arises, instead, chiefly in cases where agreement and obviousness are *absent*—and where the law must not just uphold expectations that can easily be derived from unchanging norms and social practices, but resolve a conflict between strongly held expectations which are in conflict, and each of which is consistent with the values, beliefs or goals of a section of society. As such, its defining feature is not consistency, but the deeply embedded inconsistencies and contradictions with which it must deal, and the oppositions it is called upon to overcome.

[50] On the history of this trend, see R Merkin and S Dziobon, 'Tort Law and Compulsory Insurance' in TT Arvind and J Steele (eds), *Tort Law and the Legislature: Common Law, Statute and the Dynamics of Legal Change* (Oxford, Hart Publishing, 2012).

[51] This point is strikingly made in R Merkin and J Steele, 'Insurance Between Neighbours: *Stannard v Gore* and Common Law Liability for Fire' (2013) 25 *Journal of Environmental Law* 305, 317.

[52] R Stevens, *Torts and Rights* (Oxford, OUP, 2007) 330.

The emergence of shared expectations, as has been discussed above, depends on the existence of shared frames of reference, and shared understandings of the social significance of facts.[53] But in situations where goals, norms and understandings are not shared across the entire populace (as, in a typical society, they will not be) institutional theory suggests that the expectations and ideas of acceptable and unacceptable acts which any given person holds depend upon the community with which that person identifies, and the shared vision of society, claims and resources it reflects.[54] The history of the law of obligations demonstrates how frequently it has been called upon to do precisely this, from the Statute of Labourers of 1351 and the ensuing Peasant's Revolt of 1381, where the peasants' newfound expectation of freer bargaining following the labour shortages produced by the Black Death clashed head-on with the aristocracy's expectations that the privileges afforded to them by the pre-plague status quo would continue;[55] to *Taff Vale*,[56] where the expectations of trade unions in relation to the ability to use particular forms to minimise liability came into conflict with the employers' expectations in relation to responsibility for wilful acts;[57] to *Rookes v Barnard*,[58] which brought into sharp contrast the expectation of solidarity amongst workers which the union attempted to enforce, and the opposing expectation held by employers and non-unionised workers that each individual had full freedom of action. In each case, the question for the court was which of these conflicting, but deeply rooted and value-laden, expectations had the greater claim to the law's support.[59] Conflicting expectations of this type show up in a range of contexts: the press's expectation of absolute press freedom and public figures' expectations in relation to their control over their public images; producers' expectations in relation to the ability to contractually limit responsibility and purchasers' expectations in relation to minimal levels of functionality and quality;[60] and a range of other areas.

It is this aspect of the 'law-job'[61] discharged by the law of obligations that makes the denial of the connection between it and the state particularly problematic. The task of resolving conflicting expectations is a fundamental aspect of the political life of a community, and the involvement of the law of obligations in this task suggests that it has an important constitutional role, closely related to the roles of other agencies of the state.

[53] See also J Searle, *Making the Social World: The Structure of Human Civilization* (Oxford, OUP, 2011).

[54] For a similar point made from a more traditional moral theoretical perspective, see Michael Sandel's discussion of community and allegiances, and its relation to justice, in M Sandel, *Liberalism and the Limits of Justice* (Cambridge, CUP, 1998), and Peter Gerhart's discussion of the relationship between tort law and community in PM Gerhart, *Tort Law and Social Morality* (Cambridge, CUP, 2010).

[55] See R Palmer, *English Law in the Age of the Black Death* (Chapel Hill, NC, UNC Press, 1993).

[56] *Taff Vale Railway Co v Amalgamated Society of Railway Servants* [1901] AC 426 (HL).

[57] *cf* John Morgan's description of the decision as reflecting a natural 'adjustment of law to social development' in J Morgan, *Remedies Against the Crown* (London, University of London Press, 1925) lxxvi.

[58] *Rookes v Barnard* [1964] AC 1129 (HL).

[59] A very similar point was made by the Scandinavian realist thinker Vilhelm Lundstedt in his analysis of the corresponding Swedish cases and legislation concerning the legality of strikes and picketing. See TT Arvind, 'Beyond Rights and Duty: Lundstedt's Theory of Obligations' in D Nolan and A Robertson (eds), *Rights and Private Law* (Oxford, Hart Publishing, 2012).

[60] See, eg, *L'Estrange v F Graucob Ltd* [1934] 2 KB 394. The history of various doctrines of common law and equity (from unconscionability, to *contra proferentem*, to fundamental breach) and the wildly divergent answers reached by different common law jurisdictions in England, the United States and Australia demonstrate the magnitude of the task of resolving conflicting expectations.

[61] See K Llewellyn, 'The Normative, the Legal, and the Law-Jobs: The Problem of Juristic Method' (1940) 49 *Yale Law Journal* 1355.

The question, therefore, is how the manner in which the law of obligations approaches and discharges this task relates to the approaches taken by other agencies. As we will see, the modern law of obligations has within it the potential for two distinct approaches to dealing with the problem of conflicting expectations, the first focused on the *systemic* question of risk management, and the second on the *social* question of embedded expectations. Re-examining the doctrinal structure of the law of obligations in this light helps shed light both on deeper issues underlying various convergences and divergences within the modern law of obligations, and the reasons underlying its retreat.

V. Managing Risk

Let us start with risk management. Obligations theory is today littered with dichotomies built on particular shibboleths: between principle and policy, or distributive and corrective justice, or doctrine and pragmatism. A far more pertinent, but far less considered, dichotomy is that between approaches that are social, and those that are technocratic or managerial. A significant proportion of modern approaches to the law of obligations fall within the latter camp, regardless of whether they argue in favour of either a particular approach to morality, as in theories of corrective justice, or of some particular approach to social engineering, such as modern accounts of 'resilience'. The consequence, in either case, is to argue that social expectations should be settled *not* with reference to the society itself, but with reference to the attainment of goals chosen or paths charted by a sub-sect of that society claiming a greater expertise or ability than ordinary members of that society. Whether this is because of their greater learning in Kant, Giddens or Ricardo is a matter of detail. Either way, the underlying understanding of the role of the law of obligations is the same: it is to remake society in the image of a particular vision of the great society.

Much suggests that this is the direction in which the law of obligations has been evolving over the past decades. The procedural steps that are today associated with the invocation and use of the law of obligations raise serious structural hurdles to the broad-based participation on which social embedding depends, and there appears to be little inclination to change them to facilitate—leave alone encourage—greater or more diverse participation. Consider the procedural structure of the law of obligations. Viewed in the abstract, the law of obligations is a peculiar institution, an odd mix of private self-help and public assistance. On the one hand, the state provides and funds courts and judges to hear and decide cases, and brings the full weight of its coercive power to bear upon the wrongdoer if he happens to lose the case before the courts. On the other hand, it is entirely for the private party to bring or defend his action before the courts and to amass the evidence he requires to discharge the burden of proof. If he does not have the wherewithal to sustain an action or defence through all the stages it may traverse (and in this age of shrinking legal aid budgets it is almost always the individual who must find the resources to pay either by himself or through a limited range of market-based devices), or if his means do not extend to engaging pleaders as effective as those engaged by the opponent, his wrong will go uncorrected or his privilege undefended. For all that the state is willing to put its coercive powers at his disposal once he has won, it does little to assist him until then, no matter how grave the injustice. In sharp contrast with the operation of regulatory bodies or the welfare state, that is entirely up to him and his resources as a private person, and to whatever he can obtain on the 'market' for legal services. Taken together with the procedural and substantive changes discussed in section I of this chapter, they suggest that something fundamental has changed about the way the work the law of obligations does in society and governance is conceptualised.

What is the nature of that change? A range of features of the institutions that surround the law of obligations provides a clue. Take, for example, the question of access to the civil court system. What is striking is not just the level of control that judges exercise in determining the type of cases that should come before them, or in determining what type of litigants merit the attention of the courts, but their rule-bound regularity and the economic nature of the criteria on which they are based. Take, too, the involvement of judges in 'case management', the role they increasingly adopt through reformulating the law in ways not expressly argued before them,[62] and the professionalised approach to determining who enters the judiciary with its focus on identifying those most successful in their prior career. These changes, cumulatively, paint a picture of a system of governance that is far closer to regulatory institutions, where the role of the judge is primarily as a technocrat and where judicial governance through the law of obligations is a form of technocracy, than it is to the judiciary of the seventeenth or eighteenth centuries.

The essence of technocracy is the view that experts of a particular type, by virtue of their expertise, are ideally placed to take certain types of decisions. To the extent it has become a form of technocracy, the law of obligations differs from regulation not in its approach to governance, but in the specific domain of expertise of the judges who are tasked with its operation when compared to the local officials tasked with the administration of the Environmental Protection Act 1990, or the officials tasked with the regulation of financial markets under the United Kingdom's Financial Services and Markets Act 2000. This expertise is the primary source from which the law is made and through which it develops. The legal consciousness and ideas of legality constructed by the public are not, in this model, the *source* of the content of the law. They are, rather, its *products*. Legal consciousness, and the conceptual framework of rights, duties, liabilities, legitimate entitlements, acceptable behaviour, and so on, are, as Vilhelm Lundstedt put it, 'pressed into service' by the legal system to entrench the conceptions of legality that give the law its legitimacy and power.[63]

What sort of technocracy, then, does the new common law embody? A full discussion is well beyond the scope of this chapter, although it is a topic I have discussed at great length (indeed, book length) elsewhere.[64] However, four particularly significant characteristics of this approach deserve mention, both because they are deeply embedded in common law doctrine (particularly in England and Wales, but not exclusively in that jurisdiction), and because they highlight important features of a managerial approach.

First, the structure of modern obligations doctrine reflects a preoccupation with facilitating the management of risk. The law of obligations does not itself manage risk; that is to say, its task is not primarily to decide who should bear what risk in relation to which

[62] See, eg, Richard Buxton's powerful critique of the judiciary's action in *Hedley Byrne & Co Ltd v Heller & Partners Ltd* [1964] AC 465 (HL); *Pepper v Hart* [1993] AC 593 (HL); and *Attorney-General v Blake* [2001] 1 AC 268 (HL) in R Buxton, 'How the Common Law Gets Made' (2009) 125 *LQR* 60.

[63] AV Lundstedt, *Legal Thinking Revised* (Uppsala, Almqvist and Wiksell, 1956).

[64] See TT Arvind, *The Law of Obligations: A New Realist Approach* (Cambridge, CUP, forthcoming).

action. It is, rather, to let the parties do so. Unlike the socially embedded approach which will be discussed in section VI, which is expressly focused on determining what types of *conduct* are acceptable, the focus of this approach is simply to set bounds within which one party is expected to manage the risks inherent in its interaction with another party. This is every inch as true of contract as it is of tort. The focus of the 'other' element of the test for a duty of care (whether that be the 'reason' of the *Anns*[65] approach or the 'fair, just and reasonable' limb of the *Caparo*[66] approach, or the startling and generally unremarked expansion of assumptions of responsibility into personal injury) is on the precise question of whether something in the parties' relationship has led to the responsibility for managing some aspect of the risk inherent in their interaction being transferred to one of the parties. The *Reynolds*[67] defence as applied in cases such as *Flood*[68] makes far more sense if it is viewed as being, in essence, a framework to enable newspapers to develop sophisticated risk-management strategies to inform the making of publication decisions (as, indeed, most of them have now done)—a perfect counterpart to *Royal Bank of Scotland plc v Etridge*.[69] So, too, do recent developments in the law of personal injury, including in particular the surprising spread of 'assumption of responsibility' to areas far beyond the negligent misstatement / pure economic loss cases that were its original focus, to become a central tool in determining whether a duty of care existed in personal injury cases.[70]

Secondly, a central element in the facilitation of risk management is the individuation of interaction. Virtually every interaction that takes place is embedded in a complex network of interaction: a person who is at a petrol station buying petrol to drive to a florist to buy flowers to decorate a social evening at which one guest will be a potential client with whom she is hoping to secure an important deal, which will help her to make money to invest in an important expansion of her business … and so on for each of the persons involved in each of these instances of interaction. The doctrines of the law of obligations, in contrast, take their starting point in individuation of these instances of interaction, under which each transaction is pulled out of this web and treated in splendid isolation as if it were a simple bipartite transaction unsurrounded by the flow of anterior and posterior transactions (unless those transactions are in some way incorporated into this one). Georg Simmel, whose theories on money have in recent times attracted some attention in the world of obligations theory, described this process as an isolation of instances from the flow of life, a process which he argued was accomplished through the set of concepts we bring to bear in thinking about a situation.[71] A significant proportion of the concepts that comprise the intellectual framework of the law of obligations play precisely this role. Such a representation is not an accurate one, and it periodically causes problems for the law: the *Panatown* problem,[72] as well as *Coop v Argyll*,[73] are particularly clear examples, as is the lesser known

[65] *Anns v Merton London Borough Council* [1978] AC 728 (HL).

[66] *Caparo Industries plc v Dickman*, above n 20.

[67] *Reynolds v Times Newspapers Ltd* [2001] 2 AC 127 (HL).

[68] *Flood v Times Newspapers Ltd* [2012] UKSC 11, [2012] 2 AC 273.

[69] *Royal Bank of Scotland plc v Etridge* [2001] UKHL 44, [2002] 2 AC 773.

[70] See, eg, *Ministry of Defence v Radclyffe* [2009] EWCA Civ 635; *Andrew Risk v Rose Bruford College* [2013] EWHC 3869 (QB).

[71] G Simmel, *The View of Life* (Chicago, IL, University of Chicago Press, 2011).

[72] *Alfred McAlpine Construction Ltd v Panatown Ltd* [2000] UKHL 43, [2001] 1 AC 518.

[73] *Co-operative Insurance Society Ltd v Argyll Stores (Holdings) Ltd* [1998] AC 1 (HL).

but far worse, instance of the attempt by the Irish courts in the pyrite litigation to deal in an individuated manner with complex multipartite transactions.[74] Nevertheless, this approach is overall a stable one, because it has utility from the perspective of risk management, as cases such as *BAI v Durham*[75] demonstrate.

Thirdly, individuation is of vital importance to risk management because it permits central aspects of interaction to be turned into what Karl Polanyi, a twentieth century economic anthropologist, termed 'fictitious commodities'—things which, unlike real commodities, are not produced to meet a demand for consumption, but which are nevertheless treated as if they were so.[76] The consequence of treating an aspect of the world as a fictitious commodity is to permit it to be dealt with through market-oriented techniques; and, in particular, to be regulated through the operation of a price-setting market, rather than through more direct governmental techniques. Unlike Polanyi, who was deeply sceptical about fictitious commodities, this chapter takes no position on their desirability. The point I seek to make is that this is the ordinary result of individuation. Obligations function effectively as a system of risk management because the effect of legal doctrine is to turn 'duty', 'risk' and 'damage' into fictitious commodities—things which are divisible in the way commodities are, which can in consequence be traded on a market and priced by marketised techniques (amongst which those associated with insurance occupy a central place),[77] and which are most effectively managed when they are dealt with in this way. This opens up a range of new techniques for managing risk. The rise of apportionment is a particularly clear example. Injuries and harms themselves resist division. It is in most cases impossible to say, for instance, that the victim's broken rib can be attributed to the second defendant, the broken collarbone to the first defendant, and the broken thigh to the claimant. To turn damage into a fictitious commodity, however, permits the use of techniques of apportionment without such an exercise becoming necessary. The same can be said of duty and risk, both of which can be endlessly sub-divided, transferred and manipulated using complex techniques.

Fourthly, and finally, such an approach is incompatible with any idea of relationality within the law of obligations. Much has been written about the failure of contract law to take adequate account of the relationality inherent in contracting. The discussion in this section has explained why the resulting law might be stable, even if it is based on a distortion of the true nature of the parties' relationship. If the law is not primarily concerned with setting standards of conduct, the fact that it ignores central aspects of the parties' relationship is irrelevant. What matters is not the accuracy of the legal representation of the parties' relationship, but its effectiveness in facilitating the management of risk.

Whilst relational theory is more commonly associated with contract, a far better example of the derelationalisation of the law of obligations can be found in the tort of negligence. Negligence covers, at one extreme, situations where the interaction between the parties arises purely out of the use of shared resources (two persons who happen to be on the same road at the same time, a crane hoisting a steel beam in the air) where there is no intentional engagement with the person or class of persons to whom the obligation is owed, and where

[74] *James Elliot Construction Ltd v Irish Asphalt Ltd* [2014] IESC 74; *James Elliot Construction Ltd v Irish Asphalt Ltd* [2011] IEHC 269.

[75] *BAI v Durham* [2012] UKSC 14, [2012] 1 WLR 867.

[76] K Polanyi, *The Great Transformation: The Political and Economic Origins of Our Time* (Boston, NJ, Beacon Press, 2001).

[77] On which, see R Merkin and J Steele, *Insurance and the Law of Obligations* (Oxford, OUP, 2013).

proximity is therefore purely physical, a function of the persons' shared use of a common resource ('common resource proximity'). At an intermediate level, we have persons who are linked by being part of a network of connected transactions (a producer and a consumer, a bank's valuer and a house purchaser, a builder and a subsequent purchaser) and whose proximity is a function of the nature of the network and the strength of the links between transactors on that network ('network proximity'). At the relational extreme, we have situations which involve persons whose interaction and engagement with each other occurs in a context that is far removed from that of strangers (an employer and an employee, the parents of a child and the parents of one of the classmates of that child, and so on) and whose proximity is therefore principally a function of their relationship ('relational proximity'). To use a market-based understanding of relations (thus treating one's counterparties as substitutable fictitious commodities) is to collapse these three categories into common resource negligence, even though they each naturally embody a distinctive set of social expectations and generate very different types of uncertainty. Such a representation is clearly an oversimplification, but if our purpose is simply to make risk management easier, it is a distortion that is both sustainable and likely to be long-lived.

VI. Conceptualism and Social Needs

A hallmark of the risk management approach is the relative unimportance within it of the actual task of setting standards of conduct. The law's role is not to set these standards. It is, rather, to create a framework within which they can be set. From this perspective, it is easy to see why such a law would cede an increasing amount of space to regulation, which is expressly concerned with setting such standards. It should also be easy to see why a law whose doctrines were built on such an approach would not necessarily produce salutary results if it were asserted against regulation. The experience of the pyrite litigation in Ireland is a particularly egregious example, in which the invocation of the law of the sale of goods in a complex, multi-level, multipartite and heavily insured transaction produced utter chaos which required high-level regulatory intervention to sort out.

Does this mean that the law of obligations should continue its retreat and withdrawal in the face of regulation? Or does it continue to have a role to play? It is useful to start by contrasting the operation of administrative and regulatory bodies, on the one hand, and the law of obligations, on the other. The role of administrative and regulatory bodies tends to lie at two extremes of a spectrum of discretion. Independent *regulators* such as central banks, utilities regulators and financial watchdogs lie at one end of this spectrum. They tend to be given a broad range of powers, and a lightly restrained discretion, to pursue goals which are clearly defined, but broadly phrased. In the pursuit of these goals, they both apply rules and make rules—thus, in essence, administering rules which they themselves make. They are also assigned specific objectives, which are typically expressly tied to the expectations of a particular group of society, which they are asked to champion or protect; for example, the objective of 'the protection of consumers'[78] which is often assigned to financial watchdogs. Purely *administrative* bodies, in contrast, have far more limited

[78] Financial Services and Markets Act 2000, s 2(c).

powers. Consumer watchdogs such as the UK Office of Fair Trading, for example, have the power to issue guidance, but not to make binding rules, nor themselves to directly levy fines. Their role is, rather, investigative, with the actual making and enforcement of binding rules coming from elsewhere.

The law of obligations occupies an intermediate role in this spectrum. Courts applying tort law, for instance, do more than merely enforce and the modern trend is, if anything, to reduce their role in straightforward cases of enforcement—the application of clear rules—by giving jurisdiction to other authorities. Yet the discretion of courts is limited in a way the discretion of regulatory bodies is not. Courts do not have the power to formulate elaborate systems of guidance, analogous to the rule books prepared by regulatory bodies, nor can they entirely remake the law, as regulatory bodies can in successive editions of their rule books. Instead, as the history of the law of obligations demonstrates, the law is made not by a single case, but by a chain of cases through which a court repeatedly revisits the same legal issue in a number of factual contexts. This gives the law of obligations a special character, in that the process by which it resolves conflicting expectations has the potential to be socially embedded, and context-sensitive, in a way no other arm of the state can match.

This is reflected in the manner in which the law of obligations and regulatory bodies make their decisions. The policy guidance that is given to regulatory bodies is, in effect, a directive to *always* prioritise the interests of one class over another. To task a financial regulator with the job of 'the protection of consumers' is to require that regulator to necessarily and always favour consumer expectations where they conflict with the expectations of financial service providers; for example, in a situation where the consumer's expectation in relation to the quality of advice conflicts with the financial body's expectation of being able to 'talk up' a product, so as to show it in the most favourable light.

The law of obligations, in contrast, has no equivalent. Tort law does not explain why those particular wrongs are redressed, nor does it set out what interests such redress is intended to serve. Equally, the position taken by the law is never as simple as holding that the interests of one will always prevail over the interests of another. The role of the law of obligations is, instead, to determine the specific contexts in which, and the circumstances under which, one type of interest will prevail; and this determination comes from the repeated consideration of a broad range of contexts and circumstances by different judges over a large number of cases. In the law of obligations, unlike in the operation of regulatory bodies, the setting of an expectation is the aggregate result of a series of decisions—a process which Maitland accurately described as one of 'blundering into wisdom' in an 'empirical fashion'.[79]

The result is that the concepts in which the law of obligations is expressed have a socially embedded character. The problem of liability for the negligent provision of false information provides a good example. The issue can arise in a number of different contexts, ranging from the inclusion of incorrect information in a printed reference work,[80] to an auditor's report that negligently presents a company as being sounder than it actually is,[81] or a credit rating report that negligently gives bonds a far higher rating than their underlying fundamentals merit.[82] Each of these contexts raises a complex mix of conflicting expectations.

[79] FW Maitland, 'English Law Under Norman Rule' in HD Traill (ed), *Social England: A Record of the Progress of the People*, 2nd edn (London, Cassell, 1894) 280.

[80] See, eg, *Alm v Van Nostrand Reinhold* 480 NE2d 1263 (Ill App 1 Dist 1985).

[81] *Caparo Industries plc v Dickman*, above n 20.

[82] *Bathurst Regional Council v Local Government Financial Services Pty (No 5)* [2012] FCA 1200.

Take the example of an encyclopaedia of mushrooms which wrongly portrays a mushroom as being safe when it is poisonous, or perhaps insufficiently distinguishes a safe mushroom from an unsafe one.[83] On the one hand, the purchaser has an expectation of safety—the very purpose behind buying such a book is to be able to spot dangerous mushrooms, a notoriously difficult task. On the other hand, one has the publishers' expectation that as simple non-expert intermediaries (mere 'conduits', to adopt a phrase from a different area of law) they cannot be expected to spend the time and effort checking the factual accuracy of every book they put out.[84] Finally, there are the authors' expectation (common to anyone who gives advice) that they cannot be required to verify every single fact in a book, that the potential liability from a book must be proportionate to the rewards its publication carries, that advice may be wrong, and that persons who choose to take it do so at their peril because nobody can be accurate all the time. Audited accounts and credit rating reports present similar patterns of expectations.

How might a person debating the issue in purely common-sense normative terms think about it? It is clearly not standard practice for authors to refrain from publishing unless they are certain that every single thing they say is correct. The question, therefore, is to what extent and in what circumstances we should say that this standard practice in authoring and publishing is wrong. The result might be a scale with instruction manuals for the use of medical equipment close to one end, and a blog with a travelogue about the author's visit to various beaches and the swimming conditions there close to the other.

How does this relate to the law? Reasonableness, with its seductive promise of capturing the thought-style of the man on the Clapham omnibus, is part of the answer. But the law also has its own thought-style, because the Clapham omnibus can only carry us so far. Where social expectations conflict, or are nebulous, the figure of man on the Clapham omnibus is of little use because his answer (or rather, the judge's estimate of his answer) will depend upon the particular institutional environment in which he operates and the influences this environment exercises upon him, so that different hypothetical passengers on the omnibus will give different answers. The jury system, with its multi-member jury and its safeguards against selection bias, might or might not have helped obviate this particular problem, but the limited role of civil juries in most Commonwealth countries makes that question academic. It is here, therefore, that the distinctly legal component of negligence, the duty of care, steps in. Traditionalist legal theory, and, in particular, legal theories that are based on moral accounts, are hard to reconcile with the specifics of the *Caparo*[85] approach. But seen as a form of governance oriented towards establishing social expectations, the approach is far more intelligible.

Proximity is arguably the most important and most underestimated component of that approach. At least since *Donoghue*, proximity has given legal recognition to the fact that every person has a broad range of circles of interaction of differing width, which give rise to different expectations. The focus here, therefore, is on the nature and nearness of the relationship between the parties and, thus, on the expectations to which such a degree of

[83] *Winter v GP Putnam's Sons* 938 F 2d 1033 (9th Cir 1991).

[84] This factor, in particular, has been influential in the US case law on the liability of publishers for incorrect information in printed material. See, eg, *Alm v Van Nostrand Reinhold* 480 NE2d 1263 (Ill App 1 Dist 1985); *Jones v Lippincott* 694 F Supp 1216 (D Md 1988).

[85] *Caparo Industries plc v Dickman*, above n 20.

closeness could legitimately give rise. The closest type of relationship privity, established by contract as in, for example, a report produced at the express request of the claimant will give rise to a range of duties under the contract, including unless excluded implied terms as to quality. The relationship between the publisher and the reader of a commercially produced book, in contrast, is several steps removed in terms of proximity, in that the publisher has little or no role to play in the production of the misleading information that is the subject of the claim. The author and the reader of such a book stand in a relationship of greater proximity, albeit one still some way removed from the far closer relationship between one who specially commissions the production of the report or information. Proximity, in other words, permits the courts to relationalise the manner in which they resolve conflicting expectations, by giving them a conceptual framework for examining how different types of relationships give rise to different types of expectations, and to separate out relational factors that are relevant to the generation of expectations from those that are not.

Foreseeability, similarly, puts the focus on the specific activity that the claimant carried on with the assistance of the misleading information, and on the harm that resulted. As the link between proximity and foreseeability suggest, the cumulative question is whether the degree of proximity is sufficient to create an expectation that the defendant would take steps to avert harm of that specific degree of foreseeability. The third criterion—the fair, just and reasonable analysis—reflects in this particular example the fact that different factual contexts will carry different social expectations, based on factors such as the social perception as to the importance of the defendant's activity, the seriousness of the harm that could result, and the dependence of one party upon the other. Contexts that relate to the carrying on of activities that would potentially result in personal injury if not properly informed, for instance, air navigation charts,[86] or the hypothetical book *How to Make Your Own Parachute* that is often cited in US case law,[87] are likelier to carry an expectation of care than contexts that would merely result in harm to goods or to economic loss. Put together, these concepts, as they form part of the law, provide the judge with tools that he or she can use to estimate where social expectations lie if the case relates to existing social expectations, or where they most appropriately fall in the specific social context of the case if the task of the court is to set them.

The latter task necessarily raises more complex issues. As a form of governance, the law of obligations would ordinarily be expected to work in tandem with, rather than in opposition to, other forms of governance. One would therefore ordinarily expect the underlying ideas it reflects in relation to where social expectations should be set, and where they appropriately fall, to be influenced by the policies underlying governance in the country more generally. Unlike government policy, the policies that make their way into the law of obligations will not change at every general election, but they will nevertheless necessarily have their origin in the overall framework for governance and regulation in the relevant society, and the priorities these set. To some extent, *Caparo* itself reflects this. *Caparo* was a case involving the negligent provision of untrue information, in this case, an audited set of accounts for the company that because of the auditor's negligence reflected an untrue picture of the company's financial position. As discussed in a previous section, the manner in which the House of Lords decided that it was the auditor's expectations that would

[86] *Aetna v Jeppesen* 642 F 2d 339 (1981).

[87] *Lewin v McCreight* 655 F Supp 282, 284 (ED Mich 1987).

prevail was influenced by the surrounding regulatory context, specifically, the provisions of the relevant Companies Act that mandated the auditing of accounts and their provision to shareholders, and the purpose for which these accounts were provided, through the proximity and foreseeability criteria.

Legal doctrines and concepts are in this approach institutionalised strategies for dealing with the task of managing contradictory expectations, and of determining where social expectations lie or, where they are as yet nebulous, where they more appropriately lie. In the language of the social sciences, these are tools that judges use to estimate latent variables. The principal effect of doctrine is to create (in the language of institutional theory) a distinctively legal set of 'thought styles', or ways of thinking about social expectations, social relations, and the manner in which and conditions under which the expectations of one will be required to give way to the contradictory expectations of another—one which within it embeds both interpersonal justice and community welfare,[88] not as opposites to be reconciled, but as inseparable facets of a whole. The requirement that judges must work with legal doctrine, then, plays the role of translating and transforming the social factors that are the ultimate basis of this decision into the thought styles that characterise the law, but it remains fundamentally socially embedded, and it is this social embedding that gives the law of obligations its power and its enduring relevance.

VII. Conclusion: Constitutionalising Obligations Theory

In a society as concerned with the dangers of risk, and with the top-down nurturing of resilience, the rise of the managerial approach is not entirely surprising, nor is it surprising that it has led to the slow retreat of the law of obligations, and the corresponding rise of regulation. The tone of many current debates about the current law of obligations, as well as about the nature of its past, appear at least in part to be driven by a discomfort with the managerial nature of the modern law of obligations. In seeking to recover older aspects of the law that the modern institution is said to have forgotten the trend has been to seek to return to pre-technocratic modes of governance within obligations. Yet there is nothing inherently positive or negative about technocracy. Any complex society requires a range of different types of institutions to deal effectively, and in a manner that avoids social conflict, with the problems posed by the uncertainty inherent in social existence, and the conflicting expectations that are its products. Technocratic institutions have a role to play in this mix, not least because they provide an alternate, non-ideological framework within which to discuss social issues. The implications of a turn to technocracy are, rather, constitutional. As this chapter has sought to argue, in a managerial framework, the primary factor separating civil courts from regulatory bodies is that the former possess a more widely embedded autonomy. Where this wider embedding is useful (as it is in commercial law or maritime law), the law of obligations is likely to continue to thrive. Where it is less useful than goal-driven technocratic expertise (as in securities law, environmental law or consumer law), it is likely to increasingly give way to regulatory bodies. This is more or less what we currently see in the law of obligations.

[88] A Robertson, 'On the Function of the Law of Negligence' (2013) 33 *OJLS* 31.

This chapter has sought to argue for another approach, where the law of obligations is neither subordinate nor superior to public regulation, but is seen as having very different strengths, lying in its incrementalism and its social embeddedness. As this chapter has argued, it is the ability of the law of obligations to address issues of social expectations through the manner in which it uses, develops, applies and engages with concepts that give its power, and its constitutional importance. Such an understanding implies a very different, and much broader, role for the law of obligations. Nor is it alien to legal theory. It was fundamental to Scandinavian legal realism. The Scandinavian realists held that if one accepts epistemological realism, and if one accepts (as they did) that the law is a thing that has real existence, then one can describe it in conceptual terms without being normative as long as the concepts one uses have a basis in fact. Form, concepts and doctrine represent the results of the 'social evaluations' (as Vilhelm Lundstedt put it) that are embedded in the law. To the Scandinavian realists, understanding what these evaluations are, and how they relate to the concepts used in law, was a critical part of legal analysis. The question they asked in legal analysis, in essence, was 'If a concept has reality, what are the (social) facts and evaluations to which its words correspond?'. The power of this approach lies in its ability to restate legal concepts in a way that relates them directly to the social realities to which the concepts apply. What sort of social evaluations do they reflect? What are the facts—the goals, expectations, activities, perceptions, interests, motives, outcomes, preferences—to which these evaluations relate and upon which the value choices they embody are based?

It is the refusal to accept this, and the insistence upon monist principles, that have left this peculiar gap in obligations theory, where the retreat of obligations continues for the most part unremarked. Redressing this requires asking a very different set of questions about the law as it currently is, centring around the question of why we have the rights we do but lack the rights we lack, whose expectations they protect, and why it is so. These are fundamental questions, which we must face and with which we must deal if we want to fight the corner of the law of obligations, and argue for the continuance of the common law tradition it represents.

13

Divergent Evolution in the Law of Torts: Jurisdictional Isolation, Jurisprudential Divergence and Explanatory Theories

JAMES GOUDKAMP AND JOHN MURPHY

I. Introduction

Since the first wave of law-and-economics scholarship in the United States in the early 1970s, scholars have spent a tremendous amount of time trying to come to grips with tort law from a theoretical perspective. Richard Posner was on the crest of that wave, and his voluminous writings[1] revolutionised how tort law is understood. He contended that tort law (as well as the law generally) is best explained on the ground that it maximises societal wealth. Posner, writing together with William Landes, asserted that 'the common law of torts' should be accounted for 'as if the judges who created the law through decisions operating as precedents in later cases were trying to promote efficient resource allocation'.[2] Many scholars, especially in the United States, remain in the thrall of Posner's economic model.

The main reaction to Posner's account of tort law began in the 1990s. At the forefront of this reaction was Ernest Weinrib, who in 1995 published his ground-breaking *The Idea of Private Law*.[3] In this book Weinrib attacked functionalist theories of private law, and of tort law in particular. Posner's economic theory was Weinrib's principal target. As part of that attack, Weinrib proposed a non-functionalist explanation of tort law based on the idea of corrective justice. Many other writers have made similar criticisms of Posner's treatment of tort law, although the attacks have not all come from the same direction as Weinrib's. These writers include Robert Stevens[4] and John Goldberg and Benjamin Zipursky.[5] As is

[1] For a conspectus of his work in relation to tort law, see RA Posner, 'A Theory of Negligence' (1972) 1 *Journal of Legal Studies* 29; WM Landes and RA Posner, 'The Positive Economic Theory of Tort Law' (1980) 15 *Georgia Law Review* 851; WM Landes and RA Posner, *The Economic Structure of Tort Law* (Cambridge, MA, Harvard University Press, 1987); RA Posner, 'Wealth Maximization and Tort Law: A Philosophical Inquiry' in DG Owen (ed), *Philosophical Foundations of Tort Law* (Oxford, OUP, 1995) ch 4.

[2] Landes and Posner, *The Economic Structure of Tort Law*, above n 1, 1.

[3] EJ Weinrib, *The Idea of Private Law* (Cambridge, MA, Harvard University Press, 1995).

[4] R Stevens, *Torts and Rights* (Oxford, OUP, 2007).

[5] See, eg, JCP Goldberg and BC Zipursky, 'Torts as Wrongs' (2010) 88 *Texas Law Review* 917.

the case with Weinrib, these other scholars are in large part concerned to demonstrate that Posner's explanation of tort law is unable to account for large swathes of tort law and is hence unconvincing. Like Weinrib, they also propose non-functionalist accounts of tort law, although their accounts are phrased in terms of rights rather than corrective justice.

There are obviously deep-seated disagreements between Posner, on the one hand, and Weinrib, Stevens and Goldberg and Zipursky, on the other hand, as to how tort law should be understood. Yet there are also significant disputes between Weinrib, Stevens and Goldberg and Zipursky. These disputes even include the question of whether their respective theories are materially different from each other, and if they are different, the respects in which they differ.[6] However, there are also several things that all five of these theorists have in common. First, they are all offering *explanatory* theories of tort law. They are all, in other words, offering a model of tort law that they claim enables it to be understood as it presently exists.[7] It is true that these scholars, most notably Posner,[8] also offer blueprints for the law of torts that they believe we should have. But the fact that they all make prescriptive claims does not mean that they are not also endeavouring to explain the law that we currently have. In at least the cases of Weinrib, Stevens and Goldberg and Zipursky, the explanatory part of their work is clearly the dominant one, and they may even be reluctant to admit to making prescriptive claims. Secondly, all five theorists are seeking to explain *the whole* of tort law as opposed to just one or a few parts of it.[9] None of these writers is concerned just to explain, for example, the tort of negligence, strict liability torts or torts that are actionable per se. Thirdly, all of the theorists are concerned to explain tort law not just in one jurisdiction but *in at least all of the major common law jurisdictions*. They intend their theories to be relevant across jurisdictional boundaries. Sometimes this is said expressly. Stevens, for example, contends that his book *Torts and Rights* 'would [have] look[ed] much the same if [he] had … used the case law of any … common law jurisdiction'.[10] Usually, however, the inter-jurisdictional scope of the theorists' claims is implicit from, for example, the fact that they cite as evidence in support of their accounts cases from several jurisdictions.[11] Regardless of the precise form in which the evidence comes, it is clear that the theories in question are all *universal* theories of tort law.

Elsewhere, we have shown in much more detail why it is appropriate to understand the theories of Posner, Weinrib, Stevens and Goldberg and Zipursky as we have just described

[6] Compare, eg, BC Zipursky, 'Civil Recourse, Not Corrective Justice' (2003) 91 *Georgetown Law Journal* 695 and EJ Weinrib, 'Civil Recourse and Corrective Justice' (2011) 39 *Florida State University Law Review* 273 (Zipursky contends that the civil recourse theory that he developed with Goldberg is different from Weinrib's corrective justice theory; Weinrib, replying, doubts that there is any material difference).

[7] In relation to Posner, see the quotation in the opening paragraph of this chapter. Weinrib says that he wants 'to understand tort law' (Weinrib, above n 3, 3) and that 'Tort liability reflects corrective justice' (ibid 134). Stevens asserts that '[t]he law of torts is concerned with the secondary obligations generated by the infringement of primary rights' (Stevens, above n 4, 2). Goldberg and Zipursky 'argue … for the descriptive superiority' of their civil resource theory (Goldberg and Zipursky, above n 5, 920).

[8] See, eg, Posner, 'Wealth Maximization and Tort Law', above n 1, 101–11 (addressing what he calls the 'normative theory' of his economic analysis).

[9] See the passages quoted above, n 7.

[10] Stevens, above n 4, vii.

[11] eg, Weinrib invokes many cases from Australia, Canada, the United Kingdom and the United States in support of his theory. He presumably thinks that there is sufficient uniformity in the law in these jurisdictions to entitle him to draw on materials from any of them. Given this assumption of uniformity, he must also believe that the theory that he builds from the law in several jurisdictions must in turn apply to those jurisdictions.

them, namely, as universal explanatory theories of the whole of the law of torts.[12] In that work we have also argued at length why their exceptionally ambitious claims are overstated. We incorporate that analysis by reference. Very briefly, however, we note that the essential reason why we believe that they are unconvincing is that there are many important aspects of tort law that these theories cannot explain within any given jurisdiction. The gaps between the law and the respective theoretical accounts are significant, both in their number and their size. This difficulty for the theories is magnified greatly when one tries to apply them in more than one jurisdiction. We do not re-tread this ground in this chapter. Rather, our aim here is to demonstrate that it is highly improbable that a satisfactory universal explanatory account of the whole of tort law could be developed. We cannot, of course, prove a negative. We cannot, in other words, show that a satisfactory universal explanatory theory of the whole of tort law could never be devised. But we consider the probability that such a theory could be developed to be so remote that the search for one, which has now lasted for at least four decades, will almost certainly be in vain. In all likelihood, tort law as it exists throughout the common law world cannot be reduced to a single organising concept or principle given, among other things, its immense complexity and the fact that it is the product of so many different influences, and the significant differences in tort law between jurisdictions render fanciful the suggestion that any single account is capable of providing a compelling explanation of tort law in its entirety across multiple jurisdictions. Indeed, we think that the already remote probability that a satisfactory universal explanatory theory of the full range of tort law could be devised will dwindle over time. We hold this view because we believe that the scene is set for the already significant inter-jurisdictional differences between the systems of tort law in common law jurisdictions to increase.

II. Divergent Evolution in the Law of Torts

Divergent evolution is a familiar concept in biology. It refers to the process by which a single species develops into two species due to the gradual accumulation of differences between groups of the original species. This process usually occurs when two groups of the original species are separated from each other (for example, by an ocean) so that interbreeding is impossible. Natural selection favours certain characteristics in one group and different characteristics in the other group. Animals with favoured characteristics become more populous within each group relative to those animals that lack the characteristics. The process continues and, over a long enough period of time, the accumulated differences become sufficiently significant that the two groups of animals constitute separate species.

An analogy can be drawn between divergent evolution in biology and inter-jurisdictional differences in the law of torts. We believe that common law systems have become increasingly isolated from each other with the result that local factors have been able to operate independently on tort law in these systems so as to yield distinct tort law regimes and, moreover, regimes that are likely, because of the isolation, to continue to grow further apart. The suggestion that there are distinct systems of tort law throughout the common

[12] J Goudkamp and J Murphy, 'Tort Statutes and Tort Theories' (2015) 131 *LQR* 133; J Goudkamp and J Murphy, 'The Failure of Universal Tort Theories' (2016) (forthcoming).

law world (as opposed to a law of tort that is shared by all common law jurisdictions) is not novel. Other writers have made similar claims. For example, Kit Barker, Peter Cane, Mark Lunney and Francis Trindade wrote in the fifth and latest edition of *The Law of Torts of Australia*, published in 2012:[13]

> Since the first edition of this book was written [in 1985], Australian common law in general and Australian tort law in particular have become much more independent of foreign influence, and Antipodean tort law has, in important respects, diverged from its English roots. This trend has continued since the fourth edition was prepared [in 2006]. Importantly, too, English tort law is increasingly influenced by human rights law and European Union law, and resulting changes in the law seem to be creating new divergences between English and Australian tort law.

It is clear from this passage that these authors are conscious of both the phenomenon of jurisdictional isolation and the capacity of tort law to adapt to local pressures, leading to jurisprudential divergence. In this chapter, we explain the process of isolation and identify several local factors that have resulted in the divergent development of tort law in different jurisdictions.

It might be queried whether the analogy with divergent evolution in biology that we have drawn is apt. We think that the analogy is illuminating, but do not want to push it too far. There are obvious and significant differences between the evolution of species and the way in which the law of torts has been developed in common law jurisdictions. One such difference concerns the relevant timeframe. The evolution of species is generally measured on a geological timescale whereas the law can be changed essentially overnight. Another major difference is that the evolution of species involves the gradual accumulation of almost imperceptible changes whereas a single change in the law in a given jurisdiction can result in the law in that jurisdiction diverging dramatically from the law elsewhere. A final important difference is that the evolution of species is always a result of environmental pressures whereas this is not the case in relation to changes in the law. For example, judges in a given jurisdiction might change a given rule based simply on their ideological preferences as opposed to any differences in the environment in that jurisdiction compared with the environment in other jurisdictions.

III. Jurisdictional Isolation

In this part of the chapter, we contend that, whereas in the past common law jurisdictions were very closely connected to each other, they are now quite isolated from each other, and that this isolation is entrenched. We should explain precisely what we mean by 'isolation'. When we say that one jurisdiction has been isolated from another, we mean to say that they do not share the same sources of law. By 'sources of law', we do not intend to refer to the *types* of material that are authoritative as to what the law is, such as legislation and cases. (Obviously, all common law jurisdictions sing from essentially the same hymn sheet in

[13] K Barker, P Cane, M Lunney and F Trindade, *The Law of Torts in Australia*, 5th edn (Oxford, OUP, 2012) 14 (footnote omitted). See also the analysis by Trindade, writing alone, concerning 'how indigenous, how Australian, the law of torts has become over the last three decades': F Trindade, 'Towards an Australian Law of Torts' (1993) 23 *Western Australia Law Review* 79, 79.

terms of the types of materials that they regard as being authoritative.) Rather, by sources of law, we mean to refer to the *specific manifestations* of the authority to declare the law, such as a particular judicial decision. Our claim is that common law jurisdictions today are to a large degree isolated from each other in the sense that (to continue the example of judicial decisions), judgments delivered in one jurisdiction lay down the law only in the jurisdiction in which they were delivered. This is not a bold claim. However, it is essential for us to establish it as it is a crucial step in our argument that jurisprudential divergence in the law of torts is likely to increase, which in turn has ramifications for the probability that a compelling universal explanatory theory of the whole of tort law can be developed. We also feel that the range of factors that have led to jurisdictions becoming isolated has not been properly appreciated, and so see a need to elaborate upon the process of isolation.

A great many factors have brought about the transition that has occurred throughout the common law world from interdependence to independence. We discuss some of the more interesting and significant of those factors. To be clear, we are not concerned in this chapter with the underlying political reasons that led to the current situation of jurisdictional isolation (such as, for example, a perception that it is inconsistent with the concept of nationhood for a legal system to be dependent on the sources of law of another jurisdiction, a rejection of colonialism, and so on). Rather, we are interested in the specific legal changes that took place that led to jurisdictions lacking unity in terms of their sources of law. We explore (1) the shrinking overseas jurisdiction of the Privy Council; (2) the reduced precedential force of British authority; (3) the reduced deference to British authority; (4) a tendency towards judicial parochialism in some jurisdictions; (5) harmonisation of legal systems with different legal traditions; and (6) the growth of legislation in the tort law context.

Shrinking Overseas Jurisdiction of the Privy Council

In earlier times, the Privy Council was the final court of appeal for many jurisdictions. Indeed, by almost any conceivable measure of the extent of a court's jurisdiction (eg, the number of people subject to its authority, the size of the geographical area in which its decisions apply, and so on), the Privy Council had a larger jurisdiction than any other court that has ever existed. Its position at the apex of numerous court hierarchies made a significant contribution to uniformity in the law across the common law world. Indeed, it was thought in the past that the Privy Council enjoyed a judicial function not just out of a 'desire to govern' the 'countless millions … all over the world'[14] but also as a result of a commitment to the view that there was and should be a single common law throughout the world.[15] The possibility that there could be as many systems of common law as there were common law jurisdictions was regarded as deeply repugnant. For example, in *Trimble v Hill* the Privy Council said that 'it is of the utmost importance that in all parts of the Empire where English law prevails, the interpretation of that law by the Courts should be as nearly

[14] Henry (later Lord) Brougham in the House of Commons, quoted in K Keith, 'The Interplay with the Judicial Committee of the Privy Council' in L Blom-Cooper, B Dickson and G Drewry (eds), *The Judicial House of Lords 1876–2009* (Oxford, OUP, 2009) 315.

[15] See Andrew Burrows, 'The Influence of Comparative Law on the English Law of Obligations', ch 2 of this volume.

as possible the same'.[16] As late as 1972, Lord Hailsham LC remarked in *Cassell & Co Ltd v Broome*, a decision of the House of Lords: 'I view with dismay the doctrine that the common law should differ in different parts of the Commonwealth'.[17]

It is worth observing that this understanding—that there was (and should be) a single common law throughout the world—was closely associated with the declaratory theory of the common law. According to this theory, which held a firm grip on the minds of jurists in earlier times, the common law had existed since time immemorial and the role of judges was simply to declare its content. The common law, on this account, did not change, and judges certainly did not make the common law. When the courts departed from previous authority, the common law was simply being correctly re-expressed. Of course, there are few judges or scholars who these days place any faith in this theory.[18] The declaratory theory was famously dismissed by Lord Reid in 1972 as a 'fairy tale'.[19] The view that there was but a single common law throughout the world was connected with the declaratory theory. The possibility that the common law might be different in different jurisdictions would have sat most uncomfortably with that theory.

It is important to understand exactly how the fact that the Privy Council was the ultimate appellate court for several jurisdictions had a powerful unifying effect on the law throughout the common law world. The dominant view regarding the precedential status of the Privy Council's decisions is that they have binding force not only in the jurisdiction from which a given appeal comes, but in all jurisdictions from which the Privy Council hears appeals.[20] So, if the Privy Council settles the law as being X on an appeal from jurisdiction Y, X is the law not only in jurisdiction Y but in all jurisdictions from which an appeal to the Privy Council lies. The Privy Council, when its overseas jurisdiction was at its zenith, thus contributed greatly to uniformity in the law throughout the common law world. By a single decision, the Privy Council would lay down the law for a great many jurisdictions, including, arguably, Britain.[21]

The dissolution of the British Empire and its replacement by the Commonwealth witnessed the removal of the Privy Council as the final court of appeal for many jurisdictions.

[16] *Trimble v Hill* (1879) 5 App Cas 342 (PC (Aust)), 345. Similarly, in *Wright v Wright* (1948) 77 CLR 191, 210 Dixon J wrote: 'For myself, I have in the past regarded it as better that this Court should conform to English decisions which we think have settled the general law in that jurisdiction than that we should be insistent on adhering to reasoning which we believe to be right but which will create diversity in the development of legal principle. Diversity in the development of the common law (using that expression not in the historical but in the very widest sense) seems to me to be an evil. Its avoidance is more desirable than a preservation here of what we regard as sounder principle'. In the instant case, however, Dixon J felt that it was impossible to determine what the law of England was due to conflicting cases, with the result that he felt that it was appropriate for the High Court to adhere to one of its earlier decisions rather than to a decision of the English Court of Appeal.

[17] *Cassell & Co Ltd v Broome* (1972) AC 1027 (HL), 1067.

[18] For a recent re-interpretation and defence of the declaratory theory, see A Beever, 'The Declaratory Theory of Law' (2013) 33 *OJLS* 421.

[19] Lord Reid, 'The Judge as Lawmaker' (1972) 12 *Journal of the Society of Public Teachers of Law* 22, 22.

[20] The High Court of Australia in *Morris v English, Scottish and Australian Bank* (1957) 97 CLR 624 and the New Zealand Court of Appeal in *Bruer v Wright* [1982] NZLR 77 (CA) thought that they were bound by all Privy Council decisions, including decisions on appeals emanating from other jurisdictions. In contrast, the Ontario Court of Appeal held in *Negro v Pietro's Bread Co Ltd* [1933] 1 DLR 490 (Ont CA) that it was bound only by decisions of the Privy Council brought on appeal from Canadian courts.

[21] Regarding the status of Privy Council decisions in Britain, see Lord Wright, 'Precedents' (1942) 8 *CLJ* 117, 135–36.

The precise process by which this transition occurred, which has a long history,[22] differed from jurisdiction to jurisdiction. The details are complex, and not terribly relevant for present purposes. It will suffice to make some very general remarks. In the case of Australia, the process of limiting appeals to the Privy Council was a protracted one lasting many decades.[23] It culminated with the enactment of the Australia Act 1986 (UK) and the Australia Act 1986 (Cth),[24] which, save for a merely theoretical possibility of appeals to the Privy Council on certain constitutional issues,[25] resulted in the complete termination of appeals from Australia. The process in relation to Canada was similarly tortuous.[26] Criminal appeals to the Privy Council were eliminated in 1933. Civil appeals to the Privy Council were ended in 1949, although appeals remained permissible in cases in which proceedings were commenced before this date. In 2003, the Supreme Court of New Zealand replaced the Privy Council as the ultimate appellate court for New Zealand.[27] A great many other jurisdictions have now also abolished the right to appeal to the Privy Council. As to the scale of the decline in the Privy Council's jurisdiction, one recent study observes that, at the start of the twentieth century, 25 per cent of the world's population was subject to the Privy Council's jurisdiction while today that figure has dwindled to just 0.1 per cent.[28] The Privy Council's jurisdiction 'has been reduced to a shadow of its earlier self'.[29]

Where the Privy Council has been replaced by a national court of final appeal, that national court of appeal has ultimate responsibility for the development of the law in the jurisdiction in question. Final national courts are not bound by either prior or subsequent decisions of the Privy Council.[30] This is because it is thought that it would be inappropriate for such a court to observe the decisions of the Privy Council given that the Privy Council could no longer correct what might be thought to be an incorrect decision of the national court. The freeing of many jurisdictions from the yoke of the Privy Council afforded their courts increased freedom to develop the common law in the direction that they saw fit. This development was a critical step in the process of jurisdictional isolation.

[22] As long ago as 1923, Viscount Haldane wrote that the Privy Council was 'a disappearing body': Lord Haldane, 'The Work for the Empire of the Judicial Committee of the Privy Council' (1923) 1 *CLJ* 143, 154.

[23] See, generally, A Twomey, *The Australia Acts 1986: Australia's Statutes of Independence* (Sydney, Federation Press, 2010).

[24] These Acts abolished appeals to the Privy Council from State courts. Appeals in federal matters had been abolished by the Privy Council (Limitation of Appeals) Act 1968 (Cth) and appeals from the High Court were ended by the Privy Council (Appeals from the High Court) Act 1975 (Cth).

[25] The High Court of Australia is empowered by s 74 of the Australian Constitution to issue a certificate that permits an appeal to the Privy Council on select constitutional matters. This power has only been exercised once, in *Colonial Sugar Refining Co v The Commonwealth* (1912) 15 CLR 182. The High Court has indicated that this certificate will never again be granted: *Kirmani v Captain Cook Cruises Pty Ltd (No 2)* (1985) 159 CLR 461, 464–65.

[26] The details are given in MJ Herman, 'The Founding of the Supreme Court of Canada and the Abolition of the Appeal to the Privy Council (1976) 8 *Ottawa Law Review* 7, 23–31; A Roland, 'Appeals to the Judicial Committee of the Privy Council: A Canadian Perspective' (2006) 32 *Commonwealth Law Bulletin* 569.

[27] Supreme Court Act 2003 (NZ), s 42.

[28] D Clarry, 'Institutional Judicial Independence and the Privy Council' (2014) 3 *Cambridge Journal of International and Comparative Law* 46, 48–51.

[29] Keith, above n 14, 316.

[30] See *Viro v R* (1978) 141 CLR 88, 92–94; *Reference re Agricultural Products Marketing* [1978] 2 SCR 1198, 1256–67; *China Field Ltd v Appeal Tribunal (Buildings)* (2009) 12 HKCFAR 68 [79]–[81].

Reduced Precedential Force of British Authority

Intimately related to the termination of appeals from many jurisdictions to the Privy Council is the marked weakening in the precedential force of domestic British authority as a source of law outside of the United Kingdom. When the overseas jurisdiction of the Privy Council was in its heyday, the prevailing view was that the decisions of the House of Lords were effectively binding on the courts overseas.[31] The qualifier 'effectively' appears in the previous sentence in recognition of the fact that because the House of Lords was part of the judicial system of the United Kingdom only, its decisions were not strictly speaking binding on courts other than those in the United Kingdom.[32] However, for all intents and purposes, in earlier times, the position was that decisions of both the Privy Council *and* the House of Lords were binding in jurisdictions that were subject to the Privy Council's authority. A clear statement to this effect can be found in *Piro v W Foster & Co Ltd*.[33] In this case, Latham CJ said that although the High Court of Australia is not 'technically bound by a decision of the House of Lords', it:[34]

> and other courts in Australia should as a general rule follow decisions of the House of Lords. The House of Lords is the final authority for declaring English law, and where a case involves only principles of English law which admittedly are part of the law of Australia, and there are no relevant differentiating local circumstances, the House of Lords should be regarded as finally declaring the law. ... In my opinion it should now be formally decided that it will be a wise general rule of practice that in cases of clear conflict between a decision of the House of Lords and of the High Court, this Court, and other courts in Australia, should follow a decision of the House of Lords upon matters of general legal principle.

Another well-known statement along the same lines is that of Viscount Dunedin in *Robins v National Trust Co Ltd*.[35] Lord Dunedin stated:[36]

> when an appellate Court in a colony which is regulated by English law differs from an appellate Court in England, it is not right to assume that the Colonial Court is wrong. It is otherwise if the authority in England is that of the House of Lords. That is the supreme tribunal to settle English law, and that being settled, the Colonial Court, which is bound by English law, is bound to follow it.

The fact that decisions of not only the Privy Council but also (if not de jure then certainly de facto) the House of Lords had precedential force tended to add to the uniformity in the common law that was achieved by virtue of the Privy Council's overseas jurisdiction.

Decisions of the Privy Council were of course binding because that court formed part of the judicial hierarchy of overseas jurisdictions. Decisions of the House of Lords were regarded as binding for a different reason, namely, the fact that the composition of the Appellate Committee of the House of Lords and of the Judicial Committee of the Privy

[31] Comments can be found to the effect that decisions of the English Court of Appeal were binding too: see, eg, *Waghorn v Waghorn* (1942) 65 CLR 289, 292–93.

[32] Wright, above n 21, 135–36.

[33] *Piro v W Foster & Co Ltd* (1943) 68 CLR 313.

[34] ibid 320. Parallel remarks were made by all of the other members of the Court: Rich J (at 325–26), Starke J (at 326–27), McTiernan J (at 335–36) and Williams J (at 340–42).

[35] *Robins v National Trust Co Ltd* [1927] AC 515 (PC (Can)).

[36] ibid 519. See also *Stuart v Bank of Montreal* (1909) 41 SCR 516, 548 ('A decision of the House of Lords should ... be respected and followed though inconsistent with a previous judgment of this court').

Council were substantially the same.[37] As a result of the largely common membership of the two courts, the law enunciated by the Privy Council tended to be the same as that adumbrated by the House of Lords. So courts in jurisdictions that were subject to the authority of the Privy Council could be reasonably confident that a pronouncement of the House of Lords would be followed by the Privy Council. It was thus necessary for them to them to proceed 'with one eye on the prevailing English case law on the subject'.[38]

The status in many parts of the Commonwealth, and certainly in those parts that had terminated appeals to the Privy Council, of decisions of the House of Lords changed significantly around the middle of the twentieth century. The general view that emerged was that its decisions were no longer binding, at least not on final national courts of appeal. A notable decision in this sea change is *Parker v The Queen*.[39] In this case, decided in 1963, the High Court of Australia refused to follow the decision of the House of Lords in *DPP v Smith*.[40] Dixon CJ, speaking for the court on this point, said:[41]

> Hitherto I have thought that we ought to follow decisions of the House of Lords, at the expense of our own opinions and cases decided here, but having carefully studied *Smith's* case I think that we cannot adhere to that view or policy. There are propositions laid down in the judgment ... which I could never bring myself to accept ... I think *Smith's* case should not be used as authority in Australia at all.

This retreat from the view that British authority had precedential force in Australia continued in *Uren v John Fairfax & Son Pty Ltd*.[42] In that case, the Australian High Court unanimously refused to follow the decision of the House of Lords in *Rookes v Barnard*, in which the House had famously severely restricted the availability of exemplary damages.[43] McTiernan J remarked: 'A decision of the House of Lords is not as a matter of law binding on this Court'.[44] Owen J, expanding on comments that he had made in an earlier matter,[45] opined:[46]

> if the High Court comes to a firm conclusion that a decision of the House of Lords is wrong it should act in accordance with its own view ...; and ... where a conflict exists between a decision of the High Court and one of the House of Lords I am of opinion that other Australian courts should follow the decision of this court.

[37] '[T]he board of the Privy Council is drawn practically from the same judges who take part in the judicial sittings of the House of Lords': Lord Wright, 'Precedents' (1942) 8 *CLJ* 118, 135.

[38] WMC Gummow, 'The High Court of Australia and the House of Lords (1903–2003)' in G Doeker Mach and KA Ziegert (eds), *Law, Legal Culture and Politics in the Twenty First Century* (Stuttgart, Franz Steiner Verlag, 2004) 44.

[39] *Parker v The Queen* (1963) 111 CLR 610.

[40] *DPP v Smith* (1961) AC 290 (HL).

[41] (1963) 111 CLR 610, 632 (footnotes omitted). The New Zealand counterpart to this development is *Bognuda v Upton & Shearer Ltd* [1972] NZLR 741 (CA). As a side note, *Smith* did not survive in the United Kingdom. Parliament departed from it in s 8 of the Criminal Justice Act 1967 (UK) and the Privy Council later held that it did not represent the common law: *Frankland v The Queen* [1987] AC 576 (PC (Isle of Man)), 594.

[42] *Uren v John Fairfax & Son Pty Ltd* (1966) 117 CLR 118. For a longer treatment of this case and associated decisions, see JR Lehane, '*Stare Decisis*, Judicial Policy and Punitive Damages' (1986) 6 *Sydney Law Review* 111.

[43] *Rookes v Barnard* [1964] AC 1129 (HL). The law as stated in *Rookes v Barnard* has also been rejected in Canada: *Vorvis v Insurance Corp of British Columbia* [1989] 1 SCR 1085.

[44] *Uren v John Fairfax & Son Pty Ltd* (1966) 117 CLR 118, 122.

[45] *Skelton v Collins* (1966) 115 CLR 94, 138.

[46] *Uren v John Fairfax & Son Pty Ltd* (1966) 117 CLR 118, 161 (footnote omitted).

In *Australian Consolidated Press v Uren*,[47] the High Court affirmed the departure from *Rookes v Barnard*. On appeal to the Privy Council, their Lordships said that the High Court was entitled not to follow *Rookes v Barnard*.[48] Significantly, their Lordships appeared to suggest that local judges, in at least certain legal contexts, are best positioned to decide the legal destiny of their respective jurisdictions.[49]

This reduction in the precedential force of decisions of the House of Lords in relation to Australia has occurred in many other common law jurisdictions. The details are given elsewhere.[50] It is unnecessary to delve into them here, for the critical point to grasp for present purposes is that the fact that decisions of the House of Lords are no longer binding in Commonwealth jurisdictions, at least in those jurisdictions that have terminated appeals to the Privy Council, has played an important role in facilitating jurisdictional isolation.

Reduced Deference to British Authority

Another, related factor that has led to jurisdictional isolation is that of reduced deference to British authority. Historically, judges in many Commonwealth jurisdictions placed special emphasis on British authority even when they were not formally bound by it. For example, Kitto J in *Skelton v Collins*, after arguing that the High Court of Australia was not bound by decisions of the House of Lords, nonetheless wrote that the High Court:[51] 'has always recognised [the] particularly high persuasive value [of decisions of the House of Lords]'. This approach had a certain unifying effect on the law throughout the common law world. However, this deferential attitude waned over time. It is generally true to say that, today, the persuasiveness of the reasoning of a particular decision, rather than the jurisdiction from which it emanated, determines the extent to which courts in other jurisdictions will have recourse to it.[52] This attitude is visible in, for example, the following extra-curial remark made by Sir Anthony Mason, then the Chief Justice of Australia, in 1987:[53]

> There is … every reason why we should fashion a common law for Australia that is best suited to our conditions and circumstances. In deciding what is law in Australia we should derive such assistance as we can from English authorities. But this does not mean that we should account for every English judicial decision as if it were a decision of an Australian court. The value of English judgments, like Canadian, New Zealand and for that matter United States judgments depends on the persuasive force of their reasoning.

[47] *Australian Consolidated Press v Uren* (1966) 117 CLR 185.

[48] *Australian Consolidated Press v Uren* [1969] 1 AC 590 (PC (Aust)), 644.

[49] For clear statements to this effect, see *Geelong Harbor Trust Commissioners v Gibbs Bright & Co* [1974] AC 810 (PC (Aust)), 819; *Jamil bin Harun v Yang Kamsiah BTE Meor Rasdi* [1984] AC 529 (PC (Malaysia)), 535, 538; *Hart v O'Connor* [1985] AC 1000 (PC (NZ)), 1017.

[50] In relation to Canada, see RJ Sharpe, 'Canada' in L Blom-Cooper, B Dickson and G Drewry (eds), *The Judicial House of Lords 1876–2009* (Oxford, OUP, 2009) ch 19(b), where Justice Sharpe describes the transition from what he calls 'the era of obedience' to 'the era of persuasion'. The story with respect to New Zealand is set out in MD Kirby, 'Australia and New Zealand' in L Blom-Cooper, B Dickson and G Drewry (eds), *The Judicial House of Lords 1876–2009* (Oxford, OUP, 2009) 347–50.

[51] *Skelton v Collins* (1966) 115 CLR 94, 104.

[52] *cf* the view of JW Harris, who wrote that in 1990, 'perhaps, even today, English decisions have a special primacy' in Commonwealth jurisdictions: JW Harris, 'The Privy Council and the Common Law' (1990) *LQR* 574, 588.

[53] A Mason, 'Future Directions in Australian Law' (1987) 13 *Monash University Law Review* 149, 154.

A similar statement has been made by Justice Robert Sharpe in relation to Canada. Speaking extra-judicially, Justice Sharpe wrote:[54]

> Canadian courts continue to look to the House of Lords for authoritative statements of common law principle, but have adopted a more eclectic approach [than in the past], often citing the decisions of other non-Canadian courts … English jurisprudence is no longer accorded automatic precedence, and its acceptance rests entirely upon its persuasiveness.

The increased willingness of Commonwealth courts to look other than to the jurisprudence of British courts for inspiration has diminished the unifying effect on the law to which the previous deferential approach contributed.

Judicial Parochialism

In some jurisdictions, judges have tended towards parochialism. The result of this tendency has been, at least to some degree, to cut off the jurisdiction in question from the rest of the legal universe. By far the most striking illustration of this phenomenon concerns the United States. As is well known, US judges refer almost exclusively to domestic legal sources, with the result that the United States is an exporter of law and not an importer.[55] There is a fairly widely held belief among the judiciary in the United States that it is inappropriate to take cognisance of materials from other jurisdictions, especially in certain contexts, such as that of constitutional interpretation.[56] A key reason why many judges in the United States tend to focus almost exclusively on domestic sources concerns the sheer scale on which judicial authority is produced in that country. It is difficult enough for judges to master the domestic authorities given their number, and they are hence understandably reluctant to add to their workload by making frequent recourse to foreign sources. As one commentator has put it, 'judges from other American state jurisdictions have often provided such an abundance of authority on common law issues … that reference to non-American authority has been unnecessary'.[57] Another reason for the insular attitude that exists in the United States is that comparative insights are readily available from jurisdictions that are internal to the United States. A judge sitting in, say, New York is able to look to how his or her fellow judges are proceeding in, say, California. However, the motivations of the US judiciary for putting itself into self-imposed exile are unimportant for present purposes. What matters is the fact that the judiciary in that country has substantially isolated itself from the rest of the common law world.

Judges in other major common law jurisdictions freely and frequently have recourse to foreign sources. It might be thought, therefore, that parochialism has extended only to the United States. It is impossible justifiably to reach any firm conclusions in this connection,

[54] Sharpe, above n 50, 355.

[55] Judges in other jurisdictions not infrequently have recourse to US authority. See, eg, Andrew Burrows, 'The Influence of Comparative Law on the English Law of Obligations', ch 2 of this volume, regarding the use made by the House of Lords and UK Supreme Court of US authorities.

[56] See the sources cited in RJ Delahunty and J Yoo, 'Against Foreign Law' (2005) 29 *Harvard Journal of Law and Public Policy* 291, 294–95.

[57] PE von Nessen, 'The Use of American Precedents by the High Court of Australia, 1901–1987' (1992) 14 *Adelaide Law Review* 181, 183–84.

at least without engaging in a further, very different kind of research project. For what it is worth, however, our feeling is that foreign sources are much less influential in many jurisdictions than is commonly thought. It is undeniable that judges in many parts of the common law world regularly cite foreign sources. But this fact does not mean that these sources have a significant or, indeed, any influence on the outcomes of decisions or the reasoning employed therein. Arguably, citations of foreign legal materials are to a large degree ornamental. On this view, judges canvass sources of law in other jurisdictions merely or mainly, for example, out of concern for judicial comity or to create the impression that all of the main angles to a given legal problem have been considered. If this is correct, judicial parochialism might be more widespread than is commonly thought, with important implications for jurisdictional isolation.

Harmonisation of Legal Systems with Different Legal Traditions

The previous section dealt with insular attitudes on the part of judges, which can contribute to the isolation of a jurisdiction. Paradoxically, a willingness of judges to look beyond the confines of their jurisdiction for inspiration can also contribute to isolation. A good illustration of this concerns the United Kingdom. It is probably fair to say that judges in the United Kingdom refer to a greater degree today than they did in the past to European sources of law.[58] This tendency is due at least partly to the significant efforts that have been made to harmonise the law throughout the European Union.[59] It is arguable that the increased use by the British judiciary of European sources of law has tended to make their decisions less relevant to other common law jurisdictions than might have otherwise been the case. So while the United Kingdom might be less isolated from continental jurisdictions than in former times, efforts to harmonise the law across the European Union have tended to isolate the United Kingdom from other common law jurisdictions.

Growth of Legislation

There are two central points that are worth making about legislation and isolationism. The first is that there has been a lack of source unity in terms of legislation from a relatively early stage. The reign of the British Imperial Parliament has long since come to an end, and legislatures in most common law jurisdictions are now free to specify what the law is within their respective domains, subject to local constitutional constraints. The second point concerns the rise of legislation as a source of law. As is well known, the way in which law is made has changed dramatically in the last 150 years or so throughout the common law world. Historically, the courts assumed the main responsibility for ensuring that lacunae in the law were filled and that the law served the needs of the day. The bulk of the law was,

[58] See Andrew Burrows, 'The Influence of Comparative Law on the English Law of Obligations', ch 2 of this volume.

[59] The main work in this respect in so far as the law of torts is concerned has been done by the European Group on Tort Law, the Study Group on a European Civil Code and the Joint Network on European Private Law. For details of their various projects, see P Giliker, *The Europeanisation of English Tort Law* (Oxford, Hart Publishing, 2014) 198–202.

in other words, judge-made, and the legislature was the lesser partner in the law-making enterprise. This state of affairs has been dramatically reversed. The legislatures in at least all major common law jurisdictions are now by far the dominant producers of law. Guido Calabresi encapsulated the transition from a world of primarily judge-made law to a world of statutory law in his now well-worn remark that we live 'in the age of statutes'.[60] The rise of legislation as a source of law has profoundly affected, of course, the law of torts,[61] a fact that that has not been properly recognised by many tort scholars.[62] The reasons for this role reversal are irrelevant for present purposes. What matters is the fact that it has occurred. It is a significant development because nowadays, many decisions are set against a distinctive statutory backdrop, with the result that they are less relevant to judges in other jurisdictions than might otherwise have been the case. This contributes, of course, to isolationism.

IV. Jurisprudential Divergence

The previous section described how the major common law jurisdictions have become increasingly isolated from each other. Law-makers (including judges) in these jurisdictions are now masters of their own legal destinies, subject to local political, constitutional and cognate constraints. We now show that the ability of law-makers to determine their own legal fate has enabled them to adapt tort law in response to domestic pressures. We consider a selection of such pressures here and the impact that they have had. The purpose of this analysis is not so much to show that the systems of tort law in common law jurisdictions have drifted apart from each other. Everyone knows that there is significant divergence. Rather, the aim is to continue the story that has been told to this point, namely, that jurisdictional isolation has permitted jurisprudential divergence in the law of torts.

Constitutional Arrangements and International Human Rights Commitments

A jurisdiction's particular constitutional arrangements and human rights obligations can influence the trajectory of tort law within that jurisdiction and cause it to diverge significantly from that found elsewhere. Several areas of tort law seem to be especially susceptible to such influences. We consider some of these below.

Defamation

A clear example of constitutional arrangements influencing the development of tort law concerns the First Amendment to the United States Constitution and the law of defamation.[63]

[60] G Calabresi, *A Common Law for the Age of Statutes* (Cambridge, MA, Harvard University Press, 1985).

[61] See Goudkamp and Murphy, 'Tort Statutes and Tort Theories', above n 12.

[62] Arvind and Steele justifiably complain that 'legislation tends to be left at the periphery of the subject, either unconsciously, or deliberately': TT Arvind and J Steele, 'Introduction: Legislation and the Shape of Tort Law' in TT Arvind and J Steele (eds), *Tort Law and the Legislature* (Oxford, Hart Publishing, 2013) 2.

[63] The First Amendment states: 'Congress shall make no law respecting an establishment of religion, or prohibiting the free exercise thereof; or abridging the freedom of speech, or of the press; or the right of the people peaceably to assemble, and to petition the Government for a redress of grievances'.

In *New York Times v Sullivan*,[64] the US Supreme Court decided that the existing defences to liability in defamation did not adequately secure the constitutional free-speech guarantee. Accordingly, it crafted new exclusionary rules applicable where the person defamed is a public official. The main change made was to prevent public officials from recovering 'damages for a defamatory statement unless [the public official concerned proved] that it was made with "actual malice"—that is, with knowledge that it was false or with reckless disregard of whether it was false or not'.[65] Crucially for present purposes, the Supreme Court made it clear that it was changing the law because of the First Amendment, a unique local factor. The Court stressed its 'commitment to the principle that debate on public issues should be uninhibited'[66] principally on the ground that it was vital to the achievement of democratic accountability, a central constitutional value in the United States. Our point here, we stress, is not that the First Amendment somehow dictated that precisely this rule had to be developed (plainly, it made no such demand) but, rather, that the Supreme Court developed the law of defamation on account of the First Amendment.

In the United Kingdom, against the background of the European Convention on Human Rights (ECHR), and in anticipation of the introduction of Human Rights Act 1998 (UK), the House of Lords in *Reynolds v Times Newspapers Ltd*[67] crafted a defence (which subsequently became known as the '*Reynolds* defence') that would be available in respect of statements on matters of public interest so long as those statements met the standard of responsible journalism.[68] The *Reynolds* defence was created in order to give greater weight in English defamation law to the right to freedom of expression enshrined in Article 10 of the ECHR. Judicial acknowledgement of the impact of the ECHR in this regard was supplied by Lord Phillips P in *Flood v Times Newspapers Ltd*. His Lordship stated that 'British courts … developed the defence of public interest privilege under the influence of principles laid down in the European Court of Human Rights'.[69] It is important to note that the House of Lords in *Reynolds* developed English law differently from the way in which the US Supreme Court in *Sullivan* changed the law of defamation in the United States. The difference in the legal solutions adopted is partly attributable to the fact that Article 10 of the ECHR grants a much more qualified right to freedom of expression than exists in the United States.[70] Sedley LJ captured the difference in this way: 'Where rights to reputation and privacy have wilted somewhat in the bright light of First Amendment jurisprudence, the English common law, now reinforced by the [ECHR], seeks to hold the two in a sometimes difficult balance, calibrated by the concept of responsible journalism'.[71] It is important to note that section 4 of the Defamation Act 2013 (UK) abolished the *Reynolds* defence and installed a new 'public interest' defence in its place. However, this new defence seems to

[64] *New York Times v Sullivan* 376 US 254 (1964).

[65] ibid 279–80.

[66] ibid 270.

[67] *Reynolds v Times Newspapers Ltd* [2001] 2 AC 127 (HL).

[68] Although the defence was described in *Reynolds* as one of 'responsible journalism', it was subsequently made clear that it was potentially applicable to publications by non-media company defendants in any medium: *Charman v Orion Publishing Group Ltd* [2007] EWCA Civ 972, [2008] 1 All ER 750; *Seaga v Harper* [2008] UKPC 9, [2009] 1 AC 1.

[69] *Flood v Times Newspapers Ltd* [2012] UKSC 11, [2012] 2 AC 273 [138].

[70] See further M Tushnet, '*New York Times v Sullivan* Around the World' (2014) 66 *Alabama Law Review* 337, 352–53.

[71] *Roberts v Gable* [2007] EWCA Civ 721, [2008] QB 502 [75].

be identical to the *Reynolds* defence. The Explanatory Notes to the Act stated that the public interest defence is 'based on the existing common law defence established in *Reynolds*'.[72] This understanding is reinforced by an examination of the parliamentary debates.[73] It is also shared by other writers.[74]

The law of defamation elsewhere has also been developed in unique ways due to constitutional influences. The High Court of Australia in *Lange v Australian Broadcasting Corporation*[75] recognised an implied freedom of political communication derived from aspects of the Federal Constitution providing for a system of representative democracy. According to the High Court, this implied freedom required the defence of qualified privilege to be extended to cover defamatory statements concerning 'government and political matters'. The extended privilege (the *Lange* privilege) is conditional upon the publisher of the statement having acted reasonably in publishing the statement. The key difference between the *Lange* privilege and the *Reynolds* defence is that the former is limited to political statements whereas the latter is not. This difference can be explained in part by reference to different influences at play in each jurisdiction. Freedom of political communication is an implicit constitutional liberty in Australia. There is no equivalent in Australia to Article 10 of the ECHR (recognising a more general right to freedom of speech) which, as noted earlier, underscores the *Reynolds* defence.

Different, again, are the relevant developments in New Zealand. In the leading case of *Lange v Atkinson* the New Zealand Court of Appeal crafted a narrow defence confined to 'statements which directly concern the functioning of representative and responsible government'.[76] Ostensibly, this defence bears some similarity to the *Lange* privilege in Australia. However, there is an important difference between the two defences, for the New Zealand Court of Appeal declined to follow the Australian lead of qualifying the defence with a reasonableness requirement. The case went to the Privy Council.[77] The Judicial Committee remitted the matter to the Court of Appeal for a further hearing and invited the Court to reconsider its first decision in the light of *Reynolds*. However, the Court of Appeal declined to depart from its earlier statement of the law.[78] Anthony Lester described the second decision of the Court of Appeal as follows:[79]

> [The Court of Appeal] found the constitutional air of New Zealand too pure to be contaminated by uncertain English common law restrictions on political expression ... When diplomatically explaining its reasons for departing from the English law, the Court of Appeal referred to differences between the New Zealand and the United Kingdom constitutional structures.

In Canada, a development along the lines of the decision in *Sullivan* was rejected, with the Supreme Court remarking that '[n]one of the factors which prompted the United States

[72] Defamation Act 2013 (UK), Explanatory Notes [29].

[73] During the Committee stage in the House of Lords, Lord McNally, then the Minister for Justice, suggested that 'in determining whether in all the circumstances the test is met, we would expect the courts to look at many of the same sorts of considerations as they have done before': (HL Deb 741, col GC534, 19 December 2012).

[74] See, eg, M Jones (ed), *Clerk and Lindsell on Torts* (London, Sweet and Maxwell, 2014) 1264.

[75] *Lange v Australian Broadcasting Corporation* (1997) 189 CLR 520.

[76] *Lange v Atkinson* [1998] 3 NZLR 424 (CA), 467.

[77] *Lange v Atkinson* [2000] 1 NZLR 257 (PC (NZ)).

[78] *Lange v Atkinson* [2000] 3 NZLR 385 (CA).

[79] A Lester, 'The Magnetism of the Human Rights Act 1998' (2002) 33 *Victoria University of Wellington Law Review* 53, 53–54.

Supreme Court to re-write the law of defamation in America are present in the case at bar'.[80] Subsequently, in *Grant v Torstar Corp*,[81] the Supreme Court recognised a defence of responsible communication on matters of public interest. It is somewhat similar to the *Reynolds* defence. Significantly, however, it was crafted in order to render Canadian defamation law consistent with the particular values embodied in the Canadian Charter of Rights and Freedoms rather than to keep step with developments in the United Kingdom or elsewhere. So, although in the instant case there was a significant trawl of the case law throughout the Commonwealth, the Supreme Court ultimately held that the most important impetus for change derived from the fact that, as it presently stood, Canadian defamation law did not afford sufficient weight to the Charter value of freedom of expression. McLachlin CJ (speaking for the Court) said that the 'common law defence of qualified privilege should be expanded to comply with Charter values'.[82]

Privacy

Privacy is a second area in which constitutional guarantees and human rights commitments have resulted in the differential development of tort law in the major common law jurisdictions. In the United Kingdom, there is no general tort of invasion of privacy.[83] However, privacy nonetheless receives some direct protection in the form of the tort of misuse of private information.[84] This tort, which is an offshoot of the equitable wrong of breach of confidence, was welcomed into English tort law by the seminal House of Lords' case of *Campbell v MGN Ltd*.[85] Its elements are (1) the information in question must have been of a private nature; (2) the information must have been disclosed in circumstances where the defendant knew or ought to have known that the claimant reasonably expected the information to remain private; and (3) it must not have been more important that the defendant be free to disclose the information than that it remain private.[86] Even the most cursory reading of the opinions in *Campbell* reveals that the ECHR was at the forefront of the Law Lords' minds.[87] The elements of the tort, and the third element in particular, clearly reflect the influence of Article 8 (protecting the right to privacy) and Article 10 (protecting the right to free speech).

In Australia, there is no constitutional guarantee against invasions of privacy or human rights instruments comparable to the ECHR. It is unsurprising, therefore, that the protection that Australian tort law gives to privacy interests is essentially the same as the protection conferred by English tort law prior to the incorporation of the ECHR into domestic law. An unsuccessful attempt to augment tort law's protection of privacy interests was made

[80] *Hill v Church of Scientology of Toronto* [1995] 2 SCR 1130 [139].

[81] *Grant v Torstar Corp* [2009] SCC 61, [2009] 3 SCR 640.

[82] ibid [142].

[83] *Wainwright v Home Office* [2003] UKHL 53, [2004] 2 AC 406.

[84] Beyond the direct protection afforded by this action, tort law has long since protected privacy indirectly via an array of other torts such as private nuisance, trespass to land and the action under the Protection from Harassment Act 1997 (UK).

[85] *Campbell v MGN Ltd* [2004] UKHL 22, [2004] 2 AC 457.

[86] ibid [92]–[100] (Lord Hope).

[87] We are not alone in reading the case in this way. McBride and Bagshaw, for example, argue that '[t]he most important influence on the development of the new tort has been, and remains, the right to privacy contained in Article 8 of the European Convention': NJ McBride and R Bagshaw, *Tort Law*, 4th edn (Harlow, Pearson, 2012) 592.

in *Australian Broadcasting Corporation v Lenah Game Meats Pty Ltd*.[88] In this case, the High Court of Australia strictly only ruled out the possibility of corporate entities relying on a privacy-based tort. But the general tenor of the decision was also against the development of a privacy-based tort for human claimants. Accordingly, in its recent summary of the present state of the law in Australia, the Australian Law Reform Commission concluded that '[a] common law tort for invasion of privacy has not yet developed in Australia'.[89]

The law in New Zealand is different again. In that country there is a 'tort covering the invasion of personal privacy'.[90] The elements of this tort, according to the landmark decision in *Hosking v Runting*, are (1) the existence of facts in respect of which there is a reasonable expectation of privacy; and (2) publicity given to those facts which is highly offensive according to an objective standard.[91] This is a more expansive action than its English counterpart, primarily because its elements may be satisfied even where the defendant has acted reasonably. Gault P, who delivered the main opinion in *Hosking*, was mindful of New Zealand's human rights commitments. After making the general point that '[t]he legislative landscape is important'[92] he wrote that, 'when enacting the Bill of Rights Act to affirm New Zealand's commitment to the International Covenant on Civil and Political Rights Parliament did not include among the provisions affirming specific rights and freedoms a provision corresponding to article 17 of the Covenant'.[93] In essence, that article contains a guarantee against arbitrary or unlawful interference with a person's privacy. Because the Bill of Rights Act 1990 (NZ) was silent on the right to privacy in spite of New Zealand being party to the International Covenant, Gault P thought it fell to the courts to develop the common law so as to honour New Zealand's commitment to Article 17.

It is worth noting that, more recently, the New Zealand courts have also recognised a tort of intrusion upon seclusion.[94] The elements of this tort are (1) an intentional and unauthorised intrusion; (2) upon seclusion; (3) involving the infringement of a reasonable expectation of privacy; and (4) in circumstances where the invasion would be highly offensive to a reasonable person.[95] In the foundational case, it was held that these elements were present where the defendant had spied on the claimant while she was showering. Again, this tort was developed on account of essentially the same local considerations that prompted the Court of Appeal in *Hosking* to recognise the tort of invasion of personal privacy.[96] It is clear that this tort, which involves the defendant *acquiring* information about the claimant, rather than misusing information that is already in the defendant's possession, offers protection that goes substantially beyond that which exists in the United Kingdom.

The protection of privacy under Canadian tort law has also largely been driven by local human rights guarantees. In the recent and leading case of *Tsige v Jones*, Sharpe JA (delivering the reasons of the Ontario Court of Appeal) noted '[t]he explicit recognition of a right to privacy as underlying specific Charter rights and freedoms'.[97] His Honour then argued

[88] *Australian Broadcasting Corporation v Lenah Game Meats Pty Ltd* [2001] HCA 63, (2001) 208 CLR 199.
[89] Australian Law Reform Commission, *Serious Invasions of Privacy in the Digital Era* (Report 123, 2014) [3.53].
[90] *Hosking v Runting* [2004] NZCA 34, [2003] 3 NZLR 385 [79].
[91] ibid [117].
[92] ibid [91].
[93] ibid.
[94] *C v Holland* [2012] 3 NZHC 2155, [2012] 3 NZLR 672.
[95] ibid [94].
[96] See, eg, the references to New Zealand's international obligations at ibid [67] n 93.
[97] *Tsige v Jones* [2012] ONCA 32, (2012) 108 OR (3d) 241 [46].

that 'the principle that the common law should be developed in a manner consistent with Charter values supports the recognition of a civil action for damages for intrusion upon the plaintiff's seclusion'.[98] Importantly, however, he also noted that the privacy right in the Charter should be understood as including a right to seclusion that was rather different from the one in New Zealand. What the case minted was a cause of action that lies where a defendant gains unauthorised access to a claimant's private personal records (such as the bank account, in this case). Obviously, this differs significantly from the New Zealand tort of intrusion upon seclusion. It also differs from both the New Zealand tort of invasion of personal privacy and the English tort of misuse of private information, since both of those torts require the dissemination of private information.

In the United States, the protection of privacy by tort law is of very considerable vintage.[99] The *Restatement (Second) of the Law of Torts* recognises four privacy torts: (1) unreasonable intrusion upon seclusion; (2) appropriation of another's name or likeness; (3) unreasonable publicity given to another's private life; and (4) publicity that unreasonably places another in a false light before the public.[100] This understanding of the law was endorsed by the US Supreme Court in *Cox Broadcasting Corp v Cohn*,[101] and some of these torts have been shaped by the United States Constitution. In *Cohn* itself, the third of these torts was in issue. A television company (and a reporter employed by it) were sued by the father of a 17-year-old rape victim for publishing his daughter's name. The reporter had obtained the daughter's name in open court. The father argued, relevantly, that in publishing his daughter's name his right to privacy had been violated. By way of defence, the company argued, among other things, that granting the action would infringe the First Amendment.[102] This argument was accepted by a majority of the Court. White J stated that it was constitutionally impermissible for a State to 'impose sanctions on the accurate publication of the name of a rape victim obtained from public records—more specifically, from judicial records which are maintained in connection with a public prosecution and which themselves are open to public inspection'.[103] The scope of the tort of unreasonably giving publicity to another's private life consequently had to be restricted. Leaving *Cohn* to one side, it is also notable that the United States Constitution has also influenced the first-mentioned privacy tort, which is concerned with the right to seclusion. In *Olmstead v United States*, Brandeis J, having recognised 'the right to be let alone' stated that 'every unjustifiable intrusion by the government upon the privacy of the individual, whatever the means employed, must be deemed a violation of the Fourth Amendment'.[104] We offer no comment on the merits of these developments, which are irrelevant for present purposes. We confine ourselves to the observation that these constitutional concerns have influenced the law of privacy in the United States in a unique way.

[98] ibid. For further analysis, see T Bennett, 'Privacy, Corrective Justice, and Incrementalism: Legal Imagination and the Recognition of a Privacy Tort in Ontario' (2013) 59 *McGill Law Journal* 49.

[99] SD Warren and LD Brandeis, 'The Right to Privacy' (1890) 4 *Harvard Law Review* 193 is often regarded as marking the beginning of the field.

[100] At § 652A.

[101] *Cox Broadcasting Corp v Cohn* 420 US 469, 489 (1975).

[102] See above n 63.

[103] 420 US 469, 491 (1975).

[104] 277 US 438, 478 (1928). The Fourth Amendment states: 'The right of the people to be secure in their persons, houses, papers, and effects, against unreasonable searches and seizures, shall not be violated, and no Warrants shall issue, but upon probable cause, supported by Oath or affirmation, and particularly describing the place to be searched, and the persons or things to be seized'.

Caps on Compensatory Damages

The influence of the constitutional arrangements on US tort law has not been confined to the areas of defamation or privacy. Those arrangements also constrain the freedom of State legislatures to cap compensatory damages. The relevant jurisprudence is on a vast scale, and it is both impossible and unnecessary to do more here than make a few brief observations.[105] Damages caps in the United States are widespread and are emblematic of modern tort reform efforts in that country. Sometimes, particular heads of damages are capped, such as damages for non-economic loss (as that category of damages is usually called in the United States).[106] On other occasions, caps exist on the total amount of damages.[107] Yet another variation is found in the form of caps on awards arising from a particular accident, irrespective of the number of claimants involved.[108] The constitutional validity of caps has been hotly contested and some caps have been struck down. For example, in *Ferdon v Wisconsin Patients Compensation Fund*,[109] the Supreme Court of Wisconsin held incompatible with Wisconsin's equal protection guarantees a cap on non-economic damages in medical malpractice cases. Similarly, in *Estate of McCall v United States*,[110] the Florida Supreme Court found unconstitutional a cap on wrongful death non-economic damages recoverable in a medical malpractice suit. The Court held that the cap violated Florida's equal protection guarantee. The contrast with the experience in other common law jurisdictions is stark. Statutory caps on compensatory damages are commonplace in Australia, and have existed for decades.[111] However, none has ever been struck down on constitutional grounds. Indeed, to the best of our knowledge, no Australian court has even been invited to declare any statutory cap on damages constitutionally invalid. Equally, so far as we are aware, the informal caps on general damages for pain and suffering established in the Judicial Studies Board's *Guidelines for the Assessment of General Damages in Personal Injury Cases*[112] have raised no constitutional concerns in the United Kingdom. The same is true, as we understand it, of the judicially created caps on general damages that exist in Canada.[113] In short, the unique constitutional considerations at play in the United States have created a distinct strand of tort law jurisprudence in relation to damages caps.

Reforms Resulting from Highly Publicised Legal Concerns

In all of the major common law jurisdictions, legislation has been enacted in the tort law context in response to pressing and highly publicised local concerns. Such legislation has

[105] An accessible introduction is JCP Goldberg, 'The Constitutional Status of Tort Law: Due Process and the Right to a Law for the Redress of Wrongs' (2006) 115 *Yale Law Journal* 524, especially at 621–22.

[106] See, eg, Wis Stat §§ 655.017, 893.55(4)(d) (2001–2002).

[107] See, eg, Va Code Ann § 8.01-581.15 (2000).

[108] See, eg, Fla Stat § 766.118(2); Ind Code § 34-13-3-4.

[109] 284 Wis 2d 573, 701 NW 2d 440 (2005).

[110] 134 So 3d 894 (Fla, 2014).

[111] See, eg, Civil Liability Act 2002 (NSW), s 12 (capping damages for a loss of earnings), s 16 (capping damages for non-economic loss).

[112] In *Wall v Mutuelle de Poitiers Assurances*, the quasi-statutory effect of these Guidelines was described by Longmore LJ in these terms: 'judges will tend to follow them. No doubt one can call this "soft law" rather than "hard law" but it is law nevertheless': [2014] EWCA Civ 138, [2014] 1 WLR 4263.

[113] In a trilogy of cases decided in 1978, the Supreme Court of Canada imposed caps on compensatory damages for non-pecuniary loss: *Andrews v Grand & Toy Alberta Ltd* [1978] 2 SCR 229; *Arnold v Teno* [1978] 2 SCR 287; *Thornton v School Dist No 57 (Prince George)* [1978] 2 SCR 267.

often caused tort law in the jurisdiction in question to diverge radically from that which exists elsewhere. The prime example of such legislation is the Accident Compensation Act 1972 (NZ). This Act effected the most radical reform of the common law of torts ever to have been wrought by a single statute anywhere in the world. It provided for a no-fault solution to accidents and, in doing so, rendered tort law in New Zealand a much less expansive beast than any counterpart system of tort law. Its origins can be traced to a particular local concern. In the 1960s there was widespread dissatisfaction with the workers' compensation system then in place. That dissatisfaction led to the appointment of the Royal Commission. The Commission concluded that 'the workers' compensation legislation had been put forward on a wrong principle and had since been dominated by a wrong outlook'.[114] Accordingly, the Commission recommended major changes. This recommendation, contained in the Commission's final report in 1967, provided the crucial impetus for the introduction of the 1972 Act. In short, it was primarily dissatisfaction with an existing local regime governing workers' compensation that prompted the enactment of the 1972 statute.

A similar story can be told of the far-reaching statutory reforms of tort law that occurred in Australia at the turn of the twenty-first century. The particular local concern that these reforms addressed was the 2001–02 'insurance crisis'. That crisis involved an exponential increase in premiums for liability insurance. The public outcry was deafening, and the crisis was headline news at the time. With remarkable speed (some might say too much speed), all Australian legislatures, operating on the assumption that tort law was largely or wholly to blame for these hikes in premiums,[115] legislated to curb radically both the scope of tortious liability and the quantum of damages recoverable.[116] Largely as a consequence of these reforms, the law of torts in Australia became, and remains, quite different in very important respects from the law of torts in other common law jurisdictions.

As a final example of distinctive legislation prompted by highly publicised local concerns, consider the Congenital Disabilities (Civil Liability) Act 1976 (UK). This Act changed the law in the United Kingdom in response to the prominently documented inability of the common law of torts to provide adequately for victims of Thalidomide. In particular, the *Sunday Times* campaigned vigorously for legislative reform, and the newspaper's role was acknowledged in parliamentary debates.[117] The resulting legislation, which is unique to the United Kingdom,[118] created a novel cause of action on behalf Thalidomide victims that is parasitic upon a breach of duty owed to the child's mother.

[114] *Compensation for Personal Injury in New Zealand: Report of the Royal Commission of Inquiry* (Wellington, Government Printer, 1967) 97.

[115] For an account of the crisis, see P Cane, 'Reforming Tort Law in Australia: A Personal Perspective' (2003) 27 *Melbourne University Law Review* 649, 656–60; J Goudkamp, 'The Yong Report: An Australian Perspective on the Latest Response to Britain's "Compensation Crisis"' (2012) 28 *Journal of Professional Negligence* 4, 6–7.

[116] The principal statutes are as follows: Civil Liability Act 2002 (NSW); Civil Liability Act 2003 (Qld); Personal Injuries Proceedings Act 2002 (Qld); Civil Liability Act 1936 (SA); Recreational Services (Limitation of Liability) Act 2002 (SA); Volunteers Protection Act 2001 (SA); Civil Liability Act 2002 (Tas); Wrongs Act 1958 (Vic) (as amended by the Wrongs and Other Acts (Public Liability Insurance Reform) Act 2002 (Vic), the Wrongs and Other Acts (Law of Negligence) Act 2003 (Vic) and the Wrongs and Limitation of Actions Acts (Insurance Reform) Act 2003 (Vic)); Civil Liability Act 2002 (WA); Volunteers and Food and Other Donors (Protection from Liability) Act 2002 (WA); Civil Law (Wrongs) Act 2002 (ACT); Personal Injuries (Liability and Damages) Act 2003 (NT); Personal Injuries (Civil Claims) Act 2003 (NT).

[117] Hansard, House of Lords, 6 July 1976, vol 372, cols 1137–38.

[118] In the United States, the Thalidomide tragedy prompted an amendment to the Federal Food, Drug, and Cosmetic Act, whereby regulatory requirements on manufacturers were stiffened. Similar reform occurred in

V. The Future: A Self-Sustaining Reaction

Section III of this chapter explained how the major common law jurisdictions have become effectively isolated from each other, and section IV demonstrated how this isolation has permitted local factors to influence the trajectory of tort law so that it has developed differently from one jurisdiction to another. Together, these parts of the chapter tell the tale of divergent evolution in the law of torts. One important point that we want to make by way of conclusion is that this process—jurisdictional isolation and jurisprudential divergence—is self-sustaining. As the law of torts in jurisdiction X becomes sufficiently different from that in jurisdiction Y, legal materials in jurisdiction X will become less relevant to disputes in jurisdiction Y than might have otherwise been the case, and vice versa. In turn, this increases the degree of isolation and the potential for local factors to operate separately on the different jurisdictions. The process then continues.

This hypothesis can be verified by looking at different legal systems around the world, some of which became isolated from the United Kingdom at an earlier point in time than others. The United States became isolated from the United Kingdom in terms of its legal sources earlier than the other major common law jurisdictions and, as per our hypothesis, tort law in the United Kingdom and in the United States have drifted quite far apart from each other. By contrast, Australia, Canada and New Zealand became isolated from the United Kingdom in terms of source unity much later in the day. The law in these jurisdictions is more similar, and it is unsurprising that judges in these jurisdictions look to legal sources in fellow Commonwealth jurisdictions more regularly than they turn to legal materials in The United States.

If we are correct in our claim that divergent evolution in the law of torts is a runaway phenomenon, this obviously has significant consequences for the prospect of finding a viable universal theory of the whole of the law of tort. Specifically, it means that the likelihood that a viable universal theory will be found, which is already low in our view, will dwindle over time. The point will eventually be reached, if it has not been reached already, that no single theory will be able to accommodate the diversity of rules that are found across the common law world.

Canada. For details, see HW Choi and JH Lee, 'Pharmaceutical Product Liability' in LD Edwards, AW Fox and PD Stonier (eds), *Principles and Practice of Pharmaceutical Medicine*, 3rd edn (Oxford, Wiley-Blackwell, 2010). In Australia and New Zealand, the matter was left to the common law.

14

Common Law Values: The Role of Party Autonomy in Private Law

SARAH WORTHINGTON

The purpose of this chapter is to explore the extent to which the common law adheres to party autonomy as one of its fundamental or foundational values. Its cardinal importance in the common law is often presumed: it is one of the law's ideologies.[1] But matters which are presumed may too often end up being ignored. Party autonomy is not the only value supported by the common law, but unless we know its place and significance there is a risk it will be lost sight of in the working out of our modern legal rules. Explicit acknowledgement will not diminish conflicts between competing values, but at least outcomes will be more transparently defended.[2]

The suggestion advanced here is that there is an increasing tendency to favour paternalism over autonomy,[3] but very little argument from principle or policy to support that trend. True, this reflects a social choice. Our laws could be settled in either direction. But much of moral and political philosophy asserts the importance of personal autonomy; sophisticated democracies typically strive to enhance individual freedom, not limit it.[4] Unless there are principled arguments to the contrary, this suggests any trend towards paternalism should be resisted, and party autonomy robustly reasserted.

The simple question at the heart of this chapter is obvious. How important *is* autonomy? We have any number of legal authorities telling us that 'The law is X' because party autonomy must be upheld. But we also have other authorities telling us that 'The law is Y' because party autonomy is to be overridden, dismissed in no uncertain terms. Contract

[1] See JN Adams and R Brownsword, 'The Ideologies of Contract' (1987) 7 *Legal Studies* 205, 208–10, and at fn 3, citing P McAuslan, *The Ideologies of Planning Law* (Oxford, Pergamon, 1980) xii: 'Philosophy denotes a carefully prepared and thought out set of values and ideas. Ideology on the other hand denotes values, attitudes, assumptions, "hidden inarticulate premises" that may not be well thought out and are usually disguised rather than spoken out loud'.

[2] See JN Adams and R Brownsword, *Understanding Contract Law*, 5th edn (London, Sweet and Maxwell, 2007). Even advocates of autonomy can adopt a paternalistic approach to its delivery: see, eg, S Smith, 'Future Freedom and Freedom of Contract' (1996) 59 *MLR* 167, 177 ff on the idea of autonomy, and 187 concluding that 'the state should not help individuals to limit their freedom unduly'.

[3] See Smith, above n 2, 175, while still adopting the Mill view of minimal intervention to preserve and foster autonomy. Also see generally J Morgan, *Contract Law Minimalism: A Formalist Restatement of Commercial Contract Law* (Cambridge, CUP, 2013).

[4] N Ferguson, *Civilisation* (London, Penguin, 2012) 97: 'In reality, democracy was the capstone of an edifice that had as its foundation the rule of law—to be precise, the sanctity of individual freedom and the security of private property rights, ensured by representative, constitutional government'.

terms defining the price are in the former camp: the parties have autonomy; courts will not rewrite agreements to make them fair.[5] By contrast, terms providing for penalties on breach are in the latter camp.[6] Why do we uphold autonomy in some contexts but not in others? When is autonomy important and when is it not?

The answer cannot simply be 'Because the law says so'. The answer necessarily defines a boundary, separating situations where the law gives one answer from those where it gives another. It is essential to say something about why there is a boundary at all, and what distinctions it is attempting to address. Without that, disagreement on legal outcomes is inevitable. The need for principled justifications exists even though many of these boundary issues depend on only vaguely articulated values, and often contested ones at that.[7] Here, one value in issue is party autonomy, inevitably pitched against other equally attractive values. Justifying priorities is essential.

This chapter proceeds from the general to the particular. The first section concerns the general issue of party autonomy; the next addresses general points of contract law; and the final sections then turn to implication of contract terms, and then to three aspects of agreed remedies, being exclusion clauses, termination clauses and penalties, although not all in equal detail. These final four specific areas of contract law illustrate areas of judicial intervention which can easily slip into objectionable denial of party autonomy. To pre-empt what is to come, it is suggested that only the penalties jurisdiction merits that epithet.

I. Party Autonomy

The dictionary defines party autonomy as independence, freedom, self-determination, self-rule, sovereignty, liberty: all attractive qualities. But party autonomy in the law? It sounds important, and yet a moment's thought reveals that almost every law constrains autonomy rather than advancing it. Most laws tell us what we cannot do, not what we can.

The common law is built on this foundation. The historical caricature was that the common law proceeds from the premise that 'where there is a remedy, there is a right'. The civil law adopts the opposite position, 'where there is a [codified] right, there is a remedy'. Put more vividly, in common law jurisdictions everything was allowed unless there was a settled law permitting someone to stop you; in civilian jurisdictions, nothing was allowed unless there was a settled law permitting it. It then appeared apt to suggest that in common law systems all law constrained freedom and autonomy; in civilian systems, all law supported freedom and autonomy.

Caricature or not, there is still a grain of truth there. It perhaps follows that if party autonomy is a value worth supporting at all, then its function is to require that legal intervention restricting freedom is kept to an absolute minimum. The law should interfere no more than is necessary for society to live peaceably, in harmony, and function effectively

[5] *Thomas v Thomas* (1842) 2 QB 851. This assumes there is indeed an agreement.

[6] See the discussion below, section VII.

[7] See, eg, the various competing values at play in defining the rules of contract, summarised in R Brownsword, 'The Law of Contract: Doctrinal Impulses, External Pressures, Future Directions' (2014) 31 *Journal of Contract Law* 73, especially 75–76.

and efficiently. That involves a value judgement, but at a minimum it suggests that any legal constraint should be well justified by appeal to alternative and competing values.

Some constraints on autonomy are self-evidently valuable. We might expect constraints in the interests of appropriate legal determinations of disputes. That supports the rule of law. We might also expect constraints when our choices harm others. In the private law arena, much of tort, unjust enrichment, the rules on illegal contracts and so forth fulfil such a role. These all involve competition between concerns for party autonomy and concerns for the social welfare of others. Precise boundaries are likely to be disputed, but the need for some rules, and role of party autonomy in determining the boundary lines for those rules, are clear.

II. Contract Law Generally

But when we move to contracts we have a fertile ground for testing the value placed on party autonomy. To what extent *is* it fundamental? In *Photo Production Ltd v Securicor Transport Ltd*, Lord Diplock placed autonomy very clearly to the fore:[8]

> A basic principle of the common law of contract ... is that parties to a contract are free to determine for themselves what primary obligations they will accept. They may state these in express words in the contract itself and, where they do, the statement is determinative ... [and, turning to the common law's default rules, he continued] if the parties wish to reject or modify [those default] obligations which would otherwise be so incorporated, they are fully at liberty to do so by express words.

In short, party autonomy reigns supreme in contract. Other cases are to the same effect.[9] But these suggestions of absolutism cannot hide some very obvious constraints on party autonomy, even within the law of contract.

First, there are constraints from the general law. These arise because autonomy is deemed subservient to other social values. Both the criminal law and civil law outlaw certain bargains. It is not permissible to hire an assassin; certain assets cannot be bought and sold (contracts for human trafficking or the sale of body parts); other assets can only be bought and sold at fixed or capped prices (consider the constraints on water and gas regulators, or on interest rates in standard loans); still other assets can only be bought and sold subject to protective regimes (as with the sale of guns or drugs). Whatever their history, all these rules are now typically found in legislation, not settled by the courts. They reflect social values; they are not immutable rules of law or of nature. Recall it was once possible to trade slaves; now it is not. That is a choice.

Secondly, there are constraints within the law of contract which exist precisely because individual freedom, or party autonomy, *is* so highly prized. Consent is crucial. A contract is binding only on those who have agreed or consented to its terms. It follows that strangers are not affected: bilateral contracts cannot take away third parties' rights. And even between contracting parties, the consent to the deal must be real. This is the work of the legal rules

[8] *Photo Production Ltd v Securicor Transport Ltd* [1980] AC 827 (HL), 848.

[9] See, eg, Lord Upjohn in *Chertsey UDC v Mixnam's Properties Ltd* [1965] AC 735 (HL), 764, referring to freedom of contract as 'a fundamental right ... even today'.

on capacity, duress, undue influence, particular sorts of inequality of bargaining power, misrepresentation, mistake, etc.[10] Note that the issue here is that the party's consent is real, not that the parties are free, or even equally free, of life's pressures and influences, nor that they are equally matched in their abilities to understand the facts and the risks inherent in the deal, nor even that they each fully understand and are completely at one on the precise terms of the deal and its potential ramifications in an uncertain future.[11] The issue is simply did both parties truly consent to their mutual engagement. This is implicit in the idea that contracts concern voluntarily assumed legal obligations. The agreement between the parties is upheld only *because* the parties, as autonomous individuals, have agreed to be bound. It follows that the courts should intervene where there is no consent, or no proper consent. But, equally, our well-known rules on *caveat emptor* ('buyer beware') remind us that all these interventions map flawed consent; they are not directed at ensuring good faith, or even the absence of bad faith.[12]

But this seam of concern for consent runs slightly deeper. First, the law inhibits monopolies, holding it unacceptable to limit party autonomy to a choice to deal on the monopoly's terms or go without. Secondly, most democracies accept paternalistic intervention by the legislature in contexts where consent is perhaps not truly 'free', even if it passes the legal test for proper consent. Such legislation typically regulates contract terms where there is a perceived imbalance of power, in consumer contracts, employment contracts, loan contracts with unsophisticated parties, etc.[13] But the conflict between delivering these protective rules and infringing party autonomy is plain. It is a delicate balance. In consumer contracts, for example, many of the protections are confined to transactions entered into on the basis of standard form contracts; they do not impose a comprehensive ban, conceding that the parties might specifically agree to different terms. This in itself is instructive.

Thirdly, even if consent is real, we can expect further rules for determining *what* the parties have agreed to do. In England and Wales, Lord Hoffmann is responsible for much of the modern development in this area, starting with the *Investors Compensation* case.[14]

[10] For further details on this, and on all the other general contract rules discussed throughout this chapter, see *Chitty on Contracts*, 31st edn (London, Sweet and Maxwell, 2012); E Peel, *Treitel: The Law of Contract,* 13th edn (London, Sweet and Maxwell, 2011) or any other standard contract law text.

[11] But contrast the approach in M Chen-Wishart, 'The Nature of Vitiating Factors in Contract Law' in G Klass, G Letsas and P Saprai (eds), *Philosophical Foundations of Contract Law* (Oxford, OUP, 2014) ch 15, suggesting that other principles, such as responsibility in contract formation and protection of reasonable expectations, are also factors in these rules, not merely vitiated consent. Similarly, M Chen-Wishart, 'Undue Influence: Beyond Impaired Consent and Wrong-Doing, Towards a Relational Analysis' in A Burrows and Lord Roger of Earlsferry (eds), *Mapping the Law: Essays in Honour of Peter Birks* (Oxford, OUP, 2006) 201.

[12] Although within particular relationships there are other rules that will ensure this: see, eg, the rules on fiduciary obligations and on abuse of discretionary powers.

[13] These restrictions are described in all the standard textbooks on contract law, but for an exploration of the justifications for this intervention, see M Chen-Wishart, 'Regulating Unfair Terms' in L Gullifer and S Vogenauer (eds), *English and European Perspectives on Contract and Commercial Law: Essays in Honour of Hugh Beale* (Oxford, Hart Publishing, 2014) ch 7.

[14] *Investors Compensation Scheme Ltd v West Bromwich Building Society* [1998] 1 WLR 896 (HL), 912–13. Lord Hoffmann suggested these rules merely restated orthodoxy: *Chartbrook Ltd v Persimmon Homes Ltd* [2009] UKHL 38, [2009] 1 AC 1101 [37]. Of the same view, also see K Lewison, *The Interpretation of Contracts,* 5th edn (London, Sweet and Maxwell, 2011) para 5.02; *Marley v Rawlings* [2014] UKSC 2, [2014] 2 WLR 213 [36] (Lord Neuberger). By contrast, others suggest the new rules are a radical revision, or at least a high water mark: R Calnan, *Principles of Contractual Interpretation* (Oxford, OUP, 2013); J Carter, *The Construction of Commercial Contracts* (Oxford, Hart Publishing, 2013) [5-05]–[5-19]; A Berg, 'Thrashing through the Undergrowth' (2006) 122 *LQR* 354; C Staughton, 'How Do the Courts Interpret Commercial Contracts?' (1999) 58 *CLJ* 303, 307; J Spigelman, 'From Text to Context: Contemporary Contractual Interpretation' (2007) 81 *Australian Law Journal* 322.

These rules favour party autonomy, while recognising that the search is for *agreement*, not the parties' individual and subjective understandings: the tests are objective. When contracting, we are responsible for the impression we create in others.[15] The courts' first recourse is to the objective meaning of the terms of any written agreement, only going beyond them to the background 'matrix of facts'[16] if competing meanings present themselves,[17] and only then if still other competing reasons do not preclude it.[18] This modern approach to contract interpretation has been subjected to intense scrutiny and a good deal of critical comment.[19] But for the purposes of this chapter it suffices to note that the courts' approach unequivocally supports party autonomy.[20]

Finally, since no contract will contain terms covering every eventuality, and since there are efficiencies in having default rules rather than tailor-made rules, we can expect the law to provide such rules without feeling that party autonomy is being impugned. There are very few default rules defining the parties' primary performance obligations.[21] By contrast, there are a good number providing for remedies in all their various guises. These rules are sensitive to context, providing more aggressive protection when warranted: damages, injunctions, specific performance, proprietary remedies, etc, are all part of the remedial menu. All these default rules are undeniably useful, but, on the argument advanced here, unless there is some serious justification for overriding party autonomy, these default rules ought to be optional, not mandatory.

Beyond this short list, is judicial intervention ever warranted? If the parties have agreed, and their terms are clear, should the law nevertheless intervene in certain circumstances, or should party autonomy be given free rein? To take the extreme case, where the parties are sophisticated, fully informed and well advised, should they be subject to court interference concerning the substantive terms of their engagement? The law on penalties is the most obvious illustration of a positive answer, but not the only one, and it is these several areas

[15] Although contrast Chen-Wishart, 'The Nature of Vitiating Factors in Contract Law', above n 11, suggesting this is then not about consent.

[16] With the argument being that taking account of these issues does not breach the allegedly hard line to be drawn between interpretation of the written contract and infringement of the parol evidence rule, which prevents parties adducing evidence to add to, vary or contradict the written document (*Jacobs v Batavia and General Plantations Trust Ltd* [1924] 1 Ch 287 (CA); *Shogun Finance Ltd v Hudson* [2003] UKHL 62, [2004] 1 AC 919, especially [49] (Lord Hobhouse)), since that latter rule only applies where the writing is intended to embody the entire contract, and so the rule has been described as 'a self-evident tautology' (KW Wedderburn, 'Collateral Contracts' [1959] *CLJ* 58); or as 'no more than a circular statement' (Law Commission, *Report on the Parol Evidence Rule* (Report No 154, 1986)).

[17] *Rainy Sky SA v Kookmin Bank* [2011] UKSC 50, [2011] 1 WLR 2900 [23]: ie, where the language is unambiguous, the courts adopt that meaning even when it is unlikely to reflect the parties' intentions. On the other hand, where the words are capable of more than one meaning, then the more commercially sensible meaning should be adopted.

[18] See, eg, *Mannai Investment Co Ltd v Eagle Star Life Assurance Co Ltd* [1997] AC 749 (HL), 779 (Lord Hoffmann): 'There are documents in which the need for certainty is paramount and which admissible background is restricted to avoid the possibility that the same document may have different meanings for different people according to their knowledge of the background'.

[19] The approach has been criticised generally (see above, n 14) and also specifically, eg, on whether it blurs the separate functions of interpretation and rectification.

[20] Indeed, some commentators think it goes too far in this direction at the expense of commercial certainty: Calnan, above n 14, 17.

[21] Although see, eg, the default rules on frustrated contracts (plus the Law Reform (Frustrated Contracts) Act 1943); the various default rules applying to sales of goods (Sale of Goods Act 1979); and the rules on implying 'missing' terms in specific contracts (*The Moorcock* (1889) 14 PD 64 (CA); *Liverpool CC v Irwin* [1977] AC 239 (HL)).

which are the concern of the rest of this chapter. The core issue is what justifies interference with party autonomy, and what sort of interference is seen as warranted.

III. General Issues: Judicial Interference with Contract Terms

Four areas of contract law seem especially prone to judicial interference with the parties' agreed contractual terms. The first is implied contract terms. Here the risk to autonomy is an increasing tendency to interpret and imply contract terms in order to deliver results which are seen as more substantively fair.[22] The other three areas concern agreed remedies, widely construed. Here the risk is the courts' paternalistic response to terms explicitly adopted by the parties: exclusion clauses, express termination clauses and penalties clauses.

In all four areas there is a growing clamour, especially from some commentators, for the courts to deliver outcomes which are substantively fair: they urge the courts to go beyond judicial intervention based solely on procedural fairness (ie, real consent) or on general law constraints emanating from criminal or other general laws, and to consider as well the substantive issue of fairness in the bargain.[23]

Although the argument here is that this should be resisted, and party autonomy should prevail, the clamourers have a point. Historically, the courts displayed benign uninterest in the parties' agreed performance obligations (their primary obligations), yet were vigorously exercised by agreed terms dealing with under-performance (the parties' secondary or remedial obligations). That boundary needs justifying. The clamourers want uniformity of intervention. This chapter suggests uniformity of non-intervention is preferable, and party autonomy should prevail.

But, against that, are there reasons for maintaining the status quo, distinguishing between primary and remedial obligations? Lord Diplock, in *Photo Production Ltd v Securicor Transport Ltd*, cited earlier,[24] suggests there are not. He thought this followed logically from the autonomy of the parties, an autonomy which comprehended both the parties' primary obligations and their agreed remedies. But all contract law texts quickly correct that misconception, noting various substantial qualifications on the parties' freedom to agree contractual terms relating to exclusion clauses, express termination clauses and agreed damages clauses.

Note the divide this marks. It appears that parties are fully free to agree their primary obligations but not their 'remedial' obligations; they are fully free to occupy the space where

[22] See M Bridge, 'Freedom to Exercise Contractual Rights of Termination' in L Gullifer and S Vogenauer (eds), *English and European Perspectives on Contract and Commercial Law: Essays in Honour of Hugh Beale* (Oxford, Hart Publishing, 2014).

[23] See Smith, above n 2; SA Smith, 'In Defence of Substantive Fairness' (1996) 112 *LQR* 138, and the cases and commentary cited there (although this latter piece then concludes, at 158, that this would make little difference to current contract law rules). See also Chen-Wishart, 'The Nature of Vitiating Factors in Contract Law', above n 11. By contrast, others argue with some persuasiveness that the parties are more likely to prefer legal certainty and the ability to settle their own arrangements: see, eg, H Collins, *Regulating Contracts* (Oxford, OUP, 1999); Calnan, above n 14; Morgan, above n 3.

[24] *Photo Production*, above n 8, 848. See also H Collins, *The Law of Contract*, 4th edn (Cambridge, CUP, 2003) 365.

the law has no default rules, but not where they propose to override the common law's default rules. Those default rules would have come into play if the parties had been silent. But where the parties make their own arrangements, then (pre-empting what is to come) it seems the court insists on a close alignment with its own default rules. Those default rules are then more than gap filling. They are mandatory.

If this is true, what justifies it? Notice the problem is not lack of *any* agreement (then there would be no contract), nor even lack of agreement on the practical problem in issue (then the default rules would kick in). The problem is that the parties *have* reached agreement, but on something the courts will not permit. If this is to be defended, then its rationale must be exposed. We need good reasons for overriding party autonomy in these areas. Whether or not we have good reasons is the focus of what follows.

IV. Implied Terms and Implicit Terms

This is the slipperiest of the categories addressed. Consider implied terms. Historically the courts refused to intervene in the substance of the parties' primary agreement. Provided the parties had truly consented to their deal, then the adequacy or otherwise of their agreed consideration was not of any concern to the courts.[25] Terms were implied only where essential to enable the bargain to operate. Here, and more generally, there is a very clear and principled line between interpreting contracts according to the letter of the agreement, interpreting them according to the parties' proven understanding (the 'matrix of facts'), and interpreting them according to what the courts would regard as delivering reasonable terms in the circumstances. Yet the pressure to do the last sometimes seems overwhelming.

Often it takes only seemingly small adjustments to add or remove constraints which, with the benefit of hindsight, seem fairer and more apt, but which do not form part of the terms the parties have themselves agreed.[26] A warning against just this inclination was given by Moore-Bick LJ in *Proctor and Gamble Co v Svenska Cellulosen Aktiebolaget SCA*:[27]

> [T]he starting point must be the words the parties have used to express their intention and in the case of a carefully drafted agreement of the present kind the court must take care not to fall into the trap of re-writing the contract in order to produce what it considers to be more reasonable meaning.

Succumbing to this *post hoc* impulse to imply 'helpful' terms is grounded in a desire to deliver fairer outcomes. But such interventions frustrate party autonomy. National contract laws *could* operate this way, permitting deals only on terms which the courts deem fair, with the added uncertainty for the parties that this is to be judged at some time in the future, after the event, with the benefit of hindsight, and probably qualified by the particular predilections of the presiding judges. Whatever the attractions of substantive fairness, it is difficult to conceive of an approach further from the values of autonomy espoused by liberal democracies.

[25] Of course, in certain contexts the inadequacy of consideration might indicate flawed consent: see the law on undue influence and on fair dealing. But the adequacy of consideration alone would not defeat the arrangement.

[26] See Bridge, above n 22.

[27] *Proctor and Gamble Co v Svenska Cellulosen Aktiebolaget SCA* [2012] EWCA Civ 1413 [22].

But not all intervention can be condemned in this way. The courts may properly intervene on the basis of terms which are not simply implied by the courts in the manner just considered, but which are implicit in the parties' very agreement to come together in some form of relationship. There is a difference. These implicit terms derive directly from the particular form of the relationship between the parties. For example, the parties' engagement may, or may not, be infected by the need to obey the rules of tort, especially the law of negligence,[28] or the rules on breach of confidence, or fiduciary rules, or rules on the proper exercise of discretionary powers. The list can be extended. These terms are all founded on the particular relationship between the parties, even if the parties themselves did not appreciate these various legal consequences. But equally, however, it is necessary to pay due regard to the parties' own provisions about their engagement. The label applied by the parties is not determinative of the rights and obligations operating between the parties; that is a question of law. But their explicit provisions rarely count for nothing at all.[29] For example, if the parties provide that their agreement is binding in honour only, not at law, then it is not a contract;[30] so too with 'letters of comfort' operating only by way of moral obligation.[31] More controversially, if the parties say that their relationship is not fiduciary, then, provided other features do not countermand this, it is not.[32] Of course, the parties cannot simply agree that the general laws of the land will not apply to them, nor oust the jurisdiction of the court entirely,[33] but they can undoubtedly modify their additional implicit relationship-based obligations to others.

All of this gives due accord to party autonomy. It distinguishes between terms appropriately implied as of necessity, or properly implied as a matter of general law, and, beyond that, terms which are implicit, being essential elements of the relationship between the parties. But it also alerts to the relatively easy slippage to terms implied paternalistically to deliver a fairer result.

V. Exclusion of Liability Clauses

These clauses do just what their label suggests: exclude liability. If party autonomy is to prevail, and provided the parties are allowed to agree to these ends, then their agreement

[28] See the discussion below, section V.

[29] For a familiar example, the parties may label their arrangement a lease or a licence, or a fixed charge rather than a floating one. The task of the court is then to test this categorisation, and the rights it implicitly suggests, against other supporting or conflicting rights agreed between the parties. It is then a question of law whether the parties have applied an accurate label to their relationship. See, eg, *Re Spectrum Plus Ltd (in liq)* [2005] UKHL 41, [2005] 2 AC 680 (HL).

[30] *Jones v Vernon's Pools* [1938] 2 All ER 626.

[31] *Kleinwort Benson Ltd v Malaysia Mining Corp* [1989] 1 WLR 379. But, as ever, the words 'comfort letter' are not absolutely determinative of absence of the document's legally binding nature. Similarly on the interaction between various tort obligations and the parties' own provisions, see the discussion below, section V.

[32] See *Australian Securities and Investments Commission v Citigroup Global Markets Australia Pty Ltd (ACN 113 114 832) (No 4)* [2007] FCA 963 [276]–[281], especially [280]: 'It may well be that a fiduciary cannot exclude liability for fraud or deliberate dereliction of duty but beyond that there appears to be no restriction in the law to prevent a fiduciary from contracting out of, or modifying, his or her fiduciary duties, particularly where no prior fiduciary relationship existed and the contract defines the rights and duties of the parties'. This conclusion is roundly criticised in P Finn, 'Fiduciary Reflections' (2014) 88 *Australian Law Journal* 127.

[33] *Baker v Jones* [1954] 1 WLR 1005 (QBD); *Rose & Frank v Crompton* [1925] AC 445 (HL).

should govern and liability will be excluded. True, the clause will be construed rigorously, and against the party relying on it. But that same interpretive approach is applied in all contractual disputes.[34] Subject to that, the parties' agreement should rule.

But *can* the parties agree to exclude a liability which the law's default rules would otherwise impose? One of the more compelling analyses in this area suggests a pointed distinction between two different classes of 'exclusion' clause.[35] The first class concerns agreements by the parties to vary or limit or exclude their contractual liabilities to each other. Upholding such clauses accords with party autonomy. Indeed, such clauses are better seen as clauses denying the relevant contractual obligation is ever undertaken, not clauses excusing liability for failure to meet an obligation which has not been agreed. By contrast, the second class concerns agreements by the parties which effectively assert that they will not be subject to the general law which lies beyond their contract. This they allegedly cannot do.[36] This is said to be a clear distinction of principle. It gives the parties complete autonomy over their contracting relationship, allowing them to override what would otherwise be contract law's default rules, but does not allow them to stand outside any extra-contractual laws which would otherwise bind them.

Proponents of party autonomy can have little complaint with this approach. But the clear distinction of principle is not so clear in practice. The law of negligence is a fertile ground for dispute, with such liability commonly excluded or limited by express contractual terms.[37] Provided the law permits such duties to be excluded, or liabilities to be limited, then party autonomy simply prevails when the parties elect to proceed in this way. But matters can get complicated. For example, the general law imposes liability for misrepresentation, provided there is reliance.[38] What should then happen if the contracting parties purport to sidestep this, providing explicitly in their contracts that there has been no reliance on representations outside the terms of the written agreement? If such a provision takes effect according to its terms, as party autonomy suggests, it ensures the parties know in advance precisely which responsibilities they have assumed. But in practice it is hard to deny the persuasive power of precontractual assertions. The cases in this area suggest that party autonomy has prevailed where the parties are of equal bargaining power,[39] but

[34] As noted in *Bank of Credit and Commerce International SA v Ali* [2001] UKHL 8, [2002] 1 AC 251 [57]–[62] (Lord Hoffmann). See also *Photo Production Ltd v Securicor Transport Ltd* [1980] AC 827 (HL); *British Fermentation Products Ltd v Compair Reavell Ltd* [1999] BLR 352 (QBD TCC, Judge Bowsher); G McMeel, 'The Rise of Commercial Construction in Contract Law' [1998] *LMCLQ* 382. But it is possible to take this approach to extremes. McKendrick is not the only person to suggest that the rules of interpretation have been used with 'particular venom' in order to place difficult obstacles in the way of those who seek to exclude liability towards others: see E McKendrick, *Contract Law*, 10th edn (Basingstoke, Palgrave Macmillan, 2013) 159.

[35] B Coote, *Exception Clauses* (London, Sweet and Maxwell, 1964). See also JA Weir, '[Book Review of] *Exception Clauses* by Brian Coote' [1965] *CLJ* 801.

[36] This includes legislative bars on the parties' right to exclude liability in certain contexts, as in the Unfair Contract Terms Act 1977.

[37] See generally *Chitty on Contracts*, 31st edn (London, Sweet and Maxwell, 2012) [14-005]–[14-011]. See also *HIH Casualty and General Insurance Ltd v Chase Manhattan Bank* [2003] UKHL 6, [2003] 1 All ER (Comm) 349; *George Mitchell (Chesterhall) Ltd v Finney Lock Seeds Ltd* [1983] 2 AC 803 (HL); *Lictor Anstalt v Mir Steel UK Ltd* [2012] EWCA Civ 1397.

[38] This is true of both the common law and statutory rules (Misrepresentation Act 1967, s 3).

[39] *Watford Electronics Ltd v Sanderson CFL Ltd* [2001] EWCA Civ 317, especially [39], [41] (Chadwick LJ). But the precise wording of the clause and the factual dealings between the parties can be important: see *Mears Ltd v Shoreline Housing Partnership Ltd* [2013] EWCA Civ 639; *AXA Sun Life Services Plc v Campbell Martin Ltd* [2011] EWCA Civ 133; *Springwell Navigation Corp v JP Morgan Chase Bank* [2010] EWCA Civ 1221.

the instinct to deliver more protective and allegedly fairer outcomes for consumers has persisted.[40]

This is not the place to debate the appropriate doctrinal analysis of these cases, nor the right policy balance, but there should at least be transparent acknowledgement by the courts when party autonomy is overridden in the interests of substantive fairness as judged by the courts. As Lord Hoffmann put it:[41]

> My Lords, the lesson which I would draw from the development of the rules for construing exemption clauses is that the judicial creativity, bordering on judicial legislation, which the application of that doctrine involved is a desperate remedy, to be invoked only if it is necessary to remedy a widespread injustice. Otherwise there is much to be said for giving effect to what on ordinary principles of construction the parties agreed.

And all power to that approach.

VI. Express Termination Clauses

These clauses too do just what their label suggests: they permit contracting parties to terminate their contracts in agreed circumstances.[42] In short, if they work, they allow the parties to override the restrictive common law default rules for termination.

Before considering the courts' reaction to express agreements, recall the default rules. The early common law approach was to classify all terms as either conditions or warranties, and allow termination whenever there was a breach of condition. It was irrelevant that the consequences of the particular breach might be trivial, or that the motivation for termination was not the breach itself but rather that the innocent party was on the losing side of a bargain and now had an excuse for a clean exit. The usual illustration is *Arcos Ltd v EA Ronaasen & Son*,[43] where the timber agreed to be delivered to the buyers was about 9/16 inches thick, not the agreed 8/16 inches. The difference did not affect the intended use.[44] Nevertheless, the breach of condition was enough to entitle the buyers to escape the contract and take advantage of a falling market.

The lesson often taken from this case is that the common law's default rules favour the interests of certainty too much as against the interests of justice or fairness.[45] But the lesson which ought to have been learnt is that 'descriptions' in sale of goods contracts should not automatically be classified as conditions. That lesson was learnt, eventually: 30 years later,

[40] *Raiffeisen Zentralbank Osterreich AG v Royal Bank of Scotland Plc* [2010] EWHC 1392 (Comm), especially [313]–[315] (Christopher Clarke J), noting the different interests of commercial parties and consumers. To the same effect, see also A Trukhtanov, 'Misrepresentation: Acknowledgement of Non-Reliance as a Defence' (2009) 125 *LQR* 648. On the general issues, see J Morgan, *Great Debates: Contract Law* (Basingstoke, Palgrave Macmillan, 2012) especially 80–84.

[41] *Bank of Credit and Commerce International SA v Ali* [2001] UKHL 8, [2002] 1 AC 251 [60] (Lord Hoffmann).

[42] There is a significant literature in this area. Beyond the standard contract texts, see, eg, J Randall, 'Express Termination Clauses in Contracts' [2014] *CLJ* 113; S Whittaker, 'Termination Clauses' in A Burrows and E Peel (eds), *Contract Terms* (Oxford, OUP, 2007) ch 13; H Beale, 'Penalties in Termination Provisions' (1988) 104 *LQR* 355; J Carter, 'Termination Clauses' (1990) 3 *Journal of Contract Law* 90.

[43] *Arcos Ltd v EA Ronaasen & Son* [1933] AC 470 (HL).

[44] The intended use was to make cement barrels.

[45] See, eg, E McKendrick, *Contract Law*, 10th edn (Basingstoke, Palgrave Macmillan, 2013) 180.

in the *Hongkong Fir Shipping* case, the Court of Appeal adopted the idea of intermediate or innominate terms as a more sophisticated characterisation test;[46] and 30 years after that, the UK Sale of Goods Act 1979 was amended by the insertion of section 15A to add a test of reasonableness to modify the automatic characterisation of certain terms as conditions, although only in non-consumer contracts.[47]

So much for default rules. They indicate an overwhelmingly restrictive approach to the default right to terminate. But these default rules are readily overridden. The parties are completely free to provide that particular terms are to be categorised as conditions. It is immaterial that the term would not otherwise have been regarded as a condition.[48] The justification is that there is then not the element of surprise which a default rule risks.

The only limitation is one of construction. The courts may refuse to accept that the parties genuinely intended such dramatic consequences. The classic illustration is *Schuler AG v Wickman Machine Tool Sales Ltd*,[49] where a distributor's weekly visits to certain UK manufacturers were said to be a condition of the contract. The majority of the court thought the drastic consequences of one missed visit were so unreasonable that the parties could not have used the word 'condition' in its technical sense.[50] Lord Wilberforce disagreed, expressing the view that the parties had agreed to tough terms, and that tough consequences should ensue.[51] There is much to be said for his stance. The courts are not well placed to second guess the parties' bargain, and the parties themselves will likely have self-interested recollections at the door of the court.[52] If parties can agree to terminate their contract without cause,[53] then it seems odd that they cannot equally easily agree to terminate for breach, however trivial.[54] In both cases, the advantage of easy exit is likely to have been priced into the bargain. And if there is such an explicit clause providing for an untimely end, it could hardly be argued that the disappointed party relied on the agreement running for a longer period.[55] So the only real question for the courts should be whether the parties' tough stance was indeed agreed. There is admittedly less room for error or misunderstanding in a clause which simply provides for termination at will, rather than termination on breaches of defined sorts.

Unsurprisingly, the rules are much the same with express termination clauses. Since the parties themselves can nominate any term to be a condition, it would be invidious to deny them the equivalent freedom to specify that certain breaches will entitle the innocent party to terminate the contract. This is merely longhand for 'condition'. Cases confirm that the

[46] *Hongkong Fir Shipping Co Ltd v Kawasaki Kisen Kaisha Ltd (The Hongkong Fir)* [1962] 2 QB 26 (CA), 66, 70 (Diplock LJ).

[47] Although see Bridge, above n 22, 90, suggesting the practical impact has been negligible.

[48] *Lombard North Central plc v Butterworth* [1987] QB 527 (CA) (prompt payment of instalments). The results are sometimes undesirable (W Bojczuk, 'When is a Condition Not a Condition?' [1987] *JBL* 353), but this does not alter the rule.

[49] *Schuler AG v Wickman Machine Tool Sales Ltd* [1974] AC 235 (HL).

[50] ibid 251 (Lord Reid) and 255–56 (Lord Morris of Borth-y-Guest).

[51] ibid 262–63.

[52] *Bettini v Gye* (1876) 1 QBD 183, 187 (Blackburn J): 'Parties may think some matter, apparently of very little importance, essential; and if they sufficiently express an intention to make the literal fulfilment of such a thing a condition precedent, it will be one'.

[53] *TSG Building Services Plc v South Anglia Housing Ltd* [2013] EWHC 1151 (TCC), and this is not constrained by any implied duty of good faith.

[54] The classic illustration is *Union Eagle Ltd v Golden Achievement Ltd* [1997] AC 514 (PC).

[55] *Baird Textile Holdings Ltd v Marks & Spencer Plc* [2001] EWCA Civ 274.

parties are free to agree whatever termination rules they like,[56] with no questions arising as to whether that provision is fair or reasonable, nor whether it is fair or reasonable to exercise it[57] (although see also the comments below).[58]

All of this gives very effective and unqualified support to party autonomy. So why is there so often bad press about the risks with enforcement of express termination clauses? They are not imagined. The courts have three rather effective strategies for intervening in the parties' agreed termination provisions. All need to be addressed transparently if autonomy is not to be lost sight of.

The first strategy is to suggest that there is no true agreement. This is a general limitation on all agreements, and accords completely with party autonomy. The risk is higher in non-commercial contracts, and indeed statutes in various jurisdictions go still further and impose mandatory limitations on the use of termination clauses in situations where legislative paternalism is seen as warranted.[59]

The second strategy is to hold that the clause does not provide for termination in the circumstances which have arisen. This is a common construction issue for the courts. Of course, the parties must be clear what they mean. A term which looks to visit dire consequences on one side will be construed strictly against the party to be advantaged. As with terms described as conditions, the courts take a very strict approach to interpreting the termination provision itself and to ensuring strict compliance with it and any preconditions[60] or procedures[61] for its exercise. As a consequence, the innocent party cannot anticipate the breach, even when it is an absolute certainty that the counter-party will shortly be in breach.[62] And once that time has come, the innocent party must act within a reasonable time of the default,[63] and must make it very clear that the contract is being terminated according to the rights embedded in the contract.[64]

[56] See, eg, *Bettini v Gye*, above n 52; *Sotiros Shipping Inc v Sameiet Solholt (The Solholt)* [1983] 1 Lloyd's Rep 605 (CA), 608, where Sir John Donaldson MR referred to a party's 'unfettered right' to operate or not operate an express termination clause.

[57] See, eg, *Financings Ltd v Baldock* [1963] 2 QB 104 (CA), 115; *China National Foreign Trade Transportation Corp v Evlogia Shipping Co SA (The Mihalios Xilas)* [1979] 1 WLR 1018 (HL). For the general propositions, see S Whittaker, 'Termination Clauses' in A Burrows and E Peel (eds), *Contract Terms* (Oxford, OUP, 2007) 253–54. For the rule that the innocent party need not exercise the right to terminate either reasonably or in good faith, see *Glencore Grain Rotterdam BV v Lebanese Organisation for International Commerce (The Lorico)* [1997] 4 All ER 514 (CA), 529–31. Contrast *Panchaud Freres SA v Etablissements General Grain Co* [1970] 1 Lloyd's Rep 53 (CA). See also Randall, above n 42, 117; J Carter, 'Termination Clauses' (1990) 3 *Journal of Contract Law* 90, 103.

[58] See the discussion of abuse of power below at the text accompanying nn 75–81.

[59] See, eg, Consumer Credit Act 1974; Housing Act 1996; Unfair Contract Terms Act 1977; Unfair Terms in Consumer Contracts Regulations 1999 (SI 1999/2083).

[60] *MMP GmbH v Antal International Network Ltd* [2011] EWHC 1120 [77].

[61] *Maredelanto Compania Naviera SA v Bergbau-Handel GmbH (The Mihalis Angelos)* [1971] 1 QB 164 (CA); *Afovos Shipping Co SA v R Pagnan & Fratelli (The Afovos)* [1983] 1 WLR 195 (HL).

[62] *Mannai Investment Co Ltd v Eagle Star Life Assurance Co Ltd* [1997] AC 749 (HL); *Pan Foods Company Importers & Distributors Pty Ltd v Australia and New Zealand Banking Group Ltd* [2000] HCA 20. Also see J Carter, 'Termination Clauses' (1990) 3 *Journal of Contract Law* 90, 101, suggesting some leeway on the basis of a purposive interpretation of the requirements.

[63] *Mardorf Peach & Co Ltd v Attica Sea Carriers Corp of Liberia (The Laconia)* [1977] AC 850 (HL), 872 (Lord Wilberforce); *Scandinavian Trading Tanker Co AB v Flota Petrolera Ecuatoriana (The Scaptrade)* [1981] 2 Lloyd's Rep 425 (CA), 430 (affirmed [1983] 2 AC 694 (HL) without reference to the point).

[64] *Geys v Société Générale* [2012] UKSC 63, [2013] 1 AC 523, a very strange case concerning the unsuccessful immediate dismissal of a bank employee. There is much to be said for Lord Sumption SCJ's dissent (and the clear statement of it).

All of this accords with party autonomy. But occasionally the courts go further. The strategy of insisting that the parties cannot have used some expression (such as 'condition') in its technical sense is not open here:[65] 'termination' is not a term of art. But nevertheless the courts have intervened in some cases where their motivation looks to be fairness, delivered paternalistically, in the face of the party's seemingly clear agreement otherwise.

Two cases are frequently cited: *The Antaios*,[66] in the House of Lords, and *Rice v Great Yarmouth Borough Council*,[67] in the Court of Appeal. In both cases the parties expressly agreed that breach of any term would allow the counter-party to terminate. In both cases the courts effectively countermanded party autonomy by refusing to enforce the parties' agreed terms literally, and instead construed the words allowing for termination 'on *any* breach' (or very similar words) as meaning 'on any *repudiatory* breach'.[68] Of course, the effect of this was to render that part of the express termination clause entirely redundant, since a repudiatory breach would in any event have entitled the injured party to terminate.[69]

The first case can be sidelined as weak authority,[70] but the second appears to be an unacceptable judicial rewriting of the parties' contracts.[71] The real complaint is that the precise reasons for the courts' intervention remain disguised behind 'the courts' powers of construction, supported only by general references to the parties' "intentions" and to "common sense"'.[72] As with provisions settling conditions, it is surely material that the parties have agreed that exit from their bargain will be clean and uncomplicated in defined circumstances.[73] It is not for the court to rewrite that bargain on the basis that some other provision seems to them to deliver an outcome which is more acceptably fair or reasonable.[74] And if there are better reasons, then the tension between party autonomy and those reasons should be exposed. Thankfully these cases are few in number. They serve to warn, not to damn current interpretive practices.

The third and final strategy is one to which the courts seem to be making increasing resort—usually inappropriately, it is suggested here. Express termination clauses give one party the legal right to threaten the other with early termination. This is likely to induce performance. Indeed, that is typically the intended purpose of these clauses. Commentators and courts are now increasingly interested in ways to constrain the 'unfair' exercise of such power. To this end there are attempts to 'rewrite' the parties' bargain to limit the agreed

[65] Contrast *Schuler AG v Wickman Machine Tool Sales Ltd* [1974] AC 235 (HL), described above, text accompanying nn 49–51.

[66] *Antaios Compania Naviera SA v Salen Rederierna AB (The Antaios)* [1985] AC 191 (HL).

[67] *Rice (t/a Garden Guardian) v Great Yarmouth Borough Council* [2003] TCLR 1 (CA).

[68] *The Antaios*, above n 66, 200, 205 (Lord Diplock); 209 (Lord Roskill); and *Rice (t/a Garden Guardian) v Great Yarmouth Borough Council* [2003] TCLR 1 (CA) [17]–[28] (Hale LJ).

[69] Both cases can be contrasted with a clause worded more specifically to allow for termination for 'material breach', that expression being held to expand the innocent party's rights beyond what the common law would classify as a repudiatory breach: *National Power plc v United Gas Co Ltd* [1998] All ER (D) 321 [30]–[31] (Coleman J).

[70] The case was an appeal from an arbitrator's decision. The House of Lords held the arbitrator was not manifestly wrong, and that, in any event, the arbitrator had also denied the innocent party's claim because of delay. Accordingly, the appeal was denied.

[71] J Randall, 'Express Termination Clauses in Contracts' [2014] *CLJ* 113, 124–26; S Whittaker, 'Termination Clauses' in A Burrows and E Peel (eds), *Contract Terms* (Oxford, OUP, 2007) ch 13, 279–80.

[72] Whittaker, above n 71, 283.

[73] Bridge, above n 22, 98–100.

[74] All the more so when they do this without any thought to some fair and compensatory re-pricing of the bargain.

power to terminate to instances where its exercise is seen as fair and reasonable. This is often an undisclosed attack on party autonomy.

There are two obvious routes for this sort of intervention. The courts can either uncover implied terms in the parties' express agreement which work to limit the exercise of the power to terminate, or alternatively they can resort to general law constraints which apply to the exercise of all discretionary powers.[75] Both are perfectly legitimate avenues for intervention in the appropriate context, but neither seems apt in the context of an express termination clause. The sole and very explicit purpose of an express termination clause is to allow for termination in defined circumstances. It follows that there should not be much to criticise when the power is then exercised, or even threatened to be exercised, when the defined circumstances come to pass. It is much like the right to terminate a contract without cause,[76] or the shareholders' statutory right to dismiss directors:[77] the courts should be hard-pressed to find a reason to limit those rights to being exercised only for fair and reasonable reasons.[78] Even an implied duty of good faith, where it can be found,[79] seems to add little which would be of assistance here, or which would overturn the current longstanding rules allowing termination as soon as the contractual preconditions are met, regardless of the motivation for exercise of the right.[80] The common defence of the older strict approach is that it promotes certainty.[81] But perhaps the strict approach holds true simply because the parties have agreed that it should hold true, and their autonomy is respected in circumstances where there are no good reasons to favour competing values.

Here, and probably only here, party autonomy seems potentially under threat from the paternalistic intervention of those seeking to limit straightforward powers to terminate, and doing so without articulating the competing values being advanced. Subjective views about what might have been a 'fairer' or kinder bargain do not meet that demand.

One final comment might be made. It falls outside the autonomy theme, but links with the next section on penalties. Perhaps surprisingly, what *is* left rather up in the air with express termination clauses is whether, on termination according to such a clause, the innocent party can recover expectation damages, as with breach of a condition.[82] If the

[75] See, eg, *Yam Seng Pte Ltd v International Trade Corp Ltd* [2013] EWHC 111 (QB), [2013] 1 All ER (Comm) 1321; Brownsword, above n 7, especially 84–87; M Arden, 'Coming to Terms with Good Faith?' (2013) 30 *Journal of Contract Law* 199; R Hooley, 'Controlling Contractual Discretion' (2013) 72 *CLJ* 65; R Nolan, 'Controlling Fiduciary Power' (2009) 68 *CLJ* 293; S Kos, 'Constraints on the Exercise of Contractual Powers' (2011) 42 *Victoria University of Wellington Law Review* 17.

[76] *TSG Building Services Plc v South Anglia Housing Ltd* [2013] EWHC 1151 (TCC), also not constrained by any implied duty of good faith.

[77] Companies Act 2006, s 168.

[78] See *Mid Essex Hospital Services NHS Trust v Compass Group UK and Ireland Ltd* [2013] EWCA Civ 200 [83] (Jackson LJ): 'An important feature of the above line of authorities [on the exercise of contractual discretion] is that in each case the discretion did not involve a simple decision whether or not to exercise *an absolute contractual right*. The discretion involved making an assessment or choosing from a range of options, taking into account the interest of both parties' (emphasis added).

[79] See, eg, *Yam Seng Pte Ltd v International Trade Corp Ltd* [2013] EWHC 111 (QB), especially [54]–[55], in the context of a distributorship agreement.

[80] *Bowes v Shand* (1877) 2 App Cas 455 (HL); *The Antaios*, above n 66.

[81] See, eg, *The Laconia*, above n 63, 878 (Lord Salmon): 'certainty is of primary importance'; *Union Eagle Ltd v Golden Achievement Ltd* [1997] AC 514 (PC), 519 (Lord Hoffmann for the PC): 'the parties should know with certainty that the terms of the contract will be enforced'. See also *Tradax Export SA v Dorada Compania Naviera SA of Panama (The Lutetian)* [1982] 2 Lloyd's Rep 140 (QBD), 159.

[82] Assuming this is possible, see Bridge, above n 22.

contract is silent, the fear is that causation will prove a problem unless the breach is also a repudiatory breach at common law,[83] and if the contract is explicit, the fear is that the penalty jurisdiction will deny the option.[84] There is much to be said for the Canadian conclusion that general contract law principles should be applied in both cases to allow the innocent party to claim expectation damages.[85] This would then recognise the compelling substantive similarity between terms defining conditions and terms providing expressly for termination. One is surely only shorthand for the other, and there seems little logic in refusing to align the remedies for both.

In conclusion, and despite their bad press, it would seem that express termination clauses are respected, and party autonomy survives largely unscathed. All of this makes the contrast with penalty clauses, this chapter's final category, even more stark.

VII. Penalty Clauses

Parties to contracts have an interest in keeping the other side to the bargain. That is what each party promises: 'I'll deliver my side of the bargain'. Or, more accurately, if only implicitly, 'I'll deliver, and I'll pay damages if I don't deliver'. Such damages are either pre-agreed, as liquidated damages, or established after the event using contract law's default rules.

Pragmatically, these alternatives make sense. If one party refuses to perform at all, or refuses to perform appropriately, then only rarely will compulsion be less troublesome and of greater practical benefit than simply accepting money by way of compensation for lost expectations. Given the common law's typically pragmatic style, this justifies the default rule being expectation damages, not specific performance.[86] And it is only a default rule. Where the circumstances warrant it, performance is demanded.[87] But even with expectation damages, the injured party cannot always recover damages in an amount sufficient to remedy defective performance: recall the infamous *Ruxley Electronics v Forsyth*,[88] and the six-foot-deep swimming pool rather than the agreed seven-foot-six-inch one.

So how do contracting parties get full performance? Insisting that a particular performance is wanted, and nothing else will do, does not seem to work.[89] But proper performance

[83] See J Randall, 'Express Termination Clauses in Contracts' [2014] *CLJ* 113, 130–33 and the many references cited there.

[84] *Financings Ltd v Baldock* [1963] 2 QB 104 (CA), 115; *Lombard North Central Plc v Butterworth* [1987] QB 527 (CA), 546; Whittaker, above n 71, 258. See generally, H Beale, 'Penalties in Termination Provisions' (1988) 104 *LQR* 355.

[85] *Keneric Tractor Sales Ltd v Langille* [1987] 2 SCR 440, (1987) 43 DLR (4th) 171 [25] (Wilson J).

[86] See also Morgan, above n 40, 244, suggesting higher contracting prices would inevitably be demanded for such a default rule.

[87] See, eg, *Falcke v Gray* (1859) 4 Drew 651 (Ch D). On specific performance generally, see GH Treitel, *Remedies for Breach of Contract* (Oxford, OUP, 1998) 63–74. The suggestion that specific performance orders in relation to voluntarily assumed obligations would somehow amount to quasi-slavery is not convincing, and contradicts the practical experience in civilian jurisdictions.

[88] *Ruxley Electronics v Forsyth* [1996] AC 344 (HL), especially 358. Contrast *Radford v de Froberville* [1977] 1 WLR 1262 (Ch D). See D Harris, D Campbell and R Halson, *Remedies in Contract and Tort* 2nd edn, (Cambridge, CUP, 2002) 195, explaining that nor can the parties stipulate for imprisonment of the wrongdoer.

[89] ibid. Perhaps as a result, some commentators argue in favour of specific performance as the default remedy: see, eg, A Schwartz, 'The Case for Specific Performance' (1979) 89 *Yale Law Journal* 271; L Smith, 'Understanding Specific Performance' in N Cohen and E McKendrick (eds), *Comparative Remedies for Breach of Contract*

is generally preferred. Can the parties simply agree they will perform as promised? Perhaps oddly, at first blush, it seems not. Authority suggests the parties cannot oust the court's discretion by agreeing to the remedy of specific performance.[90] Alternatively, is signalling commitment to providing full performance any easier? Can one party explicitly agree that 'I'll deliver, or I'll pay £100,000 (or some other extravagant sum) if I don't deliver'? Such assertions are intended to indicate reliability.[91] They provide a guarantee, a hostage, to proper performance. The instinct is to believe such parties are more likely to deliver than someone not giving such a guarantee. The same sort of instinct—and effect—lies behind deposits.[92] These are often not agreed damages clauses so much as guarantees of full and satisfactory performance.

Of course, this same agreement could be worded the other way around: 'You *must* pay £100,000 (or some other extravagant sum) in the event that you do not perform'. This then makes explicit the element of coercion (if only agreed coercion) in the stipulation.

It is just this form of coercion that the law has long set its face against in the penalties jurisdiction, although often with little justification for the rule other than an assumed sense of moral outrage.[93] But the outrage is directed exclusively at terms operating on breach.[94] An agreement that 'You must pay £100,000 (or some other extravagant sum) in the event that you do not perform' is unacceptable. But an agreement that 'I'll deliver, or I'll pay £100,000 (or some other extravagant sum) if I don't deliver' merits no concern. This is despite the pragmatic point that if the parties have agreed to the term, then the change in language is one of form, not substance. And if the parties really have agreed, then what is so wrong with enforcing the term?

This is the territory of the law on penalties. The orthodox penalties jurisdiction, now with the exception of Australia,[95] allows contracting parties to agree on liquidated damages

(Oxford, Hart Publishing, 2005); R Stevens, 'Damages and the Right to Performance: A *Golden Victory* or Not?' in J Neyers *et al* (eds), *Exploring Contract Law* (Oxford, Hart Publishing, 2009) 171. But ultimately the pragmatic views expressed in the preceding paragraph remain compelling.

[90] *Quadrant Visual Communications v Hutchison Telephone (UK)* [1993] BCLC 442 (CA) (Stocker LJ). The only exception is promises to pay a sum of money: these promises can be specifically enforced (with recoveries compromised if the claim puts the defendant into insolvency).

[91] *Lake River v Carborundum Co* 769 F 2d 1284, 1289 (1985) (Posner J).

[92] *Howe v Smith* (1884) 27 Ch D 89 (CA).

[93] See, eg, P Saprai, 'The Penalties Rule and the Promise Theory of Contract' (2013) 26 *Canadian Journal of Law and Jurisprudence* 443, 447, 451, 453, taking as self-evident the unfairness in enforcing a £1million penalty clause in a £50 contract with a builder.

[94] See, eg, *Exports Credits Guarantee Department v Universal Oil Products Co* [1983] 1 WLR 399 (HL); *Euro London Appointments Ltd v Claessens International Ltd* [2006] EWCA Civ 385 (CA) (a discount for early payment rather than a penalty for late payment, held not to be subject to the penalties rule). This limitation no longer applies in Australia (see below), and commentators suggest it is unwarranted elsewhere: M Chen-Wishart, 'Controlling the Power to Agree Damages' in P Birks (ed), *Wrongs and Remedies in the Twenty-First Century* (Oxford, OUP, 1996) 271, 285.

[95] Where the High Court has expanded the jurisdiction beyond clauses operating only on breach: *Andrews v ANZ Banking Group Ltd* [2012] HCA 30, (2012) 247 CLR 205. Interestingly, despite this extension, Gordon J in *Paciocco v Australian and New Zealand Banking Group Ltd* [2014] FCA 52, applying the new tests, reached identical conclusions to those reached in the initial trial applying orthodox tests: ie, of all the various banking charges in issue, only the late payment fees were illegal penalties. By contrast, honour fees, dishonour fees, overlimit fees and non-payment fees were not. On appeal to the Full Federal Court, even the former payments were held not to be penalties: *Paciocco v Australia and New Zealand Banking Group Ltd* [2015] FCAFC 50. The *Andrews* decision in the High Court has been trenchantly criticised in JW Carter *et al*, 'Penalties: Resurrecting the Equitable Jurisdiction' (2013) 30 *Journal of Contract Law* 99. The High Court justified its expanded view of the penalties jurisdiction by

clauses, but does not allow them to impose penalties, or punishments, for breach.[96] The former is a genuine pre-estimate of loss, judged at the time the contract is made, and can accommodate relevant commercial considerations.[97] The latter is an amount which is designed to deter breach,[98] and is 'extravagant and unconscionable … in comparison with the greatest loss that could conceivably be proved': *Dunlop Pneumatic Tyre Co v New Garage and Motor Co Ltd.*[99] If a clause is judged to be a penalty it will not be enforced except to the extent of the loss actually sustained.[100]

That statement ignores the many subtle accretions to the jurisdiction over its lifetime.[101] At the most basic are those involved in the balancing act required to determine quite how 'extravagant' an estimate must be before it will be judged penal, factoring in the degree of unconscionability, the extent of the deviation from normal contract damages,[102] and the possibility that there is a commercial justification for the provision.[103] But all these assessments and careful balancing exercises skirt the fundamental question: if the parties have genuinely agreed, why is enforcement *not* justified, both commercially and in good conscience, no matter how extravagant the term?

Instead, this question is ignored. The jurisdiction retains a stranglehold on the courts despite their acknowledgement that it is both 'a blatant interference with freedom of

resort to equity's historical interventions against penal bonds, but that jurisdiction had already been conceived more narrowly by the courts during the eighteenth and nineteenth centuries (DJ Ibbestson, *A Historical Introduction to the Law of Obligations* (Oxford, OUP, 1999) 213–14) before the jurisdiction was later expanded once again, but on a different basis, in *Dunlop Pneumatic Tyre Co v New Garage and Motor Co Ltd* [1915] AC 79 (HL).

[96] The foundation of the modern law is *Dunlop Pneumatic Tyre Co v New Garage and Motor Co Ltd*, above n 95, a case which makes no mention of freedom of contract. There is an enormous literature in this area: see in particular T Downes, 'Rethinking Penalty Clauses' in P Birks (ed), *Wrongs and Remedies in the Twenty-First Century* (Oxford, OUP, 1996); L Gullifer, 'Agreed Remedies' in A Burrows and E Peel (eds), *Commercial Remedies: Current Issues and Problems* (Oxford, OUP, 2003) ch 16; A Gray, 'Contractual Penalties in Australia After *Andrews*: An Opportunity Missed' (2013) 18 *Deakin Law Review* 1; E Peden and JW Carter, 'Agreed Damages Clauses: Back to the Future?' (2006) 22 *Journal of Contract Law* 189; and other references cited below.

[97] Such clauses are attractive because they provide certainty to both parties on the precise limits of their bargain: see, eg, *Philips Hong Kong Ltd v Attorney General of Hong Kong* (1993) 61 BLR 41 (PC), 54–55 (Lord Woolf). In addition, they can accommodate claims which would not otherwise be recoverable at law (see below, n 100), and will enable cost-savings in enforcement actions since the sum is agreed and therefore recoverable as a debt (A Burrows, *Remedies for Torts and Breach of Contract*, 3rd edn (Oxford, OUP, 2004) 440).

[98] *Dunlop Pneumatic Tyre Co v New Garage and Motor Co Ltd*, above n 95; *Makdessi v Cavendish Square Holdings BV* [2013] EWCA Civ 1539 [62]. Other Commonwealth jurisdictions are generally to the same effect, with the exception of Australia (see n 95 above).

[99] *Dunlop Pneumatic Tyre Co v New Garage and Motor Co Ltd*, above n 95.

[100] *Jobson v Johnson* [1969] 1 All ER 621 (CA), 633 (Nicholls LJ). See also Downes, above n 96, 253–54. It seems such recoveries may nevertheless include some losses which might not have been recoverable under the common law's default rules: see the discussion in *Robophone Facilities Ltd v Blank* [1996] 1 WLR 1428 (CA), 1447–48 (Diplock LJ).

[101] By way of illustration, note the number of paragraphs required by Christopher Clarke LJ to deliver what is nevertheless an admirably succinct account of the relevant law: *Makdessi v Cavendish Square Holdings BV*, above n 98, [44]–[104]. For comment on this case, see E Peel, 'Unjustified Penalties or an Unjustified Rule Against Penalties?' (2014) 130 *LQR* 365.

[102] On balancing these first two elements, see the compelling comments in *AMEV UDC Finance Ltd v Austin* (1986) 162 CLR 170 (HCA), 193 (Mason and Wilson JJ), cited with approval by Lord Woolf in *Philips Hong Kong Ltd v Attorney General of Hong Kong* (1993) 61 BLR 41 (PC).

[103] *Lordsvale Finance Plc v Bank of Zambia* [1996] QB 752 (QBD); *Murray v Leisureplay Plc* [2005] EWCA Civ 963; *Philips Hong Kong Ltd v Attorney General of Hong Kong*, above n 97; *United International Pictures v Cine Bes Filmcilik ve Yapimcilik AS* [2003] EWCA Civ 1669.

contract'[104] and driven by reasons which the courts find impossible to rationalise.[105] This is a recipe for disaster. Each new set of facts then requires the courts to tinker with doctrine without having any settled guidance from principle or policy.

This brings discussion full circle. If party autonomy is important, then its abrogation should be justified. This has been the courts' approach in all the areas considered so far. *Are* there real concerns which might vindicate the very selective interference with party autonomy delivered by the penalties jurisdiction? Several possible rationalisations are commonly given, although none is judged here to be even remotely compelling.

First, it is clear from all the cases that interference is directed specifically at clauses which attempt to deter breach.[106] It is occasionally recognised that this is just the flip-side of a clause attempting to secure performance.[107] No justification is given for why either goal should be seen as obnoxious.[108] Much of the wholesale and retail world works on the assumption that markets are made this way. A contract of sale which offers a 50 per cent discount on the ticketed price for purchases made before the end of the month should not be converted into an unenforceable penalty provision if worded so that higher prices are paid on breach of a monthly time stipulation. The practical consequences for the purchaser are identical. Both clauses are designed to secure early performance and deter late performance; they are designed to make the market move more rapidly.

A second and more expansive group of arguments suggests that the penalties jurisdiction is directed generally at unconscionability, or oppression, and is designed to provide some constraint on unqualified freedom of contract and the problems of inequality of bargaining power.[109] But the common law typically addresses these problems directly, as it should. It refuses to rewrite parties' contracts. Indeed, it denies any interest in the substantive fairness of the agreed terms.[110] Instead, it asks whether those terms have been properly agreed, or whether one party's consent has been unacceptably vitiated. Only then will it interfere. Imbalances in agreed terms (not merely in agreed remedies) may signal vitiated consent, but of themselves they prove nothing.[111]

[104] *Makdessi v Cavendish Square Holdings BV*, above n 98, [44]. See also, eg, *Ringrow Pty Ltd v BP Australia Pty Ltd* [2005] HCA 71, (2005) 224 CLR 656 [31]–[32]; PS Atiyah, *The Rise and Fall of Freedom of Contract* (Oxford, Clarendon Press, 1979) 414.

[105] Diplock LJ's refusal to attempt any rationalisation where so many others had failed is widely cited: *Robophone Facilities Ltd v Blank*, above n 100, 1446.

[106] For a summary, see *Makdessi v Cavendish Square Holdings BV*, above n 98, and all the authorities cited there.

[107] As recognised by the High Court of Australia in *Andrews v ANZ Banking Group Ltd*, above n 95; and *Makdessi v Cavendish Square Holdings BV*, above n 98, [125]. This is reinforced by the illustrations given in the introduction to this section: see text accompanying nn 86–94.

[108] But see W Day, 'Penalty Clauses Revisited' [2014] *JBL* 512, 516, suggesting that permitting deterrence clauses would give commercial parties 'the legitimate right … to construct a system of private financial sanctions'. But the law of contract is exclusively concerned with agreed 'private financial sanctions', whether in relation to agreed price, agreed terms of performance, and, it is suggested here, it should also be the same with agreed remedies.

[109] *AMEV UDC Finance Ltd v Austin* (1986) 162 CLR 170 (HCA), 193 (Mason and Wilson JJ), cited with approval by Lord Woolf in *Philips Hong Kong Ltd v Attorney General of Hong Kong*, above n 97, 57–58, 59. See also *Elsey v JG Collins Insurance Agencies Ltd* (1978) 83 DLR 1, 15. Favouring this, in the interests of ensuring good faith, see M Chen-Wishart, 'Controlling the Power to Agree Damages' in P Birks (ed), *Wrongs and Remedies in the Twenty-First Century* (Oxford, OUP, 1996); JW Carter and E Peden, 'A Good Faith Perspective on Liquidated Damages' (2007) 23 *Journal of Contract Law* 157. Similarly, see Day, above n 108.

[110] Although contrast J Gordley, 'Equality in Exchange' (1981) 69 *California Law Review* 1587, suggesting the courts regularly refuse to enforce contracts because they are substantively unfair.

[111] See, eg, the law on undue influence or on fair dealing.

If this approach is to be deviated from so radically in dealing with agreed damages clauses, then some reasons are needed. There is an important difference of principle at stake. The common law's general approach favours party autonomy by focusing on the quality of the parties' consent.[112] By contrast, the 'penalties' approach favours more paternalistic intervention conditioned on the substantive unfairness of the agreed terms. This is something the courts are ill-placed to judge, as they so often recognise in other contexts. Moreover, if substantive fairness is so important, then surely it is of general importance, so that all terms perceived as oppressive, unconscionable or unfair should also be swept up in the same protective endeavour.[113] But such all-embracing judicial control would effectively eliminate the very idea of contracts, which are necessarily founded on party autonomy to agree bargains.

But perhaps there is justification for paternalism in remedies clauses only. So far, however, there seems to be little of substance in any of the arguments for needing a special approach to agreed damages clauses. Take one increasingly common argument from behavioural economics. It suggests parties should be protected against the high risk of cognitive error and over-optimism in predicting the consequences of their contingent future obligations.[114] But this problem does not distinguish agreed damages clauses. It is a problem in any long-term contract, as is so frequently recognised in warnings to consumers about hire-purchase contracts and long-term loans, although the risk is equally relevant for sophisticated commercial parties dealing in volatile markets. For all these parties, obligations which seem reasonable at the outset may look dauntingly onerous when the markets, or personal circumstances, turn. And so the point made earlier remains: if consent to the deal is real, should the courts intervene? Much more would be needed to justify intervention on the grounds of substantive fairness in any event, but such reasons are unlikely to justify intervention by such a crude and formalistically selective mechanism as is embodied in the penalties rule.

A third category of arguments suggests that the purpose of the penalties rule is to prevent injured parties recovering more than would be recovered at common law under the default compensation rules.[115] It is, effectively, an argument which favours making the common law's default rules on contractual remedies mandatory. This asserts a preferred outcome, but without supporting justification.[116] And if the outcome is so important, then judicial compulsion in seeing it is delivered should not depend on the form of the parties' agreement, but only on its substance in making alternative provisions.[117]

[112] Reinforcing this, concerns about the reality of consent appear as undercurrents in a good number of penalties cases. In typically direct fashion, see Lord Denning in *Bridge v Campbell Discount Co Ltd* [1962] AC 600 (HL), 628, considering whether Bridge had consented to the term providing for 'agreed compensation for depreciation' of the car he was acquiring on hire-purchase: 'There is not the slightest evidence that Bridge ever agreed it, and I do not suppose for a moment that he did. He simply signed the printed form'.

[113] Even the Australian High Court in *Andrews v ANZ Banking Group Ltd*, above n 95, has not gone so far: its focus is directed solely against provisions which aim to deter breach. No reasons for that limitation are given.

[114] See, eg, M Chen-Wishart, 'Controlling the Power to Agree Damages' in P Birks (ed), *Wrongs and Remedies in the Twenty-First Century* (Oxford, OUP, 1996) 271, 290; H Beale, *Remedies for Breach of Contract* (London, Sweet and Maxwell, 1980) 59; SA Smith, *Contract Theory* (Oxford, OUP, 2004) 308.

[115] *Exports Credits Guarantee Department v Universal Oil Products Co* [1983] 1 WLR 399 (HL), 403 (Lord Roskill). Also A Burrows, *Remedies for Torts and Breach of Contract,* 3rd edn (Oxford, OUP, 2004) 451.

[116] See the arguments against this approach in Morgan, above n 3, 247–52.

[117] This is essentially what the HCA concluded in *Andrews v ANZ Banking Group Ltd*, above 95.

Although contractual damages are by default compensatory not punitive,[118] there is arguably no compelling reason for insisting that this rule be mandatory. Legal precedent is to the contrary. Parties can agree that losses which would not be recoverable under the default rule will be recoverable,[119] or that losses which would be recoverable will not be;[120] moreover, they can value losses at idiosyncratic personal levels rather than at market levels.[121] Despite this, what is not allowed is any broader approach which might, technically, offend the penalties jurisdiction. Sometimes 'penalty' clauses are designed to provide very practical protections for sunk investments,[122] or intellectual property or franchise agreements. In such cases the clause may be technically penal, but not truly unfair.[123] In any event, a remedies clause cannot be judged unfair simply because it fails to map onto the common law default rule. Unfairness depends on the price paid for the remedial advantage.[124] That is typically beyond the purview of the courts, and indeed often judged by the parties themselves on the basis of a complex matrix of conflicting factors, not on some standard, readily calculated formula.

But this focus on fairness as a general concern is a deviation. It harks back to the previous category of arguments. Here what is needed is some basis for thinking that the common law's default rules for remedying breach of contract should be mandatory. This is difficult. It seems impossible to argue that this particular default rule should be mandatory when there is no concern for the fairness of other contract terms. All the more so when the penalties prohibition turns out to pay no regard to the ends achieved, but only to the mechanism used to achieve them. In short, the court is not concerned with the fairness of a deal which requires A to pay an extra £100,000 to B in certain circumstances; it is concerned only if that payment is premised on breach of contract. All that well advised parties must do is concentrate on their desired ends, and ensure that they are not conditional on a breach. The rule then catches only the unwary and ill-advised. And still without justification for doing so.

Finally, and still within this category of arguments related to mandatory default rules, the economists advance a related argument. It is based on favouring 'efficient breach', since that they argue delivers the most economically efficient use of resources.[125] From that premise it follows that any clause deterring breach is inefficient: parties will then be motivated to perform inefficient contracts. But this does not quite reflect the reality. Penalty clauses do not outlaw efficient breach; they merely alter the price at which breach is efficient.[126] Moreover, the altered price is the price agreed by the contracting parties themselves, not a price derived generically from the common law's default rules. It is overtly paternalistic to unravel

[118] Or at least not punitive in England and Australia. In Canada, punitive damages for breach of contract may be awarded in limited circumstances: *Whiten v Pilot Insurance Company* (2002) 209 DLR (4th) 257, 295, 303 (Binnie J); 160 (LeBel J); *Royal Bank of Canada v W Got & Associate Electric Ltd* (2000) 178 DLR (4th) 385, 395 (McLachlin and Bastarache JJ delivering the unanimous judgment of the court).

[119] *Robophone Facilities Ltd v Blank*, above n 100, 1447–48.

[120] *Ailsa Craig Fishing Co Ltd v Malvern Fishing Co Ltd (The Strathallan)* [1983] 1 WLR 964 (HL).

[121] See the discussion in *Astley v Weldon* (1801) 2 B & P 346, 126 ER 1318 (Court of Common Pleas).

[122] B Klein, 'Transaction Cost Determinants of "Unfair" Contractual Arrangements' (1980) 70 *American Economic Review Papers* 356.

[123] H Collins, *Regulating Contracts* (Oxford, OUP, 1999) 262.

[124] ibid 260.

[125] RL Birmingham, 'Breach of Contract, Damage Measures, and Economic Efficiency' (1970) 24 *Rutgers Law Review* 273, 292; Morgan, above n 40, 238–43, summarising the arguments and criticisms.

[126] CJ Goetz and RE Scott, 'Liquidated Damages, Penalties and the Just Compensation Principle: Some Notes on an Enforcement Model and a Theory of Efficient Breach' (1977) 77 *Columbia Law Review* 554.

this arrangement and re-price the parties' bargain according to the court's perceptions of a preferable reality,[127] and all the more so to do that for ends which no court seems able to define as having any basis in legal principle or policy.[128] Better and simpler, surely, to support the parties' autonomy and allow their own agreement to govern their relationship.

A fourth category of arguments suggests that it is unattractive to support a regime where the promisee is better off if the counter-party breaches than if the counter-party performs.[129] That conclusion assumes its own facts, however: *if*, but only if, performance is valued by the promisee according to the default rules, then on that measure the promisee gains more from the breach than from performance. The same might be said of deposits.[130] In both cases, however, the promisee typically prefers performance. That is invariably what prompts inclusion of these clauses, for which the promisee is likely to have paid a premium. The rule that a penalties clause is invalid therefore penalises rather than advantages the promisee. It also delivers a double windfall to the *promisor*, who is entitled to keep the premium paid by the promisee for inclusion of the agreed penalty clause, yet is not subjected to the burden of performance on its terms.[131] Moreover, the promisor, who by definition must be in breach of the contract, may be better off than someone who performs the contract fully.[132] This hardly seems apt, especially as the two alternatives (breach or performance) are often controlled by drafting rather than by the substance of the facts in issue. As Lord Denning noted:[133]

> Let no one mistake the injustice of this. It means that equity commits itself to this absurd paradox: it will grant relief to a man who breaks his contract but will penalise the man who keeps it. If this be the state of equity today, then it is in sore need of an overhaul so as to restore its first principles.

Before taking up that point, one final argument remains. It is something of a 'two wrongs make a right' argument. It is often suggested that there is no rational way to distinguish the penalties jurisdiction and the jurisdiction to relieve from forfeitures, and since we must not get rid of the latter, we should not get rid of the former. A great deal might be said on this, but even if it is conceded that there is something of substance left in the jurisdiction to relieve from forfeiture,[134] one significant practical issue stands out. There will be no relief at

[127] Morgan, above n 40, 225–26, citing *Lake River v Carborundum Co* 769 F 2d 1284 (1985) (Posner J).

[128] In any event, the courts have in other areas shown scant regard for arguments based on economic waste or unreasonableness as justifying premature termination of an agreed deal. See, eg, *White & Carter (Councils) Ltd v McGregor* [1962] AC 413 (HL), although whether a better approach might nevertheless have met the needs in this case is an open question.

[129] It provides an incentive to the promisee to induce the promisor's breach, and that too, according to the economists, is an inefficient use of resources: KW Clarkson, RL Miller and TJ Muris, 'Liquidated Damages v Penalties: Sense or Nonsense?' [1978] *Wisconsin Law Review* 351.

[130] Which also impose the same pressure to perform: *Howe v Smith* (1884) 27 Ch D 89 (CA).

[131] AN Hatzis, 'Having the Cake and Eating it Too: Efficient Penalty Clauses in Common and Civil Contract Law' (2003) 22 *International Review of Law and Economics* 381. See also D Harris, D Campbell and R Halson, *Remedies in Contract and Tort*, 2nd edn (Cambridge, CUP, 2002) 147, suggesting the court should therefore revise the contract price downwards in applying the penalty jurisdiction.

[132] As noticed even in early modern cases: *Bridge v Campbell Discount Co Ltd*, above n 112, 613 (Viscount Simonds).

[133] ibid 629. To similar effect, see *International Leasing Corp (Vic) Ltd v Aiken* [1967] 2 NSWR 427, 442 (Asprey JA); C Conte, 'The Jurisdiction to Relieve Against Penalties and Forfeitures: Time for a Rethink' (2010) 126 *LQR* 529, 531.

[134] For the contrary argument, ie, suggesting that all the relief awarded by the courts might now be better justified on other grounds, see S Worthington, 'What is Left of Equity's Relief Against Forfeiture?' in E Bant and M Harding (eds), *Exploring Private Law* (Cambridge, CUP, 2010) ch 11.

all from forfeiture, even if relief is theoretically warranted, unless the wrongdoer can 'make good' the injured party, and can do so according to the terms of the parties' original agreement, however onerous, including paying damages for delay, also on agreed contractual terms if so provided.[135] That is a very significant acknowledgement of the power of party autonomy. What is the equivalent in the penalties jurisdiction?

From all this it is clear that this state of affairs is a mess—or, worse, a partial mess. Retaining the status quo, relieving promisors from obligations held to be penal, maintains that partial mess. The status quo is incoherent: that is Lord Denning's point.[136] To eliminate this, judicial intervention must either rewrite all offending clauses in the parties' contracts, or enforce them all.[137] No compelling justification exists for the paternalism of the former approach. Moreover, such aggressive interventionism would make English contract law so uncertain as to be completely unattractive both nationally and internationally.[138] The preferable way out of this dilemma, surely, is simply to enforce *all* the parties' agreed terms—provided they are agreed.[139]

So this, at last, is the only bad news in this story of party autonomy.

VIII. Conclusion

Much law, both public and private, is concerned with constraining party autonomy. In private law, the laws of tort and unjust enrichment are illustrative. These laws exert considerable constraints on autonomy, but arguably none that are more than necessary for the good of society. In short, other values inevitably compete with party autonomy and must be preferred in certain contexts.

However, it would seem odd to see the same paternalism operating in contract cases. Here autonomy is thought to have free rein. The courts typically confirm this, denying their ability to countermand the parties' agreement and remaining alert to rules which might simply give parties an easy exit from bad bargains.[140] All the common law rules examined in the preceding pages support this view that in the realm of contract law party autonomy reigns supreme, with the exception of the rules on penalties.

Unless compelling justifications can be advanced, something should be done about that. Although the law should undoubtedly be fair and just, it does not follow that courts can unilaterally decide what is fair and just and compel those ends without giving reasons. The law must support the sort of society we prefer to live in, and in settling legal rules the priorities implicitly given to competing values should be made explicit.

Party autonomy is one of those values. It is perhaps the easiest to lose sight of because its role is inherently negative. It tells us what the law should *not* do, where it should *not* intervene rather than where it should. But it is no less crucial for all that.

[135] *Cukurova Finance International Ltd v Alfa Telecom Turkey Ltd* [2013] UKPC 20 (PC).

[136] See above n 133.

[137] The inevitable status quo bias is to do nothing (see S Harder, 'The Relevance of Breach to the Applicability of the Rule Against Penalties' (2013) 30 *Journal of Contract Law* 52), but that only admits defeat.

[138] Lord Scott of Foscote in *Golden Strait Corp v Nippon Yusen Kubishika Kaisha (The Golden Victory)* [2007] UKHL 12, [2007] 2 AC 353 [38]: 'Certainty is a desideratum and a very important one, particularly in commercial contracts'.

[139] To the same effect, see E Peel, 'The Rule Against Penalties' (2013) 129 *LQR* 152, 156–57.

[140] Adams and Brownsword, above n 1, 209–10.

INDEX

www.ingramcontent.com/pod-product-compliance
Ingram Content Group UK Ltd.
Pitfield, Milton Keynes, MK11 3LW, UK
UKHW051449290926
15471UKWH00008B/1104

9 781509 921119